dent (Student)

Pre A	Write first name without support	Knows at least 40 letters by name	Claps words with 1, 2 and 3 syllables	Identifies some rhyming words with consonant sounds with prompting	Is hearing L to R to print with little prompting	Tracks L to R across a book with some prompting	Describes a picture in a line of print with some prompting	Maintains 1:1 on one line of print with text	Uses pictures to predict first and last word	Understands concept first letter	Understands concept first letter
DF..	Tracks L to R without prompting	Maintains 1:1 on one line of print	Uses pictures to predict, monitor and correct	Reads about 10 sight words	Writes about 10 sight words with prompting	Knows all letters by name	Hears and records initial consonant sounds with prompting	Hears and records initial and final consonants with some prompting	Orally generates rhyming string		
DRA 3-4	Maintains 1:1 on two lines of print	Gets mouth ready for first sound with prompting	Uses first letters and pictures to cross check with prompting	Hears short a and short o in and a during word work and writing with prompting	Uses consonants and short o after reading with prompting	Retells some information after reading	Reads about 20 sight words	Writes about 20 sight words	Hears and records initial and final consonants with some prompting		
	Maintains 1:1 without pointing on familiar books	Cross checks meaning and structure, and first letters to problem solve on familiar books	Reads about 30 sight words	Writes about 30 sight words	Hears and records CVC in picture sorts with prompting	Hears short vowels in picture sorts with prompting	Uses consonants and short vowels in word work with prompting	Discusses the story with prompting			
DRA 5-6	At difficulty, gets mouth ready for initial sound without prompting	Uses known words to problem solve unknown words with little prompting	Reads about 40 sight words	Writes about 40 sight words	Hears and records CVC words without prompting	Maintains meaning while problem solving	Maintains 1:1 without pointing on new books	Hears and records diagraphs with prompting	Hears and records diagraphs and short vowels to problem solve new words with prompting	Rereads to confirm meaning	Reads in short phrases
	Uses known parts to problem solve new words with prompting	Attends to endings (ed, s, ing) with prompting	Reads about 40 sight words						Uses diagraphs and short vowels to problem solve new words with prompting		

DRA Level	Descriptors
DRA 7-8	Uses known parts to problem solve new words without prompting • Covers the endings to problem solve with prompting • Maintains meaning while using several strategies to problem solve new words • Build automaticity with a large bank of high frequency words • Blends sounds in small words • Rereads to confirm meaning • Reads familiar text with fluency and expression • Reads new text with some phrasing • Attends to bold words and reads with appropriate intonation and expression • Reads contractions that contains known parts • Hears and records diagraphs without prompting • Writes CCVC words in boxes with prompting • Retells events w prompti[ng]
DRA 9-10	Maintains meaning while using known words, parts and endings to problem solve with some prompting • Uses multiple sources of information (MSV) to monitor and correct • Attends to the middle and end of words with prompting • Reads familiar books with expression and phrasing, attends to punctuation • Reads new books with some phrasing and expression • Breaks words at the onset and rime • Reads contractions with known parts • Writes CCVC words in boxes without prompting • Writes CVCC words in boxes with prompting • Retells beginning, middle and end with prompting • Writes 3 sentences (B,M,E) with prompting • Makes logical predictions while reading
DRA 11-12	Maintain meaning while quickly solving new words using known words and parts, endings and analogies with some prompting • Reads portions of new books with phrasing and expression • Uses onsets and rimes to problem solve new words with prompting • Attends to middle and end of words with little prompting • Writes CCVCC words with some prompting • Applies the silent e rule with prompting • Writes a somebody wanted but so with prompting • Retells B, M, and E without prompting • Describes characters, setting, problem and solution with prompting • Writes 3 sentences (BME) with prompting • Makes logical predictions while reading
DRA 13-14	Problem solve new words using a variety of strategies with little prompting • Reads longer portions of new books with phrasing and expression • Uses onsets and rimes to problem solve words with prompting • Attends to middle and end of words with little prompting • Writes CVCC words in boxes without prompting • Writes CCVCC words with prompting • Applies the silent e rule with out prompting • Applies the silent e rule with prompting • Writes a somebody wanted but so with prompting • Writes 3 to 5 sentences (BME) without prompting • Retells B, M and E without prompting • Writes 3 to 5 sentences (BME) with some prompting • Writes unknown words with vowel patterns by using known words with some prompting (analogy charts) • Describes characters, setting, problem and solution with prompting
DRA 15-16	Maintain meaning while quickly solving new words using known words and parts, endings and analogies with some prompting • Reads new books with phrasing and expression, stopping occasionally to problem solve • Uses onsets and rimes to problem solve words with some prompting • Attends to middle and end of words without prompting • Adds er, ly, ing, and ed to known words; Applies the silent e rule with prompting • Applies the silent e rule with prompting • Writes unknown words with vowel patterns by using known words with some prompting (analogy charts) • Writes 3 to 5 sentences (BME) without prompting • Orally retells the story using the 5 finger retell with prompting • Writes a somebody wanted but so without prompting • Describes a characters feelings with prompting

Language Development and Reading

Custom Edition for EDSE 403-503
George Mason University
Programs in Special Education

Taken from:

Teaching Reading to Students Who Are at Risk or Have Disabilities:
A Multi-Tier Approach, Second Edition
by William D. Bursuck and Mary Damer

Reading Problems: Assessment and Teaching Strategies, Sixth Edition
by Joyce Holt Jennings, JoAnne Schudt Caldwell and Janet W. Lerner

Handbook of Reading Assessment
by Sherry Mee Bell and R. Steve McCallum

Words Their Way: Word Study for Phonics, Vocabulary, and
Spelling Instruction, Fourth Edition
by Donald R. Bear, Marcia Invernizzi, Shane Templeton and Francine Johnston

Reading Problems: Assessment and Teaching Strategies, Fifth Edition
by Joyce Holt Jennings, JoAnne Caldwell and Janet W. Lerner

Contents

From: Reading Problems: Assessment and Teaching Strategies, Fifth Edition, by Joyce Holt Jennings, JoAnne Caldwell and Janet W. Lerner

Chapter 2   Early Literacy   34

From: Teaching Reading to Students Who Are at Risk or Have Disabilities: A Multi-Tier Approach, Second Edition, by William D. Bursuck and Mary Damer

Chapter 3   Beginning Reading/Early Decoding   50

Chapter 4   Advanced Word Reading   **116**

Chapter 5   Reading Fluency   158

From: Reading Problems: Assessment and Teaching Strategies, Sixth Edition, by Joyce Holt Jennings, JoAnne Schudt Caldwell and Janet W. Lerner

Chapter 6   Obtaining Background Information   201

Chapter 7   Using an Informal Reading Inventory for Assessment   218

From: Handbook of Reading Assessment, by Sherry Mee Bell and R. Steve McCallum

Chapter 8   Informal Assessment: Progress Monitoring   246

From: Teaching Reading to Students Who Are at Risk or Have Disabilities:
A Multi-Tier Approach, Second Edition, by William D. Bursuck and Mary Damer

From: Words Their Way: Word Study for Phonics, Vocabulary, and Spelling Instruction, Fourth Edition, by Donald R. Bear, Marcia Invernizzi, Shane Templeton and Francine Johnston

From: Reading Problems: Assessment and Teaching Strategies, Sixth Edition, by Joyce Holt Jennings, JoAnne Schudt Caldwell and Janet W. Lerner

Chapter 13   Literacy Instruction for Diverse Populations: Multicultural Diversity, English Language Learners, Parents and Families, Adolescents, and Adults with Reading Problems   427

George Mason University
Programs in Special Education

EDSE 403/503
Language Development and Reading

Course Description
(effective Fall 2011)

Identifies literacy skills for typical students, and describes reading, language, and writing instruction for students with mild disabilities who access the general curriculum. Topics include emergent literacy skills, phonemic awareness, vocabulary development, and comprehension.

The Council for Exceptional Children's (CEC) Special Education Content Standard #6: Language

Special educators understand **typical and atypical language development** and the ways in which exceptional conditions can interact with an individual's experience with and use of language. Special educators use individualized strategies to **enhance language development** and **teach communication skills** to individuals with ELN*. Special educators are familiar with **augmentative, alternative, and assistive technologies** to support and enhance communication of individuals with exceptional needs. Special educators match their communication methods to an individual's language proficiency and cultural and linguistic differences. Special educators provide **effective language models** and they use communication strategies and resources to **facilitate understanding of subject matter for individuals with ELN whose primary language is not English.**

*Exceptional Learning Needs

National Institute for Literacy
The Partnership for Reading

Put Reading First

Kindergarten Through Grade 3

The Research
Building Blocks
For Teaching
Children to Read

Third Edition

The Research Building Blocks for Teaching Children to Read

Put Reading First

Kindergarten Through Grade 3

Writers:

Bonnie B. Armbruster, Ph.D., University of Illinois at Urbana-Champaign,

Fran Lehr, M.A., Lehr & Associates, Champaign, Illinois,

Jean Osborn, M.Ed., University of Illinois at Urbana-Champaign

Editor: C. Ralph Adler, RMC Research Corporation

Designer: Lisa T. Noonis, RMC Research Corporation

National Institute for Literacy

The Partnership for Reading

Contents

This publication was developed by the Center for the Improvement of Early Reading Achievement (CIERA) and was funded by the National Institute for Literacy (NIFL) through the Educational Research and Development Centers Program, PR/Award Number R305R70004, as administered by the Office of Educational Research and Improvement (OERI), U.S. Department of Education. However, the comments or conclusions do not necessarily represent the positions or policies of NIFL, OERI, or the U.S. Department of Education, and you should not assume endorsement by the Federal Government.

The National Institute for Literacy

The National Institute for Literacy, an agency in the Federal government, is authorized to help strengthen literacy across the lifespan. The Institute works to provide national leadership on literacy issues, including the improvement of reading instruction for children, youth, and adults by sharing information on scientifically based research.
Sandra Baxter, Director
Lynn Reddy, Deputy Director

The Partnership for Reading

This document was published by The Partnership for Reading, a collaborative effort of the National Institute for Literacy, the National Institute of Child Health and Human Development, and the U.S. Department of Education to make evidence-based reading research available to educators, parents, policy-makers, and others with an interest in helping all people learn to read well. The findings and conclusions in this publication were drawn from the 2000 report of the National Reading Panel, Teaching Children to Read: An Evidence-Based Assessment of the Scientific Research Literature on Reading and Its Implications for Reading Instruction—Reports of the Subgroups.

The writers and editors express their sincere thanks to:
- Isabel Beck, Douglas Carnine, Deborah Simmons, and Anne Sweet for their careful reviews and suggestions
- Sandra Baxter and Andrew Hartman at the National Institute for Literacy for their guidance and support
- The Subgroup Chairs of the National Reading Panel for their thoughtful and thorough comments: Linnea Ehri, Michael L. Kamil, S.J. Samuels, Timothy Shanahan, and Gloria Correro
- Susan Klaiber, Everett Barnes, and Douglas Hamman of RMC Research Corporation for their conceptual and editorial contributions
- The teacher collaborative groups across the United States that provided valuable feedback

Introduction

In today's schools, too many children struggle with learning to read. As many teachers and parents will attest, reading failure has exacted a tremendous long-term consequence for children's developing self-confidence and motivation to learn, as well as for their later school performance.

While there are no easy answers or quick solutions for optimizing reading achievement, an extensive knowledge base now exists to show us the skills children must learn in order to read well. These skills provide the basis for sound curriculum decisions and instructional approaches that can help prevent the predictable consequences of early reading failure.

The National Reading Panel (NRP) issued a report in 2000 that responded to a Congressional mandate to help parents, teachers, and policymakers identify key skills and methods central to reading achievement. The Panel was charged with reviewing research in reading instruction (focusing on the critical years of kindergarten through third grade) and identifying methods that consistently relate to reading success.

The Panel reviewed more than 100,000 studies. Through a carefully developed screening procedure, Panel members examined research that met several important criteria:

- the research had to address achievement of ***one or more skills in reading***. Studies of effective teaching were not included unless reading achievement was measured;
- the research had to be ***generalizable*** to the larger population of students. Thus, case studies with small numbers of children were excluded from the analysis;
- the research needed to examine the ***effectiveness*** of an approach. This type of research requires the comparison of different treatments, such as comparing the achievement of students using guided repeated reading to another group of students not using that strategy. This experimental research approach was necessary to understand whether changes in achievement could be attributed to the treatment;
- the research needed to be regarded as ***high quality***. An article or book had to have been reviewed by other scholars from the relevant field and judged to be sound and worthy of publication. Therefore, discussions of studies reported in meetings or conferences without a stringent peer review process were excluded from the analysis.

These criteria are not new in the world of educational research; they are often used as a matter of course by researchers who set out to determine the effectiveness of any educational program or approach. The National Reading Panel embraced the criteria in its review to bring balance to a field in which decisions have often been made based more on ideology than evidence. These criteria offer administrators, teachers, and parents a standard for evaluating critical decisions about how children will be taught to read. In addition to identifying effective practices, the work of the National Reading Panel challenges educators to consider the evidence of effectiveness whenever they make decisions about the content and structure of reading instruction programs. By operating on a "what works" basis, scientific evidence can help build a foundation for instructional practice. Teachers can learn about and emphasize methods and approaches that have worked well and caused reading improvement for large numbers of children. Teachers can build their students' skills efficiently and effectively, with greater results than before. Most importantly, with targeted "what works" instruction, the incidence of reading success should increase dramatically.

This guide, designed by teachers for teachers, summarizes what researchers have discovered about how to successfully teach children to read. It describes the findings of the National Reading Panel Report and provides analysis and discussion in five areas of reading instruction: ***phonemic awareness***, ***phonics***, ***fluency***, ***vocabulary***, and ***text comprehension***. Each section defines the skill, reviews the evidence from research, suggests implications for classroom instruction, describes proven strategies for teaching reading skills, and addresses frequently raised questions.

Our understanding of "what works" in reading is dynamic and fluid, subject to ongoing review and assessment through quality research. This guide begins the process of compiling the findings from scientifically based research in reading instruction, a body of knowledge that will continue to grow over time. We encourage all teachers to explore the research, open their minds to changes in their instructional practice, and take up the challenge of helping all children become successful readers.

Phonemic Awareness Instruction

Phonemic awareness is the ability to notice, think about, and work with the individual sounds in spoken words. Before children learn to read print, they need to become aware of how the sounds in words work. They must understand that words are made up of speech sounds, or phonemes.

Phonemes are the smallest parts of sound in a spoken word that make a difference in the word's meaning. For example, changing the first phoneme in the word **hat** from /h/ to /p/ changes the word from **hat** to **pat**, and so changes the meaning. (A letter between slash marks shows the phoneme, or sound, that the letter represents, and not the name of the letter. For example, the letter **h** represents the sound /h/.)

Children can show us that they have phonemic awareness in several ways, including:

- recognizing which words in a set of words begin with the same sound ("**Bell**, **bike**, and **boy** all have /b/ at the beginning.");
- isolating and saying the first or last sound in a word ("The beginning sound of **dog** is /d/." "The ending sound of **sit** is /t/.");
- combining, or blending the separate sounds in a word to say the word ("/m/, /a/, /p/— **map**.");
- breaking, or segmenting a word into its separate sounds ("**Up**—/u/, /p/.").

Children who have phonemic awareness skills are likely to have an easier time learning to read and spell than children who have few or none of these skills.

Although phonemic awareness is a widely used term in reading, it is often misunderstood. One misunderstanding is that phonemic awareness and phonics are the same thing. Phonemic awareness is **not** phonics. Phonemic awareness is the understanding that the sounds of **spoken** language work together to make words. Phonics is the understanding that there is a predictable relationship between phonemes and graphemes, the letters that represent those sounds in **written** language. If children are to benefit from phonics instruction, they need phonemic awareness.

The reason is obvious: children who cannot hear and work with the phonemes of spoken words will have a difficult time learning how to relate these phonemes to the graphemes when they see them in written words.

Another misunderstanding about phonemic awareness is that it means the same as phonological awareness. The two names are ***not*** interchangeable. Phonemic awareness is a subcategory of phonological awareness. The focus of phonemic awareness is narrow—identifying and manipulating the individual sounds in words. The focus of phonological awareness is much broader. It includes identifying and manipulating larger parts of spoken language, such as words, syllables, and onsets and rimes—as well as phonemes. It also encompasses awareness of other aspects of sound, such as rhyming, alliteration, and intonation.

Children can show us that they have phonological awareness in several ways, including:

- identifying and making oral rhymes;

     "The pig has a (wig)."

     "Pat the (cat)."

     "The sun is (fun)."

- identifying and working with syllables in spoken words;

     "I can clap the parts in my name: An-drew."

- identifying and working with onsets and rimes in spoken syllables or one-syllable words;

     "The first part of sip is s-."

     "The last part of win is -in."

- identifying and working with individual phonemes in spoken words.

     "The first sound in sun is /s/."

PHONOLOGICAL AWARENESS

Phonemic awareness is only one type of phonological awareness.

Broader phonological awareness
- *Identifying and making oral rhymes*
- *Identifying and working with syllables in spoken words*

Narrower phonological awareness
- *Identifying and working with onsets and rimes in spoken syllables*
- *Identifying and working with individual phonemes in words spoken (phonemic awareness)*

Here are some definitions of terms used frequently in reading instruction.

Phoneme

*A **phoneme** is the smallest part of **spoken** language that makes a difference in the meaning of words. English has about 41 phonemes. A few words, such as **a** or **oh**, have only one phoneme. Most words, however, have more than one phoneme: The word **if** has two phonemes (/i/ /f/); **check** has three phonemes (/ch/ /e/ /k/), and **stop** has four phonemes (/s/ /t/ /o/ /p/). Sometimes one phoneme is represented by more than one letter.*

Grapheme

*A **grapheme** is the smallest part of **written** language that represents a phoneme in the spelling of a word. A grapheme may be just one letter, such as **b**, **d**, **f**, **p**, **s**; or several letters, such as **ch**, **sh**, **th**, **-ck**, **ea**, **-igh**.*

Phonics

***Phonics** is the understanding that there is a predictable relationship between phonemes (the sounds of **spoken** language) and graphemes (the letters and spellings that represent those sounds in **written** language).*

Phonemic awareness

***Phonemic awareness** is the ability to hear, identify, and manipulate the individual sounds—phonemes—in spoken words.*

Phonological awareness

***Phonological awareness** is a broad term that includes phonemic awareness. In addition to phonemes, phonological awareness activities can involve work with rhymes, words, syllables, and onsets and rimes.*

Syllable

*A **syllable** is a word part that contains a vowel or, in spoken language, a vowel sound (**e-vent**; **news-pa-per**; **ver-y**).*

Onset and rime

***Onsets and rimes** are parts of spoken language that are smaller than syllables but larger than phonemes. An **onset** is the initial consonant(s) sound of a syllable (the onset of **bag** is **b-**; of **swim**, **sw-**). A **rime** is the part of a syllable that contains the vowel and all that follows it (the rime of **bag** is **-ag**; of **swim**, **-im**).*

What does scientifically based research tell us about phonemic awareness instruction?

Key findings from the scientific research on phonemic awareness instruction provide the following conclusions of particular interest and value to classroom teachers:

Phonemic awareness can be taught and learned.

Effective phonemic awareness instruction teaches children to notice, think about, and work with (manipulate) sounds in spoken language. Teachers use many activities to build phonemic awareness, including:

- **Phoneme isolation**

  Children recognize individual sounds in a word.

  Teacher: "What is the first sound in *van*?"

  Children: "The first sound in *van* is /v/."

- **Phoneme identity**

  Children recognize the same sounds in different words.

  Teacher: "What sound is the same in *fix*, *fall*, and *fun*?"

  Children: "The first sound, /f/, is the same."

- **Phoneme categorization**

  Children recognize the word in a set of three or four words that has the "odd" sound.

  Teacher: "Which word doesn't belong? *Bus, bun, rug.*"

  Children: "*Rug* does not belong. It doesn't begin with /b/."

- **Phoneme blending**

  Children listen to a sequence of separately spoken phonemes, and then combine the phonemes to form a word. Then they write and read the word.

  Teacher: "What word is /b/ /i/ /g/?"

  Children: "/b/ /i/ /g/ is *big*."

  Teacher: "Now let's write the sounds in *big*: /b/, write *b*; /i/, write *i*; /g/, write *g*."

  Teacher: (Writes *big* on the board.) "Now we're going to read the word *big*."

- **Phoneme segmentation**

  Children break a word into its separate sounds, saying each sound as they tap out or count it. Then they write and read the word.

  Teacher: "How many sounds are in *grab*?"

  Children: "/g/ /r/ /a/ /b/. Four sounds."

  Teacher: "Now let's write the sounds in *grab*: /g/, write *g*; /r/, write *r*; /a/, write *a*; /b/, write *b*."

  Teacher: (Writes *grab* on the board.) "Now we're going to read the word *grab*."

- **Phoneme deletion**

  Children recognize the word that remains when a phoneme is removed from another word.

  Teacher: "What is **smile** without the /s/?"

  Children: "**Smile** without the /s/ is **mile**."

- **Phoneme addition**

  Children make a new word by adding a phoneme to an existing word.

  Teacher: "What word do you have if you add /s/ to the beginning of **park**?"

  Children: "**Spark**."

- **Phoneme substitution**

  Children substitute one phoneme for another to make a new word.

  Teacher: "The word is **bug**. Change /g/ to /n/. What's the new word?"

  Children: "**Bun**."

Phonemic awareness instruction helps children learn to read.

Phonemic awareness instruction improves children's ability to read words. It also improves their reading comprehension. Phonemic awareness instruction aids reading comprehension primarily through its influence on word reading. For children to understand what they read, they must be able to read words rapidly and accurately. Rapid and accurate word reading frees children to focus their attention on the meaning of what they read. Of course, many other things, including the size of children's vocabulary and their world experiences, contribute to reading comprehension.

Phonemic awareness instruction helps children learn to spell.

Teaching phonemic awareness, particularly how to segment words into phonemes, helps children learn to spell. The explanation for this may be that children who have phonemic awareness understand that sounds and letters are related in a predictable way. Thus, they are able to relate the sounds to letters as they spell words.

Phonemic awareness instruction is most effective when children are taught to manipulate phonemes by using the letters of the alphabet.

Phonemic awareness instruction makes a stronger contribution to the improvement of reading and spelling when children are taught to use letters as they manipulate phonemes than when instruction is limited to phonemes alone. Teaching sounds along with the letters of the alphabet is important because it helps children to see how phonemic awareness relates to their reading and writing. Learning to blend phonemes with letters helps children read words. Learning to segment sounds with letters helps them spell words.

If children do not know letter names and shapes, they need to be taught them along with phonemic awareness.

Relating sounds to letters is, of course, the heart of phonics instruction, which is the subject of the next section of this booklet.

Phonemic awareness instruction is most effective when it focuses on only one or two types of phoneme manipulation, rather than several types.

Children who receive instruction that focuses on one or two types of phoneme manipulation make greater gains in reading and spelling than do children who are taught three or more types of manipulation.

One possible explanation for this is that children who are taught many different ways to manipulate phonemes may become confused about which type to apply. Another explanation is that teaching many types of manipulations does not leave enough time to teach any one type thoroughly. A third explanation is that instruction that includes several types of manipulations may result in teaching children more difficult manipulations before they acquire skills in the easier ones.

SOME COMMON PHONEMIC AWARENESS TERMS

Phoneme manipulation
When children work with phonemes in words, they are manipulating the phonemes. Types of phoneme manipulation include blending phonemes to make words, segmenting words into phonemes, deleting phonemes from words, adding phonemes to words, or substituting one phoneme for another to make a new word.

Blending
When children combine individual phonemes to form words, they are blending the phonemes. They also are blending when they combine onsets and rimes to make syllables and combine syllables to make words.

Segmenting (segmentation)
When children break words into their individual phonemes, they are segmenting the words. They are also segmenting when they break words into syllables and syllables into onsets and rimes.

Questions you may have about phonemic awareness instruction

Which activities will help my students acquire phonemic awareness?

Your instruction to increase children's phonemic awareness can include various activities in blending and segmenting words. Clearly, however, you should provide your students with instruction that is appropriate for their level of literacy development. If you teach younger children or less able, older readers, your instruction should begin with easier activities, such as having children identify and categorize the first phonemes in words. When the children can do these activities, move on to more difficult ones.

Which methods of phonemic awareness instruction will have the greatest impact on my students' learning to read?

You can use a variety of teaching methods that contribute to children's success in learning to read. However, teaching one or two types of phoneme manipulation—specifically blending and segmenting phonemes in words—is likely to produce greater benefits to your students' reading than teaching several types of manipulation.

Teaching your students to manipulate phonemes along with letters can also contribute to their reading success.

Your instruction should also be explicit about the connection between phonemic awareness and reading. For example:

> Teacher: "Listen: I'm going to say the sounds in the word *jam*—/j/ /a/ /m/. What is the word?"
>
> Children: "*Jam*."
>
> Teacher: "You say the sounds in the word *jam*."
>
> Children: "/j/ /a/ /m/."
>
> Teacher: "Now let's write the sounds in *jam*: /j/, write *j*; /a/, write *a*; /m/, write *m*."
>
> Teacher: (Writes *jam* on the board.) "Now we're going to read the word *jam*."

Which of my students will benefit from phonemic awareness instruction?

Phonemic awareness instruction can help essentially all of your students learn to read, including preschoolers, kindergartners, first graders who are just starting to read, and older, less able readers.

Phonemic awareness instruction can help most of your students learn to spell. Instruction can be effective with preschoolers, kindergartners, and first graders. It can help children from all economic levels.

How much time should I spend on phonemic awareness instruction?

You do not need to devote a lot of class time to phonemic awareness instruction. Over the school year, your entire phonemic awareness program should take no more than 20 hours.

Your students will differ in their phonemic awareness. Some will need more instruction than others. The best approach is to assess students' phonemic awareness before you begin instruction. Assessment will let you know which students do and do not need the instruction, which students should be taught the easier types of phoneme manipulation (such as identifying initial sounds in words), and which should receive instruction in more advanced types (such as segmenting, blending, deletion/addition, and substitution).

Should I teach phonemic awareness to individual students, to small groups, or to the whole class?

In general, small-group instruction is more effective in helping your students acquire phonemic awareness and learn to read. Small-group instruction may be more effective than individual or whole-group instruction because children often benefit from listening to their classmates respond and receive feedback from the teacher.

Do we know enough about the effectiveness of phonemic awareness instruction for me to implement it in my classroom?

Yes. Bear in mind, however, that phonemic awareness instruction is not a complete reading program; it cannot guarantee the reading and writing success of your students. Adding well-thought-out phonemic awareness instruction to a beginning reading program or to a remedial reading program is very likely to help your students learn to read and spell. Whether these benefits are lasting, however, will depend on the comprehensiveness and effectiveness of the entire literacy curriculum.

Phonemic awareness is

- the ability to hear, identify, and manipulate individual sounds—phonemes—in spoken words.

Phonemic awareness is important because

- it improves children's word reading and reading comprehension.
- it helps children learn to spell.

Phonemic awareness can be developed through a number of activities, including asking children to

- identify phonemes,
- categorize phonemes,
- blend phonemes to form words,
- segment words into phonemes,
- delete or add phonemes to form new words, and
- substitute phenomes to make new words.

Phonemic awareness instruction is most effective

- when children are taught to manipulate phonemes by using the letters of the alphabet.
- when instruction focuses on only one or two rather than several types of phoneme manipulation.

2 Phonics Instruction

Phonics instruction teaches children the relationships between the letters (graphemes) of written language and the individual sounds (phonemes) of spoken language. It teaches children to use these relationships to read and write words. Teachers of reading and publishers of programs of beginning reading instruction sometimes use different labels to describe these relationships, including the following:

- *graphophonemic relationships*
- *letter-sound associations*
- *letter-sound correspondences*
- *sound-symbol correspondences*
- *sound-spellings*

Regardless of the label, the goal of phonics instruction is to help children learn and use the alphabetic principle—the understanding that there are systematic and predictable relationships between written letters and spoken sounds. Knowing these relationships will help children recognize familiar words accurately and automatically, and "decode" new words. In short, knowledge of the alphabetic principle contributes greatly to children's ability to read words both in isolation and in connected text.

Critics of phonics instruction argue that English spellings are too irregular for phonics instruction to really help children learn to read words. The point is, however, that phonics instruction teaches children a system for remembering how to read words. Once children learn, for example, that *phone* is spelled this way rather than *foan*, their memory helps them to read, spell, and recognize the word instantly and more accurately than they could read *foan*. The same process is true for all irregularly spelled words. Most of these words contain some regular letter-sound relationships that can help children remember how to read them.

In summary, the alphabetic system is a mnemonic device that supports our memory for specific words.

What does scientifically based research tell us about phonics instruction?

Key findings from the scientific research on phonics instruction include the following conclusions of particular interest and value to classroom teachers.

Systematic and explicit phonics instruction is more effective than non-systematic or no phonics instruction.

Systematic and explicit phonics instruction makes a bigger contribution to children's growth in reading than instruction that provides non-systematic or no phonics instruction.

How do systematic programs of phonics instruction differ from non-systematic programs? The hallmark of programs of systematic phonics instruction is the direct teaching of a set of letter-sound relationships in a clearly defined sequence. The set includes the major sound/spelling relationships of both consonants and vowels.

The programs also provide materials that give children substantial practice in applying knowledge of these relationships as they read and write. These materials include books or stories that contain a large number of words that children can decode by using the letter-sound relationships they have learned and are learning. The programs also might provide children with opportunities to spell words and to write their own stories with the letter-sound relationships they are learning.

APPROACHES TO PHONICS INSTRUCTION

Most teachers are acquainted with several approaches to phonics instruction, including those listed below. The distinctions between approaches are not absolute, and some programs of instruction combine approaches.

Synthetic phonics *Children learn how to convert letters or letter combinations into sounds, and then how to blend the sounds together to form recognizable words.*

Analytic phonics *Children learn to analyze letter-sound relationships in previously learned words. They do not pronounce sounds in isolation.*

Analogy-based phonics *Children learn to use parts of word families they know to identify words they don't know that have similar parts.*

Phonics through spelling *Children learn to segment words into phonemes and to make words by writing letters for phonemes.*

Embedded phonics *Children are taught letter-sound relationships during the reading of connected text. (Since children encounter different letter-sound relationships as they read, this approach is not systematic or explicit.)*

Onset-rime phonics instruction *Children learn to identify the sound of the letter or letters before the first vowel (the onset) in a one-syllable word and the sound of the remaining part of the word (the rime).*

Systematic and explicit phonics instruction significantly improves kindergarten and first-grade children's word recognition and spelling.

Systematic phonics instruction produces the greatest impact on children's reading achievement when it begins in kindergarten or first grade.

Both kindergarten and first-grade children who receive systematic phonics instruction are better at reading and spelling words than kindergarten and first-grade children who do not receive systematic instruction.

Systematic and explicit phonics instruction significantly improves children's reading comprehension.

Systematic phonics instruction results in better growth in children's ability to comprehend what they read than non-systematic or no phonics instruction. This is not surprising because the ability to read the words in a text accurately and quickly is highly related to successful reading comprehension.

Systematic and explicit phonics instruction is effective for children from various social and economic levels.

Systematic phonics instruction is beneficial to children regardless of their socioeconomic status. It helps children from various backgrounds make greater gains in reading than non-systematic instruction or no phonics instruction.

Systematic and explicit phonics instruction is particularly beneficial for children who are having difficulty learning to read and who are at risk for developing future reading problems.

Systematic phonics instruction is significantly more effective than non-systematic or no phonics instruction in helping to prevent reading difficulties among at-risk students and in helping children overcome reading difficulties.

Systematic and explicit phonics instruction is most effective when introduced early.

Phonics instruction is most effective when it begins in kindergarten or first grade. To be effective with young learners, systematic instruction must be designed appropriately and taught carefully. It should include teaching letter shapes and names, phonemic awareness, and all major letter-sound relationships. It should ensure that all children learn these skills. As instruction proceeds, children should be taught to use this knowledge to read and write words.

Phonics instruction is not an entire reading program for beginning readers.

Along with phonics instruction, young children should be solidifying their knowledge of the alphabet, engaging in phonemic awareness activities, and listening to stories and informational texts read aloud to them. They also should be reading texts (both out loud and silently), and writing letters, words, messages, and stories.

PROGRAMS OF SYSTEMATIC AND EXPLICIT PHONICS INSTRUCTION

Systematic and explicit phonics instruction provides practice with letter-sound relationships in a predetermined sequence. Children learn to use these relationships to decode words that contain them.

Questions you may have about phonics instruction

Do we know enough about the effectiveness of systematic and explicit phonics instruction for me to implement it in my classroom?

Yes. Many teachers are teaching phonics systematically and explicitly and have been doing so for years. Their results, along with the findings of three decades of research, confirm the importance and effectiveness of systematic phonics instruction, particularly in kindergarten and first- and second-grade classrooms.

How can I tell if a phonics program is systematic and explicit?

A program of systematic phonics instruction clearly identifies a carefully selected and useful set of letter-sound relationships and then organizes the introduction of these relationships into a logical instructional sequence. The instructional sequence may include the relationships between the sounds associated with single letters (for example, the sound /m/ with the letter *m*), as well as with larger units of written language (for example, letter combinations such as *th* or *ing* or spelling patterns such as *ea* or *ie*). Furthermore, a systematic program of instruction provides children with ample opportunities to practice the relationships they are learning.

What do non-systematic programs of phonics instruction look like?

Programs of phonics instruction that are not systematic do not teach consonant and vowel letter-sound relationships in a prescribed sequence. Rather, they encourage informal phonics instruction based on the teacher's perceptions of what students need to learn and when they need to learn it.

Non-systematic instruction often neglects vowels, even though knowing vowel letter-sound relationships is a crucial part of knowing the alphabetic system. Non-systematic programs of phonics instruction do not provide practice materials that offer children the opportunity to apply what they are learning about letter-sound relationships. The reading materials these programs do provide for children are selected according to other criteria, such as their interest to children or their literary value.

GENERAL GUIDELINES: EVALUATING PROGRAMS OF PHONICS INSTRUCTION

Effective programs offer phonics instruction that
- *helps teachers explicitly and systematically instruct students in how to relate letters and sounds, how to break spoken words into sounds, and how to blend sounds to form words;*
- *helps students understand why they are learning the relationships between letters and sounds;*
- *helps students apply their knowledge of phonics as they read words, sentences, and text;*
- *helps students apply what they learn about sounds and letters to their own writing;*
- *can be adapted to the needs of individual students, based on assessment;*
- *includes alphabetic knowledge, phonemic awareness, vocabulary development, and the reading of text, as well as systematic phonics instruction.*

What else should I look for in programs of phonics instruction?

Programs should acknowledge that systematic phonics instruction is a means to an end. Some phonics programs focus primarily on teaching children a large number of letter-sound relationships. These programs often do not allot enough instructional time to help children learn how to put this knowledge to use in reading actual words, sentences, and texts. Although children need to be taught the major consonant and vowel letter-sound relationships, they also need ample reading and writing activities that allow them to practice using this knowledge.

What kinds of reading practice materials should I look for?

Usually, practice materials are in the form of short books or stories that contain words that provide children with practice in using the specific letter-sound relationships they are learning. Most programs of systematic phonics instruction also include materials for use in practicing writing. For example, children might have activity sheets on which they write the letters and letter combinations they are learning, and then combine these into words, sentences, messages, and their own stories.

Some programs of instruction do not teach phonics explicitly and systematically.

- **Literature-based programs that emphasize reading and writing activities.** *Phonics instruction is embedded in these activities, but letter-sound relationships are taught incidentally, usually based on key letters that appear in student reading materials.*
- **Basal reading programs that focus on whole-word or meaning-based activities.** *These programs pay only limited attention to letter-sound relationships and provide little or no instruction in how to blend letters to pronounce words.*
- **Sight-word programs that begin by teaching children a sight-word reading vocabulary of from 50 to 100 words.** *Only after they learn to read these words do children receive instruction in the alphabetic principle.*

Further, adding phonics workbooks or phonics activities to these programs of instruction has not been effective. Such "add-ons" confuse rather than help children to read.

Is phonics instruction more effective when students are taught individually, in small groups, or in whole classes?

You can teach phonics effectively to the whole class, to small groups, or to individual students. The needs of the students in your class and the number of adults working with them determine how you deliver instruction.

Doesn't phonics instruction get in the way of reading comprehension?

Quite the opposite is true. Because systematic phonics instruction helps children learn to identify words, it increases their ability to comprehend what they read. Reading words accurately and automatically enables children to focus on the meaning of text. The research is quite convincing in showing that phonics instruction contributes to comprehension skills rather than inhibiting them.

Does phonics instruction slow down the progress of some children?

Again, the opposite is true. Phonics instruction contributes to growth in the reading of most children. It is important, however, to acknowledge that children vary greatly in the knowledge of reading that they bring to school. For phonics instruction to support the reading progress of all of your students, it is important to work in flexible instructional groups and to pace instruction to maximize student progress.

How does systematic and explicit phonics instruction affect spelling?

Systematic programs of phonics instruction produce more growth in spelling among kindergarten and first-grade students than non-systematic or no phonics programs. However, systematic phonics instruction for normally developing and poor readers above first grade does not produce gains in spelling. The reason may be that as students move up in the grades, spelling is less a matter of applying letter-sound relationships and more a matter of combining word parts.

How does systematic and explicit phonics instruction affect the reading and spelling of older students?

Systematic phonics instruction by itself may not be enough to significantly improve the overall reading and spelling performance of readers beyond first grade. The effects of phonics instruction on students in second through sixth grades are limited to improving their word reading and oral text reading skills. The effects do not extend to spelling and reading comprehension. For these students, it is important to emphasize reading fluency and comprehension. In addition, these students also require explicit spelling instruction to improve their spelling.

How long should phonics be taught?

Approximately two years of phonics instruction is sufficient for most students. If phonics instruction begins early in kindergarten, it should be completed by the end of first grade. If phonics instruction begins early in first grade, it should be completed by the end of second grade.

SUMMING UP

Phonics instruction
- helps children learn the relationships between the letters of written language and the sounds of spoken language.

Phonics instruction is important because
- it leads to an understanding of the alphabetic principle—the systematic and predictable relationships between written letters and spoken sounds.

Programs of phonics instruction are effective when they are
- **systematic**—the plan of instruction includes a carefully selected set of letter-sound relationships that are organized into a logical sequence.
- **explicit**—the programs provide teachers with precise directions for the teaching of these relationships.

Effective phonics programs provide
- ample opportunities for children to apply what they are learning about letters and sounds to the reading of words, sentences, and stories.

Systematic and explicit phonics instruction
- significantly improves children's word recognition, spelling, and reading comprehension.
- is most effective when it begins in kindergarten or first grade.

3

Fluency Instruction

Fluency is the ability to read a text accurately and quickly. When fluent readers read silently, they recognize words automatically. They group words quickly to help them gain meaning from what they read. Fluent readers read aloud effortlessly and with expression. Their reading sounds natural, as if they are speaking. Readers who have not yet developed fluency read slowly, word by word. Their oral reading is choppy and plodding.

Fluency is important because it provides a bridge between word recognition and comprehension. Because fluent readers do not have to concentrate on decoding the words, they can focus their attention on what the text means. They can make connections among the ideas in the text and between the text and their background knowledge. In other words, fluent readers recognize words and comprehend at the same time. Less fluent readers, however, must focus their attention on figuring out the words, leaving them little attention for understanding the text.

FLUENCY

More fluent readers
focus their attention on making connections among the ideas in a text and between these ideas and their background knowledge. Therefore, they are able to focus on comprehension.

Less fluent readers
must focus their attention primarily on decoding individual words. Therefore, they have little attention left for comprehending the text.

Fluency develops gradually over considerable time and through substantial practice. At the earliest stage of reading development, students' oral reading is slow and labored because students are just learning to "break the code"—to attach sounds to letters and to blend letter sounds into recognizable words.

Even when students recognize many words automatically, their oral reading still may be expressionless, not fluent. To read with expression, readers must be able to divide the text into meaningful chunks. These chunks include phrases and clauses. Readers must know to pause appropriately within and at the ends of sentences and when to change emphasis and tone. For example, a reader who lacks fluency may read, probably in a monotone, a line from Bill Martin Jr.'s *Brown Bear, Brown Bear* as if it were a list of words rather than a connected text, pausing at inappropriate places:

Brown/
bear brown/
bear what/
do/
you see.

A fluent reader will read the same line as:

Brown bear/
Brown bear/
What do you see?

Fluency is not a stage of development at which readers can read all words quickly and easily. Fluency changes, depending on what readers are reading, their familiarity with the words, and the amount of their practice with reading text. Even very skilled readers may read in a slow, labored manner when reading texts with many unfamiliar words or topics. For example, readers who are usually fluent may not be able to read technical material fluently, such as a textbook about nuclear physics or an article in a medical journal.

A recent large-scale study by the National Assessment of Educational Progress (NAEP) found that 44% of a representative sample of the nation's fourth graders were low in fluency. The study also found a close relationship between fluency and reading comprehension. Students who scored lower on measures of fluency also scored lower on measures of comprehension, suggesting that fluency is a neglected reading skill in many American classrooms, affecting many students' reading comprehension.

Although some readers may recognize words automatically in isolation or on a list, they may not read the same words fluently when the words appear in sentences in connected text. Instant or automatic word recognition is a necessary, but not sufficient, reading skill. Students who can read words in isolation quickly may not be able to automatically transfer this "speed and accuracy." It is important to provide students with instruction and practice in fluency as they read connected text.

What does scientifically based research tell us about fluency instruction?

Researchers have investigated two major instructional approaches related to fluency. In the first approach, repeated and monitored oral reading (commonly called "repeated reading"), students read passages aloud several times and receive guidance and feedback from the teacher. In the second approach, independent silent reading, students are encouraged to read extensively on their own. Key findings from the scientific research on fluency instruction include the following conclusions about these two approaches that are of particular interest and value to classroom teachers.

Repeated and monitored oral reading improves reading fluency and overall reading achievement.

Students who read and reread passages orally as they receive guidance and/or feedback become better readers. Repeated oral reading substantially improves word recognition, speed, and accuracy as well as fluency. To a lesser but still considerable extent, repeated oral reading also improves reading comprehension. Repeated oral reading improves the reading ability of all students throughout the elementary school years. It also helps struggling readers at higher grade levels.

Traditionally, many teachers have relied primarily on round-robin reading to develop oral fluency. In round-robin reading, students take turns reading parts of a text aloud (though usually not repeatedly). But round-robin reading in itself does not increase fluency. This may be because students only read small amounts of text, and they usually read this small portion only once.

Researchers have found several effective techniques related to repeated oral reading:

- students read and reread a text a certain number of times or until a certain level of fluency is reached. Four rereadings are sufficient for most students; and
- oral reading practice is increased through the use of audiotapes, tutors, peer guidance, or other means.

In addition, some effective repeated oral reading techniques have carefully designed feedback to guide the reader's performance.

THE DIFFERENCE BETWEEN FLUENCY AND AUTOMATICITY

Although the terms automaticity *and* fluency *often are used interchangeably, they are not the same thing.*

Automaticity is the fast, effortless word recognition that comes with a great deal of reading practice. In the early stages of learning to read, readers may be accurate but slow and inefficient at recognizing words. Continued reading practice helps word recognition become more automatic, rapid, and effortless. Automaticity refers only to accurate, speedy word recognition, not to reading with expression. Therefore, automaticity (or automatic word recognition) is necessary, but not sufficient, for fluency.

No research evidence is available currently to confirm that instructional time spent on silent, independent reading with minimal guidance and feedback improves reading fluency and overall reading achievement.

One of the major differences between good and poor readers is the amount of time they spend reading. Many studies have found a strong relationship between reading ability and how much a student reads. On the basis of this evidence, teachers have long been encouraged to promote voluntary reading in the classroom. Teacher-education and reading-education literature often recommends in-class procedures for encouraging students to read on their own, such as Silent Sustained Reading (SSR) or Drop Everything and Read (DEAR).

Research, however, has not yet confirmed whether independent silent reading with minimal guidance or feedback improves reading achievement and fluency. Neither has it proven that more silent reading in the classroom cannot work; its effectiveness without guidance or feedback is as yet unproven. The research suggests that there are more beneficial ways to spend reading instructional time than to have students read independently in the classroom without reading instruction.

Questions you may have about fluency instruction

How can I help my students become more fluent readers?

You can help your students become more fluent readers (1) by providing them with models of fluent reading and (2) by having students repeatedly read passages as you offer guidance. In addition, you can help students improve their fluency by combining reading instruction with opportunities for them to read books that are at their independent level of reading ability.

Model fluent reading, then have students reread the text on their own.

By listening to good models of fluent reading, students learn how a reader's voice can help written text make sense. Read aloud daily to your students. By reading effortlessly and with expression, you are modeling for your students how a fluent reader sounds during reading.

After you model how to read the text, you must have the students reread it. By doing this, the students are engaging in repeated reading. Usually, having students read a text four times is sufficient to improve fluency. Remember, however, that instructional time is limited, and it is the actual time that students are actively engaged in reading that produces reading gains. Have other adults read aloud to students. Encourage parents or other family members to read aloud to their children at home. The more models of fluent reading the children hear, the better. Of course, hearing a model of fluent reading is not the only benefit of reading aloud to children. Reading to children also increases their knowledge of the world, their vocabulary, their familiarity with written language ("book language"), and their interest in reading.

Have students repeatedly read passages aloud with guidance.

The best strategy for developing reading fluency is to provide your students with many opportunities to read the same passage orally several times. To do this, you should first know what to have your students read. Second, you should know how to have your students read aloud repeatedly.

What students should read. Fluency develops as a result of many opportunities to practice reading with a high degree of success. Therefore, your students should practice orally rereading text that is reasonably easy for them—that is, text containing mostly words that they know or can decode easily. In other words, the texts should be at the students' independent reading level. A text is at students' independent reading level if they can read it with about 95% accuracy, or misread only about 1 of every 20 words. If the text is more difficult, students will focus so much on word recognition that they will not have an opportunity to develop fluency.

MODELING FLUENT READING

In the primary grades, you might read aloud from a big book. A big book is an enlarged version of a commercially published book—big enough so that all students can clearly see the text. By pointing to each word as you are reading (using either a pointer or your finger), you can show students where and how you are pausing and how the text shows you when to raise or lower your voice. Occasionally, you can also explain to your students why you are reading in a certain way:

Teacher: *Did you hear how I grouped the words* **"Brown bear/ brown bear"**? *That's because the words* **brown** *and* **bear** *belong together. And then I paused a little before repeating the words.*

Teacher: *Did you hear how my voice got louder and more excited right here? That's because the author put in this exclamation mark (point to it) to show that the speaker was excited or enthusiastic about what she was saying.*

Then, have the students practice reading the same text.

Independent level text
* *Relatively easy text for the reader, with no more than approximately 1 in 20 words difficult for the reader (95% success)*

Instructional level text
* *Challenging but manageable text for the reader, with no more than approximately 1 in 10 words difficult for the reader (90% success)*

Frustration level text
* *Difficult text for the reader, with more than 1 in 10 words difficult for the reader (less than 90% success)*

The text your students practice rereading orally should also be relatively short—probably 50–200 words, depending on the age of the students. You should also use a variety of reading materials, including stories, nonfiction, and poetry. Poetry is especially well suited to fluency practice because poems for children are often short and they contain rhythm, rhyme, and meaning, making practice easy, fun, and rewarding.

How to have your students read aloud repeatedly. There are several ways that your students can practice orally rereading text, including student-adult reading, choral (or unison) reading, tape-assisted reading, partner reading, and readers' theatre.

- ***Student-adult reading.*** In student-adult reading, the student reads one-on-one with an adult. The adult can be you, a parent, a classroom aide, or a tutor. The adult reads the text first, providing the students with a model of fluent reading. Then the student reads the same passage to the adult with the adult providing assistance and encouragement. The student rereads the passage until the reading is quite fluent. This should take approximately three to four rereadings.

- ***Choral reading.*** In choral, or unison, reading, students read along as a group with you (or another fluent adult reader). Of course, to do so, students must be able to see the same text that you are reading. They might follow along as you read from a big book, or they might read from their own copy of the book you are reading. For choral reading, choose a book that is not too long and that you think is at the independent reading level of most students. Patterned or predictable books are particularly useful for choral reading, because their repetitious style invites students to join in. Begin by reading the book aloud as you model fluent reading. Then reread the book and invite students to join in as they recognize the words you are reading. Continue rereading the book, encouraging students to read along as they are able. Students should read the book with you three to five times total (though not necessarily on the same day). At this time, students should be able to read the text independently.

- ***Tape-assisted reading.*** In tape-assisted reading, students read along in their books as they hear a fluent reader read the book on an audiotape. For tape-assisted reading, you need a book at a student's independent reading level and a tape recording of the book read by a fluent reader at about 80–100 words per minute. The tape should not have sound effects or music. For the first reading, the student should follow along with the tape, pointing to each word in her or his book as the reader reads it. Next, the student should try to read aloud along with the tape. Reading along with the tape should continue until the student is able to read the book independently, without the support of the tape.

- ***Partner reading.*** In partner reading, paired students take turns reading aloud to each other. For partner reading, more fluent readers can be paired with less fluent readers. The stronger reader reads a paragraph or page first, providing a model of fluent reading. Then the less fluent reader reads the same text aloud. The stronger student gives help with word recognition and provides feedback and encouragement to the less fluent partner. The less fluent partner rereads the passage until he or she can read it independently. Partner reading need not be done with a more and less fluent reader. In another form of partner reading, children who read at the same level are paired to reread a story that they have received instruction on during a teacher-guided part of the lesson. Two readers of equal ability can practice rereading after hearing the teacher read the passage.

- **Readers' theatre.** In readers' theatre, students rehearse and perform a play for peers or others. They read from scripts that have been derived from books that are rich in dialogue. Students play characters who speak lines or a narrator who shares necessary background information. Readers' theatre provides readers with a legitimate reason to reread text and to practice fluency. Readers' theatre also promotes cooperative interaction with peers and makes the reading task appealing.

ACTIVITIES FOR REPEATED ORAL READING PRACTICE

- **Student-adult reading**—reading one-on-one with an adult who provides a model of fluent reading, helps with word recognition, and provides feedback.
- **Choral reading**—reading aloud simultaneously in a group.
- **Tape-assisted reading**—reading aloud simultaneously or as an echo with an audio-taped model.
- **Partner reading**—reading aloud with a more fluent partner (or with a partner of equal ability) who provides a model of fluent reading, helps with word recognition, and provides feedback.
- **Readers' theatre**—the rehearsing and performing before an audience of a dialogue-rich script derived from a book.

What should I do about silent, independent reading in the classroom?

Reading fluency growth is greatest when students are working directly with you. Therefore, you should use most of your allocated reading instruction time for direct teaching of reading skills and strategies. Although silent, independent reading may be a way to increase fluency and reading achievement, it should not be used in place of direct instruction in reading.

Direct instruction is especially important for readers who are struggling. Readers who have not yet attained fluency are not likely to make effective and efficient use of silent, independent reading time. For these students, independent reading takes time away from needed reading instruction.

Rather than allocating instructional time for independent reading in the classroom, encourage your students to read more outside of school. They can read with an adult or other family member. Or, they can read on their own with books at their independent reading level. Of course, students might also read on their own during independent work time in the classroom—for example, as another small group is receiving reading instruction, or after they have completed one activity and are waiting for a new activity to begin.

PROCEDURE FOR CALCULATING WORDS CORRECT PER MINUTE

One-minute reading: Total words read – errors = words correct per minute

- *Select two or three brief passages from a grade-level basal text or other grade-level material (regardless of students' instructional levels).*
- *Have individual students read each passage aloud for exactly one minute.*
- *Count the total number of words the student read for each passage. Compute the average number of words read per minute.*
- *Count the number of errors the student made on each passage. Compute the average number of errors per minute.*
- *Subtract the average number of errors read per minute from the average total number of words read per minute. The result is the average number of words correct per minute (WCPM).*
- *Repeat the procedure several times during the year. Graphing students' WCPM throughout the year easily captures their reading growth.*
- *Compare the results with published norms or standards to determine whether students are making suitable progress in their fluency. For example, according to one published norm, students should be reading approximately 60 words per minute correctly by the end of first grade, 90–100 words per minute correctly by the end of second grade, and approximately 114 words per minute correctly by the end of third grade.*

When should fluency instruction begin? When should it end?

Fluency instruction is useful when students are not automatic at recognizing the words in their texts. How can you tell when students are not automatic? There is a strong indication that a student needs fluency instruction:

- if you ask the student to read orally from a text that he or she has not practiced, and the student makes more than 10% word recognition errors;
- if the student cannot read orally with expression; or
- if the student's comprehension is poor for the text that she or he reads orally.

Is increasing word recognition skills sufficient for developing fluency?

Isolated word recognition is a necessary but not sufficient condition for fluent reading. Throughout much of the twentieth century, it was widely assumed that fluency was the result of word recognition proficiency. Instruction, therefore, focused primarily on the development of word recognition. In recent years, however, research has shown that fluency is a separate component of reading that can be developed through instruction.

Having students review and rehearse word lists (for example, by using flash cards) may improve their ability to recognize the words in isolation, but this ability may not transfer to words presented in actual texts. Developing reading fluency in texts must be developed systematically.

Should I assess fluency? If so, how?

You should formally and informally assess fluency regularly to ensure that your students are making appropriate progress. The most informal assessment is simply listening to students read aloud and making a judgment about their progress in fluency. You should, however, also include more formal measures of fluency. For example, the student's reading rate should be faster than 90 words a minute, the student should be able to read orally with expression, and the student should be able to comprehend what is read while reading orally.

Probably the easiest way to formally assess fluency is to take timed samples of students' reading and to compare their performance (number of words read correctly per minute) with published oral reading fluency norms or standards.

Monitoring your students' progress in reading fluency will help you determine the effectiveness of your instruction and set instructional goals. Also, seeing their fluency growth reflected in the graphs you keep can motivate students.

Other procedures that have been used for measuring fluency include Informal Reading Inventories (IRIs), miscue analysis, and running records. The purpose of these procedures, however, is to identify the kinds of word recognition problems students may have, not to measure fluency. Also, these procedures are quite time-consuming. Simpler measures of speed and accuracy, such as calculating words read correctly per minute, are more appropriate for monitoring fluency.

SUMMING UP

Fluency is
- the ability to read a text accurately and quickly.

Fluency is important because
- it frees students to understand what they read.

Reading fluency can be developed
- by modeling fluent reading by having students engage in repeated oral reading.

Monitoring student progress in reading fluency
- is useful in evaluating instruction, and setting instructional goals can be motivating to students.

4 Vocabulary Instruction

Vocabulary refers to the words we must know to communicate effectively. In general, it can be described as oral vocabulary or reading vocabulary. Oral vocabulary refers to words that we use in speaking or recognize in listening. Reading vocabulary refers to words we recognize or use in print.

Vocabulary plays an important part in learning to read. As beginning readers, children use the words they have heard to make sense of the words they see in print. Consider, for example, what happens when a beginning reader comes to the word *dig* in a book. As she begins to figure out the sounds represented by the letters *d*, *i*, *g*, the reader recognizes that the sounds make up a very familiar word that she has heard and said many times. Beginning readers have a much more difficult time reading words that are not already part of their oral vocabulary.

Vocabulary also is very important to reading comprehension. Readers cannot understand what they are reading without knowing what most of the words mean. As children learn to read more advanced texts, they must learn the meaning of new words that are not part of their oral vocabulary.

TYPES OF VOCABULARY

Researchers often refer to four types of vocabulary

- **listening vocabulary**—*the words we need to know to understand what we hear.*
- **speaking vocabulary**—*the words we use when we speak.*
- **reading vocabulary**—*the words we need to know to understand what we read.*
- **writing vocabulary**—*the words we use in writing.*

What does scientifically based research tell us about vocabulary instruction?

The scientific research on vocabulary instruction reveals that (1) most vocabulary is learned indirectly and (2) some vocabulary must be taught directly. The following conclusions about indirect vocabulary learning and direct vocabulary instruction are of particular interest and value to classroom teachers:

Children learn the meanings of most words indirectly, through everyday experiences with oral and written language.

Children learn word meanings indirectly in three ways:

- ***They engage daily in oral language.*** Young children learn word meanings through conversations with other people, especially adults. As they engage in these conversations, children often hear adults repeat words several times. They also may hear adults use new and interesting words. The more oral language experiences children have, the more word meanings they learn.

- ***They listen to adults read to them.*** Children learn word meanings from listening to adults read to them. Reading aloud is particularly helpful when the reader pauses during reading to define an unfamiliar word and, after reading, engages the child in a conversation about the book. Conversations about books help children to learn new words and concepts and to relate them to their prior knowledge and experience.

- ***They read extensively on their own.*** Children learn many new words by reading extensively on their own. The more children read on their own, the more words they encounter and the more word meanings they learn.

INDIRECT VOCABULARY LEARNING	DIRECT VOCABULARY LEARNING
Students learn vocabulary indirectly when they hear and see words used in many different contexts—for example, through conversations with adults, through being read to, and through reading extensively on their own.	***Specific Word Instruction*** ***Word Learning Instruction*** *Students learn vocabulary directly when they are explicitly taught both individual words and word-learning strategies. Direct vocabulary instruction aids reading comprehension.*

Although a great deal of vocabulary is learned indirectly, some vocabulary should be taught directly.

Direct instruction helps students learn difficult words, such as words that represent complex concepts that are not part of the students' everyday experiences. Direct instruction of vocabulary relevant to a given text leads to better reading comprehension.

Direct instruction includes:

- providing students with specific word instruction; and
- teaching students word-learning strategies.

Specific word instruction

Specific word instruction, or teaching individual words, can deepen students' knowledge of word meanings. In-depth knowledge of word meanings can help students understand what they are hearing or reading. It also can help them use words accurately in speaking and writing.

In particular:

- **Teaching specific words before reading helps both vocabulary learning and reading comprehension.** Before students read a text, it is helpful to teach them specific words they will see in the text. Teaching important vocabulary before reading can help students both learn new words and comprehend the text.

- **Extended instruction that promotes active engagement with vocabulary improves word learning.** Children learn words best when they are provided with instruction over an extended period of time and when that instruction has them work actively with the words. The more students use new words and the more they use them in different contexts, the more likely they are to learn the words.

- **Repeated exposure to vocabulary in many contexts aids word learning.** Students learn new words better when they encounter them often and in various contexts. The more children see, hear, and work with specific words, the better they seem to learn them. When teachers provide extended instruction that promotes active engagement, they give students repeated exposure to new words. When the students read those same words in their texts, they increase their exposure to the new words.

AN EXAMPLE OF CLASSROOM INSTRUCTION

Teaching specific words

A teacher plans to have his third-grade class read the novel Stone Fox, *by John Reynolds Gardiner. In this novel, a young boy enters a dogsled race in hopes of winning prize money to pay the* **taxes** *on his grandfather's farm. The teacher knows that understanding the concept of taxes is important to understanding the novel's plot. Therefore, before his students begin reading the novel, the teacher may do several things to make sure that they understand what the concept means and why it is important to the story. For example, the teacher may:*

- *engage students in a discussion of the concept of* **taxes**; *and/or*
- *read a sentence from the book that contains the word* **taxes** *and ask students to use context and their prior knowledge to try to figure out what it means.*

To solidify their understanding of the word, the teacher might ask students to use **taxes** *in their own sentences.*

Word-learning strategies

Of course, it is not possible for teachers to provide specific instruction for all the words their students do not know. Therefore, students also need to be able to determine the meaning of words that are new to them but not taught directly to them. They need to develop effective word-learning strategies, such as:

- how to use dictionaries and other reference aids to learn word meanings and to deepen knowledge of word meanings;
- how to use information about word parts to figure out the meanings of words in text; and
- how to use context clues to determine word meanings.

Using dictionaries and other reference aids. Students must learn how to use dictionaries, glossaries, and thesauruses to help broaden and deepen their knowledge of words, even though these resources can be difficult to use. The most helpful dictionaries include sentences providing clear examples of word meanings in context.

AN EXAMPLE OF CLASSROOM INSTRUCTION

Extended and active engagement with vocabulary

*A first-grade teacher wants to help her students understand the concept of **jobs**, which is part of her social studies curriculum. Over a period of time, the teacher engages students in exercises in which they work repeatedly with the meaning of the concept of **jobs**. The students have many opportunities to see and actively use the word in various contexts that reinforce its meaning.*

The teacher begins by asking the students what they already know about jobs and by having them give examples of jobs their parents have. The class might have a discussion about the jobs of different people who work at the school.

*The teacher then reads the class a simple book about jobs. The book introduces the idea that different jobs help people meet their needs, and that jobs either provide goods or services. The book does not use the words **goods** and **services**, rather it uses the verbs **makes** and **helps**.*

*The teacher then asks the students to make up sentences describing their parents' jobs by using the verbs **makes** and **helps** (e.g., "My mother is a doctor. She helps sick people get well.")*

Next, the teacher asks students to brainstorm other jobs. Together, they decide whether the jobs are "making jobs" or "helping jobs." The job names are placed under the appropriate headings on a bulletin board. They might also suggest jobs that do not fit neatly into either category.

The teacher might then ask the students to share whether they think they would like to have a making or a helping job when they grow up.

The teacher next asks the students to talk with their parents about jobs. She tells them to try to bring to class two new examples of jobs—one making job and one helping job.

As the students come across different jobs throughout the year (for example, through reading books, on field trips, through classroom guests), they can add the jobs to the appropriate categories on the bulletin board.

Repeated exposure to words

*A second-grade class is reading a biography of Benjamin Franklin. The biography discusses Franklin's important role as a scientist. The teacher wants to make sure that her students understand the meaning of the words **science** and **scientist**, both because the words are important to understanding the biography and because they are obviously very useful words to know in school and in everyday life.*

*At every opportunity, therefore, the teacher draws her students' attention to the words. She points out the words **scientist** and **science** in textbooks and reading selections, particularly in her science curriculum. She has students use the words in their own writing, especially during science instruction.*

She also asks them to listen for and find in print the words as they are used outside of the classroom—in newspapers, magazines, at museums, in television shows or movies, or the Internet.

Then, as they read the biography, she discusses with students in what ways Benjamin Franklin was a scientist and what science meant in his time.

Using word parts. Knowing some common prefixes and suffixes (affixes), base words, and root words can help students learn the meanings of many new words. For example, if students learn just the four most common prefixes in English (**un-, re-, in-, dis-**), they will have important clues about the meaning of about two thirds of all English words that have prefixes. Prefixes are relatively easy to learn because they have clear meanings (for example, **un-** means "not" and **re-** means "again"); they are usually spelled the same way from word to word; and, of course, they always occur at the beginnings of words.

Learning suffixes can be more challenging than learning prefixes. This is because some suffixes have more abstract meanings than do prefixes. For example, learning that the suffix **-ness** means "the state or quality of" might not help students figure out the meaning of **kindness**. Other suffixes, however, are more helpful, for example, **-less**, which means "without" (**hopeless, thoughtless**); and **-ful**, which means "full of" (**hopeful, thoughtful**).

Latin and Greek word roots are found commonly in content-area school subjects, especially in the subjects of science and social studies. As a result, Latin and Greek word parts form a large proportion of the new vocabulary that students encounter in their content-area textbooks. Teachers should teach the word roots as they occur in the texts students read. Furthermore, teachers should teach primarily those root words that students are likely to see often.

Using dictionaries and other reference aids

As his class reads a text, a second-grade teacher discovers that many of his students do not know the meaning of the word **board**, as in the sentence, "The children were waiting to board the buses." The teacher demonstrates how to find **board** in the classroom dictionary, showing students that there are four different definitions for the word. He reads the definitions one at a time, and the class discusses whether each definition would fit the context of the sentence. The students easily eliminate the inappropriate definitions of **board** and settle on the definition, "to get on a train, an airplane, a bus, or a ship."

The teacher next has students substitute the most likely definition for **board** in the original sentence to verify that it is "The children were waiting to get on the buses" that makes the best sense.

WORD PARTS

Word parts

Word parts include affixes (prefixes and suffixes), base words, and word roots.

Affixes are word parts that are "fixed to" either the beginnings of words (prefixes) or the ending of words (suffixes). The word **disrespectful** has two affixes, a prefix (**dis-**) and a suffix (**-ful**).

Base words are words from which many other words are formed.

For example, many words can be formed from the base word **migrate**: **migration, migrant, immigration, immigrant, migrating, migratory**.

Word roots are the words from other languages that are the origin of many English words. About 60% of all English words have Latin or Greek origins.

Using word parts

- A second-grade teacher wants to teach her students how to use the base word **play** as a way to help them think about the meanings of new words they will encounter in reading. To begin, she has students brainstorm all the words or phrases they can think of that are related to **play**. The teacher records their suggestions: **player, playful, playpen, ballplayer**, and **playing field**. Then she has the class discuss the meaning of each of their proposed words and how it relates to **play**.

- A third-grade teacher identifies the base word **note**. He then sets up a "word wall," and writes the word **note** at the top of the wall. As his students read, the teacher has them look for words that are related to **note** and add them to the wall. Throughout their reading, they gradually add to the wall the words **notebook, notation, noteworthy**, and **notable**.

Using context clues. Context clues are hints about the meaning of an unknown word that are provided in the words, phrases, and sentences that surround the word. Context clues include definitions, restatements, examples, or descriptions. Because students learn most word meanings indirectly, or from context, it is important that they learn to use context clues effectively.

Not all contexts are helpful, however. Some contexts give little information about a word's meaning. An example of an unhelpful context is the sentence, "We heard the back door open, and then recognized the buoyant footsteps of Uncle Larry." A number of possible meanings of **buoyant** could fit this context, including heavy, lively, noisy, familiar, dragging, plodding, and so on. Instruction in using context clues as a word-learning strategy should include the idea that some contexts are more helpful than others.

AN EXAMPLE OF CLASSROOM INSTRUCTION

Using context clues
In a third-grade class, the teacher models how to use context clues to determine word meanings as follows:
Student *(reading the text): When the cat pounced on the dog, the dog jumped up, yelping, and knocked over a lamp, which crashed to the floor. The animals ran past Tonia, tripping her. She fell to the floor and began sobbing. Tonia's brother Felix yelled at the animals to stop. As the noise and confusion mounted, Mother hollered upstairs, "What's all that commotion?"*
Teacher: *The context of the paragraph helps us determine what* **commotion** *means. There's yelping and crashing, sobbing, and yelling. And then the last sentence says, "as the noise and confusion mounted." The author's use of the words* **noise** *and* **confusion** *gives us a very strong clue as to what* **commotion** *means. In fact, the author is really giving us a definition there, because* **commotion** *means something that's noisy and confusing—a disturbance. Mother was right; there was definitely a commotion!*

Questions you may have about vocabulary instruction

How can I help my students learn words indirectly?

You can encourage indirect learning of vocabulary in two main ways. First, read aloud to your students, no matter what grade you teach. Students of all ages can learn words from hearing texts of various kinds read to them. Reading aloud works best when you discuss the selection before, during, and after you read. Talk with students about new vocabulary and concepts and help them relate the words to their prior knowledge and experiences.

The second way to promote indirect learning of vocabulary is to encourage students to read extensively on their own. Rather than allocating instructional time for independent reading in the classroom, however, encourage your students to read more outside of school. Of course, your students also can read on their own during independent work time in the classroom—for example, while you teach another small group or after students have completed one activity and are waiting for a new activity to begin.

What words should I teach?

You won't be able to directly teach your students all the words in a text that they might not already know. In fact, there are several reasons why you **should not** directly teach all unknown words.

- The text may have a great many words that are unknown to students—too many for direct instruction.
- Direct vocabulary instruction can take a lot of class time—time that you might better spend having your students read.
- Your students can understand most texts without knowing the meaning of every word in the text.
- Your students need opportunities to use word-learning strategies to learn on their own the meanings of unknown words.

You will probably to be able to teach thoroughly only a few new words (perhaps eight or ten) per week, so you need to choose the words you teach carefully. Focus on teaching three types of words:

- ***Important words.*** When you teach words before students read a text, directly teach those words that are important for understanding a concept or the text. Your students might not know several other words in the selection, but you will not have time to teach them all. Of course, you should prepare your students to use word-learning strategies to figure out the meanings of other words in the text.

- *Useful words.* Teach words that students are likely to see and use again and again. For example, it is probably more useful for students to learn the word **fragment** than the word **fractal**; likewise, the word **revolve** is more useful than the word **gyrate**.
- *Difficult words.* Provide some instruction for words that are particularly difficult for your students.

Words with multiple meanings are particularly challenging for students. Students may have a hard time understanding that words with the same spelling and/or pronunciation can have different meanings, depending on their context. Looking up words with multiple meanings in the dictionary can cause confusion for students. They see a number of different definitions listed, and they often have a difficult time deciding which definition fits the context. You will have to help students determine which definition they should choose.

Idiomatic expressions also can be difficult for students, especially for students who are English language learners. Because idiomatic expressions do not mean what the individual words usually mean, you often will need to explain to students expressions such as "hard hearted," "a chip off the old block," "drawing a blank," or "get the picture."

MULTIPLE-MEANING WORDS THAT CAN BE DIFFICULT FOR STUDENTS	EXAMPLES
Words that are spelled the same but are pronounced differently	*sow* (a female pig); *sow* (to plant seeds) *bow* (a knot with loops); *bow* (the front of a ship)
Words that are spelled and pronounced the same, but have different meanings	*mail* (letters, cards, and packages); *mail* (a type of armor) *ray* (a narrow beam of light); *ray* (a type of fish); *ray* (part of a line)

How well do my students need to "know" vocabulary words?

Students do not either know or not know words. Rather, they know words to varying degrees. They may never have seen or heard a word before. They may have heard or seen it, but have only a vague idea of what it means. Or they may be very familiar with the meaning of a word and be able to use it accurately in their own speech and writing. These three levels of word knowledge are called **unknown**, **acquainted**, and **established**.

As they read, students can usually get by with some words at the unknown or acquainted levels. If students are to understand the text fully, however, they need to have an established level of knowledge for most of the words that they read.

LEVEL OF WORD KNOWLEDGE	DEFINITION
Unknown	The word is completely unfamiliar and its meaning is unknown.
Acquainted	The word is somewhat familiar; the student has some idea of its basic meaning.
Established	The word is very familiar; the student can immediately recognize its meaning and use the word correctly.

Are there different types of word learning?
If so, are some types of learning more difficult than others?

Four different kinds of word learning have been identified:

- learning a new meaning for a known word;
- learning the meaning for a new word representing a known concept;
- learning the meaning of a new word representing an unknown concept; and
- clarifying and enriching the meaning of a known word.

TYPE OF WORD LEARNING	EXPLANATION
Learning a new meaning for a known word	The student has the word in her oral or reading vocabulary, but she is learning a new meaning for it. For example, the student knows what a branch is and is learning in social studies about both branches of rivers and branches of government.
Learning the meaning for a new word representing a known concept	The student is familiar with the concept but he does not know the particular word for that concept. For example, the student has had a lot of experience with baseballs and globes, but does not know that they are examples of spheres.
Learning the meaning of a new word representing an unknown concept	The student is not familiar with either the concept or the word that represents that concept, and she must learn both. For example, the student may not be familiar with either the process or the word photosynthesis.
Clarifying and enriching the meaning of a known word	The student is learning finer, more subtle distinctions, or connotations, in the meaning and usage of words. For example, he is learning the differences between running, jogging, trotting, dashing, and sprinting.

These types vary in difficulty. One of the most common, yet challenging, is the third type: learning the meaning of a new word representing an unknown concept. Much of learning in the content areas involves this type of word learning. As students learn about **deserts**, **hurricanes**, and **immigrants**, they may be learning both new concepts and new words.

Learning words and concepts in science, social studies, and mathematics is even more challenging because each major concept often is associated with many other new concepts. For example, the concept ***deserts*** is often associated with other concepts that may be unfamiliar, such as ***cactus***, ***plateau***, and ***mesa***.

What else can I do to help my students develop vocabulary?

- Another way you can help your students develop vocabulary is to foster word consciousness—an awareness of and interest in words, their meanings, and their power. Word-conscious students know many words and use them well. They enjoy words and are eager to learn new words—and they know how to learn them.

- You can help your students develop word consciousness in several ways. Call their attention to the way authors choose words to convey particular meanings. Encourage students to play with words by engaging in word play, such as puns or palindromes. Help them research a word's origin or history. You can also encourage them to search for examples of a word's usage in their everyday lives.

SUMMING UP

Vocabulary refers to
- the words we must know to communicate effectively.
- **oral** vocabulary refers to words that we use in speaking or recognize in listening.
- **reading** vocabulary refers to words we recognize or use in print.

Vocabulary is important because
- beginning readers use their oral vocabulary to make sense of the words they see in print.
- readers must know what most of the words mean before they can understand what they are reading.

Vocabulary can be developed
- **indirectly,** when students engage daily in oral language, listen to adults read to them, and read extensively on their own.
- **directly,** when students are explicitly taught both individual words and word-learning strategies.

5

Text Comprehension Instruction

Comprehension is the reason for reading. If readers can read the words but do not understand what they are reading, they are not really reading.

As they read, good readers are both purposeful and active.

Good readers are purposeful.

Good readers have a purpose for reading. They may read to find out how to use a food processor, read a guidebook to gather information about national parks, read a textbook to satisfy the requirements of a course, read a magazine for entertainment, or read a classic novel to experience the pleasures of great literature.

Good readers are active.

Good readers think actively as they read. To make sense of what they read, good readers engage in a complicated process. Using their experiences and knowledge of the world, their knowledge of vocabulary and language structure, and their knowledge of reading strategies (or plans), good readers make sense of the text and know how to get the most out of it. They know when they have problems with understanding and how to resolve these problems as they occur.

Research over 30 years has shown that instruction in comprehension can help students understand what they read, remember what they read, and communicate with others about what they read.

What does scientifically based research tell us about effective text comprehension instruction?

The scientific research on text comprehension instruction reveals important information about what students should be taught about text comprehension and how it should be taught. The following key findings are of particular interest and value to classroom teachers.

Text comprehension can be improved by instruction that helps readers use specific comprehension strategies.

Comprehension strategies are conscious plans—sets of steps that good readers use to make sense of text. Comprehension strategy instruction helps students become purposeful, active readers who are in control of their own reading comprehension.

The following six strategies appear to have a firm scientific basis for improving text comprehension.

Monitoring comprehension.

Students who are good at monitoring their comprehension know when they understand what they read and when they do not. They have strategies to "fix up" problems in their understanding as the problems arise. Research shows that instruction, even in the early grades, can help students become better at monitoring their comprehension.

Comprehension monitoring instruction teaches students to:

- be aware of what they **do** understand,
- identify what they **do not** understand, and
- use appropriate "fix-up" strategies to resolve problems in comprehension.

Students may use several comprehension monitoring strategies.

- Identify where the difficulty occurs **("I don't understand the second paragraph on page 76.")**.
- Identify what the difficulty is **("I don't get what the author means when she says, 'Arriving in America was a milestone in my grandmother's life.'")**.
- Restate the difficult sentence or passage in their own words **("Oh, so the author means that coming to America was a very important event in her grandmother's life.")**.
- Look back through the text **("The author talked about Mr. McBride in Chapter 2, but I don't remember much about him. Maybe if I reread that chapter, I can figure out why he's acting this way now.")**.
- Look forward in the text for information that might help them to resolve the difficulty. **("The text says, 'The groundwater may form a stream or pond or create a wetland. People can also bring groundwater to the surface.' Hmm, I don't understand how people can do that . . . Oh, the next section is called 'Wells.' I'll read this section to see if it tells how they do it.")**.

METACOGNITION

Metacognition can be defined as "thinking about thinking." Good readers use metacognitive strategies to think about and have control over their reading.

Before reading, they might clarify their purpose for reading and preview the text. During reading, they might monitor their understanding, adjusting their reading speed to fit the difficulty of the text, and "fixing up" any comprehension problems they have. After reading, they check their understanding of what they read.

Comprehension monitoring, a critical part of metacognition, has received a great deal of attention in the reading research.

Using graphic and semantic organizers.

Graphic organizers illustrate concepts and interrelationships among concepts in a text, using diagrams or other pictorial devices. Graphic organizers are known by different names, such as maps, webs, graphs, charts, frames, or clusters. Semantic organizers (also called semantic maps or semantic webs) are graphic organizers that look somewhat like a spider web. In a semantic organizer, lines connect a central concept to a variety of related ideas and events.

Regardless of the label, graphic organizers can help readers focus on concepts and how they are related to other concepts. Graphic organizers help students read to learn from informational text in the content areas, such as science and social studies textbooks and trade books. Used with informational text, graphic organizers can help students see how concepts fit common text structures. Graphic organizers are also used with narrative text, or stories, as story maps.

Graphic organizers can:

- help students focus on text structure as they read;
- provide students with tools they can use to examine and visually represent relationships in a text; and
- help students write well-organized summaries of a text.

Answering questions.

Teachers have long used questions to guide and monitor students' learning. Research shows that teacher questioning strongly supports and advances students' learning from reading. Questions appear to be effective for improving learning from reading because they:

- give students a purpose for reading;
- focus students' attention on what they are to learn;
- help students to think actively as they read;
- encourage students to monitor their comprehension; and
- help students to review content and relate what they have learned to what they already know.

Question-answering instruction encourages students to learn to answer questions better and, therefore, to learn more as they read. One type of question-answering instruction simply teaches students to look back in the text to find answers to questions that they cannot answer after the initial reading. Another type helps students understand question-answer relationships—the relationships between questions and where the answers to those questions are found. In this instruction, readers learn to answer questions that require an understanding of information that is:

- text explicit (stated explicitly in a single sentence);
- text implicit (implied by information presented in two or more sentences); or
- scriptal (not found in the text at all, but part of the reader's prior knowledge or experience).

Generating questions.

Teaching students to ask their own questions improves their active processing of text and their comprehension. By generating questions, students become aware of whether they can answer the questions and if they understand what they are reading. Students learn to ask themselves questions that require them to integrate information from different segments of text. For example, students can be taught to ask main idea questions that relate to important information in a text.

EXAMPLES OF QUESTION-ANSWER RELATIONSHIPS

Text: (from The Skirt, by Gary Soto)

After stepping off the bus, Miata Ramirez turned around and gasped, "Ay!" The school bus lurched, coughed a puff of stinky exhaust, and made a wide turn at the corner. The driver strained as he worked the steering wheel like the horns of a bull.

Miata yelled for the driver to stop. She started running after the bus. Her hair whipped against her shoulders. A large book bag tugged at her arm with each running step, and bead earrings jingled as they banged against her neck.

"My skirt!" she cried loudly. "Stop!"

Question: Did Miata try to get the driver to stop?

Answer: Yes.

Question-Answer Relationship (Text explicit, because the information is given in one sentence): "Miata yelled for the driver to stop."

Question: Why did Miata want the driver to stop?

Answer: She suddenly remembered that she had left a skirt on the bus.

Question-Answer Relationship (Text implicit, because the information must be inferred from different parts of the text): Miata is crying "My skirt!" as she is trying to get the driver to stop.

Question: Was the skirt important to Miata?

Answer: Yes.

Question-Answer Relationship (Scriptal, because the information is not contained in the text, but must be drawn from the reader's prior knowledge): She probably would not have tried so hard to get the driver to stop if the skirt were not important to her.

Recognizing story structure.

Story structure refers to the way the content and events of a story are organized into a plot. Students who can recognize story structure have greater appreciation, understanding, and memory for stories. In story structure instruction, students learn to identify the categories of content (setting, initiating events, internal reactions, goals, attempts, and outcomes) and how this content is organized into a plot. Often, students learn to recognize story structure through the use of story maps. Story maps, a type of graphic organizer, show the sequence of events in simple stories. Instruction in the content and organization of stories improves students' comprehension and memory of stories.

Summarizing.

A summary is a synthesis of the important ideas in a text. Summarizing requires students to determine what is important in what they are reading, to condense this information, and to put it into their own words. Instruction in summarizing helps students:

- identify or generate main ideas;
- connect the main or central ideas;
- eliminate redundant and unnecessary information; and
- remember what they read.

Students can be taught to use comprehension strategies.

In addition to identifying which comprehension strategies are effective, scientific research provides guidelines for how to teach comprehension strategies.

Effective comprehension strategy instruction is explicit, or direct.

Research shows that explicit teaching techniques are particularly effective for comprehension strategy instruction. In explicit instruction, teachers tell readers why and when they should use strategies, what strategies to use, and how to apply them. The steps of explicit instruction typically include direct explanation, teacher modeling ("thinking aloud"), guided practice, and application.

- ***Direct explanation.*** The teacher explains to students why the strategy helps comprehension and when to apply the strategy.
- ***Modeling.*** The teacher models, or demonstrates, how to apply the strategy, usually by "thinking aloud" while reading the text that the students are using.
- ***Guided practice.*** The teacher guides and assists students as they learn how and when to apply the strategy.
- ***Application.*** The teacher helps students practice the strategy until they can apply it independently.

Effective comprehension strategy instruction can be accomplished through cooperative learning.

Cooperative learning (and the closely related concept, collaborative learning) involves students working together as partners or in small groups on clearly defined tasks. Cooperative learning instruction has been used successfully to teach comprehension strategies in content-area subjects. Students work together to understand content-area texts, helping each other learn and apply comprehension strategies. Teachers help students learn to work in groups. Teachers also provide demonstrations of the comprehension strategies and monitor the progress of students.

Effective instruction helps readers use comprehension strategies flexibly and in combination.

Although it can be helpful to provide students with instruction in individual comprehension strategies, good readers must be able to coordinate and adjust several strategies to assist comprehension.

Multiple-strategy instruction teaches students how to use strategies flexibly as they are needed to assist their comprehension. In a well-known example of multiple-strategy instruction called "reciprocal teaching," the teacher and students work together so that the students learn four comprehension strategies:

- asking questions about the text they are reading;
- summarizing parts of the text;
- clarifying words and sentences they don't understand; and
- predicting what might occur next in the text.

Teachers and students use these four strategies flexibly as they are needed in reading literature and informational texts.

Questions you may have about text comprehension instruction

Is enough known about comprehension strategy instruction for me to implement it in my classroom?

Yes. Scientific study of text comprehension instruction over the past 30 years has suggested instructional approaches that are ready to be implemented in classrooms.

When should text comprehension instruction begin?

Even teachers in the primary grades can begin to build the foundation for reading comprehension. Reading is a complex process that develops over time. Although the basics of reading—word recognition and fluency—can be learned in a few years, reading to learn subject matter does not occur automatically once students have "learned to read." Teachers should emphasize text comprehension from the beginning, rather than waiting until students have mastered "the basics" of reading. Instruction at all grade levels can benefit from showing students how reading is a process of making sense out of text, or constructing meaning. Beginning readers, as well as more advanced readers, must understand that the ultimate goal of reading is comprehension.

You can highlight meaning in all interactions with text. Talk about the content, whether reading aloud to students or guiding them in reading on their own. Model, or "think aloud," about your own thinking and understanding as you read. Lead students in a discussion about the meaning of what they are reading. Help students relate the content to their experience and to other texts they have read. Encourage students to ask questions about the text.

Has research identified comprehension strategies other than the six described here?

The six strategies described have received the strongest scientific support. The following strategies, however, have received some support from research. You may want to consider them for use in your classroom.

- ***Making use of prior knowledge.*** Good readers draw on prior knowledge and experience to help them understand what they are reading. You can help your students make use of their prior knowledge to improve their comprehension. Before your students read, preview the text with them. As part of previewing, ask the students what they already know about the content of the selection (for example, the topic, the concept, or the time period). Ask them what they know about the author and what text structure he or she is likely to use. Discuss the important vocabulary used in the text. Show students some pictures or diagrams to prepare them for what they are about to read.

- ***Using mental imagery.*** Good readers often form mental pictures, or images, as they read. Readers (especially younger readers) who visualize during reading understand and remember what they read better than readers who do not visualize. Help your students learn to form visual images of what they are reading. For example, urge them to picture a setting, character, or event described in the text.

Which comprehension strategies should be taught?
When should they be taught?

Comprehension strategies are not ends in themselves; they are means of helping your students understand what they are reading. Help your students learn to use comprehension strategies in natural learning situations—for example, as they read in the content areas. If your students are struggling to identify and remember the main points in a chapter they are reading in their social studies textbook, teach them how to write summaries. Or, if students have read a chapter in their science textbook but are unable to answer questions about the chapter, teach them question-answering strategies. When your students find that using comprehension strategies can help them to learn, they are more likely to be motivated and involved actively in learning.

Keep in mind that not all comprehension strategies work for all types of text. Obviously, you can only teach story structure when students are reading stories, not informational text or poetry.

Text comprehension is important because
- comprehension is the reason for reading.

Text comprehension is
- purposeful.
- active.

Text comprehension can be developed
- by teaching comprehension strategies.

Text comprehension strategies can be taught
- through explicit instruction.
- through cooperative learning.
- by helping readers use strategies flexibly and in combination.

For additional copies of this document, please contact:

National Institute for Literacy at ED Pubs
PO Box 1398
Jessup, MD 20794-1398
Phone 1-800-228-8813 Fax 301-430-1244
edpubs@inet.ed.gov.

To download the document, go to the National Institute for Literacy website at www.nifl.gov. The findings described in this document were drawn from the report of the *National Reading Panel, Teaching Children to Read: An Evidence-Based Assessment of the Scientific Research Literature on Reading and Its Implications for Reading Instruction—Reports of the Subgroups.* A complete copy of the NRP report can be read, downloaded, or ordered at no cost from the NRP website at www.nationalreadingpanel.org.

Members of the National Reading Panel

Donald N. Langenberg, Ph.D., Chair
Gloria Correro, Ed.D.
Linnea Ehri, Ph.D.
Gwenette Ferguson, M.Ed.
Norma Garza, C.P.A.
Michael L. Kamil, Ph.D.
Cora Bagley Marrett, Ph.D.
S.J. Samuels, Ed.D.
Timothy Shanahan, Ph.D.
Sally E. Shaywitz, M.D.
Thomas Trabasso, Ph.D.
Joanna Williams, Ph.D.
Dale Willows, Ph.D.
Joanne Yatvin, Ph.D.

1

An Introduction to Systematic, Explicit Reading Instruction

Objectives

After reading this chapter, you will be able to:

1. State the prevalence and characteristics of students who are at risk for reading problems and which students are likely to struggle while learning to read.

2. Identify and describe five key skill areas that should comprise a reading curriculum for students who are at risk.

3. Describe the rationale for using a prevention-based multi-tier or Response to Intervention (RTI) model of reading.

4. Describe the role of assessments in a multi-tier or RTI model of reading.

5. Identify and describe ways to enhance reading instruction for students who are at risk by making it more explicit and systematic.

Sitting in the teachers' lounge, the reading coach, Mrs. Gowdy, listened to the staff discuss the new kindergartener, Bryan. *"Why didn't they just start him out in the special education program? He's going to be there by second grade anyway."* *"Our test scores are low enough anyway, and I can't imagine Bryan ever reading."* The discouraged, pessimistic teachers sitting around the table, worked in a high-poverty school tagged by the state as "failing" because so many children could not read. Over the years, the teachers had without success implemented the latest fads in reading and felt that many of the students in their school were incapable of working at grade level. Past experience led them to believe that they would be unsuccessful with a student like Bryan who took medication for attention deficit disorder resulting from Tourette's syndrome, whose lead levels were "off the charts" when he was a toddler, and whose drug-addicted mother was so negligent she lost custody. Mrs. Gowdy barely listened to the teachers' conversation because she was busy preparing the beginning-of-the-year screening tests that signaled the start of the school's new multi-tier reading program for which staff had trained that summer.

That fall, when Bryan's kindergarten teacher gave him the universal screening tests in reading, he was unable to say the sounds of any letters, blend spoken sounds into words, or name letters of the alphabet. The tests indicated that Bryan needed intensive help. By midyear kindergarten, he was working with a small group of students in a Tier 3 intensive research-based reading curriculum taught by one of the Title 1 teachers. Of all the kindergarten Tier 3 groups, his was progressing the slowest; the weekly testing that his teacher did

to monitor progress showed only small gains. Bryan's teacher referred him for special education services, but his parents did not want him tested. Mrs. Gowdy observed his instruction
and was reassured that the intensive Tier 3 reading instruction was meeting his needs.
Bryan's end-of-the-year benchmark testing showed that he had learned the sounds of only
eight letters but could blend them into words.

The pessimistic lunchtime conversations in the teachers' lounge didn't end when Bryan
started first grade, since his September testing confirmed the teachers' beliefs and showed
that the same Tier 3 group was still appropriate for him. His first-grade Tier 3 teacher was a
skilled paraprofessional supervised by the special education teacher. Using a scripted reading
program, the paraprofessional was highly motivating; she taught energetically and enthusiastically and helped the students master the reading material by providing repeated practice
on new skills. By midyear first grade, Mrs. Gowdy was elated to learn that Bryan was racing
ahead of the other students and should be moved up to a faster-moving Tier 3 group. With
the multi-tier reading model, group placement decisions like this had to be supported with testing data, so Mrs. Gowdy checked Bryan's weekly progress-monitoring tests and noted this
same growth. By the end of first grade, Bryan was reading short three-letter words and
could do all of the activities requiring him to manipulate sounds. During a team meeting,
Mrs. Gowdy and other teachers remarked that without the ongoing testing, they probably
would not have thought to move Bryan to the higher group.

That summer, Bryan went to summer school and continued in the intensive Tier 3
scripted-reading curriculum. This year the "buzz" in the teachers' lounge was about the
growth Bryan had made. His tests showed that he was still behind, but if he continued to
make these gains, he would finish second grade at grade level. Sure enough, Bryan continued
to respond to instruction and, to the staff's surprise, by the middle of the year he tested at
grade level. The slower pace and extra practice in the intensive curriculum had finally made a
significant difference. Because the multi-tier reading model was still relatively new to the
staff, they were worried that moving Bryan up to Tier 2 might set him back. Mrs. Gowdy reassured the team that when test scores indicate a child needs less support, he should be successful in grade-level reading curriculum. Besides, now that he was in Tier 2, Bryan would still
get 30 minutes of tutoring support each day, reviewing what he had learned in the larger
second-grade class.

At the end of second grade, when the students had been tested in reading, Mrs. Gowdy
was pleased to announce to the team that Bryan had finished at the top of his class, scoring higher than any other second grader. He no longer needed the 30 minutes of Tier 2 tutoring and would start third grade in Tier 1 with no extra reading support. That day in the
teachers' lounge, one of the staff said, "*You know, I've learned that if Bryan could reach
grade level, any student entering this school can.*" Another teacher remarked, "*We have to
stop making these assumptions about students and make sure that we teach reading to all
of them as if they can come as far as Bryan.*" Mrs. Gowdy reflected on how staff conversations about students were more optimistic these days. Teachers felt empowered with the
tools and structure needed to increase reading achievement. The staff anticipated that state
test scores would increase as they had the previous year and that Bryan's response to instruction was an example of why the number of students identified with learning disabilities was decreasing in their school.

*Why do you think many of the teachers initially thought Bryan should be in special educa-
tion? What factors do you think were responsible for his progress?*

> *"Some people there are who, being grown, forget the horrible task of learning to
> read. It is perhaps the greatest single effort that the human undertakes, and he
> must do it as a child."*
>
> John Steinbeck (1976)

No other skill learned by children is more important than reading, described as the gateway to all other achievement by the American Federation of Teachers (2007). Yet, despite its critical importance for success in our society, millions of children in the United States are failing to learn to read; in fact, many of them attend schools like the one in the chapter-opening vignette. The 2007 National Assessment of Educational Progress (NAEP) report indicated that 33% of fourth graders and 26% of eighth graders were below the basic level in reading, unable to demonstrate even partial mastery of fundamental knowledge and skills. Only 31% of eighth-grade students in the United States scored at or above the proficient level, which represents grade-level expectations. Rates of failure in urban areas and among Black and Hispanic children are even higher (Lee, Grigg, & Donahue, 2007). Reading problems do not just reside among schoolchildren but pervade our entire society. Experts estimate that more than 90 million adults lack a foundation of basic literacy skills necessary to function in society, losing over 200 billion dollars a year in income (Whitehurst, 2003). Given these statistics, it is not surprising to hear the current spate of literacy problems referred to as a national health problem (Lyon, 1998).

In response to public concerns about unacceptably high rates of illiteracy and demands for increased accountability, the U.S. Congress passed the No Child Left Behind (NCLB) Act in 2001. A central provision of this act was the mandate that all of our nation's children be reading at grade level by the school year 2013–2014. While the goals of NCLB are laudable, this bold legislation has rightfully raised many questions among teachers trying to meet those goals. For example, which children have more trouble learning to read and why? How can we identify them? Are there effective methods available to teach these children to read? When is the most opportune time to teach children to read? Do all children learn to read the same way? Can we really teach all children to read? Teachers need practical answers to these and other questions if they are to make a legitimate attempt to teach all children to read.

Explanations about why large percentages of students do not attain minimum literacy levels echo the reasons that students are at risk in the first place:

* These students were raised in poverty.
* Their parents never read to them as children.
* These students have learning disabilities.
* English is not their first language.
* These students were premature babies.

Although educators agree that students who come to school with some or all of these factors present greater challenges, effective reading teachers believe that there are no excuses. These teachers can and will teach every student to read. Yes, John's mother took cocaine before he was born, but he will learn to read. Yes, Marissa has an exceptionally difficult time hearing the individual sounds in words, but she will learn to read. Yes, Shyron's mother has been married three times and amid a blended family of eight kids, he's lost in the shuffle. But he will learn to read. This tenacious attitude is necessary for teachers who get all or most of their students who are at risk to read at grade level.

A tenacious attitude alone isn't sufficient for success. Because of the greater challenges in teaching students who are at risk to read, teachers need effective teaching techniques and curriculum that have a proven track record of success with these students. Students who are at risk for reading failure require more carefully coordinated curriculum and skill instruction than do other students. Fortunately for today's teachers, the reports of the National Reading Panel (NRP, 2000) and the National Early Literacy Panel (NELP, 2008) help translate research into practice. Both panels included leading reading researchers, college professors, teachers, administrators, and parents. The panels spent considerable time identifying those studies that met the highest empirical standards of scientific investigation. Those high-quality studies were used to determine the most effective ways of teaching reading to the greatest number of students and included students who were at risk, had learning disabilities, or were underachieving.

Between 2000 and 2004, we implemented Project PRIDE, a 4-year federal model demonstration project that employed evidence-based practices to prevent reading problems in children who are at risk in three diverse, high-poverty urban schools. Bryan, the subject of the vignette at the beginning of this chapter, was a student in one of our Project PRIDE schools. As the story of Bryan shows, given the right tools and a guiding and sustaining belief in evidence-based reading practices, all children can make progress toward learning to read. The assessment and teaching strategies that were successful in PRIDE are those that occupy the pages of this text.

Who Are the Students at Risk for Reading Problems?

The strategies for teaching early literacy described in this text are based on the idea that when it comes to reading instruction, "one size does not fit all." Figure 1.1 shows how many children in a typical first-grade classroom are likely to struggle while learning to read. These figures are based on research sponsored by the National Institute of Child and Health and Development (NICHD; Lyon, 1998). Looking at the chart, you can see these trends:

* About 5% of students come to school already able to read. These children learn to read naturally without any formal instruction.
* Another 20% to 30% of students learn to read with ease, regardless of the approach to reading instruction used.
* For 20% to 30% of students, learning to read will take hard work, with some extra support needed. If parents work with these students every night, reviewing books read in class and serving as tutors, the students may learn to break the code. Extra practice with a volunteer tutor may be enough to help them break the code.
* An additional 30% of students will only learn to read if they are given intensive support. These students require explicit systematic phonics instruction and extensive practice reading the new words they are learning until they are at least able to read second-grade text accurately and fluently. If they do not receive appropriate support before second grade, many of these students will have a reading level significantly

FIGURE 1.1 Typical First-Grade Classroom

behind their peers and never catch up. Some may be incorrectly diagnosed as having learning disabilities.

* The remaining 5% of students have serious, pervasive reading disabilities and are served in special education.

In high-poverty schools, the number of children who need extra or intensive support may be even higher (Bursuck and Damer, 2005). This book refers to any students who require extra support to learn as **at risk**. Regardless of the cause, these students will learn to read if a systematic, supportive approach is in place.

When Is the Best Time to Begin Reading Instruction for Children Who Are at Risk?

Years ago, educators believed that reading skills developed naturally and that as long as children were immersed in a literature-rich environment, they would eventually learn to read when they were "ready." In a system based on this belief, struggling readers were often not given extra support until second or even third grade. Since then, educators have been confronted by a large body of research that has emphasized the importance of early identification. Educators now recognize that many children who are at risk will never develop reading skills naturally. Even more disturbing is evidence that once they are behind in reading, most students do not catch up. For example, Juel (1988) found that only one in eight readers who were behind at the end of first grade would catch up by fourth grade. Francis and colleagues (1996) followed 407 children who were classified as poor readers in third grade and found that 74% of these students still remained poor readers when they reached ninth grade. Edward Kame'enui (2007) explained:

> There's a myth, and probably a popular myth, that if kids start off slow they'll eventually catch up, and what we know from the research is that that's simply not the case. Kids who start off slow, their trajectory of learning and reading continues to flatten out. In fact, their performance decreases over time. So, what we know is that we need to intervene early and we need to intervene because we don't have any time to waste. Time is precious. Kids face the tyranny of time. And in order to catch up, we have to be very strategic in what we do in the early years.

Why is later reading intervention so ineffective for students who are at risk? One key reason is that once students get behind, it takes a significant expenditure of time and resources to catch them up, resources that budget-strapped schools may not have available. For example, getting older students who have not attained reading fluency by the end of third grade to grade level costs seven to eight times as much in time and money (Wendorf, 2003). Not only do older students have to relearn ineffective habits they have acquired, they also must overcome pervasive feelings of failure and stress related to reading. Clearly, the best method is to identify children as early as possible and provide them with the supports they need to prevent reading problems in the first place. Although the teaching strategies described in this text are effective for students of all ages, they are most effective when used early.

What Essential Skills Do Students Need to Become Mature Readers?

The NRP (2000) and NELP (2009) identified five key skill areas that should comprise the reading curriculum for students who are at risk. These areas include phonemic awareness, phonics, reading fluency, vocabulary, and reading comprehension. The key skills comprising each of these areas are shown in Figure 1.2 and described in this section. The time

	Kinder Fall	Kinder Spring	First Fall	First Spring	Second All Year	Third All Year
Phonemic Awareness						
Segmenting	X	X	X			
Blending	X	X	X			
Alphabetic Principle						
LS Correspondence	X	X	X	X	X	X
Regular Word Reading		X	X	X	X	X
Irregular Words		X	X	X	X	X
Spelling	X	X	X	X	X	X
Reading Fluency				X	X	X
Vocabulary	*	X	X	X	X	X
Reading Comprehension	*	X	X	X	X	X
*Orally taught						

FIGURE 1.2   Scientifically Based Reading Curriculum

frame information in Figure 1.2 is intended to represent when each skill area is emphasized as part of a core developmental reading program. These skills are also essential for remedial readers. The only difference is that remedial readers will learn them later than their peers. Chapters in this text will provide a clear description of what is and what is not systematic and explicit reading instruction in each of the five skill areas.

Increasingly, reading researchers are questioning why the National Reading Panel did not include spelling as the sixth key skill area to investigate. The old-fashioned notion of spelling as a visual task or task of memorization does not incorporate current research indicating that effective spelling instruction enhances word reading, fluency, vocabulary, and comprehension. Because of the reciprocal relationship between spelling and reading, each chapter will also include information on how effective spelling instruction can enhance instruction in the highlighted skill area.

Publications from the NRP and reports from NELP are free and available for downloading at http://www.nationalreadingpanel.org/Publications/publications.htm and http://www.nifl.gov/nifl/NELP/NELP09.html.

Phonemic Awareness

Phonemic awareness is the ability to hear and manipulate the smallest units of sound in spoken language (Ball & Blachman, 1991). Students who are at risk are less likely to develop this important foundational skill naturally. Word play activities and language games often do not provide enough support. A considerable body of research shows that teaching phonemic awareness skills to students who are at risk within a language-rich environment makes it easier for them to learn to read (Armbruster, Lehr, & Osborn, 2001). Although there are many different phonemic awareness skills, this book stresses the two that researchers have concluded have the most value in a beginning reading program: segmenting and blending (Ball & Blachman). **Segmenting** is the ability to break apart words into their individual phonemes or sounds. A student who can segment says /f/-/i/-/sh/ when asked to say the sounds in *fish*. The ability to segment helps students strategically attack words they will be reading in text and break words into phonemes when spelling. **Blending**, the opposite of segmenting, is the ability to say a spoken word when its individual phonemes are said slowly. A student who can blend can say the word *fish* after the teacher slowly says the individual sounds /f/-/i/-/sh/. Blending enables students to read unfamiliar text by combining single sounds into new words.

Phonics

Although a small percentage of students naturally become fluent readers, many will only develop these skills through activities stressing the connection between written letters and their most common sounds. **Phonics** is the teaching strategy described in this text to teach the relationships between written letters, or graphemes, and the speech sounds, or phonemes. Programs that emphasize phonics will often refer to teaching **sound–spelling relationships** or **graphophonemic knowledge**. Both terms refer to the connection between speech sounds (**phonemes**) and letters of the alphabet (**graphemes**). Although some would argue otherwise, the English language has more than enough regularity to merit the teaching of phonics. The Research Note at the end of this section on page 9 covers this issue more in depth.

The utility of teaching phonics has been clearly established, but not all phonics approaches are equally effective. After identifying thousands of research studies and submitting them to rigorous review, the NRP (2000) and NELP (2009) concluded that systematic and explicit phonics programs are most effective for teaching students to read, particularly students who are at risk. Armbruster, Lehr, and Osborn (2001) summarized the key differences between systematic and nonsystematic phonics programs. These differences are shown in Figure 1.3. The phonics strategies described in this book are designed to be both systematic and explicit to ensure the success of students who are at risk.

Examples

Systematic programs that teach phonics effectively . . .

* help teachers explicitly and systematically instruct students in how to relate letters and sounds, how to break spoken words into sounds, and how to blend sounds to form words.

* help students understand why they are learning the relationships between letters and sounds.

* help students apply their knowledge of phonics as they read words, sentences, and text.

* can be adapted to the needs of individual students, based on assessment.

* include alphabetic knowledge, phonemic awareness, vocabulary development, and the reading of text, as well as systematic phonics instruction.

Nonexamples

Nonsystematic programs that do not teach phonics effectively include …

* **Literature-based programs** that emphasize reading and writing activities. Phonics instruction is embedded in these activities, but letter–sound relationships are taught incidentally, usually based on key letters that appear in student reading materials.

* **Basal reading programs** that focus on whole-word or meaning-based activities. These programs pay only limited attention to letter–sound relationships and provide little or no instruction in how to blend letters to pronounce words.

* **Sight-word programs** that begin by teaching children a sight-word reading vocabulary of from 50 to 100 words. After children learn to read these words, they receive instruction in the alphabetic principle.

FIGURE 1.3   Evaluating Programs of Phonics Instruction

Source: Armbruster, B., Lehr, F., & Osborn, J. (2001). *Put Reading First: The Research Building Blocks for Teaching Children to Read* (pp. 16–17). Washington, DC: Partnership for Reading.

Ehri (2005) developed a five-phase model that describes the development of word reading skills. As readers learn spelling–sound relationships fluently, they eventually are able to unconsciously and automatically recall the pronunciation and meaning of known words. This seemingly effortless process is called sight-word reading.

Phase 1. **Pre-alphabetic phase:** Students do not yet have an understanding of the alphabetic principle and read words as memorized visual forms. A student might remember the word *school* because of the two "eyes" in the middle of the word, or the word *ladder* because of the tall letters that remind him of a ladder. Students in this phase who learn words by their visual characteristics will become easily confused when encountering words that look alike, such as *school* and *shoot.*

Phase 2. **Partial-alphabetic phase:** The development of alphabetic principle allows students to begin to associate some letters with their associated sounds and use that insight to recognize words. Students at this phase might remember the word *sail* by associating the beginning *s* and the final *l* with their respective sounds. These letter–sound connections help students remember words more efficiently than in the previous phase where they had to rely on visual cues. Words that look alike and words where letters have no relationship to their common sound will still be confusing.

Phase 3. **Full-alphabetic phase:** Students have learned the most common letter–sound associations and use this knowledge to **decode** unfamiliar words. Students reading the word *pan* for the first time would scan the word from left to right, making the letter–sound connection for *p*, the vowel sound /ă/ for *a*, and the sound associated with *n* in order to read the word *pan* as a whole word. Associating the letters with the sounds that represent them helps students at this phase commit new words to long-term memory as sight words. Readers now start to learn words more quickly by sight than in previous phases.

Phase 4. **Consolidated-alphabetic phase:** Students consolidate phase 3 knowledge of grapheme–phoneme blends into larger units that recur in different words. Instead of processing individual letter sounds, they recognize multiletter sequences called chunks, such as syllables and parts of words like *ime* and *ing*, which leads them to learn longer words more easily. Instead of having to process the ten sounds in a new word like *concentrate*, a reader would probably read three chunks /con/ /cen/ /trate/. By this phase, the reader can process and read a chunk as fast as a single letter.

Phase 5. **Automatic phase:** Students recognize words as whole words quickly by sight, unconsciously associating letters with their associated sounds. Their accurate, fluent word reading in connected text allows them to focus on comprehending the meaning of the text.

If the reader has developed alphabetic principle and has adequate knowledge of letter–sound associations, when he reads a new word he forms a connection between the letters he sees in the spelling of a word and the sounds in their pronunciation. These connections secure the word in long-term memory. After several encounters reading a new word, a typical reader can then recall it by sight. Knowing how to recognize the phase at which a student is reading helps a teacher plan effective instruction for a struggling reader. For example, a teacher working with a beginning reader (Phases 1–3 in Ehri's model) would design lessons to develop alphabetic principle and letter–sound associations rather than have a student spend time arduously memorizing lists of words relying on visual memory. Sebastian Wren argues that "teaching children in the first and second grades to memorize words only detracts from one of the primary goals of reading instruction—as early as

---

Research Note

Does Teaching Phonics Make Sense?

1. We must *polish* the *Polish* furniture.
2. "Tom, go around the corner and come to me now."

Judging from these examples, teaching students to read would be much easier if there were only one symbol for each phoneme or sound in our speech. In that case, the letter *o* would have the same sound regardless of context or what letter it happened to be positioned next to in a word. Unfortunately, as these examples show, that sound (as in *polish*), depends on the meaning of the words surrounding it. In the second sentence, seven of the words contain the letter *o*, and *o* makes a different sound in each word, depending in large part on the adjacent letters. The question is, given all of this irregularity, does teaching phonics still make sense? The truth is only about 13% of English words are exceptions with highly unpredictable letter–sound relations, whereas 87% of English language words are either very predictable or consist of more complex spelling patterns that can be explicitly taught (Venezky, 1970; Wijk, 1966). In addition, many of the exceptions, such as *said* and *where,* are easier to remember when some of their sounds are taken into account. Research also shows that context clues may only be helpful 10% to 20% of the time (Gough, 1983). Add to this over 30 years of research evidence in support of teaching phonics, and the inescapable conclusion is that the teaching of phonics is definitely justified.

---

possible, children need to learn to attend to the letters within the words, and to decode the words, and children need to become so proficient at this skill that words are decoded rapidly and effortlessly" (Wren, 2000).

Phonics instruction helps students acquire skills in the following areas: identifying letter–sound correspondences, sounding out words containing letter sounds previously taught, reading text containing those words and new words with letter–sound correspondences that have previously been taught, and identifying words by sight. As noted earlier, spelling instruction should be integrated into all aspects of phonics instruction because of the benefits of having students spell words they are also learning to read. Chapters 3 to 5 will explain how learning these skills will help your students become fluent readers. Teaching students decoding skills involves some of the most difficult and precise teaching you will do. The aim of Chapter 3 is to provide information and guides for teachers so all students become automatic phase readers, whose attention and memory resources are available to focus on comprehending the meaning of the text they are reading.

Reading Fluency

Reading fluency is the ability to read text accurately, quickly, and with expression. Students who are able to read fluently can focus their energy on finding out what the text means. Conversely, students who read in a choppy, word-by-word fashion are so focused on getting the words right that they have little energy left for deciphering their meaning. Reading fluency is an important part of the reading curriculum for students who are at risk because they may not develop it naturally, even if they have attained the alphabetic principle (Speece & Ritchey, 2005). Unfortunately, teachers often omit teaching and assessing this skill, which prevents many students who are at risk from transitioning into fluid,

TABLE 1.1 Vocabulary in Oral and Written Communication

	Oral Communication	Written Communication
Receptive Vocabulary	*listening comprehension* Example: The student knows the meaning of a vocabulary word in a story that the teacher reads aloud.	*reading comprehension* Example: The student knows the meaning of a vocabulary word in a story that she reads.
Expressive Vocabulary	*meaningful speech* Example: Correctly using the vocabulary from a story, the student describes the sequence of events in the story that he read or that was read aloud.	*meaningful writing* Example: Correctly using the vocabulary from a story, the student writes a description of the events that took place in a story that she read or that was read aloud.

expressive readers. Fortunately, there is a large body of research showing that fluency can be assessed and effectively taught (Fuchs, Fuchs, Hosp, & Jenkins, 2001; Wolf & Katzir-Cohen, 2001), particularly for students reading at grade levels 1 to 6 (Edmonds et al., 2009). In Chapter 5, you will learn to do both.

Vocabulary

Vocabulary is the fourth key component of effective early literacy programs for students who are at risk. As shown in Table 1.1, vocabulary can be either receptive or expressive and oral or written. Oral **receptive vocabulary** involves understanding the meaning of words when people speak; written receptive vocabulary concerns understanding the meaning of words that are read. Oral **expressive vocabulary** means using words in speaking so that other people understand you; written expressive vocabulary is communicating meaningfully through writing.

Knowledge of the meaning of a wide variety of words enables students to identify words more easily. A student who knows the meaning of the word *skeptic* from hearing it in conversations, but who has never read the word before, will more fluently apply his decoding knowledge when reading a sentence containing that word. He will also be more apt to understand the meaning of the sentence. In turn, knowledge of letter–sound associations provides a valuable memory cue and helps students remember vocabulary words more easily (Ehri, 2005). Students who are at risk, including those in poverty, those having disabilities, or those who speak a second language, are likely to lag behind their peers in vocabulary development (Hart & Risley, 1995). Equally disturbing is that vocabulary differences grow larger over time, due to a lack of exposure at home and failure to teach vocabulary extensively at school (Beck, McKeown, & Kucan, 2002; Biemiller, 2001). Hart and Risley (1995) estimate the gap in words learned per year between students who are at risk and their peers who are not at risk amounts to more than 2,000 words per year.

The extent of students' vocabulary knowledge can have a significant impact on their early reading achievement. For one thing, reading is infinitely more meaningful and rewarding when students understand the meaning of the words they are decoding. Imagine what reading would be like if you were reading only nonsense words! A knowledge of vocabulary is also essential for reading connected text for meaning, the ultimate goal of reading instruction.

It is widely believed that most vocabulary is learned indirectly—either through speaking with others, being read to, or reading independently. However, many students who are at risk come to school with significantly less exposure to these naturalistic experiences.

Clearly, for students who are at risk, vocabulary instruction is an essential part of teaching them to speak, read, and write adequately. Vocabulary instruction should have two key emphases: direct teaching of the meanings of important, useful, and difficult words; and strategies for figuring out the meaning of words independently using context, meanings of word parts, and the dictionary (Stahl & Nagy, 2006). In Chapter 9, you will learn how to teach vocabulary so that students have the opportunity to extensively use new words in their oral language, reading, and writing.

Reading Comprehension

One area on which reading experts agree is that reading comprehension is the ultimate goal of reading instruction. Students who understand what they read are able to decode connected text accurately and fluently and know the meanings of a variety of vocabulary words. Good comprehenders also read purposefully and actively engage with and think about what they are reading (RAND Reading Study Group, 2002). Reading comprehension is a complex process because it is influenced by factors such as the person who is reading, the text being read, the task the reader is trying to accomplish, and the context in which the reading is being done (RAND Reading Study Group, 2002). Despite its complexity, the NRP (2000) and NELP (2009) identified a number of strategies that help students derive meaning from text. These strategies are as follows:

* Activate background knowledge and use it to make meaning out of text.
* Generate and ask questions while reading.
* Evaluate or draw conclusions from information in a text.
* Get meaning by making informed predictions.
* Summarize information by explaining in their own words what the text is about.
* Monitor comprehension, including knowing when they understand and do not understand, and using additional strategies to improve when understanding is blocked.
* Derive meaning of narrative and expository text by being able to identify relevant text structures.

Chapter 10 explains teaching techniques that help students who are at risk to consistently use these strategies while engaged with the content of the text.

Which Students Are Likely to Struggle When Learning to Read?

To explain the interconnection between various systems that help the reader decode and comprehend, Marilyn Adams (1990) described a processing model that she developed from a comprehensive review of the reading research literature in education, cognitive science, and psychology. Her model describes the process that occurs as fluent readers simultaneously and successfully engage the following four processors as they read text: **orthographic processor, phonological processor, meaning processor,** and **context processor.** The more fluent the reader, the more unaware he is of how his brain is coordinating information on the sounds, letter shapes, meaning of words, and context as his eyes rapidly move across the text from left to right (Adams, 1990). The work of each processor and its connections with the others was described by Adams: "As the parts of the system are refined and developed in proper relation to one another, each guides and reinforces the growth of the other" (p. 6).

When the reader sees text on a page, the orthographic processor recognizes the visual image of words as interconnected sets of letters. For example, when the reader sees the word *cat*, the orthographic processor sees the letters clustered into a spelling pattern *cat*.

The phonological processor is the system that processes the speech sounds of language. When the reader sees the word *cat*, the "inner voice," called the phonological processor, identifies and orders the sounds of the word /c/ /a/ /t/ rather than the letters *c-a-t*. In order to develop the automatic word reading described by Ehri, the phonological and orthographic processors must work together efficiently and fluently to make the graphophonemic connections that activate associations of past experiences with "cats." The meaning processor focuses on definitions rather than the letters or sounds and the reader thinks "furry four-legged pet that meows" when reading *cat*. This meaning processor works quickly for words the reader knows, but slower for unknown words as it connects parts of the word to meaning. Coordinating with the meaning processor, the context processor brings prior knowledge to bear on understanding the meaning of the word. When the reader sees *cat*, the context processor might think about his friend's cat.

Struggling readers have problems in one or more of these four processing domains, and effective interventions need to address their specific area of difficulty. Students with deficits primarily in phonological and orthographic processing have the vocabulary and conceptual knowledge to bring meaning to text read to them but cannot decode printed words accurately and fluently enough to extract meaning on their own (Foorman & Torgesen, 2001). These students require careful instruction in word reading and fluency. A second group of struggling readers includes children living in poverty who enter school with delayed development in all areas of language that prevent the efficient functioning of all four processors. These children require intensive instruction in vocabulary and language concepts as well as word reading and fluency. A third group of children have deficits in vocabulary and concept knowledge but adequate phonological and orthographic skills. This group of struggling readers, often referred to as "word callers," comprises at most 10% of struggling readers, and includes English language learners. Students in this group need carefully targeted comprehension instruction, including both vocabulary and language concepts. These three groups of struggling readers share two common characteristics: the inability to comprehend written text and the need for early identification and reading support.

Recent studies using computerized imaging show that serious reading problems may be brain-based, with the brain activity of the most deficit readers differing from those of students who are skilled readers (Shaywitz & Shaywitz, 2007). Many deficit readers show a pattern of underactivation in a region in the back of the brain that enables first accurate and then automatic reading. These brain scans, which differ from those of skilled readers, provide insight about why these students have problems learning to decode accurately and fluently (Shaywitz, 2003). Fortunately, research also shows that effective language instruction, including systematic instruction in phonemic awareness and phonics, generates repair in underactivated sections of the brain (Shaywitz, 2003; Simos et al., 2007), reinforcing the importance of early identification and remediation.

What Is the Most Effective Way to Teach Essential Reading Skills to Children Who Are at Risk?

The evidence is clear that students who are at risk benefit from reading instruction that is explicit and systematic. **Explicit instruction** is the clear, direct teaching of reading skills and strategies and includes these:

- Clear instructional outcomes (what you want the student to do with the information you've taught)
- Clear purpose for learning

* Clear and understandable directions and explanations
* Adequate modeling/demonstration, guided practice, and independent practice as part of the teaching process
* Clear, consistent corrective feedback on student success and student errors

The second-grade teachers at Fourth Avenue School use an explicit reading curriculum to teach reading. They expect their students to read at least 90 words per minute by the end of the year and to apply that skill when reading books of different genres for school assignments and for enjoyment. If the students are taking turns reading a play, the teachers explain the directions beforehand and tell students the procedure for rotating turns and for correcting errors. Because the teachers are so clear, the students, after misreading a word, have formed the habit of immediately starting again at the beginning of the sentence and rereading. The teachers always introduce new concepts by first showing the students how to do them and then supporting their learning until independence. Because the two- and three-syllable words introduced last week were difficult for many of the students, the teachers spent an extra day reviewing them so students had more practice. Whenever students make mistakes, the teachers follow the systematic error correction procedures that you will read about later in this chapter. By correcting errors using these procedures, teachers make sure that students know how to perform the skill correctly the next time they are called on.

Systematic instruction is teaching that clearly identifies a carefully selected and useful set of skills and then organizes those skills into a logical sequence of instruction. For example, Mr. Prince decides to teach his students to sound out regular words because there is not enough time for them to memorize all the words with which they come in contact. Before he works on sounding out words, Mr. Prince teaches his students to say the sounds in words they hear and to blend sounds into whole words. Gradually, he begins teaching his students letter sounds. By the time his students begin sounding out words, they will have all the skills they need to be successful.

Students vary in the amount of explicit, systematic instruction they need for learning to read. Reflect back on the typical first-grade class (Figure 1.1) with its wide range of learners. In a typical class, some students learn new material as fast as the teacher can teach it; other students need extra practice before they learn it; and a third group needs very deliberate teaching that slowly moves from easier skills to more difficult concepts. Because of these differences, schools need a range of instructional options to meet the diverse needs of their students. Teaching that provides this broader range of options is known as differentiated instruction (Friend & Bursuck, 2009).

Throughout this book, we will show you how to provide differentiated instruction through two schoolwide approaches, the **multi-tier** model and the **Response to Intervention** (RTI) model, both designed to provide support for struggling readers at the first sign of difficulty (Gersten et al., 2009). In a multi-tier model, which was the prevention-based system of delivering reading instruction in Project PRIDE, students who needed additional support in reading were identified through regularly scheduled research-based assessments of essential reading skills. Students who needed more support received additional research-based interventions of varying intensity. Varying levels of intensities are called "tiers," and in a typical multi-tier model, Tier 1 is the general classroom curriculum, Tier 2 provides additional small-group tutoring support, and Tier 3 is a more intensive alternative reading program (Hoover & Patton, 2008). The tiers depicted in Figure 1.4 are described in more detail later in this chapter. Assessments given on a weekly or monthly basis provide information about whether students are responding to the amount of support they receive, and adjustments are made as needed.

In RTI, a multi-tier system of instruction provides the foundation, but in addition, a process is included to determine whether a student is eligible for learning disability services. In RTI, a student's lack of response (i.e., lack of improvement) to several high-quality research-based Tier 2 and Tier 3 interventions can be viewed as evidence of an underlying

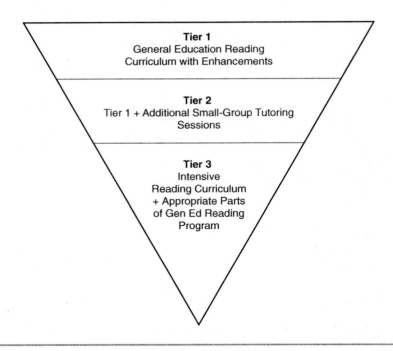

FIGURE 1.4   Multi-Tiered Model of Differentiated Instruction

Learn more about RTI at the National Center on Response to Intervention at **http://www.rti4success.org/.**

learning disability if other testing or data support that diagnosis (Brown-Chidsey & Steege, 2005). Both RTI and multi-tier models include these components:

* Research-based instruction in the general education classroom
* Ongoing student assessment—frequently monitored student progress to examine student achievement and gauge the effectiveness of the interventions
* Tiered instruction—specific research-based interventions of varying intensities matched to student need

Tier 1 Instruction

Tier 1 in a multi-tier or RTI model is the least intensive, first level of instruction and consists of the core reading program used in the classroom, whether it is basal, strictly literature-based, or a combination of the two. In Project PRIDE we added a number of research-based teaching enhancements to the core reading program that helped our students who were at risk learn more efficiently and effectively (Bursuck et al., 2004; Kame'enui, Good, Simmons, & Chard, 2002). Throughout the text we will teach you ways to use these same enhancements to maximize the effectiveness of your Tier 1 core reading program so that you can meet the needs of as many of your students as possible. Of course, more students who are at risk will learn to read successfully with the additional Tier 1 enhancements if the core reading program already reflects effective reading practices described in the NRP (2000) and NELP (2009) reports and is implemented as designed for at least 90 minutes per day (Arndt & Crawford, 2006). An effective Tier 1 program should be able to serve 80% of the students, though in schools with large numbers of students who are at risk, that number may be smaller, even with the use of enhancements (Bursuck & Damer, 2005). While instruction using small homogeneous groups of 3 to 4 students has been shown to be the most effective grouping procedure in general (Elbaum, Vaughn, Hughes, & Moody, 2000), extensive use of small groups in Tier 1 can reduce instructional time with the teacher, a key predictor of student success (Rosenshine, 1986). Also, behavior problems proliferate in classes where students work independently for more than 15 or 20 minutes, waiting for the teacher to work with their small group. In Project PRIDE, the instructional enhancements were designed to make large-group instruction more effective. Small-group instruction was then provided for those students needing additional support in Tier 2 and Tier 3, a practice recommended by Gersten et al. (2009). Regardless of the approach, the quality of the core reading program and the amount of time students receive systematic, explicit instruction with feedback from the teacher are critical features of effective Tier 1 instruction.

Tier 2 Instruction

Tier 2 in a multi-tier or RTI model consists of Tier 1 instruction plus additional daily small-group intervention sessions that provide extra practice on key skills covered in Tier 1. Students enter Tier 2 when their performance dips below benchmark scores or a set percentile on universal screening or progress-monitoring measures described later in this chapter. In Project PRIDE, Tier 2 sessions usually lasted 10 minutes in kindergarten and 30 to 40 minutes in the later grades—practices consistent with research-based guidelines recommended by the Institute for Education Sciences (Gersten et al., 2009). While the institute recommends group sizes of three to four, in Project PRIDE we were often able to accommodate slightly larger group sizes by using the same enhancements employed in Tier 1, such as unison responding. Tier 2 instruction ensures that students become fluent, accurate readers by providing extra practice on essential foundational word reading skills in the primary grades with more of an emphasis on vocabulary and comprehension skills after third grade. Word reading skills are emphasized in the primary grades because a high percentage of students who are at risk fail to comprehend what they are reading because they cannot read connected text accurately and fluently (Adams & Bruck, 1993). Their comprehension will not mature until their word reading improves, enabling them to focus more attention on the meaning of the text. Tier 2 sessions are carried out by a variety of staff, including general education teachers, Title 1 teachers, special education teachers, and paraprofessionals, all carefully prepared to ensure quality implementation. Having effective Tier 1 and Tier 2 programs in place should enable you to meet the needs of all but 5% of your students, although high-poverty schools usually have more students who require Tier 3 support (Bursuck & Damer, 2005).

Tier 3 Instruction

Tier 3 in a multi-tier or RTI model includes all of the enhancements that are in Tiers 1 and 2 plus a more systematically designed and explicitly taught reading curriculum. Students placed in Tier 3 have failed to make substantial progress despite a Tier 1 enhanced general education reading program and extra help in Tier 2 intervention groups. In Project PRIDE, Tier 3 sessions were conducted in small groups daily for 60 to 90 minutes. Research indicates that Tier 3 interventions that focus on key foundational skills and are conducted in small groups of one to four students are highly systematic and explicit and are longer in duration, resulting in increased reading achievement results (Gersten et al., 2009).

Fewer than 5% of students make little progress even in the presence of otherwise effective instruction (Torgesen, 2000). Students in this group have serious, pervasive reading disabilities and in an RTI model are more appropriately served in special education (Wanzek & Vaughn, 2008), which, depending on the specific multi-tier model, can be included as a part of Tier 3 or a separate Tier 4. These students may benefit from doubling their reading time using a practice called "double dosing." However, double dosing only works when what you are doubling is well-designed, systematic, and explicit instruction (Wanzek & Vaughn, 2008).

Some Title 1 or special education teachers work with older students on a remedial basis, but by the time their students begin instruction, typically after third grade, they are significantly behind their classmates. Although this later start to intervention poses difficult challenges, upper-grade teachers are responsible for catching up these students so they are reading at grade level. Catching up students is difficult due to limits in district time and resources, but even so, older students reading below a fourth-grade reading level should be taught for at least 2 hours per day using a well-designed Tier 3 program (Archer, Gleason, & Vachon, 2003).

Although the focus of this text is on making sure that you can teach most children using Tiers 1 and 2, experience shows that, depending on where you are teaching, at least a third of your children may need Tier 3 instruction (Damer, Bursuck, & Harris, 2008). The intensity of Tier 3 programs differs from district to district in terms of time, size of group, and curriculum. Ideally, students who do not respond to interventions in Tier 3 should receive increased intensity of services such as double dosing, the implementation of a formal motivational behavior program, reduced group size, or a change in curriculum. Districts in high-poverty areas that implement multi-tier or RTI models and identify up to 60% of second-grade or older students as so far behind that only a Tier 3 intervention will provide "catch-up," face an ethical dilemma when, because of cost, they only provide those services to the lowest performing 10% of students. Meeting the needs of a large group of older students requiring Tier 3 instruction forces schools to be creative, using new strategies such as training general education teachers to teach Tier 3 groups or enlisting everyone in the building from the principal to the music teacher to teach reading to at least a small Tier 2 reading group. When enhanced Tier 1 and Tier 2 instruction begins in preschool or kindergarten, the percentage of older students who need Tier 3 should decrease significantly.

The ultimate purpose of Tier 3 is to catch students up to their peers, which means that students need instruction that is well designed and efficiently and competently taught. Otherwise, Tier 3 groups can become a dumping ground with an irrelevant, watered-down curriculum in which students fall further behind and become at high risk for dropping out of school. Too often in the past, remedial programs have become such dead-end options. Because of potential risks associated with remedial pull-out programs, we suggest using a prepackaged, commercially produced reading program that is evidence based, has teacher-friendly formats that are relatively easy to implement, and provides scaffolding to teachers without a lot of prior experience teaching explicit reading.

How can you determine which alternative reading program will have the most success with the largest number of your students? How do you know whether the alternative program has an adequate phonemic awareness emphasis? How can you tell if the alternative program is a systematic phonics program? These questions are confusing for many educators who are faced with testimonials defending reading curricula as having research support. To assist you or your school in deciding on a Tier 3 program, toward the end of each chapter we have listed key characteristics to look for in alternative reading programs. These characteristics include the skill focus, design, and instructional approach as they relate to students who are at risk or who have disabilities. In addition, we have analyzed some commonly used alternative reading programs to determine which ones include these characteristics.

We also suggest that whenever feasible, Tier 3 groups take place in the classroom. In-class groups are preferred because they provide a valuable instructional model for general education teachers and can lead to shared responsibility for the reading outcomes of all students (Friend & Cook, 2007). Many of the intensive reading programs do not include adequate vocabulary and comprehension instruction, so students in Tier 3 need to develop those skills in the larger classroom group. As long as the teacher conducting the large group doesn't humiliate Tier 3 students by expecting them to orally read frustration-level text in front of their peers and differentiates instruction by having them listen to the text before the large group takes place, all students can participate in vocabulary and comprehension development activities. A sample schedule for a classroom using a three-tier approach is shown in Figure 1.5.

Large-Group Instruction: Tiers 1, 2, 3 students **(20 minutes)**

Who Teaches: Mrs. James
Prereading, vocabulary, carryover comprehension activities from last story/article.

Large-Group Instruction: (30 minutes)
Tier 1 and Tier 2 students work with Mrs. James on parts of core curriculum that would be at frustration level for students in Tier 3.

* Letter–sound identification

* Word reading, spelling, first read-through of the story/article in the corereading curriculum.

Small-Group Instruction: (60 minutes)
One or two small Tier 3* groups, conducted by Title 1 teacher, special education teacher, classroom aide trained to conduct scripted reading lessons, or another assigned general education teacher, work on intensive reading lessons at small tables in the room.

Small-Group Instruction and Centers: (30 minutes)

* Tier 2 support group meets to review new sounds and words taught in class and/or read decodable text. These students work with Mrs. James.

* Tier 1 students independently work on challenging center activities.

Large-Group Instruction: Tiers 1, 2, 3 students **(25 minutes)**

Who Teaches: Mrs. James
All students work on comprehension and vocabulary activities related to the story that students read earlier. Although students in Tier 3 do not orally read frustration-level text, they fully participate in all of the comprehension and vocabulary activities related to the story. Tier 1 and Tier 2 students have another opportunity to read the text with comprehension integrated at the sentence level.

Extra Small-Group Instruction: Tiers 1, 2, 3 students **(15 minutes)**

Who Teaches: Mrs. James
Other times during the day when reading instruction takes place:

* After lunch, Mrs. James reads to the students (50% of the time reads nonfiction) using graphic organizers and frequent questions to develop listening comprehension.

* During math, Mrs. James challenges advanced readers by teaching them to read the names of difficult shapes.

* During the social studies and science block, Mrs. James uses a combination of large group and centers, integrating vocabulary, reading, writing, and comprehension into her volcanoes activity.

* During "sponge times" (waiting outside the lunch room, lining up in the room), Mrs. James provides extra practice and asks students to segment words, spell words, identify vocabulary words on the word wall, etc.

FIGURE 1.5   120-Minute Core Reading Block Conducted in Mrs. James's First Grade Classroom

* For these Tier 3 students to catch up to their peers, it is recommended that in the afternoon they have another 30 minutes of intensive instruction in the same curriculum, incorporating spelling instruction.

How Do I Identify Struggling Readers, Monitor Student Progress, and Diagnose Instructional Needs in a Multi-Tier or RTI Model?

Assessments in multi-tier or RTI models serve three purposes: universal screening, progress monitoring, and diagnosis. Regardless of the purpose, the assessments used must accurately measure essential early reading skills, be easy to give, take up little classroom time, predict later classroom problems, and enable teachers to readily monitor student progress (Jenkins, 2009). In multi-tier or RTI models, criterion-referenced tests are most often used. Criterion-referenced tests compare student performance to a specific level of performance or benchmark. One particularly useful type of criterion-referenced assessment is curriculum-based measurement (CBM; Deno, 2003). CBM is an assessment method that directly measures basic academic skills. CBM is characterized by an extensive research base establishing its technical adequacy as well as tasks and scoring procedures that are brief, grounded in the classroom curriculum, standardized, and fluency based. Fluency, or how quickly a student can perform a skill or recall academic content, adds an important dimension to assessment that level of accuracy alone can't provide. Students who are fluent in a skill are more likely to retain it and master more advanced skills based on its foundation (Friend & Bursuck, 2009).

Universal screening involves identifying students who, despite a strong reading program in Tier 1, are not making adequate progress and require extra support in Tier 2 or Tier 3. Quality screening measures accurately identify students who are at risk for future reading failure, are efficient, and result in students' reading needs being met (Jenkins & Johnson, 2007). These screening measures, sometimes called "benchmark assessments," are typically administered at the beginning, middle, and end of the year to ensure that students who require increased or decreased support get it. The assessments should address skills related to both word reading and comprehension (Catts, Fey, Zhang, & Tomblin, 1999) and reflect grade-level differences. In the early grades, letter knowledge, phonemic awareness, and phonics should be stressed, while vocabulary and comprehension take on increased importance in the later grades (Jenkins & Johnson, 2007). Screening measures are best given by general education classroom teachers because they afford teachers the opportunity to learn about the attention, verbal skills, and attitudes of students not in their reading groups.

Some schools identify students who are at risk by defining deficit reading as a score corresponding to a percentile such as performing below the 50th percentile or in the bottom 10% of their school or district. Other screening assessments define deficit reading as falling below a predetermined standard, which is often a cutoff point either on a state high-stakes test or on a curriculum-based measure that is predictive of future reading problems. Universal screening identifies accurately students who are truly in need and avoids either identifying children for extra tier help who don't need it (**false positives**) or not identifying children for extra tier help who need it (**false negatives**). While too many false positives can drain resources in times of reduced funding, having too many false negatives can have more dire consequences for students whose reading needs are neglected. That is why we recommend caution when using cutoffs such as identifying only the bottom 10% or 20% of a given school or district as being eligible to receive extra Tier 3 support, particularly when engaged in screening activities in urban districts where a much higher percentage of children are likely to be at risk when a multi-tier program is first implemented.

Throughout this book, universal-screening subtests that assess the skills highlighted in each chapter will be discussed. These subtests have been selected from four larger assessment batteries because they are most frequently discussed in the RTI literature as being credible assessments, have established reliability and validity, and take a relatively short amount of time to administer. The Dynamic Indicators of Basic Literacy Skills (DIBELS),

AIMSweb, Phonological Awareness Literacy Screening (PALS), and Texas Primary Reading Inventory (TPRI) can be used as universal screeners within multi-tier or RTI models.

As much as we know about evidence-based practices in reading, we still cannot predict how each student will respond to a given instructional intervention. That is why measuring student growth is such an important part of multi-tier and RTI models. **Progress monitoring** enables teachers to make important decisions such as whether a student should remain in a tier, enter a more intensive tier, or exit into a less-intensive tier. Progress-monitoring assessments are given repeatedly over time and must be of approximately equal difficulty, a feature of CBM that makes them ideal for measuring student progress. Generally, students in Tier 1 are assessed at a minimum of three times per year, while Tier 2 and Tier 3 students can be assessed every 3 to 4 weeks (Jenkins, 2009), or more often if desired. Jenkins describes a four-step process of progress monitoring: setting growth goals, selecting progress monitoring assessments of approximately equal difficulty, measuring performance every 3 to 4 weeks to determine growth rates, and adjusting instruction when growth is inadequate. Jenkins also recommends obtaining multiple measures (at least two, ideally three) of each skill on each progress monitoring occasion to ensure the accuracy of the growth rates.

At the heart of the "one size doesn't fit all" reading model is the need to provide differentiated instruction, including materials and tasks at varied levels of difficulty and with varying levels of support through the use of multiple grouping arrangements (Friend & Bursuck, 2009). Differentiation is achieved by diagnosing the needs of students shown to be at risk on universal screening measures. **Diagnostic assessments** can be used to determine these needs:

* What skills students need to practice in Tier 2
* The reading level at which a student should be instructed
* Which letter–sound correspondences or phonemic awareness skills are in need of instruction
* Whether there is a need for fluency building in passage reading or for modeling and guided practice when students are sounding out multisyllable words
* Which students can be grouped together to work on comprehension skills, such as finding the main idea

For Tier 2 students, classroom teachers can give simple diagnostic tests or identify error patterns based on student performance on universal screeners. Two of the larger assessment batteries include diagnostic tests to help plan smaller instructional groups. In an RTI model, Tier 3 students who are not responding to interventions at an acceptable rate and whose eligibility for special education services is being considered receive further diagnostic assessment by a reading teacher, special education teacher, speech and language pathologist, or school psychologist.

> To learn more about RTI, go to the IRIS Center Web site and complete the RTI (Part 1) Overview Module at **http://iris.peabody.vanderbilt.edu/ rti01_overview/chalcycle.htm.**

What Are the Instructional Enhancements for Students Who Are at Risk?

The instructional enhancements for students who are at risk described in this section are evidence based and can provide the consistency, predictability, and structure students who are at risk need to be successful (Stichter, Stormont, & Lewis, 2009) because they are based on the principle of **universal design** of instruction (Pisha & Stahl, 2005). The idea behind universal design is that instructional materials and methods designed with built-in supports minimize the need for differentiated instruction later on (Friend & Bursuck, 2009). The enhancements include advance organizers, unison responses through the use of effective signals, perky pace, efficient use of teacher talk, increased practice, support for new learning using a My Turn–Together–Your Turn format, systematic error correction, cumulative review, teaching to success, and motivational strategies. Each of these enhancements is described in this section, and throughout this book, we provide ways for you to maximize the learning of all students by integrating them into your teaching.

Advance Organizers

When students are easily distracted or come from chaotic home environments, they want and need structure and predictability in their environment. Disorganized students often do not automatically draw connections from one part of a learning task to another. Unless the teacher has told students that the words they are reading on the board will be in that day's story, some of the students who are more disorganized will not make the connection to those words when they open their books to the new story and begin to read. Teachers establish a comfortable level of predictability when they use advance organizers at the start of each lesson by telling students what they are learning, why they are learning it, and what the behavioral expectations are during the lesson (Marzano, 2003). When these advance organizers provide the beginning organization for each day's lesson, students learn to anticipate connections between what they are learning and how they will apply the new learning to other situations. By briefly describing the sequence of activities covered during the reading lesson and checking each one off after it is completed, teachers also motivate students who are likely to tune out or act out in a part of the lesson that they find difficult. For example, reading the new long-vowel words might be difficult for Debra, but if she knows that word practice is followed by an interesting story about a lizard that bakes cakes, she will pay closer attention and work harder. Advance organizers should include a graphic depiction along with a brief verbal description, especially for younger students. A sample visually presented advance organizer for a kindergarten lesson is shown in Figure 1.6. It includes the comments the teacher makes to prepare the students to learn.

Unison Responding

Students who are at risk need more practice of the key skills they are learning than their peers who are not at risk. They need to be actively engaged with many opportunities to orally practice the new sounds, read the new words, read the longer stories, and use new vocabulary words in increasingly longer sentences (Lemoine, Levy, & Hutchinson, 1993). For example, to learn to automatically recognize a written word as a sight word, the average student requires between 4 and 14 exposures, while struggling readers need 20 or more exposures (Lyon, 1998). Students with disabilities may require 50 to 100 exposures to automatize the recognition of a new word in context (Honig, 2001). In a class of 20 or 30 students, teachers can only provide that amount of practice by having all of the students answer in unison. Rather than ask one student to say the sound of the new letter l, the teacher increases academic learning time for everyone by asking all of the students to answer at the same time.

As an added benefit, students who are actively participating are more likely to pay attention to instruction and follow classroom rules. Students who are constantly answering and reading have little time to be off task, staring out the window, or disrupting the class.

1.   Segmenting Lesson—"Let's pull some words apart!"

2.   Blending—"Next we'll put some sounds together to make words."

3.   Letter Sounds—"Then we'll work with the letter **d** and its buddies."

Working with the letter. . . **d** and its buddies.

4.   Reading Words—"Then we'll read some words."

5.   Spelling—"Then we'll spell some words."

During the lesson today I would like you to. . .
 • Sit up nice and tall in your seats.
 • Listen very closely.
 • And answer on my signal.

FIGURE 1.6   Advance Organizer—Letter and Sounds Lesson

Source: Hicks, A. (2006). Model advance organizer. Unpublished manuscript, University of North Carolina at Greensboro.

Since students who are at risk also need to have their answers carefully monitored to make sure that they are acquiring the skills that are taught, teachers are more effective if they follow each section of the lesson with a few quick, individual questions. These quick checkouts enable the teacher to provide more practice if some students still are making errors.

Effective Signals

Effective signals help a teacher get all the students to answer together, speaking in one voice as if in a choir. If students answer too early or too late, reading instruction will not be as effective. One or two students who immediately grasp the concept may answer ahead of everyone else, creating the illusion that the class does not need any more practice. Students who are at risk may answer after everyone else, relying on other students' answers and not sounding out the words by themselves. The parts of an effectively delivered signal that will get all students to answer together are described in Table 1.2.

Note that the teacher first focuses the students' attention on the question. Questions that teachers ask in beginning reading instruction include the following:

* Asking students to name letter sounds
* Asking students to sound out words
* Asking students to say all of the sounds in the words they hear
* Asking students to read simple sentences

TABLE 1.2 Effective Signals

Component	Description
1. FOCUS students' attention, and then ask your question.	The teacher gains students' attention by having them focus on the word they will read or on an oral question.
	* When asking an oral question, hold up a hand to gain students' attention and tell students what they will do. Example: Hold up a hand and say, "You are going to take some words apart. First word is *mat*."
	* If asking students to read, tell students what they will do and point a finger to the left of the first word. Example: Tell students, "Get ready to read the word when I touch it," and point to the left of the word.
2. THINK Time	A brief pause of no more than three seconds provides students with time to formulate an answer. If the questions are easy or review, the teacher gives a very short thinking pause. If the questions are difficult or new, the teacher gives a longer thinking pause.
3. SIGNAL	The teacher gives the signal that indicates everyone should answer at that very instant. The signal always comes **after** the directions, never at the same time. Thus a teacher never talks and signals at the same time. Chapter 3 describes specific signals including:
	* Hand-clap * Loop signal

Next the teacher provides think time, waiting for a few seconds after asking the question and calling on the students. The amount of think time will vary depending on the question. For new or more difficult questions, the think time is longer than for easier or review ones. Following the thinking pause, the teacher asks the question, pauses one second, and then gives the signal. The type of signal used depends on the nature of the question that students are asked. For example, when students are asked to sound out words listed on the board, the teacher points to the letters in the word signaling for students to sound them out. When asking students to orally take apart words ("What are the sounds in *fish*: /f/ /i/ /s/ /h/?"), the teacher either snaps two fingers, claps hands together, or drops a hand as the signal. Specific strategies for using signals are covered in Chapter 3. Some teachers develop their own signals, such as moving their arms as if directing an orchestra, using a clicker in the shape of a bug, moving fingers in the air, or tapping fingers on a surface.

Efficient Use of Teacher Talk

The clarity with which teachers present information to students at risk has a strong influence on their learning. Students in classrooms where teachers present material in concise statements, using language the students understand, are more likely to be on task than students whose teachers provide lengthy explanations and present information unrelated to the task at hand. Teaching in a clear and concise manner is easier said than done. We have included scripted teaching formats for all of the key skills covered in the text as a scaffold for teachers as they develop their abilities to teach more clearly.

Perky Pace

Teachers can also increase student attention and learning by employing a perky pace throughout every lesson (Englert, Tarrant, & Mariage, 1992). Teachers who use a perky pace start with a brief advance organizer and minimize the transition time between activities, as well as between each student answer and the teacher's next question. Students give more of their attention to a teacher who uses an animated teaching style, conveying her enthusiasm for what they are learning. They are less likely to waste time, be uncooperative, or tune out when a theatrical teacher uses exaggerated affect, enthusiastic voice tones, and dramatic gestures.

My Turn–Together–Your Turn Format

All students require support or scaffolding when they are learning new skills or content. Think about the frustration you felt when a math or physics teacher introduced a new concept and then, without adequately giving you practice using the new concept, expected you to apply it to that night's homework problems. As you tried to solve problems that depended on your knowledge of the new concept, your frustration and tension level increased as you stared at the work. Unless you could find a better teacher in the form of a friend, a tutor, or a detailed book, your learning was at a standstill. Students who are at risk require even more support when they are learning to read and write. An effective way to scaffold their new learning is to use the My Turn–Together–Your Turn strategy used in explicit instruction (Archer, 1995). The components of this approach are as follows:

* **My Turn:** The teacher first demonstrates how to do the new skill so that students have no difficulty understanding exactly what the new skill looks like.
* **Together:** The teacher practices the skill with his students until they are able to do it without him. Students experience a higher level of success and less frustration if

they first have the opportunity to practice with the teacher. In this way, students are prevented from practicing the errors and acquiring habits that, once learned, are difficult to break.

* **Your Turn:**   The teacher monitors students as they do the skill independently. By closely monitoring his students, the teacher can correct any errors and prevent them from acquiring habits that, once learned, are difficult to break.

Teachers who use a My Turn–Together–Your Turn format for teaching new critical skills are explicitly teaching so that students are successful from the start. These teachers know that when students inadvertently learn errors such as saying /sh/ for the /th/ sound, valuable time will be wasted reteaching. Jerry Ameis (2003) cautions, "Reteaching is a significant waste of time for students and teachers. It is far better to spend the needed time on trying *'to get it right'* the first time than to bore and/or frustrate students (and yourself) by reteaching and reteaching . . ." (Ameis, 2003). Eventually teachers move to using "Your Turns" as students' accuracy shows they have learned the new skill. Moving to "Your Turns" represents an important transition because providing more support than is needed can thwart student independence and prevent accurate progress monitoring. Indeed, when the building is complete, the scaffolds come down.

Cumulative Review

Teachers who work with students who are at risk often observe that these students have difficulty retaining new information or skills. Just when it seems that they have learned something new, the very next day they have already forgotten it. In addition to problems with retention, students who are at risk also have trouble discriminating between new information and information previously learned. For example, Delarnes learned the sound /b/ several weeks ago, but since learning other sounds has practiced it only once or twice. This week, he learned the new /d/ sound on Thursday. On Friday, he read all of the *b* words in his decodable book as if they contained the letter *d*. If Delarnes's teacher had continued to practice the /b/ sound every day after he learned it, he would have been less likely to confuse it with /d/. **Cumulative review** is a method of selecting teaching examples where the teacher adds previously learned material to examples of newly learned material. Cumulative review increases student retention and helps students discriminate between new and old learning. To use cumulative review, simply add examples of previously learned material to examples of newly learned material.

Systematic Error Correction

No matter how systematic and explicit the reading instruction, students will always make some errors. Research shows that in an effective lesson, students answer at least eight out of every ten answers correctly (McEwan & Damer, 2000). This minimum level of success instills confidence and reduces frustration for at-risk students. The way that teachers correct student errors is critical. If errors are not corrected appropriately, students continue to make the same errors and develop habits that can seriously undermine the goal of fluent, accurate reading with comprehension.

In making a **systematic error correction**, the teacher corrects the students immediately after they make the error by modeling the correct answer/skill ("My Turn"), guiding the students to correct the error as needed ("Together"), and then re-asking the same question so students have the opportunity to independently answer the question correctly ("Your Turn"). Later in the lesson, the teacher provides even more practice by asking students to answer the same question again. If students answer correctly, the teacher knows that she can move ahead in the lesson.

Teachers who use systematic error corrections provide high levels of feedback to their students, an important component of explicit instruction. According to Fisher and colleagues (1980), academic feedback should be provided as often as possible to students. When more frequent feedback is given, students pay closer attention and learn more. In their research, academic feedback was more strongly and consistently related to learning than any of the other teaching behaviors.

Teaching to Success

Children who are at risk or have disabilities often require more time to learn to read. When teaching reading to students who are at risk, teachers often need to spend more time on a given skill, continuing instruction and not moving on to the next skill until students have clearly learned the one currently being taught. Research shows that if instruction is evidence based, most children can learn, given the right amount of time (Ornstein & Lasley, 2004). For example, Mr. Lazaro's class was struggling to correctly identify the short sound for the letter a. While he had originally planned to introduce the sound for the letter p on the following day, Mr. Lazaro decided he would continue working on the sound of a, not introducing a new sound until his students could correctly identify the first one. Mr. Lazaro knew that if his students could not automatically identify the sound for the letter a, they would struggle with the many words they would subsequently be reading that contained it. Another teacher using this strategy was Ms. Gentry. Her class was orally reading the latest story in their reader. Ms. Gentry, who was keeping track of the number of words her students missed, found that they were missing more than two words per page and that their accuracy was below 90%. Before Ms. Gentry moved to the next story, she had her students practice reading the words they misread and had them reread the current story until they could read it with 97% accuracy. In the past, when Ms. Gentry had moved her students to the next story regardless of their accuracy, she found that they made more errors. Sometimes our Project PRIDE teachers repeated lessons for several extra days, even an entire week. For example, when students first learned blends such as *st, sk,* and *br,* their teacher spent an extra week having them read words with those sound patterns before moving on. During social studies, one of our teachers took two or three additional days teaching comprehension, moving through the text paragraph by paragraph using graphic organizers. Time is of the essence when students are behind in reading, and teachers cannot afford to spend the long hours that are needed to reteach a skill that a child has learned incorrectly. Zig Engelmann (2007) explains that if by fourth grade a child has learned to misread words, it will take about 400 teaching trials to reteach those words. The older the student becomes, the more difficult the task of reteaching errors, and by high school, reteaching those errors can take almost three times the effort, or more than 1,000 trials.

Student Motivational System

Students who are at risk often enter school with a more limited repertoire of appropriate social and academic behaviors. As a result, learning can initially be quite difficult for them, even when the instruction provided by the teacher is systematic and explicit. Once students experience the success that results from well-designed instruction, success alone may be enough to keep them motivated and working hard. Until then, teachers often need to use a student motivational system to maintain a positive classroom atmosphere and to strengthen key academic and social behaviors that students who are at risk often lack. When Pressley and colleagues (2001) investigated what types of teachers were most effective in teaching primary-level literacy, they found that the most effective teachers had classrooms that were positive learning environments. The authors found

In Your Classroom

Using the Teacher–Class Game

Getting a classroom of students to pay attention to the reading lesson, follow the classroom rules and procedures, and answer in unison can be challenging, especially when some students come to school without these basic behavior skills needed for learning:

- Wait for a turn to speak or act.
- Understand and follow directions.
- Actively listen.
- Work independently.
- Accept consequences of behavior.

When students are not answering in unison or when misbehavior is interfering with learning time, the Teacher–Class game teaches students these skills while enabling the teacher to maintain a positive classroom environment. To organize the game before class starts, the teacher writes a T-grid on the board so he can easily award points to the class or to himself. A sample completed grid at the end of class looks like Figure 1.7.

During the lesson introduction, the teacher informs students that they will be playing the Teacher–Class game and reminds them how they can earn points. Periodically throughout the lesson when students are following the rules, the teacher awards the class points. Whenever a student does not follow the rules, the teacher gives himself a point. The more frequently the teacher gives the class a point and compliments students on their behavior, the more motivating the lesson becomes. As students work hard to get more points than the teacher, they learn successful school behaviors in the process. On Friday during the advance organizers for reading class, Mr. Setinz introduced the game to his class sitting on the rug by saying:

"Remember to pay attention to my signals, to keep your hands and feet to yourself, and to do your

best work. We are going to play the Teacher–Class game again today. Every day this week you have earned more points than I have (exaggerated sigh of exasperation). If you beat me today, that is five days in a row, and so everyone earns an extra recess at the end of the day. You'll need to pay close attention because I am going to try my hardest to win today. I would like to win at least one day, but this class is hard to beat."

Without interrupting the flow of his teaching during the lesson, Mr. Setinz juggled paying attention to students' answers along with closely monitoring their behavior. He provided some of the following feedback as he gave or took away respective points:

"Everyone followed my signal and read those first six words, so the class gets a point."

"That's my point. Tanya and Robert, I need you to answer with everyone."

"You took out your books so quickly that I just have to give you a point."

Whether a behavior strategy succeeds or fails depends on how effectively the teacher uses it. To teach positive behaviors with this game, the following guidelines are recommended:

- **Do not give warnings about potential points lost.** If your rules are that no one gets out of his seat or talks out of turn, you need to immediately give yourself a point when a student does either of those behaviors. If you warn students by saying, *"Next time, I'm going to give myself a point,"* you are actually encouraging higher rates of misbehavior because students recognize that sometimes they get away with breaking the rules.
- **Remember to notice positive student behaviors and give points for them.** *"Row 3 has been working so hard and listening to my instructions that they've earned a point for the class."* The game helps teachers maintain a positive classroom by frequently giving feedback on the positive actions of their students.
- **Put thought into selecting rewards.** Students should want the reward they will earn so they will be motivated to do their best work. Avoid using the same award every week because it will lose its impact as students become bored with it. Some

Teacher	Class
⦀⦀ ⦀⦀⦀	⦀⦀⦀ ⦀⦀⦀⦀ ⦀⦀⦀ ⦀⦀⦀⦀
7	20

FIGURE 1.7   **The Teacher–Class Game**

rewards that Project PRIDE teachers used included these:

- The opportunity for a drawing period using the white boards
- The opportunity to go to the music room and play some instruments
- A special cartoon sticker choice
- The opportunity to have extra computer lab time
- A small box of crayons to bring home
- The opportunity to use stamping markers or to earn one to bring home
- The opportunity to fly paper airplanes
- The opportunity to earn books that the teacher had purchased at garage sales the summer before

Note: This game is as successful with older students as it is with younger ones, as long as the rewards are adjusted for that age level.

- **Give students frequent points in the beginning** so they experience success and win the game the majority of the time. Otherwise, the game will not be effective.
- **Always give feedback with the points,** describing the reason why students earned or didn't earn points. Younger students require more enthusiastic, animated feedback than older ones when they earn a point. Your positive feedback will be effective if accompanied by a change in voice or facial expression that indicates you are genuinely pleased with their success. Feedback for teacher points should be explained in a matter-of-fact, no-nonsense voice tone: *"Some students forgot to follow with their finger so I get a point. Remember to use your reading finger."*

The Teacher–Class game has many variations. Some teachers will call the game Ms. Garvey vs. the Raptors, or Mr. Wood = St. Louis Cardinals vs. Class = Chicago Cubs. Teachers can give students several points when they see more effort than usual, *"We worked so hard that we finished the lesson by 10:00 and can move on to another one. This class deserves five points."* As student behaviors improve, the game should become more challenging. The teacher can tell the class that in order to win they cannot let him win more than 5 points during the entire class; or that they must earn twice as many points as he has earned to win. Another variation that is more complicated but commonly used is dividing the class into rows or teams. The teacher draws a grid for each team and for himself. Feedback might sound like this: *"Teams 1, 3, and 4 were listening and have earned points." "I've earned a point on Teams 2 and 4's grid because some people did not remember to follow with their fingers."* In the beginning, the teacher needs to give frequent feedback, awarding points after every one or two answers. Later, when students are accustomed to answering together and rarely cause disruptions that interfere with work, the teacher can award points after an entire section of the lesson.

that these teachers frequently praised students' work and their behavior, in contrast to criticizing them.

In classrooms that are positive learning environments, teachers make three or four positive comments about students' work or behavior to every one criticism or correction (McEwan & Damer, 2000). When this ratio is reversed, the teacher is caught in a criticism trap, and students learn less and actually increase their misbehavior. If students come to school uncooperative and without school readiness skills, a teacher needs to consistently praise social behaviors such as staying in a seat, answering on the teacher's signal, and keeping hands to oneself in addition to correct answers or effort put into schoolwork. If that praise alone is not enough to maintain the necessary 3:1 ratio of positive-to-negative teacher comments, the teacher needs to develop a student motivational system. If only one or two students need the additional motivation to be successful, the teacher can plan a motivational system just for them. Otherwise, the teacher can plan a class or group strategy for injecting positive motivation. Some teachers will find that extra motivation is only necessary to diminish frustration when students are first learning new skills or when they are practicing difficult ones. Strategies for motivating students who are at risk are described throughout this book. Table 1.3 shows what to do and what not to do when using all of the teaching enhancements just described. The *In Your Classroom* feature tells how to motivate your students using the Teacher–Class Game.

TABLE 1.3 Instructional Enhancements—What to Do and Not Do

	Examples What to do	Nonexamples What not to do
Advance Organizers	The teacher starts the lesson by saying, "Today we are going to learn a new letter sound and read words the fast way. This will help you learn how to read so you can decide what kind of ice cream you want when you read the Dairy Queen menu." The teacher places symbols for activities on the board as she describes them. "First we will practice a new tiger-roaring letter sound; then you will read some words that will be in our story. Today's story is about a red rabbit that gets mixed up about everything! Remember to sit up tall, keep your hands and feet to yourself, and answer when I signal."	The teacher begins the lesson by saying, "I'll sound out a word very slowly; then you read the whole word fast, like we've done before." When the teacher says "/m/-/a/-/n/," one student shouts, "man." The teacher tells the students to start over and wait for her to clap her hands before they answer.
Unison Responding	The teacher asks all of the students in the group to sound out a word by saying the sound of each letter in the word when she touches under it. The teacher asks all of the students in the group to say the first sound in the spelling word *ran* when she drops her hand.	Individual students take turns coming to the board to sound out regular words. The teacher doesn't use a visual signal when students in unison read words that are on the word wall. Some hesitant students in the group consistently answer late, reading the words a second after the more fluent readers.
Efficient Use of Teacher Talk	Wanting students to read a row of words written on the board, the teacher points to the first word and says, "Sound it out. Get ready." The teacher then signals by touching under each letter as students sound out the word. The teacher points to the letter combination *sh* and asks, "What sound?"	Wanting students to read a row of words, the teacher points to the first word and says, "Let's sound out this word. It's one we've worked on before. See if you can remember it. Careful now. Don't forget. This word is a weird one." The teacher points to the letter combination *sh* and says, "Let's read the sound of these two letters. Remember the rhyme we always say every morning about them. Tanya, that is always your favorite rhyme! What is the sound these two letters make when they come together in a word?"
Perky Pace	The teacher points to the first sight word on the list and asks, "What word?" and then when students read it correctly moves immediately to the next word. The teacher writes the letters for the letter–sounds activity on the board before the daily reading lesson begins.	The teacher points to the first sight word on the list and asks, "What word?" The students answer correctly. The teacher pauses at least 5 seconds between the student answer and the next sight word. The delay could be due to the teacher's excessive talking, a slow reaction time, or the time required to put the next word on the board. The teacher writes the *ch* combination on the board and asks students what sound it makes. The teacher then says, "Let's try another one," and writes the next letter–sound combination on the board. The teacher continues this pattern of asking a question and writing the next letter–sound combination for the rest of the lesson.

TABLE 1.3 Continued

	Examples What to do	Nonexamples What not to do
My Turn—Together—Your Turn Format	The teacher says, "Today we are going to sound out some words for the first time," and models sounding out /m/-/a/-/n/ = *man*. Then the teacher has students sound out the word twice with him before having them sound it out on their own. The teacher provides this support for the first four new words on the list and then asks students to read the rest of the new words on their own.	The teacher says, "Today we are going to sound out some words for the first time." Then the teacher asks students to sound out /m/-/a/-/n/ = *man* one time. About 60% of the students loudly answer, and the teacher moves on to the next word.
	The teacher points to a new letter combination, *ar*, which is written on the board and says, "These letters say /ar/. Listen again: /ar/." The students then say /ar/. The teacher continues, "When I touch, you say the sound." The teacher points then touches under /ar/. "What sound?" Note that this task does not require a Together step unless students have trouble articulating the /ar/ sound.	The teacher points to a new letter combination *ar* on the board and says, "This is the sound you hear in *park*. What sound do these letters make?" The teacher then moves on to another letter sound.
Cumulative Review	The teacher just introduced regular words that begin with *s* blends such as *stop* and *slow*. When the students are able to correctly read the *s* blend words, the teacher has the students read a list of words containing *s* blends plus other previously learned words beginning with *sh* and *th*.	The teacher just introduced regular words that begin with *s* blends, such as *stop* and *slow*. When the students are able to read a list of words beginning with *s* blends, the teacher introduces words with *p* blends.
	The teacher included two more difficult words from last week's spelling list on the spelling list for this week.	The teacher's spelling list this week has fifteen new words and no review words from previous lessons.
Systematic Error Correction	During a letter–sound teaching activity, the teacher touches the letter combination *ch* and asks, "What sound?" The student says /sh/. The teacher responds, "These letters say /ch/. What sound?" The teacher then provides extra practice by alternately asking the student to say the sound for *sh* and six other sounds previously learned. Later in the lesson, she asks the student one more time to tell the sound for *sh*.	During a letter–sound teaching activity, the student says /sh/ when the teacher points to *ch*. The teacher says, "No, think about something good to eat." After the student names foods, the teacher says, "Chocolate is good to eat. What letters does chocolate begin with? Do you see those letters on the board? What sound do they make?" When the student says /ch/, the teacher moves on to the next word.
	During a sight word reading, the teacher points to the word *ghost* and says, "What word?" Several students pronounce the word incorrectly. The teacher says, "The word is *ghost*. What is this word?" When students answer correctly, the teacher returns to the top of the list of five words and has the students read all five words again, including the word *ghost*.	During a sight word reading activity, the students say *gets* when they see the word *ghost*. The teacher says, "The word is *ghost*. Let's try the next word."

Continued

TABLE 1.3   Continued

	Examples What to do	Nonexamples What not to do
Teaching to Success	The teacher introduced the *ou* sound to her students for the first time. The next day she tested her students to see if they could identify the *ou* sound when it was mixed in with the previously learned combinations of *sh, ea, ow,* and *th.* Her students made repeated errors on the *ou* sound and missed *th* and *sh* as well. The following day, the teacher decided to provide more practice on all of the sounds from the day before. She would only introduce *ar* when the students were able to identify these other sounds correctly.	The teacher introduced the *ou* sound to her students for the first time. The next day she tested her students to see if they could identify the *ou* sound when it was mixed in with the previously learned letter combinations of *sh, ea, ow,* and *th.* Her students made repeated errors on the *ou* sound and missed *th* and *sh* as well. The following day the teacher introduced a new letter combination: *ar.*
	The teacher had her students read today's story orally. The group made 20 errors, reading the story with about 88% accuracy. The following day the teacher provided a drill for the students on the words missed the previous day. She also had the students reread the story until they read it with 97% accuracy.	The teacher had her students read today's story orally. The group made 20 errors, reading the story with about 88% accuracy. The following day the teacher moved to the next story in the book.
Student Motivational System	During small-group instruction, Billy often leaves his seat. The teacher frequently praises Billy for staying in his seat and working so hard. She also praises other students for staying in their seats. The teacher seldom has to tell Billy to come back to his seat.	During small-group instruction, Billy often leaves his seat. Often when Billy leaves his seat, the teacher says, "Billy, if you can't pay attention, I'll have to call your mom." The teacher does not praise Billy when he is in his seat.
	While sight-reading a list of words, students continue to miss a number of them. Before reading through the list again, the teacher tells the students that their goal is reading every word correctly. This time, she praises the students immediately after each of the sight words is read correctly. When the list is finished, she smiles and exclaims, "I knew you could do it. Every one right! Give yourself a pat on the back!"	While sight-reading a list of words, students continue to miss a number of them. Each time they miss a word, the teacher makes a comment like, "This sure is a bad day," or "I don't know what you are all thinking about." When students continue to make mistakes, the teacher ends the lesson saying, "Maybe tomorrow you will all be awake."

APPLIED ACTIVITIES

1. Explain what is wrong about each nonexample in Table 1.3. Be sure to focus your answer on the particular enhancement in question.

2. Think of the most difficult class you had this past year. If the teacher used a My Turn–Together–Your Turn strategy to support your success in learning the material, describe how that teaching strategy was used. If the teacher did not use a My Turn–Together–Your Turn strategy, describe how that strategy could have been used to help you more successfully learn the course material.

3. Have you worked for a boss who maintained a 3:1 ratio of positive comments to critical comments? Have you worked for a boss who had a ratio of 3:1 critical comments to positive comments? How did you feel about each of these individuals for whom you worked? Who was more motivating and why? How did you behave differently for each of these individuals?

4. Describe your experience as a student with a teacher who used unison responses as part of his or her teaching technique. How did the teacher get everyone to answer and how well did you learn the material?

REFERENCES

Adams, M. (1990). *Beginning to read: Thinking and learning about print.* Cambridge, MA: MIT Press.

Adams, M. S., & Bruck, M. (1993). Word recognition: The interface of educational policies and scientific research. *Reading and Writing: An Interdisciplinary Journal, 5,* 113–139.

Ameis, J. (2003). *Early years e-text book: Three stages of teaching* [Electronic version]. Retrieved June 7, 2009, from University of Winnipeg Department of Education: http://web.archive.org/web/20070807070201/http://io.uwinnipeg.ca/~jameis/New+Pages/EYR5.html

American Federation of Teachers (2007). Where we stand: K–12 literacy. [Electronic version]. Retrieved June 7, 2009, from http://www.aft.org/pubs-reports/downloads/teachers/WWS-K12literacy.pdf

Archer, A. (Speaker). (1995). *The time is now* [Cassette recording]. Eugene, OR: World Association of Direct Instruction 21st Annual Conference.

Archer, A., Gleason, M. M., & Vachon, V. (2003). Decoding and fluency: Foundation skills for struggling older readers. *Learning Disability Quarterly, 26,* 89–101.

Armbruster, B., Lehr, F., & Osborn, J. (2001). *Put reading first: The research building blocks for teaching children to read.* Washington, DC: Partnership for Reading.

Arndt, E., & Crawford, E. (2006). Effective reading interventions: Characteristics, resources and implications for SLPs [Electronic version]. Retrieved July 27, 2009, from http://www.fcrr.org/science/powerpoint/crawford/ASHA2006presentation.ppt

Ball, E. W., & Blachman, B. A. (1991). Does phoneme awareness training in kindergarten make a difference in early word recognition and developmental spelling? *Reading Research Quarterly, 24,* 49–66.

Beck, I., McKeown, M., & Kucan, L. (2002). *Bringing words to life: Robust vocabulary instruction.* New York: The Guilford Press.

Biemiller, A. (2001). Teaching vocabulary: Early, direct, and sequential. *The American Educator, 25*(1), 24–28.

Brown-Chidsey, R., & Steege, M. (2005). *Response to Intervention: Principles and strategies for effective practice.* New York: The Guilford Press.

Bursuck, W., & Damer, M. (2005). *Project PRIDE* (CFDA 84.334T August 2005 Final Report). Unpublished manuscript.

Bursuck, B., Smith, T., Munk, D., Damer, M., Mehlig, L., & Perry, J. (2004). Evaluating the impact of a prevention-based model of reading on children who are at risk. *Remedial and Special Education, 25,* 303–313.

Catts, H. W., Fey, M. E., Zhang, X., & Tomblin, J. B. (1999). Language basis of reading and reading disabilities: Evidence from a longitudinal investigation. *Scientific Studies of Reading, 3,* 331–361.

Damer, M., Bursuck, W., & Harris, R. (2008, Spring). A year later: Performance of students who exit Tier 3 direct instruction within a multi-tier reading model. *Direct Instruction News.*

Deno, S. L. (2003). Developments in curriculum-based measurement. *Journal of Special Education, 37,* 184–192.

Edmonds, M. S., Vaughn, S., Wexler, J., Reutebuch, C., Cable, A., Klingner, J., & Tackett, K. (2009). A synthesis of reading interventions and effects on reading comprehension outcomes for older struggling readers. *Review of Educational Research, 79,* 262–300.

Ehri, L. C. (2005). Learning to read words: Theory, findings, and issues. *Scientific Studies of Reading, 9,* 167–188.

Elbaum, B., Vaughn, S., Hughes, M. T., & Moody, S. W. (2000). Grouping practices and reading outcome for students with disabilities. *Exceptional Children, 65,* 399–415.

Englert, C., Tarrant, K., & Mariage, T. (1992). Defining and redefining instructional practice in special education: Perspectives on good teaching. *Teacher Education and Special Education, 15*(2), 62–86.

Engelmann, Z. (2007). *Teaching needy kids in our backward system.* Eugene, OR: ADI Press.

Fisher, C., Berliner, D., Filby, N., Marliave, R., Cahen, L., & Dishaw, M. (1980). Teaching behaviors, academic learning time, and student achievement: An overview. In C. Denham & A. Lieberman (Eds.), *Time to learn: A review of the Beginning Teacher Evaluation Study* (pp. 7–32). Washington, DC: Department of Health, Education, and Welfare.

Foorman, B., & Torgesen, J. (2001). Critical elements of classroom and small-group instruction promote reading success in all children. *Learning Disabilities Research & Practice, 16,* 203–212.

Francis, D. J., Shaywitz, S. E., Stuebing, K. K., Fletcher, J. M., & Shaywitz, B. A. (1996). Developmental lag vs. deficit models of reading disability: A longitudinal individual growth curves analysis. *Journal of Educational Psychology, 1,* 3–17.

Friend, M., & Bursuck, W. D. (2009). *Including students with special needs: A practical guide for classroom teachers* (4th ed.) Boston: Pearson/Allyn & Bacon.

Friend, M., & Cook, L. (2007). *Interactions: Collaborative skills for school professionals* (5th ed.). Boston: Allyn & Bacon.

Fuchs, L., Fuchs, D., Hosp, M., & Jenkins, J. (2001). Oral reading fluency as an indicator of reading competence: A theoretical, empirical, and historical analysis. *Scientific Studies of Reading, 5,* 239–256.

Gersten, R., Compton, D., Connor, C. M., Dimino, J., Santoro, L., Linan-Thompson, S., & Tilly, W. D. (2009). Assisting students struggling with reading: Response to Intervention and multi-tier intervention for reading in the primary grades. A practice guide (NCEE 2009-4045) [Electronic version]. Washington, DC: National Center for Education Evaluation and Regional Assistance, Institute of Education Sciences, U.S. Department of Education. Retrieved May 28, 2009, from http://ies.ed.gov/ncee/wwc/publications/practiceguides/

Gough, P. (1983). Context, form, and interaction. In K. Rayner (Ed.), *Eye movements in reading* (pp. 331–358). Cambridge, MA: MIT Press.

Hall, S., & Moats, L. (1999). *Straight talk about reading.* Chicago: Contemporary Books.

Hart, B., & Risley, T. (1995). *Meaningful differences.* Baltimore: Paul H. Brookes Publishing.

Honig, B. (2001). *Teaching our children to read: The components of an effective, comprehensive reading program.* Thousand Oaks, CA: Corwin Press.

Hoover, J. J., & Patton, J. R. (2008). The role of special educators in a multitiered instructional system. *Remedial and Special Education, 43,* 195–202.

Jenkins, J. (2009). Measuring reading growth: New findings on progress monitoring. *New Times for DLD, 27,* pp. 1–2.

Jenkins, J., & Johnson, E. (2007). Universal screening for reading problems: Why and how should we do this? Retrieved June 11, 2009, from RTI Action Network: http://www.rtinetwork.org/Essential/Assessment/Universal/ar/ReadingProblems

Juel, C. (1988). Retention and nonretention of at-risk readers in first grade and their subsequent reading achievement. *Journal of Learning Disabilities, 21,* 571–580.

Kame'enui, E., Good, R., Simmons, D., & Chard, D. (2002). Project CIRCUITS: Toward a primary, secondary, and tertiary prevention system in schools. Paper presented at the Annual Convention of the Council for Exceptional Children, New York.

Kame'enui, E. (2007) An Interview with Edward Kame'enui [Electronic version]. Retrieved from http://www.pbs.org/launchingreaders/soundsandsymbols/meettheexperts_2.html

Lee, J., Grigg, W., & Donahue, P. (2007). *The nation's report card: Reading 2007* (NCES 2007-496). National Center for Education Statistics, Institute of Education Sciences, U.S. Department of Education, Washington, DC.

Lemoine, H. E., Levy, B. A., & Hutchinson, A. (1993). Increasing the naming speed of poor readers: Representations formed across repetitions. *Journal of Experimental Child Psychology, 55,* 297–328.

Lyon, R. (1998). Why reading is not a natural activity. *Educational Leadership, 3,* 14–18.

Lyon, R. (1998, April 28). *Overview of reading and literacy initiatives.* Statement to Committee on Labor and Human Resources, Bethesda, MD [Electronic version]. Retrieved from http://www.dys-add.com/ReidLyonJeffords.pdf

Marzano, R. J. (2003). *What works in schools: Translating research into action.* Alexandria, VA: Association for Supervision and Curriculum Development.

McEwan, E., & Damer, M. (2000). *Managing unmanageable students.* Thousand Oaks, CA: Corwin Press.

National Reading Panel. (2000). *Teaching children to read: An evidence-based assessment of the scientific research literature on reading and its implications for reading instruction.* Washington, DC: National Institute of Child Health and Human Development.

National Early Literacy Panel. (2008). *Developing early literacy: Report of the National Early Literacy Panel.* Washington, DC: National Institute for Literacy.

Ornstein, A. C., & Lasley, T. J. II (2004). *Strategies for effective teaching* (4th ed.). New York: McGraw-Hill.

Pisha, B., & Stahl, S. (2005). The promise of new learning environments for students with disabilities. *Intervention in School and Clinic, 41,* 67–75.

Pressley, M., Wharton-McDonald, R., Allington, R., Block, C., Morrow, L., Tracey, D., et al. (2001). A study of effective first-grade literacy instruction. *Scientific Studies of Reading, 5*(1), 35–58.

RAND Reading Study Group. (2002). Reading for understanding: Toward an R&D program in reading comprehension [Electronic version]. Retrieved May 17, 2009, from http://www.rand.org/pubs/monograph_reports/MR1465/

Rosenshine, B. (1986). Synthesis of research on explicit teaching. *Educational Leadership, 43*(7), 60–69.

Shaywitz, S. (2003). *Overcoming dyslexia: A new and complete science-based program for reading problems at any level.* New York: Knopf.

Shaywitz, S. E., & Shaywitz, B. E. (2007). What neuroscience really tells us about reading instruction. *Educational Leadership, 64,* 74–76.

Simos, P. G., Fletcher, J. M., Sarkari, S., Billingsley-Marshall, R. L., Denton, C. A., & Papanicolaou, A. C. (2007). Intensive instruction affects brain magnetic activity associated with oral word reading in children with persistent reading disabilities. *Journal of Learning Disabilities, 40,* 37–48.

Speece, D. L., & Ritchey, K. D. (2005). A longitudinal study of the development of oral reading fluency in young children at risk for reading failure. *Journal of Learning Disabilities, 38,* 387–399.

Stahl, S., & Nagy, W. (2006). *Teaching word meanings.* Mahwah, NJ: Lawrence Erlbaum Associates.

Steinbeck, J. (1976). The acts of King Arthur and his noble knights: Introduction to his translation of *Le Morte d'Arthur.* In *The Winchester Manuscripts of Thomas Malory & Other Sources* (pp. 3–4). Portsmouth, NH: Heinemann Publishing Company.

Stichter, J., Stormont, M., & Lewis, T. (2009). Instructional practices and behavior during reading: A descriptive summary and comparison of practices in title one and non-title elementary schools. *Psychology in the Schools, 46,* 172–183.

Torgesen, J. K. (2000). Individual differences in response to early interventions in reading: The lingering problem of treatment resisters. *Learning Disabilities Research and Practice, 15,* 55–64.

Vellutino, F. R., Scanlon, D. M., Sipay, E. R., Small, S. G., Pratt, A., Chen, R., et al. (1996). Cognitive profiles of difficult-to-remediate and readily remediated poor readers: Early intervention as a vehicle for distinguishing between cognitive and experiential deficits as basic causes of specific reading disability. *Journal of Educational Psychology, 88,* 601–638.

Venezky, R. L. (1970). *The structure of English orthography.* The Hague: Mouton.

Wanzek, J., & Vaughn, S. (2008). Response to varying amounts of time in reading intervention for students with low response to intervention. *Journal of Learning Disabilities, 41,* 126–142.

Wendorf, J. (2003, September 10). Interview: *Children of the code* [Electronic version]. Interviewer: David Boulton. Retrieved March 24, 2009, from http://www.childrenofthecode.org/interviews/wendorf.htm#TheCostsofTeachingReading

Whitehurst, G. (2003, September 10). Interview: *Evidence-based education science and the challenge of learning to read* [Electronic version]. Interviewer: David Boulton. Retrieved May 12, 2009, from http://www.childrenofthecode.org/interviews/whitehurst.htm

Wijk, A. (1966). *Rules of pronunciation for the English language.* Oxford: Oxford University Press.

Wolf, M., & Katzir-Cohen, T. (2001). Reading fluency and its intervention. *Scientific Studies of Reading, 5,* 211–238.

Wren, S. (2000). *Reading by sight* [Electronic version]. Retrieved June 6, 2009, from the Southwest Educational Development Laboratory Web site: http://www.sedl.org/reading/topics/sightwords.pdf

2 Early Literacy

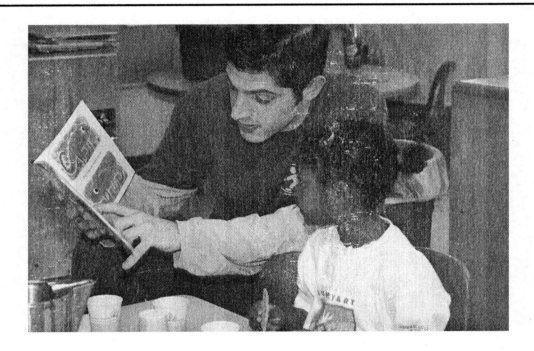

Introduction

This chapter discusses the underlying concepts that students must develop to read. The term *emergent literacy* refers to the gradual process children go through as they develop an understanding of written language.

At one time, the field of reading focused on *reading readiness* as a set of skills students needed before they could begin reading instruction. However, research has shown that children best develop the foundation for reading as they engage in activities with print. Rather than children being "ready for reading" at one point in their lives, the basis for reading is laid gradually and involves speaking, listening, reading, and writing (Strickland, Galda, & Cullinan, 2004). In a joint position statement, the International Reading Association and the National Association for the Education of Young Children (1998) identified five stages of literacy development: awareness and exploration; experimentation; early reading and writing; transitional reading and writing; and conventional reading and writing.

Unfortunately, many students with reading problems have not mastered one or more of these crucial concepts. If you have students who cannot comfortably read beginning-level books, you must determine whether they have developed the foundation needed for reading. Many such students, even those in intermediate grades, lack basic concepts about print. When these concepts are developed using books, stories, letters, and words, students improve dramatically. The tasks used to assess early literacy in the Reading Center are based on the Early Reading Screening Instrument (ERSI), developed by Darrell Morris (1998).

This chapter focuses on the first four stages of development and the concepts that children should develop as they progress through these stages. We discuss how to assess those concepts and suggest some instructional strategies to teach them. Although most students struggling in the early stages of literacy development will progress using these techniques, some students with multiple or severe disabilities need more intensive measures.

Early Literacy Concepts

Six areas are included in the early stages of literacy development:

- Oral language development
- Concepts about print
- Alphabet knowledge
- Phonemic awareness
- Letter-sound correspondence
- Beginning reading vocabulary

This section discusses each of these concepts and provides informal methods by which to assess them.

Oral Language Development

Reading, writing, listening, and speaking are all aspects of language. Students whose oral language is not well developed have difficulty with literacy.

Aspects of Oral Language Important for Literacy   To read effectively, students need to be able to express and understand ideas fully. They also need to develop language skills specifically related to stories. For example, they must understand and be able to express the structure of stories. This understanding includes realizing that stories have characters and events that occur in sequence.

Questioning is also a crucial language skill. To participate fully in lessons, students must respond to teachers' questions. They also need to ask questions to clarify their own understandings or seek information. Many students with language development problems have difficulty constructing or responding to questions.

During the "get acquainted" activity in the Reading Center, it became apparent that Sean, a third grader, had language problems. When Sean's teacher asked him for a word describing himself, he could not answer. After many probes, he finally said "boy" and "brother." When he retold *Little Red Riding Hood* in his own words, he referred to the Grandmother as "Mom" and to Little Red Riding Hood as "she." Finally, despite the many problems Sean encountered, he never asked for help in reading or writing.

Assessing Oral Language Development   Oral language development is assessed through informal teacher observations and through narrative comprehension. As you engage students in conversations and observe their conversations with others, you should notice whether students talk about their interests and activities. When you ask students about important events in their lives, are the responses full accounts or one-word answers? Can students convey events in sequential order? When students misunderstand directions or encounter problems, can they ask for help?

Before students become skilled readers, teachers can assess their narrative comprehension skills through story construction. Narrative comprehension is an important predictor of later reading success (Paris & Paris, 2003). One way to assess narrative comprehension is to read a story to students and ask them to retell it (Morrow, 2004). You can also use passages from an informal reading inventory to determine the language levels of your students. Paris and Paris (2003) have developed an assessment tool that uses wordless picture books and asks students to construct stories based on these sequential pictures. Checklists that help teachers score students' retellings and story constructions are especially useful in maintaining class records and monitoring students' progress (Gredler & Johnson, 2004; Walker, 2005).

Concepts about Print

An understanding of how print works is critical to early literacy. Students must realize that print on the page is read in a certain order and that it contains individual words.

Concepts Crucial to Reading   Students need three understandings about print:

* Print rather than pictures carries meaning.
* Reading is tracked, or followed, from top to bottom and left to right.
* In print, words are separated by spaces.

Although these concepts are typically developed in the kindergarten years, some students with reading problems have not fully mastered them in the primary grades. Kelly, a first grader in the Reading Center, traced lines backward, from right to left, as her teacher read them. Derrick, a second-grade child, thought that every spoken syllable he heard was a printed word. These children still needed to develop fundamental concepts about print.

Assessing Concepts about Print   In her *An Observation Survey of Early Literacy Achievement*, Marie Clay (1993, 2002) includes a *Concepts about Print* test using two books, *Sand* and *Stone,* that are specifically designed to measure students' understanding of how print works. These books provide teachers with the opportunity to determine students' awareness of print as meaning, ability to track words and lines in text, and knowledge of what a word is. The test also measures awareness of inverted pages, transposed words, reversed letters, mismatches between pictures and text, and sentences printed out of sequence.

Many concepts about print can be measured without formal tests just by sharing a simple book with a student. Choose an 8- to 12-page book with one or two lines of text per page. The book should contain multisyllabic words and at least one return sweep. To determine awareness of print as meaning, open the book and ask the student to point to "what we read." The student should identify print, not pictures. Next, to determine tracking, point to the print and ask the student to show you "where we begin to read," and "where we go next." Notice whether the student starts at the left for each line. Finally, for word awareness, ask the student to point to and repeat words after *you* have read each page. From this repetition, you can see whether the student can correctly identify a multisyllabic word as one word.

Alphabet Knowledge

Research shows that the ability to name letters is an excellent predictor of early reading achievement (Hammill, 2004; Trieman, Tincoff, & Richmond-Welty, 1996; Walsh, Price, & Gillingham, 1988).

Knowledge Needed for Reading   Alphabet knowledge consists of two parts: recognizing letters and writing letters. Students must identify letters automatically and must be able to name them when they are presented in random order. In addition, students must know both uppercase and lowercase letters.

Some reading disabled students, even in the third grade, still have problems with letter recognition. Allen, a third grader in the Reading Center, frequently asked the teacher how to make a *u* or a *j*.

Assessing Alphabet Knowledge   A sample of an alphabet test is given in Figure 2.1. To administer the task, ask your student to say each letter, reading across the lines. Next, ask the student to write these same letters as you say them.

Phonemic Awareness

Phonemic, or phonological, awareness is the knowledge that speech is built from sounds. For example, the word *bed* consists of three speech sounds, or phonemes: *b, short e,* and *d*. The word *sleep* consists of four phonemes: *s, l, long e,* and *p,* even though it has five letters; the *ee* combination makes only one sound. Consonants can also combine to make one sound; the word *sheep,* which is five letters, consists of three phonemes: *sh, long e,* and *p*.

Knowledge Needed for Reading   Phonemic awareness refers to students' knowledge of individual sounds in words and their ability to manipulate those segments (Hammill, 2004; National Reading Panel, 2000; Stahl & Murray, 1994). Research shows that students' abilities to identify and manipulate these sound elements are highly related to reading achievement and spelling (Ball & Blachman, 1991; Byrne & Fielding-Barnsley, 1991; Dreher & Zenge, 1990; Hammill, 2004; Muter, Hulme, & Taylor, 1998; Naslund & Schneider, 1996; Paris, 2003; Stanovich, 1988).

Phonemic awareness includes a variety of abilities. Students must be able to identify and separate beginning sounds of words, identify and separate ending sounds, and substitute sounds within a basic pattern. Finally, students need to be able to manipulate sounds by putting them together (or blending them), taking them apart (or segmenting them), and deleting and substituting them. All these abilities help students to master phonics in reading.

Assessing Phonemic Awareness   Phonemic awareness is assessed by asking students to blend and segment sounds, as shown in Figure 2.2. Other tasks include asking students to identify the first sound in a spoken word (e.g., "What is the first sound in *table*?") or to say a word without a sound (e.g., "Say *table* without the /t/.") (Paris, 2003; Stahl & Murray, 1994).

FIGURE 2.1   Alphabet Recognition Test

Letter-Sound Correspondence

To read successfully, students must be able to identify and manipulate sounds and associate these sounds with their corresponding letters (Ball & Blachman, 1991; Busin, 1997; International Reading Association, 1998; Morrow, 2004; Muter, Hulme, & Taylor, 1998; Trieman, Tincoff, & Richmond-Welty, 1996).

Relationship to Reading Achievement   Students' knowledge of letter-sound correspondence is highly related to later reading achievement (Dreher & Zenge, 1990; Morrow, 2004; Naslund & Schneider, 1996). Most important to emergent literacy is knowledge about beginning consonants.

Directions: I am going to say some words in a special code, and I want you to figure out the real word. If I say /s/-/a/-/t/, you say *sat.* If I say /p/-/i/-/g/, you say *pig.*

Teacher says:	Expected Response	Student's Response
/d/-/i/-/g/	dig	
/p/-/u/-/l/	pull	
/b/-/e/-/d/	bed	
/f/-/a/-/s/-/t/	fast	
/s/-/o/-/f/-/t/	soft	

Directions: Now we will change jobs. If I say *bat,* you say /b/-/a/-/t/. If I say *feet,* you say /f/-/ee/-/t/.

Teacher says:	Expected Response	Student's Response
can	/c/-/a/-/n/	
tell	/t/-/e/-/l/	
dust	/d/-/u/-/s/-/t/	
sit	/s/-/i/-/t/	
fog	/f/-/o/-/g/	

NOTE: The use of slashes (//) indicates that you should say the letter *sound.*

FIGURE 2.2   Assessing Phonological Awareness: Blending and Segmenting

Assessing Knowledge of Letter-Sound Correspondence   To assess students' knowledge of beginning consonants, the teacher gives them a word and asks them to identify the beginning sound of the word and the letter that corresponds to this sound. The words in the sample task in Figure 2.3 are frequently found in beginning reading materials and all begin with single-letter initial consonant sounds. The task also includes some two-syllable words.

Students' spelling of unfamiliar words also reveals important information about letter-sound correspondences (Gentry & Gillet, 1993; Paris, 2003; Roberts, 1996).

Beginning Reading Vocabulary

The earliest words children learn to read are from their environment. Children who recognize *McDonald's, Cheerios,* and *Don't Walk* are reading environmental print. As books, paper, and markers become a part of children's worlds, they make a transition from recognizing logos and signs to recognizing their names or *MOM* and *DAD.*

A child's first sight words play a critical role in emergent literacy, for emergent readers gain confidence by using their beginning sight words in reading and writing. These words also form the foundation for word analysis strategies and enable students to use known words as a basis for learning about new ones.

One way to assess early reading vocabulary is to ask students to write any words they know. This activity provides students with the opportunity to show you what they know instead of what they do *not* know.

Practice: What is the beginning sound of *mat*? (Student should say /m/.) What letter makes that sound? (Student should say *M.* If not, model and practice another word.)

Word	Beginning Sound	Beginning Letter
fish		
little		
ride		
want		
happy		

FIGURE 2.3 Assessing Letter-Sound Correspondences: Beginning Letter Sounds

Clay (1993, 2002) recommends that teachers assess beginning reading vocabulary by developing a word list using 15 high-frequency words drawn from the students' early reading materials and asking students to read these words. This method allows the teacher to discover which early reading words students know and what their strategies are for coping with unknown words. Allow 10 minutes for students to repeat this activity.

Strategies to Develop Early Literacy Concepts

This section suggests activities for developing early literacy concepts. Although in assessment, we often try to separate components of literacy development, these areas are usually learned through an integrated literate environment (Morrow, 2004). Thus, one activity may foster several areas of early literacy. As previously emphasized, early literacy understandings are best taught within the context of real reading and writing in literacy-rich environments. Because emerging into reading is a gradual process, the instructional activities used to support development overlap with those used for beginning reading and writing.

Oral Language Development

As stated earlier in this chapter, oral language development forms the basis for reading and writing. Three aspects of oral language development crucial to literacy are understanding and using oral language, understanding the structure of stories, and responding to and constructing questions.

Reading Aloud to Students Reading books aloud to children is valuable for helping them to develop language skills. Many students with reading problems have not had wide experience in sharing print with an adult. Reading to students enables them to experience the rich language of books as an adult models the process of reading. Children learn to follow a story structure and to engage in conversation about books. In the sections that follow, additional strategies are given that may be used as the teacher reads books aloud to children.

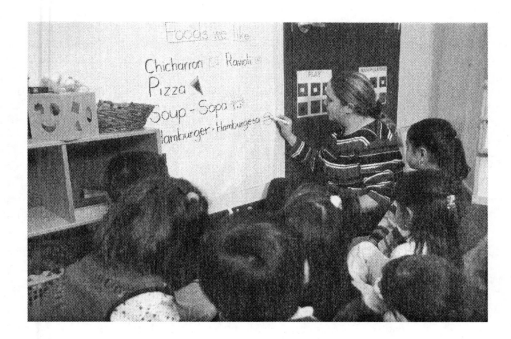

Directed Listening-Thinking Activity   Often referred to by its initials, DL-TA, this activity is a modification of the Directed Reading-Thinking Activity (DR-TA) developed by Stauffer (1975). In DL-TA, the teacher reads the text aloud, stopping at crucial points to allow students to predict what will happen next and to confirm or revise previous predictions. These predictions and confirmations (or revisions) guide the students' understanding of the story.

After students are familiar with this strategy, the teacher can alter it by stopping before the last section of text and asking students what they think will happen in the end. Ask students to draw pictures showing what they think will happen; they may then write or dictate a sentence or two about their pictures. Next, read the author's actual ending to the story and compare it with the students' endings.

Story Structure   The structure of stories can be used to guide the discussion of books a teacher reads to children. Focusing on story elements helps students learn that (1) stories are organized in a predictable fashion; (2) special terms, such as *characters, events,* and *setting,* are used for stories. These understandings will help children both to read and to write stories (Galda, Cullinan, & Strickland, 1997; Gillet, Crawford, Temple, & Cooney, 2003; Gillet & Temple, 2000; Strickland, Cullinan, & Galda, 2003).

After you read a story to your students, ask them, "Who is this story about?" or "Who are the main characters in this story?" Then ask the students, "Where does this story take place?" and "When does this story take place?" Next, ask students, "What is the main characters' problem?" and finally ask, "How do they solve the problem?"

In the Reading Center, questions are often placed on a chart. Students can answer the questions with pictures from the story or refer to the chart as they retell stories or construct their own. Learning about the *language of stories* provides an excellent foundation for the more complex story grammars and maps used in later comprehension instruction.

Shanahan and Shanahan (1997) have developed a related strategy called Character Perspective Charting. In this strategy, children track the main characters in stories and identify their perspectives in relation to story events. This strategy has proved quite effective in helping students understand stories.

Shared Book Experience   In this strategy (Button & Johnson, 1997; Holdaway, 1979; Morrow, 2004), teachers imitate the "bedtime story" experience of young children. You can use the shared book experience with whole classes, in small groups, or with individuals. Students are drawn into the shared book experience by the quality of the stories shared, by the teacher's enthusiasm, and by the "sharing" format. A shared book experience may be extended over several days, as children reread and engage in several different activities. Generally, the teacher uses predictable, or patterned, books, which contain repeated words or phrases and plots simple enough for students to predict outcomes. Some favorite predictable books include *Have You Seen My Duckling?* (by Tafuri), *Bears in the Night* (by Berenstain & Berenstain), *Where's Spot?* (by Hill), *Have You Seen Crocodile?* (by West), *The Carrot Seed* (by Krauss), *Titch* (by Hutchins), *Ape in a Cape* (by Eichenberg), *Is Your Mama a Llama?* (by Guarino), *Green Eggs and Ham* (by Dr. Seuss), *Too Much Noise* (by McGovern), and *The Very Hungry Caterpillar* (by Carle). Predictable books support students as they attempt to read on their own.

The steps in a shared book experience are:

1. *Introduce the book.* Ask students to predict what it will be about as you clarify any concepts that may be unknown. Show the pictures of the book.
2. *Read the book aloud to students.* Point to each word as you read. Read slowly but with expression rather than word by word. Position the book so that the students can see it. Then reread the book, inviting children to join you. If students do not join you in the rereading, encourage them by leaving off significant words. For example, for "I Know an Old Lady Who Swallowed a Fly," you might read:

   > She swallowed a spider
   > That wiggled and jiggled and tickled inside her
   > She swallowed the spider to catch the fly
   > But I don't know why she swallowed the fly . . .

   Who can resist joining in with "I guess she'll die"?
3. *Follow the reading with language activities.* The language-related activities developed from shared book experiences can focus on letter-sound correspondences, dramatization, learning new vocabulary, or any other aspect of literacy that the teacher chooses to develop.

   For example, if you choose to focus on letter sounds, select significant words from the story and draw pictures of them on index cards. Have students group the pictures by their beginning sounds. Next, introduce the letters that correspond to those sounds. Then, you might present a picture card and ask students to write the beginning letter.

Language Experience Approach   The shared book experience is an excellent springboard for the language experience approach (LEA) (Allen, 1976; Morrow, 2004; Stauffer, 1980; Warner, 1963). In an LEA, teachers and students compose an original story or retell a story in their own words. Generally, students dictate to a teacher, who writes down their words on a chalkboard or large piece of paper.

To try this strategy, follow these procedures:

1. *Brainstorm ideas for a story.* Topics may include shared experiences, such as field trips, science experiments, special events, or stories read aloud. Choose one topic for your story.
2. *Take dictation from students.* Ask students to tell you the words you should write. At early stages, stories should be limited to four or five sentences. Write the words in large print.
3. *Read each word as you write it.*
4. *Reread each sentence, pointing to each word as you say it.* Have students reread each sentence with you.
5. *Reread the entire story with students.*

6. *Follow up with language activities.* For example, students might select three words that they can recognize or draw pictures to go with their story. If they draw pictures, they might choose to write captions for them.

Often teachers combine the language experience activity with the shared book experience to create a cohesive lesson. One second-grade Title I teacher used this format with poetry to provide her students with rich language experiences, as seen in Strategy Snapshot 2.1.

Strategy Snapshot 2.1

A Shared Book Experience with an LEA

Ms. Burgess, a teacher in a second-grade Title I class, began with a favorite poem, *Honey, I Love* (by Greenfield), printed on chart paper. She pointed to the words and the students read along in a sing-song fashion.

Next, Ms. Burgess reread a favorite story, *Being Here with You* (by Nicola-Lisa, 1992), as part of a unit on friendship. Ms. Burgess introduced the LEA saying, "Today we're going to write a story like Mr. Nicola-Lisa's, except ours is going to be about our class and how nice it is that we are all so different, but alike."

The students brainstormed ways they were alike and different. As the students talked about what they liked to do together, they recalled a picnic at which they met their seventh-grade pen pals. The students created their own story, "Pen Pals in the Park."

Next, the class divided into teams. One team played a sorting game with the letters p and b. Another group used magnetic letters to write words selected from their story. The third group sorted picture cards under the headings "Alike" and "Different." The fourth group met with Ms. Burgess to read sentences they wrote about a previous story.

After several minutes, the students reassembled for Ms. Burgess to introduce a new book, *Three Friends* (by Kraus). As she read, Ms. Burgess pointed to the words in the text and stopped occasionally to ask the students how they thought the characters could solve their problems. When she came to a word that started with *b* or *p*, she asked the sorting group for help.

Using Wordless Books   Wordless books, which tell stories through pictures only and contain no text, can help students develop the skill of telling a narrative in sequence. In using a wordless book, you may wish to have students dictate a sentence for each picture. An alternative approach is to discuss the book with students, record their dictation, writing each sentence on a separate page, and have students illustrate the book. You can then bind the pages to create your own big book. Children can be encouraged to identify words that they know and to read their creation to others. Popular wordless books include *A Boy, a Dog, and a Frog* (by Mayer), *What?* (by Lionni), and *Apt. 3* (by Keats). Each of these authors has written additional wordless books.

Concepts about Print

The activities described in the previous sections of this chapter help to develop crucial concepts about print. This section presents some additional activities to develop these understandings.

Echo Reading or Pointing   The echo reading procedure presented earlier to evaluate concepts about print may also be used to teach these concepts. Good assessment should have much in common with instruction (Cunningham, Cunningham, Moore, & Moore, 2004; Johnston, 1997; Rasinski, 2003).

In echo reading, teachers help students match the spoken word with the printed word. To implement this strategy, select a predictable book with limited print. First, read the entire book to the students. Next, read one sentence, pointing to each word. To echo read, students reread what you have read as they also point to words. As students become more familiar with the process, the length students repeat may be increased. Monitor students' pointing carefully; make certain that they point to each *word* rather than to each *syllable* that is read.

Uhry (2002) emphasizes that this strategy is much more complex than it appears to be. Research has shown that matching speech to print is an underlying skill for specific word learning (Morris, 1993). However, both Morris (1993) and Ehri (1992) found that students who could segment phonemes were also more successful at finger-point reading. Many children involved in finger-point reading studies have reported that they used a system of "counting words" across a line of print to help them identify specific words (Uhry, 2002).

A major implication for teachers in early grades or for teachers working with older students who are at an early literacy stage of development is that these skills are interrelated. Students need to develop one-to-one correspondence so that they can match individual words in speech and print. They need to develop the alphabetic principle in order to develop letter-sound correspondence, and they need to develop phonemic awareness to segment phonemes. The instructional strategies that follow can help you foster the development of these skills.

Counting Words   In this activity (Cunningham, 2000; Cunningham, Cunningham, Moore, & Moore, 2004), students recognize words in speech, a skill that prepares them to recognize them later in print. To do the activity, give students objects (blocks, Popsicle sticks) to use as counters. The student listens as you say a sentence at a normal rate. Then say the sentence again, pausing after each word. Students should move a counter for each word you say. Next, have students make up their own sentences and count the words in them.

Jumbled Sentences   In this strategy, students count words as they reorder them. Many students who develop early reading problems need this physical separation of words to develop a strong concept of word. To try this strategy, follow these procedures:

1. *Begin with a story you have read or written with your students.* Ask students to write a sentence about the story. Most students write summary sentences. For example, in a story about a hungry dog, Ramon wrote, "Duffy gobbled up all our food." Students often draw a picture about the story and write or dictate a sentence in a practice book.
2. *Write the sentence on a large sentence strip.* Have students read their sentence to you. Next, read the sentence together as you point to each word.
3. *Have students rewrite their sentence on a small sentence strip.* Use the large sentence strip as a model. Students then reread the sentence and point to each word as they read it.
4. *Cut the large sentence strip into individual words and mix them up.*
5. *Have the students reassemble the sentence, using the small sentence strip as a model.* Then students reread the sentence.

Being the Words   In this activity (Cunningham, 2000, 2004), students actually "become" one word. To start, the teacher should write the sentences from a predictable book onto sentence strips. You may, of course, need to duplicate words that are used twice in a sentence, or write some words using both lowercase and uppercase first letters. However, you need not make copies of words that reappear in different sentences. Cut the words from two sentence strips into individual words and distribute each word to a student. Make a separate card for each punctuation mark.

Now tell the students they are going to *be* the words they are holding. Display the first two sentences of the book, and read them together. Point to the words as you read them and ask students to look at their words to see if they have any matches. Students who have the words from those sentences come forward and arrange themselves in left-to-right order. Have the other students in the class read the sentences as you point to each "student word." Continue this activity until you have made all the sentences from the book.

For older students, write the sentences on smaller cards and deal a few (like a deck of playing cards) to each student. When you display the sentence, the students must cooperate to construct it.

Alphabet Knowledge

In teaching alphabet knowledge, the teacher combines letter names with letter sounds to help students progress more efficiently.

Memory Game   Sets of cards, which can be easily made or purchased, are used in this game. A set of cards is placed face down on the table. Half contain pictures (no words) of objects, and half contain the letters representing the initial consonant sounds of those objects. Students turn pairs of cards over and try to match the beginning sound of a picture card with its letter. When a match is found, students must name the object and identify the corresponding letter name.

Using Alphabet Books   A variety of beautiful alphabet books help expand children's word knowledge and appreciation of literature as they learn letters. Some of our favorites include *Alligators All Around* (by Sendak), *ABC* (by Burningham), and *I Love My Anteater with an A* (by Dahlov). Research by Stahl (2003) indicates that children's alphabet books that provide words starting with a letter sound (such as *dog* for *d*) also help in developing phonemic awareness. Letters in an alphabet book should be shown in both upper and lower case (e.g., *D* and *d*).

Phonemic Awareness

The phonemic awareness assessment procedures presented earlier in this chapter may also be used as activities to practice phonemic, or phonological, awareness. This section describes other procedures.

Using Nursery Rhymes and Rhyming Books   Chanting nursery rhymes develops phonemic awareness and the ability to rhyme. Traditional poetry and songs are excellent resources to use with younger children.

Teachers can also use the many excellent books that focus on rhyming to help develop this ability. Begin by reading a rhyming book to students. Next, reread it, but this time, leave out the word that "completes the rhyme," and ask the students to provide it. For example, in the sentences "It is a nice day; I would like to play," you would omit the word *play* and ask the students to supply it. Students can also create their own rhymes.

Excellent books to model rhyming include *Sheep in a Jeep* and its sequels (by Shaw), *The Hungry Thing* and its sequels (by Slepian and Seidler), and books by Dr. Seuss, such as *One Fish, Two Fish* or *Green Eggs and Ham*. For older students, use collections of poetry, such as *The New Kid on the Block* (by Pretlutsky) or *A Light in the Attic* (by Silverstein).

As you read, children will naturally participate in the humorous rhyming words of Dr. Seuss's *There's a Wocket in my Pocket* or *The Hungry Thing*'s "schmancakes." Follow the readings with activities in which students create their own rhymes using common objects in the room. For example, you can have a "tock on the clock." You can wear a FEED ME sign and use plastic foods in a lunch bag to practice phoneme substitution and rhyming words (Cunningham, 2004; Yopp & Yopp, 2000).

Identifying Beginning Sounds   Yopp (1992) uses well-known tunes to help reinforce the skill of identifying initial letter sounds. One song is set to the tune of "Old MacDonald Had a Farm."

> What's the sound that starts these words:
> *Basket, bug,* and *Bill*? (wait for response)
> /b/ is the sound that starts these words,
> *Basket, bug,* and *Bill,*
> With a /b/ - /b/ here and a /b/ - /b/ there
> Here a /b/, there a /b/, everywhere a /b/ - /b/
> /b/ is the sound that starts these words, *basket, bug,* and *Bill.*

> NOTE: The use of slashes (//) indicates that you should say the letter *sound.*

Rhymes and Riddles   In the Rhymes and Riddles activity (Cunningham, 2004), teachers select two groups of words, one to rhyme with *head* and the other to rhyme with *feet.* Next, ask students a riddle so that the answer rhymes with either *head* or *feet.* The children point to the part of their bodies that rhymes with the answer to the riddle. For example, if you ask, "When you are hungry, do you want to . . . ?" students should point to their *feet,* because *eat* rhymes with *feet.* You can repeat this game with other parts of the body. For example, you can ask students to answer riddles with words that rhyme with *hand* and *knee* or *arm* and *leg.*

Counting Sounds   In this activity, students break apart words and count their sounds. To do the activity, select 10 words that contain two to four phonemes each. The words should be regular; that is, if the word has two sounds, it should have two letters. In fact, use only words with short vowels, consonants, and consonant blends (in which each consonant says a sound). Example words would be *it, man, bent, stop.*

Students listen to you pronounce a spoken word, say it themselves, and then move one object for each sound they hear. You can use craft sticks, cubes, or counters. Try to use objects that are all the same, such as blocks of one color or similarly sized paper clips.

Begin by modeling the activity. Pronounce a word. Then pronounce each sound element of the word and move a counter for each sound that you say. Finally, move the counters back together and repeat the word as a whole.

Next, repeat the procedure with the same word, but this time ask students to try the game with you. Repeat this procedure with another word. Model the segmentation task. Then ask students to join you. Stop after the second phoneme and see if your students can complete the task. If practiced over a period of several weeks, this activity has produced substantial gains for students.

Deleting Phonemes   In this relatively advanced activity, students take a word apart, remove one sound, and pronounce the word without that sound. You might introduce this activity by removing parts of compound words. For example, pronounce a word, such as *playground,* and ask students to say it without *play.* Students should say *ground.* Next, tell students to say *applesauce* without the *sauce.*

Next, ask students to say words, omitting single sounds. Ask students to say *ball* without the /b/. (They should say *all.*) Try several of these, asking students to omit the beginning sounds; then ask students to omit ending sounds. When students successfully can omit beginning and ending sounds from words, ask them to say a word, omitting a medial sound. For example, you might say "Say *stack,* without the /t/." The student should say *sack.*

Segmenting and Blending   Students must be able to segment, or separate sounds in words, and to blend, or put sounds together to make words. The ability to segment sounds usually develops earlier than the ability to blend, and segmenting the onset from the rime usually develops earlier than the ability to segment individual phonemes in words.

Games, songs, and chants that teachers and parents often sing and play with young children are easily adapted to help children learn to blend and segment.

You can begin with a simple riddle game: "I'm thinking of an animal that lives on a farm and is a /p/ - /ig/." Children are asked to blend the onset and rime into the correct word. As children become more skilled, you can segment the individual phonemes. You can also let the child who guesses the correct animal give the next riddle.

Letter-Sound Correspondence

As students develop stronger concepts about print and the ability to identify individual sounds in spoken words, they need to connect these spoken words with printed letters and words. Start with initial consonant sounds because they are the easiest sounds for students to hear and segment and they are therefore the easiest to associate to letters.

Acting Beginning Sounds   Many students have difficulty breaking words down into their individual sounds and identifying these sounds. To develop this skill, Cunningham (2000, 2004) suggests that teachers start by working with individual sounds in words. Begin by showing a specific letter, such as *b*, and having all the students engage in an activity that begins with that sound as they repeat the sound. For /b/ students bounce; for /c/ they catch. Other actions might include dance, fall, gallop, hop, jump, kick, laugh, march, nod, paint, run, sit, talk, vacuum, walk, yawn, and zip.

Manipulating Letters and Sounds   To use familiar words to figure out unfamiliar words, students need to be able to find familiar patterns and substitute individual phonemes. The foundation for this skill is laid in phoneme deletion (described earlier). Now we are ready to move to the next step of phoneme substitution. Cunningham (2004) has developed an activity called "Changing a Hen to a Fox" that provides practice in letter-sound manipulation. By changing one letter at a time, you can guide students to change from one word to another. For example, in Cunningham's "Changing a Hen to a Fox," you begin with the word *hen*, ask children to change *hen* to *pen*, then ask them to change *pen* to *pet, pet* to *pit, pit* to *sit, sit* to *six, six* to *fix*, and, finally, *fix* to *fox*. We like to use magnetic letters or magnetic letter tiles for this activity. After students practice with the magnetic letters, you can ask them to write the words. This activity is an important transition from phonemic awareness to more advanced word analysis strategies.

Spelling   Allowing students to spell words they have worked with provides practice in manipulating letters and sounds in print. As students gain in their understanding of letter-sound relationships, their writing will become more conventional. Encourage students to write freely and explore their own spelling. Try not to correct them, but rather let them explore their own understandings, whether or not they are completely accurate.

Beginning Reading Vocabulary

Many activities can encourage students to develop the first sight words on which reading is built. You may make a collection of logos and children's favorite words. Some teachers prepare flash cards with words that are common in the environment. They cut out pictures from newspaper and magazine advertisements and label them. Children often enjoy bringing in and identifying food labels and wrappers. In "print walks," children and adults walk through a building and identify all the times they see a certain type of print, such as the word *exit*, words about weather, or 10-letter words.

Many of the activities presented earlier, such as shared book experiences and language experience stories, help children develop a fund of sight words. However, students also need to directly learn a number of important words by sight. These words, at first, might include their names, addresses, and words that they frequently see in reading or use in writing. Students might keep personal cards for each word and form them into sentences using the jumbled-sentences activity presented earlier.

Summary

In early literacy, students surrounded by reading and writing gradually develop the foundation for these activities. Students with reading problems may lack some early literacy understandings. Six needed areas of knowledge include oral language development, concepts about print, alphabet knowledge, phonemic awareness, letter-sound correspondences, and beginning reading vocabulary.

In oral language development, students need to express and understand ideas fully, understand how stories are organized, and develop the ability to answer and formulate questions. Instruction in oral language development includes retelling stories, composing original stories, developing questions, reading to students, the Directed Listening-Thinking Activity (DR-TA), discussing story structure, shared book activities, language experience approach (LEA), and using wordless books.

Three concepts about print are crucial to reading: understanding that print carries meaning, knowing how print is organized, and understanding what words are. Instruction includes echo reading, counting words, jumbled sentences, and "being" the word.

Alphabet knowledge is strongly related to reading. Sounds can be taught with letter names. Instruction includes the memory game and the use of alphabet books.

Phonemic awareness refers to the abilities to manipulate sounds, including segmenting, blending, rhyming, sound deletion, sound addition, and sound substitution. Activities include using nursery rhymes and rhyming books, identifying beginning sounds, guessing rhymes and riddles, identifying sounds, counting sounds, deleting phonemes, and blending.

Letter-sound correspondences, identifying a letter and its sound, can be taught by acting as beginning sounds, manipulating letters and sounds, and practicing spelling as well as several strategies mentioned above.

Students' early reading vocabulary words come from their environments. As they are exposed to more print, students start to connect environmental print with specific words. Teachers and parents help the process by reading extensively to students, labeling objects in their environments, and collecting interesting words.

REFERENCES

Allen, R. V. (1976). *Language experiences in communication*. Boston, MA: Houghton Mifflin.

Ball, E. W., & Blachman, B. A. (1991). Does phoneme awareness training in kindergarten make a difference in early word recognition and spelling? *Reading Research Quarterly, 26*, 49–66.

Busin, R. (1997). Reading and phonological awareness: What we have learned and how we can use it. *Reading Research and Instruction, 36*, 199–215.

Button, K., & Johnson, M. (1997). The role of shared reading in developing effective early reading strategies. *Reading Horizons, 37*, 262–273.

Byrne, B., & Fielding-Barnsley, R. (1991). Evaluation of a program to teach phonemic awareness to young children. *Journal of Educational Psychology, 83*, 451–455.

Clay, M. M. (1993). *An observation survey of early literacy achievement*. Portsmouth, NH: Heinemann Educational Books.

Clay, M. M. (2002). *An observation survey of early literacy achievement* (2nd ed.). Portsmouth, NH: Heinemann Educational Books.

Cunningham, P. M. (2000). *Phonics they use: Words for reading and writing* (3rd ed.). New York: Longman.

Cunningham, P. M. (2004). *Phonics they use: Words for reading and writing* (4th ed.). Boston: Allyn & Bacon.

Cunningham, P. M., Cunningham, J. W., Moore, S. A., & Moore, D. W. (2004). *Reading and writing in elementary classrooms: Research based K-4 instruction* (5th ed.). Boston: Allyn and Bacon.

Dreher, M. J., & Zenge, S. D. (1990). Using metalinguistic awareness in first grade to predict reading achievement in third and fifth grades. *Journal of Educational Research, 84,* 13–21.

Ehri, L. C. (1992). Reconceptualizing the development of sight word reading and its relationship to recoding. In P. B. Gough, L. C. Ehri, & R. Treiman (Eds.), *Reading acquisition* (pp. 107–143). Mahwah, NJ: Lawrence Erlbaum Associates, Inc.

Galda, L., Cullinan, B. E., & Strickland, D. S. (1997). *Language, literacy and the child* (2nd ed.). Fort Worth: Harcourt Brace College Publishers.

Gentry, J. R., & Gillet, J. W. (1993). *Teaching kids to spell.* Portsmouth, NH: Heinemann.

Gillet, J. W., & Temple, C. (2000). *Understanding reading problems: Assessment and instruction* (5th ed.). New York: Longman.

Gillet, J. W., Temple, C., Crawford, A., & Cooney, B. (2003). *Understanding reading problems: Assessment and instruction* (6th ed.). Saddle River Creek, NJ: Allyn and Bacon.

Gredler, M. E., & Johnson, R. L. (2004). *Assessment in the literacy classroom.* Boston: Allyn & Bacon.

Hammill, D. D. (2004). What we know about correlates of reading. *Exceptional Children, 4,* 453–468.

Holdaway, D. (1979). *The foundations of literacy.* Portsmouth, NH: Heinemann.

International Reading Association & National Association for the Education of Young Children. (1998). *Learning to read and write: Developmentally appropriate practices for young children.* Newark, DE: International Reading Association.

Johnston, P. H. (1997). *Knowing literacy: Constructive literacy assessment.* York, ME: Stenhouse Publishers.

Morris, D. (1993). The relationship between children's concept of word in text and phoneme awareness in learning to read: A longitudinal study. *Research in the Teaching of English, 27,* 133–153.

Morris, D. (1998). Assessing printed word knowledge in beginning readers: The Early Reading Screening Instrument (ERSI). *Illinois Reading Council Journal, 26,* 30–41.

Morrow, L. M. (2004). *Literacy development in the early years: Helping children read and write* (5th ed.). Boston: Allyn and Bacon.

Muter, V., Hulme, C., & Taylor, S. (1998). Segmentation, not rhyming, predicts early progress in learning to read. *Journal of Experimental Child Psychology, 71,* 3–27.

Naslund, J. C., & Schneider, W. (1996). Kindergarten letter knowledge, phonological skills, and memory processes: Relative effects on early literacy. *Journal of Experimental Child Psychology, 62,* 30–59.

National Reading Panel (2000). *Teaching children to read: An evidence-based assessment of the scientific research literature on reading and its implications for reading instruction: Reports of the subgroups* (National Institute of Health Pub. No. 00-4754). Washington, DC: National Institute of Child Health and Human Development.

Paris, A. H., & Paris, S. G. (2003). Assessing narrative comprehension in young children. *Reading Research Quarterly, 38,* 36–76.

Paris, S. G. (2003). *What K–3 teachers need to know about assessing children's reading.* Naperville, IL: Learning Point Associates.

Rasinski, T. V. (2003). *The fluent reader: Oral reading strategies for building word recognition, fluency, and comprehension.* New York: Scholastic Professional Books, Inc.

Roberts, B. (1996). Spelling and the growth of concept of word as first graders write. *Reading Psychology: An International Quarterly, 17,* 229–252.

Stahl, S. A. (2003). Literature-based instruction in the early years. In S. B. Neuman & D. K. Dickinson (Eds.), *Handbook of early literacy research.* New York: Guilford Press.

Stahl, S. A., & Murray, B. A. (1994). Defining phonological awareness and its relationship to early reading. *Journal of Educational Psychology, 86,* 221–234.

Stanovich, K. E. (1988). *Children's reading and the development of phonological awareness.* Detroit: Wayne State University Press.

Stanovich, K. E. (1988). The right and wrong places to look for the cognitive locus of reading disability. *Annals of Dyslexia, 38,* 154–177.

Stauffer, R. G. (1975). *Directing the reading-thinking process.* New York: Harper and Row.

Stauffer, R. G. (1980). *The language experience approach to the teaching of reading* (2nd ed.). New York: Harper and Row.

Strickland, D. S., Cullinan, B. E. & Galda, L., (2003). *Language arts: Learning and teaching.* Belmont, CA: Thomson/Wadsworth.

Trieman, R., Tincoff, R., & Richmond-Welty, E. D. (1996). Letter names help children to connect print and speech. *Developmental Psychology, 32,* 505–514.

Uhry, J. K. (2002). Finger-point reading in kindergarten: The role of phonemic awareness, one-to-one correspondence, and rapid serial naming. *Scientific Studies of Reading, 6,* 319–342.

Walker, B. J. (2005). *Techniques for reading assessment and instruction.* Upper Saddle River Creek, NJ: Merrill-Prentice Hall.

Walsh, D. J., Price, G. G., & Gillingham, M. G. (1988). The critical but transitory importance of letter naming. *Reading Research Quarterly, 23,* 108–122.

Warner, S. A. (1963). *Teacher.* New York: Simon and Schuster.

Yopp, H. K. (1992). Developing phonemic awareness in young children. *The Reading Teacher, 45,* 696–703.

Yopp, H. K., & Yopp, R. H. (2000). Supporting phonemic awareness development in the classroom. *The Reading Teacher, 54,* 130–143.

Yopp, R. H., & Yopp, H. K. (2000). Sharing informational text with young children. *The Reading Teacher, 53,* 410–423.

3 Beginning Reading/Early Decoding

Objectives

After reading this chapter you will be able to:

1. Identify and describe the sequence of skills needed for students to become full alphabetic phase readers.

2. Use assessment data to identify students who need more support, diagnose specific letter–sound and word-reading difficulties, and monitor student progress in beginning word reading in a multi-tier or RTI program.

3. Implement strategies for teaching letter–sound correspondences and beginning word reading that maximize the probability of students becoming full alphabetic phase readers.

4. Implement Tier 2 strategies to provide extra support for students, and identify and describe the beginning word and passage reading instruction of five commonly used Tier 3 reading programs.

5. Identify and describe ways to help older students and English language learners become full alphabetic phase readers.

6. Describe games and activities that can be used to reinforce students' decoding skills.

Mr. Lange stared at the large rocket ship on the back wall of the classroom. "Teaching reading is rocket science; teaching reading is rocket science." The refrain echoed in his head and helped him maintain his perky teaching style while he led his students through reading that day's word list for the third time. With the energy of a football coach, he told his small group of seven students, *"If you read every word in this row correctly, it will be a 'firecracker row,' and we'll take a minute and pretend we are firecrackers going up in the air and coming down."*

Teaching kindergarten was so much easier ten years ago. Students were expected to learn through play, so much of his day was spent working in the different centers around the classroom. Mr. Lange had always been a kid at heart, and wielding a sword in the dress-up area or pretending to make bacon in the kitchen area came naturally to him. All of the students spent some time each day at the learning center, and by the end of the year most of the students could print all of the letters, knew their names, and were able to read some familiar books that the class had read together many times.

But when a multi-tier system was introduced into the school two years ago, and the literacy coach told the kindergarten teachers that the goal was to get 80% of the kindergarten students reading 15 nonsense words in a minute so that they would go into first grade with grade-level decoding skills, Mr. Lange hoped that what he regarded as one more teaching fad would disappear soon. He worked in a high-poverty neighborhood, and keeping his wiggly five-year-olds sitting and reading letter sounds and sounding out words as they followed his signals seemed impossible at first. However, when Mr. Lange listened to kindergarten teachers from similar schools talk about students' progress after beginning a multi-tiered reading program, he knew he had to try to replicate their results. His kids deserved the best, and if those teachers at Gary Elementary were saying the best was possible, maybe it was.

After attending summer training, Mr. Lange worked closely with a reading coach who came to his room every other week. After his students had learned several sounds, getting them to sound out words containing those sounds seemed to take forever. But the literacy coach wasn't satisfied with him having his students read the words only one time during the lesson. *"Your students need to practice reading these words several times if the sound-spellings are going to be stored in their long-term memory,"* the coach explained. *"As your students learn more words, they'll start learning new sounds and words more quickly."* All Mr. Lange could do was trust the coach and try to do his best with this new method.

In June, all the effort paid off when, after final benchmark testing, data showed that 85% of Mr. Lange's students had met the goal. He was as amazed as anyone, because secretly he hadn't thought it possible. He had doubted if more than three or four of his students last year would have read any of the nonsense words. When the principal asked Mr. Lange why his students were more successful than the rest of the kindergartners in the school, Mr. Lange looked at the rocket ship that he used as a reminder to teach to mastery and said, *"I just tried to follow the recommendations exactly. It was the hardest teaching I've ever done, but I've never had so many of my students pick up books that they've never seen before and read them. I thought that doing all this practice would turn them off from reading, but it's had the opposite effect. I'm so proud of them."*

What do you think was the biggest change for Mr. Lange and his students?

Why do you think more of Mr. Lange's students were able to read books they had never seen before?

What Beginning Reading Skills Do I Need to Teach?

It is important to emphasize the importance of assessing and systematically teaching phonemic awareness to students who are at risk and explaining how an understanding of the sound system of spoken language relates to reading. Although this knowledge of our system of spoken language is essential, phonemic awareness is only one component needed for developing accurate and fluent reading. An effective reading program for students who are at risk must also help them attain alphabetic principle, which is "the recognition that there are systematic and predictable relationships between written letters and spoken sounds" (Armbruster, Lehr, & Osborn, 2001, p. 12). Gaining alphabetic principle through learning letter–sound relationships is the first step that indicates students have moved out of the first prealphabetic phase of reading where they view words as memorized visual forms. This understanding of alphabetic principle provides the foundation for students to then learn how to sound out individual phonemes before blending them into a word (/k/ + /a/ + /t/ = *cat*). Eventually, they will learn to read words automatically as whole words (*cat*). As readers mature, they learn to decipher new and familiar regular words accurately and automatically. Most importantly, the fluent decoding that characterizes students who read fluently enables them to focus more thought on the meaning of the text they are reading. In this chapter the term "beginning readers" will refer to students who are still reading at the first three phases described in Ehri's phase model of word reading in Chapter 1.

Learn more about alphabetic principle and the role it plays in decoding: **http://www.readingrockets.org/article/3408/.**

The purpose of phonics instruction is to teach students the relationship between written letters, or **graphemes,** and the 41 to 44 sounds of spoken language, or phonemes. Educators who minimize the role of phonics in teaching reading argue that the English language does not incorporate a one-to-one relationship between the 41 to 44 sounds and 26 letter symbols. For example, sometimes the sound of /ĕ/, as in *red,* also appears as *ea,* as in *bread.* The sound /ā/ can be written *ay* as in *may,* *a_e* as in *made,* or *ai* as in *maid.* These critics ignore the large proportion of regularity in English that justifies the teaching of phonics, which is supported by extensive research validating its effectiveness, particularly with children who are at risk or who have disabilities.

The foundation of our approach to teaching decoding is based on a systematic and explicit phonics approach called **synthetic phonics,** in which student success and independence are emphasized through the use of carefully supported teaching strategies and curricula. A teacher using a synthetic phonics approach first teaches the most common letter–sound associations in isolation using a logical, success-oriented sequence. With carefully supported teacher instruction, students learn to apply their phonemic awareness skills and knowledge of letter–sound correspondences to sounding out words in lists and sentences as well as spelling from dictation. The teacher provides substantial practice so that students can apply their decoding skills to reading and writing. Beginning reading books and written assignments are carefully coordinated with those skills.

Synthetic phonics is not the only explicit and systematic way of teaching phonics. Other systematic and explicit phonics programs include analytic phonics, analogy phonics, and phonics through spelling. **Analytic phonics** emphasizes first teaching the whole word before analyzing letter–sound relationships. In this approach, students learn letter–sound relationships using words they already know. Letter sounds are not introduced in isolation. **Analogy-based** phonics emphasizes using known word family patterns to identify unknown words. **Phonics through spelling** emphasizes phonetic spelling as the foundation for word reading. In this approach, students learn to break apart words into phonemes and to spell words by translating the phonemes into letters. Although the many varied systematic and explicit phonics programs are based primarily on one of these categories, realistically, most of the programs incorporate strategies from some or all of these approaches. In this book, when we describe how to effectively teach synthetic phonics, we also include recommendations from spelling, analytic, and analogy phonics approaches.

The systematic and explicit phonics approach described in this text follows a logical sequence of skills needed to read **regular words** accurately and fluently. The first words taught contain the most common sounds of individual letters. Once the student can decode some basic consonant–vowel–consonant (CVC) words, a relatively small number of irregular or exception words are introduced. A list of skills in a typical systematic phonics program is shown in Figure 3.1. Three skills specifically related to beginning reading are described in the following section. Note that the first group of words is likely to appear in beginning phonics programs when students are still unable to visualize the multiletter sequences needed to perceive larger word parts. Instruction for students who are still learning beginning reading skills at the individual letter–sound level should focus on the most common letter–sound correspondences, including the short vowels. The second group of more advanced words mainly appears after students are reading at the consolidated alphabetic phase, when they begin to decode clusters as opposed to individual letter sounds.

Words for a Beginning Reader

1. CVC words beginning with a continuous sound:
   mad, mop, red, rig, sun
2. CVC words beginning with a stop sound:
   bad, did, gun, hot, jet
3. CVCC words ending with a consonant blend or double consonants:
   band, pond, jump, miss, kept
4. CCVC words ending with a consonant blend:
   clam, frog, glad, skin, step
5. CCVCC, CCCVC, and CCCVCC words beginning and/or ending with a consonant blend:
   Blink, glass, slump, split, struck
6. Compound words composed of CVC words or CVC variants such as "catnip" or "sandbox."

Words for an Advanced Reader

1. Digraphs
   ma**sh**, **ch**op, **th**is, **ch**imp
2. VCe (silent e) pattern words in which the vowel is long (VCV rule)
   * Words beginning with a single consonant (CVCe):
     hope, cute, Pete, mile, tape
   * Words beginning with a consonant blend (CCVCe):
     skate, spoke, froze, bride, stripe
   * Multisyllable words with a VCe syllable:
     Hopeless, excuse, likely, stampede, grateful
3. Letter combinations:
   r**ai**n, h**ar**m, gr**ee**n, cl**ou**d, **sh**ed
4. CVCe derivative words:
   * Words with *s* endings:
     *bite**s**, cube**s**, mope**s**, plane**s**, time**s***
   * Words with *er* endings:
     *lat**er**, smok**er**, us**er**, brav**er**, tim**er***
   * Words with *ed* endings:
     *hop**ed**, nam**ed**, smil**ed**, smok**ed**, glid**ed***
   * Words with *ing* endings:
     *nam**ing**, rid**ing**, clos**ing**, shad**ing**, bit**ing***
   * Words with *y* endings:
     *grav**y**, spic**y**, bon**y**, shin**y**, wav**y***
   * Words with *est* endings:
     *cut**est**, lat**est**, wis**est**, saf**est**, wid**est***
5. Y-derivative words:
   *fogg**iest** (foggy), funn**ier** (funny), part**ies** (party), bab**ied** (baby)*
6. Suffixes
   *cheer**ful**, ac**tion**, argu**ment**, trace**able***
7. Prefixes:
   ***a**mount, **con**duct, **mis**lead, **pro**test, **trans**late, **under**go*

FIGURE 3.1   Phonics Word Types for Beginning and Advanced Readers

Sequence for Teaching Beginning Reading

Identify the Most Common Sounds of Individual Letters in Isolation   All
systematic phonics programs identify a planned sequence for teaching letter–sound correspondences. The most common letter–sound correspondences are stressed because they lend more predictability to the beginning reading process and also lead to the eventual

identification of more words. A beginning reader who first learns both sounds of *a* does not yet have the skills to scan the whole word *plane* and automatically make the decision between reading /ă/ or /ā/. Without those skills, she is still unable to differentiate consistently between two visually similar words such as *plan* and *plane*. Unable to make the decision logically between two sounds needed for more advanced reading, she may start guessing whenever she has to determine which sound to associate with a specific letter. Learning first to associate the grapheme *a* with /ă/ and then learning to read words in which *a* is associated with its most common sound /ă/ prevents the development of guessing strategies that lead to reduced word reading accuracy in text. Note that teaching the sounds of letters is recommended before teaching letter names. Students who are at risk are more likely to come to school unable to identify the letters of the alphabet by name. Since these students may have difficulty learning the letter names and sounds at the same time, letter–sound correspondences should be taught first because they lead more directly to reading words.

An often neglected key to teaching phonics effectively is the careful pronunciation of letter sounds. In the approach to sounds recommended here, great care is taken when teaching students to pronounce consonants without adding an *uh* or schwa sound to each.

Each systematic phonics program presents its own rationale for the sequence of letter–sound correspondences that are introduced. Although the National Reading Panel report (2000) didn't address the issue, the order in which the letter sounds are taught can influence how quickly students acquire them during instruction (Carnine, Silbert, Kame'enui, & Tarver, 2010). Letter–sound correspondences are most easily learned when the sound of the letter is in the onset of the letter's name, such as *k* (*kā*) *or v* (*vē*). More difficult to learn are letter–sound correspondences where the sound of the letter is in the final position of the letter's name, such as *l* (*el*) or *f* (*ef*). Letter sounds that have no connection with their name, such as the sound for *h*, are the most difficult for students to remember (McBride-Chang, 1999). *The Reflective Teacher* summarizes the rationale behind the order in which letter–sound correspondences are taught in two systematic phonics programs.

Read CVC Words   Orally **sound out** lists of single-syllable words that contain letter–sound correspondences previously taught. As they decode a word, students say each sound in succession from left to right. Students then blend the sounds together to quickly say a word. The first words students read are often referred to as short vowel words or consonant–vowel–consonant (CVC) words, such as *mat* or *sit*. Words beginning with stop sounds (*t, d, b*) are more difficult to read than those beginning with continuous sounds (*m, s, f*). CVC words are **regular words,** meaning that they can be sounded out.

Read CVC-Variant Words   Orally sound out and read lists of single-syllable **CVC-variant** words that contain blends composed of letter sounds previously taught. Single-syllable words that begin or end with consonant blends are more difficult to read than regular CVC words. **Consonant blends,** also called **consonant clusters,** are two or three successive consonant sounds said in sequence without losing their identity. Examples of consonant blends include *st* as in *stop, nd* as in *sand,* and *st* and *nd* as in *stand.* Since each consonant in a blend retains its individual sound, the blend *st*, which has two graphemes, is a two-phoneme blend since both /s/ and /t/ have distinct sounds. Thus, the word *stop* has four phonemes, /s/ /t/ /ŏ/ /p/, while the word *stand* has five phonemes, /s/ /t/ /ă/ /n/ /d/. A three-letter consonant blend such as *str* is composed of the three phonemes /s/ /t/ /r/. Because the phonemes are blurred to make a smooth sequence, students have a more difficult time hearing and spelling these individual sounds. Shut your eyes as you say these words slowly and feel your mouth change position as you say each phoneme.

The Reflective Teacher

Sequencing the Teaching of Letter–Sound Correspondences

The order in which letter–sound correspondences are introduced can have a big impact on how easily they are learned. Described below are two different strategies for sequencing letter–sound correspondences used in reading programs shown to be successful with students who have great difficulty learning to read: *Reading Mastery* and *Lindamood®: LiPS*. Even if you don't use these programs, the rules they use for sequencing letters can be applied to adapt other programs, or, at least, give you clues to where your students might experience difficulty. As you read the descriptions of the way that letter–sound correspondences are introduced in the two programs, determine the strengths and weaknesses of each.

Rationale 1: Direct Instruction

Reduce confusion when learning letters with similar sounds or appearance.
Letters that have a similar sound or are similar in apperance should not be introduced to students at the same time. At least six letters should be introduced between them. Letters that have both a similar sound and a similar appearance should be separated by at least six letters. Carnine and colleagues (2010) further suggest that when introducing vowels, teachers should separate them by at least three letters, and that /ĭ/ and /ē/ be separated by six letters. Table 3.1 lists specific letters that students are likely to confuse and that are in need of separating when teaching.

TABLE 3.1   Letter Characteristics

Letters with Similar Sound	Letters with Similar Appearance	Letters with Similar Sound and Appearance
b and *d*	*b* and *d*	*b* and *d*
b and *p*	*b* and *p*	*m* and *n*
m and *n*	*m* and *n*	*b* and *p*
ĭ and ĕ	*q* and *p*	
k and *g*	*h* and *n*	
t and *d*	*v* and *w*	
ŏ and ŭ	*n* and *r*	
f and *v*		

Move into story reading earlier by teaching high-frequency letter sounds
Introduce more-useful letter sounds (consonant sounds such as /m/, /n/, /s/, /t/; all of the vowel sounds) before less-useful letter sounds (/x/, /z/, /q/).

Teach lowercase letters before uppercase letters
Most uppercase letters are not identical to their lowercase counterparts, and learning both at the same time can place an undue burden on a student who is at risk. Since beginning reading passages contain mostly lowercase letters, these are the letters that should be taught first.

Rationale 2: *Lindamood: LiPS*

Choose Your Approach
Depending on the needs of the students, teachers can opt for Path 1 or Path 2. In Path 1, all of the consonant sounds are taught before the vowel sounds. These sounds are then applied to manipulating phonemes, spelling, and reading. Path 1 is typically used for older students. In

Continued

Path 2, three consonant pairs (a total of six sounds) and three vowel sounds are taught and then used in manipulating phonemes, spelling, and reading. When students have success applying those letter sounds to reading and spelling, the other consonants and vowels are taught. Path 2 is more appropriate for younger children and remedial students who have experienced consistent failure (Lindamood & Lindamood, 1998).

Teach the Brothers

Teach consonant pairs called *brothers*. Each consonant pair consists of a voiced and an unvoiced consonant formed with the same mouth movements. Examples of consonant pairs are:

/p/ and /b/
/t/ and /d/
/k/ and /g/

Teach the Cousins

After students know the brothers, teach the groups of consonants called the *cousins*. Nose sounds (/m/, /n/, /ng/), wind sounds (/w/, /wh/, /h/), and lifters (/l/, /r/) fall in this category.

Teach the Borrowers

Next teach the last group of consonants, called the *borrowers* because they borrow the sounds of other letters (/c/, /x/, /qu/, /y/).

Teach the Vowel Circle

Fifteen long and short vowels are categorized into four distinct groups according to the way they are formed by the mouth and tongue. Students discover where the vowel sounds are articulated, using sensory information to organize them into the following categories: round, smile, sliders, and open. Students learn to organize the vowels into a linguistic vowel circle depicted in Figure 3.2, organized by tongue placement and shape of the mouth for each vowel.

FIGURE 3.2 Vowel Circle Map

Source: Gildroy, P. G., & Francis, S. (1999). Learning about phonemes (Module I, Lesson 2). In B. K. Lenz & P. G. Gildroy (Eds), *Beginning word reading* [Online]. Lawrence. KS: University of Kansas, Center for Research on Learning. Available online at www.academy.org.

Either just before or after consonant blends are taught, students learn to read words ending in double consonants represented by one phoneme. Students learn to say the one sound that is represented by *ll, ss, ff,* or *zz* at the end of words. The knowledge that a word like *still*, which begins with a blend and ends with a double consonant, has four phonemes, /s/ /t/ /i/ /l/, helps you teach your students to decode similar words.

CVC words containing blends are described by their consonant–vowel pattern and are termed **CVC Variants.** *Stop* is a CCVC word, *sand* is a CVCC word, and *stand* is a CCVCC word. In a multisensory reading program, these CVC and CVC-variant words are referred to as *closed syllables* because each word has only one short vowel sound. Teachers explain that the vowel says its short sound because the word is *closed* at the end by one or more consonants.

> Teach blends in isolation, just as you would teach letter sounds. Predrawn initial consonant blend flashcards can be downloaded at the following website: **http://www.firstschoolyears.com/literacy/word/phonics/clusters/worksheets/initial%20cluster%20letters.doc.**

Read a Small Number of High-Frequency Exception Words Needed to Read Passages

By teaching students a limited number of high-frequency or common exception words required for reading beginning text (for example, *the* and *have*), teachers can focus student attention on critical sounding-out strategies. **Exception** words, sometimes called irregular words, are words that cannot be conventionally sounded out and so must be learned as whole words. *From* is an exception word, because if the reader decoded it relying on the conventional letter–sound relationships, he would read the word as /frŏm/ since the short vowel /ŏ/ typically corresponds to the letter *o* in a CVC-variant word. *Said, where,* and *could* are other commonly used exception words in early reading books. If regular words have letter–sound correspondences that students have not yet learned in isolation, these words also must be learned as whole words and are considered exception words until the student has learned those letter–sound correspondences. The word *stop* is an exception word for a student who has not yet learned the sound associated with *p.* During the first two reading phases identified by Ehri (2005), before students have consolidated their letter–sound knowledge, learning to read exception words takes many exposures to the word until the word can be easily retrieved from a child's long-term memory (Reitsma, 1983). Teachers who wait to introduce most exception words until students are past the beginning reading phases save time because their students then learn these words much more quickly.

Sound Out Previously Taught One-Syllable Words in Sentences and Passages

Decodable books are those in which at least 70% of the text is composed of words that can be sounded out interspersed with a relatively small proportion of previously taught high-frequency exception words. Passage reading differs from reading lists of individual words in that students are reading connected text, scanning each word from left to right, moving from word to word, learning how punctuation marks affect meaning, and answering comprehension questions. In early passage reading, students are required to sound out words by independently moving their fingers from letter to letter as they orally sound out the words. Requiring students to move from letter to letter while pointing to each letter reinforces left-to-right reading and keeps the reader focused on each letter in the words, strengthening letter–sound associations. Because students who are at risk need more practice reading a word until its sound–spelling pattern is remembered, instruction should focus on decodable books containing mainly words that can be sounded out, with key words repeated at least several times during the passages.

Read One-Syllable Words and Passages by Sight

When students have ample opportunities to read word lists and text coordinated with letter–sound correspondences they have learned, they begin *subvocal sounding out* by silently moving their lips or silently reading the sounds before blending. Since some students will not make this leap on their own, teachers of students who are at risk will be more effective if they explicitly teach subvocal sounding out and provide practice for their students to use the new strategy. In the beginning have your students read words, first sounding them out loud orally, then subvocally, without making an audible sound, and finally by sight if their accuracy is high. Students then learn to read words by sight in lists followed by passages or connected text. Students who begin to use subvocal sounding-out are starting to become full alphabetic phase readers. Gradually, with more practice they will move to automatic word recognition.

Spelling and Writing What Is Read   Once students start reading CVC and CVC-variant words by sight, a more advanced sequence of letter combinations, rule-based reading, and structural analysis skills is taught to prepare students to read multisyllable words. Chapter 4 describes strategies to teach these more complex words.

Systematic phonics programs should also incorporate spelling and writing as soon as the students learn their first letter–sound correspondence. As students spell words, their knowledge of sound–spelling relationships improves and reading becomes more fluent (Joshi, Treiman, Carreker, & Moats, 2008). After learning to say letter sounds, students learn to write those same sounds. As students learn to read words, they are taught to spell those same words and incorporate them into their writing.

Following a skill sequence such as the letter–sound and word-reading ones described in the text does not mean that each skill is taught by itself and then dropped when the next skill in the sequence is introduced. In a systematic phonics program, newly introduced skills remain in play even as other, newer skills are introduced. For example, once students have learned a few common letter sounds, carefully planned instruction moves between applying these new sounds to reading words in lists and passages and applying them to spelling and written expression.

How Do I Assess Beginning Reading Skills in a Multi-Tier or RTI Model?

Screening Assessments

Teachers need to assess two key skills as their students develop beginning reading skills: individual letter–sound correspondences and sounding out of words. Careful assessment of individual letter–sound correspondences informs a teacher when to introduce regular sounding out of words. For example, when Ms. Remick assessed her students to determine whether they knew the six letter–sound correspondences she had taught during the first three weeks of school, almost every student in her class correctly identified the /a/, /m/, /t/, /r/, /s/, and /l/ sounds. Because previous assessments in phonemic awareness showed that her students could also segment and blend at the individual sound level, Ms. Remick knew that her students were ready to learn how to sound out CVC words beginning with continuous sounds. After giving the letter–sound assessment, Ms. Remick selected a decodable book that had only regular words containing the /a/, /m/, /r/, /s/, and /l/ sounds in addition to three exception words her students knew.

While not a skill that is initially useful in sounding out words, the ability to name letters of the alphabet or numbers rapidly is useful in identifying students who are at risk for future reading problems. These assessments of rapid automatized naming (or RAN) appear to measure **lexical retrieval,** or the efficiency with which a reader can locate and apply to reading previously learned information about letters and words stored in long-term memory. Lexical retrieval is an early indicator of fluency and is highly predictive of later reading ability (Jones, Branigan, & Kelly, 2009). In order to decode, students must retrieve sounds quickly so that they can blend them into words, and RAN assessments allow you to quickly identify students with weak lexical retrieval. Research indicates that RAN assessments requiring students to name letters or numbers are more predictive than those requiring students to name colors or objects. Among younger struggling readers, those who have stronger rapid-naming speed typically respond more quickly to intervention (Rathvon, 2004). Low scores on RAN assessments are characteristic of younger readers who need intensive intervention and of adults with reading disabilities, which is why these assessments are described in this section and should always be used to screen younger students or as part of a diagnostic testing battery for older ones.

Because RAN tests of rapid letter naming are included in many early screening assessments, sometimes teachers teach students to say letter names at a faster pace even though this instruction does not increase reading achievement and therefore wastes precious classroom instructional time. Although students can be taught to say letter names more quickly, teaching this isolated skill does not appear to translate into developing faster lexical retrieval with other naming tasks that haven't been practiced (Fugate, 1997). Such training risks invalidating student scores for any RAN test normed on a population of students who did not receive specific training in this isolated skill. In these situations, a student who has poor lexical retrieval but has had weeks of practice saying the letter names quickly might score higher on the rapid-naming test and might not appear to need support in reading because his score has been artificially inflated by the teaching.

Teachers also need to directly assess word reading to determine whether students are making progress toward reading at the consolidated phase. Although a regular word-reading assessment provides helpful information before second or third grade, a teacher doesn't know whether a child is reading these relatively easy words by applying decoding strategies or is reading them at the prealphabetic phase as visual images. A beginning prealphabetic phase reader who has memorized a large number of words in combination with guessing could do well on a regular word-reading assessment in first grade but still not have developed decoding skills. For that reason, in addition to regular word reading, students should be tested in reading nonsense words, also called pseudowords. The advantage of using nonsense words is that nonsense words can only be decoded by accurate sounding out. Nonsense words control for context as well as sight word memorization and are therefore a relatively pristine measure of a student's ability to sound out. Because nonsense words such as *vug, phlaim,* or *seeply* follow regular spelling rules, the results of a test of nonsense word reading enable the teacher to assess students' knowledge of letter–sound correspondences as well as the ability to blend letters to form words. Specific screening assessments for letter–sound correspondence, rapid automatized naming, and word sounding-out for beginning readers are described in the next section.

Letter–Sound Correspondence   The tasks for assessing letter–sound correspondence can differ greatly, as descriptions of these screening assessment subtests demonstrate. In the untimed PALS Letter–Sound subtest, students are shown 26 capital letters and asked to point to each one and say its sound. In the untimed TPRI Letter–Sound subtest, students are shown 10 upper- and lowercase letters and asked to say each letter's name and sound. Students receive a point only for correctly saying the letter sounds. The third subtest, the AIMSweb Letter–Sound Fluency subtest, is a one-minute test. Students are given a sheet of lowercase letters in rows and asked to identify as many sounds as possible in one minute. Incorrect answers are subtracted from the total. Because students need to retrieve letter sounds quickly, one would expect a letter–sound fluency test such as the AIMSweb subtest to be more predictive of reading problems than the letter-naming test described in the previous section. However, Rathvon (2004) writes that to-date research indicates that the letter-naming task is more predictive.

When Is It Routinely Given?

* The **PALS** and **TPRI Letter–Sound** subtests and the **AIMSweb Letter–Sound Fluency** subtest are routinely given in kindergarten and at the beginning of first grade.

Rapid Automatized Naming (RAN)   Because the ability to name letters of the alphabet is not needed to read beginning words, we recommend that this screening subtest, which tests a student's ability to say letter names rapidly, be used strictly as a screening measure and/or diagnostic measure and not as an outcome- or progress-monitoring measure. The validity of RAN assessments depends on some initial exposure to or knowledge of the alphabet; therefore, when students enter kindergarten without this exposure or knowledge, the measure should be given in winter of kindergarten at the earliest. The AIMSweb and DIBELS tests are almost identical. Students are given a minute to name as many of the upper- and lowercase letters of the alphabet as they can. For the DIBELS LNF assessment, students receive credit for every letter identified correctly. Desmon, the student in Figure 3.3, identified 28 letters correctly per minute in May of his kindergarten year. Locate the score in the DIBELS tables and note that a score of 28 letter names correctly read on the Letter Naming Fluency assessment indicates Desmon is at risk for future reading difficulties and thus has only a 20% chance of meeting the next benchmark without intervention. Depending on Desmon's scores in other areas such as letter–sound correspondence, DIBELS Phonemic Segmentation Fluency, and Nonsense Word Fluency, Desmon's teachers might decide to place him in a Tier 3 intensive reading program. Both the TPRI and PALS screening assessment batteries have subtests requiring students to say letter names, but because these are not timed tests, they do not assess rapid automatized naming.

When Is It Given?

* **DIBELS and AIMSweb Letter Naming Fluency:**   Beginning/end of kindergarten and beginning of first grade

Benchmark 1
DIBELS™ Letter Naming Fluency

Name: _Desmon_   Date: _May 10_

V	I	h	g	S	y	Z	W	L	N
I	K	T	D	K	T	q	d	Z	w
h	w	Z	m	U	r	j	G	X	u
g	R	B	Q	I	f	I	Z	s	r
S	n	C	B	p	Y	F	c	a	E
y	s	Q	P	M	v	O	t	n	P
Z	A	e	x	f	F	h	u	A	t
W	G	H	b	S	I	g	m	i	i
L	L	o	o	X	N	E	Y	p	x
N	k	c	D	d	y	b	j	R	v
V	M	W	q	V	I	h	g	S	y

Total: _28_

FIGURE 3.3   Sample DIBELS LNF Score Sheet (for Desmon)

Source: Official DIBELS home page: https://dibels.uoregon.edu/measures/lnf.php

Reading Pseudowords   The DIBELS and AIMSweb Nonsense Word Fluency (NWF) assessments are also almost identical. As the name suggests, in the NWF assessment students are given one minute to read a series of make-believe words, all having the most common sounds of letters arranged according to a VC or CVC word pattern. The wording and scoring for the Nonsense Word Fluency test can be a problem, because if a student reads all of the words as individual sounds rather than as words, he receives the same number of points as if he read whole words. On the DIBELS NWF assessment, students receive credit for every letter–sound correspondence identified correctly, regardless of whether the sounds are identified individually or as a part of a whole word. For example, when Jamarius came to the nonsense word *bif,* he read it as three separate sounds, /b/-/i/-/f/. He received a score of 3 for three letter sounds identified correctly. When Matoria came to the same word, she read *bif* accurately as a whole word and also received 3 points, one for each letter sound in the word. Matoria's final score of 52 sounds correct per minute, with 18 words read accurately, indicates that she decodes words so fluently that she is starting to read chunks of letters and is ready for more advanced word reading. Jamal's final score of 52 sounds correct per minute and 0 words read indicates that he is unable to decode words phonetically and needs explicit instruction in learning to sound out. In the event students score 50–60 by reading single letter sounds only, Good and colleagues have added the following criterion for meeting benchmark: Students must also read at least 15 words as whole words (Good, Kaminski, & Howe, 2005).

The standardized directions for both the DIBELS and AIMSweb Nonsense Words Fluency assessments can be misleading for students who are told that they can read either letter sounds or words. We found that teachers could get students to read whole words rather then the letter sounds by doing the following:

* Talking to students before the assessment about how they would have a chance to read those silly **words**
* Stressing *"Read as whole **words** if you can"* when they say the directions
* Giving informative feedback after the assessment about how many **words** a student read

In our work with thousands of students, we found that more students met benchmarks in first grade if we set the bar higher for nonsense word reading. Students who left kindergarten reading fewer than four words typically started to fall behind in first grade as shown by their mid- or end-year benchmark scores indicating they needed Tier 3 support. When a higher benchmark was set, these students received the support they needed earlier.

Some schools use PDAs, also called personal digital assistants, which are small handheld digital devices that store information, analyze data, and chart progress for progress monitoring. When teachers input NWF scores into PDAs, only the total scores of sounds read is recorded in the charts. Because this score can be misleading, in order to analyze NWF scores for screening, the number of words read should always be included in the analysis. Under the progress-monitoring section, Table 3.2 depicts an easy record teachers used in some of our project schools to track the number of nonsense words students read.

When Is It Routinely Given? DIBELS and AIMSweb Nonsense Word Fluency   Middle of kindergarten through the beginning of second grade

Reading High-Frequency Regular and Exception Words   Struggling readers have deficits in word reading; therefore, some beginning reading screening inventories

> At the official DIBELS website **(https:// dibels.uoregon.edu/measures/nwf. php)**, you can watch a teacher giving the Nonsense Word Fluency assessment to a student. Directions to administer and score the test are available at the same website, as are copies that can be downloaded at no charge.

TABLE 3.2   Nonsense Word Record Form

Student Name	Feb	Feb	March	March	April	April
	number of letter sounds/number of whole words read accurately					
Paula	44/10	55/10	58/12			
Pete	32/8	44/11	55/10			
Roberta	10/0	18/4	20/6			
Ted	36/8	44/10	44/11			
Steve	44/2	45/6	48/8			
Peyton	59/7	59/12	62/13			

include word reading as a subtest, either timed or untimed. The assumption is that when students read a combination of regular and exception real words, both phonemic decoding ability and automatic sight word reading are assessed. Since many students can retain up to 400 words in visual memory (Hempenstall, 2001), it is possible to do well on a real word-reading test in the early grades either by relying on phonemic decoding or by using visual memory. Not until fourth grade, when the visual memory demand increases to 4,000 words, are some students who have been relying on a strong visual memory identified as needing support when their visual memory is no longer adequate for more advanced reading (Hempenstall, 2001).

A typical word-reading test is the PALS Word Recognition in Isolation subtest. Students read high-frequency words from a list of 60 words. The TPRI Word Reading test is similar to the PALS with the exception that there are only 10 high-frequency words to read.

The Test of Word Reading Efficiency (TOWRE) has two subtests that can be used for screening. In the first 45-second subtest, Sight Word Efficiency, students read real words that range from one to four syllables. In the second 45-second subtest, Phonemic Decoding Efficiency, students read nonsense words that range from two phonemes to four syllables. For more information go to http://www.sedl.org/cgi-bin/mysql/rad.cgi?searchid=225.

When Is It Given?

* **PALS Word Recognition in Isolation:**   Optional for kindergarten; fall and spring of first through third grade
* **TPRI Inventory Word Reading:**   Fall and spring of first grade; fall of second and third grade
* **Test of Word-Reading Efficiency (TOWRE):**   Since the norming group for this fluency-based assessment includes adolescents, this test is appropriate for a wide range of students at any time during the school year.

Progress Monitoring for Beginning Word-Reading Skills

Letter–Sound Correspondence   When students are first learning letter–sound correspondences, teachers can informally monitor their progress by asking them to identify the letter sounds that they have learned after every four or five letter sounds taught in the reading program. This assessment should always include all the letter sounds taught from the beginning of the year until the time of the current assessment. Accuracy of 100% is required. By the end of October, Ms. Bolas had taught her class letter sounds for the following letters: a, h, m, d, and s. Then, in order to determine whether her instruction was effective, for two days during center time she worked with students one at a time, giving them a brief letter–sound assessment. The student test sheet, score sheet, and directions for the letter–sound correspondence assessment she gave are shown in Figures 3.4 and 3.5.

Note that in the measure, only the letters Ms. Bolas taught until the end of October were assessed. Note also that Ms. Bolas taught her students the sounds for both upper- and lowercase letters. If you are teaching your students the sounds for lowercase letters first, then your assessment should only include lowercase letters. Although some teachers add a column for letter names, the score for this assessment is based only on students' accurate identification of letter sounds necessary for word reading.

When giving the letter–sounds assessment, Ms. Bolas put a student test sheet in front of the student. Letters on the test sheet were typed in a large font matching the font used

H	h
T	t
A	a
M	m
D	d
O	o
S	s

FIGURE 3.4 Letter–Sound Assessment: Student Test Sheet

Student Name: _Caryn_   Date: _Oct. 31_

Directions: Place the Test Sheet in front of the student and hold the Record Sheet on a clipboard so that the student cannot see the scores you record. Point to the letters and say, "Look at these upper- and lowercase alphabet letters. I want you to tell me the sound that each letter makes." Cover all the letters except the first one with a sheet of paper, point to that first letter, and say, "What sound does this letter make?" If the student says the correct letter sound, write the score, slide the paper down one row, point to the next letter, and ask the same question. If the student says the letter name, say, "___ is the name of this letter. Now tell me what sound this letter makes." Uncover one letter at a time, until you have asked for the sound of every letter on the sheet. If the student says the long vowel sound, say, "That's one sound this letter makes. What is another sound this letter makes?"

Scoring: Score 1 point for every correct letter sound. Score 0 for every incorrect letter sound.

Testing Tips: The child either knows a letter sound or does not know a letter sound. Do not prompt any answers by giving hints. If a child cannot say just the letter sound, but has to say a keyword jingle that matches it ("/ă/ - apple - /ă/") or has to say the letter sound three or four times in succession (/h/, /h/, /h/), count the answer as incorrect. In order to accurately decode words, a student must be able to say the letter sound once and continue decoding.

Letter	Letter Sound
1. H h	1
2. T t	1
3. A a	0
4. M m	1
5. D d	1
6. O o	1
7. S s	1
Total Correct	6
Percent	86%

FIGURE 3.5 Letter–Sound Assessment: Teacher's Directions and Score Sheet

in classroom instruction. While the example above uses manuscript letters, if you are teaching D'Nealian, fonts in that script are available for your classroom computer.

Reading Pseudowords   Because teachers need to regularly monitor student progress in decoding, ideally a nonsense word–reading fluency assessment such as AIMSweb or DI-BELS NWF should be given at least every two to four weeks for beginning readers in Tiers 2 and 3 starting in the winter of kindergarten until the student has met benchmark and the skill is scored as "established." Once students meet the benchmark score, they do not need to be monitored with this assessment any longer because their phonological decoding of CVC words now enables them to read new CVC and CVC-variant words by sight. Reading 15 words and 50 sounds on a Nonsense Words Reading Fluency subtest lets a teacher know when to start teaching the advanced word-reading skills presented in Chapter 4. A sample score sheet for the DIBELS NWF subtest is shown in Figure 3.6.

When one or two students in a class do not make adequate progress in developing decoding skills, that lack of progress reflects their individual need for more support. When the majority of students in a class do not make adequate progress on NWF assessments, the reading curriculum, the quality of teaching, and the amount of practice for everyone needs to be investigated. Teachers often ask if they should have their students practice reading nonsense words. Although some phonics programs use a few nonsense words for occasional practice, having students decode real words is more productive. Through additional practice decoding real words, the students are more likely to eventually learn to read them by sight. As students gain skills in phonological decoding, the NWF test scores will reflect that growth.

The 25 PALS Quick Checks allow teachers to monitor progress in pseudoword decoding. These untimed assessments begin by assessing CVC words, but by Quick Check #6 include words with blends and digraphs; by #21 they emphasize words with long vowel patterns. Because the nonsense words progressively get more difficult on the later tests, these Quick Checks can be used to monitor progress for both beginning word reading and some of the

---

Name: _____   Date: _____

f a p	b o s	f i c	d i f	v i m	___/15
l o m	o v	v e f	h i z	b e j	___/14
r i z	m a g	v e g	f e v	u b	___/14
y u f	h o z	w u c	m i d	m e z	___/15
n a k	y i p	w u l	f e c	k a l	___/15
k u d	z u t	j u b	s u p	a d	___/14
t o f	n e z	l a l	d o c	b u j	___/15
r u d	p e s	s i g	n u d	z u r	___/15
a c	r i s	w o v	b o l	t a j	___/14
m o d	r o g	m o z	w u c	r o m	___/15

Total: ___

Error Pattern:

FIGURE 3.6   DIBELS NWF Assessment and Score Sheet (Blank)

Source: Official DIBELS home page: https://dibels.uoregon.edu/measures/nwf.php

earlier advanced word-reading skills. For older students, the TOWRE Phonemic Decoding Efficiency Subtest can be used for progress-monitoring nonsense word reading at "relatively short intervals" if only one alternative form A or B is given at a time (Torgesen, Wagner, & Rashotte, 1999).

Reading High-Frequency Regular and Exception Words   Another set of PALS Quick Checks allows teachers to monitor progress in reading high-frequency regular and exception words. In this untimed assessment the words range from preprimer to third grade. For older students, the TOWRE Sight Word Efficiency Subtest can be used for monitoring progress in high-frequency regular word reading at "relatively short intervals" if only one alternative form A or B is given at a time (Torgesen et al., 1999).

Diagnostic Assessments for Beginning Word-Reading Skills

By looking at individual student answer patterns as well as the cumulative score on Nonsense Word Fluency subtests, you can tell how to adapt your instruction to move the student into the next decoding phase. Student scores on Nonsense Word Fluency assessments indicate four definite patterns as students develop beginning reading skills. These patterns are shown in Figure 3.7. Note that student 1, Jervon, is still reading at the individual sound level as indicated by the scoring of his nonsense word reading. Every letter is marked because he said only the individual letter sounds as he read words on the test. Student 2, Tori, is beginning to sound out by saying the individual letter–sound correspondence in each word and then blending those letter sounds together into whole words. The third student, Yolanda, is sounding out many words as onset rime before reading them as whole words. She is beginning to read many two-letter words automatically as one word without needing to sound out. At this stage, students' scores begin to increase substantially as they develop the skills of a full alphabetic phase reader. Finally, the fourth student, Katina, represents a student who is moving into the consolidated alphabetic reading phase. Of the four students, only Katina will score at benchmark levels. She is ready to sound out more complex words like those discussed in Chapter 4 and work on fluency in grade-level text. Jervon needs more practice sounding out and blending basic CVC words. Tori needs to transition to subvocal sounding out, so she begins to read words the fast way or more automatically. Yolanda is almost there. Continued daily practice with word and passage reading will help Yolanda go that extra step and move into the advanced word reading stage that characterizes someone at the consolidated alphabetic phase.

Sounding-Out Stage
Student #1: Jervon

l i n   m u s   u k   d o v   o v

Transition Sounding-Out Stage
Student #2: Tori

l i n   m u s   u k   d o v   o v

Onset-Rime Sounding-Out Stage
Student #3: Yolanda

l i n   m u s   u k   d o v   o v

Fully Developed Alphabetic Principle
Student #4: Katina

l i n   m u s   u k   d o v   o v

FIGURE 3.7 Sample DIBELS Scoring Patterns

The Woodcock Reading Mastery Test Revised (WRMT-R) contains two word-reading subtests that are normed for individuals from 5 to 75+ years. The untimed Word Identification subtest includes high-frequency regular and exception words. The Word Attack subtest requires students to sound out a series of nonsense words of increasing complexity. While this measure lacks the fluency component of the DIBELS Nonsense Word Fluency subtest, the use of multisyllable nonsense words provides teachers with more in-depth diagnostic information for older students. For more information on the Woodcock Reading Mastery Tests, go to http://www.pearsonassessments.com/wrmtrnu.aspx. To assess word-reading fluency, the TOWRE can also be used for diagnostic assessment for a wide age range of students.

Rathvon (2004) cautions that different regular word-reading subtests used for diagnostic testing can yield significantly different scores. Therefore, corroborating your findings with other formal and informal word-reading measures is recommended, particularly when making decisions such as the identification of a learning disability. When diagnostic tests are used to determine eligibility for a learning disability in reading, tests of RAN should be included. One alternative for assessing older students is the Comprehensive Test of Phonological Processing (CTOPP), which has four rapid-naming assessments and is normed for students from 5 to 24 years of age. Another option for older students is the test of Rapid Picture Naming on the Woodcock-Johnson III Test of Cognitive Abilities, which has norms for examinees from 2 through 90 years of age.

An informal phonics diagnostic assessment can provide information for teachers whose students are beginning readers. The measure can tell you which beginning letter–sound correspondences students have learned and which CVC variants students are able to decode. This information can then be used to identify letter sounds and word types for instruction. For example, if on this assessment Grace misreads only the letter sound for x, but then misreads all CCVC words with beginning blends and the more difficult words, Mr. Farley knows to teach her the sound of x and to begin teaching her to read blends in isolation, in words, and in text.

Spelling Assessment

Three of the four assessment screening batteries have spelling tests that can be used for either screening, progress monitoring, or diagnostic purposes. AIMSweb has first- through eighth-grade spelling tests that can be used for screening or progress monitoring. The 12 words on each test represent high-frequency words, some regular and some irregular. Students have up to 10 seconds to write each word. Teachers score the tests by counting the number of correct letter sequences.

> More information on curriculum-based measurement spelling probes and how to compute correct letter sequences can be found at **http://www.jimwrightonline.com/pdfdocs/cbmresources/cbmdirections/cbmspell.pdf**.

Spelling is also assessed in the PALS Kindergarten Letter–Sound Knowledge section on an untimed test where students are asked to spell five CVC words, receiving one point for each letter sound correctly written. The Grades 1–3 PALS also includes a spelling inventory as part of the Word Knowledge screening section. Because all of the words are regular with specific types of phonics patterns (e.g., blends, digraphs, nasals, long vowels), this subtest provides diagnostic information to help a teacher plan instruction. Points are awarded for specific phonics features that are spelled correctly. Quick Checks requiring students to spell regular words that get progressively more difficult over the course of the school year allow for progress monitoring.

On the first-grade TPRI, students complete a number of spelling tasks with magnetic boards and letters. After students spell an orally dictated CVC word, they manipulate the magnetic letters to make requested final consonant substitutions, middle vowel substitutions, and initial and final blending substitutions. Both the second- and third-grade inventories include regular word-spelling tests.

How Do I Teach Beginning Reading Skills to My Students?

As emphasized in Chapter 1, the multi-tier and RTI approaches described in this text allow teachers to accommodate a range of learners. The teaching enhancements described in that chapter also apply for each of the key skill areas in beginning reading instruction. The general education reading program for children who are at risk is enhanced through the use of advance organizers, unison responding, perky pace, support for new learning using My Turn–Together–Your Turn, systematic error corrections, cumulative review, integrated motivational strategies, and teaching to success. The following formats for teaching letter–sound correspondences, word reading, and text reading are used for large-group Tier 1 instruction and also small-group Tier 2 interventions. In addition, descriptions of more intensive programs appropriate for Tier 3 are provided along with special strategies for English language learners and older students.

Identifying Letter–Sound Correspondences

Even when students can segment and blend, before learning to sound out words they must be able to automatically identify some letter–sound correspondences in isolation. For example, Carnine and colleagues (2010) recommend that at least six to eight letter–sound correspondences, including one or two vowels, be taught prior to the introduction of sounding out words. Failure to work on letter–sound correspondences in isolation prior to sounding out words can result in the problem shown in the following example:

> Keionda's teacher showed her how to sound out the word *man*, but Keionda had not learned /ă/, the most common sound of the letter *a*. Keionda's teacher had to stop the decoding instruction temporarily in order to practice the /ă/ letter–sound correspondence. Stopping to work on a letter sound that should have been learned previously slowed the pace of the lesson and diverted Keionda's attention from learning the decoding strategy. This spur-of-the-moment instruction on /ă/ did not provide enough practice for Keionda to predictably remember that letter sound the next day.

Many programs teach sounds using an indirect approach. Instead of introducing letter sounds in isolation, teachers write a list of words that begin with a new letter on the board. After asking the students what letter sound is the same in all of these words, the teacher asks the students to say the sound of the new letter. For students with disabilities or who are at risk, this approach is clearly not explicit enough. Such an approach does not provide enough practice of the new letter–sound correspondence or review of previously introduced sounds. The format in Table 3.3 directly teaches letter–sound correspondences and provides extensive student practice and review. The first part of this format introduces the new letter–sound correspondence using the My Turn–Together–Your Turn strategy shown in steps 2–5 in Table 3.3. In Part B of this format, the teacher provides practice of the new letter–sound correspondence in combination with six or seven other previously introduced sounds. In Part B, the teacher reduces scaffolding by first testing the group (Your Turn) on the new and review letter sounds before checking student mastery by calling on individual students to read the letter sounds.

Figure 3.8 shows the LOOP signal used by the teacher to elicit unison answers from the group. As shown, the teacher first points to the left of the letter, provides a thinking pause, asks "what sound?" and then loops his finger to touch underneath the letter. He pauses under the letter two

FIGURE 3.8 LOOP Signal

TABLE 3.3 Format for Teaching New Letter Sounds in the General Curriculum

Objective	After seeing a new letter, students will say its sound with 100% accuracy
Materials Needed	Board, chart paper, or overhead transparency and writing implement
Signaling	Before starting letter–sound drill, students should practice responding to your loop signal, so they learn to say the sound of the letter as long as your finger stays on the letter. Place your finger to the left of the letter. **"What sound?"** initiates the signal for unison answers.
	Signal for continuous sounds: After looping to the letter, hold your finger under it for 2 seconds as students say the sound, before looping your finger back to the starting point.
	Signal for stop sounds: After looping to the letter, immediately bounce your finger out as students say the sound, and return to the starting point.
Time	3–5 minutes

Teaching New Letter Sounds: Part A

Instructions	Teacher	Students
	1. Advance Organizer	
	2. My Turn (examples given for continuous and stop sounds). During the beginning reading phases typically only one sound would be introduced.	
	Write a lowercase letter *s* on the board and point to the letter:	
	Signal for *continuous sounds:* (finger to the left of letter) **"Here's our new sound for today."** (loop signal) **"/s/."** (loop back to starting point) **"This letter says"** (loop signal) **"/s/"** (end signal).	
	Write a lowercase letter *t* on the board and point to the letter:	
	Signal for *stop sounds:* (finger to the left of letter) **"Here's our new sound for today."** (loop signal and bounce out) **"/t/."** (back to starting point) **"This letter says"** (loop signal and bounce out) **"/t/."** (end signal).	
	3. Together	
	The teacher answers with students this time.	
	Signal for *continuous sounds:* (finger to the left of letter) **"Together. What sound?"** (loop signal) **"/s/."** (loop back to starting point) **"Yes, /s/."**	/s/
	Signal for *stop sounds:* (finger to the left of letter) **"Together. What sound?"** (loop signal and bounce out) **"/t/."** (back to starting point) **"Yes, /t/."**	/t/
	Repeat this sequence several times.	
	4. Your Turn	
	Signal for *continuous sounds:* (finger to the left of letter) **"Your turn. What sound?"** (loop signal) (answer) (loop back to starting point) **"Yes, /s/."**	/s/
	Signal for *stop sounds:* (finger to the left of letter) **"Your turn. What sound?"** (loop signal and bounce out) (answer) (back to starting point) **"Yes, /t/."**	/t/
	Repeat several times.	
	5. Individual Student Checkout	
	Signal for *continuous sounds:* (finger to the left of letter) **"Individual turns. What sound? Marissa."** (loop signal) (answer) (loop back to starting point) **"Yes, /s/."**	/s/
	Signal for *stop sounds:* (finger to the left of letter) **"Individual turns. What sound? Tonia."** (loop signal and bounce out) (answer) (back to starting point) **"Yes, /t/."**	/t/
	Call on several individual students and check accuracy.	
Error Correction	If students make an error, immediately return to a My Turn–Together–Your Turn pattern. You may need to refocus students to your mouth position as you say the letter.	

TABLE 3.3 Continued

	Teaching New Letter Sounds with Review Sounds: Part B	
Instructions	**Teacher**	**Students**
Scaffolding Reduction	1. Advance Organizer	
	2. Your Turn	
	The teacher uses an alternating pattern to teach the new letter sound by writing the new lowercase letter on the board followed by one previously taught letter, followed by the new letter, followed by two previously taught letters. This pattern is continued until five letters separate the last two new letters (for example, **s** t **s** a t **s** m t a **s** h m t a **s** a t h m f **s**). The teacher provides more practice identifying the more difficult previously taught letters and vowels by including them in the list every day.	
	Signal for *continuous sounds:* (finger to the left of letter) **"Your turn. What sound?"** (loop signal) (answer) (loop back to starting point) **"Yes, /s/."**	/s/, /t/, /s/, /a/, /t/,
	Signal for *stop sounds:* (finger to the left of letter) **"Your turn. What sound?"** (loop signal and bounce out) (answer) (back to starting point) **"Yes, /t/."**	/s/, /m/, /t/ /s/
	3. Individual Student Checkout	
	Signal for *continuous sounds:* (finger to the left of letter) **"Individual turns. What sound? Kyle."** (loop signal) (answer) (loop back to starting point) **"Yes, /s/."**	/s/
	Signal for *stop sounds:* (finger to the left of letter) **"Individual turns. What sound? Lynnette."** (loop signal and bounce out) (answer) (back to starting point) **"Yes, /ă/."** Call on several individual students to check accuracy.	/ă/
Error Correction	If students make an error, immediately return to a My Turn–Together–Your Turn pattern. Then alternate between the missed letter and familiar letters until students identify the missed letter correctly three times.	
	For example, if you are working on *a, m, r, s,* and *i,* and the students missed *s,* say, (finger to the left of letter) **"This sound is /s/."** before asking, **"What sound?"** (loop signal and end) **"Yes, /s/."**	
	Then ask the students to identify letter sounds using the following alternating pattern: **a s** m i **s** r i m **s**.	
Perk Up Your Drill	※ Vary the color of the letters.	
	※ Hold your pointer finger on a continuous sound letter for an extra second or two and praise everyone who had enough air to hold it the entire time.	
	※ Occasionally tell students that they will say the sounds in booming lion voices, in squeaky mouse voices, or in robot voices.	
	※ Occasionally signal using an unusual pointer such as a puppet's hand, a wand, or a baton. Decorate a pointer to fit the occasion; dress it up with ribbons and glitter or an appropriate theme for the time of year.	
	※ Some teachers teach their students to finger-spell the new letter as they say it. Other teachers add easier hand signals for the more difficult letters. For example, when students say /p/, the teacher has them point their finger down; when students say /i/, the teacher holds up a pretend antenna to represent an *insect.* Signals can provide extra motivation as long as teachers eventually fade them out. Signals should not interfere with the pace of instruction.	
Adaptations	※ When students have reached 100% accuracy on Part B, you can begin to use a combination of upper-case and lowercase letters.	
	※ Before teaching the new letter sound, see if students in the class can repeat the new sound after they hear you say it. Some students may need articulation practice. For example, if students have difficulty saying /p/, put your fingers to your lips and show the students how your lips pop when you say the /p/ sound. Next ask the students to put their fingers on their lips and make the same lip-popping sound. If some of the students are vocalizing the /b/ sound instead of the /p/ sound, ask students to put their hands on their necks in order to feel the difference between a voiced sound and an unvoiced sound.	

Source: This script is based on one originally developed and field-tested by Carnine, D. W., Silbert, J., Kame'enui, E. J., & Tarver, S. (2010). *Direct Instruction Reading* (5th ed.). Boston: Merrill.

to three seconds for continuous sounds and immediately bounces out for stop sounds. When he bounces off to return to the starting point or loops back to the starting point, students stop saying the letter sound. In this way, the teacher can calibrate the length of time students say the sound.

Two Best Practices for Teaching Letter–Sound Correspondences   Let's look at how Mrs. Nguyen taught letter sounds to her class, using the following effective teaching strategies.

Use Classroom Time Efficiently   Since many of Mrs. Nguyen's students came to school with limited language skills, she started teaching letter–sound correspondences by the second week of school. Although the general education curriculum was designed to teach one letter–sound correspondence a week, she knew that she could not waste any time because many of her kindergartners would need two weeks on each vowel sound and the more difficult consonant sounds. Every morning after calendar time, she immediately started her language arts instruction by following the letter–sound format in Table 3.3 for three to five minutes. When teaching a new letter–sound correspondence, Mrs. Nguyen used the format in Table 3.3 Part A: Steps 1–5 for the first two or three days. Every day after teaching the new letter sound of the week, Mrs. Nguyen reviewed the previous letter sounds. Immediately after practicing the new /b/ sound, Mrs. Nguyen used the format in Table 3.3: Part B, reviewing the /f/, /s/, /a/, and /m/ letter sounds that she had taught during the first month and a half of school.

Give More Individual Turns to Students Who Have the Most Difficulty   Shoshana, Greg, and Tracy's scores on last month's letter–sound assessment showed that they had learned the fewest sounds, so Mrs. Nguyen asked them more questions during individual student checkouts.

Writing Letter–Sound Correspondences

Students' learning of letter–sound correspondences is enhanced when they are required to spell the sounds and words they are reading. Therefore, when you are teaching letter sounds in isolation, students should also write as well as say the sounds. For example, Ms. Chapelle's students can identify the most common sounds for the following letters: *s, r, m, t, a,* and *d.* After her students practice saying the letter sounds, Ms. Chapelle has her students take out their whiteboards and write the same letter sounds from dictation using the format shown in Figure 3.9.

Louisa Moats describes why spelling (encoding) instruction helps students' ability to read (decoding) and the complementary relationship between the two:

> Ehri and Snowling (2004) found the ability to read words "by sight" (i.e., automatically) rests on the ability to map letters and letter combinations to sounds. Because words are not very visually distinctive (for example, *car, can, cane*), it is impossible for children to memorize more than a few dozen words unless they have developed insights into how letters and sounds correspond. Learning to spell requires instruction and gradual integration of information about print, speech sounds, and meaning—these, in turn, support memory for whole words, which is used in both spelling and sight reading. (Moats, 2005, p. 12)

Make sure that your teaching objectives integrate teaching students to say and to write the letter–sound associations you teach. The kindergarten teacher, Ms. Krill, would be teaching ten letter sounds in the next ten weeks. Thus, when she wrote her teaching objectives for that

---

Sound Spelling Activity: Children write /t/ and /r/.

Teacher: "You're going to write some letter sounds."
　　　　　"First sound /t/. What sound?" (signal) (answer) **"Yes, /t/."**
　　　　　"Write /t/." Check children's answers and give feedback.
　　　　　"Next sound /r/. What sound?" (signal) (answer) **"Yes, /r/."**
　　　　　"Write /r/." Check children's answers and give feedback.

FIGURE 3.9　Sound Writing Format

Source: This script was adapted from Engelmann, S., & Bruner, E. (1995). *Reading Mastery I: Teacher's guide*. Columbus, OH: SRA Macmillan/McGraw-Hill.

quarter, in addition to expecting students to look at a letter and say the most common sound associated with it, she wrote the following spelling objective: "When orally presented with the sounds /s/, /f/, /m/, /t/, /a/, /p/, /b/, /i/, /c/, and /d/, the students will write the correct letter for 10 out of the 10 sounds." Because many of Ms. Krill's students came to school unable to write their letters, she made handwriting instruction a part of sound instruction until students could reproduce the letters. For students requiring more support, she integrated handwriting into some of her Tier 2 groups.

Although none of the four assessment batteries tests spelling at the sound–symbol level, be sure that beginning readers can spell the new letter–sound correspondences you are teaching. The informal letter–sound assessment described earlier in the diagnostic section can be used to assess students' encoding of letter sounds. Give each student a sheet of paper with blank lines and ask them to write the letter that represents a sound you say.

> Read about the 12 components of research-based reading programs at the Reading Rockets website: **http://www.readingrockets.org/articles/242.**

Applying the Enhancements to a Commercial Reading Program

The following lesson introducing the most common sound for the letter *u* is a typical lesson from a commercial reading program:

> Say *us* and *under* slowly, focusing on the /u/ sound. Ask the students what sound they hear at the beginning of both words. Write a large uppercase *U* and lowercase *u* on the blackboard and say, "This is uppercase *U* and this is lowercase *u*." Tell the students that a vowel can stand for several sounds. Call on volunteers to identify words in a rhyme printed on a chart that begin with the letter *u*.
>
> Write *us* and *under* on the chart and have the students tell you other words that begin with the /u/ sound. Add these words to the chart and read them all together with the students.

This activity is likely to create several problems for children who are at risk. First, and most importantly, the lesson doesn't provide adequate practice and support by introducing the letter sound using a My Turn–Together–Your Turn strategy. Students never directly hear the sound that the letter *u* represents, nor are they given any direct practice on saying the letter sound while the teacher points to the letter. Pointing to words with *u* in the rime and volunteering words that begin with the letter *u* can all be done without making the association between the sound and the written letter *u*. If the teacher has called on individual students to answer these questions, adequate practice for everyone is not provided. Students who are at risk will be unlikely to be able to identify the short sound for the letter *u* when they come to a word that has its most common sound.

Another problem with this lesson is that the words on the chart that students read are not in any way coordinated with the letter sounds and skills they have already learned. During the previous week students may have learned the difficult letter sound /j/, which still needs daily practice. When words on the chart do not incorporate cumulative review, prior learning is frequently forgotten. Students are encouraged to memorize the words, thus promoting the idea that reading words involves memorization, not sounding out.

Enhancing this lesson for students who are at risk includes adding more My Turn–Together–Your Turn opportunities so everyone gets enough practice. The format for introducing new letter sounds in the general curriculum, which was shown in Table 3.3 (pages 68–69), can be used by teachers to instruct any new letter–sound correspondence. Once students receive more directed instruction and practice with the new letter–sound association by itself, teachers have students practice the new letter sound along with previously introduced sounds using Part B of the same format. Any teacher using a reading curriculum containing lessons similar to the example /u/ lesson can modify letter–sound activities by starting lessons using the formats included in Table 3.3. Although it is important that students directly see how the letter sounds and phonemic awareness skills they are learning relate to word reading, having students read these words as sight words can undermine their acquisition of the alphabetic principle. Instead of having students read the words, ask them to say the first letter sound when you point to and read the words on the chart. Additional ways you can help your students learn letter–sound correspondences are described in the *In Your Classroom* feature.

In Your Classroom

Helping Your Students Articulate and Differentiate Letter Sounds

The *b* vs. *d* Conundrum

When your daily teaching shows that some of the first graders are still mixing lowercase *b*'s with *d*'s, they will benefit from practicing reading words with these letter sounds. The key to this practice is focusing on accuracy. The more /b/-/d/ errors your students make, the more reteaching you have to do. Show students how the lowercase *b* looks like a bat and ball. Ask them what letter sound *bat* starts with, and then ask what letter sound *ball* starts with. Then ask, "If the letter looks like a bat and ball, what is its sound?" Make a list of six CVC words containing *d*'s or *b*'s, and before asking the students to read the word, tell them to say the first sound in the word. Each time, point out the "bat and ball" letter. Tell students they will earn a point for every word read correctly and that 6 points wins the game.

Getting Students to Hear *j*

These tips about the production of /j/ should make your task easier if students are saying a different sound for this letter. According to the Lindamood: LiPS Program, /j/ is a "Noisy Fat-Pushed Air" sound (Lindamood & Lindamood, 1998).

Why Is /j/ Noisy????

If you put your hand on your throat as you say /j/, you can feel the vibration. With quiet sounds such as /s/ and /p/, you will not feel this vibration. Help your children feel their necks vibrate as they say /j/.

What Is "Fat-Pushed Air?"

As you say /j/, hold the back of your hand in front of your mouth and feel the air push out. Unlike /s/ or

/sh/, where one's air comes out in a smooth flow, /j/ requires a fat-push of air that sprays all over.

What Else Can I Do to Help My Students Hear This Sound?

Compose a list of /j/ words that are familiar to your students with words like *jet, jump, jelly,* and *jellybean.* Following the script, say, "My turn, *jet.* First sound? /j/." Follow this with a Together and a Your Turn until the children begin to produce a clear /j/ sound. Remember to loudly and clearly say the /j/ sound, over-accentuating it. You will have to work at saying /j/ loudly and clearly so that your children distinctly hear it.

The Elusive /ĕ/

Frequently, some first graders and kindergartners confuse the sounds of /ĕ/ and /ă/. For example, when asked to blend /p/-/ĕ/-/n/, students confusing these two phonemes reply *pan.* They are likely to make the same mistake when reading the word *pan.* When asked what the new word means, they proudly explain that it is something to write with. Slipping the follow-ing activities into your day for five to ten minutes will help end the confusion:

- Play a short game where the children hold up one "man" if you say *man,* and two "men" if you say *men.*
- Ask students to say *cook* if you say *pan,* and *write* if you say *pen.*
- Make sure that students can write *e* when you say that letter sound. Expect students to sound-write all the vowels.
- Write the vowel letters in a circle on the board and have the students "say the vowel circle" as you point to the letters. Listen to be certain students are accurately saying each letter sound. Be sure that your voice and jaw go down when you say /ă/, overaccentuating the dip.
- Line up with a vowel focus: As you call students to line up, instead of saying, "Table 1 line up," ask Table 1 to first say the letter sound for *e* before lining up. Locate your students at Table 1 who still have vowel confusion and ask them to individually tell you the difficult letter sound. Example: "Table 1, tell me the sound of *e* before you line up." (signal) "Good. Jessie and Dustin, let me hear you say the sound for *a* one more time." (signal) "Table 2. . . ."

Reading Regular Words: A Three-Part Process

There are three parts to the format for reading regular words. In Part 1, students sound out each word orally before reading it as a whole word, receiving added support from the teacher using My Turn–Together–Your Turn as needed. In Part 2, students continue to sound out the words, but do so subvocally, in their heads. In Part 3 student sounding out is at an automatic level where students read each regular word by sight, without any conscious sounding out. In this section a description of each of these parts, including when to use them based on students' DIBELS and AIMSweb NWF scores, is provided.

Part 1: Sounding Out Orally   Sounding out regular words should begin as soon as possible, because phonemic awareness and knowledge of letter sounds are not sufficient for students who are at risk to learn to read. Systematic, explicit instruction in sounding out words is a key component for learning to read. Students who are at risk require extensive practice in sounding out words before they are ready for advanced word reading. Accurate, fluent sounding out and blending of regular words is a key prerequisite to the automatic sight–word reading necessary for fluent reading. When students sound out loud, the teacher can closely monitor their accuracy, providing corrections and additional teaching when needed.

You can begin teaching students to sound out words as soon as they have learned between six and eight letter sounds, including one or two common vowel sounds. Beginning sounding out is most effectively taught when word selection is first confined to the VC, CVC, and CVC-variant words. As described earlier, these are one-syllable words formed using the most common sounds of all single consonants and vowels. Some teachers may want to follow the easy-to-hard sequence of CVC words shown in Figure 3.1 (p. 53), starting with CVC words that begin with continuous sounds, because these are the words that are easiest to blend.

In Part 1 of regular word reading, students orally sound out regular words. This teaching procedure, which is shown in Table 3.4, is most helpful for students reading at the

TABLE 3.4   Format for Reading Regular Words—Part 1: Oral Sounding Out

Objective	After seeing a regular word, students will orally sound out the letter sounds before saying the word.
Materials Needed	Board, chart paper, or overhead transparency and writing implement. Write the regular words that students will read in rows on the board. For example, if students are reading eight words, write two rows of four words.
Signaling	Three-part signal: Finger is in starting position to the left of the word. **"Sound out,"** or **"What word?"** initiates the signal for unison answers.
	1. Use loop signal for orally sounding out the letter sounds in the words.
	2. As students are saying the final letter sound, immediately loop finger back to the starting point.
	3. Pause for a moment of think time before asking students **"What word?"** and side-slash to the end of the word.
Time	Depends on number of new words and difficulty level. Kindergarten students often work on this skill for between 5 and 15 minutes each day. First-grade students may need to work on this skill for up to 20 minutes if the curriculum has introduced many new words or a new letter–sound pattern.

Instructions	**Teacher**	**Students**
	1. Advance Organizer	
	2. My Turn (Note: See Ms. Elizondo's fourth tip on page 77 in the text to determine whether to start at Step 2, 3, or 4.)	
	(finger to the left of the first letter) **"My turn sounding out this word."** (loop from letter to letter) **"/f/-/ă/-/n/"** (loop back to starting point) **"What word?"** (side-slash signal) **"fan."**	
	3. Together The teacher answers with students this time:	
	(finger to the left of the first letter) **"Together, sound out this word."** (loop from letter to letter) **"/f/-/ă/-/n/."** (loop back to starting point) **"What word?"** (side-slash signal) **"fan."** (loop to starting point) **"Yes, fan."**	/f/-/ăl/-/n/ fan
	4. Your Turn	
	(finger to the left of the first letter) **"Your turn to sound out this word."** (loop from letter to letter) (answer) (loop back to starting point) **"What word?"** (side-slash signal) (answer) (loop to starting point) **"Yes, fan."** Repeat step 4 for every word in the row.	/f/-/ăl/-/n/ fan
	5. Individual Student Checkout:	
	Point to the first regular word written on the board (*fan*) and place your finger slightly to the left of the word.	
	"Individual turns. Sound out this word. Grant." (loop from letter to letter) (answer) (loop back to starting point) **"What word?"** (side-slash signal) (answer) (loop to starting point) **"Yes, fan."**	/f/-/ă/-/n/ fan
	"Sound out this word. Leila." (loop from letter to letter) (answer) (loop back to starting point) **"What word?"** (side-slash signal) (answer) (loop to starting point) **"Yes, sip."**	/s/-/ĭ/-/p/ sip
	Call on several students to check for accuracy. When students' correct answers show you that they know all of the words in the row, move to the second row of words.	

TABLE 3.4 Continued

Scaffolding Reduction	6. Be sure to move to using mainly Your Turns as soon as possible.
Error Correction	If students make an error, immediately return to a My Turn–Together–Your Turn pattern, always requiring them to sound out the word. Then return to the beginning of the row and have students reread words the fast way.
Perk Up Your Drill	Do not assume that students are connecting word reading to story reading, even when you do both activities each day. In addition to providing the rationale for word reading at the beginning of the lesson, at least once or twice during the lesson explain to your students how learning to read words will enable them to read books about interesting topics: "You just read the word *sip* all by yourself. When you read books about birthday parties, you might see the word *sip* used when everyone in the story sips some pop before eating the cake." Telling students that the words they are reading on the board will later appear in the story motivates them to do their best.
	When students are beginning readers and need to slowly sound out before blending words, you may find following this format tedious and slow going. Be assured that this is the most important drill that you can do and if you carefully follow the scripts allowing students to practice their sounding out, your class will soon acquire alphabetic principle and move on to faster word reading.
Adaptations	Although you may have readers in your class, you cannot assume that they have learned alphabetic principle, since they may have originally memorized the beginning regular words rather than learned to decode them. Thus, they will benefit from practice with decoding these words. If any readers in your class appear to be reading one or two grade levels above your other students, work with your school team to determine whether it is appropriate for them to participate in a higher grade-level reading group. Use a higher grade-level DIBELS Oral Reading Fluency assessment (Chapter 5) to determine whether the student(s) in question should move up to another reading group or a reading class in a higher grade.
	Some students can automatically read new words after one or two times of sounding them out and blending the letter sounds. Before the end of the lesson, ask these students to read the words the fast way.

Source: This script is based on one originally developed and field-tested by Carnine, D. W., Silbert, J., Kame'enui, E. J., and Tarver, S. (2010). *Direct Instruction Reading* (5th ed.). Boston: Merrill.

prealphabetic or partial alphabetic phase as represented by a score of less than 30 sounds per minute on the DIBELS or AIMSweb NWF assessment, with few if any nonsense words read as whole words. Part 1 stresses several critical skills required to sound out words: sounding out words from left to right and attending to every letter in the word before reading the whole word. Note that students are first taught to sound out words in lists so that they avoid the use of picture and context clues. Picture and context clues can undermine student acquisition of the alphabetic principle by encouraging guessing and are not recommended when teaching beginning students who are at risk to read. Reading clues will be discussed at length later in this chapter and in Chapter 4. Students should remain at Part 1 of regular word reading until they are able to sound out lists of CVC words with 100% accuracy, and without the teacher having to provide support in the form of My Turn–Together–Your Turn.

The signaling procedure for Part 1 of reading regular words is shown in Figure 3.10. First the teacher points to the left of the word to show that sounding always begins on the left side of a word and that sounding is about to begin. The teacher then uses a looping motion as she moves from letter to letter in the word.

FIGURE 3.10   Signal for Sounding Out Regular Words

Students say the letter sound as the teacher's finger rests underneath the letter for one or two seconds. As students are saying the final letter sound, the teacher immediately loops her finger back to the first letter sound. After a pause, the teacher asks students, "What word?" and side-slashes to the end of the word.

Five Best Practices for Teaching Oral Sounding Out   Let's look at how Ms. Elizondo used Part 1 of regular word reading with her students at the early sounding-out stage using the following five best practices:

Provide More Time as Needed for Teaching Difficult Skills to Mastery   Most of Ms. Elizondo's students came to first grade knowing their letter sounds. Many of them still needed more practice blending because they slowly and often inaccurately sounded out words. In order to make sure that her students were ready for advanced word reading by January, when digraphs and long vowels were introduced, she spent more time than the general education reading curriculum recommended on word reading. Every day before class, she wrote the new words presented in the regular curriculum and the new passage reading on the board and started by using the Part 1 format listed in Table 3.4 to teach them. Although the curriculum recommended a lesson a day, when the words were especially difficult, she spent two or even three days on the problematic lesson until students could sound them out quickly on their own when she pointed to them out of order. At that point, unless she was correcting an error or using a My Turn for a particularly difficult word, Ms. Elizondo never read the words with the students, because she wanted them to do their own thinking, and some of them might simply chime in after hearing her voice. Because the principal had decided that all assemblies or other activities would always be scheduled in the afternoon, she was more confident moving through the curriculum at a slower pace. With nothing interfering in the morning, she had gained more teaching days.

Avoid Adding Schwas to Stop Sounds   Ms. Elizondo was careful to avoid adding schwas to her letter sounds when using the My Turn strategy the first time through the word list. Although she had learned the correct pronunciation of letter sounds, the teaching coach had pointed out that when Ms. Elizondo was blending words, she sometimes added those cumbersome schwas. While the coach was observing her, she had actually blended *pal* as /puh/+/a/+/luh/. Sometimes bad habits pop up at the most embarrassing times. Ms. Elizondo was careful to make sure that situation never happened again.

Calibrate Think Time to Difficulty of the Task   Once Ms. Elizondo moved from the My Turn to the Your Turn step, she was careful to calibrate the amount of think time that she provided students before asking, "What word?" If she didn't pause between the time when students said the letter sounds and when they said the entire word, only her best students would answer. Ms. Elizondo knew that when those three or four louder readers answered at lightning speed, she could easily be fooled into believing that the entire class knew the new words taught that day. The first time she had students read the words on a new list, she gave more think time than the second or third time, because her goal was having students read the words faster.

When Students Are Successful in Sounding Out New Words, Reduce Scaffolding and Start Teaching at Step 4   During the first and sometimes the second time students were reading through the word list, Ms. Elizondo carefully progressed through all of the steps in Table 3.4. When her students were more proficient and orally sounding out the words independently, she phased out the My Turn and Together steps and started teaching at Step 4 (Your Turn). As soon as Ms. Elizondo noticed that her students were reading new CVC words accurately and more rapidly the first time they saw them, she began encouraging independence by also starting at Step 4 for the new word lists. After all, Ms. Elizondo knew that readers must develop confidence when sounding out new words they are seeing for the first time. When the new list had a more difficult word that she anticipated her students would miss, she continued to use the entire My Turn–Together–Your Turn sequence for that word.

Use Assessment Information to Determine Individual Turns   Every day Ms. Elizondo gave more turns during individual checkouts to her students who received the lowest scores on the DIBELS Nonsense Word Assessment. When her students were able to sound out words accurately without her help, Ms. Elizondo added Part 2 of regular word reading to her daily instruction in reading regular words.

Applying the Enhancements to a Commercial Reading Program

A typical reading curriculum details an early word-reading lesson in which the purpose of the activity is blending sounds into words using the new letter sound /n/ and several other letter sounds previously introduced. The teacher is instructed to give each student the letter cards *n, i, a, p,* and *t* and tell everyone to place each letter in their mini pocket chart. As each letter is placed in the chart, the students are to say the sound associated with it.

Next the teacher is advised to place the letters *a* and *n* in her large pocket chart and direct the students to do the same in their small ones. Instructions in the curriculum guide indicate that the teacher should demonstrate blending the word *an* by sliding her hand under the letters as she slowly stretches the sounds /ăăănnn/. She is supposed to say the word *an* naturally before asking her students to do the same.

Finally, the teacher is instructed to give the following directions before students blend letter sounds to read new words:

"Put *p* at the beginning. What word did you make?" (*pan*)

"Change the *a* in *pan* to *i*. What word did you make?" (*pin*)

"Make the *p* and *n* change places. What word did you make?" (*nip*)

The major problem with this activity is that it doesn't provide enough support for blending sounds into words. Evidently, the lesson assumes that with no guided practice, after one example students will learn to sound out these new words automatically and independently. Unless modified, this activity does not provide the support and practice that many students who are at risk need to learn to sound out words. A final problem with this activity is that students are asked to respond individually with their own letters. Managing students' behavior and monitoring their work under these conditions present additional challenges in many classrooms.

This activity could be enhanced in a number of ways. First, to avoid the behavior management and monitoring problems that can occur when using manipulatives in a large group, the teacher could have students respond in unison as she manipulates the letters on her large pocket chart. The teacher could also use the format in Table 3.4, injecting My Turn–Together–Your Turn for each of the words the first time the students blend them. The second time through the list, the teacher could switch to Your Turn for these same words, first asking students to sound out each word before reading it by sight. The teacher could also use individual turns with some of her lowest performers to make sure that all of the students acquire the emphasized word-reading skill.

Sometimes students are unable to blend past stop sounds. They can blend the sounds and read words that start with continuous sounds like *man* and *fit*, but they get stuck on words like *can* and *bit*. Teaching students to blend past all stop sounds so they learn to sound out *can* as /că/ /n/ or *bit* as /bĭ/ /t/ solves this problem. A reading program online has activities for "stopping at the vowel" where students blend all words to the vowel, as in the examples *can* or *bit*. For a student whose progress has been stalled because he can't blend past stop sounds, this approach sometimes is effective. Go to http://www.readingkey.com/demo/Files/CD-1/strategy/strategy.doc to learn more.

As we have shown, repeated practice or drill is an indispensable part of teaching students who are at risk to read, particularly when reading material for the first time (Engelmann & Bruner, 1995). Nonetheless, the use of repeated practice and drill is often criticized on the grounds that it decreases student motivation. The impact of systematic, explicit instruction on students' attitude toward reading is explained in the *Research Note*.

Research Note

Attitudes of Students Who Are At Risk

Effective teaching for children who are at risk involves providing them with frequent opportunities to practice the skills they are learning. Practice activities are most successful when a teacher is animated, teaches at a perky pace, and challenges her students without frustrating them. Still, much controversy surrounds the issue of student practice, with repeated practice activities often being referred to as "drill and kill."

Particularly challenging for teachers and students alike was having to sound out words in both lists and passages before reading them the fast way. While our students seemed to enjoy the lively pace and the reading success brought by the practice, given the controversy in the field over the use of practice, we wanted to be certain that the daily drill and decodable reading were not dampening student interest in reading.

In order to investigate exactly how our students felt about reading, we assessed our first cohort of students at the end of grades 1 and 2 using the "Elementary Reading Attitude Survey" (McKenna & Kear, 1990). In this survey, student attitudes toward both academic and recreational reading are assessed. Students are asked to circle a picture of Garfield the cat that best depicts how they feel in response to items that are read aloud by the teacher. Ten of the items assess academic reading, while another 10 assess recreational reading or reading for fun. To answer each question, students select either the "very happy" Garfield standing with a big smile, the "little bit happy" Garfield, the "little bit upset" Garfield, or the "very upset" Garfield who has a distinctive scowl. Questions such as "How do you feel about reading instead of playing?" assess students' attitudes toward recreational reading. Questions such as "How do you feel about the stories you read in reading class?" assess academic reading.

Scores for all of the instructional tiers for both grades 1 and 2 were uniformly high; students enjoyed both academic and recreational reading, scoring an average of 3 out of 4 on both types of items. Despite the frequent presence of drill in the reading instruction, students in all of the tiers liked to read, confirming our strong belief that when practice is lively and geared to student needs on skills leading to important outcomes, practice will thrill, *not* kill.

Part 2: Sounding Out Words Subvocally   A key goal of reading instruction is the accurate, fluent reading of connected text. Once students can orally decode words sound by sound independently and with a high degree of accuracy, teachers need to prepare them for the next phase of reading by adding Part 2 to their daily regular word-reading instruction: sounding out words in their heads, or **subvocal sounding out.** It was once thought that fluent adult readers relied mainly on context and background knowledge to figure out words, engaging in what was often called a guessing game as they made their way through connected text. More recent research shows just the opposite; while mature readers are fluent, they still attend to the letters in words, but at an automatic level. Pausing to look at pictures or using word attack strategies that focus on the middle or the end of the word interrupts the reading process. Consider this description by Shaywitz (2003) of a consolidated alphabetic phase reader chunking when encountering a new word.

> She sees a word and scans all the letters. Do any of the letters fall into a familiar pattern? Do they resemble letter groups—parts of words—that she has stored? If so, she is able to take these letter patterns and connect them to a known pronunciation. For example, if she sees the unfamiliar printed word *architect,* meaning a designer of buildings, she may know that the letters t-e-c-t go together and how they are pronounced. She may also know from experience that the letters a-r-c-h are often grouped together and that arch sounds either like arch of your foot or Noah's ark. She tries to pronounce the unknown word both ways, arch-itect or ar-ki-tect, and uses the surrounding text to judge which pronunciation fits. From the context, she realizes that the word is *architect,* meaning a designer of buildings, and is pronounced like ark (ar-ki-tect). Once she has successfully decoded this word, it joins the other words stored in her lexicon. (p. 104)

Note that in this example, the reader first scans the word from left to right, looking for graphophonemic clues. Only after the reader looks at the letters does she use context clues to make her final decoding decision. This example of a process happening in milliseconds demonstrates the importance of automatic decoding and why it needs to be established first before other decoding clues such as using the context are introduced.

Teachers cannot assume that most students who are at risk will make a successful transition from oral sounding out to silently reading words by sight without adding a transition step that provides subvocal sounding-out practice. Once students no longer need to say each sound aloud, their speed with word reading will increase. Part 2 of regular word reading shown in Table 3.5 is a format for helping students make the transition from sounding out loud to sounding out words in their heads. This teaching procedure is especially effective for students scoring below 30 on the DIBELS or AIMSweb NWF who are also orally sounding out each word before blending them, like the pattern shown for Student 2 in Figure 3.7 (p. 65).

The signals used for subvocal sounding out are the same as those used for sounding out words aloud. The only difference is that when the teacher engages in the looping motion from letter to letter, students are mouthing the sounds without saying them out loud. The only time the students answer out loud is when the teacher asks them to read the word.

Three Best Practices for Teaching Subvocal Sounding Out   Ms. Elizondo was delighted when she was able to add Part 2, subvocal sounding out, to her daily instruction in regular word reading. She used Part 2 when her students were able to sound out the words for the day with 100% accuracy using Part 1. She then moved to Part 2 while using these three best practices to help her students transition to subvocal sounding out:

Carefully Watch Students' Eye Movements   Ms. Elizondo carefully watched eye movement to check if students' eyes were moving from left to right as they directly looked at the words on the board. When she saw students' eyes staring into the distance, she tapped their

TABLE 3.5   Format for Reading Regular Words—Part 2: Subvocal Sounding Out

Objective	After seeing a regular word, students will subvocally sound out the letter sounds before saying the word.
Materials Needed	Board, chart paper, or overhead transparency and writing implement. Write the regular words that students will read in rows on the board. For example, if students are reading eight words, write two rows of four words.
Signaling	Three-part signal: Finger is in starting position to the left of the word. **"Ready," "Sound out in your heads,"** or **"What word?"** initiates the signal for unison answers.
	1. Use loop signal for orally sounding out the letter sounds in the words.
	2. As students are saying the final letter sound, immediately loop finger back to the starting point.
	3. Pause for a moment of think time before asking students **"What word?"** and side-slash to the end of the word.
Time	Depends on number of new words and difficulty level. Kindergarten students often work on this skill for 5 minutes each day. First-grade students may need to work on this skill for up to 20 minutes if the curriculum has introduced many new words or a new letter–sound pattern.

Instructions	Teacher	Student
	1. Advance Organizer	
	2. My Turn (Use several times until students know what to do; then eliminate and start with step 3.) (finger to the left of the first letter) **"My turn sounding out this word in my head."** (loop from letter to letter and silently mouth letter sounds /f/-/ă/-/n/) (loop back to starting point) **"What word?"** (side-slash signal) **"fan."**	fan
Scaffolding Reduction	3. Your Turn (finger to the left of the first letter) **"Your turn. Sound out this word in your heads."** (loop from letter to letter) (students mouth sounds) (loop back to starting point) **"What word?"** (side-slash signal) **"Yes, fan."**	fan
	4. Individual Student Checkout (finger to the left of the first letter) **"Individual turns. Sound out this word in your head. Maria."** (loop from letter to letter) (student mouths sounds) (loop back to starting point) **"What word?"** (side-slash signal) (answer) (loop to starting point) **"Yes, fan."** Call on several individual students to check for accuracy.	fan
	5. Read the Row: Reading the row of words by sight Note: If you provide three seconds of think time before signaling for an answer, students should be ready to read the row of words the fast way. Use the Part 3 format for this section: **"Let's read all four words the fast way this time."**	
	(think time) **"What word?"** (side-slash signal) (answer) (loop to starting point) **"Yes, fan."**	fan
	(think time) **"What word?"** (side-slash signal) (answer) (loop to starting point) **"Yes, sip."**	sip
	(think time) **"What word?"** (side-slash signal) (answer) (loop to starting point) **"Yes, let."**	let
	(think time) **"What word?"** (side-slash signal) (answer) (loop to starting point) **"Yes, cat."**	cat
Scaffolding Reduction	Be sure to move to using mainly Your Turns as soon as possible or you are just telling students the word rather than having them independently use their subvocal decoding.	
Error Correction	If students make an error, immediately return to a My Turn–Together–Your Turn pattern requiring them to sound the word out loud. Then return to the beginning of the row and have students reread words the fast way.	

TABLE 3.5   Continued

Perk Up Your Drill	✳ Students love to reach a predetermined goal. Before reading all the words in a row, tell students that their goal is reading every single word in that row. If they read the words correctly, quickly draw a star next to the row and tell them that they just earned their first "starred" row.
	✳ When students are reading with 100% accuracy, perk up the pace by giving less think time. As long as the accuracy remains high, you can comfortably move at this quicker pace.
Adaptations	✳ As your students transition to Part 3, begin to switch between the Part 2 and Part 3 scripts depending on the difficulty of the word. If your students are solid on CVC words containing any vowel but /ē/, start asking them to read those easier CVC words by sight from the beginning. When you come to a CVC word containing an /ē/, have the students subvocally sound out the word. If you anticipate that students will almost certainly make an error on a difficult word the first time they read the word, ask them to sound it out loud.

Source: This script is based on one originally developed and field-tested by Carnine, D. W., Silbert, J., Kame'enui, E. J., & Tarver, S. (2010). *Direct Instruction Reading* (5th ed.). Boston: Merrill.

shoulder or called their name to redirect them to the reading work. Because Ms. Elizondo wanted to maintain a motivating classroom, she gave students points for paying attention to the words.

When Students Are Subvocally Sounding Out New Words Accurately With Teacher Support, Reduce Scaffolding and Start Teaching at Step 4   When her students became more proficient at subvocal sounding out, Ms. Elizondo again faded out the My Turn and Together steps and started teaching at Step 4, Your Turn. She continued to use the entire My Turn–Together–Your Turn sequence for difficult new words.

Once Students Can Subvocally Sound Out Words Without Help, Add Part 3, Reading Words the Fast Way, to Your Daily Regular Word Reading   As her students moved through Part 2 reading and were able to subvocally sound out words accurately without added teacher support, Ms. Elizondo added Part 3, reading words by sight, to her daily instruction in reading regular words. It was at this point that Ms. Elizondo noticed that her students' DIBELS NWF scores were beginning to approach 30 sounds per minute, reading at least eight whole words, the point at which they would start reading CVC word lists by sight, using oral or subvocal sounding out only for more difficult words or for making error corrections.

Part 3: Reading Words by Sight   Once students are able to sound out words in their heads accurately, add Part 3 to your daily teaching. In this part, students read words by sight, sounding out at an automatic level. While interpretations of the meaning of sight reading vary, a common implication drawn from the term is that the words have been memorized first rather than sounded out. For the purposes of this text, reading by sight is preceded by sounding out, not visual memorization. When reading regular words by sight is introduced into your daily word-reading exercises, students are beginning to say the words without pausing to sound out the individual letter sounds because the process is becoming automatic. Table 3.6 describes Part 3, the format for teaching students to read words by sight. When your students' DIBELS NWF scores reach 30 sounds per minute or higher reading whole words, they are beginning to see words in chunks, rather than as individual sounds. You can detect this when you notice that your students are reading at the onset-rime stage on their DIBELS NWF (starting to read *dov* as /d//ov/ rather than as /d//o//v/). They may also be reading the nonsense

TABLE 3.6   Format for Reading Regular Words—Part 3: By Sight

Objective	After seeing a regular word, students will orally read the word the fast way.
Materials Needed	Board, chart paper, or overhead transparency and writing implement. Write the regular words that students will read in rows on the board. For example, if students are reading eight words, write two rows of four words.
Signaling	Finger is in starting position to the left of the word. **"What word?"** initiates the side-slash signal for unison answers.
Time	Depends on number of new words and difficulty level. First-grade students may need to work on this skill for up to 20 minutes if the curriculum has introduced many new words or a new letter–sound pattern. Older students with alphabetic principle may only have a few new one-syllable words that are appropriate for this format.

Instructions	Teacher	Student
	1. Advance Organizer	
	2. My Turn (use for first word only, and only for the first day or two using this format) (finger to the left of the first letter) **"My turn to read this word the fast way."** (side-slash signal) ***"fan."***	
	3. Your Turn	
	Note: For new words that you anticipate your students misreading, use the Part 1 sounding-out format the first time the word is introduced in the list.	
	"Your turn to read the rest of the words by yourself."	
	(point and pause) **"What word?"** (side-slash answer) (loop back to starting point) **"Yes, *fan.*"**	fan
	(point and pause) **"What word?"** (side-slash answer) (loop back to starting point) **"Yes, *hat.*"**	hat
	(point and pause) **"What word?"** (side-slash answer) (loop back to starting point) **"Yes, *sit.*"**	sit
	(point and pause) **"What word?"** (side-slash answer) (loop back to starting point) **"Yes, *Pam.*"**	Pam
	4. Individual Student Checkout	
	(point and pause) **"Individual turns. What word? Ali."** (side-slash answer) (loop back to starting point) **"Yes, *fan.*"**	fan
	(point and pause) **"What word? Toni."** (side-slash answer) (loop back to starting point) **"Yes, *sit.*"**	sit
	Call on several individual students to check for accuracy.	
Error Correction	If students make an error, immediately return to Part 1 sounding out aloud using a My Turn–Together–Your Turn pattern. Then return to the beginning of the row and have students reread words the fast way.	
Perk Up Your Drill	※ Tell students that words they read correctly will go in their weekly dictionaries taken home to parents. Create a sense of drama about the large number of words that are going into the dictionary. ※ Ask a student to lead the drill, signaling just as you do.	
Adaptations	※ Many students who are at risk will not automatically know the meaning of common vocabulary such as *snap, pal,* or *tap.* Connecting words to their usage or meaning will help students remember them while expanding their vocabulary. After students read a word for which they don't know the meaning, some teachers will connect the word to its meaning and use the word in a brief sentence, saying the key word louder for emphasis. **"A *pal* is a friend. In our story yesterday, Big Bear's *pal* was mouse."**	

Source: This script is based on one originally developed and field-tested by Carnine, D. W., Silbert, J., Kame'enui, E. J., & Tarver, S. (2010). *Direct Instruction Reading* (5th ed.). Boston: Merrill.

words slowly, but as whole words. When students reach this point, use Part 3 exclusively for their daily regular word reading, except for particularly difficult words, the first day when new letter sounds are introduced, or when correcting student errors.

Teachers who expect their students to read regular words by sight before they are ready risk having their students memorize the visual form of the word rather than reading it through an automatic decoding process. Students who are not ready for this format will make far more errors if expected to read new words by sight. Deciding to use this format too early can be a temptation because the instruction is far less demanding than that during earlier formats where every letter sound is articulated orally. When teachers begin to use this format they will also still be using Part I: Oral Sounding Out for new words that contain new and difficult letter–sound combinations. Mr. McCoy was able to use the Part 3 format Reading by Sight with his students for any new CVC word, but when blends such as *br, cl,* and *sm* were introduced, he knew his students would misread many of these words if they read them by sight. He adapted his teaching and went back to using the Part 1 format until his students were more accurate reading CVC-variant words with blends.

The signaling procedure for reading words by sight consists of touching to the left of the word, providing a thinking pause, saying, "What word?" and then giving the side-slash signal. Tips for teaching students to read words by sight are as follows.

Three Best Practices for Teaching Part 3: Reading Words by Sight

Note how Ms. Elizondo used the following four best practices when she used Part 3 in teaching her students to read words by sight.

Use Assessment Information to Guide Teaching

Every morning, Ms. Elizondo wrote the new words from the daily lesson on the board and presented a brief advance organizer, telling her students that first they would read words that would later appear in the new elephant story. Since almost everyone in her class had scored 50 or higher on the DIBELS NWF assessment, and was reading whole words, she used Part 3 only for her regular word reading unless the story had a particularly difficult word that needed to be sounded out, when her students made errors, or when a new letter–sound correspondence was introduced.

Gradually Decrease Your Think Time

Ms. Elizondo knew that think time was critical during this stage of reading. The first time students read through the word list, Mrs. Elizondo paused for three seconds before asking, "What word," and then giving the signal to read the word. This longer think time increased her students' success in reading the words the first time. The second time she went through the list, she paused for only one or two seconds of think time.

Preplan by Using the Optional Step for Difficult Words

To prevent errors when a difficult new word was on the list, Ms. Elizondo used the "optional step" and asked students first to orally sound out the difficult word. For example, when /str/ was introduced in the new lesson, she returned to a My Turn–Together–Your Turn Part 1 sounding-out pattern to show students how to apply the new letter sounds to *strum, strap,* and *strict.* She knew that whenever students make errors reading a word, it takes much longer for them to unlearn the error and then learn the correct word.

The process of helping students become readers at the consolidated alphabetic phase so they are ready for advanced word reading is critical, but important decisions about when to use which of the three word-reading formats, and with which students, can be complicated. A chart of how to match your students with the appropriate formats based on their scores on the DIBELS or AIMSweb NWF measure is shown in Figure 3.11.

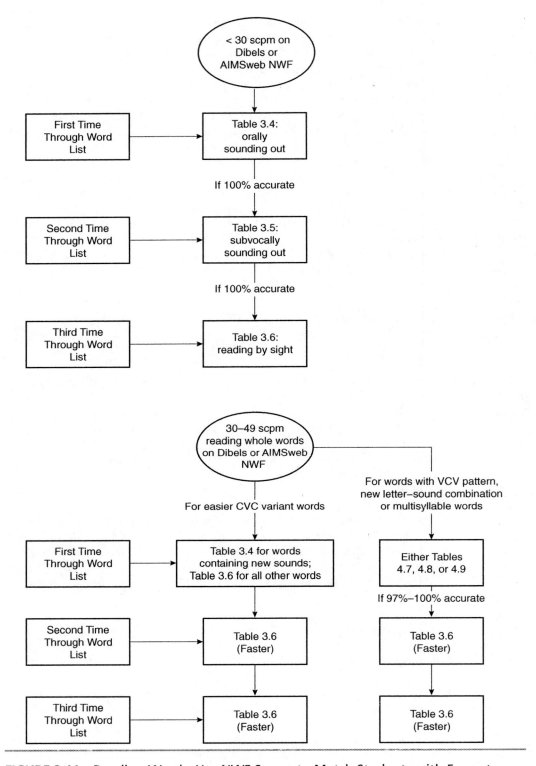

FIGURE 3.11 Reading Words: Use NWF Scores to Match Students with Formats

---

Spelling activity: Students write *in, pin, pat.*

Teacher: "You're going to write the word *in*. Listen. *In*. Say the sounds in *in*."
Signal for each sound by using a finger snap, clap, or extended finger as the children say /ĭĭĭ/ (pause) /nnn/. Repeat until firm.

Teacher: "Everybody, write the word (pause) ***in.***"
Check children's answers so you can give feedback.

Repeat for ***pin*** and ***pat.***

FIGURE 3.12   Regular Word Spelling Format

Source: Adapted from Engelmann, S., & Bruner, E. (1995). *Reading Mastery I: Teacher's Guide.* Columbus, OH: SRA Macmillan/McGraw-Hill.

Spelling and Writing Regular Words

Students benefit when they are writing or spelling the same regular words that they are learning to sound out and read. For example, Mr. Drake's students sounded out the following words in their daily lesson: *man, rap, top, pat, stop,* and *grab.* He then asked his students to spell each of these words using the format shown in Figure 3.12.

Students benefit when teachers ask them to substitute, add, and delete letter sounds in words that they spell. Hardware supply stores will cut large white boards used for showers into smaller boards your students can use for spelling instruction. Mrs. Kilroy asked her students to spell *tan.* Then she asked them to turn *tan* into *an,* and after checking their work, asked them to turn *an* into *pan.* Students were just learning how to read words that started with blends, and so before moving on to vowel substitutions, Mrs. Kilroy asked her students to turn pan into *span.*

Grapheme–phoneme mapping with small letter tiles works well as a small-group activity. Students construct the VC and CVC words dictated by the teacher. Later, students map the letter sounds on phoneme–grapheme mapping paper. You can make your own phoneme–grapheme mapping paper by printing out a table with four or five columns and one row for each word students will spell. Each letter sound representing a phoneme in the word is "mapped" in an individual square. The words *stop* and *sit* are mapped in Table 3.7. Representing the vowel with a different-colored tile than the consonant tiles helps students conceptualize the vowel decisions they will be making when they move to advanced word reading. When students map using grid paper, they can shade the vowel square(s) (Grace, 2007).

Teachers often wonder whether they should start instruction by teaching students to blend individual letter sounds into words, or start with larger units or word families and have students use them to read words. *The Reflective Teacher* helps answer this question.

TABLE 3.7   Phoneme–Grapheme Mapping for Beginning Readers

s	t	o	p
s	i	t	

The Reflective Teacher

Which Is the Best Way to Teach Beginning Readers?

Two of the most common beginning phonics approaches are letter–sound blending and word-family instruction (Wanzek & Hagger, 2003). In letter–sound blending, students are first taught the most common sounds of letters in isolation and are then taught to blend them into words. The approach that is used in this text is referred to as synthetic phonics. For example, Mr. Ellis taught his students to identify the letter sounds /m/, /s/, /t/, and /a/ in isolation. Once these letter sounds were learned, and his students could orally segment and blend, Mr. Ellis taught them to read words such as *Sam, sat,* and *mast.* Another beginning phonics approach starts by using larger units of sounds such as word families. In this approach, called analogizing, students are typically taught a rime pattern and then taught to use that known word part to form new words. This instruction forces the student to chunk the beginning letter(s) of the word and rime. For example, Ms. Calhoun taught her students to read the rime /am/. She then had her students read by sight related words such as *Sam, ham,* and *jam* that they had decoded and read in previous lessons.

If introduced after decoding is first taught, word-family instruction can help students read faster and remember spellings of words more easily (Durrell, 1963). If introduced too early, students can overgeneralize rhyming as a strategy for reading, which can lead to students reading the first sound and guessing at the rest of the word (Nation, Allen, & Hulme, 2001). The National Reading Panel (2000) found that both letter–sound blending and analogizing were effective in teaching beginning word reading to students. Which of these approaches should teachers use with their students who are at risk? Wanzek and Hagger (2003) suggest that both be used with letter–sound blending coming first because it is a necessary preskill for word reading, and word-family instruction next because it helps students better generalize their decoding skills to more complex words. Follow these guidelines for teaching analogizing to beginning readers.

- Select rimes that consist of previously taught letter–sound correspondences or letter combinations. If you have taught students to sound out and read a number of CVC words ending in the rime *an* (e.g., *can, Dan, man, pan*) using Part 1 and Part 2 of the Format for Reading Regular Words, begin your lesson by writing *an, Dan, can, man, pan* on the board. Ask students to read *an* and then show them that all the words end in *an*. Finally, ask them to read the words by sight. In order to read the words accurately, they have to read the sound of the onset letter, chunking it together with the rime. Their accuracy with word-family sight reading will tell you if they are ready for this strategy.
- Coordinate with the scope and sequence in your curriculum and select words that progress from simple onsets (*man*) to blends (*Stan*).
- Have students spell words based on the word families they are learning and have them substitute beginning, final, and middle sounds. Teacher: *"Everyone write **tap, sap,** and **map** on your whiteboards."* (Students write.) Teacher: *"Now change **tap** to **lap**."*
- At this beginning word-reading stage, teach only the following rimes for closed syllables: *ad, am, an, *ap, *at, ax, ed, eg, en, ep, et, ib, id, ig, im, *in, *ip, it, ix, od, *op, ot, ox, uf, ud, *ug, un, up, us, ut.* The rimes with stars in front of them are the most frequently used ones.

Reading Exception Words

Reading connected text, even when most of the words can be sounded out, requires recognition of the most frequently used exception words. Students who are at risk or who have disabilities need extra practice learning exception words, especially when they are beginning readers. When a new exception word is introduced, students are first told what the word is and are asked to repeat it. The students then spell the word as the teacher points to each individual letter. Finally, the students say the word again. Spelling the word reinforces the important idea that even for words that can't be sounded out, it is still important to look at all the letters of words in a left-to-right sequence.

The importance of viewing the words from left to right rather than as a picture makes sense if you think of Adams' processor model described in Chapter 1. Irregular and regular words are both stored in lexical memory in the same way (Gough & Walsh, 1991). Most letters in irregular words correspond to their associated sounds, which helps the reader connect the word's orthography to its pronunciation, just as with a regular word. Although there is some variation for this number depending upon the phonics rules taught in a curriculum, of the 150 most frequent words in printed school English according to the *American Heritage Word Frequency Book* (Carroll, 1971), only 44 are exception words, and of those words 39 have only one letter–sound association that makes the word irregular. For example, in the word *what,* only the grapheme *a* deviates from its conventional letter–sound association. The *wh* as well as the *t* are associated with their most common sounds and thus will bond in the reader's memory more easily. Ehri (2005) described this letter–sound association as the glue that binds the word to memory. Teaching students to spell the exception words that they learn creates an even stronger bond, reducing the time until students read the exception word by sight. Students reading at the final consolidated alphabetic phase learn exception words like *what* much faster than students who are reading at earlier levels because they can chunk past the irregular letter sounds. For that reason, we advise teachers to prioritize decoding for young or struggling readers and only teach exception words that are necessary for reading.

Once exception words are introduced, they are thereafter read by sight as whole words. If the student misreads one, the teacher returns to a My Turn, supplying the word and asking students to spell it just as if the word was being introduced for the first time. The format for introducing exception words is shown in Table 3.8.

Three Tips for Teaching Exception Words   Try these strategies to enhance your teaching of exception words:

Avoid Teaching Similar Exception Words Together, Such as Where and Were   Include similar exception words together only after students can automatically read each individual word when it is presented by itself.

Attach Meaning by Saying a Clear Sentence After Abstract Exception Words   Some exception words reflect abstract concepts and can be meaningless, especially to English language learners. Definitions for these words can be even more confusing. Using a clear, short sentence after introducing a vague exception word will attach meaning and make it more likely that students will remember the word. When you say the sentence to students, place more emphasis on the word in the sentence. For example, when introducing the word *would,* Mrs. Amonette pointed to the word and said, "***Would.*** *(pause) I know that Shantell **would** like to have some chocolate ice cream right now.* ***Would.***" Mrs. Amonette then continued with the format.

Provide Multiple Opportunities to Practice Exception Words   When you are teaching students a list of words, they often forget the words at the top of the list by the time you get to the end of the list. To prevent this from happening, we suggest that you "firm the list " to avoid memory slippage and the loss of time it takes to reteach those first words. You "firm a list" when, after teaching students to read the second word on the list, you have them go back and read the first word and then the second one. After students read the third word

TABLE 3.8   Format for Reading Exception Words

Objective	After seeing an exception word, students will orally read the word by sight.
Materials	Board, chart paper, or overhead transparency and writing implement. Teacher writes the new exception words in a column. The review exception words are written in another column.
Signaling	Two-part signal: **"What word?"** or **"Spell _____"** initiates the signal for unison answers. 1. After asking **"What word?"** or **"Spell _____,"** use a side-slash signal, and after students answer, loop back to the starting point before affirming the answer. 2. After saying **"Spell _____,"** point under each letter as students spell the word.
Time	3–5 minutes

Instructions	Teacher	Student
	1. Advance Organizer **Part 1: Introduction of new words.** 2. Write the new exception words from the daily story in a column on the left side of the board: for example, *today, father, strange*. Write four review exception words in a column on the right side of the board: for example, *was, isn't, should, great*. Teach the first exception sight word written on the board (*today*).	
	a. (finger to the left of the first letter) **"This word is"** (side-slash while saying **"today."**) (loop back to starting point)	
	b. **"What word?"** (side-slash-answer) (loop back to starting point) **"Yes, today."**	today
	c. **"Spell today."** (point to each letter as students answer) (loop back to starting point)	t-o-d-a-y
	d. **"What word?"** (side-slash-answer) (loop back to starting point) **"Yes, today."**	today
	e. (finger to the left of the first letter) **"This word is"** (side-slash while saying **"father."**) (loop back to starting point)	
	f. **"What word?"** (side-slash-answer) (loop back to the starting point) **"Yes, father."**	father
	g. **"Spell father."** (point to each letter as students answer) (loop back to starting point)	f-a-t-h-e-r
	h. **"What word?"** (side-slash-answer) (loop back to starting point) **"Yes, father."**	father
	i. Return to the top of the list and point to the left of the first word. Pause and ask, **"What word?"** (side-slash-answer) (loop back to starting point) **"Yes, today."**	today
	Quickly point to the left of the second word. Pause and ask, **"What word?"** (side-slash-answer) (loop back to starting point) **"Yes, father."**	father
	j. Repeat steps e–i with the remaining words until students can quickly read all of the words in the column without errors.	
	k. Individual Student Checkout: Call on between one and three students to check for accuracy.	
	Part 2: Students sight read new words and review words.	
Scaffold Reduction	3. Point to words randomly.	
	a. **"When I signal, read the word."** (finger to the left of the first letter) **"What word?"** (side-slash-answer) (loop back to starting point) **"Yes, father."**	father
	(finger to the left of the first letter) **"What word?"** (side-slash-answer) (loop back to starting point) **"Yes, was."**	was
	(finger to the left of the first letter) **"What word?"** (side-slash-answer) (loop back to starting point) **"Yes, should."**	should
	b. Individual Student Checkout: Call on between one and three students to check for accuracy.	
Error Correction	If students make an error, immediately return to a My Turn. Tell students the word, ask them to spell the exception word, to read the word (Part 2: steps a-d), and then return to the top of the list asking them to read all of the words again.	

TABLE 3.8 Continued

Perk Up Your Drill	※ On the last section of the exception word script (Part 2), tell students that you will erase every word they read correctly. The goal is to have all words erased on the first read-through. ※ If you are working with a smaller group, you can write each exception word on a large card to hold up. Construct a "we know that" box, and on the last section of the exception word script (Part 2), dramatically throw each word that students read correctly into the box.
Adaptations	※ Many students who are at risk will not automatically put exception words such as *was, where, should,* and *couldn't* into context unless you briefly add that component at the start. Connecting words to their usage or meaning will help students remember them while expanding their vocabulary. The first time they introduce a new exception word, some teachers will use the word in a brief sentence, saying the word louder for emphasis: **"This word is *should*. Your mom says, 'It's late and you *should* go to bed.'"** Later in the lesson, if students make an error, the teacher will use another sentence to connect the word to its meaning.

Source: This script is based on one originally developed and field-tested by Carnine, D. W., Silbert, J., Kame'enui, E. J., & Tarver, S. (2010). *Direct Instruction Reading* (5th ed.). Boston: Merrill.

on the list, you have them go back and read the first two words before reading the third one. Repeated practice like this makes it more likely that information is stored in **long-term memory** where, because it is readily available to the person, it can be activated automatically (Marzano, 2004). The following practice strategies will also help your students acquire the ability to read exception words by sight whenever they encounter them in text.

※ Reading a new exception word several times
※ Spelling the word so letter–sound associations are used to strengthen the word in memory
※ Connecting the word with meaning when first learning it
※ Connecting the new word with meaning when accurately reading it in a text shortly after the word-reading lesson

Additional strategies for helping students remember exception words are in the *In Your Classroom* feature.

You can learn ways to find more time for your students to practice word reading in *In Your Classroom*. Strategies for making Word Walls a part of your systematic explicit reading program are discussed in *The Reflective Teacher* feature.

Reading Decodable Sentences

After students can sound out a number of regular words and know a few exception words, they can begin reading sentences. Sentence reading provides a good opportunity to explicitly teach students to read connected text. Using this format, students quickly learn to follow a line of print, recognize that spaces mark boundaries between words, automatically move from left to right, read word by word, recognize that sentences are composed of words, and recognize final punctuation marks. If your students' DIBELS or AIMSweb NWF scores are under 30 and they are still learning new words by orally or subvocally sounding them out before reading the whole word (Tables 3.4–3.5), use those same formats during sentence reading starting with the First Reading described in Table 3.9 for story reading. When students come to an exception word, have them read it as a whole word. When students' NWF scores are still below 30 sounds per minute reading whole words, you still need to use the First, Second, and Third Readings in Table 3.9, moving from step to step on each subsequent read as long as student accuracy is high. Your students are still at the prealphabetic or partial

In Your Classroom

Finding More Time for Practice

Killer Word Boost

If your class has a "killer word" for the week, wear a scarf one day and tape the difficult word on the scarf or pin the word to your lapel. Students' eyes will alight on the word every time they look at you. Tell students you will try to trick them throughout the day by asking them to read the word at moments when they least expect that question.

Beat the Clock

If you routinely write all new exception words on large cards, you can pull these cards out when your class is waiting to get their pictures taken or you go to an assembly and have 5 minutes to fill. Each new word should be written on three cards to play this game. Select a set of exception words that students have already learned to correctly identify for the game (for example, *through, beautiful, where, enough, though*). Your goal is getting students to recognize these words more fluently.

- Include multiple cards of each word in the card deck.

- Set a goal such as 25 words correct per minute. Tell the students that you will play a game with them and that their goal is to correctly read at least 25 word cards in 1 minute.
- Start the timer or have an appointed student start it.
- Hold up the first word card so that all students can answer in unison.
- Provide quick corrective feedback whenever students make errors ("This word is *because.*").
- Continue presenting words until the timer rings.
- Put correctly identified words in the throwaway box.
- Put incorrectly read words in a pile next to you.
- At the end of 1 minute, count the number of words correct and let the class know whether they met the goal.
- Pick up the cards in the pile and review errors with the students before repeating the activity for another minute.

The Reflective Teacher

Can I Still Use My Word Wall?

A Word Wall is a group of high-frequency written words displayed in alphabetical order on a bulletin board or a section of a classroom wall. The purpose of the wall is to make the words accessible so that students can find them when reading and writing and teachers can readily focus on them when providing practice in class (Cunningham, 2000). The Word Wall gives children extra practice reading, writing, and understanding the meaning of high-frequency regular words and exception words. This purpose is consistent with the objectives of the phonics approach described in this text. In addition, the "chanting" often used when reading from the Word Wall is very similar to the unison response formats used here. Problems with the Word Wall can occur when the words on the wall are not decodable; that is, they include regular words containing untaught sounds, untaught words, or too many exception words. Here are four keys to using the Word Wall effectively with students who are at risk.

1. Select only regular words that contain sounds that have already been taught.

2. Select only exception words that have already been taught.

3. For every five regular words, select one exception word.

4. When asking your students to read the words, use teaching strategies that discourage student guessing. For example, have students sound out the regular words while they are chanting, rather than having them sight read the words if they are not yet at that phase. Try putting regular and exception words in separate colors. Use signals so everyone answers together. Calibrate your think time for students' reading ability.

TABLE 3.9   Format for Reading Stories in the Curriculum and Decodable Books: Beginning Readers

Objective	Students who have scored less than 30 letter sounds per minute on the DIBELS or AIMSweb NWF assessment will read a book containing words or word patterns taught in class, sounding out the words before reading them with 100% accuracy. Students who score between 30 and 49 on DIBELS or AIMSweb NWF reading whole words will read words by sight using the procedures described in the third reading.
Materials Needed	Use decodable text or text containing regular and exception words that the students are capable of reading with at least 90% accuracy.
Signaling	Finger-snap or hand-clap. **"Sound it out."** or **"What word?"** initiates the signal for unison answer.
Time	Between 15 and 30 minutes

Instructions	Teacher	Students
	Advance Organizer	
	Steps to reading stories and books (Prealphabetic Principle):	
	First Reading(s)	
	1. Suggested wording for focusing students to follow along: **"We are first going to sound out each word and then we will read it the fast way. When I clap, say the sound of the first letter. When I clap again, move your finger and say the next sound. When you are at the end of the word, move your finger back to the beginning of the word so you can read it the fast way. Watch me do it first."** (You will need to use a finger snap with your nondominant hand as you show students how you follow along to the signal, sounding out and reading the words.) **"Everybody, put your finger under the first letter of the very first word."**	Students touch under the first letter of the first word.
	2. Focus students on accurate reading and tell them the goal you've set: **"Our goal is to miss no more than one word today."**	
	3. Pause 1 second and then say, **"Sound it out"** and clap for the first sound. After 1 to 1½ seconds, clap for the next sound. One to 1½ seconds later, clap for the last sound. When students have said the last sound correctly, make sure that they move their finger back to the left of the word. Ask, **"What word?"** and clap. Students side-slash their finger as they read the word the fast way. Then they immediately move their finger to the left of the next word.	Students say sounds, pointing under the letters as they say them; they move their finger back to the beginning of the word before orally reading the word at a normal rate.
	4. Pause 1 second and then say, **"Sound it out"** and clap for the first sound. After 1 to 1½ seconds, clap for the next sound. One to 1½ seconds later, clap for the last sound. When students have said the last sound correctly, make sure that they move their finger back to the left of the word. Ask, **"What word?"** and clap. Students side-slash their finger as they read the word the fast way. Then they immediately move their finger to the left of the next word.	
	5. For exception words, avoid sounding out. When students move their fingers to the left of an exception word, say, **"What word?"** and clap to signal students to say the word.	Students read the whole word without sounding it out.
	6. Continue using this format to the end of the story or to the end of the page.	
	7. Wrap Up: Have students reread the story, sounding out each word until the error limit is met. When the error limit is met, give individual turns. Do not move on to the second reading format until the error limit is met.	

Continued

TABLE 3.9   Continued

Second Reading(s)

1. Repeat Steps 1–5, but have students subvocally sound out the words as in Stage 2 regular word reading (Table 3.6). At the end of the story have students practice reading any missed words. Do not move on to the third reading format until the error limit is met.

Students subvocally sound out before saying the word at a normal rate.

Third Reading(s)

1. Repeat Steps 1–5, but have students read words the fast way as in Stage 3 (Table 3.7) word reading.

2. Use individual checkouts to determine whether students are solid on reading the story. Have each student read one sentence.

Students read the words in the story the fast way.

Error Correction	When students make a sounding-out error, immediately say, **"My Turn,"** and sound out the word correctly. Move into a **"Your Turn"** and ask students to sound out the word before always going back to the beginning of the sentence. Any error (missed word, plural ending left off, etc.) is treated as an error.
Perk Up Your Drill	▪ Approach each story with a high degree of enthusiasm. If you convey your interest in the characters and plot, no matter how simple the story, the students' interest level and motivation will be heightened. During the second or third reading of the story, you will need to model voice inflection to match punctuation and emphasis in the story. Then ask students to reread the same text using an appropriate tone of voice.
	▪ If students grumble about reading a story one more time, reminding them that their accuracy will determine when they move to the next story empowers them and motivates them to do their best.
	▪ The day that students take home the story they have learned to read, ask them to whom they will read it. Encourage them to think about reading to a younger sibling, a parent, a grandparent, or a cousin. At the start of the next day's lesson, be sure to ask students about their story reading at home.
Adaptations	▪ Kindergartners and first graders who are still scoring under 30 on the DIBELS NWF assessment may need to repeat the first reading steps several times until they are ready to subvocally sound out the same words.
	▪ If your students are at Part 2, subvocal regular word reading, begin the story with the second reading format. When your students come to a difficult word, move back into first reading sounding out for that word.
	▪ If your students are nearing alphabetic principle (DIBELS NWF scores in the 30–49 range and nonsense words read as whole words) and they read most CVC-variant words as whole words, read new stories starting at the third reading procedure.

Source: This script is based on one originally developed and field-tested by Carnine, D. W., Silbert, J., Kame'enui, E. J., & Tarver, S. (2010). *Direct Instruction Reading* (5th ed.). Boston: Merrill Prentice Hall.

alphabetic phase of reading and need to sound out words a number of times until they finally learn them automatically as sight words.

Once your students' NWF scores are higher than 30 sounds per minute reading whole words, you can start reducing the scaffolding and gradually phase out First Readings, eventually having students read whole words in text the first time through it. Your students will quickly start reading the sentences in unison, but expect that the first few times your pace will slow as you teach students to follow the signals when reading an entire sentence. If you maintain high expectations for students to read together, they will quickly adopt the habit during this part of instruction. If you do not start with a clear signal for each word (*"What word?"*), your best readers who do not need as much think time will jump ahead with the word, and students who need an extra second or two will soon stop trying and coast by echoing the faster readers. You will be fooled into thinking that students are fluently reading when, in reality, three or four of the best readers are doing all the work for the rest of the class.

From the time your students begin to read sentences, connect meaning to what they are reading by asking questions. Chapters 9 and 10 discuss vocabulary and comprehension, but students need to develop the habit of actively thinking about what they are reading as soon as they begin reading connected text. If students still have difficulty answering concrete lower-level questions (*who, what, where* questions) where the answers are given in the sentence, ask that type of direct question. As soon as those questions become too easy, start asking inferential ones as described in Chapter 10 in the section on teaching comprehension at the sentence level (pp. 337–341). In the most basic decodable sentence, *"Matt ran and got the ham,"* you can ask students whether Matt was moving very slowly and what word in the sentence gave the clue for the answer. Or you could ask whether Matt went and got a vegetable. Inferential questions like these can be difficult for younger students who are at risk.

Tips for Teaching Decodable Sentence Reading   The curriculum that Ms. Elizondo was using in her class introduced sentence reading by the middle of September, so she wrote two or three sentences on the board each day. When her students were still sounding out words (DIBELS NWF < 30), she had them sound out each word before reading it in the sentence: *"Sound out." "What word?" "Sound out." "What word?" "Sound out." "What word?"* If she didn't have students sound out the words on the first read, some students were unable to apply their decoding skills. Although she sometimes felt like a broken record signaling across the sentence, she knew that with enough practice, students would soon develop the automaticity necessary to move into reading words by sight, reading their sentences without sounding out each word. By the third time students read each sentence, Ms. Elizondo had students read the sentences by sight, using normal intonation. At that point, she asked at least one inferential question for every sentence. She wanted her students to think of themselves as detectives, finding the clue word that let them know the answer and ultimately the meaning of the text.

Reading Decodable Passages in Beginning Reading

"The average child needs between four and fourteen exposures to automatize the recognition of a new word. Therefore, in learning to read it is vital that children read a large amount of text at their independent reading level (95% accuracy) and that the text format provides specific practice in the skills being learned" (Lyon, 1998; p. 6). Students who are at risk often need even more opportunities to practice reading books that contain the words they have learned in class. The texts used in classes today often provide fewer opportunities than many students need to read new words and map letter–sound associations until those new words become sight words. Supplementary decodable books can provide that practice. Decodable books contain a high percentage of regular words composed of sounds the students have learned plus a few high-frequency exception words. For example, Ms. Rodriguez's students had learned the most common sounds for *s, c, n, a, r, t, l, b,* and *i.* They also learned the exception words *the, a, said, were, to,* and *is.* The following sentence represents decodable text for her students:

Nat ran to the bin.

The students would be able to sound out the regular words *Nat, ran,* and *bin* and read the exception words *to* and *the.* The following sentence, while including high-frequency words, would not be decodable for the same group of students:

Come here, Bob.

In this sentence the sight words *come* and *here* haven't been learned yet. Students have also not learned the most common sound of the letter *o* and would not be able to sound out the word *Bob*. This sentence is not decodable. For information on how to select decodable books for your students, see the feature on decodable books later in this chapter.

During the first half of first grade, before students typically score 50 on the DIBELS or AIMSweb NWF assessment reading whole words, the teacher has students read in unison so they get the most practice possible on sounding out and reading regular words, developing the necessary connections between Orthographic and Phonological processors. When students are explicitly taught to read connected text, they quickly learn to follow a line of print and recognize that spaces mark boundaries between words. They automatically move from left to right, read word by word, recognize that sentences are composed of words, and identify final punctuation marks.

The actual steps of the passage reading format are described in Table 3.9. For students whose scores on the DIBELS or AIMSweb NWF are less than 30 scpm, the teacher uses all three readings described in the format, as follows. On the first reading, the students sound out all words in unison except for exception words, which are read by the group as whole words. If students read with 97% accuracy or higher, the teacher moves to the second reading. If students read below 97% accuracy, they sound out the story again, orally. During the second reading, the students subvocally sound out each word in the decodable text before saying it. For the third reading, students read each word in unison by sight. If the teacher has selected a book that matches the students' word-reading skills, this third reading is usually done accurately the first time through. As was done with the first reading, the second and third readings are repeated if student accuracy is less than 97%. The same recommendations for integrating comprehension with sentence reading apply to passage reading. Typically, we recommend that teachers ask questions after each sentence or paragraph when students are reading text, but asking comprehension questions of beginning readers whose cognitive resources are focused on decoding words diverts their attention away from the text. Beginning readers slowly decoding will misread more words and will not be able to answer the comprehension questions. Thus, at this beginning reading stage, we recommend that comprehension questions follow an accurate whole-word reading.

You learned earlier that students whose scores on the DIBELS or AIMSweb NWF assessment are between 30 and 49 scpm reading whole words are now beginning to read whole words in their list reading. Therefore, their passage reading begins with the third reading on Table 3.9, reading words by sight in unison. Students read the story through two times in unison as a group, reading each word by sight with the teacher and building fluency by gradually decreasing the thinking time required over the course of the two readings. If students perform fluently with 97% accuracy the second time through, the teacher gives individual turns, with each student reading one sentence. Check comprehension during this third reading. Once students reach benchmark levels on the NWF assessment, they are ready to read stories in a more traditional fashion by taking individual turns as described in the SAFER oral-passage-reading format in Chapter 5 (see Table 5.3, p. 175).

We found that one of the most difficult decisions for teachers was determining when to reduce scaffolding. Some teachers provide too little support and move into whole-word sight reading too quickly. When this happens, students make many errors and do not comprehend the text. Other teachers provide too much support and always start with First Readings, even when the DIBELS scores indicate that students no longer need that much support. To help the teachers determine when to reduce scaffolding when students are reading text, we developed these guidelines reflected in Figures 3.13 and 3.14. Reduce scaffolding and start with the Third Reading if the following apply:

※ Students are scoring above 30 sounds per minute reading whole words on the DIBELS or AIMSweb NWF assessment.

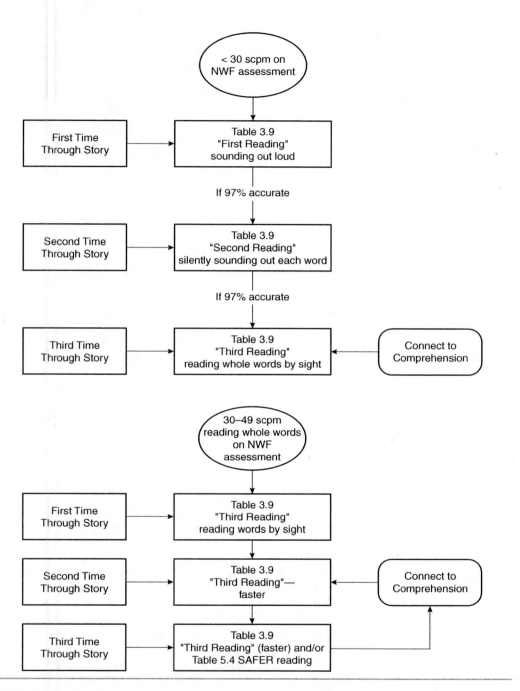

FIGURE 3.13 Passage Reading: Use NWF Scores to Match Students with Formats

- ※ You pretaught letter sounds and words in the story that contain those sounds to mastery by having students sound out the words in lists before whole-word reading. Students should then be able to read those same words in the story by sight.
- ※ Student accuracy is at or above 97% during the unison word reading. If not, return to sound-by-sound reading.

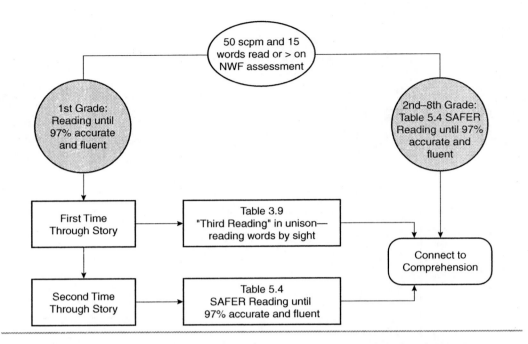

FIGURE 3.14 Passage Reading: Use NWF Scores to Match Students with Formats

During whole-word text reading, have students sound out and read any misread words so that they develop automatic decoding as their first strategy when confronting new difficult words in text.

Tips for the Transition from Words to Passages   These tips will help move students successfully from word reading to decodable passage reading.

1. Although your students will quickly start reading the sentences in unison, expect that the first few times your pace will slow as you teach students to follow the signals while they follow with their fingers and turn pages of the book.
2. Take time to teach students how to follow the text with the pointer finger of their dominant hand. When students are following along with their fingers, whether reading in unison or when another child is reading, you know they are paying attention. Since consistently following the text will be difficult for your most inattentive students, provide an incentive with the Teacher-Student game in the beginning for consistent finger pointing: *"The class just earned another point because everyone remembered to follow with their fingers."* Teachers in one of our schools reminded students before they began reading to use their "smooth reading finger." Teachers in classrooms with older students frequently complained about students whose previous teachers had not encouraged a smooth reading finger. These students followed text with a finger that bounced on every word, that was turned in an awkward position following on the tops of words, or that covered the text as they read. Breaking this ingrained habit of older students was difficult.
3. Some teachers clarify key vocabulary when students first read words they do not know during the first read-through. Other teachers focus exclusively on sounding out words or

reading during a first read and wait until the second reading to ask comprehension questions and discuss vocabulary. Other teachers preteach the meaning of vocabulary words that they anticipate the children will not know. Chapter 9 discusses strategies to teach vocabulary explicitly.

An additional consideration when moving from words to passages is whether the passage should include pictures. The role that pictures play in beginning passage reading is discussed in the *Research Note*.

Research Note

Should I Use Pictures with My Beginning Readers?

Teachers are often confused about how to use pictures in their beginning reading programs. Some experts say that pictures are an important motivator for students and that they also help students with comprehension. Other experts warn that pictures can impede progress toward attaining the alphabetic principle by sending students the message that the text is not the primary source for decoding words. Current optical brain research about how skilled readers approach text provides the rationale for directing the beginning reader's attention to the text rather than interrupting that focus by having students move their eyes back and forth between pictures and text. A skilled reader's eyes move from left to right, word by word, only occasionally skipping function words such as *in* or *to*, visually processing each individual letter, recognizing each word within milliseconds as the brain translates speech to print. Rather than flow smoothly across the page, the eyes rapidly dart about seven to nine letters before stopping for approximately 200–250 msec (Larson, 2007; Rayner, Chace, Slattery, & Ashby, 2006). Figure 3.15 shows the course of typical eye movements called saccades, represented by arcs, and the stopping points called fixations, where two arcs intersect.

About 10% to 20% of the time, when the reader approaches a difficult word or has difficulty comprehending text, his eyes move in a backward saccade to reread the text, as happened in the second section in Figure 3.15. During the fixations when the eyes pause, readers process text and comprehension occurs. The brain first takes in the orthographic information, but within about five or ten milliseconds converts it to a phonological pattern (Larson, 2007; Rayner et al., 2006). As could be expected, beginning readers and students with reading disabilities have longer fixations and shorter saccades. Their saccades move backward more frequently as they relook at words or text to comprehend (Rayner et al., 2006; Rayner, Foorman, Perfetti, Pesetsky, & Seidenberg, 2001). When teachers ask beginning readers to move their eyes between

Current optical and brain research about how skilled readers approach

text, provide the rationale for directing the beginning reader's attention

FIGURE 3.15   Saccades

Continued

the text they are reading and pictures, to routinely skip words, or to skip ahead to the end of the sentence, this normal reading pattern is interrupted.

Can teachers resolve this dilemma with beginning readers, using pictures to motivate and clarify meaning, yet without the side effect of interfering with the teaching of systematic sounding out? Yes—simply by having pictures follow text rather than having them occur on the same page. Pictures that are shown after text is read can function as a reward for accurate reading as well as a stimulus for discussing the meaning of the text. Teachers further discourage guessing for early readers when they expect students to point to each word with their fingers and continually remind them to look at the letters in the word.

Selecting Decodable Books

The role of decodable books in beginning reading instruction remains a contentious topic (see *The Reflective Teacher* on pp. 99–100). Unfortunately, the National Reading Panel report provides no direct guidance and instead recommends that more research is needed to investigate this question (National Reading Panel, 2000). Meanwhile, since most explicit and systematic phonics curricula use decodable texts as a key part of beginning reading instruction, teachers of students who are at risk need to familiarize themselves with decodable materials and investigate the issues for themselves.

Moats (2000) explained that decodable books serve as "a bridge between phonics instruction and the reading of trade books" (p. 148). Why are decodable books so important for beginning readers? Decodable books provide more practice opportunities for students who are learning to decode letter–sound patterns. As noted earlier in this chapter, the average child needs between 4 and 14 exposures to a new pattern before it is identified automatically. Students who are at risk are likely to need even more exposure.

After Mr. Jerry's class successfully read the list of words starting with *st*, *tr*, and *d* consonant blends, he wanted to give his students more practice reading these same words in connected text. He knew that if the next story his students read contained only one or two words beginning with these new consonant blends, many students would not get enough practice and would be unable to identify the pattern successfully when it appeared in the next week's story.

Leveled texts, an option for passage reading used in many classrooms, provide much less support than decodables for struggling readers' word recognition and no support for developing decoding skills. For example, when the books in a typical kindergarten curriculum were recently analyzed, 51% of the words appeared fewer than three times, with 25% of the words appearing only once (Hiebert, 2008). Struggling readers need more practice reading words than that.

Because decodable books incorporate words or sounds that students have already learned in class, students typically are highly successful reading decodable books, even for the first time. By providing students with the opportunity to read successfully on their own, decodable books can help students develop confidence and a more positive attitude toward reading (Bursuck et al., 2004; Stanovich, 1993/1994).

While most comprehension instruction for students at the beginning reading stage is done through listening and discussing different genres of children's literature, if used correctly, decodable books can also provide opportunities for comprehension development. A creative teacher can draw out several questions even from a short decodable story. For example, after reading the decodable book *Frank the Fish Gets His Wish*, Mr. Jerry had his students identify main characters, explain why Frank was lonely, sequence events in the story, visualize how they would feel if they were the fish, and talk about the fantasy aspects of the book. When students reread the story the second time, they used fish voices and tried to express fear when knocked out of their fishbowl.

TABLE 3.10   Selecting Decodable Books Based on Word Difficulty

Skill	Examples
VC and CVC words that begin with continuous sounds	*it, fan*
VCC and CVCC words that begin with a continuous sound	*lamp, ask*
CVC words that begin with a stop sound	*cup, tin*
CVCC words that begin with a stop sound	*dust, hand*
CCVC words	*crib, blend, snap, flat*
CCVCC, CCCVC, and CCCVCC words	*damp, spent, scrap, scrimp*
Long vowels and short vowel combinations	*late, stand, stay, Pam*

Teachers selecting supplementary decodable books need to systematically match the sequence of letter sounds and word patterns taught in their classroom with text in decodable books. Because some books selling as decodables include a relatively high percentage of exception words, teachers cannot assume that a book labeled as such is decodable. Put simply, many books advertised as decodables frequently are not. Table 3.10 lists a common scope and sequence listing increasingly difficult words that you can use as a guide for selecting decodable books.

> For specific information about how to teach decoding and use decodable readers, visit the *Teaching Decoding* website: **http://www.aft.org/pubs-reports/american_educator/spring_sum98/moats.pdf.**

When selecting additional books, consider these questions:

* Are the students beginning readers and able to follow only one or two lines of text on a page?
* Do flashy pictures interrupt the students' concentration when sounding out the words?
* Are the students older readers who need a decodable chapter book with a more mature look to it?
* Are full pages of text needed because the students are ready to transition to chapter books?
* What letter–sound correspondences and types of words have the students learned to decode? What exception words do students know? Does this book match their skills?

Some reading experts advocate the use of predictable books with beginning readers (Yopp, 1995). Predictable books (also called pattern books) are texts that contain repeated phrases and language patterns (Maring, Boxie, & Wiseman, 2000). These patterns allow students to read the books successfully by guessing based on the context and/or pictures. The purpose of the predictable books is to provide a successful early reading experience for students. The issue of whether to use predictable or decodable books with beginning readers is discussed in *The Reflective Teacher*.

The Reflective Teacher

Should I Use Predictable Books?

Struggling readers often overuse the context to recognize unknown words. For example, students with reading problems tend to guess when they come to a word they don't know by using the context ("*What word makes sense?*") or by looking at the first letter of a word ("*This word*

Continued

begins with sss,"). Research shows that content words, those that are most important for text comprehension, can be predicted from the surrounding text only 10% to 20% of the time (Gough, Alford, & Holley-Wilcox, 1981). Predictable books are designed to make guessing pay off, giving students the idea that they don't have to look at all parts of words when figuring them out. Students who are at risk need to develop a consistent sounding strategy before they are taught to use the context. This means that their early reading experiences should involve as little guessing as possible. If students are required to sound out words in one setting and guess in another, they are likely to be confused and may not learn a systematic sounding strategy at all. Therefore, the use of predictable books with students who have yet to attain the alphabetic principle is not recommended. Decodable text based on the letter–sound correspondences the students are learning is much more likely to result in a strategic reader as opposed to a guesser.

If you must use predictable texts:

1. Avoid having students reread the texts if they are beginning to memorize the story.

2. Prior to having them read the story, circle words that students can decode (either a regular word for which they know the sounds or an exception word). As you read the story, students can be responsible for reading the decodable words. If decodable words are missed, make sure you use sounding out as part of your correction procedure.

3. Occasionally model sounding out when reading predictable texts. Through your example, students see that reading is not all memorization.

Divide your class into two groups. Use predictable books with the higher groups and decodable books with your students who are below the DIBELS benchmarks.

What Can I Do for Students Who Are Not Learning Beginning Reading Skills Even with Enhancements?

Students' scores on the informal letter–sound correspondence assessment let you know who needs extra Tier 2 practice reviewing letter sounds. Student scores on the DIBELS or AIMSweb NWF assessment as well as the PALS or TPRI word reading lists inform you who needs extra Tier 2 practice with decoding skills. Tier 2 intervention sessions vary, depending on whether students are just working on letter sounds or are also learning to decode.

For students just learning letter–sound correspondence in kindergarten, small-group Tier 2 sessions last between 5 and 10 minutes. Students whose letter–sound assessment indicates that they know fewer than 90% of the letter sounds taught by the teacher should receive Tier 2 intervention immediately, so that they don't fall too far behind the class. Because many kindergarten students who need letter–sound practice also need phonemic awareness practice, you can combine the two skills into one short tutoring session. During the Tier 2 tutoring group session, practice with the same letter–sound format (Table 3.3) that was used during large-group Tier 1 instruction. Each day students practice one letter, continuing to practice that same letter each day until mastery. The class may have learned sounds for the letters *s, t, a, m, f, b, i,* and *l,* but if Keivon does not know the sounds for *f, b,* and *l,* the teacher has him identify the sound of *f* every day until he knows it. Each day she also reviews the sounds he knows. After Keivon learns the sound for *f,* she begins working on the sound for *b.* Teaching more than one letter sound at a time to students who are not keeping up with the pace of the class is not effective because it is likely to be confusing, particularly for students in the primary grades.

Students learning to blend letter sounds into words need longer daily 30-minute Tier 2 tutoring sessions in which they can practice new letter sounds, regular and exception words, and passage reading. Some teachers like to schedule small Tier 2 groups before reading class so that the students who just practiced the material can participate more fully with the class. Other teachers prefer to schedule Tier 2 groups just after lunch. These teachers like to have the students' practice spaced so that there are morning and afternoon practice sessions. Since beginning decoding tutoring sessions last longer, some schools elect to have another teacher or trained paraprofessional work with each small group, taking them to a relatively quiet location. Although small groups of three to four students are ideal (Gersten et al., 2009), some schools with many students who are at risk do not have enough personnel for such small groups. In our project schools we found that having six or fewer students in each Tier 2 intervention group worked well. Tier 2 groups at our three schools were taught by a music teacher, a French teacher, a Spanish teacher, a former *Reading Recovery* teacher, a librarian, a special education teacher, a Title 1 teacher, or a paraprofessional. Each of these individuals first learned to teach the same scripts used by the classroom teacher so that they used the same signals, said the same letter sounds, and followed the same formats. These are the scripts included in this text.

Some Tier 2 groups are able to keep up with the pace of the classroom and practice the same skills and words that were taught in class that day. Other tutoring groups fall behind when difficult new patterns such as *ch* are introduced. These groups continue to practice the earlier lessons until they have success. Because Tier 2 teachers can fit only letter–sound practice, regular word reading, exception word reading, and sentence reading into the 30-minute sessions, often there isn't enough time for reading decodable books. Some school teams used tutors or paraprofessionals to provide additional time for Tier 2 students to read more decodable text.

What Can I Do for Students Who Are Not Learning Beginning Reading Skills Even with Tier 2 Support?

There can be a need for more intensive Tier 3 instruction for some students in kindergarten who are particularly at risk. However, not all students who need Tier 3 enter it in kindergarten. Some enter in first grade, as well. Later placements into Tier 3 can occur for a number of reasons. Some students manage to acquire enough segmenting, blending, and letter–sound correspondence skills to remain in Tier 2 in kindergarten, but exhibit much difficulty moving past the partial alphabetic phase in grade 1. Other students may move into your school from a school that did not stress phonemic awareness and letter–sound skills in kindergarten.

Compare the NWF guidelines with recommendations listed below for placement into Tier 3 developed by Good, Simmons, Kame'enui, and Wallin (2002):

* In September of Grade 1, the student scores below 13 letter sounds per minute on DIBELS NWF, or less than 25 letters correct per minute on the DIBELS Letter Naming Fluency, or less than 10 segments correct per minute in DIBELS Phonemic Segmentation Fluency.

- In January of Grade 1, the student scores below 30 letter sounds correct per minute on the DIBELS NWF, or less than 20 words correct per minute on DIBELS Oral Reading Fluency (ORF is discussed in Chapter 5).
- In May of Grade 1, the student scores less than 30 letter sounds correct per minute on the DIBELS NWF, or less than 20 words correct per minute on DIBELS Oral Reading Fluency. The DIBELS recommendation at less than 20 is based on an end-of-first-grade benchmark of 40. Chapter 5 provides discussion about why a year-end benchmark of 60 may be more desirable.

While the decision rules described are research-based and generally accurate, experience dictates that teacher judgment be part of the decision-making equation as well. For example, in some cases teachers have requested that the assessments be given again because the scores did not reflect students' performance in class. In other cases, students who had borderline scores and who also presented behavior problems in class were placed into Tier 3 because their behavior and attention were improved in a small-group setting. Table 3.11 describes how beginning reading skills are taught in each of the five alternative programs.

How Can I Teach Beginning Reading Skills to English Language Learners?

Systematic and explicit phonics benefits English language learners whether they are first taught to read in English or in their native language. Numerous research studies in the United States and England demonstrate that when young English language learners receive explicit teaching of the alphabetic principle, they outperform their peers in word recognition and comprehension (Francis, Rivera, Lesaux, & Rivera, 2006; Gunn, Biglan, Smolkowski, & Ary, 2000.) Even when students are not yet fluent in English, explicit practice in sounding out words develops both English reading skills and English speaking skills, if explicit vocabulary instruction accompanies the phonics. Teachers who show pictures or use gestures to depict the meaning of unfamiliar words after students decode those words are teaching both alphabetic principle and comprehension. English language learners also require extra practice learning to articulate letter sounds that have no equivalent in their native language. The length of time learning explicit phonics may be crucial for grade-level reading, with many English language learners requiring two years to catch up to their English-speaking peers.

Fortunately, "cracking the code" in one language often expedites learning to read in a second language. If students first read at the full alphabetic phase in their native language, their ability to decode can transfer to later English reading (Durgunoğlu, 2002). This transference will be more difficult for students who have had trouble learning to read in their native language, and these same students will be at high risk for reading failure in English unless they get intensive support (Gersten, 1996). English language learners who need additional support learning to read can be identified as early as kindergarten through phonemic awareness, graphophonemic knowledge, and rapid naming screening assessments. The four test batteries identified in this book either have or are developing equivalent versions in Spanish. Unfortunately, at this point in time, we simply don't know under what circumstance, if any, reading instruction for English language learners should begin in the student's primary language (Goldenberg, 2008). Too often, an ELL student's reading intervention is delayed because the assumption is that the root cause of the reading difficulty is

TABLE 3.11 Comparison of Five Common Tier 3 Approaches

	Direct Instruction: Reading Mastery	Lindamood: LiPS Program	Reading Recovery	Wilson Reading System	Language!
Do lessons introduce a predesigned sequence of letter sounds?	Yes	Yes	No	Yes. However, several sounds are introduced within one substep.	Yes
Does curriculum specifically coordinate letter sounds taught in isolation with first words read in isolation and later in passages?	Yes	Yes	No	Yes	Yes
Do students practice letter sounds and word reading, only moving to the next lesson after they are successful?	Yes	Yes	No	Yes	Yes
Are phonics clues encouraged as the primary method for reading unfamiliar words?	Yes	Yes	No	Yes; pictures are never used in this program.	Yes
Do lessons introduce a sequence of regular words that are increasingly difficult to decode? (Example: VC or CVC followed by CVC variants)	Yes	Yes	No	Yes	Yes
Are students discouraged from guessing at words as one strategy for word reading?	Yes	Yes	No	Yes	Yes
Is decodable reading used to help students apply the letter–sound knowledge they have learned?	Yes. Program includes decodable reading books that are coordinated with letter sounds and words taught to students.	Yes. Teachers select decodable reading that is coordinated with letter sounds and words taught to students.	No. Program discourages decodable reading.	Yes. Decodable reading in sentences and passages is coordinated with letter sounds and words taught to students.	Yes. Program includes decodable reading books that are coordinated with letter sounds and words taught to students.

Continued

TABLE 3.11 Continued

	Direct Instruction: Reading Mastery	Lindamood: LiPS Program	Reading Recovery	Wilson Reading System	Language!
What is the amount of time spent on development of learning letter sounds, sounding out words, writing them, and sounding out words in passages?	After first 30 lessons, almost the entire daily lesson is spent on learning these skills. Comprehension development is also included in lessons.	Beginning lessons are split between phonemic awareness and development of alphabetic principle.	The use of magnetic letters and word boxes to analyze words comprises a small proportion of the 30-minute lessons, which cover seven activities each day.	Between 66% and 90% of lesson is devoted to learning these skills. Some lessons also include listening comprehension development.	Each literacy lesson is divided into 10 sections and is designed to take between 90 to 180 minutes. Of those 10 sections, four are devoted to these skills.
Are sight words pretaught before they appear in reading passages?	Yes	Yes	No	Teachers are encouraged to preteach.	Yes
Are the first sight words taught limited to high-frequency words necessary for story reading?	Yes	Yes	No	No. Both real and nonsense words are taught.	Yes
Is left-to-right blending stressed throughout all word- and passage-reading activities?	Yes	Yes	No	Yes	Yes
Do students write words that they are learning to read?	Yes	Yes	Yes	Yes	Yes
How are students assessed?	Short mastery tests of word or passage reading given to students approximately every five lessons determine whether students are ready to move to the next lesson or move to a faster- or slower-paced group.	Ongoing observation of the students' daily performance on reading tasks during lessons provides the foundation for decision making about how quickly to move through the program.	Teachers keep daily running records, notating errors that students read in predictable books.	Specific criteria are set for reading and spelling per lesson/per substep. Students are post-tested at the end of every step. Assessment determines how quickly student moves through curriculum.	Each unit of 10 lessons contains mastery tasks for the skills presented in that unit. Students are expected to achieve 80% on all tasks in order to proceed to the next unit.

that English is not the student's primary language. Developing English skills is prioritized and reading is deemphasized while waiting for the oral skills to develop. Meanwhile, valuable time is lost because English language learners who struggle with reading, whether they are from nonalphabetic or alphabetic backgrounds, need explicit, systematic, and intensive instruction in reading, and they need that intervention sooner rather than later. Becoming more proficient in English will not help a student who has poor phonological skills associate sounds with the letters they represent. In Chapter 1 you learned that students in a typical first-grade classroom needed a range of supports in order to learn to read. English language learners need that same support (Francis et al., 2006). Fortunately, research has shown that students can develop oral language and reading skills simultaneously, and that the more students read, the more language they learn (Goldenberg, 2008).

When you listen to an English language learner read, you may have difficulty determining whether a misread word is an actual error or just an articulation difference. Becoming aware of articulation patterns in students' native languages will help your analysis in these situations. Table 3.12 details pronunciation difficulties that native Spanish speakers may have when reading English text.

> For many practical ideas on teaching reading to English language learners, go to **http://www.colorincolorado. org.**

TABLE 3.12 Potential English Pronunciation Problems for Native Speakers of Spanish

Consonants	Vowels
/v/ is often pronounced as /b/ or a sound close to /w/; *vase* becomes *base.*	/ă/ is often confused with /ĕ/; *mat* becomes *met.*
At the beginning of a word, /p/ is often pronounced as /b/; *pet* becomes *bet.*	/ē/ is often pronounced as /ĕ/; *meet* becomes *mit.*
At the beginning of a word, /t/ is often pronounced as /d/; *tap* becomes *dap.*	/ă/ is often pronounced as /ā/; *make* becomes *mek.*
At the beginning of a word, /k/ is often pronounced as /g/; *kit* becomes *git.*	/oo/ is often pronounced as /ōō/; *book* becomes *bōōk.*
/sh/ is usually pronounced as /ch/; *ship* becomes *chip.*	
/y/ is often pronounced as /j/; *yell* becomes *jell.*	
/z/ is often pronounced as /s/; *zig* becomes *sig.*	
/m/, /n/, and /ng/ may be substituted for each other; *ping* becomes *pin.*	
When words begin with consonant clusters (*pr, cl, pl, sl*), an extra vowel is often inserted at the beginning of the word; *speak* becomes *espeak.*	
When words end with consonant clusters, the final consonant sound is often omitted; *fast* becomes *fas.*	
When a voiced /th/ occurs in the middle or the end of a word, /d/ is often substituted; *mother* becomes *moder.*	

Source: Adapted from Avery, P., & Ehrlich, S. (1992). *Teaching American English Pronunciation.* New York: Oxford Press, pp.149–153.

How Important Are Beginning Reading Skills for Older Learners?

While systematic phonics instruction produces the biggest impact on growth in reading when it begins in kindergarten or Grade 1 (National Reading Panel, 2000), teachers are responsible for bringing significant numbers of struggling older readers to proficient levels of reading. The National Assessment of Educational Progress 2007 Report indicated that 33% of fourth graders and 26% of eighth graders fell below the basic level in reading, unable to demonstrate even partial mastery of reading (Lee, Gregg, & Donahue, 2007). These students do not have the skills to acquire new knowledge from text (Lee et al., 2007).

It is often difficult to determine whether a struggling older reader has learning disabilities or has not been effectively taught. According to Roberts, Torgesen, Boardman, and Scammacca (2008), "Many older struggling readers are victims of poor early reading instruction. They were not taught or were insufficiently taught the basic skills necessary for fluent reading and deep processing of text. Some of these students are able to catch up in critical reading skills if provided with additional, sustained instruction in small, focused instructional groups" (p. 63). The authors go on to explain that a second group of older readers struggle despite having received research-based reading instruction taught well. Typically, diagnostic testing or intervention in an RTI model reveals that students in this second group have learning disabilities. If they are fortunate enough to get research-based intervention of sufficient intensity, they will respond more slowly to that instruction than many of the students in the first group.

Studies investigating older students and adults who have reading problems reveal that most have basic deficits in decoding skills. Of those older students with decoding deficits, there appear to be two groups (Archer, Gleason, & Vachon, 2003). Older students in one group, the smaller of the two groups, read at the first- and second-grade level. These students are still beginning readers without adequate skills for fluent sight reading. The second group are those reading between the third- and fifth-grade levels. While these students read single-syllable words and some high-frequency words by sight, they struggle to decode multisyllable words and have considerable difficulty reading connected text fluently. The needs of the smaller group of students who have yet to attain the alphabetic principle are addressed in this chapter. The needs of the larger group of older students with decoding problems are discussed in Chapters 4 and 5.

Share & Stanovich (1995) have aptly pointed out that it is tempting to focus reading instruction for older students on whole-word recognition because beginning phonics strategies appear to be babyish. In addition, progress in developing systematic word-attack skills can be slow at first, as guessing habits acquired during many years of previous instruction are difficult to unlearn. Slow progress combined with student reluctance can act to weaken teachers' resolve to stay the alphabetic principle course. Nonetheless, teachers are urged to use with these older readers curricula that systematically and explicitly provide practice reading words to link their spellings to their pronunciations, while adding meaning through having students read the words in connected text. Otherwise these students will remain stuck in the word-guessing mode for the rest of their lives. Interventions stressing word study can increase reading achievement both in word reading and comprehension, though less so in comprehension (Roberts et al., 2008; Wexler, Edmonds, & Vaughn, 2007). Providing systematic explicit instruction in vocabulary and comprehension is recommended as well.

The teacher's only productive option when teaching decoding to older learners is to step back and teach phonemic awareness, letter–sound skills, regular word-reading skills, and coordinated passage-reading skills previously described in Chapter 3. However, doing so presents two challenges. The first is to find a text that is not only explicit and systematic but also has age-appropriate stories and doesn't look "babyish." Three evidence-based programs that have these features are *Corrective Reading* (Engelmann, Carnine, Johnson, Meyer, Becker, & Eisele, 2008), *Language!* (Greene, 2009), and *Wilson Reading System* (Wilson, 2004). The second challenge is to find enough instructional time during the school day. Programs such as the three identified here are designed for a minimum of an hour and a half to two hours of intensive teaching each day.

> This article by Louisa C. Moats, "When Older Students Can't Read," explains some of the benefits that result from teaching phonics to older struggling readers: **http://www.cdl.org/resource-library/articles/older_read.php.**

Computer-assisted instruction is a potentially powerful way to teach word identification skills to students of all ages. The effectiveness of computer-assisted instruction in teaching beginning word identification is discussed in *Technology*.

Technology

Beginning Word Reading

Because there is so little published research investigating the effectiveness of computer-assisted phonics instruction, the National Reading Panel could only conclude that computer technology appears to hold promise for reading instruction (National Reading Panel, 2000). To date, computer software designed to improve reading instruction is still in its infancy and is most appropriately used in classrooms to supplement or reinforce a systematic, explicit phonics program. A 2007 study commissioned by the federal government testing the effectiveness of reading software programs on reading achievement over a two-year period of time showed almost no improvement in classrooms with computer-assisted instruction over classrooms where the software programs weren't used (Dynarski et al., 2007). Complaints were lodged about factors that weren't controlled for, such as the amount of time students used the software and how well the teacher integrated it into their classroom. The lesson to be learned is that simply purchasing a reading software program, even if it is of high quality, and putting students in front of a computer without feedback from an adult or monitoring of mastery is not sufficient to predictably increase reading achievement.

Teaching students who are at risk to move from letter sounds to the consolidated alphabetic stage requires extremely careful, coordinated instruction. *More* instruction is not always *better* instruction, especially when poorly designed activities contribute to mistakes that the student will later have to unlearn. Teachers who are evaluating software to supplement their instruction in letter sounds, word reading, or passage reading should consider the following factors:

- How closely coordinated is the teaching of letter sounds with the students' daily reading curriculum? Check the order in which the letter sounds are introduced. If the order is different, reorder the sequence presented in the computer program. If the computer software program includes digitized speech, the letter sounds should match your articulation. For example, letter sounds should be articulated without schwas. Finally, check the intelligibility of the synthesized speech. Although the quality of synthesized speech continues to improve, the longer sentences are sometimes unintelligible.
- How well do the games and activities involving regular word reading reflect skills that students have learned? For example, if students have not yet learned to decode consonant blends, they should not be expected to read consonant blend words while playing a computer game. If the skills stressed in the games and activities do not match your reading curriculum, find out whether the design allows you to modify types of words and text that are read.
- Does the program introduce regular words composed of letter sounds that the students can identify? Are those same words practiced later in sentences, paragraphs, or stories? If not, the activities are likely to be of little benefit in strengthening skills covered in the daily reading curriculum.

Continued

- Is the phonics program systematic and explicit? Computer-assisted instructional phonics programs may include nonsystematic phonics activities reminiscent of those in the most tedious workbooks of years past. Computer phonics programs may also undermine your systematic phonics program by encouraging students to guess at words and memorize too many whole words. Finally, since students aren't using their fingers while reading, monitoring left-to-right reading is difficult, if not impossible.
- Does the software program include performance checks to ensure that students reach mastery before moving on to a more difficult skill?
- Does the program have a built-in monitoring system that allows you to evaluate how the student is progressing?

What Games and Activities Reinforce Students' Beginning Reading Skills?

Once your students are decoding CVC and CVC-variant words, use every opportunity to take advantage of the school environment for more practice. Using the words your students can decode, make posters with short poems or captions describing a funny picture, and display these posters in areas where your students routinely wait—outside the bathroom, in the lunchroom waiting line, near the library. Draw your students' attention to the posters, asking them questions about content. You will help your students feel like readers, actively applying their reading to the outside world.

For a closer look at well-designed computer software in teaching beginning reading skills, download free samples at Headsprout, **http://www.headsprout.com/school/**; Funnix, **http://www.funnix.com/**; and Waterford Early Learning, **http://www.waterfordearlylearning.org/**.

After students have successfully read a decodable book, play "Landing on Mars" with them. Ask them to turn to a page in their book and hold up their index finger as the rocket. When you call out a word that is on the page, they are to launch their rocket into the air and land it on the word you named. Say, for example, "Find *shut*." (pause) "Find *pigpen*." (pause) "Find *rack*." (pause) "Yes! This class landed on Mars all three times!" Students will work their hardest to find the words quickly, speeding up the rate at which they are decoding.

By midyear of first grade, students on track to read at grade level should be starting to move into the consolidated alphabetic phase, indicating that they are ready to read more difficult words containing long vowels, more advanced sound clusters such as *tch*, and multisyllable words. Students will advance more quickly if they have the opportunity to receive feedback and help when needed by reading aloud to the teacher, tutors, parents, or older siblings. Some classrooms have successfully used First-Grade Peer-Assisted Literacy Strategies (PALS) (Grade 1–Grade 2) to provide more oral reading practice of connected text. In these classrooms, a stronger reader is paired with a weaker reader to coach him or her. Students are taught to cooperate with their partners, praise their partners, and work steadily at reading. Student coaches learn to teach and practice letter–sound identification, word reading, and connected text reading. By the time they begin working independently with their partners, these students have even learned to give a My Turn–Your Turn response any time the weaker student makes an error. The positive feedback and effective error correction are critical elements in this process (Mathes & Babyak, 2001). A similar PALS strategy has also been effective with weaker high school readers (Fuchs, Fuchs, & Kazdan, 1999).

Connecting reading to spelling and, ultimately, students' writing further develops reading skills. Not only should students be able to read CVC and CVC variants by sight no later than December of first grade, but they should also accurately spell regular CVC words, where the letters match the sounds. Once students can read words that contain *blends*, they should also write words that contain those same patterns. Rather than having to memorize words such as *plot, clam, send,* and *stand*, students should learn to automatically spell them by sound once they have learned to read similar words containing blends. The teacher who then tells her students to write a story about a big fat red bug extends her students' new learning even further. Shortly after the beginning of first grade is also the time to begin teaching the spelling of a few of the most common exception words that students are reading in their stories. The more students read, formally spell, and use these words in their writing, the more automatically they will recognize them in text.

The Word Box Game

The Word Box Game is a fun way to connect reading and spelling for your students. Put several clear word-building boxes on an accessible shelf so that students can play Word Box when they have completed other work.

Prepare the Game   Put the following inside each box:

* Lowercase letters of only the letter sound correspondences you have taught your students. All the vowels should be a distinctive color or marked with a distinctive tape.
* A laminated grid that students use to make words, placing a letter on each square (Figure 3.16)
* A pencil
* A "rocket" sheet that students can use for writing their words (see Figure 3.17)

FIGURE 3.16   Grid

FIGURE 3.17   Rocket Sheet

Prepare the Students

1. Tell students to bring a pencil and piece of paper when they play Word Box.
2. Teach the game to students, showing them how to put a letter in each box. Tell students to always put a marked vowel in the middle box.
3. After students put a letter into each box, ask them to say the letter sound correspondences quietly before blending them into a word.
4. Tell students to write the word they read on their paper, reading it out loud one more time after they write it.
5. Show students how to write their grand total on the page. Enthusiastically describe how, as they learn more and more words, their total numbers will get bigger and bigger.
6. Monitor students carefully as they play the game during this teaching phase to ensure that they will follow all the steps when they independently take out the word boxes.

Strategies for supporting student behaviors that are conducive to learning are described in the *In Your Classroom* feature.

In Your Classroom

Strategies to Encourage Positive Behavior

- Ms. Larson used the Teacher's Rocking Chair game to teach self-control to her kindergartners and help them learn to sit quietly for short amounts of time. Before she started playing the game with her students, when a parent, the principal, or a special education teacher would walk into the kindergarten and need a minute to talk to Ms. Larson, a few students, noticing that the teacher was occupied, would become loud or misbehave to get her attention. Ms. Larson wanted to teach everyone to sit for a few quiet moments without interrupting. During the rocking chair game, all of the children sat in rows on the carpet. One student was selected to sit in the teacher's large rocking chair in the front of the room. The selected student sat in the rocking chair surveying everyone else to determine the "quietest" student, who would get the next turn to sit in the chair. When Ms. Larson said, *"Your turn is up,"* the student in the chair picked another quiet student. Everyone wanted to be selected for the rocking chair. Students knew that if they talked during the transition when the next student was walking to the chair, they would lose their chance to sit in the chair. After starting to use the game, Ms. Larson established the rule that *"girls pick boys and boys pick girls,"* so that everyone would have a chance. Often Ms. Larson instructed students to *"pick someone who hasn't had a turn,"* or *"pick someone by the time you've*

counted to 20." Even after students had learned to quietly wait for short time periods, Ms. Larson continued to use the game because students asked for the opportunity to play it. Students learned self-control playing the game and applied these skills to other situations during the day such as waiting for their turn when answering questions about a story the teacher was reading.

- Ms. Buddin brought several large bowling trophies to her class to encourage students to follow the classroom rules when working at their tables. Quiet talking was allowed, but students were expected to finish their work or project and to ask permission if they needed to leave the table. When Ms. Buddin noticed everyone at a table following the rules, she put a bowling trophy on the surface. When someone didn't follow a rule, the trophy was removed. Gradually, working quietly became routine and the trophies were no longer needed.

- Ms. Gibbs wanted her students to become more aware of the impact their behavior had on other individuals in their community. She knew that some of her students had little experience receiving positive feedback from adults and needed to learn the feeling of pride for doing a good job that others appreciated. Thus Ms. Gibbs hung a "Compliments Chart" in the front of her classroom. Anytime the students, collectively or individually, received a compliment from anyone in the building—the principal, the custodian, another

Continued

teacher, a parent—a tally mark was put on the compliment chart. When the hundredth tally mark was put on the chart, the class earned a special surprise, which might be a pizza party or the opportunity to have a picnic lunch outside. Students who left the classroom for reading group looked forward to earning points for the class on days when their reading teacher complimented them during the lesson.

- Ms. Foley set up an "office" space where Terrance, a distractible student, could go to do his best work. By having a student desk and chair surrounded on two sides by dividers in the quietest part of the room, she could redirect him to work in the office when he could not complete independent work in a larger group. She would redirect him by saying, *"Terry, take your journal to the office where you can do your best work."* Rather than a punishment area, the "office" provided a quieter, less distracting place to complete work. Ms. Foley's goal was to get Terrance to independently go to the office when he realized that he wasn't focused on a paper or project.
- Every teacher periodically used group clapping, pats on the back, and thumbs-up to acknowledge effort, hard work, and rule following during reading class.

"Sharnicca, give yourself a thumbs-up. You wrote so much in your journal today."

"Everybody, pat yourself on the back, because you just read every word without even one mistake."

- Mr. Mixay recognized that his class liked challenges and they especially liked "fooling" the teacher and surpassing his expectations. After the students had just learned something new and still needed to use all of their concentration for success, he would often set up a challenge. Thus, when Mr. Mixay's class was supposed to spell the six irregular plural words, he said, *"This is very hard for students in your grade. Can you spell these very hard words? You will have to think very hard so I don't trick you, giving you these hard words."* Naturally the students did their best work, and Mr. Mixay shook his head and exclaimed how amazed he was that they had learned to spell such hard words. During review sessions, Mr. Mixay told his students that he was going to try to trick them by giving them difficult words to read. He smiled as he said that he was sure that they could not remember all those difficult words. Consequently, his students always rose to the challenge and read every word.

APPLIED ACTIVITIES

1. Four fact-or-fiction questions about teaching beginning word reading to students who are at risk are included below. Pair up with a partner and take turns defending your position for one of them using research sources cited in the chapter, journal articles, or information from the website resources listed in the sidebars.
   a. Beginning reading programs should stress using the context to figure out words because that is what skilled readers do. Is this fact or fiction? Explain why.
   b. An effective reading program for students who are at risk should include a high proportion of high-frequency exception words, since these are the kinds of words they are most likely to find in print. Is this fact or fiction? Explain why.
   c. Drill on word-reading skills reduces student motivation to read. Is this fact or fiction? Explain why.
   d. Decodable books are boring for children and reduce their motivation to read. Is this fact or fiction? Explain why.

2. A sample sequence of letter–sound introduction for a beginning reading program is shown below. Critique the sequence using guidelines proposed by Carnine and colleagues (2010) described in Table 3.1. Include in your critique any changes you would make.

   h t b o a d p j x e q n s f k i c y m z w u l g r v

3. In the list of words below, circle the consonant blends.

sand	clap	look	tramp	strap	stand	spat
clunk	ship	skin	think	slam	swap	grin

4. Following is a list of CVC variants. Label each as to the type of CVC word it exemplifies. For example, sat would be labeled CVC; trip would be labeled CCVC.

pen ____	mask ____	brand ____	must ____
drag ____	scrap ____	pest ____	smeil ____
spank ____	mist ____	tip ____	plan ____

5. Say the following consonant blends in unison as a group without adding schwas:

   gl br st pr str cl sn fr

6. Mr. Hayes introduced the letter sound /h/ yesterday. In the past few weeks he has taught his students to identify /m/, /a/, /s/, /f/, /t/, and /b/. Demonstrate how you would instruct Mr. Hayes's class today using the format in Table 3.4: Part B to teach the new and review sounds.

7. How would you enhance the following lesson designed to introduce the /t/ sound? Show students a piece of poster board on which is displayed the letter *t* along with a picture of a tent. Explain that the letter *t* stands for the /t/ sound as in *tent*. Write the words *tiger* and *fast* on the board. Ask the students to read the two words. Distribute the *t* letter card. Have the children put the letter in their mini pocket charts and say the *t* sound.

8. Shown below are the results for three students on the DIBELS NWF measure given in January. Identify the student who is performing at benchmark levels (see Figure 3.7 on page 65). How would you characterize the particular skill level for the two students not at benchmark levels? Identify specific teaching formats from the chapter that would help these two students attain benchmark levels.

DIBELS Nonsense Word Fluency Assessment and Score Sheet

Name: Shelby   Date: Dec. 5

w a b	p e v	yil	b u f	h u z	9/15
l e n	y o c	z o v	t o c	a b	6/14
l e b	o m	m i s	z i v	h u v	___/14
m a j	n e p	i v	n o c	k i g	___/14
				Total:	15/57

DIBELS Nonsense Word Fluency Assessment and Score Sheet

Name: Tyrone   Date: Dec. 5

W a b	p e v	y i l	b u f	h u z	15/15
l e n	y o c	z o v	t o c	a b	14/14
l e b	o m	m i s	z i v	h u v	5/14
m a j	n e p	i v	n o c	k i g	___/14
				Total:	34/57

DIBELS Nonsense Word Fluency Assessment and Score Sheet

Name: Shanique   Date: Dec. 5

w a b	p e v	y i l	b u f	h u z	14/15
l e n	y o c	z o v	t o c	a b	14/14
l e b	o m	m i s	z i v	h u v	13/14
m a j	n e p	i v	n o c	k i g	11/14
				Total:	52/57

---

9. Shown below are the scores for Mrs. Green's first-grade class on the DIBELS NWF assessment in January. Identify which students are at benchmark, which students will need a Tier 2 intervention, and which students, pending further testing, might be eligible for an alternative, intensive program in Tier 3.

Student	Nonsense Words: January Letter Sounds Correct per Minute
Maria	28
Ladariu	42
Skylar	50
Tylar	17
Jatavia	45
Jaylin	38
Dezazh	66
Andrew	21
Delundre	72
Shanteria	40
Brant	56
Jarnecia	39
Christopher	48
Bryce	29
Erionah	66
Trae	78
Joshua	35
Marquez	29
Shaheed	77
Vantrell	47

10. Ms. Munoz wanted her students to practice reading the following words on the chalkboard. Demonstrate how she would teach these words using the format described in Table 3.4.

| hop | sip | fin | tin |
| hot | sap | fox | can |

11. The reading curriculum informs Ms. Foley that students need to learn the following exception words, which will be in the next story: *bough, buy,* and *month*. She plans to have students practice the following review words that came from last week's story: *ghost, steak*. Demonstrate how you would instruct Ms. Foley's class using Table 3.8 for teaching exception words.

12. Karisha is a beginning reader who has learned the following beginning reading skills:

    Letter sounds: *a s m i t r b l w n f k h g*
    Sight words: *a is his the*

    Shown below are representative passages from three decodable books. Select the passage that would be most appropriate for Karisha. Indicate why.

Passage 1

Sam hit Kit in the hip. Sam is a big brat and will ram Matt.

Passage 2

Ed did run past his Dad. He ran fast and had fun.

Passage 3

Tom did help Mom. Tom went to get milk and a big box of hot nuts.

13. Passages from two hypothetical reading programs are shown below. By the end of November, Ms. Tonnato's students, whose DIBELS NWF scores range between 18 and 25, have learned all the short vowel sounds and the consonant sounds listed on the letter–sound chart at the end of Chapter 1. Ms. Tonnato wants to provide extra decodable reading for her students. Which passage would be more likely to lead to student success? Justify your answer.

Passage #1

The girl looked out the window. The sun was shining in the sky. "I think I will go outside today," she said. She left the house. She walked past a food stand. There was a big pile of donuts at the stand. She walked past the apple tree. There was a big cow under the apple tree. So she went home to get some lunch. I will get a sandwich, some juice, and an orange to eat.

Passage #2

Fran is fast. She can jump and hop and run fast. She gets to the swing first. I am mad. I can not jump and hop and run fast. But then I stop and think. I can hum and sing and skip. I sing for Gramps and hum for Mom. I skip up and down the steps. I will be pals with Fran. I can help Fran hum and sing and skip. Fran can help me jump and hop and run fast.

REFERENCES

Archer, A. L., Gleason, M. M., & Vachon, V. L. (2003). Decoding and fluency: Foundation skills. *Learning Disability Quarterly: Journal of the Division for Children with Learning Disabilities, 26*(2), 89 (28 pp.).

Armbruster, B., Lehr, F., & Osborn, J. (2001). *Put reading first: The research building blocks for teaching children to read.* Washington, DC: Partnership for Reading.

Avery, P., & Ehrlich, S. (1992). *Teaching American English pronunciation.* New York: Oxford Press.

Bursuck, B., Smith, T., Munk, D., Damer, M., Mehlig, L., & Perry, J. (2004). Evaluating the impact of a prevention-based model of reading on children who are at-risk. *Remedial and Special Education, 25,* 303–313.

Carnine, D. W., Silbert, J., Kame'enui, E. J., & Tarver, S. (2010). *Direct instruction reading* (5th ed.). Boston: Merrill.

Carroll, J., Davies, P., & Richman, B. (1971). *American Heritage Word Frequency Book.* Boston: Houghton Mifflin.

Cunningham, P. (2000). *Phonics they use: Words for reading and writing.* New York: Longman.

Durgunoğlu, A. (2002). Cross linguistic transfer in literacy development and implications for language learners. *Annals of Dyslexia, 52*(1), 189–206.

Durrell, D. (1963). *Phonograms in primary grade words.* Boston: Boston University.

Dynarski, M., Agodini, R., Heaviside, S., Novak, T., Carey, N., Campuzano, L., et al. (March, 2007). *Effectiveness of reading and mathematics software products: Findings from the first student cohort.* Report to Congress (Document No. PR07-04).

Ehri, L. C. (2005). Learning to read words: Theory, findings, and issues. *Scientific Studies of Reading, 9,* 167–188.

Ehri, L., & Snowling, M. (2004). Developmental variation in word recognition. In C. Stone, E. Silliman, B. Ehren, & K. Apel (Eds.), *Handbook of language and literacy* (pp. 433–460). New York: The Guilford Press.

Engelmann, S., & Bruner, E. (1995). *Reading Mastery I: Teacher's guide.* Columbus, OH: SRA Macmillan/McGraw-Hill.

Englemann, S., Carnine, L., Johnson, G., Meyer, L., Becker, W., & Eisele, J. (2008). *Corrective reading.* Columbus, OH: SRA/McGraw-Hill.

Francis, David J., Rivera, M., Lesaux, N., & Rivera, H. (2006). Research-based recommendations for instruction and academic interventions. *Practical guidelines for the education of English language learners.* Retrieved April 11, 2008, from http://www.centeroninstruction.org/files/ELL1-Interventions.pdf

Fuchs, L. S., Fuchs, D., & Kazdan, S. (1999). Effects of peer-assisted learning strategies on high school students with serious reading problems. *Remedial and Special Education, 20,* 309–318.

Fugate, M. (1997). Letter training and its effect on the development of beginning reading skills. *School Psychology Quarterly, 12,* 170–192.

Gersten, R. G. (1996). The double demands of teaching English language learners. *Educational Leadership, 53*(5), 18–22.

Gersten, R., Compton, D., Connor, C. M., Dimino, J., Santoro, L., Linan-Thompson, S., & Tilly, W. D. (2009). Assisting students struggling with reading:

Response to intervention and multi-tier intervention for reading in the primary grades. A practice guide (NCEE 2009-4045) [Electronic version]. Washington, DC: National Center for Education Evaluation and Regional Assistance, Institute of Education Sciences, U.S. Department of Education. Retrieved August 29, 2009, from http://ies.ed.gov/ncee/wwc/pdf/practiceguides/rti_reading_pg_ 021809.pdf

Goldenberg, C. (2008, Summer). Teaching English language learners: What the research does and does not say. *American Educator, 32*(2), 8–23, 42–44.

Good, R. H., Kaminski, R. A., & Howe, D. (June, 2005). *What data tells us about children and how to support their success.* Presented at AZ Reading First Conference, Phoenix, AZ.

Good, R. H., Simmons, D., Kame'enui, E. A., & Wallin, J. (2002). *Summary of decision rules for intensive, strategic, and benchmark instruction recommendations in kindergarten through third grade* (Technical Report No. 11). Eugene: University of Oregon.

Gough, P. B., Alford, J. A. Jr., & Holley-Wilcox, P. (1981). Words and contexts. In O. J. L. Tzeng & H. Singer (Eds.), *Perception of print: Reading research in experimental psychology*. Hillsdale, NJ: Erlbaum.

Gough, P., & Walsh, M. (1991). Chinese, Phoenicians, and the orthographic cipher of English. In S. Brady & D. Shankweiler (Eds.), *Phonological processes in literacy* (pp. 199–209). Hillsdale, NJ: Erlbaum.

Grace, K. (2007). *Phonics and spelling through phoneme-grapheme mapping*. Longmont, CO: Sopris West.

Greene, J. (2009). *Language! The comprehensive literacy curriculum*. Longmont, CO: Sopris West Educational Services.

Gunn, B., Biglan, A., Smolkowski, K., & Ary, D. (2000). The efficacy of supplemental instruction in decoding skills for Hispanic and non-Hispanic students in early elementary school. *Journal of Special Education, 34*(2), 90–103.

Hempenstall, K. (2001). School-based reading assessment: Looking for vital signs. *Australian Journal of Learning Disabilities, 6*, 26–35.

Hiebert, E. (2008). Finding the right texts. In *The (mis)match between texts and students who depend on schools to become literate* (Chapter 1). New York: The Guilford Press.

Institute of Education Sciences of the National Center for Education Statistics. (2007). National Assessment of Educational Progress. Washington, DC: U.S. Department of Education. Retrieved from http://www.isbe.state.il.us/assessment/pdfs/naep_natl_rpt_reading_2007.pdf

Jones, M. W., Branigan, H. P., & Kelly, M. I. (2009). Dyslexic and nondyslexic reading fluency: Rapid automatized naming and the importance of continuous lists. *Psychonomic Bulletin & Review, 16*(3), 567–572.

Joshi, R. M., Treiman, R., Carreker, S., & Moats, L. (2008). How words cast their spell: Spelling instruction focused on language, not memory, improves reading and writing. *American Educator, 32*(4), 6–16, 42–43.

Larson, K. (2007). *The science of word recognition or how I learned to stop worrying and love the bouma.* Retrieved September 8, 2007, from http://www.microsoft.com/typography/ctfonts/WordRecognition.aspx

Lee, J., Grigg, W., & Donahue, P. (2007). *The nation's report card: Reading 2007* (NCES 2007-496). National Center for Education Statistics, Institute of Education Sciences, U.S. Department of Education, Washington, DC.

Lindamood, P., & Lindamood, P. (1998). *The Lindamood phoneme sequencing program for reading, spelling, and speech.* Austin, TX: PRO-ED.

Lyon, R. (1998). *Overview of reading and literacy initiatives.* Statement to Committee on Labor and Human Resources, Bethesda, MD [Electronic version]. Retrieved April 28, 1998, from http://www.dys-add.com/ReidLyonJeffords.pdf

Maring, G. H., Boxie, P., & Wiseman, B. J. (2000). School-university partnerships through online pattern books. *Reading Online, 4*(5). Retrieved November, 2000, from http://www.readingonline.org/articles/art_index.asp?HREF=/articles/maring/index.html

Marzano, R. (2004). *Building background knowledge for academic achievement.* Alexandria, VA: ASCD.

Mathes, P., & Babyak, A. (2001). The effects of peer-assisted literacy strategies for first-grade readers with and without additional mini-skills lessons. *Learning Disabilities Research & Practice, 12*(1), 28–44.

McBride-Chang, C. (1999). The ABC's of the ABC's: The development of letter-name and letter-sound knowledge. *Merrill-Palmer Quarterly, 45*, 278–301.

McKenna, M.C., & Kear, D. J. (1990). Measuring attitude toward reading: A new tool for teachers. *The Reading Teacher, 54*(1), 10–23.

Moats, L. (2000). *Speech to print: Language essentials for teachers.* Baltimore, Paul H. Brookes.

Moats, Louisa C. (2005/2006, Winter). How spelling supports reading. *American Educator, 29*(4), 12–43.

Nation, K., Allen, R., & Hulme, C. (2001). The limitations of orthographic analogy in early reading development: Performance on the clue-word task depends on phonological priming and elementary decoding skill, not the use of orthographic analogy. *Journal of Experimental Child Psychology, 80*, 75–94.

National Reading Panel. (2000). *Teaching children to read: An evidence-based assessment of the scientific research literature on reading and its implications for reading instruction.* Washington, DC: National Institute of Child Health and Human Development.

Rathvon, N. (2004). *Early reading assessment: A practitioner's handbook.* New York: The Guilford Press.

Rayner, K., Chace, K., Slattery, T., & Ashby, J. (2006). Eye movements as reflections of comprehension processes in reading. *Scientific Studies of Reading, 10*(3), 241–256.

Rayner, K., Foorman, B., Perfetti, C. A., Pesetsky, D., & Seidenberg, M. S. (2001). How psychological science informs the teaching of reading. *Psychological Science in the Public Interest, 2,* 31–74. (A monograph from the American Psychological Society) Retrieved May 28, 2009, from http://www.psychologicalscience.org/journals/pspi/pdf/pspi22.pdf

Reitsma, P. (1983). Printed word learning in beginning readers. *Journal of Experimental Child Psychology, 36,* 321–339.

Roberts, G., Torgesen, J., Boardman, A., & Scammacca, N. (2008). Evidence-based strategies for reading instruction of older students with learning disabilities. *Learning Disabilities Research & Practice 23*(2), 63–39.

Share, D., & Stanovich, K. (1995). Cognitive processes in early reading development: Accommodating individual differences into a mode of acquisition. *Issues in Education: Contributions from Educational Psychology, 1,* 1–57.

Shaywitz, S. (2003). *Overcoming dyslexia: A new and complete science-based program for reading problems at any level.* New York: Alfred A. Knopf.

Stanovich, K. E. (1993/1994). Romance and reality. *The Reading Teacher, 47,* 280–291.

Torgesen, J., Wagner, R., & Rashotte, C. (1999). *TOWRE: Test of word reading efficiency examiner's manual.* Austin, TX: PRO-ED.

Wanzek, J., & Hagger, D. (2003). Teaching word recognition with blending and analogizing: Two strategies are better than one. *Teaching Exceptional Children, 36,* 32–38.

Wexler, J., Edmonds, M. S., & Vaughn, S. (2007). Teaching older readers with reading difficulties. In N. Mather (Ed.), *Evidence based interventions for students with learning and behavioral challenges* (pp. 193–214). Mahwah, NJ: Erlbaum.

Wilson, B. (2004). *Wilson reading system.* Millbury, MA: Wilson Language Training Corporation.

Yopp, H. K. (1995). Read-aloud books for developing phonemic awareness. *Reading Teacher 48,* 538–542.

4 Advanced Word Reading

Objectives

After reading this chapter you will be able to:

1. State a rationale for teaching advanced word-reading skills and identify a sequence of essential advanced word-reading skills.

2. Assess students' advanced word-reading and spelling skills in a multi-tier or RTI model.

3. Implement strategies for teaching letter combinations and affixes as preskills for reading multisyllable words.

4. Implement strategies for teaching advanced words and multisyllable regular words, structural analysis, and corresponding spelling skills in a multi-tier or RTI model.

5. Teach advanced word-reading skills to English language learners and older learners.

6. Implement games and activities that reinforce students' advanced reading skills.

Teaching Multisyllable Words

Mr. Turner wanted his students to have a high level of success reading the new story, so he carefully spent time before the lesson planning how to introduce the new difficult words from the text. Dividing multisyllable words into parts is challenging when teaching advanced word reading for the first time. Mr. Turner needed to determine how to divide each word strategically so that students were more likely to read it correctly when they combined the parts. Wednesday morning before school, Mr. Turner wrote the words he planned to teach that day on the board. Let's take a look at his thought process and how he decided to teach these words from the story students read later that day.

regular words:

fleet   flock   glide   places
hoping   biking   making
prob·ably   ad·ven·ture   pre·scrip·tion   ner·vous·ly   hor·i·zon

exception words:

papayas   chief

Mr. Turner wrote all words that he expected his students could read without any extra support as whole words in the first row. In the next row, Mr. Turner wrote the words containing a VCe pattern with an -ing suffix (*hoping, biking, making*). After his students said the rule related to these words and identified whether the vowel sound was long or short, Mr. Turner planned to ask his students to read each word as a whole word.

Since Mr. Turner's goal was to gradually increase the length of the word parts that students read, he decided to underline larger chunks in the next group of words. Although most of these chunks were also syllables, if Mr. Turner had divided all the words into syllables, he would have divided *ably* into two parts instead of one. He had already taught his students *horizon* as a vocabulary word and believed that his students could easily apply their decoding strategies to read it. Even though the second *o* in this word is represented by a schwa sound /ū/ instead of /ŏ/, because he had pretaught students the meaning of this word and used it in discussion, he anticipated that when students read the word by sight they would probably read *horizon*. Mr. Turner divided the word this way: <u>hor</u> i <u>zon</u>.

Finally, Mr. Turner taught *papayas* and *chief* as exception words. Since the word *papaya* was pivotal in the story, he planned to talk about the meaning when he introduced the word, providing vocabulary practice on the spot. On Friday, as a reinforcer, he planned to have some papayas cut so his students could taste them. Even if they were not brave enough to eat them, at least they would see what papayas look like, because the story had only a crude black-and-white line drawing of them.

Why do you think Mr. Turner chose the words that would require the least teacher support first?

Why might students need a rule to be able to decode words such as biking, hoping, and making?

Why did Mr. Turner go beyond teaching his students to decode papaya and clarify its meaning?

You learned about teaching strategies that help students develop beginning reading skills. By the end of first grade, students should be able to sound out CVC words in their heads, reading 50 or more letter sounds per minute on the DIBELS or AIMSweb Nonsense Word Fluency assessment with at least 15 words read as whole words (Good, Gruba, & Kaminski, 2002). Students should also be able to read first-grade passages accurately and at a rate of at least 40 to 60 words correct per minute, reading at the Consolidated Alphabetic Phase and instantly recognizing many words by sight. Instead of sounding out the word *slink* as five phonemes /s/ /l/ /i/ /n/ /k/, they are more likely to process it as two chunks /sl/ /ink/. Despite the significance of this accomplishment, if students are to become fluent enough decoders to tackle the reading comprehension demands of third grade and beyond, they still need to learn to apply their phonics skills to increasingly difficult words. Students need to learn to recognize and use larger letter patterns such as the *ous, tin, pre,* and *ly* to decode words. The purpose of this chapter is to provide you with explicit, systematic teaching strategies for advanced word reading. Chapter 5 will extend this focus on accuracy by providing explicit strategies for developing reading fluency. Because accuracy and fluency are closely connected, your instruction for students with advanced word-reading skills will emphasize both skills.

Why Teach Advanced Word-Reading Skills?

In a perfect world, written English would be completely regular; there would be one written symbol or grapheme for each sound in spoken English. In such a world, students who could sound out words in their heads and meet benchmark levels on the DIBELS Nonsense Word Fluency assessment would be ready to work almost exclusively on reading fluency and comprehension. Unfortunately, spoken English has 41 to 44 sounds and written English only has 26 written letters. Readers rarely encounter letters that have one unique sound in all words. Sometimes the sound of a letter depends on the adjacent letter. For example, when *t* comes before *h,* the two letters sound like /th/ in *thing* or *that;* the letter *a* is sometimes silent when it comes after an *e* in a word like *each.* Other times a letter's sound depends on letters appearing later in a word such as *made,* where the silent *e* at the end of the word results in the vowel sound /ā/. An additional source of confusion occurs when letters in a word are not logically connected to sounds, such as the *ai* in *said.*

Students who are ready to move beyond the beginning reading stage are likely to encounter other difficulties besides rule changes and irregularities. They must also be able to address the increasing prevalence of multisyllable words. Look at the following passage from an elementary school history textbook in which we have underlined all of the words containing three or more syllables.

> <u>Militiamen</u> were given little training. <u>Occasionally regiments</u> would meet at the town green where an <u>officer</u> would try to teach his men British battle <u>formations.</u> Training wasn't taken very <u>seriously.</u> <u>Officers</u> didn't demand <u>discipline</u> from their men because they were all friends. (Egger-Bovet & Smith-Baranzin, 1994)

Ask yourself, "Would I be able to understand this passage if I were unable to read all or most of the multisyllable words?"

What Advanced Word-Reading Skills Do I Need to Teach?

Clearly, readers who are at risk need to learn strategies to decode words containing more complex combinations of letters as well as words that contain multiple syllables. As with other steps in the process of learning to read, students who are at risk require more explicit teaching of these strategies. Two approaches have proven effective in teaching advanced word reading. The first approach emphasizes identifying known word parts, and the second approach emphasizes decoding syllable types. In the first approach, students are taught to identify one or more parts in the word, read the known parts first, and then read the whole word. For example, in order to read words like *production,* students first are taught the suffix *-tion.* Then in another lesson they are taught the prefix *pro-.* Finally, when learning this new word for the first time, they read the word parts /pro/ /duc/ /tion/ before reading the whole word *production.* Similarly, for the more simple word *such,* students learn to read the letter combination *ch* first, and then the whole word (Engelmann et al., 1999).

In the syllable approach, students are taught six common syllable types that occur in written English (Archer, Gleason, & Vachon, 2003; Greene, 2004; Moats, 2001; Wilson, 1996). These six syllable types, shown in Table 4.1, provide students with clues for figuring out the vowel sounds within the syllables. For example, a vowel within a syllable containing

TABLE 4.1   Six Syllable Types Used in Syllable-Type Instruction

Syllable Type	Examples	Description of Syllable Type
Closed	ra<u>bb</u>it de<u>pen</u>dent re<u>jec</u>tion	A syllable having a short vowel and ending in a consonant (VC, CVC, CCVC, CVCC).
Open	<u>ta</u>ble <u>de</u>fame star<u>va</u>tion	A syllable with a long vowel sound that is spelled with a single-vowel letter (CV, CCV).
Vowel Combinations	can<u>teen</u> pro<u>claim</u> un<u>speak</u>able	A syllable with a vowel combination such as *ai, oa, ea,* or *oi* (CVVC, CCVVC, CVVCC).
R-controlled	va<u>por</u>ize <u>sur</u>render <u>per</u>fection	A syllable with a vowel combination such as *ar, or, er, ir,* or *ur.*
Vowel-consonant-e	es<u>cape</u> obso<u>lete</u> window<u>pane</u>	A syllable with a long vowel sound with a consonant and final *e* (VCe, CVCe, CCVCe).
Consonant-le	pu<u>ddle</u> rum<u>ble</u>	A final syllable containing a consonant before *le.*

Source: Archer, A. L., Gleason, M. M., & Vachon, U. L. (2003). Decoding and fluency: Foundation skills for struggling older readers. *Learning Disability Quarterly, 26,* 89–101.

a consonant and final *e* would be long or say its name, as in *escape.* Once students are taught the syllable type, they learn to identify words by first identifying the syllable and then reading the whole word. For example, in *escape,* they would read /es/ then /cape/, and then the entire word, *escape.*

The approach for advanced word reading taken in this text is the part-by-part method, which is consistent with the synthetic phonics approach described in Chapter 3. While the syllable approach is also research-based (Archer et al., 2003; Bhattacharya, 2006), its use of multiple rules may be too difficult for younger children who are at risk because they are likely to have oral language difficulties. On the other hand, the syllable approach may be adequate for older students or those who have reading disabilities with no problems in oral language. Examples of evidence-based syllable-based programs include *Language!* (Greene, 2004) and *Wilson Reading System* (Wilson, 1996).

Letter Combinations and Affixes

To read advanced words, students need the ability to decode clusters of letters. **Letter combinations** are one type of cluster formed when two or more adjacent letters make one distinct sound. The *ch* in *church, ar* in *mart, oi* in *boil,* and *ee* in *meet* are all examples of letter combinations. Adjacent letters in a cluster can be vowels, consonants, or a combination of both. A list of common letter combinations, along with key words guiding their pronunciation, is shown in Table 4.2. These letter combinations occur frequently in common words. Included among these phonics patterns are digraphs and diphthongs. **Digraphs** are two successive letters articulated as a single phoneme. Examples of digraphs include *ch* as in *chop, th* as in *this,* and *oo* as in *book.* Another type of letter

> Practice saying the sounds for letter combinations at the Tampa Reads website where you can listen to them: **http://www.tampareads.com/ realaudio/tests/indexrm.htm.**

TABLE 4.2 Letter Combinations

Letter Combination	Phonetic Pronunciation	Voiced or Unvoiced	Articulation	Stop or Continuous Sound ⚠ = Don't Add a Schwa	When Students Have Difficulty Saying the New Letter Sound:
ai	as in *tail*	voiced	More open smiling mouth position; tongue in middle of mouth; increased mouth tension	continuous	Same as /ā/
al/all	as in *call* and *royal*	voiced	Same as /au/ + /l/	continuous	Have students say "All Done-All," moving their hands apart as they say "all."
ar	as in *hard*	voiced	Tongue is curled back toward the /r/ position	continuous	Elongate this *r*-controlled vowel for 2 to 3 seconds so the student clearly hears both sounds pronounced and sees that the mouth begins in a smiley position. Prompt with a mirror if needed. In cued speech for individuals with a hearing loss, this sound is designated as a combination of the /ah/ vowel with a following /r/.
au	as in *fault*	voiced	Rounded lips; tongue moves back in mouth; increased mouth tension	continuous	English language learners often confuse this sound with /ŏ/. The /au/ sound is produced farther back and higher in the mouth. Ask students to pretend they are sadly saying, "/Au/, the poor kitty."
aw	as in *lawn*	voiced	Rounded lips; tongue moves back in mouth; increased mouth tension	continuous	Same as /au/
ay	as in *gray*	voiced	Same as the /ā/ sound in *trail*	continuous	Same as /ā/
ch	as in *chair, munching,* and *such*	voiceless	Tip of tongue briefly contacts roof of mouth: lips forward; burst of air expelled with sound	stop ⚠	Model how your lips come forward when you say the sound. Ask students to pretend they have a cold and make a /ch/ sneeze.
dge	as in *fudge*	voiced	Tip of tongue briefly contacts the roof of mouth; a burst of air is expelled with sound	stop ⚠	Same as /j/

TABLE 4.2   Continued

Letter Combination	Phonetic Pronunciation	Voiced or Unvoiced	Articulation	Stop or Continuous Sound ⚠ = Don't Add a Schwa	When Students Have Difficulty Saying the New Letter Sound:
ea	as in *meat** *ea* says /ē/ in 60% of words containing this combination.	voiced	Smiling mouth position with lips open wide; tongue high in mouth near front; increased mouth tension	continuous	Same as /ē/
ea	as in *bread*	voiced	Smiling mouth position; tongue centered in the mid front	continuous	Same as /ĕ/
ee	as in *keep*	voiced	Same as the /ea/ sound in *meat*.	continuous	Same as /ē/
er	as in *jerk*	voiced	Tongue is in center of mouth curled back toward the /r/ position	continuous	Mouth is slightly rounded for this r-controlled vowel sound. Have your students listen and then say the sound they hear for /er/ at www.thefreedictionary.com/er
ew	as in *stew*	voiced	Rounded lips; back of tongue in highest position; increased mouth tension	continuous	Same as /o͞o/
igh	as in *night*	voiced	Smiley face; tongue and jaw raise to a high position	continuous	Same as /ī/
ing	as in *dusting*	voiced	Glide from the the /ĭ/ sound to /ng/	continuous	Same as /ĭ/ + /ng/
ir	as in *bird*	voiced	Same as /er/	continuous	Same as /er/
kn	as in *knit*	voiced	Front of tongue behind upper teeth toward front of mouth: air expelled through nose	continuous	Same as /n/
le	as in *wiggle*	voiced	Tongue lifts behind upper teeth; air passes over sides of tongue	continuous	Same as /l/

Continued

TABLE 4.2   Continued

Letter Combination	Phonetic Pronunciation	Voiced or Unvoiced	Articulation	Stop or Continuous Sound ⚠ = Don't Add a Schwa	When Students Have Difficulty Saying the New Letter Sound:
ng	as in *sing, singer,* and *bring*	voiced	Back of tongue in contact with the soft palate toward the back of the mouth; air expelled through the nose	continuous, nasal	Point out that the back of the tongue makes the sound, while the front stays down. Have students make silly /ng/ singsongs varying intonation. For example, they could sing /ng/ to the tune to "BINGO."
oa	as in *soap*	voiced	Rounded mouth that shuts like a camera shutter; tongue in middle; increased mouth tension	continuous	Same as /ō/
oi	as in *join*	voiced	Tongue glides from low back to high front; jaw rises with the tongue; an oval-shaped mouth position to a smiling position; increased mouth tension	continuous	Begin with the /au/ sound (as in *awful*) and immediately slide into the /ee/ sound. Have students look at their mouths in the mirror as they form this sound.
o͝o	as in *book*	voiced	Slightly rounded parted lips; back of tongue high; re-laxed facial muscles	continuous	Ask students to pretend that they are using all their energy while pushing a heavy elephant, saying this sound.
o͞o	as in *boot*;* *oo* says /o͞o/ in 59% of words containing this combination.	voiced	Rounded lips; back of tongue in highest position; increased mouth tension	continuous	Ask your students to pretend they just received their favorite toy as a birthday present as they say this sound of delight.
or	as in *corn*	voiced	The vowel glides toward the /r/ position	continuous	Elongate this *r*-controlled vowel for 2 to 3 seconds so the student clearly hears both sounds pronounced and sees that the mouth starts in a rounded position. Prompt with a mirror if needed.
ou	as in *cloud*	voiced	The mouth move-ment glides from one articulation position to another; jaw and tongue rise as the sound is said; lips move from open to a rounded position; increased mouth tension	continuous	Ask students to pretend they just bumped their foot into the table and because it hurts they say, "ow."

TABLE 4.2   Continued

Letter Combination	Phonetic Pronunciation	Voiced or Unvoiced	Articulation	Stop or Continuous Sound ⚠ = Don't Add a Schwa	When Students Have Difficulty Saying the New Letter Sound:
ow	as in *grow*; ow* says /ō/ in 50% of words containing this combination.	voiced	Rounded mouth that shuts like a camera shutter; tongue in middle; increased mouth tension	continuous	Same as /ō/
ow	as in *clown*	voiced	Same as /ou/ as in *cloud*	continuous	Same as /ou/
oy	as in *joy*	voiced	Same as for /oi/	continuous	Same as /oi/
ph	as in *phone*	unvoiced	Upper front teeth on lower lip: air gust expelled	continuous	Same as /f/
qu	as in *queen*	unvoiced	/qu/ sounds like /kw/. Refer to the description of those letter sounds and say this sound, quickly blending them together into one sound.	continuous	Ask students to make the sound of a cuckoo clock: "kwoo-kwoo."
sh	as in *show, ashes,* and *dish.*	unvoiced	Air passes between rounded lips; teeth close but not touching;	continuous	Ask students to put their fingers in front of their mouths to feel the air as they say the sound. Show students how /sh/ is the typical "be quiet" sound and ask them to make the sound with their pointer finger raised in front of their mouth.
tch	as in *catch*	unvoiced	Tip of tongue briefly contacts roof of mouth: burst of air expelled with sound	stop ⚠	Same as /ch/
th	as in *thimble, nothing,* and *path*; th* says this sound in 74% of words containing this combination.	unvoiced	Tip of tongue between the upper front teeth as air expelled	continuous	Ask students to stick out their tongues and silently blow.
th	as in *then, mother,* and *bathe*	voiced	Tip of tongue between the upper front teeth as air expelled	continuous	Ask students to stick out their tongues and blow. Emphasize that this sound tickles their tongues.

Continued

TABLE 4.2 Continued

Letter Combination	Phonetic Pronunciation	Voiced or Unvoiced	Articulation	Stop or Continuous Sound ⚠ = Don't Add a Schwa	When Students Have Difficulty Saying the New Letter Sound:
ur	*hurt*	voiced	Same as /er/	continuous	Same as /er/
wh	as in *when*	voiced	Same as /w/ since now most native English speakers pronounce /w/ the same as /wh/**	continuous	Same as /w/

*Percentages for letter–sound combinations having two sounds come from Hanna, Hanna, Hodges, & Rudloff (1966) as cited in Carnine, Silbert, Kame'enui, & Tarver. (2010). *Direct instruction reading* (5th ed.). Boston: Merrill Prentice Hall; and Celce-Murcia, Brinton, Goodwin, & Goodwin. (1996). *Teaching pronunciation: A reference for teachers of English to speakers of other languages.* New York: Cambridge University Press.

**Celce-Murcia et al., 2002.

combination, **diphthongs,** are vowel blends in which the first sound seems to glide into the second sound. Examples of diphthongs include *ou* as in *mouse* and *oi* as in *boil.*

One-Syllable Words Containing a Letter Combination

After students have learned a particular letter combination, the teacher supports them as they decode words that contain the combination or affix. For example, Ms. Bland introduced the letter combination *ch* to her students. They were able to read the new sound correctly for two days in a row when it was mixed in with the previously introduced combinations of *ai, ar, th,* and *sh.* Ms. Bland then began to teach the class how to read one-syllable words with *ch,* such as *much, champ,* and *rich.* After students have learned to decode words with a specific letter combination, if that letter combination is contained in one of the most common word families, the teacher should teach students to read and spell related words in that family. The most common word families for advanced readers are: *ack, all, ank, ash, aw, ay, eat, ell, est, ick, ight, ill, ing, ink, ir, ock, or, ore, out, ow, uck, ump, unk,* and final *y* in one-syllable words such as *fry, shy,* and *try.*

Two-Syllable Words Containing Closed Syllables

Students begin to expand their knowledge of VC, CVC, and CVC variant words and learn to read two-syllable words comprised of two closed syllables. Now that they read letter chunks, words like *frantic* are more easily decoded as two chunks, such as /fran/ /tic/. Students begin to read words with double consonants represented by one sound in the middle of a word, such as *muffin* or *mitten.*

Words with Rule-Based Sounds

Once students can read the CVC variant words, they are ready to read words that have long vowels, including words having the **vowel-consonant-vowel pattern.** While the approach to phonics instruction taken in this text has been to avoid teaching too many rules to children who are at risk, some rules are simple enough and work often enough to make their teaching worthwhile (Johnston, 2001; Linan-Thompson & Vaughn, 2007). The VCV rule fits into this category. Students are taught the rule that if there is a vowel-consonant-vowel pattern, the first vowel says its name. Because this rule applies to multisyllable words as well, it is introduced from the beginning when students are learning easier VCe words. Examples of easier words having the VCV pattern are words that have the vowel-consonant-silent *e* pattern (**VCe words** also called silent *-e* syllables) such as *make* and *like*. Often teachers first teach the Vowel-Consonant-e rule for the words that end in silent *-e*, but that rule only applies to one-syllable words. Students then have to learn other strategies for making long vowel/short vowel decisions when reading longer multisyllable words. Since the VCV rule applies to both one- and multisyllable words, we recommend using it. After students are taught to apply the VCV rule to reading one-syllable VCe words, they learn to differentiate these words from CVC words, a difficult discrimination for many students who are at risk. To provide practice, teachers ask students to read words with short-vowel/long-vowel contrasts like *made* and *mad* or *glade* and *glad*. When students are able to decode CVC and CVCe words at a mastery level, they are ready to learn the most common word families with VCV patterns: *ake, ale, ame, ate, ice, ide, ine* and *oke*.

Initially students learn the most common sounds for the letters *c* and *g* in one-syllable words, but as they move into advanced word reading, they are often faced with making a decision between the two sounds that represent each of these letters. When we coached teachers, we observed that those who taught their students the following rules reduced student errors reading unknown words: "When *c* is followed by *e, i,* or *y*, it usually says /s/" and "When *g* is followed by *e, i,* or *y*, it usually says /j/." When students are consolidated alphabetic phase readers, they view the entire word or word part as a unit and are able to determine the sound of *c* or *g* based on the vowel that follows it. When teaching any rule, first have the students independently say the rule and then practice applying it to words. Later, when the student misreads the *g* or *c* in a word, prompt the student to read the word correctly by asking her what the *g* rule is before asking her to reread the whole word. By using a rule-based correction for misread words, the teacher encourages students to develop the habit of applying the rule to unknown words.

A final rule helps students determine the sound of *y* as a vowel at the end of words: "A final *y* says the /ē/ sound in two-syllable and longer words and /ī/ in short one-syllable words." Knowing this rule makes the sound of *y* more predictable in words like *funny, sandy,* and *shy*.

Applying Structural Analysis to Reading Regular Words

Structural analysis involves using prefixes, suffixes and root words to determine the meaning and pronunciation of words (Nagy, Winsor, Osborn, & O'Flahavan, 1993). Teaching students the most common affixes and their meaning before having them apply that knowledge to reading multisyllable words helps them decipher those words and their distinctive meanings more readily. Structural analysis skills are first introduced when students are reading at a mid-first-grade level, and by the time they are reading at a third-grade reading level, structural analysis skills are emphasized more than phonological ones. Instruction in structural analysis develops students' skills in reading multisyllable words by sight as well as by recognizing their part of speech and knowing their meaning. These skills are necessary for fluency and comprehension when reading increasingly difficult texts in social studies and science. When explicit instruction in structural analysis skills is paired with oral reading for second- and third-grade students with reading problems, reading accuracy and fluency can significantly increase (Vadasy, Sanders, & Peyton, 2006). Usually the first two-syllable words that students read are **compound** words such as *hatbox* in which two words combine to form one with a distinct meaning. Gradually contractions such as *aren't* and *shouldn't* are introduced as they become more frequent in text that the students are reading.

When students can automatically read new one-syllable words accurately, differentiating between long or short vowel sounds, teach them to apply the VCV rule to two- and three-syllable words to which **inflectional** endings have been added. Inflectional endings are suffixes such as *-ed, -es, -ing,* and *-s* that indicate tense, number, possession, or gender when added to the end of a base word. These words can present unique spellings or reading difficulties because an inflectional ending can have more than one sound or the ending can change the spelling of the base word.

One way to divide and analyze words is by breaking them into syllables. You can easily clap out the four syllables in the word *unbeliever* as *un•be•liev•er.* If, instead of syllables, you decide to divide a word into its smallest units of meaning, you have three **morphemes** (the smallest parts of words that have a distinctive meaning):

un•believe•er

* *un* means *not*
* *believe* means to accept as real
* *er* means a person who does something

In this example word, *believe* is the foundational morpheme that establishes the basic meaning of the word. Because *believe* is a complete word that can stand by itself, it is called **a base word.** When the foundational morpheme is not a complete word, such as *struct* in the word *construction,* it is called a **root.** All multisyllable words have at least one base word or root. Morphemes that precede the root or base word are called **prefixes;** morphemes that are added to the end of the root or base word are called **suffixes.** In our example, *un-* is the prefix and *-er* is the suffix. Both suffixes and prefixes are categorized as affixes. For example:

reseat, seating, reseating

* The word *reseat* contains the morphemes *re* + *seat.* The prefix is *re-; seat* is the base word. The prefix *re-* is also categorized as an affix.
* The word *seating* contains the morphemes *seat* + *ing.* The suffix is *-ing;* again, *seat* is the base word. The suffix *-ing* is also categorized as an affix.
* The word *reseating* contains the morphemes *re* + *seat* + *ing.* Both the prefix *re-* and the suffix *-ing* are categorized as affixes; again the base word is *seat.*
* The base word *seat* contains the letter combination *ea.*

desirable, undesirable

* The word *desirable* contains the morphemes *desire* + *able.* The suffix is *-able; desire* is the base word. The suffix *-able* is also categorized as an affix.
* The word *undesirable* contains the morphemes *un +desire* + *able.* Both the prefix *un-* and the suffix *-able* are categorized as affixes; again the base word is *desire.*

pendant, dependent

* The word *pendant* contains the morphemes *pend* + *ant.* *Pend* is the root word meaning "to hang." The suffix *-ant* is also categorized as an affix.
* The word *dependent* contains the morphemes *de* + *pend* + *ent.* Both the prefix *de* and the suffix *-ent* are categorized as affixes; again the root word is *pend.*

For a list of the most common prefixes, suffixes, and roots along with their meanings, visit: **http://www. englishclub.com/vocabulary/ prefixes.htm** and **http://www. dummies.com/WileyCDA/ DummiesArticle/id-1186.html.**

The careful teaching of affixes as preskills to multisyllable word reading is a key feature of effective advanced word-reading programs (Archer et al., 2003). As with letter combinations, spend your limited class time teaching the affixes that most frequently are used in common words. A list of some of the more common beginning affixes and their meaning is provided in Table 4.3. You will notice that two letter combinations, *er* and *ing*, are also affixes.

> Learn how to use structural analysis circles and the word builder strategy at: **http://forpd.ucf.edu/strategies/ stratstructural_analysis.html.**

Words with Two or More Syllables and One or More Irregular Parts

As students read increasingly difficult passages, they encounter multisyllable words that have one or more irregular parts. Usually these irregular parts involve vowels that do not say their most common sounds. For example, in the word *obeyed*, students should be able

TABLE 4.3 Affixes

Affix	Meaning	Phonetic Pronunciation	Affix	Meaning	Phonetic Pronunciation
a	without/not/to	aside	**less**	without	restless
able/ible		drinkable, incredible	**ly**	characteristic of	happily
anti	against	antigravity	**ment**	action or process	movement
al/ial	having the characteristic of	personal, special	**mid**	middle	midterm
de	opposite	defrost	**mis**	wrongly	misjudge
dis	not, opposite	disarm	**ness**	state of, condition of	kindness
en,em	cause to	enable	**non**	not	nonsense
er/or	comparative, one who	helper, actor	**ous/eous/ious**	having the qualities of	joyous, courageous, conscious
fore	before	forecast	**over**	over	overhand
ful	full of	thankful	**pre**	before	predetermine
ic	having the characteristics of	scientific	**re**	again	retake
il/ir/in/im	not	illegal, irrational, injustice, impossible	**semi**	half	semicircle
ing	verb form	helping	**sub**	under	substation
inter	between	intermix	**super**	above	superstar
ion/tion/ation	act, process	attraction, gradation, occasion	**s/es**	more than one	banks, boxes
ity/ty	state of	honesty, gravity	**un**	not	unbeatable
ative/itive/ive	adj. form of a noun	cooperative, sensitive, festive	**under**	under	Underworld
			y	characterized by	grumpy

to read the -*ed* ending but are likely to have difficulty decoding the letters *ey*. Words having a single consonant between two vowels in a word can also be problematic when they don't follow the VCV rule. For example, students may read the word *panic* as having a long *a* because of the seeming presence of a VCV pattern in the word. Fortunately, students can also apply their decoding skills to learn these new longer words. Many times the exception sound is a schwa /uh/ such as the *e* in *totem* or the *a* in *important*. After students sound out the parts of the word, they naturally substitute the schwa when they read the word as a whole, especially if the word is in their speaking vocabulary.

One- and Two-Syllable Exception Words

Some words are so irregular that it makes sense to introduce them in the same way that exception words were introduced in beginning reading. Examples of these irregular words include *chaos, stomach,* and *chief.* These words can be introduced by telling students the word, having them spell the word, and then having them read the word again (see Table 3.8: Format for Reading Exception Words).

Spelling Exception Words: Rule- and Pattern-Based Spelling and Morphographic Spelling

Students reading at the consolidated alphabetic phase learn to spell irregular words more quickly. Their spelling instruction should mirror their new reading skills, with words they are learning to spell organized into patterns. For example, they learn that in words ending in *ack, eck, ick, ock,* and *uck,* the ending sound /k/ is spelled *ck.* Instruction should gradually introduce high-frequency prefixes, suffixes, and base words as well as more irregularly spelled words. Most spelling programs used in the general education curriculum are based on high-frequency words and do not have this careful design. In our project schools, we found that we could modify the beginning phonetic spelling programs to make them more effective, but that for advanced word readers, none of our modifications could compensate for the lack of a well-designed spelling program based on structural analysis skills. Reading skills do not directly transfer to spelling. But because the two skills are interdependent, explicit instruction in spelling benefits reading as well as spelling. When spelling a word correctly, students first search memory for the spelling. If unsuccessful, they segment the word's phonemes to write their corresponding graphemes. Finally, students look at the written word to check if it matches the form of the word stored in memory or if it matches the phonemes they hear in the word (Ehri, 1989).

How Do I Assess Advanced Word-Reading Skills in a Multi-Tier or RTI Model?

Older struggling readers have gaps in the letter–sound and structural analysis skills that they have learned to mastery. Sonnie, a student in Tier 2, may still have two digraphs that she continues to confuse, and when she reads a word with both a prefix and suffix, she tends to guess at the suffix. Before you can use your small-group time with her to fill in these holes, you first have to identify them using a diagnostic assessment to pinpoint what skills your students still have not mastered and where your reading instruction should start. Pinpointing error patterns is critical so that you can determine whether the student has difficulty reading words with inflected endings or confuses long and short vowels in multisyllable words. If inflected endings are difficult for several Tier 2 students, your small-group practice will include teaching that skill. If another group of students is unable to read words with some of the basic prefixes, you can form another group to practice reading words with those problematic prefixes.

Once students are consolidated alphabetic phase readers, the primary way to monitor their reading progress is through assessing oral passage reading and comprehension. Strategies for using assessments in these areas are described more fully in Chapters 5, 9, and 10. However, there are students who, despite your best teaching efforts, may struggle learning letter combinations and affixes. These are students who tend to read grade-level passages slowly and with more errors. They are likely to be your students in Tier 2 or Tier 3. By assessing them directly on their advanced sounds, you can find out which sounds need more instruction. Additional instruction can then be provided during differentiated small-group instruction. You can assess your students on all of the common affixes and letter combinations. A shorter way to assess student knowledge of combinations and affixes is to check your reading series and identify which letter combinations and affixes have been taught up to the time of the assessment. For example, by November, Ms. Mobley had taught the letter combinations *ch, sh, th, ea, ar, ur,* and *ow* and the affixes *a, -ing, be, -est,* and *-ly.* When she decided to assess her students in Tier 2 to see whether they had learned these sounds, Ms. Mobley selected a key word to assess each sound. She selected the word *chin* for *ch,* for *ar* she selected *part,* and for *ing* she selected the word *rusting.* She then developed a typed list of the keywords, asking her students individually to read each word on the chart in Figure 4.1. As her students read, Ms. Mobley marked her score sheet, shown in Figure 4.2, with a plus if a student read the word correctly and a 0 if not.

When scoring her students' answers, Ms. Mobley was careful to score a response as incorrect only if the student missed the targeted sound. For example, Deanna in Figure 4.2 read word number two as *bash,* rather than *dash.* Although Ms. Mobley wrote the incorrect word that Deanna read as a reminder for herself, she still scored Deanna's answer as correct because she read the *sh* sound correctly. After giving this assessment to all of the students in her class, Ms. Mobley developed a group score sheet to help her make instructional decisions about which skills to teach using more group instruction. Table 4.4 depicts the group score sheet she used to summarize the class results.

chin	grow
dash	amaze
math	rusting
real	become
farm	funniest
turn	hardly

FIGURE 4.1 Informal Assessment of Letter Combinations and Affixes (Student Sheet)

Student: Deanna   **Date:** Oct 23
Teacher: Ms. Mobley

1. **ch**in +   7. gr**ow** 0 grew
2. da**sh** + bash   8. **a**maze +
3. ma**th** +   9. rust**ing** +
4. r**ea**l +   10. **be**come +
5. f**ar**m 0 firm   11. funni**est** +
6. t**ur**n +   12. hard**ly** +

FIGURE 4.2 Informal Assessment of Letter Combinations and Affixes (Teacher Score Sheet)

TABLE 4.4 Class Score Sheet for Assessment of Letter Combinations and Affixes

Date: <u>Oct 23</u>   Teacher: <u>Mrs. Mobley</u>

Sounds	Darrell	Gabriella	Deanna	Otis	Alexis
ch	+	+	+	o	+
sh	+	+	+	+	+
th	+	+	+	o	+
ea	+	+	+	+	+
ar	o	o	o	o	o
ur	+	+	+	o	+
ow	o	o	o	o	o
a_e	+	+	+	+	+
ing	+	+	+	+	+
be	+	+	+	+	+
est	+	+	+	+	+
ly	o	o	+	o	o

Use the lists available at this website to generate word lists containing specific letter combinations or specific syllable patterns: **http://www.resourceroom. net/readspell/wordlists/default.asp.**

Some of the word-reading, screening, and progress-monitoring assessments described in Chapter 3, "Beginning Word Reading," are appropriate for assessing word reading until the end of third grade. For older students, the TOWRE and Woodcock Reading Mastery word-reading assessments are recommended for evaluating word reading both with real words and more advanced nonsense words.

How Can I Assess Students' Advanced Spelling Skills?

Spelling assessments described in Chapter 3 included skills through the end of third grade with the exception of AIMSweb, which includes spelling skills through eighth grade. Using traditional norm-referenced diagnostic spelling assessments can be problematic (Rathvon, 2004). For example, the relatively few words at each level on most spelling assessments makes identifying error patterns for instruction difficult. Also, some tests simply require students to select a spelling word out of a group of words rather than have them produce the word in writing, the latter being the response mode required most often. Finally, scores can vary significantly on different diagnostic tests. Unlike other spelling tests, the Word Identification and Spelling Test (WIST) Regular Word Spelling subtest can be used to identify error patterns and plan instruction for students from the age of 7 through 18. On this assessment, students spell 100 one-syllable to four-syllable regular words, and scores include a record of errors for each of the six syllable types. Learn more about this assessment at http://www.proedinc.com/customer/Product View.aspx?ID=2031.

A kindergarten–fifth grade spelling assessment that records errors in terms of missed patterns (ex. digraphs, inflected endings) is available online at: **http:// www.csus.edu/indiv/s/ sellensh/319A%20materials/ Primary% 20Spelling%20Inventory. pdf.**

How Can I Teach Students to Decode Advanced Words and Words with Multiple Syllables?

In Chapters 1 and 3, a multi-tiered instructional approach was described that allows teachers to accommodate a range of learners who are at risk. The enhancements described in those chapters also apply to teaching the advanced word-reading skills just described. No matter what reading program you are using, your likelihood of success with students who are at risk will increase with the use of advance organizers, unison responding, perky pace, support for new learning using My Turn–Together–Your Turn, systematic error corrections, cumulative review, integrated motivational strategies, and teaching to success. The formats for teaching advanced word reading in this chapter can be used for large-group Tier 1 instruction as well as small-group Tier 2 intervention sessions.

Identifying Letter Combinations and Affixes Introduced in the Curriculum

Teaching your students to identify common letter combinations and affixes in isolation before they read them in words greatly enhances their chance of success reading multisyllable words. The format for teaching combinations and affixes in isolation is shown in Table 4.5. This format is similar to the one used for teaching single-letter sounds (Table 3.3). Advanced readers learn letter combinations at a more rapid rate. Students who needed to practice new letter sounds like /b/ or /j/ for a week when they were younger now learn the sound for a new letter combination after only one or two days of practice. Because students now have more experience and knowledge with letter sounds, the teacher can introduce a new letter combination by telling students the sound and then asking them to say the sound by themselves. Togethers are only used as needed at this stage of skill development. The new sound is then practiced along with a number of previously introduced sounds using an alternating pattern. For example, when the new combination *ar* was first introduced, it was practiced using the following alternating pattern: *ar, ea, ar, th, ing, ar, ent, ea, sl, ar, br, ai, ea, ing,* and so on. Note that both letter combinations and affixes previously covered are reviewed in a typical daily lesson.

The Suffix -*ed*

Unlike the other affixes and letter combinations, the suffix -*ed* can't be introduced cleanly in isolation because it has three different sounds. The sound that -*ed* makes depends on the base word to which it is added. Therefore, teach -*ed* separately by using your students' oral language to help them determine which sound of *ed* to use rather than scalloping under the -*ed* suffix. Carnine and colleagues (2010) suggested writing the -*ed* ending on the board before presenting a series of examples to demonstrate the three different *ed* sounds. For example, Mrs. Gibbs pointed to the information in Table 4.6 when she gave instructions to students to do the following activity: First she asked students to read the word *jump.* After pointing to the -*ed* ending in the word *jumped,* she told students that *jump* plus *ed* = *jumped* (where *ed* takes on the sound of /t/). She then had the students read the word *land* before telling them that *land* plus *ed* = *landed* (where *ed* is a second syllable /ĕd/). Next, she had the students say the word *fill,* and told them that *fill* plus *ed* = *filled* (where *ed* takes on a /d/ sound with no extra syllable). Finally, Mrs. Gibbs tested the students' understanding by asking them to add -*ed* to a series of orally presented words (What's *lift* plus *ed?* What's *kill* plus *ed?* What's *skip* plus *ed?*)

TABLE 4.5 Format for New Letter Combinations and Affixes Introduced in the Curriculum

Objectives	After seeing a new letter combination or affix, students will say its sound with 100% accuracy.
Materials Needed	Board, chart paper, or overhead transparency and writing implement. Write the letter combinations and affixes that will be reviewed with the new letter sound. Use an alternating pattern to teach the new letter combination or affix by writing it on the board followed by one review letter combination/affix, followed by the new letter combination/affix, followed by two review letter combinations/affixes. This pattern is continued until five letter combinations or affixes separate the last two new ones (examples: **ar** ea **ar** th ing **ar** ent ea re ou **ar** ai ea ing oo _le **ar**).
Signaling	*Loop signal for continuous sounds:* After looping to the end of the letter combination, hold your finger for two seconds as students say the sound before looping your finger back to the starting point. *Loop signal for stop sounds:* After looping to the end of the letter combination, bounce your finger out as students say the sound and return to the starting point.
Time	3–5 minutes

Instructions	Teacher	Student
	1. Advance Organizer	
	2. My Turn (Examples given for continuous and stop sounds.) Point to the new letter combination or affix.	
	continuous sound: (finger to the left of letter) **"My turn. Here's our new sound for today."** (loop signal) **"/ar/."** (loop back to starting point)	/ar/
	stop sound: (finger to the left of letter) **"My turn. Here's our new sound for today."** (loop signal and bounce out) **"/ch/."** (back to starting point)	/ch/
	3. Your Turn	
	continuous sound: (finger to the left of letter) **"Your turn. What sound?"** (loop signal) (answer) (loop back to starting point) **"Yes, /ar/."**	/ar/
	stop sound: (finger to the left of letter) **"Your turn. What sound?"** (loop signal and bounce out) (answer) (back to starting point). **"Yes, /ch/."**	/ch/
	4. Individual Student Checkout	
	continuous sound: (finger to the left of letter) **"Individual turns. What sound? Inez."** (loop signal) (answer) (loop back to starting point) **"Yes, /ar/."**	/ar/
	stop sound: (finger to the left of letter) **"Individual turns. What sound? Shan."** (loop signal and bounce out) (answer) (back to starting point). **"Yes, /ch/."**	/ch/
Scaffolding Reduction	5. Your Turn to Read the Row (new plus previously learned letter combinations and affixes) Starting at the first letter combination/affix move through the row of letters on the list, signaling for each letter combination/affix just as you did in Step 3. As you move through the list say, **"What sound?"** for each letter combination/affix.	/ar/ /ea/ /ar/
	6. Individual Student Checkout Point to random letters. Starting at the first letter combination/affix, move across the row of letters on the list, signaling for each letter combination/affix just as you did in Step 5. As you point to random letter combinations/affixes on the list say, **"Individual turns. What sound? Carmella."**	/ing/, /ar/, /ent/ . . .
Error Correction	If an error occurs at Step 3, immediately return to a My Turn–Your Turn pattern. If an error occurs at Step 5 or 6, immediately return to a My Turn–Your Turn pattern. Then alternate between the missed letter and familiar letters until students identify the missed letter correctly three times.	

TABLE 4.5   Continued

Adaptations	⁕ When teaching two sounds for the same letter combination (e.g., /ē/and /ĕ/for *ea*), ask students to say two sounds for the combination, saying the most common sound first. If you introduce the letter combination in this way from the start, students will have a higher probability of accurately reading an unknown word containing the letter combination. You can point to the letter combination and signal: **"Say the two sounds. First sound."** (student answer) **"Second sound."** (student answer)

Source: This script is based on one originally developed and field-tested by Carnine, D. W., Silbert, J., Kame'enui, E. J., & Tarver, S. (2010). *Direct instruction reading* (5th ed.). Boston: Merrill.

Many students who are at risk have difficulty doing this oral task. They may be influenced by their native language and routinely add a syllable to indicate past tense; they may use a dialect that does not routinely add past tense to verbs; or they may have articulation problems that make this task more difficult. These students need daily practice until they begin to hear and say these past-tense endings. Since -*ed* has three sounds, you should never expect students to read the separate -*ed* ending as a "stand-alone." Instead, have students read the base word and then the whole word. For students who do not routinely use -*ed* past-tense verbs in their oral communication, learning to read these words is as much a language task as a decoding one. After teaching students to read the word *gasp* and discussing its meaning, the teacher would do the following when she instructs the word *gasped:*

Written on board:

gasped

1. Teacher loops under "gasp" and says, *"Read the base word"* (Students read *gasp.*)
2. Teacher loops back to the beginning of the word and says, *"Now read the whole word."* (The teacher slashes under word from left-to-right as the students read *gasped.*)

Error Correction   If students can't read the word *gasped*, chances are that they are not familiar with the past tense of *gasp* as a vocabulary word. Thus the teacher should first say the word correctly (*"gasped"*) before using it in a sentence loudly emphasizing the word ending. For example, the teacher says, *"Right now, I gasp because I'm thinking of all the work I have to do, but yesterday I gasp**ed** when I saw that spider in the room. Everyone say the word gasp**ed**."* After students say the word, the teacher asks them to read it once more. Note that sometimes the teacher needs to articulate the word with students. For example, saying /pt/ at the end of a word is difficult, and students with weaker phonemic awareness skills might not hear the two sounds.

Reading One-Syllable Words with Letter Combinations

Once students can read a letter combination in isolation, teach them to read it in words using the format shown in Table 4.7. In this approach, the teacher uses strategic underlining and a part-whole strategy to focus student attention on the new combination. The teacher begins by underlining the letter combination in the first three or four words. Students first read the underlined letter combination and then the entire word. After doing this procedure for the first three to four words, students then read the rest of the words in the list by sight at least two

TABLE 4.6   Action Words with *ed* Endings Tell Us What Happened in the Past

Base Word	Base Word: Past	Sound
jump	jumped	/t/
land	landed	/d/ + syllable
fill	filled	/d/

TABLE 4.7   Format for Reading One-Syllable Regular Words with Letter Combinations

Objectives	After seeing a one-syllable regular word that contains a letter combination, students will orally read the word the fast way.
Materials Needed	Board, chart paper, or overhead transparency and writing implement. Write the regular words that students will read in rows on the board. For example, if students are reading eight words, write two rows of four words. On the first day, underline the new letter combinations before students read words containing them.
Signaling	Two-part signal: **"What sound?"** or **"What word?"** initiates the signal for unison answers.
	1. Loop signal. **"What sound?"** initiates the signal for unison answers.
	2. Side-slash-signal. **"What word?"** initiates the signal for unison answers.
Time	Depends on the number of words with new letter combinations introduced in the reading curriculum.

Instructions	**Teacher**	**Student**
	1. Advance Organizer	
Scaffolding Reduction	2. Your Turn with Sound Prompting	
	a. (finger just to the left of underlined sound) **"Your turn. What sound?"** (loop signal) (answer) (loop back to starting point). **"Yes,** (loop signal) **/sh/."** (loop back to the left of the word)	/sh/
	b. (pointing to the left of the word.) **"What word?"** (side-slash-answer) (loop back to starting point). **"Yes, *ship.*"**	ship
Further Scaffolding Reduction	3. Your Turn without Sound Prompting	
	After the first three or four words on the list, omit the sound prompting. Remember to use a longer think time the first or second time students read words on the list.	
	"What word?" (side-slash-signal under the entire word–answer) (loop back to starting point) **"Yes, *shall.*"**	shall
	"What word?" (side-slash-signal under the entire word–answer) (loop back to starting point) **"Yes, *wish.*"**	wish
	Teach between 3 and 10 other words with the same letter combinations.	
	4. Individual Student Checkout	
	"What word? Bethany." (side-slash-signal under the entire word–answer) (loop back to starting point) **"Yes, *wish.*"**	wish
	Call on between one and three students to check for accuracy.	
Error Correction	If students make an error reading the new sound combination, ask them to tell you the sound and then read the word again. If students still make a mistake, move into a My Turn–Your Turn pattern. Then return to the beginning of the row and have students reread the words.	
	If students make an error reading another sound they have previously learned, immediately have them sound out loud and then read the whole word. If they still make an error, return to a My Turn–Your Turn. Once the error is corrected, return to the beginning of the row and have students reread the words.	
Perk Up Your Drill	Some teachers send home a list of the words with their students for extra practice. On Friday afternoon, the class splits into assigned pairs. First one student reads to her partner who marks every correct word. Then the pair switches. The teacher monitors closely for any questions. Students keep track of their cumulative score from week to week by charting it on a thermometer.	
Adaptations	The first two or three times through the word list, give longer think time as students sound out the words with the new combination.	

Source: This script is based on one originally developed and field-tested by Carnine, D. W., Silbert, J., Kame'enui, E. J., & Tarver, S. (2010). *Direct instruction reading* (5th ed.). Boston: Merrill.

times. The first time through the list, the teacher provides more think time, gradually reducing the amount each time thereafter to build fluency. At least one third of the words in the list should have the new letter combination because newer skills require more practice. The remaining words should contain review letter combinations to build student retention. A loop signal is used for reading the underlined combination; a side-slash signal is used for reading the whole word. These are the same signals shown in Figure 3.10.

Reading One-Syllable Words Ending in VCe

Reading VCe words is difficult for students because it is the first time they encounter long vowels that are not part of a vowel combination. After saying the rule, the teacher guides the students by applying it to four or five VCe words as shown in Table 4.8. After the rule has been successfully applied to each word, the students read each word by sight. If the students make an error while reading words by sight, the teacher guides them as they reapply the rule, reread the word, and then go back to the beginning of the list and read the words by sight again. The goal for this activity is 100% accuracy.

Once students are able to read lists of VCe words without error, they are presented with a mixture of VCe and CVC words to ensure that they apply the VCV rule only when appropriate. A common problem among children who are at risk is that once they learn to read long vowel words, they have a tendency to make all vowels long, whether they are or not. For example, after Mr. Gagliano taught his students the VCV rule, he noticed that during passage reading they were reading the words *hop* as *hope*, *tap* as *tape*, and *rip* as *ripe*. Including Part B in this format is helpful for preventing this kind of vowel confusion.

In Part B of the VCV format, the teacher asks the questions that students will need to ask themselves in order to apply the rule independently to words and read them accurately. After the students have applied the rule to the list of words, they read the list of words by sight until they are 100% accurate. As with Part A, errors are corrected by having students reapply the rule and then go back to the beginning of the list. Once again the goal is 100% accuracy for a given list of words. Since this reading skill is especially difficult for students who are at risk, teachers often spend several days practicing reading a mixture of CVC and VCe words until students are successful. Eventually, once students learn to apply the rule, they automatically learn to distinguish VCe and CVC words without conscious thought.

With regard to signaling, a finger snap or hand clap is used for all rule application questions such as, *"Is there a vowel-consonant-vowel?"* The side-slash signal is used when it is time for students to read the word. When the teacher asks, *"So, do we say /ā/ or /ă/ for this letter?"* a snap or clap is used.

/Ū/ presents additional challenges because there are two sounds associated with it. In words like *duke*, the sound is represented by the $\overline{oo}$ sound, but in words like *mule* and *cube*, the *u* says its name /yū/. Students who are at risk may have difficulty with this distinction. Fischer (1993) recommended teaching /yū/ for /ū/ and explained:

> I have found it unnecessary to teach both sounds explicitly. When sounding out words such as flute, rude, and June, a brief discussion of the use of /oo/ usually is sufficient for prompting the students to switch from long /u/ to long /oo/. (In fact, they have fun trying to use /u/ in those words!) (p. 130)

TABLE 4.8   Format for Reading One-Syllable Words That End with VCe: Part A

Objective	After seeing one-syllable words that end with VCe, students will orally read the words the fast way.
Materials Needed	Board, chart paper, or overhead transparency and writing implement. Write the regular words that students will read in rows on the board. In this beginning format, the word list should only contain VCe words. On the first day, underline the two vowels before students read words containing them.
Signaling	Two-part signal: 1. A finger snap 2. Side-slash signal: **"What word?"** initiates the signal for unison answers. In Part B, a looping signal is used after the teacher asks, **"What sound?"**

Instructions	Teacher	Student
	Note: The first few times you read VCe words, use a My Turn to show students how you apply the rule and read the words.	
Preskill 1	Teach students the rule for one-syllable words that end in VCe. **"When it's vowel–consonant–vowel, the first vowel says its name."** Don't move on to Step 2 until students can say this rule.	When it's vowel–consonant–vowel . . .
Preskill 2	Teach students to identify which letters are vowels and consonants.	
Format	1. Point to the first word and ask, **"Does this word have a vowel–consonant–vowel?"** (pause) (finger snap) (answer) (point to VCV letters as you affirm) **"Yes, this word has a vowel–consonant–vowel."**	yes
	2. Point to the first vowel and ask, **"So does this letter say its name?"** (pause) (finger snap) (answer) **"Yes, this letter says its name."**	yes
	3. Point to the first vowel: **"Say the name of this letter."** (finger snap) (answer) (point to the first vowel) **"Yes, /ā/."**	/ā/
	4. Point your finger to the left of the first letter in the word, pause and ask, **"What word?"** (side-slash signal under the entire word–answer) (loop back to starting point) **"Yes, name."**	name
	5. Repeat this pattern for all of the words.	
	6. After students read all of the words on the list, start at the beginning and read all of the words the fast way.	
	(point and pause) **"What word?"** (side-slash signal under the entire word–answer) (loop back to starting point) **"Yes, name."**	name
	(point and pause) **"What word?"** (side-slash signal under the entire word–answer) (loop back to starting point) **"Yes, gate."**	gate
	(point and pause) **"What word?"** (side-slash signal under the entire word–answer) (loop back to starting point) **"Yes, sale."**	sale
Reduce Scaffolding	Gradually fade out your prompts. On day 2 or 3, you might begin omitting Step 3. If students are not successful, add that prompt for several more days. Once students can read the long vowel words when you omit Step 3, also omit Step 2 during the first time through the words.	
	7. Individual Student Checkout	
	(point and pause) **"Individual turns. What word? Austin."** (side-slash signal under the entire word–answer) (loop back to starting point) **"Yes, gate."**	gate
	(point and pause) **"What word? Chan."** (side-slash signal under the entire word–answer) (loop back to starting point) **"Yes, sale."**	sale
	Call on between one and three students to check for accuracy.	

TABLE 4.8 Continued

Error Correction	If an error occurs at any step, immediately repeat steps 1–6. Repeat the rule as in step 1 if necessary.

Format for Reading a Mixture of One-Syllable CVC Words and Words That End with VCe: Part B

Objective	After seeing a combination of one-syllable CVC words and words that end with VCe students will orally read the words the fast way.
Materials Needed	Board, chart paper, or overhead transparency and writing implement. Write the regular words that students will read in rows on the board. The word list should contain a mixture of words that end in VCe and CVC words in random order.
Signal	Three-part signal: 1. A finger snap. 2. Loop signal. **"What sound?"** initiates the signal for unison answers. 3. Side-slash signal. **"What word?"** initiates the signal for unison answers.

Instructions	Teacher	Student
	1. **What's the vowel–consonant–vowel rule?** (signal 1)	When it's vowel–consonant–vowel . . .
	2. Point to the vowel. **"Does this say its name or sound?"**	
	3. **"What Word?"**	
	4. Gradually reduce your scaffolding until students can read a list of words with a combination of one-syllable CVC words and words that end with VCe with 100% accuracy.	

Error Correction	Repeat steps 1–3 with missed word and start at the beginning of the word list.
Perk Up Your Drill	If students read interspersed VCe and CVC words on a first read with at least 90% accuracy, you can play the "I'll try to trick you" game. When students first see the new word list, tell them that each year you like to trick your students and have put up a challenging list of words to try to trick them. Using an animated tone of voice and gestures, tell the students that they will read the word list and try not to be tricked by any of the words. Students will use all of their effort to avoid mistakes so the teacher can't trick them. You will find that your students never tire of these challenges.

Adaptations	※ Check to see whether students who have difficulty reading the words with long vowels are confusing the terms *name* and *sound*. In the beginning exercises, you may need to overemphasize the word *name* when you ask, **"Say the NAME of this letter."**
	※ Students who are most at risk may need to learn the following preskills:
	    ※ to identify letters as vowels or consonants
	    ※ to tell the difference between a letter name and a letter sound

Source: This script is based on one originally developed and field-tested by Carnine, D. W., Silbert, J., Kame'enui, E. J., & Tarver, S. (2010). *Direct instruction reading* (5th ed.). Boston: Merrill.

Reading Regular Words with Two or More Syllables

The format for reading regular words with two or more syllables, which is shown in Table 4.9, teaches students to see words as parts rather than as a collection of individual letters. Regular words with two or more syllables are words that can be broken into parts that can be

TABLE 4.9 Format for Reading Regular Words with Two or More Syllables

Objective	After seeing a regular word that contains two or more syllables, students will orally read the word the fast way.
Materials Needed	Board, chart paper, or overhead transparency and writing implement. Write the regular words that students will read in rows on the board. For example, if students are reading eight words, write two rows of four words. On the first day, underline each part of the word before students read. *Reading* is written as <u>read</u> <u>ing</u>. *Portion* is written as <u>por</u> <u>tion</u>.
Signaling	Two-part signal: 1. Loop signal. **"Read this part"** initiates the signal for unison answers. Repeat for each part of the word, moving from left to right. 2. Side-slash signal. **"What word?"** initiates the signal for unison answers.
Time	Depends on the number of words introduced in the reading curriculum.

Instructions	Teacher	Student
	1. Advance Organizer	

Scaffolding Reduction	2. Your Turn with prompting of word parts
	"First you're going to read the parts of the word and then you'll read the whole word."
	  a. Place your finger to the left of the first underlined part of the first word written on the board (<u>read</u> <u>ing</u>).
	  "First part?" (loop signal under the underlined part)
		read

	b. Point to the left of the second underlined part of the word. **"Next Part?"** (loop signal under the underlined part)	ing
	c. Loop your finger to the left of the word. **"What word?"** (side-slash signal under the entire word–answer) (loop back to starting point) **"Yes, *reading."*** Repeat this pattern for all of the multisyllable words on the list.	reading
	3. Your Turn without prompting of word parts After reading all of the multisyllable words on the list, start again and read the words by sight without prompting the parts. (point and pause) **"What word?"** (side-slash signal under the entire word–answer) (loop back to starting point) **"Yes, *reading."***	reading
	(point and pause) **"What word?"** (side-slash signal under the entire word–answer) (loop back to starting point) **"Yes, *shelter."*** **Teach between 10 and 15 words.**	shelter
	4. Repeat 3, even faster.	
	5. Individual Student Checkout (point and pause) **"Individual turns. What word? Johnny."** (side-slash signal under the entire word–answer) (loop back to starting point) **"Yes, *candle."***	candle
	(point and pause) **"What word? Greta."** (side-slash signal under the entire word–answer) (loop back to starting point) **"Yes, *tailor."***	tailor
Error Correction	If students make an error reading the individual parts, immediately have them first orally sound out that part of the word and then read the entire part as a whole. Ask students to read the whole word one more time. Finally, return to the beginning of the row and have students reread all the words to that point. If students make an error reading the whole word the fast way, immediately tell students the word; then ask them to read the word parts again before reading the whole word. Once the error is corrected, return to the beginning of the row and have students reread all of the words.	

TABLE 4.9   Continued

Perk Up Your Drill	Every time students read two rows of words correctly, have them raise their hands as if a fireworks display is rising into the sky. In unison, make the gentle sound of fireworks drifting back to the ground.
Adaptations	If students have had difficulty reading words with a new sound like /tion/, once they are reading the words accurately, find decodable books that emphasize that sound for more practice.
	If students have difficulty determining whether the vowel in an open syllable says its name or its sound, you can tell students that when you put a line above a letter, the letter says its name. Use this strategy when you anticipate that students will be unable to decode a new word such as *starvation* = star vā tion

Source: This script is based on one originally developed and field-tested by Carnine, D. W., Silbert, J., Kame'enui, E. J., & Tarver, S. (2010). *Direct instruction reading* (5th ed.). Boston: Merrill.

readily decoded as long as students have the prerequisite decoding skills. For example, the word *returning* can be broken up into the parts *re + turn + ing.* As long as students are capable of decoding all three parts, they can be taught how to attack the word. In this format, the teacher uses a loop signal under each decodable part as students read the parts, and then side-slashes as students read the whole word. Students read all of the words by sight after they have first read them in parts.

When students misread the part or the whole word, the teacher must instantly analyze their mistake in order to select the appropriate error correction. Her error correction will depend on whether they misread a word part or the entire word. If students misread a part of the word, the teacher supports the students by having them read the part phoneme-by-phoneme before reading that whole word part. Once students have read the missed part correctly, the teacher points slightly to the left of the word and has them once again begin reading the parts of the same word to give them some more immediate practice. When Mrs. Dettman came to the third word on Tuesday's list (*constrictor*), which she had underlined as *con strict or,* she asked everyone to read the first part, which they did with no problem. When she asked them to read the second part, they said, "*sicker,*" so she immediately put her finger slightly to the left of the *s* and asked them to sound out that part. As she looped from part to part, the students replied, "/str/ + /i/ +/ct/. Now when she asked them to read that part, they correctly answered *strict.* Mrs. Dettman enthusiastically told the group, "*Yes, this part is* **strict**," before saying, "*Let's read this word one more time. Read the first part.*" Her students then quickly read each part, *con + strict + or,* so she asked them to read the whole word, which they accurately did. Instead of having students move down the list and read the fourth word, Mrs. Dettman said, "*Starting over. Let's start at the top of the list and see if this time we can get every word correct the first time.*" By returning to the top of the list and giving the students this slightly delayed practice reading *constrictor* again, she ensured that they would be likely to read it correctly when they opened their books and read the boa constrictor snake story. Of course, if word lists are long and students miss a word toward the bottom of the list, merely go up three or four words rather than returning to the top.

The second type of error correction is used when students read the parts correctly but blend them into a different word. If Mrs. Dettman's students had decoded the parts *con + strict + or* correctly, but then read the word as *contraction*, they would have made this second type of error. Recognizing the second type of error, Mrs. Dettman would switch to a My Turn strategy and tell students the word (*constrictor*). For immediate practice she would then ask her students to read the parts of the word (*con + strict + or*) before reading the whole word again (*constrictor*). Just as with the first error, Mrs. Dettman would say "*Starting over,*" and return to the top of the list so her students practice reading all of the words again. Students should now move quickly through

TABLE 4.10   Is Your Phonics and Word Study Instruction Research Based?

	Research-Based	**Not Research-Based**
Phonics and Word Study	Explicit, systematic, cumulative teaching of phoneme-grapheme (sound-symbol) correspondences, syllable types, and meaningful word parts (prefixes, suffixes, roots, and base words); word-reading skills applied in text reading; "Sound it out" comes before "Does it make sense?"	Children directed to pay attention to the sense of a sentence before guessing at a word from context and the first letter; "sounding out" whole word is de-emphasized; no systematic presentation of sound—symbol correspondences; avoidance of decodable text; use of leveled books without phonetically controlled vocabulary.

Source: Adapted from Moats, L. (2007). *Whole-language high jinks: How to tell when "scientifically based reading instruction" isn't.* Washington, DC: Fordham Foundation.

the list reading these words by sight since they have had more practice decoding them. Of course, if students failed to blend word parts into the whole word *constrictor* correctly because they hadn't heard of that word before, Mrs. Dettman would also teach the meaning of the word *constrictor* since understanding the meaning of the word would help students remember that word the next time they saw it in print. Table 4.10 compares systematic and explicit scientifically based research instruction in phonics and word study instruction described in Chapters 3 and 4 with other commonly used teaching methods that are not research-based.

How Do I Teach Students to Apply Structural Analysis Skills to Reading Regular Words?

When teaching students how to apply structural analysis to reading regular words, your instruction should be as explicit as when teaching beginning decoding skills. When we expanded one-day structural analysis activities in the general education curriculum to five-day lessons, teachers told us that adding four days of practice still didn't provide enough support for their students when learning to apply a rule or the meaning of a suffix to a word. As a result, our teachers often doubled that amount of time. The teachers found that if they left the skill before students were at mastery, the rule or meaning of a prefix was quickly forgotten. They told us that the structural analysis part of the lesson needed more review than most other skills they taught during reading. Expecting students to answer in unison is also important, because only a small percentage of students have the opportunity to apply the rules otherwise. Procedures to teach contractions, prefixes, and dividing words into syllables are described next.

Teaching Contractions

Preskill   Teach your students to say the definition for a ***contraction.*** *"A contraction is a short way of saying and writing two words."* Teaching the definition may take some "My

Turn–Together–Your Turn" practice, and you might want to teach the definition by clapping it out or having students say it in rhythm. Students should also be able to say the definition independently as well as say the word *contraction* when you tell them the definition.

1. Write the following words on the board:
   a. we'll = we + will
   b. I'll = I + will
   c. isn't = is + not
   d. can't = can + not

2. MY TURN: Point to the first word and explain that *we'll* is a short way of saying *we will*. Point out the apostrophe. Another one of your goals for these structural analysis activities is to make sure that all of your students can say *apostrophe* when you point to that punctuation mark.

3. TOGETHER: First, ask students to read *we'll* = *we will;* Next, erase *we* + *will* and ask them what *we'll* means (*we will*). Finally, add meaning and say, "*We will go to the store. How can I say that sentence a different way?*" (answer: "*We'll go to the store.*")

4. YOUR TURN

   Ask: "*What does we'll mean?*"

5. Repeat for second word. Thereafter, before teaching another new contraction, always return to the top of the list and have the students read each contraction already taught and tell you what it means.

Your students have mastered the skill when they can tell you what a specific contraction means at the start of a lesson with no support, or when a student answers your question about the meaning of a contraction in the text she is reading. Students should learn to spell the contractions at the same time they are learning to read them.

Teaching Affixes

Preskill   Several preskills are needed before teaching students to apply the meaning of prefixes and suffixes. If you are teaching students about prefixes, they should be able to read the base or root word as well as the prefix you are teaching them. If you are teaching a prefix, then they need to know its definition. Teach the definition with My Turn–Together–Your Turn until students can say it independently. "*What's a **prefix**?*" (answer: "*A prefix is a word part added to the beginning of a base word that changes its meaning.*") The same preskills apply to teaching suffixes. "*What's a **suffix**?*" (answer: "*A suffix is a word part added to the end of a base word that changes its meaning.*") The following lesson teaches students word building with two prefixes. A lesson focused on suffixes or both would follow the same pattern. Teach only one or two prefixes or suffixes to mastery before introducing others. Add prefixes and suffixes you have taught to your word wall for easy review.

Many students need several days of instruction at the My Turn-Together level before you can add new words or reduce scaffolding. These activities require manipulating language and are more difficult than expected. Do not underestimate how difficult learning how to apply prefixes and suffixes to base and root words is for your students who are at risk. This lesson teaches the prefix *re-*, though you can teach up to two affixes during a given lesson using the same wording.

1. Write the following on the board:

   Definition: *Re-* means *again*

   He retells the story.

   Shavon reset the alarm clock.

2. Ask your students: "What's a prefix?" (answer: *A prefix is a word part added to the <u>beginning</u> of a base word that changes its meaning.*") Reteach this definition if students have forgotten it.

3. Ask your students to read the definition "***Re-*** means ***again***." Ask students what *re-* means. Ask them to shut their eyes and tell you what *re-* means.

4. MY TURN: Ask students to read the first sentence. Circle the prefix, and remind students, "***re-*** means ***again***." Tell students that, because *re-* means *again*, *retells* means *tells again*. Explain that if Martina tells her mom what happened at school and then she tells her mom again a second time, she tells the story again or she **retells** the story. Ask if anyone knows someone who retells a lot of stories or information. Ask the students if *re-* is a prefix or a suffix and why. Ask the students one more time what *re-* means. Ask the students one more time what *retells* means. Erase the definition.

5. TOGETHER: Ask students to read the second sentence. Circle the prefix and ask students what *re* means. Ask students if *re* is a prefix or suffix. Then ask, "*If re means **again**, what does **reset** mean?*" If students are unable to answer, increase scaffolding and use a My Turn to explain. If students answer correctly, say, "*So we know that Shavon set the alarm clock once and then he set it again. He **reset** the clock. Do any of you have an alarm clock that you have to reset each day?*" Ask someone who answers what time he or she reset the clock to. Finish by saying, "*Tell me one more time what **reset** means.*"

If students struggle with a lesson, use the same base words the next day; otherwise, select new ones. When students read words in text that have the prefix *re-* or other prefixes and suffixes taught, ask them to apply the rule and tell you what the word means and why. Select words comprised of base words and affixes that your students can already spell and add them to the spelling list. Your goal is teaching the prefix *re-* at the **Your Turn** level by the third or fourth day. At that point, you will start the lesson by first asking students what *re-* means and then asking them what a new word like *redo* means. Their independent accurate answers will let you know that they were ready for that reduced support.

Dividing Words into Syllables

If you are teaching advanced word reading using syllables, these tips will lead to more effective instruction:

1. Explicitly teach each syllabication rule before asking students to apply it. When you start teaching syllabication, have students put a dot or *v* under every vowel sound before dividing the word into syllables. Remember that vowel combinations such as *ai* count as one vowel sound. Careful use of My Turns, Togethers, and Your Turns will result in higher accuracy as you gradually reduce the scaffolds to your instruction.

2. During word-reading instruction, scallop under syllables rather than word parts. Either before or after students read the words, ask them what kind of syllables they will be reading.

3. When you have your students do phoneme–grapheme mapping described in the following spelling section, ask students to draw scallops under each syllable.

4. Give the students syllable sorts (e.g., "Put all closed syllables in one pile."), which you monitor so that you can provide immediate feedback for errors.

5. If students misread r-controlled syllables, syllables with VCe endings, or syllables with letter–sound combinations, go back a step and teach students to read the letter combinations or learn the associated rule first.

How Can I Teach Rule- and Pattern-Based Spelling and Morphographic Spelling

While the processes are similar, spelling is more difficult than reading (Ehri, 2005). Ehri explained:

> The reason is that more bits of information must be remembered for correct spelling than for correct reading. When a student remembers how to read a familiar word, he or she accesses essentially one bit of information from memory, an amalgam consisting of the word's spelling, pronunciation, and meaning. However, when the student remembers how to spell a familiar word, he or she must access several bits of information from memory consisting of individual letters in the proper order. (p. 27)

Spelling instruction that is systematic and explicit leads to what have been described as "exceptional" gains in reading and writing (Ehri, 2005). While we know less about effective spelling instruction than reading, research shows that certain ways of teaching spelling, while frequently used, are ineffective. Studies also provide guidelines for how to teach spelling more systematically and explicitly. Both types of teaching strategies are described in Table 4.11.

Table 4.12 presents one format for teaching exception spelling words developed by Kinder (1990). Students can learn to conduct practice sessions following this format to provide additional practice and motivation in peer practice sessions. Although students need to learn high frequency exception words, morphographic spelling, which teaches the meaning and spelling of prefixes, suffixes, root and base words, provides the foundation for spelling thousands of new words.

Spelling instruction should only include high utility rules that have few exceptions. We identified the following ten spelling rules most commonly taught in spelling programs used in our project schools:

1. Because words don't usually end in *v*, always add an *e* after a final *v* such as in *dove*.
2. When words end in *ack, eck, ick, ock,* and *uck*, /k/ is spelled *ck*.
3. When words end in /j/ as in *adge, edge, idge, odge,* and *udge*, /j/ is spelled *dge*.
4. When words end in *atch, etch, itch, otch,* or *utch*, /ch/ is spelled tch.
5. The floss rule: After a short vowel at the end of the word, a final *f, s,* or *l* is doubled.
6. Final e Rule: When a word ends in *e* and you add a morphograph that begins with a vowel letter, drop the *e*.
7. Doubling Rule: When a short word ends in CVC and the next morphograph begins with a vowel, double the final consonant.
8. Plural Variation Rule: When a word ends in a "hissing" sound (/s/, /z/, /x/, /ch/, /sh/), add an -*es* to form the plural.
9. Changing *y* to *i* rule: When a word ends in consonant and *y*, to make the plural change the *y* to *i* before adding -*es*. Variation of rule: When a word ends in consonant and *y*, change the *y* to *i* before adding -*ed,- es,- er,* or -*est*.
10. Changing *f* rule: For words that end with the /f/ sound, change the letter *f* to *ves* when spelling the plural form. You can always hear the sound /v/ in the plural.

The following format for the *y* to *i* rule for plurals can be used to teach any of these spelling rules. As with teaching structural analysis in reading, students often need weeks of practice applying the rule to new words with frequent review of previously learned rules and words.

Teaching the Changing *y* to *i* Rule for Plurals

Preskill: Teach your students to independently say the *y* rule: "*When a word ends in* **consonant** *and* **y,** *to make the plural change the* **y** *to* **i** *before you add* **es.** Until students

TABLE 4.11   Systematic, Explicit Spelling Instruction

Ineffective	Why It's Not Effective	Effective
Giving weekly tests of 20–25 words at the end of each week	Most students retain spelling words in long-term memory better if they learn to spell 15 or fewer words a week. Lists of words for students who struggle the most with spelling should be limited to between 6 and 12 words per week.	Select 15 or fewer words per week and review those words frequently. Give students who struggle the most with spelling 6–12 words per week.
Writing words many times	This practice does not ensure words are in long-term memory because students often do this aversive task robotically without thinking about the words.	Use word-study procedures that involve seeing, hearing, saying, and writing the spelling words. Students need immediate corrective feedback from someone when they misspell a word.
Randomly selecting spelling words from lists of high frequency words or choosing words from mistakes in students' work	Poor spellers do not naturally develop strategic skills in recognizing common rule-based and morphographic spelling patterns. They need explicit instruction in phonetically spelling words, recognizing patterns, and learning morphographs.	Use a well-designed scope and sequence and common examples for spelling. Spelling instruction should progress from phonetic spelling to rule-/pattern-based spelling to morphographic spelling. 84% of words have basically regular spellings with no more than one exception sound-spelling.
Teaching students too many rules for spelling	Students can't remember numerous rules, and there are frequent exceptions to many of them.	Teach the 10 rules shown on page 143 that apply to a large number of words.
Giving students words with multiple spellings of the same letter sound in the same lesson	If students study words in the same week with four different ways to spell one sound, they become confused, and this absence of any patterns leads to increased errors.	Introduce sound patterns sequentially, coordinated with the reading program.
Expecting everyone in the class to learn the same words	Since students' skills in spelling vary as widely as they do in reading, giving everyone the same spelling words will not meet the needs of many students in the class.	Assess spelling frequently and differentiate instruction as needed.
Spelling is not integrated with reading, vocabulary, and writing	Students need to fluently retrieve correct letter sequences from long-term memory when writing. Spelling is not just a visual memory task. Integration of the phonological, orthographic, meaning, and context processors will help students generalize spellings to their writing.	Students learn to spell the words they are learning to read. Word study including the meaning of morphographs is stressed during spelling instruction. Writing topics are designed to provide students with the opportunity to use words they have learned to spell in their writing.
Spelling instruction is conducted infrequently	Students need enough practice so the words they learn are not easily forgotten. As Hunter (2004) writes: "Don't just cover material. If you do, use a shovel, cover the material with dirt, and lay it to rest, for it will be dead as far as memory is concerned." (p. 129)	Daily practice in spelling with new spelling words practiced for several days is more effective. Students orally spell words as well as write words with the opportunity for immediate feedback for errors.
After the end of the week, words learned that week are rarely if ever reviewed	Cumulative review is an essential teaching strategy for struggling learners.	Every day, several words from past spelling lessons are reviewed and if students misspell then they are retaught.

Source: Adapted from Allal (1997); Dixon & Englemann (2007); Graham (1999); Hunter (2004); and O'Connor (2007).

TABLE 4.12   Spelling Exception Words

The teaching procedure for exception words involves repeated practice, both oral and written. In this format typically four to six words are learned at a time. Some students may be able to learn only three words at a time; higher performing students may be able to learn up to ten words with good retention.

ORAL EXERCISE

(Write on the board:)	enough	touch
	said	monk
	where	

(Teacher points to *enough* and asks students to read the word.)
WHAT WORD? (signal) "enough"
SPELL *ENOUGH* AS I POINT TO THE LETTERS, (signal) "e-n-o-u-g-h"
SPELL *ENOUGH*, (signal) "e-n-o-u-g-h"
ONCE MORE. SPELL *ENOUGH*, (signal) "e-n-o-u-g-h"
(Teacher erases enough.)
SPELL *ENOUGH*, (signal) Students visualize word and spell "e-n-o-u-g-h."

(Teacher points to *said*.)
WHAT WORD? (signal) "said"
SPELL *SAID* AS I POINT TO THE LETTERS, (signal) "s-a-i-d"
SPELL *SAID* (signal) "s-a-i-d" **ONCE MORE. SPELL *SAID*,**
(signal) "s-a-i-d" (Teacher erases said.)
SPELL *SAID*, (signal) Students visualize word and spell "s-a-i-d." (After each new word taught, the teacher always returns to the first word in the list and asks students to spell it and then all the other words that have been introduced during the lesson up until the new word. This extra practice with the new words is called part firming because students are firming up that part of the lesson to mastery.)
SPELL *ENOUGH*, (signal) Students visualize word and spell "e-n-o-u-g-h."
SPELL *SAID*, (signal) Students visualize word and spell "s-a-i-d."

Teacher goes to third word when the first two words are spelled correctly.

(Teacher points to *where*.)
WHAT WORD? (signal) "where"
SPELL *WHERE* AS I POINT TO THE LETTERS, (signal) "w-h-e-r-e"
SPELL *WHERE*, (signal) "w-h-e-r-e" **ONCE MORE. SPELL *WHERE*.**
(Signal) "w-h-e-r-e" (Teacher erases where.)
SPELL *WHERE*, (signal) Students visualize word and spell "w-h-e-r-e." (The teacher part firms and returns to the beginning of the list.) **NOW SPELL *ENOUGH*,** (signal) Students visualize word and spell "e-n-o-u-g-h."
SPELL *SAID*, (signal) Students visualize word and spell "s-a-i-d." **SPELL *WHERE*,** (signal) Students visualize word and spell "w-h-e-r-e."

The teacher repeats this sequence for the remaining words. She ends the lesson by dictating all the words to students. When dictating the words, she adds meaning by saying a clear sentence after saying the word. Two or three review words are always added to this part of the lesson. After students write the words, the teacher dictates a sentence that contains at least one of the new words.

Correction When students misspell a word, the teacher writes it on the board, and teaches it again before saying "Start over," and having students spell all the words on the list.

Source: Kinder, D. (1990). *Format for spelling irregular words.* Unpublished manuscript, Northern Illinois University.

can say the rule from memory, don't continue. Use several My Turn–Togethers until they can say the rule fluently. If students have difficulty memorizing the rule, have them clap it or say it rhythmically at first.

1. Write these words on the board. Every student should have a small whiteboard, marker, and eraser.

   cr<u>y</u> = cries

   cit<u>y</u> = cities

   candy = candies

   pry =

   try =

2. MY TURN: Explain to students that *cry* ends with a "**consonant** and **y**" (point to the letters as you talk); "*I change the **y** to **i** before adding **es** to make the plural. "Spell **cries** with me.*" (Students spell word)

   "*How do you make **cry** plural?*" (answer: "*Change the **y** to **i** before adding **es**.*") Ask students to spell *cries* orally. Ask them to write *cries* on their whiteboards without looking at the board. Walk around and monitor. (note: Depending on your group, you may need to do several My Turns the first day.)

3. MY TURN: Ask students if *city* ends in **consonant** and **y**." (Students answer "yes.") Point to the letters as you say, "*I change the **y** to **i** before adding **es** to make the plural. Spell **cities** with me.*" (Teacher and students spell *cities*.) "*What did you do to make the plural of city?*" (Students say the rule.) If students answer correctly, ask them to spell *cities* orally before writing it on their whiteboards. Correct any misspellings immediately.

4. TOGETHER: Ask students if *candy* ends in "**consonant** and **y**." (Students answer "yes.") Then ask, "*What do you do to make the plural of a word that ends in **consonant** and **y**?*" If students answer correctly and say, "*Change the **y** to **i** before adding **es**,* ask them to spell *candies* orally before writing it on their whiteboards. Correct any misspellings immediately. If students aren't accurate, increase support to the My Turn level.

5. If students are accurate with the last two words, tell them you will make it harder by listing two words, one that ends in consonant *y* and one that doesn't. (Write *horse* and *penny*. Don't move beyond the Together level at least on the first day and repeat the same steps as in #4.

6. Each day, gradually reduce scaffolding with the new words for that day until students can write the plurals for a list of words, some ending in consonant and *y* and some ending in *vowel* plus y, with 100% accuracy.

A detailed article synthesizing effective word study procedures for spelling can be found at: **http://www. thefreelibrary.com/LANGUAGE-BASED+SPELLING+INSTRUCTION:+ TEACHING+CHILDREN+TO+MAKE . . . a063652399.**

Phoneme–grapheme mapping first described in beginning reading in Chapter 3 can also be used to reinforce advanced word-reading skills. A student's mapping of the words *match, knee,* and *unite* is shown in Figure 4.3. Because the /ī/ in *unite* results from the silent *e* at the end of the syllable (or if you are teaching word parts, because of the VCV pattern), a line is drawn to show the connection. The letter *e* is silent and thus is graphed in the same box as the /t/. As students learn to

m	a	tch			
kn	e̅e̅				
ū	n	ī	te		

FIGURE 4.3 Phoneme–Grapheme Mapping

map letter sounds, rule-based patterns, and syllables, they develop **metacognitive skills,** a term for the awareness of one's thought processes in thinking about how to spell advanced words (Grace, 2007).

Applying the Teaching Enhancements to a Commercial Reading Program

In this four-part activity from a general education curriculum, students are introduced to reading VCe words involving the vowels *a, o,* and *i.* Read it carefully and consider whether you would use it without modification—and why or why not.

1. Hold up a Big Book, displaying the text as you read the rhyme. Ask the students to listen for words that have the /ă/ sound as in *Sam,* and the /ā/ sound as in *name.* Repeat the process for words with long and short *i* and *o.*
2. Give letter cards to the students, read a series of words, and have students tape their letter cards to the board, spelling out the words.

   at-ate; tap-tape; cap-cape; dim-dime; kit-kite; hid-hide; not-note; rod-rode; hop-hope.

3. Ask students to read the following words and phrases.

dive	bat	home	big
came	bit	rim	gave
stop	can	make	hand

Rob's robe	Tim has time.
Smile and grin	Dave and Meg rode bikes.
Can of canes	Ken gave his mom a gift.

Analysis of Activity   The transition from long to short vowels is a difficult one for students who are at risk. First-grade teachers in Project PRIDE had to work extra hard each year helping students acquire this skill. Unfortunately, the instruction provided in Parts 1–3 is unlikely to prepare students to read the words, phrases, and sentences in Part 4. Even students in Tier 1 are likely to be confused by this lesson. Part of the problem is that expecting students to complete Part 4 successfully is too big of a goal, considering that this is the first day that the VCV rule is introduced. A more realistic goal would be to have the students apply the rule to word lists first. Only after they were successful on the word lists would the teacher move on to phrases and sentences. Students who are at risk may need several days of list practice before they are ready for the phrases and sentences.

Another major problem with this lesson is that the instruction isn't explicit enough. Although the teacher points out VCe and CVC patterns, she never demonstrates with a My Turn to show how the silent *e* rule is applied to reading words, nor are the students guided by the teacher as they apply the rule using a series of Togethers. This lesson could be easily adapted for your students who are at risk by using the format in Table 4.8.

The three-part lesson also is inefficient. If the purpose of Part 1 is to help students discriminate between long and short vowels, this skill could be taught more directly using the vowel-consonant-vowel teaching format shown in Table 4.8. In Part 2, the use of letter cards with individual students coming to the board to make words takes a lot of time and is difficult to manage. A more efficient approach would be to have students read word pairs on the board using a unison-response format. In addition, the word list in Part 2 is too predictable; the short vowel word in the word pairs always comes first, allowing students to guess the correct vowel sound without having to apply the rule.

In Your Classroom

Enhancers for Advanced Word Reading

1. Effective teaching of reading multisyllable words is enhanced by ongoing vocabulary instruction like Mrs. Gibbs's weekly "$100 words." Every Monday, Mrs. Gibbs selects a challenging multisyllable word related to positive character development. First she writes the word on the board and shows students how to decode it before giving them practice reading the new word. Mrs. Gibbs tells students what the word means before using it in sample sentences. Some students then have the opportunity to use the word in an original sentence they compose on the spot. At least once during the week, Mrs. Gibbs makes sure that students spell the word and use it in their writing. Each morning starts out with reading and discussing that week's $100 word. When Mrs. Gibbs has an extra 2 or 3 minutes during the day, she asks everyone to read in unison all of the $100 words taught from the beginning of the year and displayed on the blackboard.

   Students are eager to learn these words, because if they find an opportunity to use them in context during the day, Mrs. Gibbs gives them a fake $100 bill that can be used toward items in the treasure chest that she bought during summer garage sales. Latecia was delighted when her *Reading Mastery* teacher reminded the group that they needed to read the story one more time until they met their goal. This gave Latecia the opportunity to respond, "So, you want us to be *tenacious.*" When her *Reading Mastery* teacher exclaimed about her use of such a big word, Latecia smiled and told her that it was one of their $100 words. When Latecia returned to the room, her *Reading Mastery* teacher told Mrs. Gibbs about Latecia's use of *tenacious* so she could get her bill. Throughout the year, students learned to read and understand words like *cooperation, diligence,* and *compassion.*

2. In the afternoon, Mr. Szymck teaches a thematic unit, integrating science and social studies. He finds that during his unit, he has the opportunity to provide his students with extra review reading letter combinations that they have learned in reading. When he previews his lesson plans, he looks for any words that have patterns that his students have learned. At the start of the activity he has them read those new science words. During his unit on "Spring as a Time of Growth," he wrote the words *puddles* and *raindrops* on the board and asked students to read them. When the unit moved from the topic of water to trees, he selected the following words: *treetop, maple,* and *branches.*

Sometimes it is unclear to teachers how advanced reading fits within a daily reading lesson. Students who are learning advanced word reading also need fluency instruction to increase their reading speed. Chapter 5 will explain how a typical classroom day looks when advanced word reading and fluency are the critical skills. More suggestions for enhancing advanced word reading are in the feature, *In Your Classroom.*

What Can I Do for Students Who Are Not Developing Advanced Word-Reading Skills Even with Tier 2 Support?

Descriptions about how each tier can meet the needs of individual students as well as decision-making rules for any tier changes are detailed in Chapter 5. Table 4.13 depicts how advanced word-reading skills are taught in each of the five intensive, alternative Tier 3 programs described in previous chapters.

TABLE 4.13   Comparison of Five Common Tier 3 Approaches

	Direct Instruction: Reading Mastery	**Lindamood® LiPS**	**Reading Recovery**	**Wilson Reading System**	**Language!**
Does curriculum introduce advanced word-reading skills, explicitly, first presenting letter combinations, affixes, or syllables in isolation and then in words?	Yes	Yes	No	Yes. In addition Wilson has recently added a program *Wilson Just Words* for students in grades 4–12, which emphasizes word study in reading and spelling.	Yes
Does curriculum explicitly teach students to read multisyllable words by using prefixes, suffixes, and known word parts?	Yes	Emphasis is on syllables.	No	Emphasis is on syllables.	Emphasis is on syllables.
Does curriculum explicitly teach students to read multisyllable words by first teaching syllable rules and then providing practice applying them?	Emphasis is on morphemes/logical word parts.	Yes	No	Yes	Yes
Is connected text that contains advanced words students have learned part of the curriculum?	Yes	No, but it is encouraged.	No	Yes	Yes
Does curriculum incorporate spelling to reinforce word analysis? After students can read words, do they write the words?	Yes	Yes	Sometimes this occurs.	Yes, they are taught together, simultaneously.	Yes
Are decodable words that appear frequently in grade-appropriate reading text emphasized?	Yes	Both real and nonsense words/word parts are used.	No	Both real and nonsense words are used.	Yes
Are exception words pretaught before appearing in connected text?	Yes	Not a part of the LiPS program, but teachers are encouraged to do this.	No	Yes	Yes
Does daily instruction include a review of decodable and sight words recently learned?	Yes	This is up to teacher's discretion.	No	Yes	Word forms and phoneme-grapheme relationships taught are reviewed, but not the exact words previously taught.

How Can I Teach Advanced Word-Reading Skills to English Language Learners?

Since the regular past-tense ending -ed can be pronounced as a syllable (/ed/), as /t/, or as /d/, English language learners usually have difficulty determining what to say. If none of your strategies for teaching -ed has worked, try helping students learn and apply the following rules (Avery & Ehrlich, 1992, p. 48). Your students will need a chart listing all of the unvoiced sounds.

A.   If a verb ends with /t/ or /d/, the past tense is pronounced /ed/. An example is *wanted.*
B.   If a verb ends with a voiced sound, the past tense is pronounced /d/. An example is *bagged.*
C.   If a verb ends with an unvoiced sound, the past tense is pronounced /t/. An example is *baked.*

If you have a few minutes at the end of the day, the **Yesterday game** provides extra practice using past-tense verbs. Write two sets of regular verbs on large cardboard cards: (*bake, bunt, hang, ski, arrive, ask, cross,* and *invent*). Once you have taught students irregular verbs, you can also add those words to the list. Divide your class in half and explain that everyone will be going back in time to yesterday. Assign a card holder for each team and ask that student to sit on a chair in front of her team and hold up one card for each person. You will need to monitor both teams and award points on a clipboard, so stand in the middle. Since everyone is symbolically going back in time, when you say "Start," one person from each team walks backwards to the card holder. Once that person arrives at the card holder, she has to turn around and say a sentence that begins with "*Yesterday, I…*" If the card holder is displaying the word *bake,* the student might say, "*Yesterday, I **baked** a cake.*" When you hear the correct past-tense word used in a sentence, give a point to that team. The person then runs forward and taps another team member, and the game continues. The rules are that everyone gets a turn, and that running or walking backwards in a silly or dangerous manner forfeits one point for the team. Keep track of words that students miss so you can review them later.

> Internet resources for teachers working with English language learners are listed at this website. Links are provided to journal articles and Internet resources: **www.iteachilearn.com/uh/ guadarrama/sociopsycho/paper. htm#research%20journals.**

How Important Are Advanced Word-Reading Skills for Older Learners?

Most older learners who struggle with reading are challenged by multisyllable words. Only through explicit instruction will they acquire and learn to apply the word-analysis skills of recognizing and understanding morphemes, prefixes, and suffixes. Without word-analysis knowledge, reading more difficult text becomes increasingly frustrating. Struggling older readers often guess at words from the first sound, a difficult habit to break. The reading level of text becomes a critical issue for older learners who often have developed anxiety and avoidance toward all text because of a history of frustrating and embarrassing experiences. In addition to the difficulty of words, teachers should also consider simplicity of sentence structure and number of clauses, lengths of sentences and paragraphs, and whether the story or book includes subheadings that organize the information. Some teachers find that carefully selected newspaper and magazine articles with an easier reading level are useful age-appropriate reading materials. With such uncontrolled text, the burden is on the teacher to make sure that the text is not at a frustration level for the student. Other teachers

Resources for older struggling readers are found at: **www.balancedreading. com/Feldman.pdf.**

select decodable chapter books that are written for older students. The older learner has expended hours of energy trying to hide reading difficulties from peers and teachers and most likely will reject books that are perceived as "babyish." Although the text is at an easier level, none of the decodable books designed for older learners looks like the picture books or books with large fonts that are written for younger students. Table 4.14 summarizes instructional needs for older learners in a multi-tier or RTI model depending on their reading level.

TABLE 4.14 Three-Tier Instructional Plan

Secondary Level 8–12	Tier 1: Grade Level English/Language Arts	Tier 1: Grade Level Content Courses	Tier 2: Strategic Instruction	Tier 3: Intensive Intervention
Learners	All students	All students	Students who need additional structured support and are between a 3rd and 7th grade reading level	Students, who have marked difficulties learning to read and are reading at lower than a 3rd grade level
Instructional Leader	Classroom/core teacher	Content teacher	Specialized reading teacher or specifically trained classroom teacher	Specialized reading teacher or special education teacher
Time Allocation	One instructional period	Scheduled content-area classes	60 minutes daily strategic reading and spelling instruction to support skills taught in core classes	Alternative, intensive, research-based reading and spelling intervention for 90–120 minutes daily
Instructional Components	Fluency, vocabulary (including work on word/root origins), background knowledge, and comprehension. Scaffolding for Tier 2 and Tier 3 students through use of graphic organizers, books on tape, assistive technology, etc.	Focus on content vocabulary and comprehension skills needed for reading expository text. Scaffolding for Tier 2 and Tier 3 students through use of graphic organizers, books on tape, AT, etc.	Advanced word reading skills/spelling, structural analysis, comprehension/ fluency and reading text at instructional level. Curriculum such as *REWARDS*, *REWARDS +Science*, *REWARDS + Social Studies*, *Morphographic Spelling*, or fluency programs like *Read Naturally.*	Intensive word recognition (sound/ symbol, decoding regular words, common irregular words), fluency building, spelling, reading text at instructional level. Curriculum recommended: *Wilson, Corrective Reading, Morphographic Spelling*, or *Language!*
Grouping Structure	Flexible: whole group, small group, partners	Flexible: whole group, small group, partners	Flexible homogeneous group of not more than 6 students.	Flexible homogeneous groups of 3 or fewer students

Source: Adapted from Feldman (1999); Geiger, Banks, Hasbrouck, & Ebbers (2005); Roberts, Torgesen, Boardman, & Scammacca (2008).

Technology

Advanced Word-Reading Skills

In his fifth-grade classroom, Mr. Benvenuti had a student, Maia, who was identified as having learning disabilities. Although Maia continued to receive daily systematic phonics instruction, she had not yet caught up to her peers. One of the recommendations on Maia's IEP indicated that with an **assistive technology** accommodation, Maia could independently read textbooks above her reading level. Mr. Benvenuti knew that assistive technology includes a wide variety of technology applications designed to help students with disabilities learn, communicate, enjoy recreation, and otherwise function more independently by bypassing their disabilities, but he was not aware of any technology other than taped readings that would help in this situation.

When the special education teacher told Mr. Benvenuti that she was going to try having Maia use a QuickLink Reading Pen in class and at home, Mr. Benvenuti decided to learn more about the device. He knew that few scientifically based research studies have been done investigating whether technology devices and applications improve reading. Maia's special education teacher had explained that the QuickLink wouldn't explicitly teach Maia to read more difficult words, but it should help her function more independently in content-area classes.

Mr. Benvenuti learned that the pen, powered by two AA batteries, is a portable assistive device that the student runs over words just like a highlighter to scan either a word or line of text. The pen then reads the text aloud or converts it to text in Windows. In addition, the pen can display the syllables of a scanned word and display the dictionary definitions of the word on its small screen. Mr. Benvenuti was relieved to hear that headphones could be used so that only Maia would hear the speech. As he read the descriptions, Mr. Benvenuti listed the positive and negative aspects of the pen:

Positive Aspects to the Reading Pen
1. Great accuracy with little practice.
2. No need to press a button while scanning.
3. Comes with extensive software and built-in tools.
4. The pen can be adapted for either right-handed or left-handed individuals.

Negative Aspects to the Reading Pen
1. Cumbersome interface.
2. Editing text can be frustrating.
3. Reading different fonts can pose problems.

After looking at his list, Mr. Benvenuti decided that trying this assistive technology accommodation was a reasonable option when Maia was able to read material independently with 90% accuracy or better. His biggest concern was whether operating the pen would be frustrating or slow her reading down so much that comprehension was negatively affected.

Assistive-technology strategies for older students who do not yet have the advanced word-reading skills needed to read textbooks in social studies and science are highlighted in the *Technology* section.

What Games and Activities Will Reinforce Students' Advanced Word-Reading Skills?

Here are two games that can be adapted to a wide range of topics. The first game uses a science topic, but you can modify it to fit your curriculum.

Word Race

After students have learned to decode six difficult words from a reading selection describing ocean pollution and they accurately but slowly read them in the science story, use those words for a drill game so students get practice reading them at faster rates. Construct a table on your word-processing program with five rows and six columns. Type each of the six words into a box in every row, placing each one in a different column. Divide your students into pairs and give each pair a word-table sheet and an inexpensive sand timer that can be flipped for a 1-minute timing. When you say "Go," one student in each pair will flip the timer; the other student will begin reading all of the words starting in the upper left corner. If a student misreads a word, his partner will ask him to sound out the word and then he'll try again until he reads all of the words in less than a minute.

Short or Long Sort

When you are working with a small group, the Short or Long Sort provides extra practice for students who have learned a new long-vowel pattern. Make several sets of word cards with words containing short a and long a sounds and put each into an activity box. Select words similar to these:

rack	date	tank	play	grant
game	slap	pace	hail	safe

First, have students sort words into /ă/ or /ā/ piles. After students have sorted the cards, they should write each word in the correct column on the paper. Since you will not be able to monitor errors, select words that students can read with at least 95% accuracy. The *In Your Classroom* feature describes other motivational strategies that you can add to the Teacher–Class game.

In Your Classroom

Extending the Teacher–Class Game

Depending on the age and maturity level of your students, you can use your creativity to spice up the Teacher–Class Game and further increase the motivation level of your students. Your reading instruction will be more effective when paired with a system to encourage on-task behaviors. Research informs us that struggling readers in first grade are more likely in third grade to have poor self-control, off-task behaviors, and both externalizing and internalizing behavior problems (Morgan, Farkas, Tufis, & Sperling, 2008).

Younger Students

One of the simplest adaptations to the Teacher–Class Game is the use of a *Good Work Week* award sheet (see Figure 4.4). Every day that students win the game, the teacher puts a sticker or stamped mark next to that day of the week on their chart. On Friday, students who earned all five stickers receive a special reward or activity, which might be a selection of a prize box item, a special activity during the last twenty minutes of class on Friday, a note home to parents telling about the students' hard work, or the opportunity for the class

Good Work Week

Name: _____

Monday

Tuesday

Wednesday

Thursday

Friday

FIGURE 4.4 Good Work Week Award Sheet

Continued

FIGURE 4.5 Climb the Mountain to the Castle Game

to read a section of the latest story, which is videotaped for viewing immediately afterwards.

Another adaptation for younger students is called the *Climb the Mountain to the Castle* game (Figure 4.5). Before starting the game, the teacher needs between 15 and 20 large cutouts that can be taped to the wall along with colorful construction-paper circles with large numbers printed on them (numbers 10–20–30, etc.). Cutouts needed for this motivation game include a castle, fairy tale characters (some menacing and some friendly), and an interesting animal character for each team or row of students. The castle is taped at the top of the classroom wall just below the ceiling, and the numbered circles are taped up the side of the wall, creating a path from

the floor to the castle. The animal figures, which represent the student teams, all start on the beginning circle, 0. Fairy tale images are taped along the path to create interest: *"Team 4 is about to go past the spooky forest. I hope they earn enough points to go right past it without stopping."* As the teams earn points, their animals advance up the path toward the castle. When all of the teams reach the castle, the teacher gives everyone a reward or conducts a fun activity.

At the end of each class, the teacher subtracts the number of points she earned from the points earned by each of the teams. That number is added to the cumulative total and the team animal advances the number of points earned that day. The classroom wall should look like Figure 4.5. The teacher can use this game with any theme. Students can scuba dive past sharks and jellyfish to reach a treasure chest, or they can be mountain climbers attempting to climb the path going to the top of Mt. Everest.

Older Students

Teachers can combine reading and math by having students earn play money in a simulated banking experience. When students win the Teacher–Class Game, they earn play money that later can be exchanged for privileges or items. Students can collect the play money or keep track of their totals in a bankbook. Older students enjoy earning the privilege to omit one homework assignment, or earn a few minutes of extra chat time with friends. Other motivators include "work and eat" days, the opportunity to help younger students, and the opportunity to work to music. A variation on the Climb the Mountain to the Castle game for older students is creating a simulated *Carmen Sandiego* game. Display a world map with an adventure trail across the continents. Students can earn points to travel past geographical barriers such as the raging Amazon River or Mt. Everest. For more of a political science focus, students can move past political hotspots around the world until they reach their destination. Clues to their secret mission are taped to different countries that they pass, and intermittently spaced *hot* cards tell them to move back a few spaces. The final destination spot card should inform students of the surprise they have been working for.

APPLIED ACTIVITIES

1. Answer this fact-or-fiction question about advanced word reading using references from research sources cited in the chapter or from information on the website resources listed in the sidebars.
   - Phonics instruction is no longer necessary when students who are at risk have learned all of the single-letter sounds and can fluently decode one-syllable words. Is this fact or fiction? Explain why.

2. In the list of words below, underline all of the prefixes and circle the suffixes.

boyish	watering	displeased
prejudge	undesirable	writer
mistreatment	government	gently

3. Divide the following words into their morphemes. Circle all affixes.

government	deregulated	wonderful
disagreement	rewritten	reshaped

4. You wonder if your students are ready for a story about a little boy who goes to Atlantic City. Although they have learned all of the single-letter sounds, they still do not know all of the letter combinations. Your first step in analyzing whether they are ready to read this story is to identify all of the letter combinations and affixes. Underline all of the letter combinations in the following sentences and circle the affixes. As some letter clusters can be an affix in one word and a combination in another, be sure that all clusters identified as affixes directly affect the meaning of the word. For example, *er* in *her* is a letter combination because it doesn't affect the meaning of the word; however, *er* in *faster* does affect the meaning of the base word *fast* and thus is an affix.

   > Shawn looked up at the stars and wished he had fudge to eat. Whenever he went to the beach with his mom and dad, Shawn liked to get fudge. Shawn looked at his mom and said, "I am thinking about fudge now. You might think I want to play, but all I want is fudge. I do not want to go on the boat right now. A sailor needs fudge. Please go and bring me some fudge that will be chewy and hard to eat."

5. Two multisyllable words that your students will encounter in their next story are *carelessly* and *sodium*. Identify which of these words would be more difficult for students to learn. Explain your answer.

6. Map the phonemes in each of the following words. The first one is completed for you:

glade	g	l	ā	d				
bread								
grander								
bounty								
splashed								
gladden								
retake								
shoulder								
knight								
battle								
judged								
grassier								

7. Ms. Wilson gave her three Tier 2 students the test of affixes and letter combinations just described. Their results are as follows.

Sounds Known:
ed, s, dge, er, ch, oo, oa, ou, ow, ay, or

Sounds Unknown:
aw, ar, sh, wh, ea, th, ing, igh, ai, ee, y, ew

Using the passage in Applied Activity 3, identify which words containing letter combinations and/or affixes that Ms. Wilson's Tier 2 students will not be able to decode.

8. The purpose of the following lesson from a commercial reading program is to teach the affixes *-ful, -ly,* and *-ness.* Identify how this lesson may be problematic for students who are at risk. Describe how you would enhance the lesson to increase the likelihood of student success.

Lesson: Theme 5–Selection 4: Day 5

- Read a big book to the class. When you come to the word *beautiful,* show students the word and explain that when they come to a larger word that looks new, they can try looking for a base word they know and see if an ending has been added to it.
- Display a transparency that defines a suffix as "one kind of word ending that adds meaning to the base word." The transparency includes three examples broken into parts that are listed in columns. Read each example for the students.

Base Word	+ Suffix =	New Word
joy	ful	joyful (full of joy)
neat	ly	neatly (in a way that is neat)
sad	ness	sadness (being sad)

- Introduce a story about a boy who brings his pet mouse to school. In this story, three words are related to the examples above: *fearful, softly,* and *darkness.* When you come to these words, ask the students to identify the base word, the suffix, the new word, and its meaning.

9. New words in Tuesday's reading lesson include:

sighed	flights	brighter	frightened
salesman	watchman	amazing	admiring
topple	shoppers	mattress	button

Demonstrate how you would teach these new words using the format in Table 4.9.

10. Ms. Carrier has just introduced to her students the *ou* letter combination in isolation. For the first day of word reading with *ou,* she selected the following words as examples: *sound, cloud, our, through, proud,* and *though.* Critique Ms. Carrier's choice of examples.

REFERENCES

Allal, L. (1997) Learning to spell in the classroom. In C. Perfetti, L. Rieben, & M. Fayol (Eds.), *Learning to spell: Research, theory, and practice.* Mahwah, NJ: Lawrence Erlbaum (pp. 129–150).

Archer, A. L., Gleason, M. M., & Vachon, V. L. (2003). Decoding and fluency: Foundation skills for struggling older readers. *Learning Disability Quarterly, 26,* 89–101.

Avery, P., & Ehrlich, S. (1992). *Teaching American English pronunciation.* New York: Oxford Press, p. 48.

Bhattacharya, A. (2006). Syllable-Based Reading Strategy for Mastery of Scientific Information. *Remedial Special Education, 27*(2), 116–123.

Carnine, D. W., Silbert, J., Kame'enui, E. J., & Tarver, S. (2010). *Direct instruction reading* (5th ed.). Boston: Merrill.

Celce-Murcia, M., Brinton, D., Goodwin, J. M., & Goodwin, J. (1996). *Teaching pronunciation: A reference for teachers of English to speakers of other languages.* New York: Cambridge University Press.

Dixon, R., & Engelmann, S. (2007). *Spelling mastery.* Desoto, TX: SRA/McGraw-Hill.

Egger-Bovet, H., & Smith-Baranzini, M. (1994). *USKids history: Book of the American Revolution* (p. 11). New York: Little Brown & Company.

Ehri, L. (1989). The development of spelling knowledge and its role in reading acquisition and reading disability. *Journal of Learning Disabilities, 22,* 356–365.

Ehri, L. (2005). Learning to read words: Theory, findings, and issues. *Scientific Studies of Reading, 9*(2), 167–188.

Engelmann, S., Carnine, L., Johnson, G., Meyer, L., Becker, W., & Eisele, J. (1999). *Corrective reading: Decoding.* Columbus, OH: SRA/McGraw Hill.

Feldman, K (1999) The California Reading Initiative and special education in California developed by the Special Education Reading Task Force. Retrieved on April 3, 2009, from http://www.calstat.org/publications/pdfs/ca_reading_initiative.pdf

Fischer, P. (1993). *The sounds and spelling patterns of English: Phonics for teachers and parents.* Farmington, ME: Oxton House

Geiger, S., Banks, A., Hasbrouck, J., & Ebbers, S. (2005). Washington State K-12 Reading Model Implementation Guide. Olympia, WA: Office of Superintendent of Public Instruction. Retrieved from http://www.k12.wa.us/Curriculuminstruct/reading/pubdocs/K-12ReadingModelFINAL6105.pdf

Good, R. H., Gruba, J., & Kaminski, R. A. (2002). Best practices in using dynamic indicators of basic emerging literacy skills (DIBELS) in an outcomes-driven model. In A. Thomas & J. Grimes (Eds.), *Best practices in school psychology IV* (pp. 699–720). Bethesda, MD: National Association of School Psychologists.

Grace, K. (2007). *Phonics and spelling through phoneme-grapheme mapping.* Longmont, CO: Sopris West.

Graham, S. (1999). Handwriting and spelling instruction for students with learning disabilities: A review, *Learning Disability Quarterly, 22*, 78–98.

Greene, J. F. (2004). *Language! A literacy intervention curriculum.* Longmont, CO: Sopris West Educational Services.

Hanna, P., Hanna, J., Hodges, R., & Rudloff, E. (1966). *Phoneme-grapheme correspondences as cues to spelling improvement.* Washington, DC: U.S. Government Printing Office.

Hunter, R. (2004) *Madeline Hunter's Mastery Teaching: Increasing instructional effectiveness in elementary and secondary schools.* Thousand Oaks, CA: Corwin Press.

Johnston, F. (2001) The utility of phonic generalizations: Let's take another look at Clymer's conclusions. *The Reading Teacher, 55*(2), 132–142.

Kinder, D. (1990). *Format for spelling irregular words.* Unpublished manuscript, Northern Illinois University.

Linan-Thompson, S., & Vaughn, S. (2007). *Research-based methods of reading instruction for English language learners, grades K-4.* Alexandria, VA: ASCD.

Moats, L. (2001). When older students can't read. *Educational Leadership, 58*(6), 36–40.

Moats, L. (2007). *Whole-language high jinks: How to tell when "scientifically based reading instruction" isn't.* Washington, DC: Fordham Foundation.

Morgan, P., Farkas, G., Tufis, P., & Sperling, R. (2008). Are reading and behavior problems risk factors for each other? *Journal of Learning Disabilities, 41*(5), 417–436.

Nagy, W., Winsor, P., Osborn, J., & O'Flahavan, J. (1993). Structural analysis: Guidelines for instruction. In F. Lehr & J. Osborn (Eds.), *Reading, language, and literacy: Instruction for the twenty-first century* (pp. 45–58). Hillsdale, NJ: Erlbaum.

O'Connor, R. (2007). *Teaching word recognition: Effective strategies for students with learning difficulties.* New York: The Guilford Press.

Rathvon, N. (2004). *Early reading assessment: A practitioner's handbook.* New York: The Guilford Press.

Roberts, G., Torgesen, J., Boardman, A., & Scammacca, N. (2008). Evidence-based strategies for reading instruction of older students with learning disabilities. *Learning Disabilities Research & Practice, 23*(2), 63–69.

Vadasy, P., Sanders, E., & Peyton, J. (2006). Paraeducator-supplemented instruction in structural analysis with text reading practice for second and third graders at risk for reading problems. *Remedial and Special Education, 27*(6), 365–378.

Wilson, B. (1996). *Wilson reading system.* Millbury, MA: Wilson Language Training.

Wilson, B., & Felton, R. (2004). *Word Identification and Spelling Test (WIST).* Austin, TX: PRO-ED.

5 Reading Fluency

Objectives

After reading this chapter, you will be able to:

1. Use oral reading fluency assessment data in a multi-tier or RTI model to screen students at risk, diagnose their skill needs, place them into curricular materials, and monitor and chart their reading progress.

2. Implement the SAFER (Successful, Anxiety-Free, Engaged Reading) strategy for conducting group oral passage reading sessions.

3. Implement strategies for building student reading fluency using repeated readings and other research-based methods.

4. Implement strategies for working with older readers with fluency problems and teaching expressive reading skills to English language learners.

5. Describe the main components of a Tier 1 and Tier 2 reading lesson.

6. Identify and describe the approaches to teaching fluency of four commonly used Tier 3 programs.

7. Use games and activities to reinforce students' fluency skills.

Mr. Rundall had taught third grade for ten years. Every summer when the state returned test score results, he was disappointed that more students in his class did not meet the state standards. He was teaching the advanced phonics strategies suggested by the school literacy coach, but his students' scores hadn't improved. After attending a summer inservice on teaching fluency, Mr. Rundall realized that he was not teaching this skill explicitly. The workshop leader stressed that if teachers used the suggestions from the workshop to increase fluency, students' comprehension would also improve. That made sense. How can students think about the meaning of what they are reading when they are spending so much time trying to decipher the larger words?

At the start of the school year Mr. Rundall was determined to use the new fluency building strategies he learned at the summer workshop. He knew finding enough time would be a problem; the school expected him to cover so much content in so many areas! His oral reading fluency screening assessments in the fall showed that almost half the scores for his class were unacceptably low, falling under the 50th percentile on the AIMSweb Oral Reading Fluency assessment. Mr. Rundall was able to set aside a 20-minute block of time after lunch three days per week for fluency building, but he realized there wouldn't be nearly enough time to get to each and every student, even in three days. He remembered a 15-minute paired-practice repeated reading strategy that the workshop leader had suggested that allowed all the students to practice at the same time. So Mr. Rundall paired his students, organized the materials needed for tutoring, and carefully trained his students to do the tutoring. He always monitored his students' tutoring so they performed their tutoring roles effectively. He noticed that the students enjoyed tutoring each other and were excited to see their reading rates increase on the charts they completed each day. Mr. Rundall also began to see a corresponding increase in his students' reading rates on their bimonthly progress monitoring. At the end of the year, he was overjoyed when the number of students meeting standards on the state test finally increased.

Why do you think Mr. Rundall hadn't done fluency building with his students before?

Why do you think Mr. Rundall's students' scores on the state test improved?

This vignette shows that as with phonemic awareness and word reading, gains in reading fluency for students who are at risk are not likely to occur naturally. According to recent results on the National Assessment of Educational Progress (NAEP), 44% of a representative sample of the nation's fourth graders were low in fluency (Lee, Grigg, & Donahue, 2007). Until Mr. Rundall started explicitly teaching his students to become more fluent readers, many did not develop this skill. In order to meet grade-level benchmarks, students must increase their fluency levels from 40 to 60 words correct per minute in Grade 1 to 90 wcpm by the end of Grade 2, and to 110 wcpm by the end of Grade 3. By the end of sixth grade students should reach the important milestone of reading 150 wcpm, described as the point when reading instruction shifts from "learning to read" to "reading to learn" (Good, Simmons, Kame'enui, & Wallin, 2002; Hasbrouck & Tindal, 2006). Students who are at risk need systematic, explicit teaching if they are to make this progress and move beyond beginning reading accuracy to become fluent, accurate readers.

What Is Reading Fluency, and Why Do I Need to Teach It?

In May, Ms. Dornbush had two of her second-grade students, Darrell and Damon, read out loud from a Grade 2 passage. When Ms. Dornbush recorded the percent accuracy for the two boys, she found that both of them read the passage with 94% accuracy. Ms. Dornbush was surprised at these results because she had thought Darrell was a better reader than Damon. Darrell read more words, and his good expression indicated that he understood what he was reading. Damon, on the other hand, read haltingly, sounding out some of the words as he read. His reading lacked appropriate phrasing, he frequently failed to stop at periods, and he read with little expression overall. Ms. Dornbush wondered, "How could two students who read so differently both score the same on a sample of their oral reading?"

The answer is that Ms. Dornbush's measures failed to take **fluency** into account. On a subsequent assessment, Ms. Dornbush recorded the number of words the boys read correctly per minute, a measure of their accuracy and fluency. This time the results revealed the differences between their reading levels. Darrell read the Grade 2 passage at a rate of 94 words correct per minute and made six errors. Damon read 68 wcpm and made four errors. Again, both read at 94% accuracy, but this time the results showed that there were major differences in fluency between the two boys. Darrell's rate exceeded the benchmark of 90 wcpm for the end of Grade 2. This score indicated that Darrell is likely to have fewer problems reading fluently and comprehending Grade 3 material. Damon's lower rate indicated he is likely to have problems in Grade 3 unless he builds his reading fluency. By initially failing to take fluency into account, Ms. Dornbush left out a key piece of assessment information, without which program planning and progress monitoring would have been difficult.

Reading fluency is the ability to read text accurately, quickly, and with expression. All three of these elements—accuracy, speed, and expression—are essential so that students can apply their fluency skills during silent reading and comprehend the text (Pikulski & Chard, 2005). In the example just described, Damon was reasonably accurate in his reading but had to focus so intently on decoding the words that he had little energy left to think about and understand what he was reading. Darrell, on the other hand, read with accuracy, speed, and expression. When reading, he could devote most of his attention, working memory, and cognition to making connections among the ideas in the text as well as between those ideas and his background knowledge. As a result, Darrell was much more likely than Damon to understand what he was reading. Chard, Ketterlin-Geller, Baker, Doabler, and Apichatabutra (2009) summarized the issue:

> If attention is consumed by decoding words, little or no capacity is available for the attention-demanding process of comprehending. Therefore, automaticity of decoding—a critical component of fluency—is essential for high levels of reading achievement. (p. 264)

Fluency becomes increasingly important as students move through the grades. As students get older, they are expected to read greater amounts of more difficult material in less time. Students who read slowly, regardless of accuracy, have little chance of keeping up with their peers. They are also less likely to practice their reading, choosing other ways to spend their time such as watching television and being with friends (Archer, Gleason, & Vachon, 2003). This lack of practice further widens the academic gulf between slow readers and their more fluent classmates in a "rich-get-richer" scenario (Stanovich, 1986).

Although fluency as discussed in this chapter involves reading connected text, fluency involves many more skills and processes with comprehension as the ultimate goal. Therefore, the approach to building fluency must be broad-based, encompassing activities to strengthen students' capacity to process information accurately and efficiently, not just at the orthographic and phonological levels, but at the contextual and meaning-based levels as well (Adams, 1990). While the theme of this chapter is building fluency, the teaching strategies described in all the other chapters directly relate to building fluency as well. Not until students attain levels of automaticity in these more foundational skills can they read connected text fluently and with understanding.

How Do I Assess Students' Reading Fluency in a Multi-Tier or RTI Model?

The ability to read passages accurately, fluently, and expressively requires that the reader engage in a number of complex processes at the same time. The reader must translate letters into sounds, blend sounds into meaningful words, access words without thinking, make meaningful connections within and between sentences, relate text meaning to prior knowledge, and make inferences to supply missing information (Fuchs, Fuchs, Hosp, & Jenkins, 2001). The beauty of oral reading fluency assessments is that in minutes the teacher is given a quick snapshot of the extent to which all of these processes are working in concert. It is not surprising that students who are able to read accurately and fluently are also likely to understand what they read (Fuchs et al., 2001; Fuchs, Fuchs, & Maxwell, 1988). Since oral reading fluency develops gradually over the school years, student scores on oral reading fluency assessments over time provide teachers with a measure that can be used for screening, diagnostic, and progress-monitoring purposes. The measures of oral reading fluency described here are DIBELS Oral Reading Fluency (DORF), AIMSweb, TPRI, and PALS. These oral reading fluency instruments are based on measures originally developed by Deno (1985).

> Visit the official DIBELS website and view a teacher giving an oral reading fluency assessment to students. Directions to administer and score the test are available at the same website, as are copies that can be downloaded at no charge. **http://reading.uoregon.edu/ video/ORFEstablishedReader.mov.**

Administering and Scoring Oral Reading Fluency Measures

Directions for administering and scoring the DIBELS Oral Reading Fluency assessment are shown in Figure 5.1. Directions for giving the AIMSweb and TPRI measures are similar. The teacher takes three 1-minute oral reading samples, using three passages at the student's grade level. The teacher places the passage in front of the student and begins timing as soon as the student reads the first word. As the student reads, the teacher puts a slash through any words that are read incorrectly or omitted. Self-corrections and the insertion of

---

Directions for Administering and Scoring the DIBELS Oral Reading Fluency Assessment

Oral Reading Fluency

Materials: Unnumbered copy of passage, numbered copy of passage, stopwatch, tape recorder[a] (optional)

Directions:

Place the unnumbered copy in front of the student.

Place the numbered copy in front of you but shielded so the student cannot see what you record.

Say these specific directions to the student for each passage: **"When I say 'begin,' start reading aloud at the top of this page. Read across the page."** (Demonstrate by pointing.) **"Try to read each word. If you come to a word you don't know, I'll tell it to you. Be sure to do your best reading. Are there any questions?"** (Pause.) **"Begin."**

Say **"Begin"** and start your stopwatch when the student says the first word. If the student fails to say the first word of the passage after *3 seconds,* tell him the word and mark it as incorrect, then start your stopwatch.[b]

Follow along on your copy. Put a slash (/) through words read incorrectly (see scoring procedures).

If a student stops or struggles with a word for *3 seconds,* tell the student the word and mark it as incorrect.

At the end of *1 minute,* place a bracket (}) after the last word. You may allow the student to complete the last sentence he was reading when time expired.

[a]Tape recorders facilitate error analysis.

[b]On rare occasions the student may speed-read (i.e., read the passage very fast and without expression). If this occurs, tell the student, "This is not a speed-reading test. Begin again, and be sure to do your best reading."

FIGURE 5.1 Directions for DIBELS Oral Reading Fluency Assessment

Source: https://dibels.uoregon.edu/measures/orf.php

Stars of the Sea

What fish looks like it belongs more in the sky than in the   12
sea? The answer is a starfish. Most starfish have five arms, but   25
some have many more. If a starfish loses an arm, it grows a new   39
one. A starfish can lose one or two arms and still be just fine.   53

A starfish can stretch its arms to as long as two feet. The   66
starfish uses its arms to move through water or along rocks. A   78
starfish has tiny tubes on the undersides of its arms. The tubes   91
are like sticky suction cups. The starfish can hold onto rocks   103
even in the waves. The tubes work like hundreds of tiny feet.   115
Starfish crawl along the ocean bottom, but they don't move very   126
fast.   127

A starfish eats tiny fish and plants. Its mouth is on the   139
bottom, in the center of the star. Their favorite food is shellfish,   151
and they can eat a lot. The starfish eats during high tide, when   164
the waves bring in lots of food. During low tide you might find   177
them holding onto the rocks and waiting for the tide to change.   189

Starfish come in many colors, including yellow, orange, red,   198
blue, purple, pink, and brown. They come in all sizes, from tiny   210
to very large. When many different ones are in the same area,   222
they look like a rainbow under water.   229

Total words: _29_

Total correct: _28_   Total incorrect: _1_

FIGURE 5.2   DORF Assessment Passage 1: Cierra

additional words are not counted as errors. The teacher stops the assessment at the end of 1 minute and puts a bracket after the last word read. The total number of words read, number of errors, and number of words read correctly per minute (WCPM) are then calculated. After the three passages are read, the student's median or middle score is noted. That **median score** of words read correctly per minute is the score used in instructional decision making.

Sample score sheets for Cierra, a second-grade student, on the fall DORF assessments are shown in Figures 5.2–5.4. Note that Cierra scored 28 words correct per minute on the first passage, 38 wcpm on the second passage, and 43 wcpm on passage three. Cierra's median score of 38 is the one that will be used in instructional decision making. Another important indicator provided by this assessment shows that Cierra's median errors per minute are two. This score shows that Cierra is reading with a high degree of accuracy.

> Create your own reading fluency score sheets by going to **http://www.interventioncentral.org** and clicking on the OKAPI Reading Probe Generator.

Using Oral Reading Fluency Assessment to Screen Students

The DORF, AIMSweb, and TPRI can be used to screen students who are at risk and, once they are identified, monitor their progress. Calculating fluency is optional on the PALS passages, but they can also be used this way if the teacher times the students' reading.

Twins

Six years ago my family grew from two people to four	11
people in one day. That was the day my sister and I were ~~born~~.	25
That was the <u>day</u> Mom and Dad had to start b<del>uy</del>ing two of	38
everything. My mom and dad say we were much more than	49
twice the work of one baby. They also said we gave back more	62
than twice as much love and fun.	69
We look just alike because we are identical twins, but we	80
don't act just the same. My sister likes peas and beans and I hate	94
them. I like grape juice and she likes apple juice. She likes to	107
read. I would rather climb a tree than read a book.	118
Mom and Dad are the only ones who can tell us apart when	131
we dress the same. They know the secret. I have a mole on my	145
ear and my sister doesn't. We look so much alike that we can	158
even fool Grandma and Grandpa.	168
It's nice to be a twin sometimes. We always have someone	174
our own age who will share our secrets. Sometimes we don't	185
want to share everything. Sometimes it is nice to have my mom	197
or my toys all to myself. Dad says we aren't really that much	210
alike because no person is exactly like anyone else.	219

Total words: __40__

Total correct: __38__   Total incorrect: __2__

FIGURE 5.3   DORF Assessment Passage 2: Cierra

Oral Reading Fluency: Screening

When is it given?

* The AIMSweb ORF assessments are given at the beginning, middle, and end of first through eighth grade; the DIBELS ORF assessments are given midyear and end of year first grade and three times a year from second through sixth grade.

* The TPRI *screening* assessment does not have an oral reading fluency measure, but the TPRI oral reading fluency *inventory* assessment is commonly given to all students and can be used as a screening measure at the end of Grade 1 and at the beginning and end of the year in Grades 2 and 3. Screening word identification lists are used to place students in inventory passages determined by the highest level at which the student can read the word list with 90% accuracy.

* The PALS measures passage accuracy beginning in the fall of Grade 1 through Grade 3. Fluency is optional. Students first read word lists; the highest level at which they are able to read 15 or more words determines which passage they read, and those results are used. Passages are read orally and scored for accuracy using a running record.

Students who score as *low risk* on the DIBELS Oral Reading Fluency assessment have met the benchmark and are on track for reading at grade level. For example, Rudy, who scored 62 wcpm, met the first-grade benchmark at the end of the year and is at low risk for failing to read at benchmark by the end of second grade. Cierra, the second-grade student shown in Figures 5.2–5.4, had a median score of 38 wcpm in the fall of the year. This score indicates that

---

Riding the Bus to School

I ride a big yellow bus to school. I stand on the corner of our	15
street with my friends and we wait for the bus. My friend's	27
grandma waits with us. When it's raining, she holds an umbrella	38
to keep us dry. Sometimes when it's cold she brings us hot	50
chocolate.	51
I leave my house to walk to the bus stop after my parents go	65
to work. I watch the clock so I know when to leave. Sometimes	78
mom phones me from her office to remind me. Sometimes she	89
can't call, so I have to be sure to watch the time.	101
Our bus driver puts his flashing yellow lights on and then	112
stops right next to us. When he has stopped he turns the red	125
lights on so all the cars will stop. He makes sure we are all	139
sitting down before he starts to go. He watches out for us very	152
carefully.	153
My friends and I are the first ones to be picked up by the bus.	168
We like to sit right behind the bus driver and watch while he	181
picks up all the other kids. We know where everyone lives. By	193
the time we get to our school, the bus is almost full. Sometimes	206
the kids get noisy and the driver has to remind us to keep it	220
down. He says their noise makes it hard for him to concentrate	232
and drive safely. I am glad that our bus driver is so careful.	245

Total words: __45__

Total correct: __43__   Total incorrect: __2__

FIGURE 5.4 DORF Assessment Passage 3: Cierra

Cierra is at *some risk*, and we would predict she might not reach a benchmark score of 90 words correct per minute by the end of second grade unless she receives extra support in fluency building. While the DORF benchmarks are generally comparable to TPRI and AIMSweb benchmarks as well as other published oral fluency norms such as those researched by Hasbrouck & Tindal (2006), the DORF end-of-first-grade benchmark of 40 wcpm to 50 wcpm is considerably lower than the TPRI benchmark of 60 wcpm. In our estimation, a score of 40 wcpm should be viewed as a minimum, because our data have shown that the rate of growth needed to move from 40 wcpm, and even 50 wcpm, to the end-of-second-grade benchmark of 90 wcpm is challenging for many students who are at risk. O'Connor (2007) describes scores below 40 wcpm in May of first grade as "dangerous" because they indicate that the odds are that students scoring that low will continue to struggle with reading in fourth grade. Hasbrouck and Tindal's widely used national norms for oral reading fluency are reported according to 25th, 50th, and 75th percentiles. Crawford (personal communication, 2004) has proposed a more simplified system for identifying children who are at risk. He set ranges for each grade that represent normal growth over the course of the year. These are: Grade 1, 0–50 words correct per minute; Grade 2, 50–100 wcpm; Grade 3, 100–150 wcpm.

> Hasbrouck and Tindal's norms can be accessed online at **http://www.readnaturally.com/howto/orftable.htm.**

Oral reading fluency concerns do not end at third grade. Readers face increasingly higher fluency challenges as they mature. The DORF tables extend up to Grade 6, while

Hasbrouck and Tindal's and AIMSweb norms extend through Grade 8. Unless the student is reading the passage for the first time during the screening assessment, the results are invalid.

> The Gray Oral Reading Test-4 (GORT-4) is a standardized test of oral reading fluency whose norms are appropriate for students from 6 years of age to 18 years, 11 months. In this assessment, which can take up to 20 minutes to administer, students read passages that increase in length and difficulty. The final score reflects both rate and accuracy.

Using Oral Reading Fluency Measures to Monitor Students' Progress

The key to accurate progress monitoring of oral reading fluency is that the passages given over time should be of comparable difficulty. Progress, or the lack of it, must result from student reading skill, not passage difficulty. Both DORF and AIMSweb have numerous graded passages available for use in progress monitoring. Other sources for progress-monitoring passages are listed at the end of this section. Teachers can use these passages to monitor the progress of students performing at or close to their natural grade levels within their developmental reading program or remedial students who have fallen behind their classmates.

By the middle of first grade, progress charts based on oral reading fluency assessments can be used to determine who needs extra support. In addition to helping monitor progress, progress charts help facilitate parent understanding and motivate students to improve. Figure 5.5 shows an example of a progress chart for a second-grade student. Misuou's chart shows that he started second grade at benchmark for reading at 60 wcpm. His teacher drew an **aimline** from his first score in September to the final benchmark score of 90 wcpm needed in May. This sloping aim line enabled her to determine when he was on track for meeting the year-end benchmark. ORF scores that were above the aim line indicated that Misuou was on track. Likewise, the teacher could see when Misuou's progress stalled. The chart showed that beginning in November, Misuou was no longer on track to meet the May benchmark. As soon as his teacher saw that by January 4 his scores were below the aim line, she switched Misuou into a Tier 2 intervention group so he could get more support. Misuou's chart shows that the extra support was beneficial, and by May he was at benchmark.

Using Excel (© Microsoft Corporation), you can make a progress-monitoring chart like the one depicted for Misuou. Students move into Tier 2 when their ORF scores are below the progress line, indicating that they are not on track for reading at grade level by the end of the year. Although students at benchmark might take the ORF assessment only two or three times a year, anyone who is in Tier 2 can take the test anywhere from once a week to once a month (Jenkins, Graff, & Miglioretti, 2009). However, if teachers monitor progress using one passage each time, as opposed to taking the median of three separate passages, monitoring progress every week or two is recommended. Frequent progress monitoring helps the teacher determine when scores are back on the growth line so Tier 2 can be discontinued.

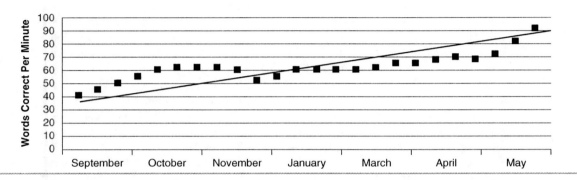

FIGURE 5.5 Grade 2 Oral Reading Fluency Progress Chart: Missuou

More resources on progress-monitoring oral reading fluency are available at the National Center for Progress Monitoring website at **http://www. studentprogress.org/weblibrary.asp.**

Once a Tier 2 student scores above the aimline four consecutive times, he is ready to move back to Tier 1 and continue without the additional support. More importantly, the teacher can also identify someone who has plateaued (scoring below the aim line for four consecutive assessments) and analyze whether difficulties with advanced word reading or fluent reading of text are contributing to the lack of progress. If a student has prepared the passage used for progress monitoring, the results are invalid.

Setting Goals and Monitoring the Progress of Students Who Are Significantly Below Grade Level

The rate at which students normally make gains in reading follows a pattern (Shaywitz, 2003), with the greatest gains occurring in the early school years, then lessening with each subsequent grade. The rate of growth also differs within each school year, with maximum growth occurring at the beginning of the year and then tapering off toward spring (Shaywitz, 2003). Shown below are expected growth rates in oral reading fluency. Rates are displayed in words correct per minute per week. Note that the *realistic* rates reflect the growth rates for typical children moving through the reading curriculum. The more *ambitious* rates apply to students who are behind in reading, as they need to make even greater gains in order to catch up. For example, Grazia is in second grade and performs at grade level. We would expect her rate of growth to be at least 1.5 words correct per minute per week. LaBron is also in second grade but is reading at a low first-grade level. In order for him to catch up, a more ambitious rate of growth of two words correct per minute per week is required.

Grade	Realistic	Ambitious
1	2.0	3.00
2	1.5	2.00
3	1.0	1.50
4	.85	1.10
5	.50	.80
6	.30	.65

Source: Fuchs, L. S., Fuchs, D., Hamlett, C. L., Walz, L., & Germann, G. (1993). Formative evaluation of academic progress: How much growth can we expect? *School Psychology Review, 22*(1), 27–48.

To demonstrate how these growth rates can help you measure the progress of your students who are lagging behind, take the case of Daquan, a fourth grader whose median DORF score at the beginning of the year was 75 wcpm, making him at some risk and eligible for Tier 2 support. Daquan's rate of accuracy in Grade 4 material was 93%, so his reading instruction used Grade 4 material, and his expected growth was based on his performance on Grade 4 passages. (See the section on placing students into the right reader on pp. 172–173.) Daquan's teacher set an ambitious growth rate of 1.10 more words per week for him. This meant that after 10 weeks she expected Daquan to be reading 11 more words correct per minute in Grade 4 material (75 wcpm + (1.10 × 10) = 86 wcpm). At the end of the 10-week period she had Daquan read a Grade 4 passage and he scored 83 wcpm, a little below what was expected. As a result, the teacher added one more extra small-group Tier 2 fluency-building session per week for him.

Another example is Carly, a fifth-grade student who is in Tier 3. In the fall, she read Grade 5 material at a rate of 47 wcpm; her rate of accuracy was 79%. Her teacher, Mr. Braden, continued to "back-test" and assess her on increasingly easier passages at lower grade levels until

---

In Your Classroom

Using Oral Reading Fluency to set IEP Goals and Objectives

Because oral reading fluency encompasses so many reading skills and is so closely related to reading comprehension, it is an ideal measure to use for setting annual goals and short-term objectives in reading. Here is an example of how oral reading fluency data were used to set annual goals and short-term objectives on the IEP for Ramone, a fifth-grade student with a reading disability. Ramone's instructional level at the beginning of the year was Grade 3. Instructional level is the highest grade level at which he was able to read passages with 90%–94% accuracy. Ramone's median fluency score on third-grade passages was 83 wcpm. Ramone's teacher used an ambitious rate of growth for him of 1.5 words per week to narrow the reading gap between Ramone and his peers. Ramone's goal was to read Grade 3 material at a benchmark rate of 110 words correct per minute by the end of the 18-week term. His short-term objectives were based on growth for two 9-week marking periods: 9 weeks × 1.5 words

correct per week = growth of 14 words correct per minute, per marking period.

Objective 1:

Given three passages at the Grade 3 level, Ramone will read the passages orally with a median rate of at least 97 words correct per minute by the end of the first marking period.

Objective 2:

Given three passages at the Grade 3 level, Ramone will read the passages orally with a median rate of at least 111 words correct per minute by the end of the second marking period.

Because he met benchmarks in Grade 3 passages, when Ramone's second objective was met, a new one was set based on his performance on fourth-grade material.

---

he determined that she could read third-grade passages with 91% accuracy (instructional level) and 81 wcpm ("some risk" for end of third grade), establishing Grade 3 as her instructional level (see pp. 172–173). Mr. Braden set Carly's growth at an ambitious 1.5 words per week in Grade 3 material. After 4 weeks, he checked her fluency on Grade 3 passages to see if she had made the expected growth of 6 wcpm (a score of 87 wcpm). When he found that she had, he felt comfortable keeping her current instructional supports in place.

For students such as Daquan and Carly who are behind their classmates in reading, short-term instructional progress can be evaluated using passages at their instructional level and the expected growth rates shown above. However, it is important to remember that only oral reading fluency scores at students' chronological grade/age levels show whether they are at benchmark. Thus, Mr. Braden also made sure that Carly was assessed three times per year using benchmark assessments for Grade 5. A way to use oral reading fluency data to set annual goals and short-term objectives on the Individualized Education Plans (IEPs) of students with disabilities is described in the *In Your Classroom* feature.

How Can I Use Oral Reading Fluency to Diagnose Student Reading Needs?

Information gathered from oral reading fluency assessments can help teachers diagnose student skill needs so that more support can be provided if needed. In this section, the collection of three types of diagnostic information is described: reading with expression, diagnosing student error patterns, and placing students in the right reader.

> Other sources for graded oral reading passages are available at Edcheckup (**http://www.edcheckup.com**) and Yearly Progress Pro (**http://www. mhdigitallearning.com**). For a Web-based application that creates progress-monitoring graphs, go to Chart Dog at **http://www. interventioncentral.org.**

TABLE 5.1 Prosody Chart

	Expressive Readers	Nonexpressive Readers
Stress (loudness)	※ Use weak stresses throughout reading. ※ Stress increases at end of exclamatory sentences.	※ Often stress every word. ※ Sometimes use more than one stress per word.
Variations in pitch (intonation)	※ Have greater variations in pitch—rise and fall in voice pitch. ※ Use a rising pitch at the end of a sentence that asks a question or that exclaims. ※ Use a downward pitch for a sentence making a statement.	※ Have inappropriate pitch changes. Either sustain the same pitch for longer periods or use a rising pitch where a falling one is appropriate.
Duration (how long a word is pronounced)	※ Lengthen the word/vowel that precedes a comma. Lengthen the last word of a sentence.	※ Often lengthen other unexpected words in a sentence. ※ Often do not lengthen words/vowels preceding commas or at the end of a sentence.
Chunk words into appropriate phrases	※ Use few pauses within sentences. ※ Use shorter pauses between sentences; shorter pauses after page turn. ※ Pause at commas. ※ Use punctuation to group words into natural units. ※ Often pause at the end of clauses.	※ Pause between words and within words more frequently; pauses can last longer; often pause after every word; awkward word groups. ※ Are vulnerable to disruptions in text such as page turns. ※ Chunk words with little attention to punctuation or clauses within the sentence.

Source: Based on information from Cowie, R., Douglas-Cowie, E., & Wichmann, A. (2002) and Dowhower, S. (1991).

Reading with Expression

Although there is a strong relationship between students' oral reading fluency and reading comprehension, the extent to which students read with expression, using a level of **intonation** that reasonably approximates everyday speech, is also related to how well students comprehend what they are reading (Tindal & Marston, 1996). This ability to read text orally using appropriate phrasing, intonation, and attention to punctuation is termed **prosody.** Table 5.1 lists reading behaviors for students who read fluently and with expression compared to those who do not.

Tindal & Marston (1996) validated an assessment for expressive reading that is highly related to standardized tests of reading comprehension and that can be used along with the DIBELS Oral Reading Fluency assessment just described. After students read a passage, the teacher scores their expression using the following 5-point scale:

1 = Reads single words. No "flow." Very choppy.

2 = Some phrasing is noted (2–3 words), but still choppy.

3 = Pauses for ending punctuation. Inflection changes may not be present.

4 = Appropriate "flow" and phrasing is noted as well as attention to punctuation, with pauses and appropriate inflection most of the time.

5 = Reading generally "flows." Voice changes to reflect meaning changes. Appropriate ending inflections.

Although standard norms are not available for the scale, the student averages for fall in grades 1–8 are shown in Figure 5.6.

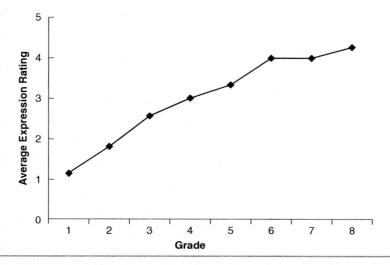

FIGURE 5.6 Average Reading Expression Ratings—Grades 1 to 8, Fall

Source: Tindal, G. & Marston, D. (1996). *Technical adequacy of alternative reading measures as perform-ance assessments.* Exceptionality, 6, 201–230.

It is recommended that you practice scoring with a colleague before you use the results to guide your instruction. During the practice session, you and a colleague should score a student's expressive reading together and compare your ratings, continuing this process until you have 90% agreement. Rating audio- or videotapes of students reading may be more convenient and easier than practicing live.

Diagnosing Student Error Patterns

Information from oral reading fluency assessments, along with the results from the expressive reading scale, helps teachers diagnose specific error patterns so that the appropriate support can be provided. The various error patterns that can be gleaned from the results of these measures are described next. Remember that when interpreting the results of your oral reading fluency and expressive reading assessments, ask yourself this important question before you intervene: Is the information I have collected consistent with the child's everyday performance? If not, you should reassess before using the interventions suggested below.

Low Accuracy, Below Benchmark for Fluency, and Low Prosody Score   Often students with low scores in all three skill areas do not have phonemic awareness and beginning decoding skills, so instruction needs to focus on developing those skills. Students who have those foundational skills but still have low accuracy and fluency typically perform well on CVC words and high-frequency sight words, but tend to make errors on words containing letter combinations and multisyllable words. Shown in Figure 5.7 is the passage-reading performance for Titus on a Grade 1 passage in May. Also in May, Titus scored 57 letter sounds correct per minute with 20 words read as whole words on DIBELS Nonsense Word Fluency.

For students such as Titus, assess knowledge of letter combinations and affixes using an assessment. The results let you know which letter combinations and affixes need to be taught. Titus can then be taught to decode single- or multisyllable words having these sounds. Practice should include reading the words in both lists and passages. Because of Titus's low accuracy and fluency, one would expect that he would also have low prosody.

Visiting Aunt Rose

My ~~Aunt~~ Rose ~~invited~~ me to ~~spend~~ the ~~weekend~~. ~~Aunt~~ Rose   11
doesn't have kids. She said I could be her kid for two days. She's   25
like my big ~~sister~~.   29

I [like] to go to visit my Aunt Rose's home. She likes to do the   44
same things I like. I like to go swimming. So does my Aunt   57
Rose. The pool where she goes also has a hot tub. I like to sit in   73
the hot tub. So does my Aunt Rose. I always bring my swimming   86
suit when I visit.   90

Our weekend was perfect. On Saturday we went out for   100
breakfast. I had strawberry pancakes with whipped cream. Then   109
we went shopping. She bought me a pink shirt. Then we went   121
swimming and sat in the hot tub.   128

On Sunday she helped me make oatmeal cookies. Then we   138
painted each other's nails. Our fingers and toes match. They are   149
bright pink. Then we went to the movies. We saw *The Lion*   161
King.   162

Aunt Rose drove me home. I handed my mother a plate of   174
the oatmeal cookies. I showed my brother my new shirt. Dad   185
admired my bright pink nails.   190

"Dad," I asked, "could I live at Aunt Rose's?"   199

"No," he said. "If you went there all the time, it wouldn't be a   213
special treat."   215

Total words: __31__

Total correct: __25__   Total incorrect: __6__

FIGURE 5.7   DORF Progress Check: Titus

Although the teacher can use some of the fluency practice sessions as an opportunity to increase Titus's awareness of punctuation and how it alters reading, at this stage of reading the focus should center on developing accuracy and fluency.

High Accuracy, Below Benchmark for Fluency, and Low Prosody Score   These students can read grade-level material accurately but slowly. Their oral reading usually lacks expression because they are so preoccupied with identifying each word, and they are unable to think about the meaning of what they are reading. Typical ratings on the expression scale would likely be between 1 and 2. Damon, the student described at the beginning of this chapter, has this type of problem. Students like Damon benefit from a combination of fluency building and practice in developing expression.

At Fluency Benchmark but Low Prosody Score   This smallest group of students read at a rate that is at or above benchmark for their grade, but their expression ratings are below average for their grade level. They show few indications that they are thinking about what they are reading. Problems with expression can include one or more of the following indicators: does not pay attention to punctuation, fails to group words together in meaningful chunks, and intonation shows little resemblance to live speech.

Although Kassandra met the ORF benchmark and decoded all the words, she read the passage in a choppy, monotone voice:

"Six . . . . . . year . . . . s ago my . . . . . . fam . . . ily . . . . grew from two . . . . . . people to four . . . . . people in . . . . one day. That . . . . . . was the day my sister . . . . . . and I were . . . . . born. That was the . . . . . . day Mom . . . . and Dad had . . . . . to start . . . . ."

As she read, Kassandra did not use appropriate inflection at the end of sentences and did not adapt her reading to account for punctuation. Although she used some phrasing, she frequently paused in the middle of prepositional phrases or verbs. Kassandra would benefit from some of the expression-building activities described in the next section of this chapter. If her lack of expression is due to an oral language deficit or because English is not her primary language, Kassandra will also benefit from oral language activities that build vocabulary and grammatical structures.

Lacking Specific Skills   As you are scoring a student's oral reading performance, you may detect patterns of student errors that indicate difficulty with a particular letter combination, affix, or sight word. For example, when Dominique was reading, he missed the words *coat* and *throat*, pronouncing them as *cot* and *that*, respectively. His teacher Ms. Sanchez detected a skill pattern; Dominique could not decode the letter combination *oa*. Ms. Sanchez noticed that several other students in class were having difficulty with this letter combination as well. Therefore, Ms. Sanchez decided to reteach the *oa* combination, first reintroducing it in isolation using the format in Table 4.5, and then integrating *oa* into the daily word lists using the format in Table 4.7. Ms Sanchez also informally assessed letter combinations and affixes because she realized that there were likely to be other combinations and affixes that her students didn't know but that didn't appear in the oral reading passages. Another teacher, Mr. Utomwen, noticed that many of his students were repeatedly missing the word *chaos* in a new story they were reading. Mr. Utomwen retaught the exception word *chaos* using the format for teaching exception words in Table 3.8.

Over- or Underdependence on Context   Sometimes students reading orally make errors that point to no obvious skill deficit. For example, Trais missed 6 words out of 100, but all the words contained different sound patterns. His teacher, Mr. Nguyen, noticed that for all of the errors except one, the word Trais substituted made sense in the context of the sentence but was still incorrect. For example, he read the sentence "Leon laid the book on the table" as "Leon left the book on the table." This pattern of errors revealed that Trais was overly dependent on context. The word *left* made sense but was incorrect and didn't convey the same meaning as *laid*. Students who are overly dependent on context benefit from being rewarded for accuracy in order to break this reading habit. For example, Mr. Nguyen was able to reduce Trais's context errors by rewarding him for accurate reading. He first told Trais, "Your goal is to read these three pages making no more than one error. You'll earn two points for meeting your goal." When Trais was working toward earning points for extra time on the class computer, he was motivated to read more carefully and look at the sounds in the words rather than leaping to conclusions based on what made sense.

Another student, Evan, read the sentence "Simone ran to the *waterfall*" as "Simone ran to the *warning*." Unlike in the previous example, the word Evan substituted did not make sense in context. Evan's teacher, Ms. Williams, had noticed that Evan made this type of error at least three times for every hundred words he read. To help Evan and two other students who had a similar problem, Ms. Williams formed a small group, and for 5 minutes daily she read pairs of sentences to Evan and his classmates in the group. One sentence made sense and one didn't, as in the following examples: "The dog licked his master's hand" and "The dog licked his master's here." The students were required to identify and repeat the sentence that made sense. This simple exercise, originally suggested by Carnine, Silbert, Kame'enui, and Tarver (2010), helped Evan and his classmates begin to think about the meaning of the sentences rather than thinking about them merely as strings of words.

Assigning Students to the Right Reader   Over the course of a typical school day, students are required to read a variety of books for a number of different purposes. The classroom basal reader provides a context for teacher-directed instruction of reading skills. As they read their basals, students are typically provided with instructional support that comes in the form of instruction in word reading, vocabulary, and comprehension. Classrooms with literature-based programs may use trade books as the context for instruction rather than basals. Theoretically, in literature-based programs, students receive similar teacher support but on an individual basis. Teachers may also use these instructional readers with their students to develop fluency, or they may select books specifically for that purpose. Independent reading includes all books students select to read for pleasure or to complete assignments. As these activities are done independently, students are expected to carry them out with minimal teacher support.

> Lexile measures can help teachers match students to the appropriate reading material. For more information, go to **http://www.Lexile.com.** You can find book-level equivalencies for PALS and six leveling systems (Basal Level, Guided Reading, Reading Recovery, DRA, Rigby PM Bench, and the Lexile framework) at **http://www. readingrockets.org/articles/21939.**

Selecting reading material at a level of difficulty appropriate to the activity is important. For example, text that students read with teacher support can be somewhat more difficult than material that students are expected to read independently. In either case, the material cannot be so difficult that students become frustrated.

Armbruster, Lehr, and Osborn (2001) ascribe three levels of difficulty to classroom books or passages: independent-level text, instructional-level text, and frustration-level text. Independent-level texts can be read with at least 95% accuracy on an unrehearsed or "cold read," with no more than 1 in 20 words being difficult for the student. Material at the independent level is appropriate for fluency training as well as any reading task receiving little teacher support. Instructional-level text is unrehearsed material the student can read with at least 90% accuracy, with no more than 1 in 10 words being difficult for the student. Material at the instructional level is appropriate for basal texts or literature-based tasks as long as students get full instructional support as they navigate through the reading.

Frustration-level text is read with less than 90% accuracy. Text at this level is too difficult under any circumstance unless there is a provision for having the material read to the student. Because of their frustration, students who are reading text at this level are likely either to fidget excessively by squirming in their seats or to tune out, looking away from their reading. With leveled books, readability and word difficulty can vary considerably among books designated at one specific level, so teachers cannot assume that because one level J book is at an instructional level for a struggling reader, another level J book is (Mesmer, 2008). Partially because of this variance, caution is advised when using the results of level tests such as the DRA for determining reading level (Rathvon, 2006). Before assigning a book, scan the text to see if it appears to be at the right level. When in doubt, have the student read a representative passage and calculate the percent correct.

Occasionally you will encounter students who can read material as difficult as the third-grade level fluently and accurately, yet their DIBELS NWF scores show they are still at the beginning reading stage. For these students we suggest a careful assessment of their phonics skills along with considerable practice sounding out words and reading decodable text. An example of how to determine whether a book is appropriate for a student is shown in Figure 5.8.

If time permits, you will improve the accuracy of your findings by taking three reading samples from the text and using the median or middle score in deciding on the appropriateness of the book. Table 5.2 shows that Mr. Haas assessed Abdul on three passages from a book and found that his percentages correct were 91, 93, and 95. The median score was 93%, indicating that the book was at Abdul's instructional level. Mr. Haas knew that he would need to provide Abdul with some help if he was to successfully read and comprehend this book, and the book wouldn't be too frustrating for him.

Ms. Luden wanted to see whether a book was appropriate for her student Akayla. Here is what she did.

1. Ms. Luden selected a representative passage of about 200 words from the book and had Akayla read orally for 1 minute. She scored Akayla's performance the same way she did when giving DIBELS Oral Reading Fluency (DORF).

2. Ms. Luden calculated the number of words Akayla read, the number of errors she made, and the number of words she read correctly. The results were as follows:

   Total Words Read = 93
   Errors = 3
   Words Correct = 90

3. Ms. Luden calculated Akayla's percentage correct by dividing the number of words read correctly (90) by the total number of words read (93). Akayla's percentage was 97%, two percentage points above the 95% cutoff for the independent level. The book is appropriate for Akayla to read independently or to build Akayla's fluency.

FIGURE 5.8   Placing Students in the Right Reader

How Do I Teach My Students to Read Passages Accurately and Fluently?

Reading fluency can be viewed within the classic *good news–bad news* framework. The bad news is that reading fluency does not develop naturally for many students. If left alone, it is *not* likely to increase. The good news is that reading fluency can be increased with practice, provided that practice is guided by someone, be it a teacher, classmate, parent, or classroom aide. The two most common techniques used to provide students with reading practice are oral passage reading and strategies that encourage students to read silently, such as Sustained Silent Reading (SSR). In their report, the National Reading Panel (2000) concluded that despite its broad intuitive appeal, at the present time no evidence supports the use of silent reading of material of interest, either in or out of class. Although future studies may show otherwise, this finding seems to make sense when it comes to students who are at risk. These students may be reluctant to put much effort into their silent reading because reading is such a struggle for them. The fact that they are likely to select books that are too difficult or easy for them can further undermine their motivation to read. Finally, students who are learning to read need feedback on their performance, and teachers cannot closely monitor silent reading. For all of these reasons, the teaching strategies for building passage-reading accuracy and fluency covered in this text stress oral passage reading, a method of building fluency for which there is considerable research support. The passage-reading strategy described here includes what is referred to in this text as Successful, Anxiety-Free, Engaged Reading (SAFER).

SAFER Passage Reading

As you learned in Chapter 3, during oral passage reading conducted in the beginning stages of reading development, students read decodable books and respond in unison, sometimes

TABLE 5.2   Calculations for Abdul's Reading Samples

	Words	Errors	Words Correct	% Words Correct
Reading Sample 1	93	8	85	85/93 = 91%
Reading Sample 2	89	6	83	83/89 = 93%
Reading Sample 3	91	5	86	86/91 = 95%

sounding out each word before reading them by sight (see Table 3.9, pp. 91–92). However, once students' NWF scores are at or above 50 sounds per minute with at least 15 whole words read, they are processing sounds in chunks and able to read multisyllable words. Stories become longer, as do sentences. Traditionally at this consolidated alphabetic stage, oral passage reading in general education classes has been conducted using what is commonly called a **round-robin** approach. In this method, all students in the class read aloud from the same book, regardless of their reading levels. The teacher calls on individuals to read, following a predetermined order. Round-robin reading has been correctly criticized in a number of areas. First, when students of varying reading levels all read from the same book, it will be too difficult for some and too easy for others. The students for whom the reading is too easy are likely to become bored. Students called on to read material that is too difficult are likely to become embarrassed and frustrated. Second, when students are called on in a predetermined order, they tend to pay attention to the part they are scheduled to read and ignore the other parts of the passages. Thus, the level of practice the students actually engage in is minimal. If the goal of oral reading is to provide students with a successful experience while building their reading fluency, it is unlikely this goal will be met using round-robin reading.

This text recommends the SAFER procedure as a more effective, high-success, low-stress approach to providing students with needed reading practice. SAFER is based on procedures for instructing group oral reading originally developed by Carnine and colleagues (2010). The SAFER group oral reading procedure incorporates many of the Tier 1 enhancements described in previous chapters and is done with groups of students having similar reading levels. The text read is carefully matched to students' reading levels using an approach described earlier in this chapter. Thus, every student in the group who is asked to orally read text is capable of reading the passages successfully. Using SAFER, students are called on in random order and asked to read amounts of text that vary from one to three sentences, following along with their fingers as other students read. These SAFER components maximize student practice by encouraging students to be attentive even when it is not their turn. They also allow the teacher to monitor student performance. SAFER is also carried out at a perky pace. Teacher talk is kept simple, students are called on quickly and efficiently, comprehension questions focus on key main ideas and supporting details, and errors are corrected quickly yet systematically. Finally, increased practice is provided on an as-needed basis by requiring that students reread stories when their accuracy as a group falls below criterion levels. The teaching procedures for SAFER are shown in Table 5.3.

In Part 1 of SAFER, students read the story orally using the procedures just described. Students are expected to follow along with their fingers when other students in the group are reading, because that ensures that they are paying attention. Finger pointing also allows the teacher to monitor whether they are following along as directed. Before reading the text, the teacher announces the oral reading goal, which is to read the story as a group with at least 97% accuracy. This goal means that for every 100 words read, students are allowed to make three errors. If the accuracy of the group is below 97%, students reread the story. Staying with text until students read it at mastery is important because students should be solid on skills they have learned thus far before moving to a new story, which has even more challenging skills. Sometimes the group scores below 97%, but the errors are due to the performance of only one or two students. In that case, schedule extra passage reading for them instead of requiring the entire group to reread the story. When an error occurs, first let the student read several more words to allow for self-correction. If the student fails to self-correct, the teacher has two options: He can tell the student the word or have the student use the sounding-out strategy. When students misread exception words, the teacher tells students the word. When they misread regular words, students are encouraged to sound out the word or to apply a rule like the VCV or c-rule. The sounding-out correction has to be concise because lengthy corrections can cause the other students in the group to go off task. If a student struggles sounding out the word, the teacher immediately tells the student the word and writes it down so that later she can review the missed word. After reading the word correctly, the student returns to the beginning of the

TABLE 5.3 Format for SAFER (Successful, Anxiety-Free, Engaged Reading)

Objective	Students who have scored 50 sounds per minute or more on a Nonsense Words Fluency assessment reading at least 15 read as whole words or who are reading second-grade or higher leveled text will read a book at their instructional level with at least 97% accuracy.
Materials Needed	Use text that is at the students' instructional level.
Signaling	None
Time	Between 15 and 30 minutes

Instructions	**Teacher**
	Advance Organizers: When you tell students your behavior expectations, remind them that they must use a pointer finger to follow along with the reading.
	Steps to reading stories in the curriculum and decodable books:
	1. Conduct prereading comprehension activities.
	2. Tell students the error limit for the story. The error limit is based on the number of words in the story. When children exceed the error limit, discontinue reading and have them practice the words they missed before resuming the story.
	3. Call on individual students randomly and have them read between 1 and 3 sentences of the story. Expect the other students to follow along with their fingers.
	4. If student accuracy is high enough, include comprehension instruction. First determine whether students need questions asked after each sentence, paragraph, or page.
	5. Call on students quickly and avoid unnecessary tangential teacher talk by focusing discussion on content, vocabulary, and comprehension strategy(ies) you are teaching or reviewing. (Refer to comprehension and vocabulary strategies in Chapters 9 and 10.)
	6. Write missed words on the board. At the end of the story have students sound out each missed regular word and read it. If the word is an exception word, use the initial exception word teaching format to review the word, having students orally spell it.
	7. Move on to the next story when students read the story with between 97% and 100% accuracy and they have completed the planned comprehension activities related to the story.
Error Correction	a. When a student makes an error, let the student read several more words, then say, **"Stop."** Do not use an abrupt or loud voice. By waiting you are giving the student a chance to self-correct.
	b. Point out to the student what error was made, indicating whether he misidentified a word, skipped a line, or omitted a word.
	c. Model the correct pronunciation of the word, or have the student sound it out. Then, ask the student to read from the beginning of the sentence. Treat omitted words as errors.
	d. Remember to write the missed word on the board for later practice, as described in Step 6 above. Use the list of story errors as an opportunity for extra word-reading practice.
Perk Up Your Drill	▓ When students finish a story, talk briefly about the next story they will read in order to heighten their curiosity and enthusiasm.
	▓ Most students want the attention they get through answering a question. Instead of looking for students with hands raised to answer your questions, tell your class that you are looking for students who followed along during story reading.
Adaptations	▓ Whenever possible, coordinate other activities during the day with the current story. If the story is about growing bean seeds, integrate related activities into your science period. If the story is about a historical character, try to expand on the students' knowledge by developing a related social studies lesson.
	▓ During story reading, if a student consistently does not follow with her finger, try having her sit next to you so you can redirect more often with a touch on the shoulder or a point to the page. If the tactic still does not work, look at her Oral Reading Fluency scores. Students who are reading text at a frustration level are usually unable to follow along after the first few sentences.

Source: This script is based on one originally developed and field-tested by Carnine, D. W., Silbert, J., Kame'enui, E. J., & Tarver, S. (2010). *Direct instruction reading* (5th ed.). Boston: Merrill Prentice Hall.

sentence and rereads. Making the student reread the sentence allows for immediate practice rereading the word and also enables the student to reestablish the word-reading flow necessary for comprehension. Encouraging accurate reading during SAFER reading sessions helps students who are at risk to develop the habit of paying careful attention to text.

In a study with third-grade children who had learning disabilities, Pany and McCoy (1988) found that students who previously made many oral reading errors significantly improved both on accurate word reading and on comprehension when immediate corrective feedback was given after every oral reading error. In contrast, feedback that was given only on errors related to the meaning of the text had no impact. A rationale for why correction procedures should stress having students look carefully at the word missed is in the *Research Note* feature.

Research Note

Correcting Errors During Oral Passage Reading

An approach commonly recommended by teachers for correcting students' oral reading errors is called the *three-cueing system*. This strategy is based on the assumption that efficient readers use three different systems to attack words: graphophonemic, syntactic, and semantic. **Graphophonemic strategies** involve looking at the letters in words by breaking a word into parts or matching letters and letter combinations with the sounds they make. **Syntactic strategies** involve figuring out whether the word sounds right in the sentence, as if someone were talking. **Semantic strategies** focus on whether or not a word makes sense in a sentence. Advocates of the three-cueing system assume that poor readers miss more words because they are overly dependent on graphophonemic cues or the letters and sounds in words. As explained in the following example, this is not the case.

The purpose of error corrections in the three-cueing system is to focus student attention on syntactical and semantic cues and to de-emphasize looking at the letters in words. After a student error, teachers using the three-cueing system are likely to say, "Does that word make sense?" Then they direct students' attention to the meaning of the words surrounding the missed word or the word order of the sentence. Students are told to look at the letters in the word only as a last resort. In the three-cueing system, only errors that change the meaning of the text are corrected. For example, consider these two student errors in reading the sentence:

The man rode his horse to town.

Student 1 read the word *horse* as /pony/. Student 2 read the word *horse* as /house/. In the three-cueing approach, the first error, identifying the word *horse* as /pony/ would not be corrected because the meaning of the sentence was unchanged. In contrast, the error made by student 2 indicated an overreliance on graphophonemic cues; student 2 would be corrected by being told to use semantic or syntactic cues to figure out the word (Hempenstall, 1999).

Adams (1998) has pointed out that the three-cueing system makes sense from the standpoint of reading comprehension; to get meaning from written text, readers need to use all three types of cues. However, as an approach to word identification, the three-cueing system is not consistent with the research (Adams, 1998). Research comparing the reading errors of good and poor readers has repeatedly demonstrated that proficient readers rely primarily on the letters in words when trying to identify them. The errors of proficient readers show that they most frequently attempt to decipher unknown words by using graphophonemic strategies, in contrast to poor readers, who tend to guess by looking at pictures or using the context (Adams, 1990).

This research, when applied to classroom practice, indicates that when word identification is the objective, graphophonemic cues should be stressed. When students make an error during oral passage reading, regardless of type, the teacher should prompt them to look at the letters in the word and/or sound out the word. This correction discourages guessing by sending the message to learners that it is important to carefully read every word.

Once students are reading longer stories, determining a 97% accuracy level becomes more challenging. A general rule of thumb is that two or fewer errors on a longer page of text is acceptable. Once the students have made between 5 and 10 word-reading errors, stop the oral reading and immediately teach those missed words using the procedures in Table 5.3:

Learn more about the three-cueing strategy at **http://www.sedl.org/reading/topics/cueing.html.**

* Students sound out each missed regular word and read it.
* Teacher uses the initial exception-word teaching format to review exception words, having students spell them.

After students have practiced reading the missed words, resume reading from the beginning of the story. This time students should read with a higher level of success.

As individual students in the group read and you record their errors, you are able to detect error patterns that may require new teaching. For example, Mr. Sax's students missed the following words during passage reading: *around, sound,* and *loud.* They struggled with the /ou/ sound in each of these words. Before the students reread the story, Mr. Sax conducted a mini review, first reteaching /ou/ in isolation (see Table 4.5) and then in a word list (see Table 4.7). Just before reading the story, Mr. Sax directed the students' attention to each of the three words in context and had them read each word before starting the story.

If no obvious error patterns are present, it is still helpful to practice missed words in a list before the story is reread. Do not include missed articles or connecting words such as *a, and,* or *the* in lists. Instead point out to the students that one of them was missed and ask the student to reread the sentence. Then remind students about the importance of reading each word in the passage carefully.

A final useful feature of SAFER is that it lends itself readily to including comprehension instruction. As comprehension instruction is covered in more detail in Chapter 10, we only provide several examples here of how it can be integrated into the SAFER reading format. Before students read the passage, teachers use prereading activities related to comprehension. Then, when students can read the passage with 97% accuracy, comprehension instruction is integrated during the passage reading. In many circumstances, when teachers have instructed the more difficult words before students read the text, comprehension can be integrated on the first reading. During SAFER the teacher stops frequently to clarify vocabulary or ideas, model comprehension strategies by thinking out loud, and guide students to monitor their strategy use. Teachers also use graphic organizers and ask students questions related to them. Including comprehension in SAFER has two advantages. First, through modeling, clarifying, and questioning, the teacher is modeling what a good reader does in the active thinking needed for comprehension. Students who are at risk need carefully crafted explicit models for comprehension. In addition, the act of clarifying content as it is read, sentence by sentence, paragraph by paragraph, or page by page, ensures accurate comprehension by preventing misconceptions or correcting them as soon as they occur.

SAFER and round-robin reading are sometimes confused because in both strategies students read text out loud, and the teacher is able to work with a large group of students at one time. Yet, as we have indicated, these two methods differ significantly. The differences between SAFER and round-robin reading are summarized in Table 5.4.

TABLE 5.4   Differences Between Round-Robin and SAFER Reading

Round-Robin Reading	SAFER Reading
1. Students who read out loud are grouped heterogeneously. The text is at a frustration level for some students.	1. Students who read out loud are grouped homogeneously. Although some students who are in Tier 3 may sit in the group to participate in comprehension activities, all students who read out loud can read the text at least at an instructional level.
2. Students are called on to read in a predictable order. Students can anticipate when their turn will occur.	2. Students are called on to read in random order. On any given day, a student may read twice as many times as another student. Students never can anticipate when their turn will occur.
3. Students read large chunks of text, typically a paragraph or a page. Other students can become bored or distracted when someone else reads.	3. Students never read more than three sentences of text and the class moves at a far perkier pace.
4. The teacher corrects errors by telling students the correct word. The student then continues reading. Sometimes the teacher waits a long time for the student to struggle reading the word.	4. The teacher never waits more than 3 seconds to correct the word, so that the student doesn't unduly struggle. The teacher's precise error correction depends upon whether the word is a sight word or a decodable word (see pp. 174–175).
5. Students are not expected to follow text with their fingers and often do not pay attention when other students read.	5. The teacher expects all students to follow the text with their fingers. Students are reinforced for following along with their fingers. Students pay attention and get more practice reading the words silently as other students read out loud.

How Do I Teach Oral Reading Fluency and Expressive Reading?

When the oral reading fluency scores of Tier 2 and Tier 3 students don't increase, fluency training is usually the missing ingredient. Although accuracy in reading is important, often it is not sufficient for fluency. Many students who are at risk require additional practice sessions to develop automatic reading with increasingly more difficult text. As you work to improve your students' reading fluency, remember that activities designed to increase fluency always involve reading aloud. Ideally these fluency sessions are brief activities and involve having students read or reread passages at their instructional level with feedback (O'Connor, White, & Swanson, 2007). You have learned that fluent reading is also dependent on student performance on key phonological, phonic, vocabulary, and syntactical skills (Pikulski & Chard, 2005; Wolf & Katzir-Cohen, 2001). Teachers must take great care to teach these foundational skills to automaticity using the teaching strategies described throughout this text for growth in reading fluency.

Repeated Readings

This method of building student fluency can be done individually or in small groups. It only works if the students have previously read the material at an accuracy rate of 95% or higher.

1. Select a 100–300 word passage from the story just read or from other material.
2. Set a daily goal for each student that is 40% above the students' most recent fluency figure (Carnine et al., 2010). For example: Ray scored 54 words correct per minute on his most recent DORF assessment, so 40% higher than his current rate would be 54 + (54 × .40), or 54 + 22 = 76. Ray's fluency goal is 76 words correct per minute.
3. Time the student's reading of the selected passage for 1 minute. Tell the student that his goal is to read the passage at 76 words correct per minute. If the student meets the goal on the first reading, move to another passage or another student. If the student does not meet the goal, have him continue reading until he meets the goal. It may take between three and five tries to meet the goal.
4. Let the student chart his score to provide extra motivation in the form of a visual record of his progress. See Figure 5.9 for an example of a speed chart.

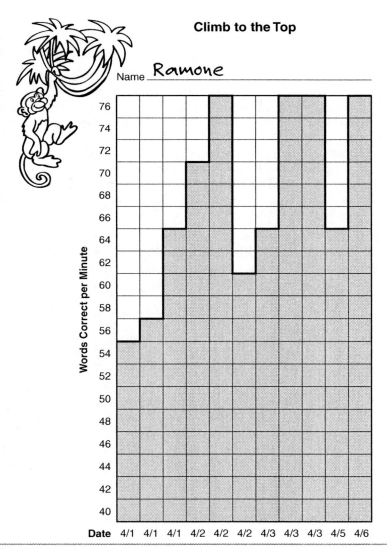

Climb to the Top

Name _Ramone_

FIGURE 5.9 Chart for Speed Drills

5. Use one or more of the following strategies along with the rereadings when the goal you set is not reached on the first reading:

* Model reading the passage for the student before he rereads the passage. This model can be provided by the teacher, another student, or a taped recording.
* Allow the student to silently read the passage prior to rereading it.
* Provide drill on missed words or phrases after each reading.

Taped Readings

Ask the student to silently read a short passage that she can read with at least 95% accuracy before allowing her to read the passage into a tape recorder. Have her replay the tape so she can follow along with the text in order to listen to how her reading sounds. Encourage her to record the passage again and listen to the improvement.

Partner Reading

Since you are only one person, you cannot schedule enough one-on-one fluency sessions to meet the needs of a classroom where many students are at risk. You can overcome this problem by carefully organizing partner readings.

* Pair students whose reading levels are in the top half of your class with students whose levels are in the bottom half and adjust according to personality issues.
* Select reading material for this activity that the lower-performing student can read with at least 95% accuracy.
* Tell your students that they will be reading partners for the next three weeks.
* Designate the more advanced reader as the first-read partner and always have that student read first to model how the text should be read.
* Give both students the opportunity to read as well as to be tutors.
* Use partner reading to conduct student speed drills or other fluency activities.

An example of partner reading is a routine called Fifteen Minutes to Fluency (adapted from *The Six Minute Solution*, http://www.fcrr.org/FCRRReports/PDF/SixMinuteSolution.pdf). The steps involved in implementing Fifteen Minutes to Fluency are as follows:

Minute 1	Setup: Students get their folders and sit next to an assigned partner.
Minutes 2–6	Practice read for Student 1: Timer set for 5 minutes; Student 1 reads each sentence three times correctly with feedback from Student 2 for errors.
Minute 7	Best read: Timer is set for one minute; Student 1 is reminded to read carefully, but as quickly and smoothly as he can. Student 2 records data during the reading.
Minute 8	Student 1 finds out how many words he correctly read per minute so he can graph his score.
Minutes 9–15	Repeat process with Student 2.

Fifteen Minutes to Fluency requires careful teacher preparation and organization prior to the start of the program. In addition, partners need to be thoroughly taught to assume their role as tutor, and their performance needs to be regularly monitored. Throughout the session, the teacher walks around the room providing specific feedback to students.

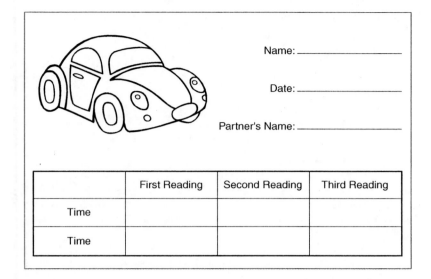

	First Reading	Second Reading	Third Reading
Time			
Time			

FIGURE 5.10 Page Races Worksheet

Page Races

This variation of student speed drills works well with partners. Give each pair of students a timer that you have taught them how to use, a grid for marking times, and a page of independent-level reading. The timer starts when the student begins reading and stops when she reaches the end of the page. The student who is timing tells the reader how fast she read the page before recording the time on the chart depicted in Figure 5.10. The reader's goal is to improve on that time for the second reading. If any words are skipped or missed, the reader starts again.

Echo Reading

Read one sentence of text aloud with appropriate intonation and phrasing. Ask the student to imitate this oral reading model. Continue this pattern of reading until the student can imitate more than one sentence at a time.

Choral Reading

Give your students a short poem or song that they can read with at least 95% accuracy. Practice reading the text in unison until everyone is reading it together as a chorus. Later you can divide the students into groups and assign various parts of the passage to each. Invite the principal to your room and give a short demonstration.

Think About Your Reading

Buy some cheap clipboards at a dollar store and put one copy of the reading fluency chart in Table 5.5 on each clipboard. After giving everyone a copy of the last book they read accurately, a clipboard, and a pencil, demonstrate how a good reader uses expression and phrasing. Then demonstrate how a choppy reader reads the same pages. Tell students that everyone will have a turn to be a listener and a reader, and explain what they will be looking for when their partners read. Divide the students into pairs and have the first reader begin reading. During the first read-through, the listener identifies any words that have been omitted or misread. The second time the story is read, the listener checks off each

TABLE 5.5   Reading Fluency Chart

My Partner_____:

After the second reading:

Yes	No	Read every word correctly.
Yes	No	Read without skipping any words.
Yes	No	Read faster.
Yes	No	Read with more expression.

Source: Adapted from Murray, B. (1999). *Developing reading fluency. The reading genie.* Auburn University. Retrieved August 28, 2009, from http://www.auburn.edu/%7Emurraba/fluency.html

quality on the checklist. Before switching roles, the listener shows the checklist to the reader and explains the markings.

Reading in Chunks

Write a sentence on the board or on student worksheets in chunks of text that match how one would read it aloud. Poems and song lyrics work well for this kind of activity. Model how you read the sentence, pausing at the end of lines, before having everyone read it in unison with you. Practice reading text like this one with the students until you are all reading with one voice:

> "Help! Help!"
> cried the Page
> when the sun got hot.
> "King Bidgood's in the bathtub,
> and he won't get out!
> Oh,
> who knows what to do?" (Wood & Wood, 1985)

Scallop the Text

Take a page of text that students can accurately read and draw scallops connecting phrases that logically are read as a unit. If doing this activity with one student, give him a copy of the page so he can follow the scallop pattern with his fingers as he reads. If doing this with the class, put the page on an overhead transparency so students can follow your finger scoops. Reread the text until the sound, the speed, and rhythm are acceptable. Then ask the student to read the same text without the scallop marks

> "Do you want some catnip?"   said Hank.   Lifting it up   on his wing,
>
> he put it   on the rock   next to Flash.   Flash   held up the catnip.
>
> "No,   no,"   she said.   "I couldn't have it
>
> just for myself.   You and Hank and I   will have the catnip.

(Rasmussen & Goldberg, 2000, p. 73)

An alternative to scallops is to embed slash marks called phrase boundaries into the text at phrase junctures (Rasinski & Padak, 2008). An illustration of the use of phrase boundaries developed by Hudson, Lane, and Pullen (2005) is shown below. Note that single slashes represent shorter pauses and double slashes indicate longer pauses.

My favorite season / of the year / is summer. // I am so glad / we don't have school / in the summer. // I would rather / spend my time / playing, / and reading. //

Readers' Theatre

As long as students can read them accurately, plays work well for repeated readings with an emphasis on expression. If you are working with a large class, you can divide the students into small choral reading groups to minimize waiting time. The first one or two times through the play, whenever a group reads without expression, model how the group can make the reading sound more lively.

Teaching Intonation

Blevins (2001; cited in Hudson et al., 2005) described a number of ways to teach intonation explicitly. One way is to teach students to recite the alphabet by pretending that it is a conversation to show inflection (e.g., ABCD? EFG! HI? JKL. MN? OPQ. RST! UVWX. YZ!). A similar approach can be used to show the importance of punctuation to meaning by saying the same sentence using different punctuation (e.g., Dogs bark? Dogs bark! Dogs bark.). After modeling each sentence by exaggerating your intonation, ask your students to read and mirror your inflection. Do this type of activity until your students no longer need your modeling to phrase new sentences.

Duet or Shared Reading

In duet reading, the teacher and student sit next to each other and alternate reading words from the same story that has already been read (Engelmann, 2009). The teacher reads the first word, the student reads the next word, and so forth. With younger students or students new to the exercise, the teacher points to the words. Older and more experienced students can point to the words on their own. Duet reading is effective for a number of reasons. First, it is very motivating; students enjoy doing it. Duet reading also provides a built-in model for fluent reading by having the teacher read every other word. Finally, duet reading teaches students to look ahead to anticipate the next word that will be read, a key skill fluent readers possess (Rayner, 1998). Duet reading can also be done with entire groups, with the teacher reading one word and then the class reading the next in unison. Jones and Bursuck (2007) successfully used duet reading with high school students who have learning disabilities as peer partners.

> The websites for the following fluency-building programs contain useful information and tips for developing fluency: Read Naturally **(http://www.readnaturally.com)**; Great Leaps **(http://www.greatleaps.com)**; Jamestown Timed Readings Plus **(http://www.glencoe.com/gln/jamestown/reading_rate/timed_readings_plus_science.php)**; and Wilson Fluency **(http://www.wilsonlanguage.com/Fluency_description.html)**.

Although related, the strategies used to develop fluency differ from the SAFER strategy used to teach passage reading accuracy described earlier in the chapter. Does teaching passage reading accuracy ultimately improve fluency? Of course. But to be effective, research-based strategies must be applied to learning activities where they are consistent with student objectives. If not, otherwise effective teaching strategies can undermine student progress. When you teach passage reading using SAFER, the immediate objectives are student accuracy and comprehension. When the objective is developing fluency, the focus becomes reading the text accurately and quickly without interruption. Problems can develop when fluency-building activities are substituted for strategies such as SAFER. In Table 5.6, the disadvantages of using fluency-building

TABLE 5.6   Disadvantages of Using Fluency-Building Activities to Teach Passage Reading Accuracy

Fluency-Building Method	What Is It?	Disadvantages
Reading Text to Students Before They Read	Teacher reads the story or has students listen to it on tape.	⁂ Students hear all the unusual new words before reading the story and do not have to decode them. The teacher can be fooled about the students' actual ability to read the text. ⁂ This strategy provides too much support for a homogeneous group of students who can read the text at an instructional level.
Choral Reading	Teacher leads the entire class or group in reading aloud in unison.	⁂ The teacher is unable to hear students' errors and thus cannot correct them systematically. ⁂ The teacher can be fooled about the students' actual ability to read the text.
Echo Reading	Teacher reads a sentence and then the class rereads it aloud.	⁂ Same disadvantages as with reading text to students before they read it.
Partner Reading	Pairs of readers alternate reading aloud by a set protocol.	⁂ Unless one student in the pair is as accurate a reader as the teacher, and both students have been taught the protocol and follow it exactly, student errors are not corrected.
Whisper Reading or Silent Reading	Each child reads aloud (but not in unison) in a quiet voice.	⁂ Teachers are unable to provide the immediate feedback for word-reading errors. ⁂ The teacher can be easily fooled that students were able to read the text when they answer comprehension questions that could be answered without reading the story.
Orally Reading to Teacher in Small Groups	Students do SAFER reading in small groups.	⁂ Although small-group reading instruction is effective, its use increases the amount of time in which other students in the class do independent work without a teacher's direct instruction. Behavior problems and off-task behaviors often increase when students are not directly working with the teacher for more than 15–20 minutes.

activities as substitutes for teaching passage reading using an oral reading method such as SAFER are identified. All of these fluency-building strategies can be more appropriately used to develop fluency *after* students have read the text with 97% accuracy using SAFER.

Strategies for finding time for fluency building during a busy school day are in the *In Your Classroom* feature.

How Important Is Fluency for Older Learners?

Because significant numbers of older students do not read at grade level, many teachers in schools with large numbers of students who are at risk confront the same dilemma as this eighth-grade teacher faced each day:

> This year our district is emphasizing literacy. They gave me a two-hour reading/language arts block. I got a set of eighth-grade literature books and a set of eighth-grade grammar

In Your Classroom

Making Time for Oral Reading

Fluency will only improve if students have the opportunity to read out loud and receive feedback on their reading. You cannot afford to skip oral reading time. Squeeze more oral reading time into the day when you have a few minutes to fill before moving to a new activity.

- When students go to the computer lab, work individually with those at-risk students whose fluency has plateaued.
- If you have a morning field trip, fit reading into the afternoon. Because everyone will be tired, you will need to be especially energetic as you motivate students to do their best work. Reading should never be skipped during a scheduled school day.

- When gym class is canceled for the day, do more oral reading.
- If your students need more oral reading time, make those activities a priority rather than art projects or watching a video.
- If you play a video for your class, pull out one or two students for more oral reading practice. Most of your students would prefer having concentrated time and attention with a teacher rather than watching a video.
- If you have a sustained silent reading time for your class, use the time to work with one to three students for oral reading. If you have the students use their quiet voices and work in a corner of the room, you will not disturb the other students.

books. There are thirty-four kids in the block. Only one or two can actually read the eighth-grade literature book . . . you know, Edgar Allan Poe short stories. It's ridiculous. These kids can't read this stuff. Lots of these kids can't read at more than about third-grade level, if that. I've brought in a lot of books my own kids had when they were little, just to try to get them reading. (Greene, 1998)

One of the greatest challenges for subject-area teachers of older students with reading problems is obtaining reading material that is at students' instructional or independent reading level. Frustration-level text will only result in higher anxiety levels or tuning out. To solve this problem, some teachers scour the Internet and school libraries to find subject-area text that they can photocopy for their students and use for fluency practice.

If previous teachers have not expected older learners to orally read passages accurately in the past, students will initially complain that your high expectations are "picky." In response to the complaining, stop a student after a word-reading error that affects the meaning of the text and point out exactly how the wrong word or omission of the word changes the meaning of the text. Teachers help their students strategically think about the importance of careful reading by periodically explaining that accurate reading is essential for success on the job, for success on quizzes in classes, and for following directions. Because fluent, accurate reading requires so much concentration for the older learner who is not reading at grade level, charting progress on a graph can inject much-needed motivation. Charting progress on a predrawn graph or an Excel (© Microsoft Corporation) program helps students see their progress more concretely.

When content-area text in subjects such as social studies and science is routinely at a frustration level for older students, teachers cannot use the text to improve the students' reading skills. Only oral reading of instructional-level text benefits struggling older readers. However, there are times when students are unable to read their textbooks but need them to gain access to class content. These same students also experience problems communicating what they have learned because they can't read classroom tests. One promising software program to help with these problems is Read & Write Gold Scanning (http://www.readwritegold.com/). This program allows teachers to scan any paper-based document and convert it into an audio file. Students can then listen to their textbooks and tests. Although this method does not provide systematic instruction to increase the reading skills of older learners, the assistive technology allows students full access to the general education curriculum and a fair and equitable way to demonstrate what they have learned. More information about using assistive technology with struggling readers is in the *Technology Note*.

Technology Note

Assistive Technology in Reading

Despite years of remedial intervention aimed at improving their reading skills, reading problems experienced by children and adolescents persist into their preteen and adolescent years. At the same time, these students are spending more time in general education classes where access to content depends largely on reading texts at their frustration level. While attempts to remediate their skill deficits need to continue, **assistive technology** (AT) offers a viable supplement to alternative approaches. AT does not try to improve deficits that have shown resistance to remedial approaches, but rather provides a compensatory approach that circumvents, or "works around," deficits while capitalizing on strengths. AT can allow students to access content independently. With independence comes higher self-esteem, confidence, and the ability to navigate the road to adulthood more successfully (Patton & Polloway, 1992).

For students who are unable to read text in their content-area classes accurately and fluently but have good listening skills, a text-to-speech screen reader can be a bridge between the written text and the students' ability to process information aurally. The particular screen-reading tool required depends on how it is to be used. The various uses for screen-reader programs, along with corresponding examples of AT tools are shown below (Bisagno & Haven, 2002).

Use	AT Tool
Read aloud large volumes of straight text from the computer screen	Simple text (Apple) ReadPlease (PC)
Navigate and search the Internet	eReader (CAST.org) Home Page Reader (IBM)
Provide real-time aural feedback on written text that the student types	Co: Writer 4000 (Don Johnston) WordSmith (textHELP)
Customized visual presentation of text as well as read-aloud	Kurzweil 3000 (Kurzweil Educational Systems) WYNN (Freedom Scientific)
Ebook readers	Kindle (Amazon) Sony 505 Digital Reader

Bisagno and Haven have several additional suggestions when using AT for print access. Using a screen reader requires having an electronic version of the text to be read. E-text can be obtained from online sources such as Bookshare.org. To convert course readers and text not available electronically to e-text, a scanner, OCR software, and adequate editing time are needed. For students who prefer a human to a computerized voice, prerecorded tapes, CDs, or MP3 downloads are available from organizations such as Recording for the Blind and Dyslexic or public and college libraries. CDs have the advantage of being more navigable; a student can go directly to a page without rewinding or fast-forwarding. If a recorded version of a book is not available, an alternative is to have the book read by a volunteer or paid reader. For more technical texts such as science and math, using a human reader who has knowledge of the subject is preferable.

Finally, research suggests that repeated reading interventions to build the reading fluency of older students are less likely to result in gains in comprehension (Edmonds et al., 2009). Students who gain in comprehension are those who are taught to comprehend text directly. Therefore, along with instruction in foundational skills, be sure to provide systematic explicit instruction in comprehension strategies for your older students, always within the context of content-area material and discipline-specific literacy (National Joint Committee on Learning Disabilities, 2008).

Putting the Pieces Together: What Does a Tier 1 Classroom Look Like?

By now the major elements of word reading have been covered including phonics, advanced word reading, and fluency. Here's how all of these pieces can be put together as part of effective Tier 1 instruction.

First and Second Grade

After Christmas, most of Ms. Erdmann's first-grade students in Tiers 1 and 2 met the DIBELS Nonsense Word Fluency benchmarks. Although she encouraged them to sound out longer words, they could easily read only three- and four-letter words with short vowels. Still, adapting the general-education reading curriculum for a class of students who are at risk takes pre-planning. If Ms. Erdmann was going to maintain a perky pace throughout her lessons, she needed to know exactly what sounds and words to teach and review. Our teachers have found that summary daily lesson guides help them teach the essential skills each day. Many of the large reading curriculum series include a confusing array of teacher guides, supplementary books, and workbooks. Selecting key skills to cover each day is a daunting task. The summary guides make planning easier, ensure teachers do not omit key words, and help the flow of instruction. One of Ms. Erdmann's daily lesson plans is displayed in Figure 5.11.

On this day, and every day, Ms. Erdmann started with a brief practice of the new letter combination or affix introduced in the curriculum and a review of recently learned ones. These are shown in the letter–sound correspondence section of the lesson outline. Although not shown here, Ms. Erdmann also wrote a list of CVC, VCe, and long-vowel letter combinations so that students had extra practice differentiating *make* from *mash*, *play* from *plan*, and *can* from *cane*.

About 5 minutes after the lesson started, Ms. Erdmann was ready to begin teaching the new words for the day. Before she went through the list, she taught one of the two new vocabulary words (*hatch*) that were in the lesson's story. In addition to teaching students how to decode the targeted vocabulary word, she also taught its meaning.

Then Ms. Erdmann walked to the whiteboard, where she had written the targeted words earlier in the morning. By this time of the year, the new words always included words with new letter combinations and affixes, increasingly more multisyllable words, and a few exception words. On this day, the *ou* and *ow* combinations were being practiced. All of the day's exception words were review words. Ms. Erdmann used word-reading formats from Chapters 3 and 4 to teach these words.

Word reading was followed by reading a decodable story about a hound dog, which provided more practice on the new letter combinations. Ms. Erdmann was glad when second semester came because she preferred the easier SAFER reading format to the earlier unison format. Although she focused on accuracy the first time through the story, Ms. Erdmann also integrated comprehension questions. From past years she knew that decodable stories sometimes needed a little livening up, so she hammed up the dialogue when modeling how a sentence could be read for expression. Ms. Erdmann believed that she could make any story interesting, but sometimes she had to be more theatrical and discuss more background knowledge.

Although she preferred to do more than one reading of the story, Ms. Erdmann still had to include spelling and writing in the literacy schedule. The shopkeeper story was not difficult, so she planned to have her students do partner reading right after lunch. Since her students in Tier 3 were reading different stories, she paired them up to read a story from their reading series. As she began to emphasize fluency more, she had to devise ways to fit in short rereadings. Although she could not count on all her parents, several would listen to their children read if the stories were sent home. Ms. Erdmann encouraged the other students to read to a younger sibling or grandparent so that they could get more practice.

Phonemic Awareness: (already mastered: now embedded in word-reading tasks)

Letter–Sound Correspondences (Table 4.5)

Intro: ou   ow (2)

Review: oo (2) sh ew tch ing ue o_e o igh ing ang ung

Regular Words (Tables 4.7 and 4.9)

Intro: br<u>ow</u>n, f<u>ou</u>nd, h<u>ow</u>, cr<u>ow</u>n, sc<u>ou</u>t, <u>ou</u>t, c<u>ow</u>, sh<u>ou</u>t, l<u>ou</u>d,
   r<u>ou</u>nd, d<u>ow</u>n, cr<u>ow</u>d, n<u>ow</u>, st<u>ou</u>t, gr<u>ou</u>nd, t<u>ow</u>n, h<u>ou</u>nd

   <u>pic</u> <u>nic</u>, <u>rab</u> <u>bit</u>, <u>up</u> <u>set</u>, <u>nap</u> <u>kin</u>, <u>prin</u> <u>cess</u>, <u>bas</u> <u>ket</u>,
   <u>hap</u> <u>pen</u>, <u>in</u> <u>vent</u>, <u>ten</u> <u>nis</u>, <u>traf</u> <u>fic</u>, <u>down</u> <u>town</u>

Review: playing, splash, moaned

Exception Words (either not decodable or students have not learned to decode letter–sound combinations in these words; Table 3.8)

Intro: no new words

Review: about, because, teacher, could, under, water, through, there

Passage Reading (Table 5.4)

Phonics Library: *The Stout Hound*

Error Limit: 2

Vocabulary (Figure 9.1)

hatch: *Hatch* means to come out of an egg. What does *hatch* mean?

* The egg started to move around because a baby dinosaur was going to come out of it. Was the baby dinosaur going to *hatch* or *not hatch*? Why?

* The green stem of a daisy plant grew out of the ground. Was the plant *hatching* or *not hatching*? Why?

* The baby alligator has a special egg tooth to cut through the egg it has been living in. Does the baby alligator have an egg tooth so he can *hatch* or *not hatch*? Why?

* Desiree slipped on a banana peel when she was running through the cafeteria and landed on the ground. Did Desiree *hatch* or *not hatch*? Why?

* Fish often come out of their eggs in open water. Do the fish *hatch* or *not hatch* in the open water? Why?

* I forgot to water my cactus plant and it died. Did the cactus plant *hatch* or *not hatch*? Why?

* What does *hatch* mean?

Spelling:

Regular Words (Figure 3.12)

   Intro: grab grim trap trip

   Review: (none)

Irregular Words (Table 3.8 adapted)

   Intro: cow, down, now

   Review: (none)

   Challenge Words: crowded

Comprehension: Complete all of the comprehension and vocabulary activities listed in the book that *will extend students' understanding of the passage and mastery of comprehension strategies and vocabulary.* Many of the grammar and spelling activities contain related comprehension skills.

FIGURE 5.11 First Grade Summary, Daily Lesson Guide 8, Theme 8: Selection 2: Day 1

Beyond Second Grade

By the middle of second grade, students in Tier 1 have learned to decode a large percentage of the most common affixes and letter combinations. Word reading increasingly focuses on teaching students to decode more difficult multisyllable words. Although the classroom routine will be structured like that for first grade, the emphasis on specific activities shifts. Students know their basic phonics skills but still need to apply them to more difficult words. By the middle of second grade, teachers begin to spend a larger percentage of time on vocabulary instruction and comprehension in addition to fluency-building activities.

What Can I Do for Students Who Still Aren't Learning to Read Fluently Even with Enhancements?

By the middle of first grade, progress charts based on oral reading fluency assessments can be used to determine who needs the extra support of Tier 2 (see the earlier assessment section). In Chapter 3 we described a typical first-grade Tier 2 intervention group that meets for 30 minutes as a small group outside the classroom. In the winter semester, when daily words begin to include more long vowels and multisyllable words, first-grade students continue to practice decoding those more difficult words in their Tier 2 sessions. In addition, teachers use extra moments during the day to develop fluency by providing extra decodable reading to students in Tier 2. Any extra volunteers are assigned to provide even more oral reading time. By January, any first-grade student who scores between 30 and 49 wcpm on the DIBELS Nonsense Word Fluency assessment and/or in the "some risk" category on the DIBELS Oral Reading Fluency assessment should receive Tier 2 support. Lower scores indicate that Tier 3 intensive support is needed. Teachers using TPRI, AIMSweb, or PALS need to develop similar decision rules using norms for those measures.

Beginning in second grade when students know the majority of letter combinations, Tier 2 intervention sessions shift their focus almost exclusively to developing fluency by providing an opportunity for rereading stories in the curriculum. Classroom teachers now conduct the Tier 2 sessions by scheduling a daily small reading group at a time of day when other students are independently working or silently reading. If accuracy is high, the teacher might schedule student speed drills one day, do closely monitored partner reading the next day, and do chunk reading on the third day.

What Can I Do for Students Who Still Aren't Learning to Read Fluently Even with Tier 2 Support?

A small group of first-grade students will stay on track for grade-level reading with Tier 2 support as they learn phonemic awareness skills and begin developing alphabetic principle. However, the progress of some students stalls when their DIBELS Nonsense Word Score is in the 20s or low 30s. These students plateau at that level, and even with additional time reading decodables, they are unable to automatically read simple CVC words. Unless these students are moved into a more intensive reading program, they will continue to laboriously sound out each word before reading it. Students who have been in a differentiated instructional program since kindergarten and have not needed intensive support will rarely if ever move to Tier 3 once their decoding skills are established. With explicit teaching they should learn to apply these skills to increasingly longer words. Decision rules for placement into Tier 3 are based on norms for the DIBELS assessments. As recommended for Tier 2 decisions, teachers using TPRI, AIMSweb, or PALS need to develop similar decision rules using norms for those measures.

Table 5.7 describes how fluency is taught in several of the alternative Tier 3 programs described in previous chapters. The REWARDS program, designed to increase

TABLE 5.7   Comparison of Four Common Tier 3 Approaches

	Direct Instruction: Reading Mastery	Wilson Reading System	Language!	REWARDS
Does curriculum incorporate fluency practice into lessons after students read stories with high accuracy?	Yes, assessments are timed. In order to move to the next lesson, students must meet the specified accuracy and rate criteria set for the passage.	Emphasis is on prosody rather than on time. Students orally read text while scooping meaningful chunks.	Three "fluency builders" consisting of phonetically predictable words based on skills taught are included in each unit.	Teachers are instructed to have students read carefully selected passages from content-area text. Students record the number of correctly read words on the last timing and transfer the information to a fluency chart.
Are fluency practice sessions scheduled at least several times a week?	Yes, fluency is integrated throughout the curriculum. Performance on timed assessments is graphed.	A minimum of 2–3 lessons per substep is recommended, with the first lesson introducing the concept, the second lesson building accuracy, and the third lesson building fluency.	Yes, 1-minute timings on selected skill drills are done daily until a goal is reached. Performance on timed assessments is graphed.	Fluency practice is included in each of the twenty 40- to 50-minute lessons.
Do fluency practice sessions gradually become more challenging?	Yes, passages include more-difficult words in longer sentences as students progress through the curriculum.	Fluency is not considered to be the number of wcpm, but rather the effortless and accurate decoding of more challenging words.	Words become more challenging, but the basic format of the drill—isolated words—remains the same.	As students learn to read more multisyllable words, teachers are able to select increasingly more difficult content-area text for fluency practice.
Are specific word-per-minute goals established?	Word-per-minute goals are set for reading assessment passages. Recommendations are that first graders finish Reading Mastery 11 by the end of first grade to have grade-level fluency.	No.	Separate fluency goals are set for phonetic words and sight words. Students are expected to reach the goals for 2 out of 3 days for each drill page.	Yes. The wcpm goals are: Grades 4–5: 120–150 Grades 6–8: 150–180 Grades 9–12: 180–200
Is fluency assessed regularly?	Yes, there are assessments every few lessons on passage reading.	No.	Yes, daily through 1-minute timed drills on isolated words.	Yes, daily.
Is fluency practiced with passages and stories that students have previously read with high accuracy?	Yes.	Each sentence and story/passage is read silently, then orally while scooping with finger or pencil.	No.	Accuracy is always stressed before fluency. Students decode difficult words before reading them in passages.

the fluency of struggling older readers who can read at a fourth-grade or higher level, is included in this section for the first time.

In RTI models, Tier placement decisions are based on data, and are typically made by a team consisting of teachers, administrators, and support staff such as school psychologists and speech and language pathologists. A look at how one of our Project PRIDE teams made decisions using data from DIBELS assessments is in the *In Your Classroom* feature.

> Read an evaluation of the add-on fluency program for Wilson Language (Wilson Fluency Basic Kit) at **http://www.fcrr.org/FCRRReports/PDF/WilsonFluencyBasic72707.pdf.**

In Your Classroom

A Team Uses Data-Based Decision Making

In January, the first- and second-grade teaching teams looked at the latest DORF scores to plan for Tier changes based on the assessment. Ms. Shackmann served as the recorder so she could compile a master list of changes and photocopy them for everyone. After Christmas, the team realized that a student whose assessment results indicated he should move to Tier 2 for more support had never been moved. The team recognized that improved communication was necessary to avoid such slipups. In order to prevent any other student from slipping through the cracks, the team members each had a form like the one shown in Table 5.8. They used the DIBELS Second Grade Benchmarks to determine who was in Tier 1, Tier 2, or Tier 3. During their team meeting, they filled out the last two columns once they made individual student decisions.

TABLE 5.8 Second-Grade Data

Student Name	Teacher	Sept. DIBELS ORF	Nov. DIBELS ORF	Jan. DIBELS ORF	Tier for Dec.	Tier for Jan.	Changes for Jan.
Tony	Jones	50	54	59	1	2	move to 2
Greg	Jones	65	92	106	1	1	—
Jalisha	Jones	9	12	15	3	3	move to a smaller Tier 3 group
Serabia	Jones	50	50	52	2	3	move to 3
Sonya	Jones	55	87	89	1	1	—
Taylor	Jones	43	69	79	2	1	move to 1
Justin	Jones	23	31	47	3	3	—
Simone	Jones	32	43	55	2	2	—
Lanecea	Jones	24	53	73	3	2	move to 2
John	Entwistle	60	66	91	1	1	—
Carrie	Entwistle	38	64	78	2	1	move to 1
Shantrel	Entwistle	46	48	56	1	2	move to 2
Mike	Entwistle	46	53	69	1	1	—
Tan	Entwistle	37	47	61	2	2	—

Continued

Based on the tests scores and confirmation by the teachers that further testing was not needed, the following changes were made:

Lanecea (second grade) moved from Tier 3 to Tier 2. Test results showed that her progress had dramatically increased these past few months, and she was now reading second-grade text at 73 wcpm, a level of performance warranting a move back into the general-education curriculum. However, Lanecea's Reading Mastery teacher was anxious about her moving into Tier 1, afraid that because Lanecea was shy, Tier 1 instruction within the larger class might not provide her with enough support to maintain her success. Although Lanecea's DORF score indicated that she could be placed into Tier 1, the team moved her into Tier 2 to provide her with extra support for the first few months. The team decided that if, following the next progress-monitoring period, Lanecea maintained her current progress in the general-education curriculum, they would move her into Tier 1. The general-education teacher said she thought Lanecea was ready for the move to Tier 1 because she had noticed Lanecea had begun to read the science and social studies materials used in class. The teacher suggested assigning a volunteer tutor to Lanecea for some extra support. Meanwhile, the Reading Mastery teacher would contact Lanecea once a week and ask her about stories she was reading in the new class.

Serabia (second grade), a student diagnosed with ADHD, needed to make a move in the opposite direction from Lanecea. After summer school, Serabia, who had been in Tier 3, was reading at grade level, and after much discussion was moved into Tier 2. In the early fall, she continued to make progress, so the decision seemed appropriate.

However, Serabia's DORF scores were unchanged since November, and she was rapidly falling behind. The team hypothesized that because she was so distractible, the small group had helped her pay more attention to the lessons. Whatever the reason, Serabia needed that extra support and so was moved back to the fastest-moving Tier 3 group.

The team wanted to discuss Jalisha, who was not progressing in her intensive Tier 3 group and whose DORF scores were virtually unchanged. The teaching coach agreed to watch her during reading group to determine if the teaching strategies needed fine-tuning. Following the observation, the coach felt that Jalisha would benefit from working in a smaller group, so a backup plan was worked out. One of the trained paraprofessionals who was an experienced Tier 3 teacher would begin working with Jalisha and another student in a group of two. The team agreed to check back on Jalisha in a month to see if the smaller group had triggered more progress.

Tony and Shantrel needed to move from Tier 1 to Tier 2 because they were still scoring in the 50s on the DORF, below the January cutoff for Tier 1 of 68. Taylor and Carrie no longer needed Tier 2 support. For two assessments in a row, their DORF scores were above the aimline. It was agreed that their general-education teacher would monitor them closely, giving another DORF next month to be sure that they continued making progress without Tier 2 support.

At the end of the team meeting, Ms. Shackmann summarized the changes to make sure her notes were accurate. Because it was Thursday, the team agreed that all the group changes would begin the following Monday.

How Can I Help Develop the Expressive Reading Skills of My English Language Learners?

Many English language learners first need to recognize rhythmic features in spoken English. In some other languages, changed word order indicates emphasis, in contrast to English, which often relies on intonation and stressed words (Celce-Murcia, Brinton, & Goodwin, 1996). Students can easily miss keys to comprehension when listening to a conversation, such as when a sarcastic sentence is interpreted as a statement of fact. Shades of meaning are lost when word emphasis is not interpreted. For example, the meaning of the word *okay* is affected by the way it is said. A reluctant worker who does not want to do a job may say *okay* in a resentful tone of voice, drawing out each syllable. Another person hearing about plans for a much-awaited vacation is likely to enthusiastically respond *okay!* in a thumbs-up tone of voice, signaling approval. A disgruntled teenager who knows she has no other choice but to babysit her brother on a Friday night might roll her eyes and say *okay* in a somewhat sarcastic tone of voice. Interpreting the intention of the speaker and the meaning behind what he is actually saying is a challenge for English language learners. This first step of interpretation is necessary before English language learners can reproduce these expressions in their own speech or in reading dialogue.

You can use dialogue in stories to help develop your English language learners' attention to the meaning of what they are reading. Bring the characters to life and point out expressive changes in their speech, changes that you want your students to hear in their heads as they read the text. For example, in the book *Where the Wild Things Are*, when you come to the passage

> his mother called him "WILD THING!"
> and Max said "I'll EAT YOU UP!"
> so he was sent to bed without eating anything.

you should model the rude, defiant tone that Max used when he talked back to his mother and then go an extra step by explaining that his mother sent him to bed for talking so rudely to her. Model how you overemphasize the word "anything," using hand gestures and facial expressions to convey the concept of *nothing*. Ask everyone to read the sentence using the tone of voice you did. You might want to take the lesson a step further and ask, "Did Max eat bread?" and "Did Max eat dessert?" Expecting your students to reply in full sentences provides even more directly related language practice.

In *Teaching American English Pronunciation* (1992), Avery and Ehrlich suggest these additional activities for helping students develop more expression.

Up and Down the Scale

Students whose first language is not English may need practice saying words with different pitches. When your class is reviewing vocabulary (see Chapter 9), you can use this 1-minute activity portrayed in Figure 5.12. On the board draw an upward-facing arrow alongside the numbers 1 through 5 written in a vertical column. Point to the bottom number (1) and model saying a word in a low pitch before having the student repeat. Point to number 2 and repeat at a slightly higher pitch. Go all the way up the scale until you reach number 5. Then reverse and move down pitch levels. Emphasis is on producing and hearing different levels of pitch and developing vocal muscles necessary to use in speech.

Turn Up the Volume

Show students how to say a letter sound or word, take a breath and say it louder, take a breath and say it louder, and finally take a breath and yell it out. This activity works well for everyone when the class needs a 1-minute break to release energy.

5

4

3

2

1

FIGURE 5.12
Up–Down
Scale

Variety Is the Spice of Life

Have your students memorize a sentence or short poem before changing how they recite it. First ask them to change one thing about their oral presentation. For example:

a. First read the poem *slowly* before reading it *quickly*.
b. First read the poem *quietly* before reading it *loudly*.
c. First read the poem in a *high pitch* before reading it in a *low pitch*.

Once students can change one dynamic, have them change two. For example, ask them to read *slowly* and *quietly* before reading *quickly* and *loudly*. Try some other combinations. Finally, ask students to change three dynamics. Ask them to read the poem *quickly*, *quietly*, and with a *low pitch*. Ask them to read it *quickly*, *loudly*, and with a *high pitch*.

What Games and Activities Will Reinforce Students' Fluency Skills?

Once students are fluent with a poem, story, or play, search out opportunities for your students to read the text aloud. Kindergarten teachers may appreciate it if you volunteer a pair of readers each day. Obtain a plastic microphone that plugs into a radio and let students pretend that they are recording on TV. The microphone can also serve as a motivator when students are reading a story for the third time. Poems read by your students can enliven morning announcements. Some schools allow students to read to other students in the lunchroom. Videotape your class reading and let them watch the tape to see themselves. Invite the principal or custodian into class in order to watch a choral reading. Parents always enjoy seeing their children perform. Take your students' fluent reading to the next step and encourage them to read proudly for an audience.

If younger students routinely read past final punctuation as if it is not there, spend a few days conducting punctuation walks. The first time you do this activity, you will need to show your students how you walk your fingers, starting at the beginning of the text and stopping at final punctuation. Ask students to put their two walking fingers on the first word in the sentence. When you say "sentence," tell them to walk their fingers to the end of the sentence, stopping at the punctuation mark. When you repeat the word "sentence," they should walk their fingers to the end of the next sentence. Continue in this pattern until the end of the story. Once students can easily do a basic punctuation walk, you may want to ask them to name the punctuation mark when they reach it. For added emphasis, you can have them say "period" in a matter-of-fact tone of voice; "question mark" with the rising inflection one uses at the end of a questioning sentence; and "exclamation mark" in a dramatic, exclamatory tone.

In this chapter we have covered all the elements that go into teaching reading fluency systematically and explicitly within a multi-tier/RTI system of instruction. A key assumption of RTI is that all Tiers are comprised of research-based practices. Moats (2007) provides a useful comparison between research-based and nonresearch-based strategies for building fluency in Table 5.9.

The effective implementation of RTI depends on teachers having expert classroom management skills. Strategies for making students' independent work more productive are in the *In Your Classroom* feature.

TABLE 5.9 Is Your Fluency Instruction Research-Based?

Research-Based	Not Research-Based
※ Explicit, measurable goals by grade level for oral-passage reading fluency and related subskills.	※ Reading practice in "leveled" books that provide little support for developing decoding skills.
※ Performance criteria established by research.	※ Focus on "miscue analysis" rather than words read accurately; stresses guessing rather than careful decoding.
※ Uses validated techniques such as rereading, partner reading, and reading with a model.	※ No emphasis on building fluency in subskills such as letter sounds and word reading.
	※ Avoids measurement of words correct per minute.
	※ Believes students learn to read by reading, not by instruction on specific skills.

Source: Adapted from Moats, L. (2007). *Whole language high jinks: How to tell when "scientifically-based reading instruction" isn't.* Thomas B. Fordham Institute (ERIC Document Reproduction Service No. ED 4980005).

In Your Classroom

Working Independently

When a teacher works with one group of students on fluency practice, the other students need to be engaged in productive work that will not disrupt the reading group. One key to conducting smaller reading groups is to recognize that some students have never learned to work independently. Independent work skills require specific instruction and practice, just as other classroom skills and knowledge do. Six steps used to teach independent work skills are listed, followed by more detailed descriptions for each step:

1. Identify and explain the skills and rules necessary to work independently.
2. Show students what working independently looks like.
3. Give students practice working independently in small groups with well-defined activities while you monitor closely. Use a timer to establish a clear concrete beginning and end to the independent work-time practice.
4. When working with a small reading group, sit facing students who are working independently in order to maximize monitoring. Use the timer until students no longer need it as a reminder.
5. Provide feedback and reward students for working independently.
6. Make adaptations for individual students when necessary.

Prepare for Teaching Students to Work Independently

Before you begin teaching students to work independently, determine several activities students can complete independently with at least 90% success. Students will not work quietly if they are frustrated. If Ms. Legolis introduced describing words on Monday and Tuesday and on the same days asked her students to work independently on a worksheet that required them to find describing words in sentences, many of the students would still not have the skills to do that work. The

ensuing frustration could lead to off-task behaviors. In contrast, if Mr. Dane gave his students a review sheet requiring them to circle the nouns and verbs, a skill that they learned well but still needed to review, the students would have the skills to do that work. Giving students a task to complete when they do not have the skills to complete it independently sets them up for failure.

Step 1: Identify and explain the skills and rules necessary to work independently.

Establish and enforce rules for independent work times. You might want to use the following rules:

- Respect others by keeping hands, feet, and personal objects to yourself.
- Once the timer is set, no talking is allowed until the timer rings. Don't interrupt the teacher when she is working with a group. For 15 minutes no one is allowed to talk.
- Work on your assigned activity at your assigned spot until the timer rings. If you are working at the tables and finish your work, then select one of the books in the middle of the table to silently read/scan.
- If you follow the rules after the timer is set, you'll earn 5 points when the timer rings.

Some classes require very tight rules and don't allow talking or laughing during this independent work time. Teachers who decide to set such stringent rules know that in their class a quiet giggle can turn into raucous laughter, disturbing everyone's work, or that a quiet request for help from one's neighbor can easily turn into shoving. In other classes, students can sharpen pencils when needed or quietly ask a neighbor for help. The teacher has to determine the maturity level of the class before establishing rules. Students typically will fit into one of the three categories described in Figure 5.13.

The Project PRIDE teachers found that students willingly worked quietly in order to earn a point for their

---

☺ Those students whom you encourage to **neatly complete** all work.

☺ Those students whom you encourage to complete **all** work.

☺ Those students who are still working on **following the quiet rules** while sitting with their work. You know that it is a challenge for these students to sit quietly and hope to increase the quality of their independent work gradually.

FIGURE 5.13   Expectations for Independent Work

Continued

team or table. A display chart on the wall was used for the cumulative point totals. Some teachers used a more concrete award after teams earned 20 or 30 points. Other teachers found that students were motivated by the rising point totals on the displayed chart.

Step 2: Show students what working independently looks like.

Your students who have the greatest need to learn independent work skills are those who will profit least from your verbal descriptions. Show these students what working independently looks like. Tell your students that you want to show them what quiet working looks like and sit at a desk with a pencil and paper. After quietly working for several seconds, tell students what you are doing and refer to the rules: *"This is quiet working. Mrs. Bara is quietly working until the timer rings."* Move to a computer and work quietly for a few seconds, once again telling students, *"This is quiet working. Mrs. Bara is working without interrupting the teacher."* Return to a table and read a book before telling students, *"This is quiet working. Mrs. Bara finished her work and took a book on the pile next to the table."* Your lesson will make more of an impression on students if you also include nonexamples. At this point you can add a bit of humor and theatrics for motivation. Sit next to one of the students at a table and start chatting with him. Tell your students, *"This is not quiet working. Mrs. Bara forgot and is talking."* If students are not supposed to go to the pencil sharpener during quiet work time, pretend you are a student who has left her seat to do that, and once again say, *"This is not quiet working. Mrs. Bara forgot that she isn't supposed to sharpen pencils during quiet work time."*

After showing the students examples and nonexamples, ask them more abstract questions and tell them to put their thumbs up or down depending on the answer:

- *"Should I talk to my neighbor and ask for her pencil?"* Dramatically shake your head "no" and expect that the students have their thumbs down.
- *"Should I work like this?"* As you quietly work, look to see all thumbs up.
- *"Should I get up and go to the sink?"* Another emphatic head-shaking "no."

Step 3: Give students practice working independently in small groups with well-defined activities while you monitor closely.

If simply talking about and watching the teacher model good behavior were enough, schools would have far fewer discipline problems. However, as with any skill, learning how to work independently takes practice. First, ask three or four students to come up and show everyone else how they can quietly work on a paper while everyone else watches. After 2 or

3 minutes, praise their quiet working and ask the rest of the class to clap for them.

After the small group has modeled quiet, independent working, tell the class that it is now their turn to practice. Set the timer for a predetermined number of minutes. Give the students a worksheet or project they can easily do. Before you set the timer, remind the students of the rules. For kindergarten, set the timer for only 1 minute; for second grade and above, set it for 3 or 4 minutes. You need everyone to be successful this first time. As students work, closely monitor as you walk around the room so you can redirect anyone who is not following the rules. Any time students break a rule, remind them that they are not working and must get back to work. When the timer rings, praise the students who have followed the rules and give team points to rows of students who worked diligently. In a matter-of-fact tone of voice, tell teams that haven't earned points why they didn't earn them: *"Two students at table four were talking. That team doesn't earn a point."* If students were not successful, tell the class that they need to practice again until they are successful, and repeat the process.

Practice quiet independent work using the timer at least twice a day. Gradually increase the time until students can work independently for longer periods of time.

Step 4: When working with a small reading group, sit facing students who are working independently in order to maximize monitoring. Use the timer until students no longer need it as a reminder.

Once students can independently work for 10 minutes, you can begin holding reading groups during that time. Sit facing the class with your all-seeing eye focused to catch any rule infractions. If you are successful in teaching your students to work independently, you should rarely need to say anything.

Step 5: Provide feedback and reward students for working independently.

Always provide verbal feedback at the end of the independent work time and award points. When students reach second grade, a 20-minute stretch of independent work is realistic.

Step 6: Make adaptations for individual students if necessary.

Even when you have followed all these steps in teaching students to work independently, some students may still need a little extra structure. For example, if you have an extremely impulsive student who needs more monitoring, pull up a desk near you and have that student work in closer physical proximity to your booster group. The student can still earn the point for working, as long as he can follow the rules in the period during which the timer is set.

APPLIED ACTIVITIES

1. Two fact-or-fiction questions about reading fluency are included below. Pair up with a partner and take turns defending your position for one of these questions using references from research sources cited in the chapter or from information on the website resources listed in the sidebars.
   a. Student ability to read passages accurately and fluently is highly correlated to scores on high-stakes state tests of reading comprehension. Is this fact or fiction? Explain why.
   b. It is not necessary to correct student errors in oral passage reading when those errors retain the meaning of the passage. Is this fact or fiction? Explain why.

2. Use the DIBELS tables to identify which of the following students' May oral reading fluency scores are at benchmark:

Marissa	Second Grade ORF	=	65 wcpm
Phil	Third Grade ORF	=	111 wcpm
Zion	First Grade ORF	=	36 wcpm
Sean	Fourth Grade ORF	=	112 wcpm
Grayson	First Grade ORF	=	61 wcpm
Mario	Second Grade ORF	=	93 wcpm
Glenn	Fourth Grade ORF	=	122 wcpm
Jaquesia	Third Grade ORF	=	101 wcpm
Jolynn	Fifth Grade ORF	=	129 wcpm
Christopher	Fourth Grade ORF	=	131 wcpm
Leroy	Third Grade ORF	=	98 wcpm
Won Chui	Second Grade ORF	=	82 wcpm
Tameka	First Grade ORF	=	33 wcpm

3. Replicate Misuou's ORF progress chart that appears on page 165.

4. A third-grade student, Juan, read 62 wcpm on the DIBELS Oral Reading Fluency assessment he took during the first week of September. When he was retested 6 weeks later, his teacher, Mr. Staley, used the *rate of expected weekly growth* chart on page 166 to determine whether Juan's score of 75 wcpm showed progress similar to a *typically successful* child in third grade. What did Mr. Staley find?

5. Because Ruben, a first grader, is behind his peers in oral reading fluency, Mrs. Wasmullen wants to make sure that his weekly gain in words read correctly per minute is at least at the *"ambitious"* level noted on the *rate of expected weekly growth* chart. If Ruben is reading 15 wcpm in January, how many words per minute should he be reading 10 weeks later to show a rate of progress at the *ambitious* level?

6. Latisha is a second-grade student in Ms. Carter's class. Latisha scored 45 words correct per minute on the January administration of the DIBELS Oral Reading Fluency assessment. This score was well below the January benchmark of 68 words correct per minute. Describe the steps Ms. Carter needs to take as she uses *repeated readings* to build Latisha's fluency.

7. In December, Sara's third-grade teacher gave her three passages to read aloud, in order to assess her fluency. On the first passage Sara made nine errors, reading a total of 83 words; on the second passage Sara made 10 errors, reading a total of 67 words; on the third passage Sara made eight errors, reading a total of 94 words. What was Sara's median words-correct-per-minute score? Identify Sara's areas of need. What other assessment that you have learned about in this book would you also give to Sara, and why?

8. Form a group with three other students from your class, select a page from this book, and take turns conducting a SAFER reading group using the format from Table 5.3. One person in the group should be designated to miss three words. After each person has a turn teaching the group, give feedback on how closely he followed the format. Was the error-correction procedure followed? Was the pace perky? Were turns between one and three sentences? Did you write missed words so you could practice them after the reading?

9. Select three sequential reading lessons from a first-grade regular-education reading curriculum and develop a guide sheet for each lesson to accompany that day's lesson. Use the adapted lesson guide in Figure 5.11 as your model to identify critical reading skills.

10. Mr. Orcutt is a second-grade teacher. In December he noticed that many of his students were below the aimline for reading at grade level by the end of the year. He decided to set aside 15 to 20 minutes every day for fluency activities. As of Friday, his students read a long story about a mountain lion with 97% accuracy. Develop a week's worth of lesson plans for the fluency portion of his reading period based on his teaching 26 pages about mountain lions. How many pages will students read for fluency development? Will they practice fluency activities with the same or different pages every day? Adjust your plans so you are prepared to account for student success or failure.

11. *First Step:* Make a progress chart for Janelle, who is a fourth grader. Include an aimline based on her September assessment. Use the following information to get started:

    You plan to give Janelle an ORF assessment in September, November, January, and May. Her first score in September is 80 wcpm. She is a relatively accurate reader, missing only two words.

Second Step: Once you have developed the progress chart that includes an aimline, fill in the following information:

> Janelle's November score was 89 wcpm, her January score was 88 wcpm, and her May score was 102 wcpm. All her readings continue to show a high rate of accuracy.

Third Step: Determine whether Janelle met the fourth-grade benchmark. Was there any point during the year when you would have recommended more support for Janelle? If so, describe in detail what type of support you would have provided. What Tier placement do you think would provide appropriate support based on the ORF scores?

12. Break up into groups of three and discuss your experiences of learning a foreign language. When you read aloud in the foreign language, how did your prosody and speed compare with those in English? When you spoke the language you were learning, how did your fluency compare to your everyday language? Did any teaching techniques that the foreign-language teacher used help you become more fluent? What were some strategies that the foreign-language teacher could have used to help your prosody?

13. Identify which error pattern each of the following students display. Also describe what teaching format from the text you would use to remediate.

a. Dasia was reading Grade 2 passages and missed the following words (what Dasia said is in parentheses):

couch (cook)   round (ruined)
sound (send)   ground (grinned)

b. Esmerelda is a third-grade student who is unable to read even Grade 1–level material accurately and fluently. Her most recent score on DIBELS NWF was 37. Esmerelda still confuses long and short vowels.

c. Ramona scored at the benchmark level of 110 on Grade 3 material. However, when she reads she fails to address punctuation and reads with little intonation.

REFERENCES

Adams, H. (1990). *Beginning to read: Thinking and learning about print.* Cambridge, MA: MIT Press.

Adams, M. J. (1998). The three-cueing system. In F. Lehr and J. Osborn (Eds.), *Literacy for all issues in teaching and learning* (pp. 73–99). New York: The Guilford Press.

Archer, A. L., Gleason, M. M., & Vachon, V. L. (2000) *REWARDS: Reading Excellence: Word Attack and Rate Development Strategies multisyllabic word reading strategies.* Frederick, CO: Sopris West–Cambrium Learning Group.

Archer, A. L., Gleason, M. M., & Vachon, V. L. (2003). Decoding and fluency: Foundation skills. *Learning Disability Quarterly, 26*(2), 89.

Armbruster, B., Lehr, F., & Osborn, J. (2001). *Put reading first: The research building blocks for teaching children to read.* Washington, DC: Partnership for Reading.

Avery, P., & Ehrlich, S. (1992). *Teaching American English pronunciation.* New York: Oxford Press, p. 48.

Bisagno, J. M., & Haven, R. M. (2002, Spring). Customizing technology solutions for college students with learning disabilities. International Dyslexia Association quarterly newsletter, *Perspectives,* 21–26. Retrieved February 10, 2010, from LDOnline: http://www.ldonline.org/ld_indepth/technology/customizing_technology.html

Blevins, W. (2001). *Building fluency: Lessons and strategies for reading success.* Scranton, PA: Scholastic.

Carnine, D. W., Silbert, J., Kame'enui, E. J., & Tarver, S. (2010). *Direct instruction reading* (5th ed.). Boston: Merrill Prentice Hall.

Celce-Murcia, M., Brinton, D., & Goodwin, J. (1996). *Teaching pronunciation: Reference for teachers of English to speakers of other languages.* Cambridge: Cambridge University Press.

Chard, D. J., Ketterlin-Geller, L. R., Baker, S. K., Doabler, C., & Apichatabutra, C. (2009). Repeated reading interventions for students with learning disabilities: Status of evidence. *Exceptional Children, 75,* 263–281.

Cowie, R., Douglas-Cowie, E., & Wichmann, A. (2002). Prosodic characteristics of skilled reading: Fluency and expressiveness in 8–10-year-old readers. *Language and Speech, 45*(1), 47–82.

Crawford, D. (2004, May). (personal communication).

Deno, S. L. (1985). Curriculum-based measurement: The emerging alternative. *Exceptional Children, 52*(3), 219–232.

Dowhower, S. (1991). Speaking of prosody: Fluency's unattended bedfellow. *Theory into Practice, 30*(3), 165–175.

Edmonds, M. S., et al. (2009). A synthesis of reading interventions and effects on reading comprehension outcomes on older struggling readers. *Review of Educational Research, 79*(1), 262–287.

Engelmann, S. (2009). Improving reading rate of low performers. Retrieved July 21, 2009, from http://www.zigsite.com/PDFs/readingrate.pdf

Engelmann, S., & Bruner, E. (1995). *Reading Mastery I: Teacher's guide.* Columbus, OH: SRA Macmillan/McGraw-Hill.

Fuchs, L. S., Fuchs, D., Hamlett, C. L., Walz, L., & Germann, G. (1993). Formative evaluation of academic progress: How much growth can we expect? *School Psychology Review, 22*(1), 27–48.

Fuchs, L. S., Fuchs, D., Hosp, M. K., & Jenkins, J. R. (2001). Oral reading fluency as an indicator of reading competence: A theoretical, empirical, and historical analysis. *Scientific Studies of Reading, 5*(3), 239–256.

Fuchs, L. S., Fuchs, D., & Maxwell, L. (1988). The validity of informal reading comprehension measures. *Remedial and Special Education, 9*(2), 20–28.

Good, R. H., Simmons, D., Kame'enui, E. A., & Wallin, J. (2002). *Summary of decision rules for intensive, strategic, and benchmark instruction—recommendations in kindergarten through third grade* (Technical Report No. 11). Eugene, OR: University of Oregon.

Greene, J. (1998). Another chance: Help for older students with limited literacy. *American Educator,* Spring/Summer, 1–6. Retrieved June 12, 2009, from http://www.aft.org/pubs-reports/american_educator/spring_sum98/greene.pdf

Greene, J. (2009). *Language! The comprehensive literacy curriculum.* Sopris West Educational Services. Longmont, CO. Available at www.sopriswest.com

Hasbrouck, J. E., & Tindal, G. (2006). Oral reading fluency norms: A valuable assessment tool for reading teachers. *The Reading Teacher, 59,* 636–644.

Hempenstall, K. (1999). Miscue analysis: A critique. *Effective School Practices, 17*(3), 85–93.

Hudson, R. F., Lane, H. B., & Pullen, P. C. (2005). Reading fluency assessment and instruction: What, why, and how? *The Reading Teacher, 58,* 702–714.

Jenkins, J. R., Graff, J. J., & Miglioretti, D. L. (2009). Estimating reading growth using intermittent CBM progress monitoring. *Exceptional Children, 75,* 151–163.

Jones, A., & Bursuck, W. (2007). Use of a variation of duet reading to increase the reading fluency of two high school students with learning disabilities. *Direct Instruction News: Effective School Practices, 7*(3), 12–15.

Lee, J., Grigg, W., and Donahue, P. (2007). *The nation's report card: Reading 2007* (NCES 2007-496). National Center for Education Statistics, Institute of Education Sciences, U.S. Department of Education, Washington, DC.

Mesmer, H. (2008). *Tools for matching readers to texts: Research-based practices solving problems in the teaching of literacy.* New York: The Guilford Press.

Moats, L. (2007). *Whole language high jinks: How to tell when "scientifically-based reading instruction" isn't.* Thomas B. Fordham Institute (ERIC Document Reproduction Service No. ED 4980005).

Murray, B. (1999). Developing reading fluency. The Reading Genie. Auburn University. Retrieved August 28, 2009, from http://www.auburn.edu/academic/education/reading_genie/fluency.html

National Joint Committee on Learning Disabilities. (2008). Adolescent literacy and older students with learning disabilities. *Learning Disability Quarterly, 31,* 211–218.

National Reading Panel. (2000). *Teaching children to read: An evidence-based assessment of the scientific research literature on reading and its implications for reading instruction.* Washington, DC: National Institute of Child Health and Human Development.

O'Connor, R. (2007). *Teaching word recognition: Effective strategies for students with learning difficulties.* New York: The Guilford Press.

O'Connor, R. E., White, A., & Swanson, H. L. (2007). Repeated reading versus continuous reading: Influences on reading comprehension. *Exceptional Children, 74,* 31–46.

Pany, D., & McCoy, K. M. (1988). Effects of corrective feedback on word accuracy and reading comprehension of readers with learning disabilities. *Journal of Learning Disabilities, 21,* 546–550.

Patton, J. R., & Polloway, E. A. (1992). Learning disabilities: The challenge of adulthood. *Journal of Learning Disabilities, 25,* 410–415, 447.

Pikulski, J. J., & Chard, D. J. (2005). Fluency: Bridge between decoding and reading comprehension. *The Reading Teacher, 58,* 510–519.

Rasinski, T. V., & Padak, N. D. (2008). *From phonics to fluency: Effective teaching of decoding and reading fluency in the elementary school.* Boston: Pearson/Allyn & Bacon.

Rasmussen, D., & Goldberg, L. (2000). *A king on a swing.* Columbus, OH: SRA, 73.

Rathvon, N. (2006). *Developmental reading assessment.* Retrieved from http://www.natalierathvon.com/images/DRA_Review-08-25-2006.pdf

Rayner, K. (1998). Eye movements in reading and information processing: 20 years of research. *Psychological Bulletin, 124*(3), 372–422.

Shaywitz, S. (2003). *Overcoming dyslexia: A new and complete science-based program for reading problems at any level.* New York: Alfred A. Knopf.

Stanovich, K. E. (1986). Matthew effects in reading: Some consequences of individual differences in the acquisition of literacy. *Reading Research Quarterly, 21,* 360–407.

Tindal, G., & Marston, D. (1996). Technical adequacy of alternative reading measures as performance assessments. *Exceptionality, 6,* 201–230.

Wiederhold, J., & Bryant, J. (2001). *Gray Oral Reading Tests: GORT-4.* Austin, TX: Pro-Ed.

Wilson, B. (2004). *Wilson reading system.* Millbury, MA: Wilson Language Training Corporation.

Wolf, M., & Katzir-Cohen, T. (2001). Reading fluency and its intervention [Special Issue on Fluency]. *Scientific Studies of Reading, 5,* 211–238.

Wood, A., & Wood, D. (1985). *King Bidgood's in the bathtub.* New York: Harcourt Brace Jovanovich.

6 Obtaining Background Information

Introduction

Accurate assessment helps teachers plan the best possible instruction for students. This chapter provides information on gathering and analyzing data about students and their reading. Chapter 6 discusses background information while Chapter 7 concentrates on the assessment of reading abilities. Both kinds of information are essential to good teaching.

This chapter examines ways to obtain a broad understanding of a student's background. Background information is divided into two parts: (1) the student's environments, including home, school, social, and cultural and (2) background factors within the individual, including emotional, potential (intelligence), physical, and language development. Specific methods of gathering information also are discussed.

Background factors can profoundly affect a student's reading. Some students' environmental backgrounds may not foster reading development. For other students, problems in reading seem to come from within the individual.

At times, identified problems can be corrected. For example, a student with visual difficulties may be referred to an eye doctor, receive corrective lenses, and show immediate reading gains.

However, many students face problems that cannot be resolved easily. For example, a teacher has little ability to affect a difficult home situation—but even in that instance, a teacher can make a difference. During a time of family turmoil, a student may need a compassionate, understanding adult. Knowing background information enables teachers to deal sensitively with a fragile human being and to adjust instruction to special needs.

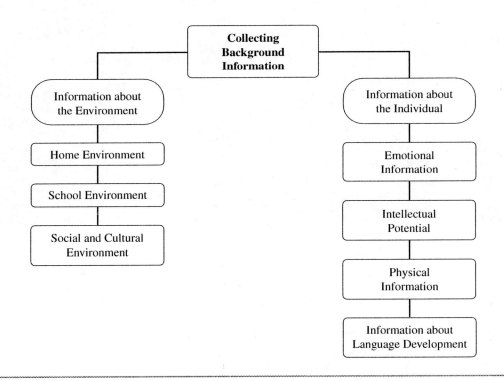

FIGURE 6.1 Collecting Background Information

The discussion of background factors in this chapter is oriented to the immediate, practical needs of teachers.

When dealing with background factors, teachers must remember that these factors have a complex relationship to reading problems. A factor may coexist with a reading problem but not actually cause that reading problem. For example, some students manage to achieve well in school despite difficult home lives. For other students, however, problems at home may impede learning. Thus, interpreting background information judiciously is important.

Information about the Environment

Students live in several environments: the home, the school, and the social and cultural environment. Each of these environments influences how students think about reading, the desire to learn, and access to reading materials. In addition, these environments interact. For example, a difficult situation at home may contribute to difficulty making friends in the social realm and to trouble in cooperating with teachers at school.

Home Environment

The home exerts a powerful influence on the development of reading and writing. Parents play an important role in modeling the value of literacy and bringing children to books, and the general home situation can influence a student's academic achievement. Events such as divorce or a move to a new neighborhood can affect a student's ability to profit from school reading instruction.

Parents as Models for Literacy   Parents are a child's earliest and most important literacy role models. If parents read for both recreation and information and provide many reading materials at home, the child learns to value literacy. Parents also stimulate a love of books by reading to their children, taking them to the library, and buying books as gifts. A home environment that is rich in books and in literacy activities fosters success in reading.

A reading teacher can determine whether the home supports and values literacy by interviewing the parents or by asking them to fill out a questionnaire. What information is helpful? Some of the questions to ask parents about their own reading habits are the following: Do they read regularly? Do they subscribe to newspapers and magazines? Do they buy books? Next, parents should be asked about literacy interactions with their child. Do they regularly read to their child? Do they encourage their child to read? Do they take their child to the library or buy books for the child? Do they subscribe to any children's magazines? Do they limit television viewing? Responses to such questions indicate how parents and other family members, including grandparents and older siblings, foster literacy at home.

Information obtained directly from a student can also give insights into how literacy is modeled at home. As you gather information from interviewing and working with your students, you learn whether they have books at home and if reading is done regularly.

What can a reading teacher do if the home does not nurture literacy? Many parents are grateful for teacher suggestions about improving literacy in their homes. Often, the parents of students with reading problems are worried about their child's future and have misgivings about their own parenting skills. A few suggestions often help foster a sense of family security and enhance literacy. For some families, these suggestions reinforce the good things they are doing already:

* Provide a good reading-studying environment. Advise parents to provide a quiet, stable, well-lighted place in which their child will study. Supplies (paper and pencils) and reference materials (dictionaries, maps) should be located near this area. Make sure that the television is off during homework or reading time.

* Share literacy with the child. When parents read to young children, they promote an interest in reading, foster language development, and share close family experiences. If the child is older, parent and child can share reading time as they each read silently. Students of all ages enjoy reading material that they have mastered to a parent who listens enthusiastically. Encourage parents to take children to a local library and to look for a helpful children's librarian, who will aid them in locating suitable books.

* Accept the child as he or she is. Admitting that one's own child has a problem is often difficult. Some parents deny that difficulties exist or hold unrealistic expectations for their child. Children are sensitive to their parents' disappointments. To prevent a reading problem from becoming a family problem, children must know that parents accept and love them as they are.

* Help the child to feel secure and confident. Encourage activities that a child does successfully. Playing baseball or basketball, taking cooking lessons, or just being dad's special helper may acquire a special meaning for a child with reading problems.

When parents are unable to provide literacy experiences at home, teachers must nurture a love of literacy during instruction. Classrooms filled with different types of books and magazines, invitingly displayed, show students that literacy is important. Give students time to browse through and share these materials. Teachers can also read to students on a regular basis and ask them to share their own thoughts and feelings about the selections.

General Home Situation   Children are profoundly affected by what happens to their families. They are often dramatically touched by a move to a new location, divorce or separation of parents, the deaths of relatives, or older siblings leaving home. A child may not be able to pay attention to reading instruction when the father has just moved out or the mother has taken a new job and will no longer be at home after school.

A parent interview is often the means of collecting helpful information about a family. This information includes the names, ages, and occupations of the parents; the number and ages of siblings; names of other family members living in the home; and the members of the nuclear family (parents, siblings) who are not living at home. During this interview, ask parents to share any other information that might help to explain their child's difficulties. Often parental insights give valuable ideas for cooperation between a reading teacher and the family.

Occasionally, the parent interview reveals that a family situation is causing stress for the student and contributing to difficulty in school. Although teachers cannot intervene in a divorce or prevent an impending move to a new neighborhood, they can be sensitive to a student's feelings and emotional needs. At such critical times, the reactions and guidance of an understanding teacher may be more important for the child than direct instruction in reading. Work with Shannon at the reading center illustrates this point. When Shannon's parents separated, she reacted with fits of crying and withdrawal from other children. The teachers realized that certain topics might upset her, so they allowed her to select her own materials for instruction. Shannon avoided books about families. Instead she chose nonsense books such as *Chicken Soup with Rice* (Sendak) and books featuring brave young children, such as *Hatupatu and the Birdwoman* (Cowley) and *Where the Wild Things Are* (Sendak). These selections proved to be key elements in improving her reading.

Teachers can help students cope with difficult home situations by:

* Being sensitive. Sensitivity in talking to students and allowing them to express their feelings is extremely important.

* Reducing demands. Teachers may want to "go easy" on students for a while by reducing both academic and behavioral demands.
* Being aware of the student's living situation. Teachers should be knowledgeable and understanding about the student's living and legal custody arrangements. If parents do not live together, make sure the appropriate parent receives communications. With permission from the custodial parent, both parents may be informed.

School Environment

Many factors in the school environment can influence reading achievement. Information about educational history, school attendance, and instructional methods helps teachers understand the student's problem and forms a basis for cooperation among all the professionals who are helping a student.

Educational History   By gathering information about a student's educational history, teachers learn what the youngster has already experienced and are able to select new options for instruction. Students differ widely in their educational histories. For some, first grade is the initial instructional experience; others enter first grade with a rich history of preschool and kindergarten. Some students are barely 6 years old when they first encounter formal reading instruction; others are almost 7. Some students have repeated a grade or have received an extra year of kindergarten instruction. Some children have received private tutoring; some have been placed in special school programs.

Educational history may offer some hints about the seriousness of a student's problem. For example, a student who has had many enriching experiences, such as preschool education and previous tutoring, and still has difficulty in reading probably has a serious problem. In contrast, a student who comes with no preschool education or history of special reading help may simply have lacked the opportunities needed for learning to read.

Educational history is gathered from many sources: interviews with parents or guardians and students, teacher interviews and questionnaires, cumulative school records that follow the student from year to year, portfolios, and report cards. If you are not a staff member at the student's school, you must obtain written permission from parents before contacting school personnel.

A complete history of schooling covers several areas:

* Ask about preschool experiences, including the length of nursery or preschool education and kindergarten attendance.
* Ask about the student's early reading and writing instruction and the age and grade at which such instruction began. Children's early literacy instruction must be considered in conjunction with their age and development (International Reading Association, 2005; Venn & Jahn, 2004; Teale & Yokota, 2000; International Reading Association & National Association for the Education of Young Children, 1998).
* Ask if the student has ever repeated a grade; if so, try to determine the cause of retention.
* Ask if the student is currently in, or has ever been in, a special school program. Placement in such programs as special education, special reading, or Title I can influence the type of instruction and attention a student receives. If the student is in a special program, is the placement full time or part time? Does the student receive supportive help in a resource room setting or in the regular classroom?
* If previous diagnostic work has been done for the student through the school or a private agency, ask the parents to bring in a copy of the findings. You must have written consent from parents or guardians to contact these professionals.

School Attendance   Absence from school and frequent transfers can be harmful to a student's progress. Some children are absent from school for weeks at a time, missing critical instruction. Other students change schools several times during the year, resulting in abrupt changes in instructional approaches and materials.

Information about school attendance can be obtained from parents, teachers, and cumulative school records. Try to determine how many times the student has been absent in the current school year and in earlier years. Instruction missed in first and second grade seems to have a particularly damaging effect on reading progress. Extended absences are also harmful. Try to determine how long the student has been in a particular school, and how many different schools the student has attended. Ask about the reasons for frequent absences or transfers.

School Instruction   Reading instruction dramatically affects students' success in reading. Research has shown that a balanced approach to literacy instruction is highly effective (Samuels & Farstrup, 2002; Anderson, Hiebert, Scott, & Wilkinson, 1985). Components of a balanced approach include reading, writing, speaking, and listening presented in a culturally sensitive, multifaceted program that is responsive to individual and developmental needs (Cunningham, Cunningham, Moore, & Moore, 2005). Thus, teachers need a strong repertoire of instructional strategies and approaches in word knowledge, comprehension, and writing. Further, although many students learn word recognition and comprehension strategies through extensive literacy experiences, struggling students may need guided instruction that supports them as they apply strategies (Duffy, 2002; Strickland, Ganske, & Monroe, 2002). Effective instruction for struggling readers must be carefully matched to individual students' needs (Allington, 2005; Duffy, 2001; Short, Kane, & Peeling, 2000).

Struggling readers are often given books that are too hard for them. Because most classrooms use basal programs as the primary instructional material for teaching literacy, it is important to examine the characteristics of these materials (Hiebert & Mesmer, 2006; Hiebert & Martin, 2001). In response to a mandate for more literature-based teaching practices and materials, the basal reading series of one publication contained more difficult words, complex concepts, and longer selections than earlier series (Hoffman, McCarthey, Abbott, Christian, Corman, Curry, et al., 1994). Studies indicated that this series contained more engaging, predictable content than the previous skills-based series. However, many students struggled with the more difficult texts. Analyses of the basal programs indicated that the 1994 programs had little regard for decodability or controlled vocabulary (Hoffman, McCarthey, Elliott, Bayler, Price, Ferree, et al., 1998). In the subsequent revision, the trend shifted back to the more decodable texts for beginning instruction (Hoffman, Sailors, & Patterson, 2002). Yet, if the whole class is using one text, lower-achieving readers may not be able to read the material successfully. Even teachers who organize students into small groups may still have one or two students who struggle with materials that are easy for their classmates. Basal reading programs published in recent years have attempted to provide a comprehensive approach to literacy instruction while providing materials teachers can use to differentiate instruction. These new reading programs integrate the instructional anthology with accompanying sets of leveled books for guided reading instruction (Houghton-Mifflin, 2008; Scott Foresman, 2008; Macmillan/McGraw-Hill, 2006; Rasinski & Padak, 2004).

Information about a student's first experiences with reading instruction may provide insights into how a problem developed. Was the initial method suited to the student's needs and level of development? Did the reading problem start in first grade, or were the student's early experiences successful? Reading problems that begin in first and second grade often involve word recognition abilities; problems that develop in the intermediate grades (or later) tend to focus on comprehension and language abilities.

Information about school instruction can be obtained from school personnel, parents, and students. The school is a particularly valuable source. For most reading teachers, the school is the primary source of information. It is typically the classroom teacher who approaches the reading teacher with concerns about individual students. Teacher interviews and questionnaires, school records, and information about schoolbooks and assignments all provide insight into instruction. In gathering information from the school, the reading teacher should try to get a full picture of instruction and progress. Is the student receiving specific reading instruction, or is reading and writing instruction addressed within the context of other subjects, such as social studies and science? If reading is taught as a subject, is a reading textbook series used? If so, which one, and at what level is the student placed? If novels and trade books are used, which ones has the student read? Is the class organized into reading groups, or is the whole class instructed together? Are word recognition and comprehension strategies taught explicitly? Are students taught strategies for reading in social studies, health, and science books? Is the class provided time for independent or recreational reading? If so, are books provided at the student's level? Is writing encouraged? How is the student performing in areas such as math, science, social studies, art, and physical education?

The student's own perceptions about reading instruction can also offer valuable insights. Interviews and informal conversations provide information about whether a student likes reading class (or instruction) and whether the books and stories are easy and interesting to read. Ask the student what activities take place during reading instruction. Are stories and novels read orally or silently? We have found that students with reading problems often would like to change something about their instruction. For this reason, the students often are asked, "If you could change one thing about reading class, what would it be?" A student's perceptions of reading can also be revealing. You might ask the student what reading is or what makes a good reader (Johnson, 2005).

Parents' perceptions of the school environment come from their child's comments, homework examples, report cards, and teacher conferences. During an interview, ask the parents to describe the type and amount of homework their child is given. Ask parents if the student brings books home from school to read. Parents often have strong feelings about instructional factors that may have contributed to their child's reading problems. Obtaining this information from parents is important in fostering a cooperative spirit between the school and home.

Sometimes, the information suggests that school factors may have indeed contributed to the reading problem. What can you, as a reading teacher, do? You cannot change the past. Furthermore, assigning blame to a particular school or teacher is not helpful. A classroom teacher may have difficulty responding to the special needs of an individual when coping with a group of 25 to 35 students. A reading teacher can make helpful suggestions to the school and can foster cooperation among all of the professionals who are trying to help the student. For example, one reading teacher suggested the titles of easy books for a low-achieving student to read during recreational reading time in his class. Another reading teacher worked with the classroom teacher to adjust difficult homework assignments for a special-needs student.

In some cases, information about past instruction is helpful in planning an effective current reading program. Ten-year-old Gregg loudly stated that he hated school reading class and "all those hard worksheets." Gregg defined reading as "saying the words right," which explained his lack of interest and enthusiasm for it. To help him overcome negative past experiences, his reading teacher avoided any tasks that resembled rote instruction and emphasized comprehension rather than accurate word pronunciation. Gregg selected the stories that he and his teacher read together. They paused periodically to discuss and predict what might happen next. Because Gregg enjoyed art, the tutor encouraged him to illustrate parts of the story and vocabulary words. At the end of the semester, Gregg proclaimed that these lessons "weren't real reading classes, but I learned to read better."

Social and Cultural Environments

Reading is a social process because during reading, an author communicates his or her ideas to the reader. Because of the social nature of reading, a student's relationships with parents, teachers, and peers can affect reading achievement. Social interactions occur through specific personal relationships and through the student's general cultural environment (Gillet & Temple, 2000).

Successful social interactions can provide the student with feelings of high self-esteem and confidence that encourage reading achievement. Unfortunately, many poor readers experience difficulties in social interactions. Students with reading problems often are rejected by their classmates and viewed with disfavor by their teachers. They may be a source of concern to their parents. As a result, poor readers often have difficulty relating to others.

In today's schools, reading instruction tends to be a social experience. Students often read orally in pairs or groups, sharing thoughts and feelings about a novel or working in cooperative groups. These activities can be burdensome to a student who lacks ability in social interactions. Students who are poor readers may withdraw in shame when they have to share their reading. The student's cultural environment may also affect reading progress. Some students are surrounded by peers who do not value literacy. In addition, the student's cultural background may make asking a teacher for help a difficult and uncomfortable experience. When a student's culture does not value academic achievement, instruction can be made relevant by having the student read and write about interesting topics, such as popular TV programs and movies, video games, and favorite musicians or comedians.

Reading teachers should gather background information about both the student's social and cultural environments. Often the parents' description of their child's social interactions is informative. Ask the parents to describe their child's relationships with them and with siblings. Does the student have many friends? Do these friends value education? What is the student's relationship with the teacher and classmates? Does the student willingly join in group activities or prefer to work alone? Is the student shy and withdrawn or outgoing?

Interviewing the student about friends and interests can also be useful. Does the student see reading as something that friends and family value? Does the student spend time with friends? What are the student's interests? Such information provides hints about how to make reading a motivating experience.

At times, the investigation of a student's social relationships indicates cause for concern. However, teachers often find that these relationships improve when academic problems are alleviated. When students read better, their feelings of success make them more confident in social interactions. Thus, by offering good instruction, reading teachers often can affect both a student's achievement and her or his social relationships.

At other times, a teacher's use of a student's interests may draw him or her more comfortably into social interactions. Eamon, the poorest reader in his third-grade class, seldom interacted with his peers. During recess, he stood in the corner of the playground; at lunch, he usually sat and ate alone. To help him, the reading teacher made a point of talking to Eamon alone whenever possible. Discovering that Eamon was passionately interested in snakes and had two pet reptiles at home, she gave him several books about snakes and asked him to bring his pets to school. The eager fascination of the other children motivated Eamon to talk about the care of his pets and how they should be handled. The teacher also read several books about snakes to the class and encouraged Eamon to critique them. Were the facts accurate? Had Eamon ever seen a snake do that? As Eamon became the class snake expert, he gradually increased his willingness to participate in class activities and to seek out the company of his peers.

Carefully planned reading with peers can promote social and reading competence. Jennifer, a sixth-grade student in the reading center, was reading at the third-grade level and had a history of negative social interactions. To improve reading and social skills,

Jennifer was paired with Samantha, a fifth-grade student. The two girls read *Charlotte's Web* (White) at home and returned to the reading center to discuss difficult words, the characters in the book, and the plot. Sharing the reading experience helped Jennifer overcome her shyness. Jennifer and Samantha became good friends as they enjoyed the positive social experience of reacting to good children's literature.

Information about the Individual

Many of the factors that contribute to reading problems are found within the individual student. This section discusses information about emotional status, potential (intelligence), physical health, and language development.

Emotional Information

Poor readers often display emotional problems that impede learning. Not surprisingly, many students who have problems in their social environments (discussed in the previous section) also display emotional problems.

For some students, problems with learning to read may result in emotional problems. For example, some children withdraw and refuse even to attempt to read or write. Seven-year-old Carlos eagerly participated in classroom activities that did not involve reading or writing. However, when the teacher asked students to take out their books, Carlos would either put his head down on the desk or turn his chair away from the teacher. To avoid repeated failure, Carlos had decided not to read anymore.

If learning has been a painful experience, some students develop a block against all school activities. Others react by becoming hostile or aggressive. Still others develop self-images of poor readers; because these students believe that they are "dumb," they give up trying to learn. Other students become overcome with anxiety and may start to shake or stutter when asked to read.

For other students, the reading problem may be a result of an underlying emotional problem. For example, some students first develop problems with literacy just as their parents are separating or going through a divorce.

Teachers, parents, and students themselves can all offer insights about emotional factors that may affect reading achievement. The teacher, who sees the child in class, can note reactions to instructional activities. The parents can describe the child at home and with peers. Finally, the perceptions of the student are perhaps the most revealing.

What types of school information are useful in determining a student's emotional state? Knowing whether the student works independently in class is helpful. Does the student cooperate well with others? Does the student pay attention and follow directions? Does the teacher see evidence of emotional outbursts, inappropriate behavior, or depression? Does the student willingly participate in reading activities? How does the student interact with others?

Through parent interviews, the reading teacher can also gain insight into a student's interactions, behavior, and attitudes within the family and with friends. For example, can the child take enough responsibility to do chores and complete work? Does the youngster often withdraw from peer groups? Does the child seem unhappy?

Of course, simply observing and interacting with a student also gives much information. Observation of a student's behaviors and attitudes during reading class can make you aware of that student's emotional state. Finally, as you interact with a student, you will be able to judge the appropriateness of responses.

At times, you may suspect that emotional factors may be affecting reading. However, because a reading teacher is not a psychologist or psychiatrist, directly addressing emotional problems is not appropriate. Rather, a reading teacher may best address these problems by planning sensitive instruction.

Donny, one student in a group of five, was quite hostile during reading instruction. He accused the teacher of liking the other children better and of thinking that he was "dumb." He deliberately dropped books and pencils, loudly complained of a stomachache, and refused to answer questions or read orally. In fact, his behavior totally disrupted group activities. To help Donny, his reading teacher made a special effort to spend some time with him alone. She read orally with Donny, praising him when he was successful and gently helping him when he had difficulties. Donny enjoyed this private attention, away from the possibly negative reactions of others. Slowly, Donny's trust in his teacher developed into an improved self-concept, and he became more cooperative during group reading activities.

Information about Potential (Intelligence)

A student's potential for learning affects his or her ability to read. Potential for learning is often measured by tests of intelligence; however, an individual's total potential cannot be fully captured in a test.

Physical Information

Many physical factors, including hearing problems, vision problems, general health problems, and neurological dysfunction, affect a student's ability to read. This section provides a brief overview of these factors.

Hearing Problems   A hearing loss, even if it is moderate or temporary, can greatly impede reading instruction. A student who cannot hear the teacher or who cannot differentiate the sounds needed for phonics instruction will often develop reading problems. However, the most serious effect of hearing loss is that it impedes normal language development, which is the basis of reading.

When students cannot hear adequately, all of their communication skills are impaired. The result can be problems with vocabulary, grammar, and verbal thinking skills. Hearing loss is most devastating if it occurs during the language acquisition years (between the ages of 2 and 4).

Because of the importance of adequate hearing, students need to be screened for possible hearing impairment. Often schools do this testing, or preliminary screening may be done by a reading teacher.

Additional information can also help pinpoint a hearing problem. The reading teacher can ask the parents if they have observed any speech problems, such as slurred speech or difficulty in making sounds. Has the student suffered frequent ear infections? Does the student turn her or his head to one side while listening? Does the student seem inattentive or ask for information to be repeated? Does the student fail to respond immediately when called? Of course, if you observe such behaviors during your own work with a student, you should immediately request a screening for hearing loss.

What should be done if a teacher suspects a hearing problem? As mentioned, many schools and reading centers have devices for screening students. However, because the testing of hearing is complex and the results may vary from time to time in children, a reading teacher cannot make a definitive diagnosis. Rather, if screening devices or symptoms suggest a hearing loss, the parents or school should be referred to a professional in the field, such as an audiologist.

Teachers can also adjust their instruction to meet the needs of a student with a hearing loss or a suspected hearing loss. Remember to sit close to and face the student directly when speaking. If the student does not respond directly to questions or comments, try to repeat them in a cheerful fashion. Let the student watch you pronounce the words.

Vision Problems   The ability to see clearly is critical to the reading process. Vision problems may be quite complex, involving difficulties in seeing close up or far away or in focusing both eyes together. In addition, certain students may have difficulties with glare, fluorescent lights, and distinguishing colors. Because vision changes rapidly for children, it should be tested often.

As with possible hearing loss, a reading teacher should try to determine whether the student has a vision problem. School records or parents can provide the results of recent vision screenings. Reading teachers can also administer vision-screening tests.

Visual behaviors that indicate problems include:

* Avoidance of reading and writing
* Holding a page very close or at an unusual angle
* Losing one's place while reading
* Frowning, squinting, or scowling during reading
* Headaches, rubbing the eyes, or covering one eye

What can a teacher do to help a student with a suspected vision problem? If a screening test or student behaviors indicate a vision problem, the youngster should be referred to a vision professional (optometrist or ophthalmologist) for further testing.

If a reading teacher is dealing with an uncorrected vision problem, certain accommodations will make the student more comfortable. Use books with larger type if they are available. Some computer software allows the teacher to adjust the size of the print. In addition, the teacher may record some of the student's books on audiotape.

General Health Problems   Because learning is an active process, it requires that a student be alert, energetic, and able to concentrate for long periods. Poor physical health can impair the ability to concentrate. Through parent interviews and questionnaires, reading teachers can determine whether the child has any medical conditions that may affect learning or if the child suffers from conditions or takes medications that affect the ability to concentrate.

What can a teacher do when a student suffers from health problems? Sensitivity to the needs of the student is often crucial. Meghan suffered from severe allergies, and the strong medication that she took during certain times of the year tended to make her lethargic. Knowing this situation, her reading teacher praised Meghan for the work she completed and never suggested that Meghan was not trying her best.

Neurological Problems   All learning, including the ability to learn to read, is neurologically based. The reading process demands an intact and well-functioning nervous system; a neurological dysfunction can destroy reading ability.

Children with atypical neurological systems are often "hard-core" disabled readers, who have extreme difficulty learning to read (Vellutino, Scanlon, Sipay, Small, Chen, Pratt, et al., 1996) or are labeled dyslexic. Thus, if assessment of a student's reading suggests a serious reading problem, a teacher might consider the possibility of referring the student for a neurological examination.

To probe further, ask the parents if any other member of the family has experienced a serious reading problem. A history of a difficult pregnancy and delivery may also point to neurological dysfunction. Certain studies suggest that 50 to 70 percent of reading disabilities may be hereditary (Torgesen, 2004). Other signs of possible neurological dysfunction include slow physical development and accidents that have involved damage to the brain.

Evidence indicates that attention deficit hyperactivity disorder (ADHD), a problem that affects the ability to concentrate, is caused by neurological problems (Lerner & Kline, 2006). Students who have ADHD are often prescribed medications, such as Ritalin, to help control their behavior. Finally, many practitioners believe that children with learning disabilities may also have subtle problems in their neurological functioning. Students with learning disabilities are entitled to special services under the provision of the 2004 reauthorization of the Individuals with Disabilities Education Improvement Act (IDEA).

Information on possible neurological problems can be gathered from the parents, school records, and specialists (such as physicians) who have been consulted by the child's parents. If students with suspected neurological problems have been diagnosed as having ADHD or a learning disability, the school will have already gathered much information about these students. For example, thorough testing is required for every special education student to comply with IDEA regulations. With parental consent, these records can be released to a reading teacher.

What can be done if a teacher suspects that a student may have a neurological dysfunction? If students need further testing, they should be referred to physicians specializing in pediatrics and neurology or to appropriate professionals in their schools.

However, teachers are still responsible for teaching these students to read. Can they help them? The answer is a resounding yes. At one time, educators believed that very specialized methods were required to teach students with neurological difficulties to read. More recent studies suggest that the same methods that are effective with all students who have reading problems will also work with those who have a neurological dysfunction (Cunningham & Allington, 2006). A reading teacher who concentrates on effective and motivating methods will often help these students make substantial gains. Be aware, however, that students with neurological problems (or suspected neurological problems) may improve at a slower rate and may need longer and more intense instruction than most reading-disabled students.

Information about Language Development

Because reading is language expressed in written form, a student's language development forms the basis for all reading. The ability to express and receive thoughts through language is fundamental to being able to read. A student who is confused about oral language sounds will have difficulty pronouncing written words. A student who does not know many word meanings will gain little information from reading, even if he or she can pronounce all of the words. In other instances, a student's language patterns may be mature but may differ from the language used in school. Many students come to school speaking languages other than English. They need rich experiences in learning English, plus experiences reading in their native languages, to develop high-level comprehension. Students who speak nonstandard dialects may lack both exposure to more standard English language patterns and a feeling of pride and proficiency in their own dialect.

A reading teacher can easily obtain background information about a student's language. Simply listening to or conversing with a student gives many valuable insights. A student who speaks in long sentences, provides full answers to questions, and is able to use many words probably has an excellent language base for reading. Unfortunately, many students with reading problems speak haltingly in short sentences and use just a few words.

Joey, for example, was in kindergarten, yet his language patterns resembled those of a 3- or 4-year-old. He often used his name instead of a pronoun or used pronouns incorrectly. "Joey needs crayons" or "Me need crayons" were typical utterances. Similarly, 8-year-old Paul had difficulty dictating even a single sentence to his reading teacher. In addition to observation, interview questions can reveal much about a student's language. Ask the parents whether their child's language development was slower than that of other children or was within a normal range. Did their child experience any speech difficulties? Has the child had any language or speech therapy? To obtain information about language differences, ask parents what languages are spoken in the home and whether the child knew English when entering school. A history of class placements, including bilingual services or ELL, often gives much information about a student's proficiency in English.

What can be done if a teacher suspects that language problems are affecting a student's reading? At times, evaluation by a language professional (speech therapist or language specialist) may be needed to pinpoint the precise source of the difficulty. However, in many other instances, a reading teacher can foster the development of rich language by employing enjoyable instructional strategies, such as reading language-rich storybooks to the student, encouraging conversation, and developing knowledge of abstract concepts.

Twelve-year-old José, a student in the reading center, could speak and understand basic English, but he lacked the English skills to read more sophisticated material. His tutor began by reading selections from the daily newspaper that focused on news about Mexico, his homeland. José enjoyed helping his tutor with the pronunciation of Spanish names. They then discussed what was happening in Mexico and read portions of the articles together several times. Finally José attempted to read articles alone. At one point, he joyfully exclaimed, "That's what NAFTA looks like!" José and his tutor continued this process, moving gradually into other familiar topics such as television and sports. As he did this, José began to locate cognates—words that are the same in Spanish and English—to help his tutor learn Spanish.

Methods of Collecting Information

As shown, a wealth of important background information may be collected about a student with reading difficulties. This information helps teachers understand the factors that contribute to a reading problem. It also aids us in planning effective and motivating instruction.

Generally, background information is collected at the beginning of a teacher's work with a student. The assessment tools most frequently used are (1) interviews and questionnaires, (2) informal talks with the student, parents, and professionals, (3) records of previous testing, school achievement, or report cards, and (4) observation. In the school setting, the classroom teacher usually initiates the process by contacting the reading teacher for help with a student who is struggling in reading and writing. In many reading centers, parents or school literacy specialists may make the initial contact and provide the first source of information. In both situations, it is important for the reading teacher to collect information from the classroom teacher and the parents as well as the student.

Interview and Questionnaire

Interviews and questionnaires with informed and concerned people yield information about the student that cannot be obtained in any other way. In these two formats, those concerned with a student's reading problem are able to state important information frankly and fully.

Interview   In an interview, a reading teacher follows a prescribed set of questions, asking them orally of the person who is being interviewed. A reading teacher can interview parents, the student, or the classroom teacher. The personal and informal atmosphere of an interview encourages the sharing of valuable information in a sympathetic setting. We interview the parents separately from the student and use different interview forms. A reading teacher who works outside the student's school may get valuable information from interviewing the classroom teachers and other professionals in the school. However, written permission must be obtained from the parents before a student's school may be contacted. Some important procedures ensure a successful interview:

* Begin by telling the parents, student, or classroom teacher that this information will be kept confidential.
* Strive for an amiable, open atmosphere. Briefly discussing a neutral topic, such as the weather or sports, can reduce initial fears or discomfort about the interview process.

- Avoid indicating disapproval of responses.
- Follow a directed plan. You should know what questions to ask before the interview begins. These questions should be in front of you so they will not be forgotten.
- Take notes, because remembering everything that was said is difficult. Explain why you are taking notes. If the person being interviewed asks about what he or she said, cheerfully read the notes back aloud.
- Because of important legal and moral considerations involved in the interview, it must be kept confidential. If you wish to tape the interview, you must obtain written consent from parents, guardians, or the professionals involved. The presence of another individual during the interview also requires consent. Finally, information shared during an interview or any other part of the assessment procedure cannot be released to another agency without parental permission.

Questionnaire   Like an interview, a questionnaire consists of a group of questions to which parents, a student, or another professional respond. However, the list of questions is responded to in writing. A questionnaire may simply be mailed to the respondent, filled out, and mailed back. Alternatively, it may be filled out in the presence of the reading teacher.

Questionnaires are valuable when a face-to-face interview is not feasible. In the reading center, we often mail questionnaires to the classroom teachers of the students we serve because they have difficulties coming in for interviews. In addition, because questions are responded to independently, the use of a questionnaire enables parents, students, and classroom teachers to formulate thoughtful responses and take the time to gather valuable information about developmental history, school attendance, and grades. However, questionnaires may be unproductive with parents and children who find writing difficult.

Parent Background Information Form   A sample form for gathering background information from parents is provided on the website for this book. Please feel free to download the document and adapt it for your own context. We suggest that, if possible, this form be used as an interview, rather than as a questionnaire.

Student Background Information Form   A student information form for younger students that can be used either in an interview or as a questionnaire is provided on the website for this book. A parallel form for older students is also provided. Questions about student interests help to establish rapport with a student and give the teacher information to motivate and personalize reading instruction. You can download the documents and modify questions to suit your locality (for example, adding skiing or surfing).

A final section gives information on how the student thinks about reading (Johnson, 2005). Often, low-achieving students think that reading is just saying words; not surprisingly, they do not focus on meaning. These questions also explore the student's reading strategies. Many students with reading problems will simply "sound it out" as the only strategy they use to cope with an unknown word; they do not realize that meaning can also be used. Other low-achieving students have unrealistic pictures of good readers and believe that such readers know all the words and never make mistakes.

School Information Form   A form for collecting information from the student's school is provided on the website for this book. Please download the form and add questions that may be pertinent to your setting. If you are working in a setting other than a school, remember that written permission from parents or guardians is needed whenever you contact a student's school.

Informal Talks

In addition to interviews and questionnaires, informal conversations throughout the year can keep providing valuable insights. Twelve-year-old Adam continued to share his frustrations with homework assignments through the school year, thus enabling us to help his classroom teacher modify them.

The parents of another child revealed, over an informal cup of coffee, that he had had extensive difficulties immediately after birth. This information, which was not given in an initial interview, was shared only as the parents became more comfortable with us. The reading teacher or the classroom teacher should be alert to opportunities to gather information through these continuing, informal means. Keeping in touch with parents as instruction continues is important. Equally important is the sharing of information between the classroom teacher and the reading teacher. Informal, but professional interactions between colleagues can often reveal important information and lead to increased effectiveness in providing instruction.

Continued contact with parents provides teachers with valuable information about how students are reacting to instruction, whether they are improving, and if their attitudes toward reading are becoming more positive. Finally, contact helps families to encourage children to read at home.

School Records and Materials

School records, previous diagnostic reports, report cards, and *student portfolios* (organized collections of student's work kept in school) are all valuable sources of information. In addition, cumulative records, which detail a student's progress over a number of years, provide information about the history of a reading problem. Reports, such as an individualized educational program (IEP) prepared for special education students under the provisions of the IDEA, are also valuable sources of information. Reading teachers in schools have access to this information. If you are a reading teacher working in a setting outside of the student's school, ask parents to allow you access to school information because it enables you to gain a more thorough and balanced view of a child's reading problem.

Observation during Reading Lessons

In the discussion of background information, many types of information were presented that could be gathered through direct observation of your student. Direct observation provides insight into students' social interactions and language development. As a reading teacher, you can make observations and enter anecdotal records as you work with a student. However, if possible, observe the student in many different settings. Student reactions and behaviors often vary according to the environment in which they are observed. A student who is quiet and cooperative in individual instruction may be noisy and defiant in a large class. In fact, sometimes a description of one student in these two settings is so different that teachers wonder if the same individual is being observed. To gain a realistic picture of students, observe them in natural settings (at parties, on the playground, in their general education classes) as well as in special reading classes. As a school-based reading teacher or literacy specialist, observations of the student in a variety of learning contexts is crucial to supporting teachers as they plan instruction for the student.

As you make observations, be sure to note them in writing for future reference. Understanding the instructional context is crucial in providing support for classroom teachers. Remember that, even if the student receives supplemental support, the vast majority of instruction for most struggling readers and writers occurs within the general education classroom setting. Thus, an important role of the reading specialist is to provide instructional support to the classroom teacher (Strickland, et al., 2002).

Summary

This chapter discusses collecting background information on students with reading problems, including information about the environment and the individual. Background factors interact with reading problems in complex ways; a background factor can coexist with a reading problem and yet not cause that problem.

Environmental factors include the home, school, and social and cultural environments. The home influences a child as parents serve as role models for literacy and provide a general environment that nurtures the child. The child's school history, attendance, and school instruction also affect a reading problem. Often, students who have reading problems are not receiving instruction that meets their needs. Students with reading problems also tend to have social difficulties. They may also come from a culture that does not support literacy.

Individual factors include emotional status, potential or intelligence, physical health, and language development. Students with reading problems may have emotional difficulties. Sometimes these emotional problems are alleviated as reading improves. Physical factors include hearing problems, visual problems, general health problems, and neurological problems. Students with ADD and learning disabilities may have subtle neurological problems. Students with reading problems may also have difficulties with language development.

Information may be collected through interviews, written questionnaires, informal talks, school records and materials, and observation.

REFERENCES

Allington, R. L. (2005). *What Really Matters for Struggling Readers: Designing Research-Based Programs.* Boston: Allyn & Bacon.

Anderson, R. C., Hiebert, E. H., Scott, J. A., & Wilkinson, I. A. G. (1985). *Becoming a Nation of Readers.* Washington, DC: National Institute of Education.

Cunningham, P. M., & Allington, R. L. (2006). *Classrooms that Work: They Can All Read and Write* (4th ed.). New York: Allyn & Bacon.

Cunningham, P. M., Cunningham, J. W., Moore, S. A., & Moore, D. W. (2005). *Reading and Writing in Elementary Classrooms: Research Based K-4 Instruction* (5th ed.). Boston: Allyn & Bacon.

Duffy, A. M. (2001). Balance, literacy acceleration, and responsive teaching in a summer school literacy program for elementary school struggling readers. *Reading Research and Instruction, 40,* 67–100.

Duffy, G. (2002). Direct explanations of strategies. In C. Block and M. Pressley (Eds.), *Comprehension Instruction: Research-Based Best Practices,* pp. 28–41. New York: The Guilford Press.

Gillet, J. W., & Temple, C. (2000). *Understanding Reading Problems: Assessment and Instruction* (5th ed.). New York: Longman.

Hiebert, E. H., & Martin, L. A. (2001). The texts of beginning reading instruction. In S. B. Neuman & D. K. Dickinson (Eds.), *Handbook of Early Literacy Research,* pp. 361–376. New York: Guilford Press.

Hiebert, E. H., & Mesmer, H. A. E. (2006). Perspectives on the difficulty of beginning reading texts. In D. K. Dickinson & S. B. Neuman (Eds.), *Handbook of Early Literacy Research,* Volume 2, pp. 395–409, New York: Guilford Press.

Hoffman, J. V., McCarthey, S. J., Abbott, J., Christain, C., Corman, L., Curry, C., et al. (1994). So what's new in the basals? A focus on first grade. *Journal of Reading Behavior, 26,* 47–73.

Hoffman, J. V., McCarthey, S. J., Elliott, B., Bayler, D. L., Price, D. P., Ferree, A., et al. (1998). The literature based basals in first-grade classrooms: Savior, Satan, or same-old, same-old? *Reading Research Quarterly, 33,* 168–197.

Hoffman, J. V., Sailors, M., & Patterson, E. U. (2002). Decodable tests for beginning reading instruction: The year 2000 basals. Report #1-016. Ann Arbor: University of Michigan, Center for the Improvement of Early Reading Achievement.

Houghton-Mifflin. (2008). *Houghton Mifflin Reading.* Boston: Houghton-Mifflin Publishing.

Individuals with Disabilities Education Improvement Act of (2004), Public Law 108-446.

International Reading Association. (2005). *Literacy Development in the Preschool Years: A Position Statement of the International Reading Association.* Newark, DE: International Reading Association.

International Reading Association & National Association for the Education of Young Children. (1998). *Learning to Read and Write: Developmentally Appropriate Practices for Young Children.*

Johnson, J. C. (2005). What makes a "good reader? Asking student to define "good" readers. *Reading Teacher, 58,* 766–773.

Lerner, J. W., & Kline, F. (2006). *Learning Disabilities and Related Disorders: Characteristics and Teaching Strategies.* Boston: Houghton-Mifflin Co.

Macmillan/McGraw-Hill. (2005). *Treasures Reading Program.* New York: McGraw-Hill Publishing.

Maslin, P. (2007). Comparison of readability and decodability levels across five first grade basal programs. *Reading Improvement, 44*(2), 59.

Rasinski, T., & Padak, N. (2004). Beyond consensus—beyond balance: Toward a comprehensive literacy curriculum. *Reading and Writing Quarterly, 20,* 91–102.

Samuels, S. J., & Farstrup, A. E. (eds.). (2002). *What Research Has to Say About Reading Instruction* (3rd ed.). Newark, DE: International Reading Association.

Scott Foresman. (2008). *Scott Foresman Reading Street.* Boston: Pearson Education.

Short, R. A., Kane, M., & Peeling, T. (2000). Retooling the reading lesson: Matching the right tools to the job. *The Reading Teacher, 54,* 284–295.

Strickland, D. S., Ganske, K., & Monroe, J. K. (2002). *Supporting Struggling Readers and Writers: Strategies for Classroom Intervention.* Newark, DE: International Reading Association.

Teale, W. H., & Yokota, J. (2000). Beginning reading and writing: Perspectives on instruction. In D. S. Strickland and L. M. Morrow (Eds.), *Beginning Reading and Writing.* New York: Teachers College Press.

Torgesen, J. K. (2004). Learning disabilities: An historical and conceptual overview. In B. Y. L. Wong (ed.), *Learning About Learning Disabilities* (3rd ed., pp. 3–34). San Diego, CA: Academic Press.

Vellutino, F. R., Scanlon, D. M., Sipay, E. R., Small, S. G., Chen, R., Pratt, A., et al. (1996). Cognitive profiles of difficult-to-remediate and readily remediated poor readers: Early intervention as a vehicle for distinguishing between cognitive and experiential deficits as basic causes of specific reading disability. *Journal of Educational Psychology, 88,* 601–638.

Venn, E. C., & Jahn, M. D. (2004). *Teaching and Learning in Preschool: Using Individually Appropriate Practices in Early Childhood Literacy Instruction.* Newark, DE: International Reading Association.

CHAPTER

7 Using an Informal Reading Inventory for Assessment

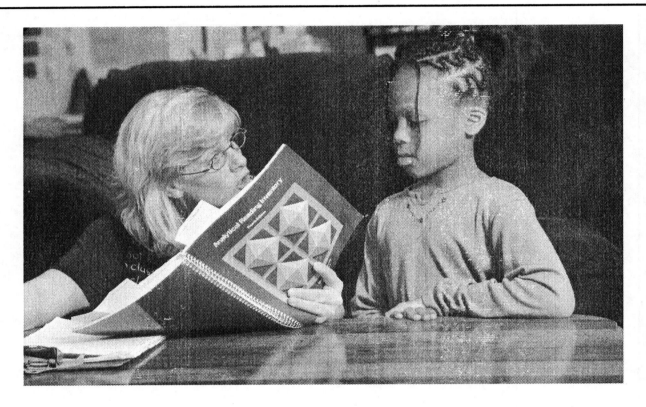

Introduction

This chapter describes the process of assessing a student's reading performance using an informal reading inventory. It begins by presenting two general questions that are critical to assessment of literacy progress. The chapter focuses on the informal reading inventory, a fundamental tool that gives many insights into a student's reading. It describes how to administer and score this instrument.

General Assessment Questions: An Overview

The process of assessing reading involves more than giving tests. In fact, a good reading teacher uses tests, background information, and observation to formulate answers to questions about a student's progress as a reader. Reading assessment thus represents a thoughtful synthesis and interpretation of all the information that is collected about a student.

Assessing a student's reading achievement involves answering three general questions: (1) Does the student have a reading problem; (2) how severe is it?; and (3) what is the general area of the reading problem? You can answer these questions by observing and working with a student and by administering a variety of assessment tools. Often, an informal reading inventory can answer both questions as well as provide much additional information about a student.

Does the Student Have a Reading Problem and How Severe Is It?

To determine the existence and severity of a reading problem, a teacher needs to determine at what level a student is reading and to compare this level with the level at which that student should be reading. Thus, compare

* The student's current reading level to
* The student's appropriate reading level

By appropriate level, experts mean the books and stories that are used in the student's classroom, both for reading and for content area instruction (math, social studies, science). Usually, appropriate materials mean those at a student's grade level. However, if the student's class is reading at a higher level, then appropriate materials are at that higher level.

However, the opposite is not true. Children who are experiencing problems in school are often placed in special classes where they read materials well below their grade level. For example, a fourth grader might be in a special class that is reading second-grade material. In this case, second-grade text is *not* an appropriate level; the appropriate level for this student would be the fourth-grade level, the actual grade placement.

A student who can read at an appropriate level with acceptable word recognition and comprehension does not have a reading problem. However, a student who cannot read appropriate materials has a reading problem; the next step is to determine the severity of that problem. The difference between the student's grade placement and the grade placement of the texts he or she can read shows us how severe the reading problem is.

How does a teacher know whether a student's problem can be classified as severe? Guidelines provided by Spache (1981), presented in Table 7.1, compare a student's current grade

TABLE 7.1   Criteria for Determining a Severe Reading Problem

Student's Grade Placement	Difference between Grade Placement and Reading Level
Grades 1, 2, 3	One year or more
Grades 4, 5, 6	Two years or more
Grades 7 and above	Three years or more

Source: Spache (1981).

placement to the student's reading level. As you can see, the younger the student, the less difference is needed to define a reading problem as severe.

Using these criteria, a student who is placed in fourth grade but is reading at the second-grade level would have a reading problem that is severe. A fourth-grade student reading at the third-grade level would have a reading problem, but not a severe one. A fourth-grade student reading at the fourth-grade level would not have a reading problem.

The severity of the student's reading problem helps determine what type of special instruction is most effective. Students with severe reading problems may require long and intensive intervention in daily classes with individual instruction. In contrast, students with less-severe problems may blossom in small group settings that meet once or twice a week.

What Is the General Area of the Reading Problem?

Reading consists of many different components, or areas. Problems with reading fall into several general areas:

* Emergent literacy
* Word recognition accuracy
* Reading fluency
* Comprehension
* Language and meaning vocabulary

Some students may have problems in only one of these general areas. Other students may have problems in a combination of areas. Deciding the general area of a student's reading problem is important, because this information helps you, as a reading teacher, deliver the most effective instruction.

Problems with Emergent Literacy   Emergent literacy refers to the understandings and skills that underlie reading. These skills include the knowledge that print stands for meaning, the recognition of alphabet letters, and the ability to discriminate letter sounds. Although most students have acquired emergent literacy skills by the time they enter first grade, some students with reading problems continue to lack them long after formal reading instruction has begun.

Problems with Word Recognition Accuracy   Many students with reading problems cannot recognize words accurately. They lack strategies for identifying unfamiliar words. For example, trying to read a passage about farms, 9-year-old Carlos pronounced the word *farm* as *from, form,* and *for.*

Without accurate word identification, a student cannot comprehend a passage. For example, Carlos's summary of the farm passage was "They—the kids—were going someplace."

Problems with Reading Fluency   In addition to recognizing words accurately, readers need to identify them quickly. Words that we recognize instantly, without any need for analysis, are often called *sight vocabulary*. When we read fluently, we read text without stopping to analyze words. Fluency is important because human beings have limited memories. If we direct all our attention to figuring out the words, we will have difficulties understanding what the author is saying because we will have no resources to devote to comprehension (National Reading Panel, 2000; LaBerge & Samuels, 1974). Only if we recognize words quickly can we devote attention to comprehension. One student, Sofia, did a flawless oral reading of a story about Johnny Appleseed. However, because she labored over many words, she read slowly and without expression. As a result, she could answer only 3 of 10 comprehension questions.

Problems with Comprehension   Many students have problems comprehending what they read. At times, youngsters do not actively construct meaning but simply read to pronounce words or answer questions; thus, they are not reading to comprehend. Comprehension occurs at different levels. Literal comprehension includes understanding content that is explicitly stated in the text. Higher-level comprehension includes organizing what is read, drawing inferences, and thinking critically.

However, at times, poor understanding of text may be rooted in causes other than comprehension. For example, a student who lacks adequate word recognition may not be able to comprehend material. Sofia, mentioned previously, could not comprehend material because she lacked reading fluency. Similarly, apparent problems in reading comprehension may actually be caused by underlying problems in understanding language and word meanings.

Students need comprehension strategies when they read storylike or narrative text. Learning from informational text, or studying, is also part of comprehension; many students with reading problems do not know how to summarize, take notes, or prepare for multiple-choice and essay examinations.

Problems with Language and Meaning Vocabulary   Because reading is a language process, the ability to read cannot exceed the language we can understand and the word meanings we already know. Students who can pronounce words as they read but cannot understand them are not really reading. Aushabell, a second-grade student, had recently arrived from Turkey. She could read orally with amazing accuracy. However, she had little idea of what she was reading, because she lacked an understanding of such common English words as *mother*, *school*, *run*, and *night*. Many other students may speak English fluently but lack the rich language patterns and meaning vocabulary needed to read more sophisticated stories, novels, and textbooks. In fact, problems with underlying language and word meaning have been recognized as an extremely important factor in reading disabilities for intermediate and upper-grade students beyond third grade (National Reading Panel, 2000; Stanovich, 1986).

Overview of Informal Assessment Measures

Informal assessments are instruments that can be modified to suit the needs of students and the information teachers want to gather. The three key differences between formal and informal measures are:

* Student scores on informal measures are not based upon comparison to the scores of a norm group; that is, the average score of the norm group is not used as a reference point for a student's score.

* Informal measures are flexible and teachers are free to make modifications in procedures, adapting them to serve specific needs. On the other hand, formal measures are standardized and the administration process must remain the same across all students. Informal measures often represent a more authentic task.
* Authentic assessments are measures that are similar to actual reading tasks. In such measures, students read longer selections, summarize them, and answer questions just as they would in a typical classroom or when reading for their own information or enjoyment. In contrast to this, many formal tests only measure the student's ability to read short passages and answer multiple-choice questions.

To summarize, informal measures allow teachers the flexibility to adapt assessment so that it gives maximum information about how students, materials, and classroom situations interact to affect a reading problem. In this way, teachers can best determine how students can meet the demands of school reading.

Informal Reading Inventory

The informal reading inventory (IRI) is one informal assessment instrument that is widely used in reading assessment. The IRI is one of the best tools for observing and analyzing reading performance and for gathering information about how a student uses a wide range of reading strategies.

The IRI is administered to students individually. In an IRI, a student reads graded passages orally and/or silently and answers questions about them. As a student reads, the teacher records performance in word recognition and comprehension. Generally, IRIs contain passages at the preprimer, primer, first-grade, and all other grade levels through the eighth grade. Some IRIs contain high school passages. In addition, many inventories contain graded word lists, which are used to help select appropriate passage levels for students to read.

Passages in IRIs are representative of textbooks at different grade levels. Thus, a teacher can see how a student functions with classroom-like materials (Johnson, Kress, & Pikulski, 1987). Because it is classroom based, the information gained from an IRI is often more useful and realistic than the results of a standardized test. An IRI is also effective for assessing both short-term and long-term growth (Leslie & Caldwell, 2005; Leslie & Allen, 1999; Caldwell, Fromm, & O'Connor, 1997–1998).

A teacher can use an IRI to assess student reading achievement at different times during the school year. After a student has participated in an intervention program, an IRI can be used to measure the student's reading growth.

There are many different types of IRIs. A IRI is included on the website for this book. Whatever IRI you choose, remember that it is an informal measure you can adapt for different purposes and needs.

Obtaining Answers to General Assessment Questions

The IRI helps teachers obtain information on the three general assessment questions presented in the beginning of this chapter: (1) Does the student have a reading problem? (2) How severe is it? (3) What is the general area of the student's reading problem?

To answer the first question, the reading teacher determines an *instructional* reading level for the student. At this level, the student can read with instructional support, such as that provided in a typical classroom. The reading teacher then compares the instructional level on the IRI to the level of reading appropriate for the student. This comparison shows the existence and the severity of the reading problem. For example, a student who has an instructional level of fifth grade on the IRI and is in fifth grade does not have a reading problem. On the other hand, a fifth-grade student who has an instructional level of first grade has a severe reading problem.

The IRI can also help reveal the general area of the reading problem. Through listening to a student read orally, the teacher can determine whether the student's problem is word recognition or reading fluency. By asking questions and having students retell passages that have been read, the teacher can assess comprehension. By having the student listen to a passage and respond to questions, the teacher can determine whether language and meaning vocabulary are problems.

Finally, because the IRI is an individual test, a teacher has opportunities during its administration to make diagnostic observations that answer many different questions. Does the student read better orally or silently? Become easily frustrated? Point to each word or regularly lose the place in reading? Does the student have particular difficulty with drawing conclusions in material? The IRI is a rich source of these and many other insights.

However, like all other assessment tools, IRIs have some limitations. For example, examiners, especially untrained ones, can miss some problems with oral reading (Pikulski & Shanahan, 1982). In addition, a student's performance on a passage may be affected by the amount of personal interest in the subject, background knowledge, and text organization (Leslie & Caldwell, 2005; Caldwell, 1985; Lipson, Cox, Iwankowski, & Simon, 1984). Finally, the shortness of IRI selections (often a few hundred words) may not allow teachers to determine how well a student reads a multipage selection.

To obtain the greatest assessment value, teachers need to prepare carefully for administering an IRI. They need to use professional observation and judgment in effectively translating IRI results into instructional decisions.

Administering and Scoring the Informal Reading Inventory

Each published IRI comes with directions for administration that may vary in detail from other IRIs. All IRIs have some common features, however, and the directions given in this chapter are based on these similarities (See Table 7.2).

The IRI consists of a series of graded reading selections followed by questions. Some IRIs, such as the one provided on the website for this book, also contain graded word lists. The teacher can use these lists to decide which passage to administer first. The student reads passages (orally or silently) at different grade levels and stops when the material becomes too difficult. After the student reads each passage, the teacher asks comprehension questions. For passages read orally, the teacher records reading errors, or *miscues*, which are deviations from what is written. The teacher also records the time needed to read the passage and student responses to the questions. For passages read silently, the teacher records the time needed for reading and the responses to questions. In addition, the teacher may wish to ask students to retell a selection in their own words.

The percentage of reading miscues determines word recognition accuracy. The time needed for reading, which determines reading fluency, may also be used to judge passages. The responses to questions determine the comprehension score. In turn, word recognition and comprehension scores determine three reading levels for the student:

* *Independent:* the level at which a student can read without teacher guidance. Use this level for recreational reading.
* *Instructional:* the level at which a student can read with teacher support. Use this level for reading instruction.
* *Frustrational:* the level that is too hard for the student. Avoid this level or, if the student must read text at this level, read it to him or her.

TABLE 7.2   Procedure for Informal Reading Inventory Administration

Administer word lists.	Determine percentage of words read correctly on each list. Stop when student scores below 60 percent.	Use word list performance to select a beginning point for passage administration. Begin at a level where the student scores 90 percent on word list.
Administer passages in oral or reading format.	Record reading errors and determine independent, instructional, and/or frustration levels for word identification.	Record time needed to read each passage.
	Ask questions about the text and determine independent, instructional, and/or frustration levels for comprehension.	
	Stop when material becomes too difficult.	
Administer passages in silent reading format.	Ask questions and determine independent, instructional, and/or frustration levels for comprehension.	Record time needed to read each passage.
	Stop when material becomes too difficult.	

Each level is expressed as a grade level (from preprimer through eighth grade). Teachers can use these three levels to determine the severity of a reading problem as well as to select reading materials for various purposes.

Materials and General Preparation   To give an IRI, select a period of about an hour to work with an individual student. For younger students and students who are extremely nervous, you may want to divide the testing into two periods.

Materials you will need usually include:

* Student copy of the IRI word lists and passages
* Protocol (or teacher copy) of word lists and passages
* Stopwatch or watch with a second hand
* Tape recorder and audiotape
* Clipboard

Seat the student across from you and hand him or her the student copy of the passage to read. The student copy contains only the passage, without the questions. Record oral reading miscues and responses to questions on a teacher copy, referred to as a *protocol*. The protocol also contains questions to ask the student. Place the protocol on a clipboard for ease in handling.

Even experienced examiners find that taping the entire session is helpful so that they can refer to it later. Explain to the student that you are taping because you can't remember everything. Then place the tape recorder off to one side to reduce its intrusion into your testing situation. Because using the tape recorder often makes students nervous, you might ask your student to state his or her name and the date and then play these back to test the tape recorder.

If you wish to record the speed of your student's reading, you will need a stopwatch. Again, explain what you are doing, allow your student to handle the stopwatch for a short time, and then place it off to one side.

To help prepare a student for the IRI, explain that he or she will read passages both orally and silently and answer questions after each passage. Finally, tell the student that the material will become progressively more difficult.

Administering Word Lists Many IRIs provide a set of graded word lists. A student's performance on reading these word lists provides a quick way to determine which passage in the IRI the student should read first. Word lists generally start at the preprimer level and continue through the sixth-grade level. Each level usually has 20 to 25 words.

Students usually begin by reading the easiest list. As your youngster reads from the student's copy, record the responses on your teacher's copy. If the student recognizes a word *instantly*, mark a "+" in the timed column. If the student must analyze the word, mark a "+" in the untimed column. Administer the graded word lists until the student scores below 60 percent on any list (for example, misses 11 or more words out of 25 on the timed words or 8 or more out of 20). Begin the oral reading passages at the highest level on which the student scores at least 90 percent (no more than two miscues). If students score low on the word lists, begin testing at the preprimer level or eliminate the IRI and use emergent literacy assessments.

For example, fourth-grade Reyna's scores on the IRI word lists follow:

Preprimer: 90%   Grade 2: 80%

Primer: 100%   Grade 3: 55%

Grade 1: 80%

The primer level is the highest level at which Reyna scored 90 percent or above. Therefore, the teacher should begin testing Reyna at the primer level.

In addition to determining which passage to administer first, a student's performance on word lists can provide important diagnostic information about word recognition abilities. By looking at incorrect responses on a word list, you can gain insights about how a student analyzes words. You can see, for example, whether students are matching letters and sounds (phonics). You can also determine if they use structural analysis, such as examining prefixes and suffixes. Figure 7.1 shows Reyna's responses to the second-grade word list. If you look at Reyna's incorrect responses, you can see that she is able to use sounds (such as *t, dr, wh*) at the beginnings of words but does not always use correct vowels and ending sounds. This information provides the reading teacher with suggestions of phonics strategies that need to be taught.

Some children score much lower on word lists than they do when reading a selection. This situation suggests that the student is using the context of the passage as an aid to word recognition. Although this strategy is normal for beginning readers, older and skilled readers do not use context for word pronunciation, and poor readers often overuse it (Stanovich, 1993–1994; 1991).

Administering Reading Passages If you have given a word list, you will know the passage level to administer first. If not, start at a level that you think will be easy for the student. Sometimes information from other testing or classroom performance can suggest a beginning passage level. Remember that beginning too low is better than beginning too high. Students who have difficulty on the first IRI passage they read often become nervous. If you find that the first passage you have chosen is too challenging, stop the reading and immediately move down to an easier level.

Most IRIs provide passages for both oral and silent reading. Administer all of the oral passages first then administer the silent passages and obtain reading levels for this mode. (For an alternative plan, see the section in this chapter on Special Issues and Options in Using IRIs.)

The following steps are appropriate for administering passages for many other published IRIs:

1. Before reading, orally give the student a brief introduction to the topic: For example, say, "This story is about a girl who wanted to become a champion skater."

| | Target Word | Student's Attempt | | Knew in Context (in oral passage) + or – |
		Timed Presentation	Untimed Presentation	
Oral Passages	camp	+		
	year	+		
	spend	+		
	whole	what	when	
	week	will	+	
	packed	pick	+	
	clothes	clap	+	
	dressed	dr...	drossed	
	brushed	+		
	teeth	test	tooth	
	kitchen	+		
	eggs	+		
	toast	test	+	
	seemed	s...	+	
	forever	+		
	hundreds	+		
	shorts	+		
	shirts	shark	shirk	
	tent	+		
	knew	k...	know	
Silent Passages	teacher	+		
	world	work	+	
	playground	+		
	classroom	+		
	card	+		
Results		# Correct	Multiplied by 4	% Correct
Timed Presentation		14	x 4	56
Untimed Presentation		6	x 4	24
Total		20	x 4	80

FIGURE 7.1   Reyna's Scored IRI Word List, Level 2

2. Ask a background question to determine how familiar the student is with the topic: "What do you know about championship skating?" Answers to such questions allow you to determine whether problems with reading might be due to lack of background knowledge. (The IRI on the website provides instructions and background questions.)

3. Hand the student copy to the student to read. State that you will ask questions after reading is completed. Have the student read orally (for oral passages) or silently (for silent passages). If the passage is to be read orally, tell the student that you will not be able to help with words and that he or she can say "pass" if a word cannot be figured out. (See Special Issues and Options in Using IRIs later in this chapter for a discussion of teacher aid.) If the passage is to be read silently, ask your student to look up immediately when finished so that you can record the time correctly.

4. For oral reading, record any differences between the text and the student's reading on your protocol. If you want to record reading speed, time the student with a stopwatch.

5. After the student finishes, take away the passage and ask the comprehension questions. If you want additional information, you may also ask the student to retell the passage in his or her own words.

6. Continue testing until you have determined the independent, instructional, and frustrational levels for your student. For example, if a student scores at an independent level for third grade, have the student read the fourth-grade passage. Continue moving up until you reach the student's frustrational level. If a student scores at a frustrational level on the first passage read, move down until you reach the independent level. The next section explains how to determine these levels.

Reading Levels Obtained from the IRI   Using an IRI, a reading teacher can determine the student's independent, instructional, and frustrational reading levels. The instructional level is particularly critical because the severity of a student's reading problem is determined by *comparing the instructional level with the level at which the student should be reading* (usually the student's grade placement). For example, if a student's IRI instructional level is third grade but he is in a sixth-grade class, he would have a severe reading problem.

How do we calculate reading levels? As stated earlier, reading levels on an IRI are determined by performance on the passages, not scores on the word lists.

The level of an orally read passage is based on (1) the word recognition accuracy score for the passage and (2) the comprehension score. The level of a silently read passage is based on the comprehension score.

The word recognition score comes from the number of miscues, or errors, that the student makes while orally reading a passage. The comprehension score comes from the number of correct responses on the comprehension questions. Table 7.3 lists the criteria suggested for the different IRI levels.

Scoring Word Recognition Accuracy   A word recognition score is obtained from the student's oral reading of passages. To obtain this score, you must code and score this oral reading.

TABLE 7.3   IRI Passage Criteria for Three Reading Levels

Reading Level	Word Recognition Accuracy (%)		Comprehension (%)
Independent	98–100	and	90–100
Instructional	95–97	and	70–89
Frustrational	Less than 95	or	Less than 70

Your first step is to code the oral reading. As the student reads, you need to mark all miscues using a standard system so that you can later determine exactly what the student said. Commercial IRIs generally provide their own coding systems. Teachers who construct their own IRIs or use the one provided with this book should use the coding system presented in Figure 7.2.

Omissions, additions, substitutions, and reversals usually count as word recognition errors. You might, in addition, want to *record* repetitions, hesitations, omissions of punctuation, and spontaneous corrections of errors. Because these four things do not usually alter the meaning of text, experts do not recommend counting them as errors (McKenna, 1983). However, they can provide additional information about a student's word recognition strategies.

After coding the oral reading, you need to score it. The easiest and most reliable way to score the oral reading is to assign one point to each omission, addition, substitution, and reversal (Leslie & Caldwell, 2005). Extensive field testing (Leslie & Caldwell, 2005) indicate that this scoring system places students at appropriate instructional levels. However, some alternatives for scoring miscues are discussed in the section Special Issues and Options in Using IRIs.

Certain scoring problems may arise during an IRI. Some propose solutions to some of these based on field testing by Leslie & Caldwell (2005):

* If a student repeatedly mispronounces the same word, count it as incorrect each time. If a student were reading an assignment in school, each mispronunciation would affect comprehension.
* If a student omits an entire line or phrase, count it as one miscue. In this situation, the student simply lost his or her place.
* Proper names are difficult for students because they often do not follow regular phonics patterns. Do not count a mispronunciation of a proper name as incorrect unless it

---

1. *Omissions:* Circle.
   □ on (the) table

2. *Insertions:* Insert the added word above a caret.
   □ on the ⌃big table

3. *Substitutions, mispronunciations:* Underline the word in the text and write the word that the student said above the word in text.
   □ on the <u>table</u> *tablet*

4. *Reversals:* Same as substitutions.

5. *Repetitions:* Draw a line with an arrow below the words.
   □ on the table ⟵

6. *Words pronounced correctly but with hesitations:* Write an *H* over the word.
   □ on the table (H)

7. *Lack of punctuation:* Circle ignored punctuation.
   □ I saw Mary(.) She was happy.

8. *Student corrections:* Cross out any previous responses and mark with *SC*.
   □ on the ~~tablet~~ *SC* table

FIGURE 7.2 Coding System for Scoring IRI Passage Miscues changes the sex of the character. For example, do not count the substitution of *Mary* for *Maria*. However, do count the substitution of *Mark* for *Maria*. Sometimes students use a nonword to pronounce a proper name such as *Manee* for *Maria*. If the student says this consistently throughout the passage, do not count it as an error. If, however, the student pronounces it differently on other occasions, count it as incorrect each time. Follow these guidelines for names of places.

* Miscues that reflect a student's speech patterns should never count as errors. In other words, mispronunciations resulting from dialect differences, speaking English as a second language, immature speech patterns, or speech impediments do not count as errors. For example, a student who speaks a dialect other than standard English might pronounce the word *tests* as *tes*, both in speaking and in reading an IRI passage. In such miscues, readers are simply recoding the written word into their own pronunciation. Pupils should never be penalized for such recoding.

After you have counted all of the errors on an individual passage, total them. Then compute the percentage of words read correctly in the passage. In the coded and scored passage in Figure 7.3, the student had four errors, and 92 correct words in the total 96 words. The percentage correct is 96 percent, an instructional level.

$$\frac{92 \text{ Words Correct}}{96 \text{ Total Words}} \times 100 = 96\%$$

Nick's Trip to the Lake

Nick and his dad like animals. <u>One</u> ⟨day⟩ *Once* Nick and his dad went to the lake. They

went to see the animals. They sat next to the lake. They were very still.

Then Nick saw a big duck. He saw the duck swim ∧ *out* to a big rock in the lake. ∧ *Then* Some-

thing made the duck fly away fast.

Nick asked his dad, "Why did the duck fly away?"

Nick's dad said, "Look over there." He showed Nick something in the lake. Nick
H
thought he would see something big.
SC
What a surprise to see a little green ~~frog~~!

Scoring System

Omissions: ◯	Repetitions: ←⏋
Insertions: ∧	Hesitations: H
Substitutions: Write the word and underline	Student corrections: SC

Words in passage	96
Errors	4
Oral Reading Accuracy Score	96%

FIGURE 7.3 Student's Coded Oral Reading of a Primer-Level IRI Passage

To make this process easier, use Table 7.4. Simply find the intersection between the number of words in the passage and the error count. For example, if the passage contains 103 words and the error count is nine, then the percentage correct is 91, a frustrational level.

After you have determined a percentage of words read correctly, translate this percentage score into a level (independent, instructional, or frustrational) by using Table 7.3.

Grading Comprehension   After the student reads each passage, the teacher asks questions to check comprehension. If the student's answer is incorrect, the teacher writes the

TABLE 7.4   Percentages for Word Recognition Accuracy Scores (*Each Number Indicates Percentage Correct*)

Number of Errors

Number of Words in Passage	1	2	3	4	5	6	7	8	9	10	11	12	13	14	15	16	17	18	19	20	21	22	23	24	25	26
28–32	97	93	90	87	83	80	77	73	70	67	63	60	57	53	50	47	43	40	37	33	30	27	23	20	17	13
33–37	97	94	92	89	86	83	80	77	74	72	69	66	63	60	57	54	52	49	46	43	40	37	34	32	29	26
38–42	98	95	93	90	88	85	82	80	78	75	72	70	68	65	62	60	58	55	52	50	48	45	42	40	38	35
43–47	98	96	93	91	89	87	84	82	80	78	76	73	71	69	67	64	62	60	58	56	53	51	49	47	44	42
48–52	98	96	94	92	90	88	86	84	82	80	78	76	74	72	70	68	66	64	62	60	58	56	54	52	50	48
53–57	98	96	95	93	91	89	87	86	84	82	80	78	77	76	73	71	69	67	66	64	62	60	58	56	55	53
58–62	98	97	95	93	92	90	88	87	85	83	82	80	78	77	75	73	72	70	68	67	65	63	62	60	58	57
63–67	98	97	95	94	92	91	89	88	86	85	83	82	80	78	77	75	74	72	71	69	68	66	65	63	62	60
68–72	99	97	95	94	93	92	90	89	87	86	84	83	82	80	79	77	76	74	73	72	70	69	67	66	64	63
73–77	99	97	96	94	93	92	91	89	87	86	85	84	83	81	80	79	77	76	75	73	72	71	69	68	67	65
78–82	99	98	96	95	94	92	91	90	89	88	86	85	84	82	81	80	79	78	76	75	74	72	71	70	69	68
83–87	99	98	96	95	94	93	92	91	89	88	87	86	85	84	82	81	80	79	78	76	75	74	73	72	71	69
88–92	99	98	97	96	94	93	92	91	90	89	88	87	86	84	83	82	81	80	79	78	77	76	74	73	72	71
93–97	99	98	97	96	95	94	93	92	91	89	88	87	86	85	84	83	82	81	80	79	78	77	76	75	74	73
98–102	99	98	97	96	95	94	93	92	91	90	89	88	87	86	85	84	83	82	81	80	79	78	77	76	75	74
103–107	99	98	97	96	95	94	93	92	91	90	90	89	88	87	86	85	84	83	82	81	80	79	78	77	76	75
108–112	99	98	97	96	95	94	93	92	91	91	90	89	88	87	86	85	85	84	83	82	81	80	79	78	77	76
113–117	99	98	97	97	96	95	94	93	92	91	90	90	89	88	87	86	85	85	84	84	83	82	81	80	79	77
118–122	99	98	98	97	96	95	94	93	92	92	91	90	89	88	88	87	86	85	84	83	82	82	81	80	79	79
123–127	99	98	98	97	96	95	94	94	93	92	91	90	90	89	88	87	86	86	85	84	83	82	82	81	80	79
128–132	99	98	98	97	96	95	95	94	93	92	92	91	90	89	88	88	87	86	85	85	84	83	82	82	81	80
133–137	99	99	98	97	96	96	95	94	93	93	92	91	90	90	89	88	87	87	86	85	84	84	83	82	81	81
138–142	99	99	98	97	96	96	95	94	94	93	92	91	91	90	89	89	88	87	86	85	85	84	84	83	82	81
143–147	99	99	98	97	97	96	95	95	94	93	92	92	91	90	90	89	88	88	87	86	86	85	84	83	83	82
148–152	99	99	98	97	97	96	95	95	94	93	92	92	91	91	90	89	89	88	87	87	86	86	85	84	83	83
153–157	99	99	98	97	97	96	95	95	94	94	93	92	92	91	90	90	89	88	88	87	86	86	85	85	84	83
158–162	99	99	98	98	97	96	96	95	94	94	93	92	92	91	91	90	89	89	88	88	87	86	86	85	84	84
163–167	99	99	98	98	97	96	96	95	95	94	93	93	92	92	91	90	90	89	88	88	87	87	86	85	85	84
168–172	99	99	98	98	97	96	96	95	95	94	94	93	93	92	91	91	90	89	89	88	88	87	86	86	85	85
173–177	99	99	98	98	97	97	96	95	95	94	94	93	93	92	91	91	90	90	89	89	88	87	87	86	86	85
178–182	99	99	98	98	97	97	96	96	95	94	94	93	93	92	92	91	91	90	89	89	88	88	87	87	86	86
183–187	99	99	98	98	97	97	96	96	95	95	94	94	93	92	92	91	91	90	90	89	89	88	88	87	87	86
188–192	99	99	98	98	97	97	96	96	95	95	94	94	93	93	92	92	91	91	90	89	89	88	88	87	87	86
193–197	99	99	98	98	97	97	96	96	95	95	94	94	93	93	92	92	91	91	90	90	89	89	88	88	87	87
198–202	100	99	98	98	98	97	96	96	96	95	94	94	93	93	92	92	91	91	90	90	89	89	88	88	87	87
203–207	100	99	99	98	98	97	97	96	96	95	95	94	94	93	93	92	92	91	91	90	90	89	89	88	88	87
208–212	100	99	99	98	98	97	97	96	96	95	95	94	94	93	93	92	92	91	91	90	90	90	89	89	88	88
213–217	100	99	99	98	98	97	97	96	96	95	95	94	94	93	93	93	92	92	91	91	90	90	89	89	88	88
218–222	100	99	99	98	98	97	97	96	96	96	95	95	94	94	93	93	92	92	91	91	90	90	90	89	89	88
223–227	100	99	99	98	98	97	97	96	96	96	95	95	94	94	93	93	92	92	92	91	91	90	90	89	89	88
228–232	100	99	99	98	98	97	97	97	96	96	95	95	94	94	94	93	93	92	92	91	91	90	90	90	89	89
233–237	100	99	99	98	98	98	97	97	96	96	95	95	95	94	94	93	93	92	92	92	91	91	90	90	89	89
238–242	100	99	99	98	98	98	97	97	96	96	96	95	95	94	94	94	93	93	92	92	92	91	91	90	90	89

exact student response; if the response is correct, simply mark a +. The teacher obtains a percentage score: for example, if the student answers three of four comprehension questions correctly, the comprehension score would be 75 percent on that selection. Table 7.5 provides the percentage of correct scores for different numbers of comprehension questions. Translate the percentage score on comprehension into a level (independent, instructional, or frustrational) from Table 7.3.

Determining Passage Levels   Once you have scored both word recognition accuracy and comprehension, you are ready to determine a *total level for that passage*. For a silent passage, a student has only one score that determines passage level: the comprehension score. Leslie, for example, read a fourth-grade passage silently and achieved at an instructional level for comprehension. Therefore, her level for that passage was instructional.

However, if a student has read a passage orally, the teacher has both a word recognition accuracy score and a comprehension score to determine whether the passage is at a student's independent, instructional, or frustrational level. If a student achieves the same level for both word recognition accuracy and comprehension, determining the level is easy. For example, on a second-grade passage, Leslie achieved at an independent level for both word recognition and comprehension. Therefore, the second-grade passage was at an independent level.

However, students sometimes have different levels for word recognition accuracy and comprehension. In this case, use the lower level to determine passage level. For example, on a third-grade passage, Leslie achieved at an instructional level for word recognition accuracy but an independent level for comprehension. Therefore, the third-grade passage was at an instructional level. Table 7.6 helps you to assign levels to oral passages.

At times, a student may achieve at the independent or instructional levels on two (or even more) passages. For example, a student reading oral passages might achieve an instructional score on the primer, first-grade, and second-grade passages. If this situation happens, the *highest* level is the instructional level. In this case, the instructional level is second grade.

Combining Oral and Silent Levels into One Overall Level   Determine the levels for oral reading and then determine the levels for silent reading. Students often perform differently on oral and silent reading and so may achieve different levels for each one.

TABLE 7.5   Percentages for Comprehension Scores (*Each Number Indicates a Percentage-Correct Score*)

		Number of Correct Responses											
		1	2	3	4	5	6	7	8	9	10	11	12
	1	100											
	2	50	100										
	3	33	67	100									
	4	25	50	75	100								
Number of Questions	5	20	40	60	80	100							
	6	17	33	50	67	83	100						
	7	14	26	43	57	71	86	100					
	8	12	25	38	50	62	75	88	100				
	9	11	22	33	44	56	67	78	89	100			
	10	10	20	30	40	50	60	70	80	90	100		
	11	9	18	27	36	45	55	64	73	82	91	100	
	12	8	17	25	33	42	50	58	67	75	83	92	100

TABLE 7.6 Criteria for Assigning Levels to Oral Reading Passages

Comprehension	Word Recognition	Passage Level
Independent	Independent	Independent
Independent	Instructional	Instructional
Independent	Frustrational	Frustrational
Instructional	Instructional	Instructional
Instructional	Independent	Instructional
Instructional	Frustrational	Frustrational
Frustrational	Frustrational	Frustrational
Frustrational	Independent	Frustrational
Frustrational	Instructional	Frustrational

However, to make instructional decisions, you should combine your results for both modes of reading.

To combine oral and silent levels, first put the level of each oral and silent passage side by side according to grade level. Then, if the two levels are different, choose the *lower* level for the total reading level.

For example, Leslie, who is in the fifth grade, achieved these levels on *orally* read passages:

Grade 2—Independent

Grade 3—Instructional

Grade 4—Frustrational

In this case, Leslie's *oral reading levels*, which are quite easy to determine, are:

Grade 2—Oral Independent Reading Level

Grade 3—Oral Instructional Reading Level

Grade 4—Oral Frustrational Reading Level

On *silently* read passages, Leslie received these levels:

Grade 2—Independent

Grade 3—Independent

Grade 4—Instructional

Grade 5—Frustrational

Based on these passages, Leslie's *silent reading* levels are:

Grade 3—Silent Independent Level

Grade 4—Silent Instructional Level

Grade 5—Silent Frustrational Level

To determine Leslie's *combined* reading levels, place the results from each silent and oral passage side by side and then choose the lower level.

Oral Reading Passages	Silent Reading Passages	Combined Level
2 Independent	2 Independent	2 Independent
3 Instructional	3 Independent	3 Instructional
4 Frustrational	4 Instructional	4 Frustrational
5 (not given)	5 Frustrational	

Based on this information, Leslie's total reading levels are:

Grade 2—Combined Independent Reading Level

Grade 3—Combined Instructional Reading Level

Grade 4—Combined Frustrational Reading Level

Assigning a combined reading level is helpful in situations where you need a general level for assigning school materials. For example, because Leslie's combined reading is instructional at the third-grade level, she should be reading a third-grade book.

Interpreting the Scores of the IRI

The IRI is a rich source of information about a student's reading, and it can provide detailed answers to the two diagnostic questions asked earlier in this chapter: (1) Does the student have a reading problem and how severe is it? and (2) What is the general area of the reading problem? Answering these two questions requires adding some procedures to ones already given. These procedures provide options for enriching the information obtained from an IRI.

How Severe Is the Student's Reading Problem?   To estimate the severity of a reading problem, the teacher should examine the gap between a student's highest instructional level on the IRI and the level of text that would be appropriate for that student.

Let's consider the case of Subash, a sixth grader whose IRI summary is presented in Table 7.7. His teacher reported that Subash's class is reading sixth-grade material. On the IRI, Subash's combined independent level is 2. Because he scored at an instructional level on both Grades 3 and 4, his instructional level is the higher level (4). His frustrational level is 5. The gap between Subash's appropriate reading level (6) and his highest instructional level on the IRI (4) indicates that he has a severe reading problem, according to the criteria by Spache (1981) mentioned earlier in Table 7.1.

We now move to the second diagnostic question: determining the general area(s) of the reading problem. To answer this question, we will consider the areas one by one.

What Is the Nature of Word Recognition Accuracy?   The student's word recognition accuracy score is generally based on passages because reading a passage is a more authentic task than reading a word list. However, the teacher should be aware that certain

TABLE 7.7   IRI Summary for Subash

| Level | Oral Passages | | | Silent Passages | Combined Reading | Listening |
	Word Recognition Accuracy Level	Comp Level	Passage Level	Comp & Passage Level	Passage Level	Passage Level
Preprimer	—	—	—	—	—	—
Primer	—	—	—	—	—	—
1	—	—	—	—	—	—
2	Ind	Ind	Ind	Ind	Ind	—
3	Ind	Ins	Ins	Ins	Ins	—
4	Ind	Ins	Ins	Ins	Ins	—
5	Ind	Frus	Frus	Frus	Frus	Ind
6	—	—	—	—	—	Ins
7	—	—	—	—	—	Frus
8	—	—	—	—	—	—

things, such as context of the passage, the familiarity of the topic, and the presence of pictures, may inflate a student's score (Leslie & Caldwell, 2005). Rhyme or repetition of phrases in the passage can also aid word recognition. If time permits, the teacher should verify the word recognition level with another passage at the same level. A word recognition accuracy score below the third-grade level on IRI passages is one sign that the primary nature of the reading difficulty is word recognition.

Judging a student's word recognition accuracy also involves determining the strategies the student uses to recognize words. Only by knowing the tools that students use to identify words can the teacher help them develop missing skills. Miscues, which are mismatches between the text and what the student says, provide opportunities to analyze these strategies.

Some miscues show that the student is using meaning or context clues. A student using context might substitute a word that makes sense in the context, for example, *Kleenex* for *handkerchief*. Readers bring a vast store of knowledge and competence to the reading act. When students use context clues, they are using this store of information to bring meaning to reading. The use of context clues shows a positive effort to preserve comprehension (Goodman & Gollasch, 1980–1981; Goodman, 1976; Goodman, 1965).

Other miscues show that the student is using phonics clues to recognize words. A student who uses phonics clues makes miscues that contain many of the same sounds as the words that are in the passage. However, the miscues will often not make sense in context. In fact, sometimes they are not even real words.

An exact recording of oral reading can be analyzed to see which strategies a student tends to use. We call this *miscue analysis* (Goodman, 1969). Some forms of miscue analysis are complex; others are simple. However, they all share a common purpose: to determine the reader's strategies for identifying words. Almost all try to determine whether the reader pays primary attention to letter-sound matching, to meaning, or to both as skilled readers do.

To help analyze a reader's strategies, look at a form of miscue analysis adapted from Leslie (1993) and Leslie and Caldwell (2005). Table 7.8 presents the miscue analysis worksheet.

Ask three sets of questions about each miscue:

1. Is the miscue similar in sounds to the original word?
   * Does it begin with the same sound?
   * Does it end with the same sound?
   If the answers are yes, the student is paying attention to phonics when reading. Beginning and ending similarity is sufficient to determine whether the student is paying attention to letter-sound matching. Do not consider middle sounds because these sounds are often vowels, which have highly variable sounds.
2. Does the miscue retain the author's meaning?
   If the answer is yes, the reader is paying attention to meaning and using it to help recognize words.
3. Did the reader correct the miscue?
   Self-correction can indicate two things. The self-correction of an acceptable miscue, which is one that does not change meaning, suggests that the reader is paying attention to letter-sound matching. Self-correction of a miscue that changes text meaning suggests that the reader is paying attention to meaning during the reading process.

To examine reading patterns, choose about 25 miscues from the instructional-level text. Record and analyze them on the sheet provided in Table 7.8. Now you can look for patterns. Several patterns typical of students with reading problems follow:

* If the student has a large number of miscues that do not change the author's meaning, the student is using the meaning (or context) of a passage as a clue to recognizing words. Another indication that the student is using the meaning of the passage as a clue is the self-correction of miscues that do not make sense.

TABLE 7.8 Miscue Analysis Work Sheet

Word in Text	Miscue	Sounds Alike		Meaning Is Retained	Corrected
		Begin	End		
_____	_____	_____	_____	_____	_____
_____	_____	_____	_____	_____	_____
_____	_____	_____	_____	_____	_____
_____	_____	_____	_____	_____	_____
_____	_____	_____	_____	_____	_____
_____	_____	_____	_____	_____	_____
_____	_____	_____	_____	_____	_____
_____	_____	_____	_____	_____	_____
_____	_____	_____	_____	_____	_____
_____	_____	_____	_____	_____	_____
_____	_____	_____	_____	_____	_____
_____	_____	_____	_____	_____	_____
_____	_____	_____	_____	_____	_____
_____	_____	_____	_____	_____	_____
_____	_____	_____	_____	_____	_____
Column Total	_____	_____	_____	_____	_____

* If the student has a high number of miscues that are similar in sound and a small number of miscues that retain the author's meaning, the reader may be paying more attention to phonics clues than to the meaning. Some readers show a large number of miscues that are similar in sound to the beginning of the text word and a small number that are similar at the end. Examples are pronouncing *when* for *wanted*; *dog* for *don't*; *live* for *liked*; and *truck* for *teach*. In this case, instruction should focus on guiding the reader to look at all the letters in a word.
* If the worksheet shows a pattern of miscues that do not contain the same sounds as the text words as well as a small number of acceptable miscues or self-corrections, the reader may be a wild guesser, one who is not using either phonics or context effectively.

In the examples presented in Figure 7.4, the first student is using meaning clues and the second is using phonics.

What Is the Nature of Reading Fluency?   To assess reading fluency, calculate the reading rate, or the number of words per minute, for oral and silent passages. To determine the reading rate, take the number of words in the passage, multiply by 60, and divide

---

Example 1.   Use of Context Clues

---

                                                    sea   *lots of*

Kim lives on an island far out in the <u>ocean</u>. You may think that it would befun to live

                      unhappy

on an island. But Kim is <u>miserable</u>. Kim hasn't seen her friends in a year. There is no

one to play with or talk to. There isn't even a school!

Example 2.   Use of Phonics Clues

---

    likes   *open*

Kim <u>lives</u> on an island far out in the <u>ocean</u>. You may think that it would be fun to live

                mysterious   *family*   *Then*

on an island. But Kim is <u>miserable</u>. Kim hasn't seen her <u>friends</u> in a year. <u>There</u> is no

                      Then

one to play with or talk to. <u>There</u> isn't even a school!

FIGURE 7.4   Examples of Oral Reading Patterns

by the number of seconds required by the student to read the selection. This calculation yields a word-per-minute score.

$$\frac{\text{Number of words} \times 60}{\text{Number of seconds to read}} = \text{Words per minute}$$

For example, Tammie read a second-grade passage that contained 249 words in 2 minutes and 15 seconds (or 135 seconds). Two hundred and forty-nine multiplied by 60 equals 14,940. Divide this number by 135 seconds. Tammie's reading rate for that passage is 110 words per minute.

Some have argued that a words per minute score is primarily an indicator of reading speed and they suggest that measuring rate as correct words per minute (CWPM) addresses both speed and accuracy (Kame'enui & Simmons, 2001; Fuchs, Fuchs, Hosp, & Jenkins, 2001). To compute CWPM, take the number of words in the passage and subtract the number of miscues to arrive at the number of words read correctly. Multiply by 60 and divide by the number of seconds the student took to read the passage. For example, Tammie made 12 miscues as she read the 249 word passage so the number of words read correctly was 237. Two hundred and thirty-seven multiplied by 60 equals 14,220. Divide this by 135 seconds and Tammie's rate is 105 corrected words per minute.

What is a normal rate for different levels of passages? Guidelines for reading rates, based on normal students at their instructional level, are given in Table 7.9 (Leslie & Caldwell, 2005). Notice that the ranges for reading rate at each grade level are quite wide because individuals tend to have very different rates of reading (Carver, 1990).

When you have determined a student's reading rate at a certain grade level of the IRI, use Table 7.9 to compare your student's rate with the acceptable range provided. For example, Arliss read a third-grade oral passage at 65 words per minute. This rate is within the normal range of the third-grade level: 51–97 words per minute.

However, the guidelines in Table 7.9 are only advisory. Reading rate must always be interpreted in relation to comprehension. A student who reads below the lowest reading rate given for a passage level probably needs work in reading fluency, especially if comprehension is poor. A slow reader who cannot comprehend adequately is probably concentrating all of his or her attention on recognizing the words. This situation strongly suggests a

TABLE 7.9   Reading Rates at Instructional Levels

Level	Oral WPM	Oral CWPM	Silent WPM
Preprimer	22–64	11–59	
Primer	28–66	10–52	
First	37–77	20–68	
Second	43–89	19–77	
Third	51–97	32–86	
Fourth	55–105	27–87	
Fifth	61–133	30–114	73–175
Sixth			91–235
Upper Middle School			105–233
High School			65–334

need for fluency instruction. However, fluency instruction may be less important for a student who reads slowly but comprehends well.

At times, the teacher may only need to listen to a student to determine that the need is reading fluency. Slow, hesitant, expressionless reading that is filled with pauses suggests that a student is working hard to identify words and lacks the fluency essential for making sense of the author's message.

What Is the Nature of Comprehension?   If both word recognition and comprehension levels are at the frustrational level on a passage, the comprehension problems are probably due to poor word recognition. Because of this relationship, the student needs to concentrate on improving word recognition accuracy or fluency.

However, if word recognition accuracy and fluency are good but comprehension is poor, the student probably has a comprehension problem and needs to focus on comprehension strategies. If the problem is comprehension, careful analysis of an IRI can provide some important instructional hints.

Some students have problems in comprehension because they believe that reading is "getting all the words right." These readers are often extremely accurate and tend to self-correct miscues that do not change meaning. As a result, they do not actively construct meaning as they read. For example, Susan was asked to read an IRI passage containing the following sentences: "Bill's mom saw the dog. Bill asked, 'May I keep it?' " She read, "Bill's mother saw the dog. Bill asked, 'Can I have it?' " Then she paused and went back, carefully correcting each miscue. Susan's comprehension of the total passage was poor, probably the result of her concern with accuracy. For a reader like Susan, the teacher should emphasize that reading is meaning, not just saying words.

An analysis of IRI questions may also provide insight into comprehension patterns. In the IRI presented on the website, for example, questions are divided into literal and inferential categories. Comparing the percentages correct on these two types of questions helps determine whether the reader is focused on factual information or able to draw inferences. You might also note whether a student appears to get the central focus of the passage or is more observant of details.

If you ask a student to retell a passage after reading it, you can see exactly how he or she constructs meaning. In judging a retelling, use these questions as guidelines for a narrative or story:

* Does the retelling contain the central events of the passage?
* Does the student remember the most important facts?
* Is the student able to retell the events in sequence?

The IRI can also give insights into the adequacy of the student's background information. If you begin each selection by asking the student questions to assess background, you have a good idea of the richness of a student's prior knowledge. If you find that the student has problems with the background for several passages, your comprehension instruction may concentrate on enriching background information and applying it to reading.

Finally, when students read both oral and silent passages, you can determine whether they comprehend better after oral or silent reading. Young or very disabled readers are usually able to comprehend better after they have read orally. These students need practice to increase their comfort in silent reading. More mature readers comprehend better after silent reading than after oral reading.

Most IRIs are based on narrative passages; that is, passages that tell stories. Although these passages allow you to assess comprehension, it is more appropriate to judge study strategies from informational passages. In the section that follows, we address the use of IRIs that contain informational passages.

Extending the IRI to Examine the Nature of Studying Informational Text

Students who have problems studying can often comprehend narrative (storylike) text but have problems with informational text. Typically, IRIs focus on narrative passages. However some, like the *Qualitative Reading Inventory-4* (Leslie & Caldwell, 2005), offer both narrative and informational passages at all levels.

If the IRI you are using does not have both types of passages, use the narrative passages, which all IRIs have, to determine an instructional level for your student. Then, have your student read expository material at the instructional level to see how he or she handles material commonly used for content area instruction.

Modifying the typical IRI procedure can often answer important questions about a student's ability to study. One extension of the IRI procedure can determine whether students can locate information to answer questions. Give the student an IRI passage that was previously read so that he or she can look at it. Then ask the questions that were missed during the original administration and see whether the student can use the passage to locate the answers to these questions.

Other modifications allow a teacher to assess the student's ability to locate main ideas and take notes. To evaluate the ability to determine main ideas, give the student an instructional-level informational passage and a pencil. Then ask him or her to underline the most important parts of the selection. To investigate study strategies, ask the student to take notes on the passage as if he or she were studying for a test. A teacher can use these procedures with any text, not just an IRI.

What Is the Nature of Language and Meaning Vocabulary: Determining the Listening Level

Because reading is a language process, people read only as well as they can understand language and word meanings. An IRI enables a teacher to determine a student's language level by *finding a student's listening level.*

To do this, the teacher reads aloud IRI passages at the reading frustrational level and asks the comprehension questions about the passage. The highest level at which the student gets 70 percent or more of the answers correct is the listening level.

The listening level provides an estimate of the student's listening, or language, comprehension level. If a student's listening level is lower than his or her grade level, that student needs to develop better language skills. Instruction should then focus on developing rich language and learning more word meanings.

In contrast, the example of Subash, the sixth grader whose IRI summary sheet is presented in Table 7.7, shows a student who has a good language base. Subash's high-listening level (6) but lower instructional reading level (4) indicate a 2-year gap between his current reading level and his language level. The fact that his listening level is equal to his grade level indicates that his language base is sufficient for reading at grade level. No language development is needed for him; instead, he needs to work on reading.

You can also use the IRI to directly assess knowledge of meaning vocabulary. After the student has read and answered the questions in a passage, ask the student to define (or use in a sentence) key vocabulary words in the passage. Remember that you may have to pronounce words that the student has not read correctly in the passage. A student who knows the meanings of difficult words in a grade-level passage has a strong vocabulary base. A student who cannot define these words or use them in a sentence needs more development of meaning vocabulary. If a student cannot define a word in isolation, you might ask him or her to reread the sentence in the passage to see if context helps the student with word meaning.

Special Issues and Options in Using IRIs

The informal nature of an IRI allows many options for administration and adaptation to the special needs of students. At times, you may face some difficult decisions. This section discusses some of these issues and, in addition, presents some alternatives for administering and interpreting the IRI.

Pronouncing Words for Students   When reading IRI selections orally, a student may sometimes become "stuck" on a word. The teacher may be tempted to supply this word to make the student more comfortable and able to continue. However, pronouncing words for the student may inflate the student's comprehension score, because understanding the passage depends on reading the words accurately. To obtain the most accurate assessment, teachers are strongly discouraged from supplying words. Tell students to say "pass" for unknown words, and score these passes as omission errors. Also encourage students to try pronouncing a word before they give up. However, some guidelines for IRI administration permit teachers to aid students.

Alternate Administration of Oral and Silent Passages   Administer all the oral passages first to determine the oral reading levels before administering the silent passages. Then combine oral and silent reading levels into a total reading level. Some reading teachers prefer a different administrative procedure. They alternate oral and silent passages at each grade level to determine the student's reading levels.

Unclear IRI Results   When administering an IRI, you may sometimes have difficulty determining a stable level. What are some of the things that can happen? A student may score just slightly below the criteria for a specific level, for example, scoring 94 percent for word recognition accuracy on one passage, only slightly below the frustrational cutoff of 95 percent. At other times, a student may not do well on a certain topic. Should the teacher count these passages as frustrational and simply discontinue testing? If you are unsure of the correct decision, you should continue to gather information by testing at higher levels or administering another passage at the same level.

At times, however, you will not be able to come to a perfectly clear-cut decision and may have to make exceptions to some of the scoring criteria. Because the IRI is an informal instrument, you should feel free to modify criteria by using your own judgment. You should, however, note that you have made an exception to the scoring criteria and explain the reason for this exception.

Alternative Ways to Score Miscues   As stated earlier, scoring each miscue as one error is the best and most reliable way to reach an appropriate reading level for your student. This recommendation has been verified with extensive field testing.

However, miscues that do not change the author's meaning suggest that the student is comprehending the passage. For example, consider the following sentence: *The teachers divided the children into four groups.* A substitution of *put* for *divided* would not affect meaning. On the other hand, the substitution of *from* for *four* does distort meaning. Some reading teachers prefer to count miscues that retain meaning (*put* for *divided*) less severely than miscues that change meaning (*from* for *for*). If you wish to do this, count a miscue that retains the original meaning as one-half error. If a miscue changes the meaning, however, count it as one full error.

Which option should you use? Because the IRI is an informal instrument, you are free to choose the scoring system that makes you most comfortable. However, once you choose the scoring system that best fits your needs, you should use it consistently.

Alternative Norms   As with many informal measures, alternative criteria for determining reading levels have been suggested by some reading experts. Based on field testing, the criteria suggested in this chapter for word recognition accuracy and comprehension place students at appropriate reading levels. These criteria reflect the authors' experiences in developing an IRI with students who have reading difficulties.

Allowing Students to Look for Answers   Another option in administering an IRI is to use *look-backs*. After scoring the questions and determining the comprehension level, you can ask the student to look back in the text to locate or correct answers. This procedure allows you to note the difference between comprehension during reading and memory after reading. A student may read a passage and understand it fully. However, when asked questions following reading, the student may forget certain parts. Hasn't this happened to you? If a student can locate or correct answers, you can assume that he or she understood the passage. If a student is unable to successfully use the look-back strategy, perhaps the problem is one of basic comprehension during reading.

Leslie and Caldwell (2005) found that students reading at the third-grade level and above could effectively use look-backs to raise their comprehension score. This situation was most evident in upper middle school and high school passages. Students who scored at the frustrational level for comprehension often raised their scores to an instructional or independent level following look-backs. In fact, Leslie and Caldwell (2005) recommend that comprehension levels for upper level text (sixth grade and above) be determined following look-backs. Actually, the look-back strategy parallels what students are asked to do in school. Rarely are they expected to answer questions without the support of the text.

If you wish to use look-backs, first ask and score the questions to arrive at a comprehension level without look-backs. Then ask the student to look back and score the results of his or her efforts. A comprehension score with look-backs represents the total of all questions answered correctly for both procedures.

Using an IRI to Measure a Student's Growth   If you are measuring classroom growth or growth following an intervention program, decide when you wish to assess the student. Every three or four months is a realistic interval for a classroom. Intervention program intervals can be of short or long duration.

Choose an IRI passage to administer prior to instruction. Obtain a score for both word recognition and comprehension. If the student scores at an independent level, continue at higher levels until you reach the student's frustrational level. Then, when the classroom interval is over or the intervention is completed, administer the same passage as a posttest measure.

You have another option. You can administer a different IRI passage for the pretest and the posttest. This option is preferable if the duration between pretest and posttest is short and you think that memory for the initial passage may inflate the results. Of course, the two passages should be as alike as possible. They should be at the same level and have the same structure: narrative or expository. They should both be relatively familiar to the student.

Levels of Questions on IRIs   Most IRIs have two types of questions: literal (or explicit) and inferential (or implicit). However, there are multiple levels of inferential questions (Caldwell & Leslie, 2005; Ciardiello, 1998). Appplegate, Quinn, and Applegate (2002) describe three basic types: low-level inference items, high-level inference items, and response items. The answers to low-level inference items are not stated in the text, but they are relatively obvious. Some may require the reader to identify information that is stated in different words from the question. Others may require identification of simple relationships such as a causal relationship that is not marked by the signal word *because*. High-level inference items ask the reader to identify an alternative solution, offer a plausible explanation, or predict past or future actions. Response items ask the reader to defend an idea and react to the passage as a whole. Applegate, Quinn, and Applegate (2002) caution that IRIs may contain a variety of such disparate items loosely grouped under the heading of inferential, or implicit, questions. To put it simply, some inference questions are more difficult than others.

What does this variety of inferential questions mean for IRI administration? You should be aware that all questions are not the same level of difficulty and take this into account when you assess a student's comprehension. Dewitz and Dewitz (2003) carefully analyzed a student's responses on an IRI and divided them into several categories: failing to link ideas across a passage, difficulty with causal inferences, excessive elaboration or overreliance on prior knowledge, problems with vocabulary, and problems with syntax. Using these categories, they designed a program of instruction for each student based on areas of need.

We do not necessarily advise you to construct such elaborate classifications of inference difficulties. However, if you decide to further analyze a student's answers, we suggest a simpler classification scheme than those just described. You can use question answer relationships (QARs) strategy as devised by Raphael (1982, 1986). This strategy provides you with two pieces of information: a system for classifying students' answers and a procedure for teaching students how to locate answers to four different kinds of questions: right there questions, think and search questions, author and me questions, and on my own questions.

Combining IRI Assessment with Think-Alouds

Assessment does not need to involve special instruments such as word lists or IRI passages. You can learn much about students' reading abilities by reading any text with them and asking pertinent questions. When students meet an unfamiliar word, you can ask how they will go about pronouncing it. If the students pronounce the word correctly but do not know its meaning, you can probe to discover what strategies they use. In talking about a selection, you can ask the students how they arrived at answers to questions. You can ask them to explain what is in their minds at that point. Basically, you are asking students to stop at various points during reading and think out loud. The *think-aloud* process has been examined by a variety of researchers who agree that it offers an interesting opportunity to observe the thinking that occurs during reading (Pressley & Afflerbach, 1995).

The think-aloud approach works only if you know exactly what you are looking for. For example, Harmon (2000) listed a variety of strategies that students might use to determine the meaning of an unfamiliar word. They could examine sentence context or the distant context of the entire selection. They could make connections to events in the text, to text and language structures, to the author's style, or to ideas beyond the text. They could use word-level strategies, such as sounding out or structural analysis, the dictionary, or other outside sources. By asking students to think aloud when they met an unfamiliar word, Harmon was able to determine the strategies they used or ignored as they attempted to determine the meaning of unfamiliar words.

The think-aloud process can also be used to examine students' comprehension. Leslie and Caldwell (2005) identified several types of think-aloud comments that suggest understanding or lack of understanding on the part of the reader. They found that think-aloud comments indicating understanding were positively and strongly related to comprehension after reading.

Think-aloud statements that indicate understanding include:

* **Paraphrasing or summarizing.**   The student retells the contents of the text in his or her own words.
* **Making new meaning.**   The student draws an inference, reaches a conclusion, or engages in reasoning of some sort.
* **Questioning that indicates understanding.**   The student asks a question, but the question clearly indicates that he or she understood the text. For example, the student may question a character's motives or ask if the content would apply to another situation.
* **Noting understanding.**   The student indicates that he or she understood what was read.
* **Reporting prior knowledge.**   The student indicates that he or she knew this information before reading or thought something different.
* **Identifying personally.**   The student relates the text to personal experiences in some way, such as stating agreement or disagreement, like or dislike, interest or lack of interest.

Think-aloud statements that indicate lack of understanding include:

* **Questions that indicate lack of understanding.**   The student's questions indicate that the student does not understand the text. For example, the student asks about the meaning of an unfamiliar word, phrase, or sentence.
* **Noting lack of understanding.**   The student states that he or she is confused or does not understand the text.

Students exhibit a variety of think-aloud patterns. Some use one comment exclusively. For example, when Jared read a selection on clouds, every comment involved a paraphrase of the text content. Some students make a variety of comments. While reading the same cloud passage, Ryan offered several paraphrases, commented on what he knew and did not know about different cloud types, and reacted quite personally to clouds that signal the possibility of severe weather, tying it to some recent tornadoes in his state. Such diverse comments certainly suggest an extremely interactive reader.

How often should you stop to ask a student to think aloud? There are no set guidelines. The text should be long enough to present enough content to think about, but you shouldn't have to stop so often that the process becomes laborious. Because there are no definitive guidelines, experiment with different text segments. Of course, segments will vary in length with the age of the reader and level of the text.

You can set up the process in different ways. One way is to mark the text with stop signals: either the word *Stop* or a colored dot. The students read orally or silently, and when they reach the signal, they stop and think aloud. You can also read orally with the students in an assisted format and stop at points of your choosing. Another way is to ask the students to read silently and stop after each paragraph or at the end of each page. You can also read to the students and use think-aloud statements to evaluate the nature of their listening comprehension processes. All methods work; choose the one that works best for you and your students.

What are you looking for? You are looking for some evidence of interaction with the text. Too many readers have difficulty thinking aloud, which suggests a lack of active comprehension processing.

Contrast the following two students who both read an article on ancient Egypt (see pages 243–244) (Leslie & Caldwell, 2005).

Using the list of think-aloud statements as a guide, you can see that John's interaction with the text is limited and minimal compared to Brittany's.

Text Segment 1

Brittany: They built pyramids to bury the pharaoh and they put them there with all their possessions because they would use them in the afterlife. *Summary/paraphrase*. Do you think they put all the pharaohs in the same pyramid? What if he died before they finished building it? Where would he go? *Questions that signal understanding*.

John: They built pyramids and used them, like tombs, they used them and they buried the kings there. *Summary/paraphrase*.

Text Segment 2

Brittany: They mummified the kings to preserve their bodies. *Summary/paraphrase*. I know all about that! They wrap them up in bandages. I saw a movie where one came to life. *Reporting prior knowledge*.

John: They made the king a mummy. *Summary/paraphrase*. Why did they do that? It seems dumb. *Question that indicates lack of understanding because the text clearly indicates the rationale for mummification*.

Text Segment 3

Brittany: Yuk, this is really gross. *Identifying personally*. They took out all the organs except the heart, rubbed the body with stuff and wrapped it. *Summary/paraphrase*. I wonder if they took out the brain. *Question that indicates understanding*. I would think the brains should have been left in so the pharaoh could think in his afterlife. But maybe they didn't know what the brain did. *Making new meaning*.

John: It took 70 days and they rubbed oil on the body and wrapped it up like a mummy. *Summary/paraphrase*.

Text Segment 4

Brittany: Farmers helped to build the pyramids when they couldn't work in their fields and they weren't slaves. *Summary/paraphrase*. If they didn't use slaves to build the pyramids, I wonder how much they paid the farmers. *Question that indicates understanding*.

John: Farmers helped to build the pyramids. *Summary/paraphrase*. What is this word? I can't pronounce it (points to *archaeologists*). *Noting lack of understanding*.

Text Segment 5

Brittany: They dragged all the stones with ropes and it was dangerous and a lot died. *Summary/paraphrase*. I bet sometimes the stones fell and crushed them. If they were going up hill and the rope broke, that could wipe out a bunch of workers. *Making new meaning*.

John: They cut stones and worked for 8 days. *Summary/paraphrase that actually contains an error; the text states the workers worked for 10 days in a row*.

> **Text Segment 6**
>
> **Brittany:** They were paid with food, and they had to work fast in case the pharaoh would die. *Summary/paraphrase.* Why weren't they paid with money? *Question that indicates understanding.* I would rather have money so I could buy the food I wanted. *Identifying personally.* Maybe there weren't many stores back then. *Making new meaning.*
>
> **John:** Nothing really, just about food and working fast. *Summary/paraphrase.* Why did they have to be courageous? They were just building something. *Question that indicates lack of understanding; the text clearly outlines the dangers.*

Summary

Assessing reading achievement involves answering two questions: How severe is the student's reading problem? and What is the general area of the reading problem?

Informal measures have not been normed on large populations as have standardized formal measures. Therefore, they may be used more flexibly and may be adapted to the needs of the student and the demands of the diagnostic situation.

The informal reading inventory (IRI) consists of a series of graded reading selections. The student reads increasingly difficult material until a frustrational level is reached. IRIs measure both oral and silent reading. Three levels of reading are obtained: independent, instructional, and frustrational. These levels are based on the student's word recognition accuracy and ability to comprehend passages. Generally, separate passages are provided for oral and silent reading.

The IRI provides information about the existence and severity of a reading problem and its general area(s). Careful analysis of the IRI can suggest whether a student is having problems with word recognition accuracy, reading fluency, comprehension, language base and meaning vocabulary, or studying. Miscue analysis, the analysis of a student's oral reading deviations, allows the reading teacher to examine the strategies that a student uses to recognize words.

Special issues and options in using IRIs involve pronouncing words for students, alternating oral and silent passages, finding unclear results, using alternative miscue scoring procedures or norms, allowing students to look back for answers, levels of questions, using an IRI to assess student growth, and employing the think-aloud procedure.

R E F E R E N C E S

Applegate, M. D., Quinn, K. B., & Applegate, A. J. (2002). Levels of thinking required by comprehension questions in informal reading inventories. *The Reading Teacher, 56,* 174–180.

Caldwell, J. (1985). A new look at the old informal reading inventory. *The Reading Teacher, 39,* 168–173.

Caldwell, J., Fromm, M., & O'Connor, V. (1997–1998). Designing an intervention for poor readers: Incorporating the best of all worlds. *Wisconsin State Reading Association Journal, 41,* 7–14.

Caldwell, J. & Leslie L. (2004/2005). Does proficiency in middle school reading assure proficiency in high school reading? The possible role of think-alouds. *Journal of Adolescent and Adult Literacy, 47,* 324–335.

Carver, R. B. (1990). *Reading Rate: A Review of Research and Theory.* San Diego, CA: Academic Press.

Ciardiello, A. V. (1998). Did you ask a good question today? Alternative cognitive and metacognitive strategies. *Journal of Adolescent and Adult Literacy, 42,* 210–219.

Dewitz, P., & Dewitz, P. K. (2003). They can read the words, but they can't understand: Refining comprehension assessment. *The Reading Teacher, 56,* 422–435.

Goodman, K. S. (1969). Analysis of oral reading miscues. *Reading Research Quarterly, 5,* 9–30.

Goodman, K. S. (1965). A linguistic study of cues and miscues in reading. *Elementary English, 42,* 639–643.

Goodman, K. S., & Gollasch, F. V. (1980–1981). Word omissions: Deliberate and non-deliberate. *Reading Research Quarterly, 14,* 6–31.

Goodman, Y. M. (1976). Miscues, errors and reading comprehension. In J. Merritt (Ed.), *New Horizons in Reading.* Newark, DE: International Reading Association.

Harmon, J. M. (2000). Assessing and supporting independent word learning strategies of middle school students. *Journal of Adolescent and Adult Literacy, 43,* 518–527.

Johnson, M. J., Kress, R. A., & Pikulski, J. L. (1987). *Informal Reading Inventories* (2nd ed.). Newark, DE: International Reading Association.

Kame'nui, E. J., & Simmons, D. (2001). Introduction to this special issue: The DNA of reading fluency. *Scientific Studies of Reading, 5,* 203–210.

LaBerge, D., & Samuels, S. M. (1974). Toward a theory of automatic information processing in reading. *Cognitive Psychology, 6,* 293–323.

Leslie, L. (1993). A developmental-interactive approach to reading assessment. *Reading and Writing Quarterly, 9,* 5–30.

Leslie, L., & Allen, L. (1999). Factors that predict success in an early literacy intervention project. *Reading Research Quarterly, 34,* 404–425.

Leslie, L., & Caldwell, J. (2005). *The Qualitative Reading Inventory IV.* New York: Longman.

Lipson, M. Y., Cox, C. H., Iwankowski, S., & Simon, M. (1984). Exploration of the interactive nature of reading: Using commercial IRI's to gain insights. *Reading Psychology: An International Quarterly, 5,* 209–218.

McKenna, M. C. (1983). Informal reading inventories: A review of the issues. *The Reading Teacher, 36,* 670–679.

National Reading Panel (2000). *Teaching Children to Read: An Evidence-Based Assessment of the Scientific Research Literature on Reading and the Implications for Reading Instruction.* Washington, DC: National Institute of Child Health and Human Development. Available at www.nichd.nih.gov/publications/nrp/smallbook.htm.

Pikulski, J. J., & Shanahan, T. (1982). Informal reading inventories: A critical analysis. In J. J. Pikulski & T. Shanahan (Eds.), *Approaches to the Informal Evaluation of Reading,* pp. 94–116. Newark, DE: International Reading Association.

Pressley, M., & Afflerbach, P. (1995). *Verbal Protocols of Reading: The Nature of Constructively Responsive Reading.* Mahwah, MJ: Erlbaum.

Raphael, T. E. (1986). Teaching question-answer relationships, revisited. *The Reading Teacher, 39,* 516–522.

Raphael, T. E. (1982). Question-answering strategies for children. *The Reading Teacher, 36,* 186–190.

Spache, G. D. (1981). *Diagnosing and Correcting Reading Disabilities.* Boston: Allyn and Bacon.

Stanovich, K. E. (1993–1994). Romance and reality. Distinguished educator series. *The Reading Teacher, 47,* 280–291.

Stanovich, K. E. (1991). Word recognition: Changing perspectives. In R. Barr, M. L. Kamil, P. Mosenthal, & P. D. Pearson (eds.), *Handbook of Reading Research* (Vol. II), pp. 418–452. New York: Longman.

Stanovich, K. E. (1986). Matthew effects in reading. Some consequences of individual differences in the acquisition of literacy. *Reading Research Quarterly, 21,* 360–406.

8 Informal Assessment: Progress Monitoring

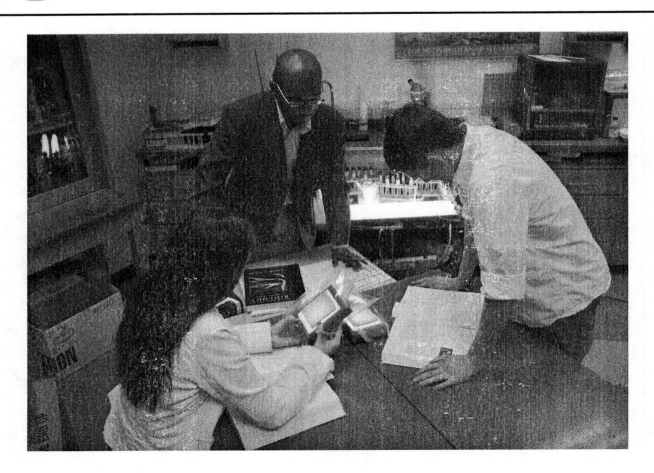

We have considered assessments used most often in the classroom, by general and special education teachers to guide instruction. In this chapter, we consider informal tests that have some characteristics of "formal" instruments. These instruments are not teacher constructed; they may have time limits, they follow standard administration procedures, and they typically provide a score that is evaluated against a criterion, benchmark, or cutoff.

Informal assessment measures that directly inform instruction and are most closely related to the actual act of reading, the outcome, arguably yield the most authentic information. However, they tend to be subjective and appropriate interpretation is based heavily on the teacher's experiences, training, and dedication.

Assessments of skills less tied to specific classroom instruction, such as recurring probes of oral reading fluency, offer more objectivity and increasingly are used for monitoring student progress. Such tests, as described in this chapter, often are administered in classroom settings by teachers, special educators, reading specialists, and sometimes, by educational diagnosticians or school psychologists. Unlike the high-stakes and norm-referenced tests, these tests are used primarily to determine whether students have mastered certain skills or are performing at specified levels on various types of reading tasks. The information gleaned from these assessments is used to determine whether instruction is effective and whether it should be continued, intensified, or changed.

The Assessment Continuum

As implied previously, some informal assessment measures are standardized (administered according to prescribed directions and time limits), yet they yield primarily criterion-referenced data, information about whether students have mastered a particular skill or set of skills. Unlike norm-referenced tests, however, the focus is on individual students' mastery of specific skills relative to some criterion. As tests become more sophisticated, the distinction between formal and informal and criterion and norm-referenced assessments become blurred. It is increasingly difficult to compare and contrast types of assessment, because current technology allows test publishers to combine elements of several types in one package. Figure 8.1, a graphic organizer, depicts a range of reading assessments. However, keep in mind that some assessments may yield more than one type of information, which we refer to as "hybrid" measures.

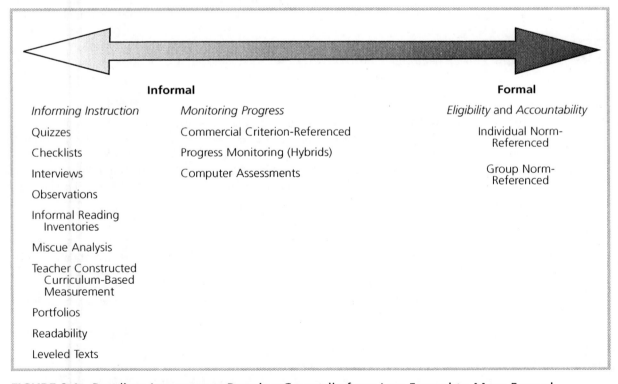

FIGURE 8.1 Reading Assessments Ranging Generally from Less Formal to More Formal

Reliability and Validity

Before considering various types of hybrid assessments, we discuss briefly two essential aspects of tests—reliability and validity—two important concepts that provide background knowledge. Remember the importance of building vocabulary and background knowledge to reading comprehension? Similarly, knowledge of these terms will give you background needed for understanding, evaluating, and using published assessments.

Reliability

Reliability is typically defined as the extent to which a test yields consistent scores and is directly related to test error. In fact, reliability is technically defined as:

> 1 — error

Conversely, error is defined as:

> 1 — reliability

Reliability is defined technically from one of several possible formulas and may range from 0 to 1, although in reality, no test will exhibit perfect reliability. For illustrative purposes, assume that the manual of a particular reading test reports a reliability of .91. In this case, 91 percent of the variability (relative placement of scores within a distribution) earned on the test can be attributed to a systematic or "real" cause, say ability to decode if that is the purpose of the test. Conversely, 9 percent of the variability is unsystematic $(1 - .91 = 9)$, cannot be predicted, and consequently represents error.

Traditionally, test authors use reliability estimates, calculated from specific formulas, as numerical indicators of the quality of a test. Certain types of reliability are based on the correlation coefficient as a starting point. The higher the reliability, the better the test. According to Salvia and Yesseldyke (1998), tests that yield a reliability index of .90 and higher can be used for important decisions such as special education placement; those that yield scores from .80 to .90 can be used for screening; those that yield scores of .60 or better can be used for research purposes.

Types of Reliability   As indicated earlier, various statistical estimates of reliability can be calculated and each is related to a slightly different type of reliability, although all estimates reference the extent to which the test produces consistent or systematic measurement.

Table 8.1 provides a description of the main types of reliability, including inter-rater reliability, intra-rater reliability, alternate forms reliability, internal consistency reliability, and

TABLE 8.1   Types of Reliability

Type of Reliability	What Is Measured?	How Is It Calculated?
Inter-Rater	Consistency between two or more raters or observers	Percentage agreement
Intra-Rater	One rater's consistency in scoring across different assessments	Percentage agreement
Alternate Form	Consistency of scores over two alternate or equivalent forms of same test	Pearson *r* coefficient
Internal Consistency	Consistency of scores on items within same test	Spearman Brown; Cronbach's alpha
Test-Retest	Consistency of scores from one testing time to another, usually within a few weeks	Pearson *r* coefficient

test-retest reliability. All these variations are tied to somewhat unique specific data analyses and statistical procedures, but all the analyses are based on determining the extent to which there is consistency within or between raters or between items. Consistency between different examiners or raters is called **inter-rater reliability,** and consistency over time by the same rater(s) is called **intra-rater reliability.** Consistency among items, which can be determined by comparing scores across two halves of the same test, is called **internal consistency reliability.**

Consistency among items can also be estimated by **test-retest reliability,** which is determined by administration of the same test twice to the same individuals within a relatively short period of time, and **alternate forms reliability,** which is obtained by administration of parallel or equivalent forms of a test at the same time to the same individuals. Intra-rater reliability and inter-rater reliability estimates typically are determined by calculating the percentage of agreement by the raters on the total number of items rated. Consistency or reliability of items typically is determined by the results of calculation of a Pearson Product Moment correlation coefficient, or r, or some reliability estimate using the Pearson r as a starting point, such as the Spearman-Brown formula. The specific procedures associated with calculating the Pearson r and related reliability formulae are beyond the scope of this book, but they can be found in many introductory measurement texts (for example, Payne 2003).

Validity

Just as reliability indexes represent the extent to which a test yields consistent measurement across examiners and items, validity indexes represent the extent to which the test assesses what it was designed to assess. Validity is the "most fundamental consideration in developing and evaluating tests" according to the Standards for Educational and Psychological Testing (American Educational Research Association [AERA], American Psychological Association [APA], & National Council on Measurement in Education [NCME], 1999, 9). There are various strategies for determining validity, including content validity, construct validity, predictive validity, and treatment validity. For informal tests, content and treatment validity are perhaps the most critical types. **Content validity** refers to the extent to which a test reflects the content that the teacher or school district considers important. **Treatment validity** refers to the extent to which a test yields information that relates directly to instruction. See Table 8.2 for a summary of validity types and some techniques used to determine them.

TABLE 8.2 Types of Validity

Type of Validity	What Is Measured?	How Is It Determined?
Content	How well do items assess the desired content	Expert review Test blueprint
Construct	How well do the items assess a particular construct, domain, or skill area	Correlation coefficients with other measures of the same construct or other measures of intent
Concurrent	How well do two or more measures of same construct agree (administered at same time)	
Predictive	How well do two or more measures of same construct agree (one administered several months or years before the other)	
Treatment	How well do the items predict students' learning gains	Analysis of gain scores following instruction

Content Validity Content validity evidence typically is determined by examining the items contained within a test and the extent to which they reflect knowledge of interest. Usually this is determined by creating a test blueprint. Figure 8.2 shows a blueprint for a test we designed with a colleague to assess teachers' knowledge of reading instruction and assessment practices. You will see that items were developed to assess mastery of knowledge at a basic recall or recognition level and at a more advanced application level in the areas of alphabetics, fluency, vocabulary, and comprehension. A quick glance at the test blueprint provides a visual summary of the number of items assessing each category. By using a blueprint, test authors can ensure a balanced coverage of the content they wish to assess.

	Alpha-betics	Fluency	Vocabulary	Comprehension	General	Total
Assessment						
# of Items	2	2	2	2	2	10
Knowledge	21, 70	53, 63	19, 69	48, 79	3, 45	
# of Items	3	3	3	3	3	15
Application	10, 42, 44	1, 12, 23	18, 9, 43	28, 30, 81	20, 61, 67	
Total per Scale/ Assessment	5	5	5	5	5	25
Instruction						
# of Items	5	5	5	5		20
Knowledge	8, 25, 31, 35, 38	14, 29, 41, 50, 66	17, 22, 39, 52, 80	6, 36, 55, 58, 76		
# of Items	9	9	9	9		36
Application	7, 11, 13, 46, 56, 59, 62, 65, 77	4, 16, 32, 37, 40, 47, 68, 71, 74	24, 26, 27, 49, 54, 57, 73, 75, 78	2, 5, 15, 33, 34, 51, 60, 64, 72		
Total per Scale/ Instruction	14	14	14	14		56
Total per Scale	19	19	19	19	5	
Total						81

FIGURE 8.2 Sample Test Blueprint

Source: Ziegler, M., Bell, S. M., & McCallum, R. S. (in press). Test Blueprint for *Assessment of Reading Instructional Knowledge-Adults.* National Institute for Literacy.

Construct Validity   Another type of validity, **construct validity,** can be determined by evaluating the relationship between the test of interest and other established measures of the construct of interest. One type of construct validity is **concurrent validity;** in this case, the measures are administered to the same examinees at approximately the same time. In our case, if an author wants to determine the validity of a newly developed informal reading test, the author may administer the new test and an older well-constructed test measuring the same or similar content to a group of students on the same day. The scores then are subjected to a statistical formula, in this case, the Pearson Product Moment correlational procedure. A high positive score, approaching 1, is an indication that the newly constructed test has construct validity because it measures the same construct as the older, established measure. For example, correlations between measures of oral reading fluency, such as those used in AIMSweb (Edformation 2001; Harcourt, 2007) and DIBELS (Good and Kaminski 2002) with the Woodcock Reading Mastery Test (Woodcock 1987/1998) were .91 and higher, according to information from the AIMSweb Training Workbook, published on the AIMSweb Web site (www.aimsweb.com). Another type of construct validity is predictive validity. **Predictive validity** is the extent to which a test predicts success on some variable of interest. For example, the goal for developing an informal test of reading might be to predict reading success in class, as represented by a language arts grade. In this case, a Pearson r might be calculated to determine the relationship between the test score and grades; and if the Pearson r yields a score approaching positive 1, the author would conclude that the test has solid predictive validity.

Treatment Validity   Treatment validity is the extent to which a test yields information that is useful in treatment, or, in the context of this book, reading instruction. Although treatment validity is more difficult to establish than other types, there are two strategies to achieve the goal. First, treatment validity may be determined by examining the specific content assessed by test items and relating that content to a teacher's instructional goals. For example, remember Misha in Ms. Crockett's first grade class? She reads slowly and haltingly. The most appropriate type of assessment is one that allows Ms. Crockett to hear her read and assess her rate and accuracy. A procedure that allows Ms. Crockett to gain information about the specific skills in question is more appropriate than a generic test, such as one that requires the student to read words from an oral word list and allows her to target specific instruction.

A second way to determine the treatment validity of a test is to evaluate how well the test predicts progress or gains made by students, based on the information taken from the test. That is, the extent to which a test predicts instruction gain may be evaluated by assessing students' achievement gain scores over a prescribed period of time during which the test results were used to guide instruction. For example, assume that Misha is targeted for extra instruction (Tier 2 in a multi-tiered instructional approach) based on her oral reading fluency scores from the DIBELS. According to this *rate* measure, Misha needs instruction designed to increase reading rate. In Tier 2 instruction, she gets lots of practice reading books at her instructional reading level, a strategy designed to increase rate. If, after eight weeks of Tier 2 instruction, her oral reading fluency score on the DIBELS improves, we can assume that the DIBELS oral reading score has treatment validity in this limited context (as a measure for determining the need for fluency instruction). Statistically, the relationship between Misha's DIBELS score on measures of oral reading fluency and her grades after instruction could be established by calculating a Pearson r between the test scores and grades after instruction.

In the remaining sections of this chapter, we address three types of commercially available assessments that are used primarily to gauge student progress: (a) criterion-referenced, (b) progress monitoring, and (c) computerized.

Criterion-Referenced Assessment

Special educators, educational diagnosticians, and others who work in remedial programs often use commercially published criterion-referenced assessments that measure a wide variety of academic skills across many grade levels. These instruments have been particularly useful for (a) assessing mastery of objectives as determined in the Individual Education Program (IEP) of students in special education; (b) determining present levels of performance, as required in federal special education law, and (c) establishing specific curricular objectives.

Criterion-referenced assessments have been extremely useful in establishing IEP objectives for students below grade level or with inconsistent performance across different types of academic skills. For example, Mr. Haywood, our special education teacher, has used the BRIGANCE® Diagnostic Comprehensive Inventory of Basic Skills–Revised (CURRICULUM ASSOCIATES®, Inc.© 1999, 1983) for the past five years with his special education students. The BRIGANCE® Inventories have been used primarily in special education to determine student mastery on a wide variety of academic skills dating back to the 1970s. These assessments have been used by thousands of special educators to determine student progress toward specific curriculum goals. An example of a specific reading goal might be: *the student demonstrates ability to substitute initial consonant sounds in words.* This specificity allows teachers to set particular educational goals and gauge progress.

All teachers conduct some type of criterion-referenced assessment. The unit tests and worksheets used by our first-grade teacher, Ms. Crockett, are criterion-referenced in that they provide information about how well a student can perform a specific skill or task, such as matching words that rhyme or choosing the correct definition for a word read in context. Criterion-referenced tests, as the name implies, tell the teacher the extent to which a student has mastered specific criteria, including curriculum objectives. These tests are used to assess student mastery of the curriculum rather than to compare a student's performance to that of other students. Most reading instructional programs include criterion-referenced assessments to measure skill mastery as students progress through the instruction. Classroom teachers typically use these assessments routinely.

In contrast to classroom teachers, special education students historically have used a variety of instructional materials, often different from or in addition to the core program used in the regular classroom. And formal instruction in reading often ends at about sixth grade. Consequently, adolescents and adults with low reading levels may not receive instruction from a basal reader or a core reading program. To gauge progress of primary students in special education and older students reading below grade level, there are numerous commercially available criterion-referenced measures that are not tied directly to a given set of instructional materials. The BRIGANCE® Inventories are the most comprehensive and are widely used in special education programs across the United States (Overton 2006). Next, we specifically describe some of the BRIGANCE® Inventories.

The BRIGANCE® Inventories

Several BRIGANCE® instruments are available, but not all are directly relevant for reading assessment. Some are designed as screening instruments (including BRIGANCE® K & 1 Screen II [2005]; BRIGANCE® Preschool Screen II [2005]) and are often administered when children first enter a school setting. Preschool, kindergarten, and first-grade classroom teachers often administer these instruments at the beginning of a school year, when a child enters a program, and sometimes to assess progress in a program. Other BRIGANCE® instruments are designed for secondary-level special education and vocational education students (such as the BRIGANCE® Life Skills Inventory 1994). Most relevant for our purpose are the BRIGANCE® Diagnostic Inventory of Early Development—Second Edition (IED-II; CURRICULUM ASSOCIATES®, Inc.© 2004, 1991, 1978) and the BRIGANCE® Diagnostic Comprehensive Inventory of Basic Skills—Revised (CIBS-R; CURRICULUM ASSOCIATES,® Inc.© 1999, 1983). These provide in-depth assessment of reading, reading readiness, and reading-related skills as well as many other academic skills. Rather than provide an exhaustive review of these instruments, our goal is to inform teachers and other assessment specialists about the basic structure and utility of the instruments, particularly about administration guidelines, depth and breadth of reading-related content, and usefulness of the information the instruments provide.

Structure Typically, the BRIGANCE® Inventories contain multiple subtests; each inventory is contained within a large, ringed binder that resembles a traditional notebook. These binders contain examiner and examinee pages that can be removed from the notebooks for ease of administration. For any particular student, only selected subtests should be administered. In addition, there is a student record book in which the teacher/examiner records specific information about the student's performance. On the first page of the student record book, the teacher circles the skills the student masters and underlines the skills to be targeted as objectives. In addition, the system allows the same student booklet to be used up to six times, with the teacher using a pen of a different color each time the student is assessed. This system works well for students in special education, whose progress needs to be assessed frequently throughout a given school year. See Figures 8.3 and 8.4 for examples of the student profile and examiner record book pages.

As is apparent from Figures 8.3 and 8.4, the tasks are clear and straightforward and each skill area to be assessed is described. Each skill is tied to an objective, and the objective

---

G. WORD ANALYSIS (CONTINUED)

Assessment	Page			
G-12	217–219	**READS SUFFIXES:**		

(page 217)	(page 218)	(page 219)
[1]1. s	13. est	25. ous (drop final *e*)
2. ed with *t* sound	14. y to i and add *es*	26. ment
3. 's	15. y to i and add *est*	27. al
4. ed with *d* sound	16. remove y and add *ily*	28. drop final *e* and add *ation*
5. ing	17. n	[4]29. ward
6. es	18. en	30. ist (drop final *e*)
7. double final consonant and add *ing*	[3]19. ful	31. less
8. double final consonant and add *ed*	20. *f* to *v* and add *es*	32. ian (remove y)
9. drop final *e* and add *ing*	21. or	33. able (drop final *e*)
[2]10. er	22. th	34. ship
11. y	23. ness	35. ance (drop final *e*)
12. ly	24. ion	[5]36. ish[6]

G-13	220	**READS PREFIXES:**

[2]1. un	3. re	5. in	[4]7. en	9. inter	[5]11. mis	13. pre
[3]2. dis	4. im	6. non	8. super	10. de	12. fore	14. ir[6]

G-14	221	**DIVIDES WORDS INTO SYLLABLES:**

[2]1. one vowel sound	5. one consonant between two vowels
2. like consonants between vowels	6. suffixes
3. unlike consonants between vowels	[3]7. three vowel sounds
4. consonant blends and digraphs between two vowels	8. ending *le*
	9. prefixes[4]

FIGURE 8.3 Page from Student Record Book, BRIGANCE® Diagnostic Comprehensive Inventory of Basic Skills–Revised

Source: Brigance, A. H. Page from Student Record Book of the *BRIGANCE® Diagnostic Comprehensive Inventory of Basic Skills–Revised.* © 1999, 1983. N. Billerica, MA: CURRICULUM ASSOCIATES®, Inc. Reprinted/Adapted by permission.

G-13   READS PREFIXES

SKILL: Reads words with prefixes when the base words are pronounced.

STUDENT RECORD BOOK: Page 17.

CLASS RECORD BOOK: Page 23.

ASSESSMENT METHOD: Individual oral response.

MATERIALS: S-220.

DISCONTINUE: Your discretion, or after failure on three consecutive prefixes.

TIME: Your discretion.

ACCURACY: 2/2 (100%) for each prefix.

NOTES:

1. **Referencing and Sequencing of Skills:** See page 166 in the Introduction to this section.

2. **Supplemental and Related Lists/Skill Sequences:** This assessment includes the more basic prefixes—those introduced in most reading programs and those frequently added to base words. For a list of more advanced or lower-frequency prefixes, see G-13S, Prefixes, on page 224, for supplemental skills and knowledge related to prefixes you may wish to include in an assessment or to add to your curriculum.

STUDENT-PAGE FORMAT AND SKILL ANALYSIS FOR S-220

DIRECTIONS

This assessment is made by pronouncing each base word—the first word in each pair—and asking the student to pronounce the base word with the prefix added—the second word in the pair.

Point to the words on S-220, and

Say: **The words in each pair are alike, except the second word has a beginning added to it. I am going to say the first word in each pair and I want you to say the second word.**

Point to the word *happy*, and

Say: **This word is *happy*. What is this word?** Point to the word *unhappy*.

Pause for student's response. If the student responds correctly, continue with the same procedure for the other items in the assessment.

NOTES: *(continued)*

You may wish to assess the student's comprehension of the meanings of the prefixes. This may be done by informally asking the student the meaning of individual prefixes. For a list of some of the more basic prefixes and their meanings, see G-13R, Comprehends Meanings of Prefixes, on page 224, for supplemental skills and knowledge related to comprehending the meaning of prefixes you may wish to include in an assessment or to add to your curriculum.

3. **Correlated BRIGANCE® Prescriptive Teaching Material:** Pages 481–500 of the *BRIGANCE Prescriptive Word Analysis: Strategies and Practice*, Volume II.

OBJECTIVE

By ____(date)____, when seeing a base word and the base word with a prefix, and after hearing the base word pronounced, ___(student's name)___ will pronounce the base word with the prefix. This task will be performed with an accuracy of 2/2 (100%) for ___(quantity)___ of fourteen prefixes.

FIGURE 8.4   Page from Examiner Book, BRIGANCE® Diagnostic Comprehensive Inventory of Basic Skills–Revised

Source: Brigance, A. H. Examiner Page from *BRIGANCE® Diagnostic Comprehensive Inventory of Basic Skills–Revised* © 1999, 1983. N. Billerica, MA: CURRICULUM ASSOCIATES®, Inc. Reprinted/Adapted by permission.

is provided with blanks embedded and to be completed by the examiner, showing the projected date of completion and the criterion required for mastery. Some of the subtests yield norm-referenced information, such as standard scores (with a mean of 100 and a standard deviation of 15), grade/age equivalents, and percentiles. The primary purpose of the administration, however, is to obtain information about students' present levels of performance and to aid in developing instructional goals and monitoring progress.

Perhaps the most widely used inventory, the CIBS-R, contains three global components that can be used to screen, determine readiness for kindergarten or first grade, and assess specific skills for students performing at instructional levels typical of students in grades 1 through 6. Because special education students are generally performing below typical grade-level expectations in one or more areas, the CIBS-R may be used with older students or even adults, depending on instructional level.

Administration   As mentioned earlier, not all sections should be administered to particular students. The examiner selects the skills areas to be assessed, presumably relative to teacher and curricular goals. Specific administration directions are provided, as are suggestions about scoring criteria, administration time, discontinue rules, and so on (see Figure 8.4).

Content BRIGANCE® Inventories are designed to provide in-depth information sufficient to inform instruction. In fact, teachers are encouraged to use the information to set instructional objectives, particularly for IEPs required for special education students. The reading and reading-related skill areas assessed by the CIBS-R include: readiness, speech, listening, word recognition, oral reading, reading comprehension, word analysis, functional word recognition, spelling, writing, reference skills, graphs, and maps. Within the functional word recognition skill area, the following specific content can be assessed: basic sight vocabulary, direction words, number words, warning and safety words, information sign words, warning label words, and food label words. Within the direction word area are specific word lists related to writing, speaking, physical activities, and studying. Additional supplemental sections include content assessing contractions, abbreviations, and so on. So assessment data can be very specific and may be tied directly to specific classroom goals.

Usefulness BRIGANCE® data can inform specific reading goals, based on direct assessment of what the student can and cannot do. Use of the system allows examiners to create very specific learning objectives. Multiple assessments can be generated to chart progress and determine ultimate mastery of the objectives. So **intra-individual comparisons** are readily available. **Inter-individual comparisons** are also available for some subtests and some ages, based on norm-referenced scores.

Psychometric Integrity **Psychometric** data are available in standardization and validation manuals. Data show moderate to good test-retest, internal consistency, inter-rater, and alternative forms reliabilities, as well as evidence for various types of validity. For example, robust correlations are shown between examinee raw scores and age. (Because achievement should progress steadily with development, this relationship between age and raw scores is expected). Several correlation coefficients show evidence for concurrent validity between the BRIGANCE® scores and related instruments, such as the Peabody Individual Achievement Test-Revised (Markwardt 1989) and the Wide Range Achievement Test-3 (Wilkinson 1993). Although appreciable psychometric data are available in the

CIBS-R Standardization and Validation Manual, not all agree on its merits. For example, according to a review of the CIBS-R by Cizek (n.d.) "Overall, the level of content validity evidence provided falls short of 'abundant' as claimed in the technical manual" (Validity section ¶ 1). Cizek calls for the collection of additional information to support content validity claims and the mastery/nonmastery cutoffs provided, as well as the development of new items that more clearly differentiate between the constructs assessed. Finally, Cizek (n.d.) recommends cautious use of the standardization data for making eligibility decisions; rather, the BRIGANCE® is best used as an information gathering tool. In that role, it appears to be strong indeed, and it can help teachers determine instructional goals and monitor progress of those goals.

Let us look at an example of a BRIGANCE® assessment for a student from Mr. Haywood's special education class. Shelby, a fifth-grade student who receives reading instruction from Mr. Haywood, was administered an informal reading inventory by the reading specialist at the beginning of fifth grade. According to results from the IRI, Shelby's instructional reading level is 3, even though she is in fifth grade. Mr. Haywood is responsible for much of Shelby's reading instruction and, consequently, wants more in-depth information about her reading. From the CIBS-R, he chooses several sections to obtain a more in-depth picture of Shelby's skills in reading; based on this assessment, he will set goals that are reflected in Shelby's IEP. He will assess her progress every six weeks, in accordance with state and federal special education guidelines, and will set new goals as she masters current ones. Figure 8.5 depicts a section from the CIBS-R and shows Shelby's performance the first time she was assessed by Mr. Haywood.

FIGURE 8.5 Shelby's Scores on Selected Sections of the BRIGANCE® Diagnostic Comprehensive Inventory of Basic Skills–Revised

Source: Brigance, A. H. *BRIGANCE® Diagnostic Comprehensive Inventory of Basic Skills–Revised* © 1999, 1983. N. Billerica, MA: CURRICULUM ASSOCIATES,® Inc. Reprinted/Adapted by permission.

Progress Monitoring

The passage of the Individuals with Disabilities Education Improvement Act (IDEA 2004) in late 2004 provides a strong impetus for collaboration of educators across disciplines to assess and gauge progress of all students, particularly in the area of reading. IDEA 2004 calls for early intervention for those at risk for academic failure and demands that educators track students' instructional responsiveness. The intent is to prevent academic failure, especially in reading, and consequently reduce the percentage of students ultimately identified as eligible for special education.

Recall the multitiered model of reading instruction and the Response to Intervention (RTI) model. The success of these models relies on two important components: (a) effective instruction and (b) accurate assessment. Our first-grade teacher, Ms. Crockett, uses a core reading program that is generally effective with most of her students. However, some fail to progress with their peers. Some enter first grade knowing only a few letters and sounds, and others enter with limited English proficiency. Occasionally, she has a student with enriched oral vocabulary who has extreme difficulty mastering phonics and remembering words automatically. For these students, early intervention is essential. Most students who do not read well by the end of third grade will never read well (Badian 1988). Consequently, there is a strong need for accurate monitoring of student progress, particularly in the early grades.

Ideally, teachers are well-informed about assessment and instruction. In many cases, effective use of the assessment techniques will provide teachers with the knowledge needed to determine when students need additional or different types of instruction. However, teacher knowledge and expertise in the use of informal classroom techniques is extremely variable. Because too many students reach middle and upper grades with inadequate reading skills, large-scale progress monitoring is included in the multitiered model RTI models. The rationale is to assess students several times per year. Their progress on certain key indicators of reading (including quick oral reading of words at grade level) is compared to the typical progress of students in the same grade. Students whose progress is below the typical performance of students in the same grades are targeted for more intensive instruction, and their progress is gauged more frequently. The National Center on Student Progress Monitoring has been established as a resource for educators, and information about progress monitoring tools is available at: www.studentprogress.org/chart/chart.asp#.

Benchmarks are expected levels of performance; for example, at the end of first grade, the average student typically can read orally about 50 words per minute (Hasbrouck and Tindal 1992). **Slope** is actually a term taken from the element of a graph that shows the relationship between performance (say oral reading fluency—defined as number of words read correctly per minute) and instructional time. Using this example, the steepness of the line showing rate of oral reading progress relative to time spent in instruction is called the slope. Consequently, we can graph the performance of Jesse in Ms. Crockett's class to see whether he is making progress consistent with expectations for his age and grade. We know that the average first-grader acquires 1.75 new sight words per week (Fuchs and Fuchs 2005). Figure 8.6 shows progress monitoring for Jesse. We can see that he appears to be making adequate progress. He generally increases his oral reading speed by about two words per week.

Because progress monitoring provides information about the student's level of performance—such as how many words the student can read in a minute and rate of acquisition (slope)—implications for instructional placement are pretty straightforward. If the child is below benchmark (i.e., expected performance at some given time) but rate is adequate, current instruction is probably effective. However, if the child performs below benchmark and rate is also slower than typical, instruction needs to be intensified. In this case, the child would begin receiving supplemental instruction (Tier 2 in the context

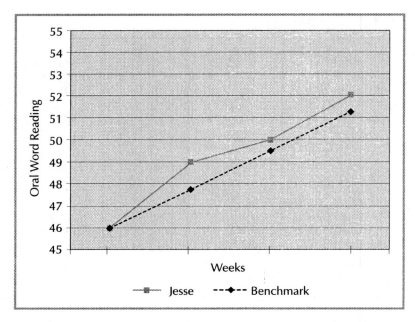

FIGURE 8.6 Oral Reading Fluency (Words Correct Per Minute) for Jesse, a First Grader

of multi-tiered instruction). For effective progress monitoring, tools should be reliable (consistent) and valid (accurate). These measures should also provide measures of discrete skills so that teachers can target instruction.

In order to meet the multiple needs of informal assessment, hybrid measures have emerged that combine some characteristics of informal and formal assessment. Curriculum-based measures (CBM) historically have been developed by teachers using actual school curriculum. However, according to Fuchs and Deno (1994), curriculum-based measurement may actually be more effective when not derived from the actual curriculum in use. There is an increasing trend toward use of standardized skills assessments in which a student's performance is compared to the typical performance for his or her grade. In this scenario, students are screened three to four times per year on one or more key measures of reading. If progress is within expected range, great! If not, students are targeted for more frequent instruction and assessed much more frequently (e.g., once per week). Two assessments that are widely used are the AIMSweb progress monitoring system (Edformation 2001) and the Dynamic Indicators of Basic Early Literacy Skills, or DIBELS (Good and Kaminski 2002).

AIMSweb

AIMSweb (www.aimsweb.com) is published by Edformation, Inc., which was acquired in 2007 by Harcourt Assessment, and is updated regularly. AIMSweb is the name of a software assessment system that can be used by school systems and individual teachers to assess, monitor, and track student progress. Also, it can be used to track students in systems that already use DIBELS (addressed in the following section of this chapter); alternatively, system personnel have the option of using unique but somewhat similar measures built into the AIMSweb system. In fact, AIMSweb includes unique measures of reading fluency, comprehension, early literacy skills, Spanish early literacy skills, early numeracy skills, mathematical computation, spelling, and written expression. These measures are curriculum-based in the sense that they are designed to assess real-world skills that teachers consider essential in the classroom and are appropriate for assessing benchmarks for students in grades K–8 and for progress monitoring for students of any age. According to the authors, AIMSweb provides a proactive, evidence-based solution for universal screening, strategic assessment, progress monitoring, and special services eligibility.

Structure   AIMSweb provides not only testing materials, but also a tracking service. Typically, system administrators or other personnel make a decision to "subscribe" to AIMSweb services, which are differentially priced depending on system needs. For example, according to the AIMSweb Internet site, a system site license can be purchased for a small fee per student, which varies depending on the type of service needed. Additional site or individual licenses can be purchased and, as with the others, prices depend on the services, academic areas assessed, and data needed (such as preservice instructor package, benchmark data package, progress monitoring data package, and RTI data package). The prices include computer scoring and monitoring, downloadable test materials, manual, online support, and training. Directions for administering the materials and tracking the scores are provided.

Administration and Scoring   Teachers or other personnel individually administer assessments to students; each assessment takes from one to five minutes, administration is fairly straightforward. The tests can be administered by a teacher or other educator or by a trained paraprofessional. Hand scoring is necessary, but it is easy to master. Analyses are conducted via the computer tracking system. Raw scores may be transformed into percentiles, age and grade equivalents, and standard scores and may be referenced in graph form to data showing an error line, goal line, and trend line. Benchmark assessments are administered three times a year, and typically, systems determine a criterion score to be used for assigning "at-risk" status to students. For example, students who score in the bottom 10 percent of other students in the system (or school) may be designated "at risk." The progress of the at-risk students is assessed more frequently; the progress monitoring probes of AIMSweb are administered once per week. In addition to low performance (i.e., scores in the bottom 10 percent), a second criterion may be added to define which students go on to more focused and presumably more powerful instruction. For example, those students whose rate of progress (slope) falls within the lowest 25 percent and who still score within the lowest 10 percent of the class may be considered eligible for a Tier 2 intervention. Systems may use continued progress monitoring to determine which students are targeted for consideration for special services, including special education eligibility.

Using the scenario created for determining Tier 1 and Tier 2 eligibility (mentioned earlier), those who continue to fall short based on the criteria—including those who continue to score within the lowest 10 percent of all students at the school and show a rate of progress consistent with the lowest 25 percent—may be referred for more in-depth academic, cognitive, or social/emotional assessment to rule out or rule in problems such as mental retardation, emotional disturbance, and learning disabilities.

Content   AIMSweb materials are designed to provide two levels of assessment specificity for reading fluency, reading comprehension (using a maze or cloze procedure), early numeracy (oral counting, identifying numbers, missing numbers, and quantity), math computation (facts and calculation), early literacy (letter and nonsense word naming, letter sound fluency, phoneme segmentation, (with a similar Spanish version)) spelling, and written expression. First, benchmark materials that are designed to be administered three times per year provide a global assessment. Benchmark data are appropriate for screening in the academic areas. Progress monitoring probes that are designed to be administered once a week are useful for tracking more specific skill acquisition. These measures tap skills that are similar to those taught in the classroom, but the particular skills measured are not tied directly to any particular curriculum. Consequently, even though probe data are more specific than benchmark data, probes will not inform instruction in a direct manner. Even though the AIMSweb system sometimes is touted as a curriculum-based assessment device, the data generated are not likely to align with a particular teacher's classroom goals and may not correspond closely to end-of-the-year, norm-referenced achievement test scores.

Usefulness   The AIMSweb system has been adopted by many school systems across the country, presumably because it provides methods for universal screening and tracking progress to conform to the No Child Left Behind mandates and related legislation, such as the Individuals with Disabilities Education Improvement Act (IDEA 2004). The ultimate utility of the system remains to be seen. On the surface at least, the data generated can be helpful to system personnel as they track system-wide student gains and at-risk student progress. It can be implemented system wide, on a school-by-school basis, or even by individual teachers or tutors. To obtain maximum use of the system, considerable assessment time and management expertise are required. For example, just ordering the materials needed for a particular school or system is somewhat daunting, requiring a solid familiarity with the components. Systems considering adopting AIMSweb must be prepared to invest significant time and energy in training, assessment, and management.

Psychometric Integrity   Although the origin of the AIMSweb system can be traced back to work of Germann and colleagues in the 1970s, and more recently Shinn (see the AIMSweb site for related literature), the current application is relatively new. Even so, its developers have not ignored the need to support its use by generating psychometric data. For example, for oral reading fluency, authors report inter-rater reliability coefficients in the high .90s; test-retest reliabilities (from 2 to 10 week periods) ranging from .84 to .97; alternate forms reliabilities (with tests administered one week apart) ranging from .84 to .94; and concurrent validity data with correlations ranging from .26 to .91 with various tests of reading, such as the Woodcock Reading Mastery Test (Woodcock 1987/1998) and the Gates-MacGinitie Reading Test (MacGinitie, MacGinitie, Maria, and Dreyer 2000) (www.aimsweb.com/research/). These data are impressive; however, they were collected using a wide variety of sources for the reading passages.

The origin of data specifically used to generate AIMSweb psychometric estimates is not easy to find on the Web site. As the system becomes increasingly popular, independent data will be generated by practitioners and researchers. Some recent research has addressed the need to provide more sophisticated psychometric data for confident interpretation of trend line scores that use repeated measures (i.e., probes). For example, Poncy, Skinner, and Axtell (2005) demonstrated that multiple probes are necessary before trend lines can be interpreted confidently. This is necessary because of the error associated with each probe. As you may remember from our earlier discussion of reliability, there is some error contained in every score and when examiners use multiple scores to make decisions, the error rate is compounded. Thus, to overcome this limitation, many measures are required.

In summary, although initial data are encouraging, further independent research will be helpful in ensuring confident use of the AIMSweb system. Further, the academic tasks in the various screening and probes tend to represent somewhat discrete academic skills, but they do not give teachers specific information about what to teach next, as does the BRIGANCE®. Rather, they simply provide information about a child's performance in a particular area defined by the authors (such as oral reading fluency), show comparability to that of peers, and track changes over time as a function of instruction.

Although the AIMSweb system offers school systems several advantages, implementation is expensive and time intensive. Administrators will need to evaluate whether their particular school system can afford the time required of school personnel to generate the massive and ongoing database produced by the multiple probes, and in fact, whether the system requires such an extensive database.

The Dynamic Indicators of Basic Early Literacy Skills

The Dynamic Indicators of Basic Early Literacy Skills, or DIBELS (Good and Kaminski 2002; https://dibels.uoregon.edu/) provide direct assessment of prereading and reading skills of students in kindergarten to sixth grade. Originally conceptualized as a curriculum-based measure, DIBELS continues to be updated and includes measures that can be aligned with the areas of reading targeted by the National Reading Panel (NRP, National Institute for Child Health and Human Development [NICHD] 2000):

* Phonemic awareness—Initial Sounds Fluency (ISF) and Phoneme Segmentation Fluency (PSF)
* Phonics—Nonsense Word Fluency (NWF)
* Fluency—Letter Naming Fluency (LNF) and Oral Reading Fluency (ORF)
* Comprehension—Retell Fluency (RTF)
* Vocabulary—Word Use Fluency (WUF)

Although not all measures are administered to all ages, the measures can be used to: (a) identify children at risk for reading failure, (b) monitor progress as students acquire literacy skills, and (c) evaluate intervention effectiveness. Two types of measures are available, including benchmark tasks which can be administered to all students three times per year, and progress monitoring tasks which can be administered more frequently.

Structure All measures are designed to be administered in one minute. The benchmark materials consist of scoring booklets, reusable student stimulus materials, and examiner scoring and recording forms. Progress monitoring probes include examiner forms and twenty alternate forms of student material per measure. A manual describing administration and scoring is available. All these materials are free and downloadable from the DIBELS Web site given earlier. Alternately, they are available for purchase from Sopris West Publishing Company. Examiners must supply a clipboard and colored pen for administering the Retell Fluency and Word Use Fluency tasks.

Content All seven DIBELS measures are described in Table 8.3. As is obvious from reading these descriptions, students are expected to produce a product, hence the use of the term "fluency" as part of the name of every measure. For example, students must identify one of four pictures that begin with a target sound and produce initial sounds of orally presented words that correspond to the pictures for the Initial Sound Fluency measure. They also must segment words into individual phonemes for the Phoneme Segmentation Fluency measure, name letters for the Letter Naming Fluency measure, call pseudowords for the Nonsense Word Fluency measure, read a passage for the Oral Reading Fluency measure, retell a passage for the Retell Fluency measure, and use a word in a sentence for the Word Use Fluency measure. For students whose first language is Spanish, there is a Spanish version, *Indicadores dinámicos del éxito en la lectura.*

Administration and Scoring Probes are administered individually and take three to five minutes each. Administration of the complete set of benchmark measures takes about ten to twenty minutes. DIBELS authors recommend that probes be administered as frequently as two times per week or as needed to monitor progress. Teaching items typically are provided, as are discontinue rules. Smooth administration requires careful attention to detail (such as pacing of stimuli, determining correctness of responses, recording scores, and timing latency to response), so practice is required. Fluency measures are scored (e.g., number of correct initial sounds and words read correctly per minute). Scoring can be somewhat difficult. For example, on some tasks, students are given three seconds to respond, and on others, they are given five seconds. To aid the examiner, specific guidelines are provided to help in determining errors, such as inaccuracies, omissions and

TABLE 8.3   Description of DIBELS Measures by NRP Domains

NRP Domains	Phonemic Awareness	Phonics	Fluency	Vocabulary	Comprehension
Measure(s) and Grade-Level Guides	Initial Sound Fluency (K)	Nonsense Word Fluency (K–2)	Letter Naming Fluency (K–1)	Word Use Fluency (grades 1–6)	Retell Fluency (grades 1–2)
	Phoneme Segmentation Fluency (K–1)		Oral Reading Fluency (grades 1–6)		
Units of Measure	Number of onsets correct per minute for the set of picture probes	Number of correct letter sounds in one minute	Number of correct letter names in one minute	Number of words in correct utterances in one minute	Number of relevant words provided in one minute
	Number of correct phonemes in 1 minute		Number of correct words in one minute; median of three passages		
Skills Targeted	Phonemic awareness	Connecting letters with sounds	Knowledge of alphabet	Semantic usage	Recalling and recounting ideas from oral reading
		Recoding phonologically	Reading ongoing text with accuracy and fluency		

Note: Adapted from Rathvon, N. (2004). *Early Reading Assessment: A Practitioner's Handbook.* Description of the DIBELS Measures by Domain, p. 208. New York: The Guilford Press.

substitutions, mispronunciations, and so on, but each task has its own set of complexities. Examiners should engage in several practice sessions before administering DIBELS for classroom use. To ease the burden of scoring and reporting, computer software is available to convert raw scores to percentiles and to provide a summary of the meaningfulness of the scores obtained.

DIBELS can be used for making comparisons using local norms based on at least three administrations per year: fall, winter, and spring. If local norms are used, a categorizing system of at-risk status is suggested. Students who perform below the twentieth percentile are considered to be "at risk"; those who perform between the twentieth and fortieth percentile are considered to be at "some risk." Those scoring above the fortieth percentile are assumed to be at low risk. Based on group performance, some performance indicators have been generated for teachers to use as rough measures of acceptable progress. Benchmark goals and risk indicators for the measures used in grades Kindergarten through six are available on the Web site https:/dibels.uoregon.edu/. It is important to note that these benchmarks are updated periodically.

Usefulness   According to its authors, DIBELS is not intended to be a comprehensive or diagnostic battery, but rather a set of quick, efficient, indicators of literacy development, which are particularly valuable for monitoring progress. The materials were developed with several criteria in mind. Some of the most important include brevity, ease of administration, and sensitivity to growth. Many school systems across the country have adopted DIBELS, in part because the authors were successful in meeting their criteria (for development of the instrument), but also, in part, because the instrument is inexpensive to acquire (downloads are easily accessible online and free of charge). Because alternate forms are available and the system is sensitive to assessing a continuum of reading skills, it has been adapted for use in screening for at-risk status and then used to monitor responsiveness to intervention. DIBELS appears to be well suited for these goals, and the data generated are readily available not only for use by classroom teachers but they may also be assimilated for determining classroom, school, and even system-wide accountability. Finally, the DIBELS authors relate the results to a five-step problem-solving model with direct implications for intervention (Kaminski and Good 1998). DIBELS measures can be administered by licensed/certified teachers or other trained personnel and screening data can be obtained for a classroom within a short time.

Psychometrics Much of the DIBELS technical adequacy data have been generated by the authors and their colleagues (Good and Kaminski 2002) and are available on the DIBELS Web site, though specific reliability and validity information is somewhat cumbersome to find. And, according to Rathvon (2004), these data are somewhat limited (e.g., some studies were conducted with older versions of some tasks, some studies do not show sample sizes, and there is limited evidence for intra-rater reliability). In her review of the reliability evidence, Rathvon noted reliabilities from .72 to .99, and concluded that the reliabilities vary considerably as a function of task and type. Similarly, concurrent validity indexes vary, with values typically ranging from the mid-.30s to mid-.70s when the DIBELS tasks are correlated with similar tasks or subtests, for example with subtests taken from the Stanford Diagnostic Reading Test (Karlsen, Madden, and Gardner 1985), the Woodcock-Johnson Psycho-Educational Battery-Revised (Woodcock and Johnson 1989), and with teacher ratings. Others have found similar correlations; for example, Elliot, Lee, and Tollefson (2001) report correlations ranging from .60 to .70 between the DIBELS and standardized measures of phonological awareness and teacher ratings of achievement.

DIBELS authors report that most measures are sensitive to grade and age changes, as expected, and the more academically sophisticated students become, the higher their scores become. DIBELS is sensitive also to the regression in scores as a function of summer layoffs (e.g., lower scores are obtained from a fall grade 1 administration, relative to the spring of the kindergarten year; similar declines are found for the higher grades). Finally, some of the tasks show floor effects for some students (for example, PSF for fall and winter administrations for kindergarten students and ORF for many first-graders). **Floor effects** occur when a measure does not have sufficient items to tap lower- or beginning-level skills for weak students. According to Rathvon (2004), the instrument simply seems too hard for these students, in part because of insufficient experience with the content at those ages.

Limitations of DIBELS Despite positive features of the DIBELS measures (such as short assessment time and low cost), they are not without critics. It is important to note that although DIBELS has achieved wide use for progress monitoring of reading, some experts including Pressley, Hilden, and Shankland (2006) have questioned the psychometric integrity of DIBELS. In fact, Brunsman and Shanahan, in a 2006 review of the test, indicated that "documentation of reliability of scores and evidence of validity for the described purposes of the DIBELS is woefully inadequate" (Comment Section, ¶ 1). Some experts question its utility for informing instruction (McGill-Franzen, personal communication, June 9, 2006). For example, when teachers administer the Letter Naming Fluency measure to kindergartners, teachers learn how quickly students can name letters but they do not learn what letters students do and do not know. DIBELS has been used as the evaluation tool in many federally-funded Reading First initiatives. However, some of the individuals involved in administering these programs have been accused of pressuring states and systems to use DIBELS (Grunwald 2006; "Two Inquiries" 2005/2006). And, Goodman (2006), along with several colleagues, has written a critical review of DIBELS questioning its reliability and usefulness. A criticism is that because DIBELS scores are based on timed performance, their use may pressure teachers to focus instruction too heavily on reading rate at the expense of other skills, particularly comprehension. Educators are encouraged to observe DIBELS in use before making decisions about adopting it in their own systems.

Interestingly, DIBELS is included in a comprehensive reading program called the Voyager Universal Literacy System (www.voyagerlearning.com/literacy/overview.jsp), but is referred to within the Voyager system as the Vital Indicators of Progress (VIP). According to information in the Assessment and Progress Monitoring section on the Voyager Web site, VIP is equivalent to DIBELS but is designed to assess progress specifically within the Voyager curriculum.

Adequacy of Progress Monitoring Systems

Advocates of the multitiered model of instruction and RTI argue that these approaches will meet the needs of a majority of students (Fletcher, Coulter, Reschly, and Vaughn 2004). Assessment plays an integral role, identifying those students who successfully respond to instruction by comparing student performance to typical performance in specific skill areas. However, not all students respond positively to intervention. Further, there are many technical and practical challenges associated with large-scale implementation of RTI. Some questions that must be addressed if RTI is to be implemented successfully include:

a. Who will administer the assessments?
b. Who will be responsible for scoring, graphing, and managing the data generated from the assessments?
c. Specifically how will the information from the assessments be tied to instruction?
d. How can assessment be scheduled to minimize disruption of student instruction?

A drawback to the use of progress monitoring is the limited amount of information provided. For example, a teacher may learn that a student is below benchmark expectations based on his or her reading fluency rate. However, this information does not tell the teacher exactly where to focus instruction. Consequently, it is likely there will be an ongoing need for criterion-referenced testing as described in the first section of this chapter.

Computer-Based Assessment of Reading

Computers are a part of everyday life. Many children in the United States use computers before entering school (Judge, Puckett, and Bell 2006). Consequently, students (and their teachers) are becoming technologically savvy and increasingly are able to take advantage of the incredible efficiency of computer learning programs, related computer peripherals, and the World Wide Web. Currently, it is possible to obtain a reading assessment using computers. But from a teacher's perspective, how does a computerized assessment help? Is computerized assessment efficient; in other words, does it free the teacher to do other things? Does it provide information unobtainable from other sources? Does it provide the specificity needed to guide instruction? Are the psychometric properties of computerized assessments acceptable? As you might guess, the answers change as a function of the particular question asked, but in general, many questions such as these can be answered with a qualified "yes." Consequently, teachers and administrators are motivated to investigate the possible benefits of computerized assessment. In the following section, we provide answers to some of the important questions teachers ask about computerized assessment of reading and we focus on the results this type of assessment generates, rather than on the use of the computer to track student and classroom progress from pencil-and-paper administration. Examples of computerized tracking systems were discussed in earlier sections of this chapter (e.g., AIMSweb).

Is Computerized Assessment Efficient?   Obviously, no innovation comes without cost. So the answer to this question is not as straightforward as it first appears. Any new technique requires not only money (to acquire it), but also time (to learn to use it effectively). Computerized assessment is no different. In order to use computerized assessment, teachers must learn how to help their students engage the computer programs. The particulars vary by product. Some computerized assessments are completely Web-based and can be accessed without having to purchase additional software, hardware, or printed materials (such as Total Reader, a Web-based benchmarking system using the Lexile framework, by EdGate 2006), which can be found online at: www.totalreader.com/index.php?fuseaction=home.faq.

Total Reader can be accessed from any computer with Internet capability and can be used for students in grades 3 through 12; it provides an individual record for progress monitoring using content-appropriate materials and allows students to access a variety of reading materials independently. Each student's level of reading is determined by an initial diagnostic test, the results of which can be printed in a report format. The report produces a Lexile measure, a score ranging from 200 (beginning reading) to 1,700 for advanced readers. This system can be used to track reading progress for an individual student's entire school career. Reading materials are provided based on that information. These passages are aligned to Lexile scores using two indicators of passage difficulty: semantic difficulty related to frequency of use and syntactic complexity related to sentence length. Using this system, students can read fiction or nonfiction passages taken from appealing real-world sources at the appropriate level. The authors of Total Reading claim that it can be used to help track students' adequate yearly progress (AYP) required by the NCLB legislation because student progress can be compared to the progress of peers within a school or system. Once students have been taught to use the Total Reader system, they can work relatively independently and teachers can use the report generated to gauge progress. Consequently, this system does provide efficient assessment and can save the teacher time once its use is automated within the classroom.

The Total Reader system is only one of several computerized assessment systems that may be used to increase efficiency in reading assessment. One of the most widely used computerized assessment systems—STAR Reading (2006; Renaissance Learning; www.renlearn.com/starreading/software/) also provides an efficient assessment of reading. STAR combines measures of vocabulary and comprehension to yield an index of student reading levels. In the "Vocabulary In-Context" section, students read a short sentence with a missing word and select the missing word from a set of four choices, as in Figure 8.7, which was taken directly from the STAR Reading Web site.

Using a similar assessment strategy for the "Authentic Text" sections, students read a passage with a missing word and select the missing word from a set of four choices, as shown in Figure 8.8, also taken from the STAR Reading Web site.

According to information provided on the Web site, any student with a reading vocabulary of one hundred words or more can take the STAR assessment. Based on the data generated, a report is produced, which includes information about the skill level of the particular student assessed and an assessment of that student's level compared to peers (e.g., percentile ranks and grade equivalents). The scores allow comparisons with classmates and same-grade peers across the country. In addition, the STAR Reading Diagnostic Report also includes narratives describing strengths and weaknesses, as well as recommendations. We reproduce an example of a STAR report in Figure 8.9 (p. 267).

Vocabulary In-context Questions

The student must actually interpret the meaning of (in other words, comprehend) the sentence in order to choose the correct answer because all of the answer choices "fit" the context sentence either semantically or syntactically.

FIGURE 8.7   STAR Reading Vocabulary

Source: STAR Reading (2006). Excerpt from *STAR Reading* "Vocabulary In-context" Assessment. Renaissance Learning. *www.renlearn.com/starreading/software/samplescreens.html*

Authentic Text Questions

To answer the question, the student selects the word from the list of answer choices that best completes the sentence based on the context of the paragraph. The correct answer choice is the word that appropriately fits both the semantics and the syntax of the sentence, and the meaning of the paragraph. All of the incorrect answer choices either fit the syntax of the sentence or relate to the meaning of the paragraph. They do not, however, meet both conditions.

FIGURE 8.8   STAR Authentic Text

Source: STAR Reading (2006). Excerpt from *STAR Reading* "Authentic Text" Assessment. Renaissance Learning. *www.renlearn.com/starreading/software/samplescreens.html*

STAR Reading®
Diagnostic Report
Monday, December 12, 2005 3:27:15 PM
Test Date: December 12, 2005 3:18:30 PM

East Elementary School

Callicutt, Dylan   **Teacher: DeMarco, Corey**
Grade: 3   **Class: Mr. DeMarco Class B**   **ID: dcalli**

This report presents diagnostic information about the student's general reading skills, based on the student's performance on a STAR Reading test.

Time for First Part: 4 minutes 45 seconds   Time for Second Part: 2 minutes 38 seconds

SS	GE	PR	PR Range	Below Average	Above 50	Above Average	NCE	IRL	ZPD
372	3.1	46	34–59		——◆——		47.9	3.2	2.6–3.7

This student's Grade Equivalent (GE) score is 3.1. His or her reading skills are therefore comparable to those of an average third grader after the first month of the school year. Dylan also achieved a national Percentile Rank (PR) of 46. This score is in the average range and means that Dylan scored greater than 46% of students nationally in the same grade. The PR Range indicates that, if this student had taken the STAR Reading test numerous times, most of his or her scores would likely have fallen between 34 and 59. It reflects the amount of statistical variability in a student's PR score.

These scores indicate that Dylan is likely starting to place less emphasis on identifying words and more emphasis on understanding what he or she reads. Students at this level select fewer picture books for their own reading. They start to challenge themselves with longer picture and chapter books. Dylan is also probably aware of his or her abilities and interests in choosing books to read. He or she is increasingly able to select books and take tests independently.

For optimal reading grown, Dylan needs to:

* Practice reading independently every day
* Continue reading aloud and reading with others
* Develop additional strategies for acquiring vocabulary in context

Dylan's Zone of Proximal Development (ZPD) for independent reading is 2.6–3.7. If Accelerated Reader® reading management software is being used in your classroom or school, Dylan should be encouraged to select books with book levels in the ZPD. These books will provide optimal reading challenge without frustration. The ZPD, however, is approximate. Success at any book level also depends on the student's interest and prior knowledge of a book's content.

The following techniques will also help ensure Dylan's continued growth in reading:

* Guide reading practice so that Dylan maintains an average score of 85 percent or higher on Accelerated Reader Reading Practice Quizzes.
* Use the Accelerated Reader Diagnostic Report and Student Record Report for more detailed information about the student's reading practice.
* Teach Dylan how to select books throughout his or her ZPD.
* Help Dylan establish a minimum book level, minimum percent correct, and point goals for each marking period.

FIGURE 8.9   STAR Diagnostic Report

Source: STAR Reading (2006). Sample Report from the *STAR Reading* Assessment. Renaissance Learning. *www.renlearn. com/starreading/software/samplescreens.html*

Renaissance Learning also publishes computerized assessments of early literacy (STAR Early Literacy). The areas of general readiness, graphophonemic knowledge, phonemic awareness, phonics, comprehension, structural analysis, and vocabulary are assessed.

Computerized assessment is also provided by the "Let's Go Learn" and the Diagnostic Online Reading Assessment system, or DORA (2006; www.letsgolearn.com/). As the name of the system implies, it allows online assessment and generates a report. Scores are provided as grade-level equivalents for a number of reading assessments in the following areas: graphophonics; high-frequency words; word recognition (phonetically irregular words); phonics (ability to sound out words); phonemic awareness (ability to manipulate sounds); spelling; and semantics, including oral vocabulary **(receptive vocabulary)** and reading comprehension (comprehension of silently read passages). DORA provides a rather extensive narrative describing these areas, along with recommendations.

As is probably apparent, there are many computerized assessments available, with accompanying and related intervention packages. In addition to those already mentioned, several others are designed for specific populations and are focused on specific skill areas via the Internet, including the Lexia Program, designed specifically for teachers who provide phonics-based literacy instruction to students with dyslexia and other learning difficulties (www.lexianet.org/). Read 180 (http://teacher.scholastic.com/products/read180/overview/) is described as an intensive reading program that helps educators confront the problem of adolescent illiteracy on several fronts. Also, the Northwest Evaluation Association (NWEA) uses several state-aligned computerized adaptive assessments (Measures of Academic Progress, for example) to determine the instructional level of students and measure growth over time (www.nwea.org/assessments/).

Can Computerized Assessment Guide Instruction?

As is apparent by now, computerized assessment systems provide information about the reading skills of students, and in some cases, the information is very specific (e.g., measurement of beginning sounds via assessment of graphophonics from the DORA). So in some cases the information is specific enough to provide teachers with helpful information to guide instruction, much like information that could be obtained from the administration of tests such as those described earlier in this chapter (e.g., BRIGANCE® Inventories). However, in some cases, the information obtained is not linked to any specific reading curriculum and therefore may not be specifically related to classroom goals. In other cases, such as Total Reader, the assessments are an integrated part of a total reading program. Hence, the answer to the question "can computerized assessment guide instruction?" is a qualified "yes."

Does Computerized Assessment Provide Unique Information?

As before, the answer to this question is a qualified "yes." Some of the computerized systems offer somewhat unique results. For example, the STAR Reading Diagnostic Report provides information that is uniquely linked to the Accelerated Reader (Renaissance Learning 2006). In other words, the STAR Report yields a grade-level reading range, which describes the examinee's instructional level. This range of appropriate materials is described in terms of grade-level equivalents and is called the Zone of Proximal Development (ZPD). The ZPD of Dylan Callicult, the example shown in Figure 8.9, is 2.6 to 3.7. The report encourages Dylan's teacher to help him select books with these levels. Of interest, the ZPD is based on Vygotsky's social development theory (1978) that to-be-learned content can be optimally matched to the sophistication level of the student. This idea is akin to a similar principle advanced by other developmental psychologists (such as the "problem of the match" by Hunt 1972) acknowledging the importance of providing instruction consistent with the readiness level of the learner, a rule well known by all successful teachers.

Lexiles

Another increasingly valuable contribution offered by some computer-based/Web-based assessment packages, including for example, the Total Reader system, is the "Lexile Framework." The Lexile Framework is a system that allows scores, called Lexiles, to be generated via the computer allowing teachers and administrators to gauge an examinee's reading ability and success across the examinee's school career. These scores range from 200 to 1,700, typically. Although they can be used to characterize a student's reading ability, the scores are not like traditional reading level scores; that is, they do not refer to grade-level performance nor can they be compared meaningfully to a psychometric scale with the population mean set to a familiar value, such as 100.

If Lexiles reference an unfamiliar scale, how can they be used? Consider, for example, a second-grader who may earn a score of 325; this score can be compared to a score earned by the same student as a ninth grader, say 990. These scores, at both grades, can be compared to Lexile means generated by the system to determine how the examinee compares to others in the school system. In addition, teachers eventually develop knowledge of how these scores are arrayed in their school across grade levels. Consequently, suppose one of Dr. Charles' high school students, Emilio, earns a Lexile score of 490. Dr. Charles, who is familiar with the range of Lexile scores, realizes that such a score is typical of middle fourth-graders. This information lets him know that Emilio likely will have trouble reading the high school biology text independently.

Perhaps the most useful feature of the Lexile Framework is that the scores provide a built-in strategy for helping teachers match students to books along the same continuum of Lexile scores. As mentioned earlier, Lexiles are assigned to the performance of a particular reader based on reading ability; Lexiles are also assigned to a text, based on the difficulty of the text. In this manner, a common language is created for students, teachers, and parents to use, not only to characterize or order the student's reading ability but also to match that ability to the difficulty of books. The difference between a reader's Lexile and a particular text's Lexile can be used to predict the reader's level of comprehension with that text. Many standardized tests yield Lexile scores—and not only those administered via computer. Further, many basal readers and trade books have been assigned Lexiles.

In order to use the Lexile Framework, a tool called the Lexile Calculator has been created. The Calculator predicts a reader's level of comprehension on a particular text and is used as follows: If a reader with a Lexile of 1,000 is given a text with a Lexile of 1,000, the reader is predicted to read that text with 75 percent comprehension. In this case, the difference between the ability of the reader and the text difficulty is "0." This relationship (and the 75-percent difficulty level set to a difference score) was chosen purposely because it is presumed to be somewhat optimal for instruction. A comprehension rate of 75 percent assures that the reader can follow the theme of the text, but still requires that the student work to acquire meaning (from the text). When the Lexile difference between the text calibration and the ability of the reader is −250, the text is more difficult than the reader is capable of reading, and the rate of predicted comprehension falls to 50 percent. On the other hand, if the Lexile rate is 250, the reader is more capable than the text is difficult, and the rate of anticipated comprehension increases to 90 percent. If a teacher wishes to use reading materials that a particular reader can comprehend at the 85 percent level, the teacher would select the material based on a Lexile difference of 150 points; that is, the material would show a Lexile score of below the Lexile established by the reader. The general relationship between predicted comprehension rate relative to the reader-text difference (in Lexiles) is expressed in Figure 8.10.

How are Lexiles Determined for Text Material?   Obviously, Lexiles are based on difficulty level, and as you know by now, difficulty level of a passage may be established

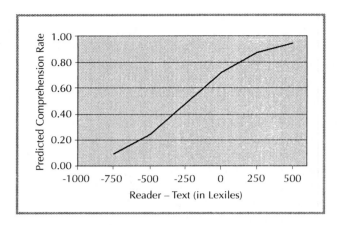

FIGURE 8.10   Predicted Comprehension Rate
Based on Reader Minus Text Lexiles

by determining the semantic sophistication (difficulty and frequency of the vocabulary words) and the syntactic complexity (average sentence length). Lexiles reflect these influences and can be created by a specific computer program called a Lexile Analyzer. Once any text is typed or scanned into the Analyzer (minus headings, titles, etc.), Lexiles can be generated. Teachers can access this program by simply logging on to www.lexile.com/EntrancePageHtml.aspx?1, registering at the site, and (without charge) determining within seconds the Lexile level of a text. Lexile levels of many textbooks are already available on this site, and others can be added quickly. Researchers have investigated the relationships between standardized test scores and Lexiles and between basal readers and Lexiles (Stenner 1996). The relationships reported in these studies provide support for the use of Lexiles.

In summary, most of the computerized assessment systems have somewhat unique features, but many of those features are not truly new for the most part and may not be unique just to computerized administered tests; hence, the appropriateness of the qualified "yes" in response to the question, "Does computerized assessment provide unique information?"

Are the Psychometric Properties of Computerized Tests Acceptable?   Again, the answer is a qualified "yes." Just as do authors of pencil and paper tests, some authors of computerized tests take seriously the need to provide psychometric data to users. And some do not. So it is not always easy for educators to find data supporting the use of a particular computerized assessment system. In other cases, the data are more accessible. For example, for the STAR Reading system reliability and validity data are available from Renaissance Learning. Reliability data include split-half and test-retest correlations that are generally acceptable, ranging from .70s to .90s. Concurrent validity data obtained from correlations of STAR Reading components with other tests are generally acceptable (e.g., ranging from .40s to .80s). Similarly, data from the STAR Early Literacy measures are available from the authors from a sample of approximately 11,000 children in grades K–3 from 84 school districts in the United States and Canada. Measures of split-half and test-retest range from .68 to .90. Standard errors of measurement are also reported and are generally acceptable. We are not aware of any independent studies showing psychometric properties of the STAR, and such studies are needed, not only for the STAR Reading system but for all the computerized systems. As with every other test, the user must take responsibility for determining whether or not the instrument is supported by reliability and validity data. (AERA 1999). Obviously, this process is facilitated by authors and publishers who make psychometric data readily available, as well as by independent researchers and other users who generate psychometric data.

The psychometric adequacy of the Lexile system was evaluated by a committee commissioned by the National Center for Educational Statistics (2001). In general, the committee indicated the system has technical adequacy for determining an individual's reading capacity, though the report focused primarily on issues related to assigning Lexiles to reading material of different types and levels. Interested readers can find detailed information about technical aspects of Lexiles at www.lexile.com.

Reliability and validity information for DORA is available online at www.letsgolearn.com/. Though moderate-to-strong correlations are reported between subsections of DORA and several well-known measures of reading, the sample size is small (e.g., twenty students) and the data used in some of the calculations appear to be taken from various versions of the DORA. So it is unclear how this reliability and validity information relates to versions currently in use.

Special Considerations for Adult and English Language Learners

We conclude the discussion of progress monitoring and hybrid assessments with particular suggestions for adult learners and for ELL students. These are presented in Boxes 8.1 and 8.2, respectively.

Box 8.1

Progress Monitoring Assessment Tips for Adult Learners

1. Assess adult learners' educational histories, background experiences, and interests as well as specific reading skills.
2. Because criterion-referenced and progress monitoring measures focus on mastery of specific skills and generally are not normed, some criterion-referenced measures, such as the BRIGANCE® Inventories, may be appropriate for adults.
3. Consider using instruments that assess functional and workplace literacy skills, such as the BRIGANCE® Diagnostic Life Skills Inventory and BRIGANCE® Diagnostic Employability Skills Inventory.
4. When using materials designed for younger students with adult learners, ensure that the reading material is age-appropriate.
5. Use of computerized assessments may be appropriate for adults, assuming the reading material is age-appropriate.
6. Because most adult learners have limited time to spend on academic tasks, monitor progress frequently to ensure instructional strategies are effective.

Box 8.2

Progress Monitoring Assessment Tips for English Language Learners

1. Because of the nature of progress monitoring assessments, such assessments may be more appropriate for ELL students than formal, standardized tests.
2. Frequent progress monitoring is especially important for ELL learners.
3. Be sure to establish rapport and put ELL learners at ease before beginning assessment.
4. At times, it may be helpful to assess ELL students' native language proficiency.
5. Consider using native language assessments, such as the BRIGANCE® Diagnostic Comprehensive Inventory of Basic Skills–Revised Spanish Edition and/or the Spanish language measures from AIMSweb or DIBELS, for students whose first language is Spanish.

Summary

In this chapter, we described tests that incorporate some aspects of informal and formal assessment, tests that typically are given within the context of either a general or special education classroom, and that are used primarily to monitor progress. First, we discussed commercially available criterion-referenced measures not tied to a specific curriculum, in particular the BRIGANCE® Inventories, which are used extensively in special education to determine progress and to set instructional goals. Next, we described hybrid assessments that have roots in teacher-generated curriculum-based methods. However, these hybrids are not actually rooted in a particular curriculum; rather, they measure discrete skills (including oral reading fluency of letters, words, and passages) and provide scores that can be compared to benchmarks to determine whether students are making adequate progress. Two of the most widely used hybrids (AIMSweb and DIBELS) include computer management systems that allow students' progress to be graphed and compared to the performance of other students and to the individual student's own progress over time. Despite increasingly widespread use, both tests have been criticized for limited evidence of reliability and for lack of usefulness for planning instruction. Finally, we addressed computerized assessment, some of which use sophisticated, but user-friendly, Lexile systems to track student progress over time and to link students to appropriate level texts. Unlike the BRIGANCE® Inventories, DIBELS, and AIMSweb, these assessments are administered and managed via computer. We expect computerized assessment to become increasingly available and integrated into traditional instruction.

A summary of characteristics of some of the most commonly used progress monitoring and criterion-referenced assessments and the specific areas of reading assessed by each are presented in Table 8.4 on page 273. Information on technical qualities (such as reliability and validity) and types of scores are presented in Table 8.5 on page 274.

TABLE 8.4 Informal Reading Assessment 1: Characteristics of Informal Assessment and Progress Monitoring Measures

Name of Technique or Measure	Publisher/Source/Date	Grades/Ages	Administration Time	Administration Format	Basic Reading Skills — Sight Recognition	Basic Reading Skills — Phonics/PA	Basic Reading Skills — Fluency	Reading Comprehension — Vocabulary	Reading Comprehension — Comprehension
Criterion-Referenced Assessments (non–curriculum-based)									
BRIGANCE® Diagnostic Inventory of Early Development, 2nd ed.	Curriculum Associates, 2004	Age Birth–6	Varies depending on measures given	Individual	X	X			
BRIGANCE® Diagnostic Comprehensive Inventory of Basic Skills–Revised	Curriculum Associates, 1999	PreK–9	Varies depending on measures given	Individual (includes some group screening tests)	X	X		X	X
Hybrids									
AIMSweb	Edformation, 2006	K–8	Series of 1 minute assessments	Individual	X	X	X		X
Dynamic Indicators of Basic Early Literacy Skills, 6th ed. (DIBELS–6)	University of Oregon, 2005	PreK–6	Series of 1 minute assessments	Individual	X	X	X	X	X
Computerized Assessments									
Diagnostic Online Reading Assessment (DORA)	Let's Go Learn	PreK–12	Varies depending on measures given	Individual	X	X		X	X
STAR Early Learning	Renaissance Learning	PreK–3 and above	Varies depending on measures given	Individual	X	X		X	X
STAR Reading	Renaissance Learning	1–12	10 minutes	Individual	X			X	X
Total Reader	EdGate	3–12	Varies	Individual				X	X

Note: PA = Phonemic Awareness.

Information is based on a combination of published and online materials (including independent test reviews, content from tests and test manuals, and publisher/author promotional materials). Strenuous efforts were made by authors to ensure accuracy but information may contain errors and omissions due to updates in the tests reviewed, errors in published materials, and conflicts in reported information. Lists are not exhaustive.

TABLE 8.5 Informal Reading Assessment 2: Psychometric Properties of Informal Assessment and Progress Monitoring Measures

Name of Measure or Technique	Reliability Reported				Validity Reported			Type of Scores
	IC	TT	AF	IR	CON	PRE	CNC	
Criterion-Referenced Assessments (non-curriculum-based)								
BRIGANCE® Diagnostic Inventory of Early Development, 2nd ed.	X	X	X		X		X	Criterion-referenced; grade equivalents
BRIGANCE® Diagnostic Comprehensive Inventory of Basic Skills–Revised	X	X	X	X	X	X	X	Criterion-referenced; grade equivalents
Hybrids								
AIMSweb	X	X	X	X	X		X	Reading rate
Dynamic Indicators of Basic Early Literacy Skills, 6th ed. (DIBELS–6)	X	X	X		X	X	X	Reading rate
Computerized Assessments								
Diagnostic Online Reading Assessment (DORA)		X			X	X	X	Grade equivalents
STAR Early Learning	X	X					X	Grade equivalents; percentiles
STAR Reading	X	X					X	Grade equivalents; percentiles
Total Reader					X		X	Lexiles

Note: IC = Internal consistency; TT = Test/retest; AF = Alternate forms; IR = Inter-rater; CON = Content; PRE = Predictive; CNC = Concurrent.

Information is based on a combination of published and online materials (including independent test reviews, content from tests and test manuals, and publisher/author promotional materials). Strenuous efforts were made by authors to ensure accuracy but information may contain errors and omissions due to updates in the tests reviewed, errors in published materials, and conflicts in reported information. Lists are not exhaustive.

REFERENCES

AIMSweb. (2007). San Antonio, TX: Harcourt Assessment. Retrieved June 4, 2007, from www.aimsweb.com

American Educational Research Association, American Psychological Association, and National Council on Measurement in Education. (1999). *Standards for educational and psychological testing.* Washington, DC: American Educational Research Association.

Brigance, A. H. (1994). *BRIGANCE® life skills inventory.* N. Billerica, MA: CURRICULUM ASSOCIATES®.

Brigance, A. H. (1999). *BRIGANCE® comprehensive inventory of basic skills—revised.* N. Billerica, MA: CURRICULUM ASSOCIATES®.

Brigance, A. H. (2004). *BRIGANCE® inventory of early development* (2nd ed.). N. Billerica, MA: CURRICULUM ASSOCIATES®.

Brigance, A. H. (2005). *BRIGANCE® K and I screen.* N. Billerica, MA: CURRICULUM ASSOCIATES®.

Brigance, A. H. (2005). *BRIGANCE® preschool screen.* N. Billerica, MA: CURRICULUM ASSOCIATES®.

Brunsman, B., & Shanahan, T. A. (n.d.) Review of the dynamic indicators of basic early literacy skills. In *Buros Mental Measurements Yearbook,* 16. Retrieved June 5, 2007, from http://web5.silver platter.com.proxy.lib.utk.edu:90/webspirs/start.ws? customer5c14360anddatabases5S(YB)

Cizek, G. J. (n.d.). Review of the BRIGANCE® diagnostic inventory of basic skills. In Buros Mental Measurements Yearbook, 14. Retrieved June 5, 2007, from http://web5.silverplatter.com.proxy.lib.utk.edu: 90/webspirs/start.ws?customer5c14360anddatabases 5S(YB)

Diagnostic Online Reading Assessment System (DORA) by Let's Go Learn. (2007). Retrieved June 4, 2007, from www.letsgolearn.com/

Edformation. Retrieved June 4, 2007, from www.aimsweb.com/index.php

Elliott, J., Lee, S. W., & Tollesfson, N. (2001). A reliability and validity study of the dynamic indicators of basic early literacy skills—modified. *School Psychology Review, 30,* 33–49.

Fletcher, J. M., Coulter, W. A., Reschly, D. J., & Vaughn, S. (2004). Alternative approaches to the definition and identification of learning disabilities: Some questions and answers. *Annals of Dyslexia, 54*(2), 304–331.

Fuchs, L. S., & Deno, S. L. (1994). Must instructionally useful performance assessment be based in the curriculum? *Exceptional Children, 61*(1), 15–24.

Fuchs, L. S., & Fuchs, D. (2005). Response to intervention as a method of LD identification: four case studies. Retrieved June 5, 2007, from http://tennessee.gov/ education/speced/doc/seoperrtifuchcase.pdf

Good, R. H., & Kaminski, R. A. (2002). *DIBELS* Oral reading fluency passages for first through third grades.

(Technical report no.10). Eugene, OR: University of Oregon. https://dibels.uoregon.edu/

Goodman, K. S. (2006). *The truth about DIBELS: What it is, what it does.* Portsmouth, NH: Heinemann.

Grunwald, M. (October 1, 2006). Special report: *Reading First* under fire. *The Education Issue: Washington Post,* B01.

Harcourt (2002). *Stanford achievement tests* (10th ed.). San Antonio, TX: Author.

Hasbrouck, J. E., & Tindal, G. (1992). Curriculum-based oral reading fluency norms for students in grades 2 through 5. *Teaching Exceptional Children, 24*(3), 41–44.

Hunt, J. McV. (1972). The role of experience in the development of competence. In J. McV. Hunt (Ed.), *Human intelligence.* Brunswick, NJ: Transaction Books.

Individuals with Disabilities Education Act Amendments (IDEA) of 2004, 20 U.S.C. (2004).

Judge, S., Puckett, K., & Bell, S. M. (2006, September/ October). Closing the digital divide: An update from the Early Childhood Longitudinal Study. *Journal of Educational Research, 100*(1), 52–60.

Kaminiski, R. A., & Good, R. H. (1998). Assessing early literacy skills in a problem-solving model: Dynamic indicators of basic early literacy skills. In M. R. Shinn (Ed.), *Advanced applications of curriculum-based measurement* (pp. 113–142). New York: Guilford Press.

Karlsen, B., Madden, R., & Gardner, E. (1985). *Stanford diagnostic reading test* (3rd ed.). San Antonio, TX: The Psychological Corporation.

MacGinitie, W. H., MacGinitie, R. K., Maria, K., & Dreyer, L. (2000). *Gates-MacGinitie reading tests* (4th ed.). Itasca: IL: Riverside Publishing Company.

Markwardt, F. C. (1989). *Peabody individual achievement test–revised.* Circle Pines, MN: American Guidance Services.

McGill-Franzen, A. (2006). Kindergarten literacy: Matching assessment and instruction in kindergarten. New York: Scholastic.

National Center for Education Statistics (2006). *National assessment of adult literacy.* Retrieved June 4, 2007, from http://nces.ed.gov/nationsreportcard/itmrls/

National Center for Education Statistics (2006). *The nation's report card: Reading.* Retrieved June 4, 2007, from http://nces.ed.gov/nationsreportcard/ reading/

National Institute of Child Health and Human Development. (2000). *Report of the national reading panel: Teaching children to read* (NIH Publication No. 00–4769). Washington, DC: U.S. Government Printing Office.

No Child Left Behind Act of 2001, PL 107–110, 115 Stat. 1425 (2002).

Overton, T. (2006). *Assessing learners with special needs: An applied approach* (5th ed.). Upper Saddle River, NJ: Pearson Prentice Hall.

Payne, D. A. (2003). *Applied educational assessment* (2nd ed.). Belmont, CA: Wadsworth/Thomson Learning.

Poncy, B. C., Skinner, C. H., & Axtell, P. K. (2005). An investigation of the reliability and standard error of measurement of words read correctly per minute using curriculum-based measurement. *Journal of Psychoeducational Assessment, 23,* 326–338.

Pressley, M., Hilden, K. R., & Shankland, R. K. (n.d.). An evaluation of end-grade–3 dynamic indicators of basic early literacy skills (DIBELS): Speed reading without comprehension, predicting little. East Lansing, MI: Michigan State University, College of Education, Literacy Achievement Research Center (LARC). www.msularc.org/dibels%20submitted.pdf

Rathvon, N. (2004). Early reading assessment: A practitioner's handbook. New York: Guilford Press.

Salvia, J., & Yesseldyke, J. E. (1998). *Assessment* (7th ed.). Boston: Houghton Mifflin.

STAR Reading (2006). Renaissance Learning. Retrieved June 4, 2007, from www.renlearn.com/starreading/software/

Stenner, A. J. (1996). *Measuring reading comprehension with the Lexile framework.* Durham, NC: Metametrics.

Total Reader by Edgate. (2006). Retrieved June 4, 2007, from www.totalreader.com/index.php?fuseaction5 home.faq

Two inquiries underway on Reading First questions. (December 2005/January 2006). *Reading Today, 23*(3), 3.

Voyager Universal Literacy System®. (n.d.) Retrieved June 4, 2007, from www.voyager learning.com/literacy/overview.jsp

Wilkinson, G. S. (2006). *Wide range achievement test* (4th ed.). Lutz, FL: Psychological Assessment Resources.

Woodcock, R. W. (1987/1998). *Woodcock reading mastery test–revised/normative update.* Circle Pines, MN: American Guidance Service.

Woodcock, R. W., & Johnson, M. B. (1989). *Woodcock-Johnson III pscyhoeducational battery–revised.* Allen, TX: DLM Teaching Resources.

Ziegler, M., Bell, S. M., & McCallum, R. S. (in press). *Assessment of reading instructional knowledge–adult.* Washington, DC: National Institute for Literacy.

9 Vocabulary Instruction

Objectives

After reading this chapter, you will be able to:

1. State guidelines for deciding which vocabulary words to teach and how to assess them.

2. Implement strategies for teaching new vocabulary directly and indirectly.

3. Implement strategies to teach students to answer vocabulary questions on high-stakes tests.

4. Describe ways to provide extra vocabulary practice for students in a multi-tier or RTI program.

5. Describe strategies for teaching vocabulary to older students and English language learners.

When Ms. Reed's students read the story *Coyote Places the Stars* (Taylor, 1993), she knew that many of them didn't know the meaning of *bounded* in the following sentence:

Bears *bounded* out of their dens.

Ms. Reed told her students, *"Bound**ed** means jumped lightly along. When the bears bound**ed** out of their dens, they jump**ed** lightly along out of the dens."* She emphasized the past tense ending to the verb as she described the action. She further explained that the bears were bounding along because they were curious to see what the Coyote had done with the stars. Ms. Reed pointed to the word *bounded* that she had printed earlier on the whiteboard, asked the students to read it, and then had Delarnes, one of her students who received extra Tier 2 support, print the word on a sticky note and put it on the word wall. Before the students lined up for lunch she had Delarnes and one or two other students "walk the wall," asking them to read all the new vocabulary words for the week, including *bounded,* and explain their meanings. Ms. Reed's students in Tier 3 also participated, but they were only required to tell the meanings of the words. When her students came in from recess, Ms. Reed pointed out how she saw Josie and Raymond *bounding* over to the door from the swings. Sam, with a proud, expectant look on his face, raised his hand and asked whether *bounding* was like bouncing. Ms. Reed complimented him on recognizing such a good synonym. Later that afternoon during writing, she noticed that one of the students had used the word *bounded* in his story. Ms. Reed praised him and taped his paper to the "Good Work" board.

In a younger classroom down the hall, Ms. Falth's Tier 3 students were reading *Lad and the Fat Cat,* one of the beginning decodable *Bob* books (Maslen & Maslen, 2006). One of the pages shows a cat sitting in a box with the words *The cat is Kit. Kit sat in a box.* After students read this page, Ms. Falth engaged them in a discussion about the word *independent.* She explained that cats are very *independent* and asked the students to say the new vocabulary word. Ms. Falth then explained that the word *independent* means doing things on your own. She described ways that her cat at home showed his independence. She then asked her students to give examples from their own lives about independent cats they had known. Ms. Falth then showed students the picture of the cat in the box and asked how they thought the cat felt about being in the box, given its independent nature. She concluded the discussion by asking students about things they liked to do independently, on their own. When students answered in partial sentences, she modeled a full sentence before asking them to repeat it so that they had the opportunity to use the word *independent* as part of the answer.

How are Ms. Reed and Ms. Falth similar in their approach to teaching vocabulary?

What teaching behaviors are likely to expand the vocabularies of students who are at risk?

Y̶ou learned how to teach students to read accurately and fluently. While accurate, fluent reading is necessary for reading with understanding, it is not sufficient. Students also need to know the meanings of the words they are reading. As students move into reading third- and fourth-grade-level text, a larger percentage of your instruction will shift toward teaching students to comprehend increasingly difficult text. Their success in understanding text hinges on knowing the meanings of the words they now can decode. In Chapter 9 you will learn about the key role that vocabulary instruction plays in reading.

Both decoding and comprehension are easier when students have an extensive vocabulary. If students already know the meaning of a word, they can blend words more readily after reading the individual parts, particularly for multisyllable words. For example, Alex was trying to read the word *hilarious.* He was able to read the regular parts /hil/ and /ous/. He then began to try different sounds for the irregular vowels in the middle of the word. After trying several sounds, he was able to make the connection between his oral knowledge of the word *hilarious* and the written word *hilarious* because the word was part of his oral vocabulary. Of course Alex's previous knowledge of the word *hilarious* could have also helped him decode the word using context clues. Decoding, vocabulary knowledge, and context clues enable the reader to read the new word quickly and accurately at this level of reading.

This relationship between decoding and vocabulary knowledge is reciprocal. Ehri (2000) explains that seeing a new vocabulary word activates the connections between its written letters and their sounds. As a result of making this automatic graphophonemic connection, a student is more likely to remember the word and its meaning than if he had not seen the word's spelling. The implication is that vocabulary instruction is more effective when the written word is included because of the association between the letters and sounds representing the word and their connection to memory (Ehri, 2005). Increasing the likelihood that a student will retain a new vocabulary word in long-term memory is not the only contribution that graphophonemic connections contribute to learning vocabulary. Joshi, Treiman, Carreker, & Moats (2008–2009) explain:

> Good spellers not only demonstrate a good sense of the sounds in words, they also have a good sense of the meaningful parts of words (e.g., *un-, desir[e], -able*), the roles words play in sentences (e.g., *packed* is a past-tense verb, but *pact* is a noun), and the relationships among words' meanings that exist in spite of differences in their sounds (e.g., *image* and *imagination*).

What Is Vocabulary Instruction and Why Do I Need to Teach It?

Knowledge of vocabulary is also related to reading comprehension. As students learn to decode text of increasing difficulty, they are more likely to encounter words that are not part of their oral language, especially when reading expository text. As a result, students often need instruction in key vocabulary to make sense of what they are reading. Often a significant gap in vocabulary knowledge separates students who are at risk from their classmates. A large percentage of students who are at risk start school with considerably smaller vocabularies. Some of these differences are attributed to poverty. Before entering school, young students whose parents have jobs categorized as "professional" can be exposed to twice as many words as students whose parents are on welfare, and 50% more words than students whose parents are considered "blue collar" (Hart & Risley, 1995). Children from poverty are more likely to have less time and fewer opportunities for speaking, listening to conversation, and listening to stories read aloud. Students who come from households where English is not the first language may be just beginning to develop skills in learning and understanding English. For other students, speech and communication problems may increase the difficulty in learning more abstract words. Louisa Moats describes this gap in vocabulary knowledge as "word poverty," estimating that students who enter Grade 1 with linguistic advantages know approximately 20,000 words, while those who are linguistically disadvantaged know only about 5,000 words (Moats, 2001).

During the school day, students learn vocabulary in two ways: directly and indirectly. Because the majority of words are acquired indirectly through independent reading, when students lack the reading accuracy and fluency necessary to engage in high levels of independent reading, this source of vocabulary enrichment is closed off. Stanovich (1986) describes the rapidly widening gap between students who read independently and those who don't as the **Matthew Effect,** loosely translated as "the rich get richer and the poor get poorer." Students who read more learn more vocabulary words and acquire more background knowledge. In contrast, students who have reading problems often find reading so frustrating that they develop attitudinal problems and rarely or never choose to read independently. One research study showed that students who read independently for just 10 minutes per day experience higher rates of vocabulary growth than students who do little independent reading (Jitendra, Edwards, Sacks, & Jacobson, 2004). In addition to independent reading, listening to books and participating in daily conversation are two main sources for indirect vocabulary acquisition during the school day.

Students who are at risk are also unlikely to use context clues strategically to learn the meaning of vocabulary words on their own (Pany, Jenkins, & Schreck, 1982). In order to use context clues to figure out unknown words when reading or listening, students must understand the meaning of at least 95% of the words in the communication (Hirsch, 2003). When students with limited vocabularies do not understand basic story words such as *pal, branches, barn,* or *choose,* they are unlikely to figure out the meanings of more challenging words introduced in a new story or an explanation of a story related by the teacher. Factors that influence whether a student will learn a word from context include the following:

* The difficulty of the text and decoding skills of the reader
* Comprehension skills of the reader
* The number of times the word is encountered in the text
* The conceptual difficulty of a word
* Whether the word is important for comprehending the text

* Age of the student, with younger students having less than a 10% chance of learning the meaning of a word from context
* Prior knowledge the student has about the topic or theme of the text
* Whether the reader is an English language learner (Scott, 2005; Sousa, 2005)

While this lack of vocabulary knowledge accounts for many of the increased challenges behind teaching students who are at risk, it does not present an insurmountable obstacle. Vocabulary, like fluency, is too often ignored as part of ongoing reading instruction. If taught, vocabulary instruction often consists of "much mentioning and assigning and little actual teaching" (Beck & McKeown, 2007; p. 252) even though directly teaching new words is highly effective. Research shows that students who are at risk learn new words at the same rate as other students if they are directly taught vocabulary in school (Silverman, 2007). The challenge lies in catching them up to their peers by increasing that rate of learning. Only a teacher-directed curriculum emphasizing vocabulary has a chance of bridging the gap (Beck & McKeown, 2007; Biemiller, 2001). Students need to be taught the meanings of some words directly, and they must be taught how to figure out words on their own using the context, morphemic analysis, and the dictionary. Equally important, students must be inspired to appreciate words through word consciousness strategies such as those used by Ms. Reed and Ms. Falth in the opening vignette. Furthermore, the language interaction surrounding effective vocabulary instruction serves as a form of virtual experience, adding to student background knowledge, a critical contribution to reading comprehension (Marzano, 2004). In this chapter, strategies for assessing vocabulary knowledge and selecting and teaching essential vocabulary words are described in hopes of not just increasing the vocabulary knowledge of students, but raising their consciousness of words as well. Both strategies are necessary if we are to attain the ultimate goal of helping students read for meaning.

> Learn more about the research support behind effective vocabulary instruction at this website: **http://idea.uoregon.edu/~ncite/documents/techrep/tech13.html.**

What Vocabulary Words Do I Choose for Instruction?

Teaching vocabulary explicitly and systematically takes time and effort, both in planning and in teaching. Because of the time and effort involved in teaching vocabulary, the number of words that can be taught directly is limited. It is estimated that teachers can realistically teach 300 words per year, which translates to about 8 to 10 per week (Armbruster, Lehr, & Osborn, 2001). This limitation makes the selection of which words to teach an important responsibility of the teacher.

Armbruster and colleagues suggest that you should teach your students three kinds of words: important words, useful words, and difficult words. Important words are words that students need to know to understand the particular text they are reading. Useful words are high-frequency words that the students are likely to see repeatedly in their reading. Difficult words are words that are hard for students to understand such as words that have multiple meanings; these are words that are either spelled the same but pronounced differently, such as *invalid* (not true) and *invalid* (weak or ill), or that are spelled and pronounced the same but have different meanings, such as *fix*, as in *fix* a car, *fix* a sporting event, *fix* a cat, and so on.

Consider Mr. Halpern, who was selecting words to prepare his students to read the story "The Golden Goose" (Adams & Bereiter, 1995). The following words were underlined by the publisher as being possible vocabulary words: *Simpleton, cider, jug, feasted, inn, innkeeper, sexton, hayfields, pastor, cellar, disappeared,* and *court.* Mr. Halpern decided to spend two days preparing his students to read the story. He knew that realistically he could present no more than two words per day, so he had to decide which four words he would teach his Grade 2 students directly. He eliminated *cider* and *jug* because he felt that these were common words that his students would already know. He decided not to teach *inn* and *innkeeper* because he felt these words could be easily figured out from their context. Mr. Halpern made a mental note to make sure to include these terms in his questions after the story reading. He eliminated *pastor* and *sexton* because these words were not common and were not important for the meaning of the story. He wasn't sure whether his students, who were from the city, would know *hayfields,* but he decided not to teach it anyway because it was not important for the meaning of the story. Mr. Halpern settled on *Simpleton,* because *Simpleton* was the main character and the personal qualities that led him to be called *Simpleton* were important for the meaning of the story. Mr. Halpern also decided to teach *disappeared* and *feasted* because these were high-frequency words. *Court* was the fourth word he opted to teach because it was high frequency and, with its multiple meanings, would be difficult.

After words are selected, the question arises as to when to teach them: before, during, or after the text is read. We suggest that words essential to the meaning of the text be taught directly prior to reading but that no more than two be presented at a time. Mr. Halpern, in the example above, decided to directly teach the word *Simpleton* because of its importance to the meaning of the story. Terms in expository text that comprise needed background knowledge for comprehending the content would also qualify for teaching before reading the text.

Beck, McKeown, and Kucan (2008) point out that vocabulary should also be taught during reading. When teaching vocabulary during reading, the goal is to clarify the meaning of the word without taking students' attention away from the text. They suggest using a strategy called "Explain quickly and go on reading." For example, they clarify the word *prescription* as follows: "The doctor tore off the prescription—a prescription is a small piece of paper that a doctor writes his directions on" (Beck et al., 2008; p. 20). Vocabulary embedded in expository text may require more expansive explanations, but diverting students' attention from the story line is not an issue. Vocabulary can also be taught after reading the text, when time is less of an issue. Beck and colleagues encourage saving this time for words that are of high utility, yet robust, or full of meaning. Students who are at risk are not normally exposed to these words that are needed to provide the foundation of knowledge required for reading comprehension. Mr. Halpern selected *feasted* and *disappeared* for instruction after his students had read the story.

In the process of selecting vocabulary, recognize that a student's reading vocabulary, speaking vocabulary, and listening vocabulary are not the same and that principles that apply to one do not necessarily apply to the other. In this book, our main focus is reading vocabulary, although effective teaching of vocabulary also involves speaking vocabulary, listening vocabulary, and writing vocabulary. A teacher reading a book about volcanoes to students is enriching their listening vocabularies when emphasizing *lava* and *cinders.* Later, when students use those terms to describe the papier-mâché volcanoes they have made, they are engaging their speaking vocabularies. When those same students read a story about a child whose eyes are tearing from a *cinder* as she runs down the mountain attempting to escape the *lava* flow, the words are becoming part of their reading vocabulary. If the teacher makes *lava* one of the week's spelling words and assigns students to write a paragraph about how they would escape a lava flow in their town, that word is used in their writing vocabulary. Because research indicates that for increased comprehension students need at least 12 encounters with a new word, teachers cannot afford to miss opportunities to teach vocabulary in a variety of contexts throughout the school day (McKeown, Beck, Omanson, & Pople, 1985).

How Do I Assess My Students' Vocabulary Knowledge?

Vocabulary assessment presents more challenges than other assessments previously discussed in this book. The assumption behind vocabulary testing is that the more words on a test that students identify, the larger their vocabulary. Because only a small sample of words represent the thousands of possible vocabulary words for an assessment, the words selected have to represent a wide body of knowledge. The first question teachers should ask when assessing vocabulary is whether the test provides information on the intended vocabulary they want to test. The answer to that question depends largely on the nature and purpose of the test being considered.

Standardized norm-referenced tests of vocabulary assess general vocabulary knowledge and allow us to determine how a student's vocabulary knowledge compares to that of her peers. Using norm-referenced vocabulary assessments as screening instruments helps answer the question of whether a student's vocabulary problems are small or are large enough to warrant additional intervention (Klingner, Vaughn, & Boardman, 2007). In addition to screening, standardized measures help diagnose the specific nature of vocabulary problems such as whether the student has more difficulty with expressive or receptive language. Standardized vocabulary tests also can serve as year-end outcome measures to determine whether students have achieved grade-level performance as part of school- or district-wide accountability efforts. Because there is so much variation among vocabulary tests, when selecting one you must first examine the types of assessment tasks on the test and whether they match what you need to assess. For example, a vocabulary assessment in which students name pictures or provide oral definitions for words is assessing their speaking vocabulary, whereas a multiple-choice assessment in which students circle the correct definition of words is assessing their reading vocabulary. Teachers should always determine whether the test is assessing a skill other than vocabulary. For example, on a multiple-choice assessment, students who know the meaning of the words but cannot decode many of them are penalized for reading mistakes. Their low score may reflect a decoding deficit rather than limited vocabulary.

Teachers also need to consider whether the vocabulary assessment is testing expressive or receptive vocabulary. For example, a test requiring students to actively write or say the word or definition is measuring expressive vocabulary. Because students' receptive vocabulary is usually higher than their expressive vocabulary, they will often get higher scores on assessments in which they have to only select an answer from ones that are provided. A final concern related to standardized vocabulary assessments is the time that it can take to administer them in contrast to the other brief assessments discussed thus far in this book. Some of the tests have to be given individually and can take from 10 to 30 minutes or longer. If the teacher has no support to help assess students, classroom instructional time can be compromised.

While standardized tests are useful for screening, diagnostic, and accountability purposes, they may not capture knowledge of words taught in your classroom. As Beck et al. (2008) point out, the fact that students don't improve on standardized vocabulary tests doesn't necessarily mean they haven't learned the vocabulary words you taught them. Because general vocabulary tests usually do not include the specific words you have taught, curriculum-based assessments are more appropriate for measuring student progress because the words you assess are those you have instructed.

For young children, vocabulary knowledge can be assessed expressively by simply asking them to tell you the definition of a word (e.g., *"What does the word **feasted** mean?"*). In one recommended scoring system, first record the student's response verbatim. If the student doesn't respond after 5 seconds, or replies, *"I don't know,"* ask, *"Can you tell me anything about the word **feasted**?"* Give the student 2 points for a complete response (e.g., *"**Feasted** means to eat a very big meal."*). Score 1 point for a partial or related response (e.g., *"**Feasted** means food."*); (Coyne, Loftus, Zipoli, & Kapp, 2009).

Pictures used as prompts provide an alternative method to assess young children's knowledge of the vocabulary words you have taught (Beck & McKeown, 2007). Display a picture that represents the targeted vocabulary word you taught along with three other distraction pictures and ask students to select the correct picture (e.g., *"Which picture shows someone who is **feasting**?"*). Another option is using a verbal format such as one developed by Beck and McKeown (2007) in which children are asked to respond to pairs of *yes* or *no* questions about each word. In one type of question children are asked whether a presented meaning matches a given word (e.g., *"Is a **feast** a big special meal?" "Is a **feast** a light snack?"*). Another type of question is designed to assess the word in multiple contexts; students are asked to judge whether a brief context exemplifies a word's meaning (e.g., *"Would it be **feasting** if people were having Thanksgiving dinner?" "Would it be **feasting** if Dominic and his brother were eating a peanut butter sandwich?"*).

One method of assessing older students is using true/false and multiple-choice questions (Beck et al., 2008). These questions are most helpful if you want to know if students can recognize the meaning of a word or indicate whether a taught word fits a particular situation. True/false and multiple-choice questions are easy or difficult depending on the depth of understanding you expect from students. In our view, teachers should always aim for the greatest depth of understanding since therein lies the link to reading comprehension (Stahl & Fairbanks, 1986). Nonetheless, knowing a vocabulary word is not an "all or nothing" proposition. For example, students may know a word when it is presented in context, but still be unable to use it spontaneously (Beck, McKeown, & Kucan, 2002; Carey, 1978). Thus there may be times when using easier items is more appropriate, such as after words have first been introduced. To illustrate, here are two true/false items for the word *disappear:*

If someone disappears, it means they can no longer be seen. T or F

The word *disappear* is related to the visual sense. T or F

Note that the second example is more abstract, requiring a deeper understanding of the word. Consider the following two multiple-choice questions developed by Beck et al. for the word *diligent.*

1. Which word means *diligent?*
   fast
   hardworking
   lost
   punished
2. Which phrase means *diligent?*
   making a lot of money
   working at an interesting job
   always trying your best
   remembering everything (p. 37)

The first question is more obvious, while the latter requires deeper thought because the answer is not clearly stated. The student has to infer the answer, logically integrating information he knows about the definition with clues provided in the correct phrase. In addition to requiring deeper thinking, more challenging questions also reduce the possibility of students getting an answer correct by guessing. Although true/false and multiple-choice tests are more efficient because you can give them to the entire class at the same time, be sure that students' incorrect answers result from a lack of vocabulary knowledge, not an inability to decode the question. When in doubt about whether students are able to read the items, administer the assessment orally.

Beck et al. (2008) recommend using more challenging tests to measure students' deep knowledge of vocabulary. When students process words deeply they connect new and known learning using critical thinking (Stahl & Fairbanks, 1986). To measure the deeper processing of vocabulary, ask questions like the following ones that require students to design examples, situations, and contexts for words taught.

What might an *ally* do for you? Why might someone need an *ally*?

What is something someone might do that would be *devious*? What might give you a clue that someone was being *devious*?

Why might someone say a house is *typical*?

What is something you might want to be *inspired* about?

Tell about a time you tried to act *nonchalantly*. (Beck et al., p. 38)

Another way to assess older students' vocabulary is determining whether they can apply morphographic rules to words making connections related to the meaning of the morphographs. Examples of morphology-based questions one teacher asked included:

"Four of our target words this week were *pollution, population control, public transportation,* and *pesticides.* In what ways could all of these terms be connected to a larger concept?"

"The concept we discussed this week was *prejudice.* How could we use the prefix and the root word for this word to help us understand its meaning?" (Allen, 1999, cited in Klingner et al., 2007, p. 50)

Espin, Busch, Shin, and Kruschwitz (2001) developed and validated a 5-minute vocabulary matching assessment to measure student knowledge of vocabulary covered in social studies. Sample items from a student-read probe are shown in Table 9.1. This assessment can be read by students or by the teacher. For the student-read assessment, the vocabulary terms are listed vertically in alphabetical order along the left side of the page, and definitions are placed in random order on the right side. Students are given 5 minutes to match

TABLE 9.1 Sample Items from a Student-Read Vocabulary Probe

5. colloid	1. substance with atoms that are all alike
3. conductor	2. compounds with identical chemical formulas but different molecular structures and shapes
1. element	3. material, such as cooper wire, in which electrons can move easily
2. isomers	4. matter consisting of positively and negatively charged particles
4. plasma	5. heterogeneous mixture whose particles never settle
6. solenoid	6. a wire wrapped in a cylindrical foil

Source: Adapted from Espin, C. A., Busch, T. W., Shin, J., & Kruschwitz, R. (2001). Curriculum-based measurement in the content areas: Validity of vocabulary-matching as an indicator of performance in social studies. *Learning Disabilities Research & Practice, 16*(3), 142–151.

the terms with their definitions. When the teacher reads the assessment, no definitions are provided on the right side. The teacher first reads the entire list of terms to the students and then reads the definitions at 15-second intervals. Students mark the term corresponding to each definition.

Because cumulative review increases student retention of new material and helps students discriminate between new and old learning, we recommend systematically including review words in all vocabulary progress monitoring assessments. In addition to providing you with valuable information about student retention, incorporating review questions into your assessments sends a signal to students that remembering what they are learning is important.

What Methods Do I Use to Teach Key Vocabulary Words?

Once you have selected the key words in a story, the next step is to decide whether to teach the word directly or indirectly. Direct teaching of vocabulary involves teaching students the meaning of vocabulary using examples, synonyms, definitions, *text talk,* graphic organizers, and key words. Indirect methods include teaching students to use strategies such as context clues, morphemic analysis, or dictionary usage so that they can determine the meaning of a word on their own. Strategies for teaching students vocabulary both directly and indirectly are described in this section.

Selecting Examples for Direct Instruction of Vocabulary

Ms. Vetrano was a kindergarten teacher in an at-risk school who was teaching her students the color red. She showed her students the following examples of red: red play dough, red car, a doll with a red dress on, and a red ball. Ms. Vetrano then pointed to her red dress and asked the children if it was an example of red. Most of the children answered, "No." Ms. Vetrano then pointed to a blue ball and asked whether it was red, and this time many students replied, "Yes." Frustrated by her students' lack of basic knowledge, Ms. Vetrano might shrug and blame the parents or preschool for not getting her students ready for kindergarten. She might also attribute the lack of learning to the students having a bad day or the moon being full. However, a close look at Ms. Vetrano's examples shows that her students were simply responding based on the examples they were given. First, Ms. Vetrano taught the concept of red using only examples that were toys. Selecting play dough, a toy car, a doll, and a ball for examples probably gave her students the false impression that only toys could be red. When she pointed to her red dress and asked the students whether it was red, the students didn't think so because her dress wasn't a toy. Logically, the students now believed that if something wasn't a toy, it couldn't be red. Ms. Vetrano could have improved her teaching of red by using a wider range of red things as examples: red clothes, red books, red crayons, etc. Unlike Ms. Vetrano, when Mr. Lopez was teaching his students the meaning of the word *cautious,* he made sure that his examples represented people who were cautious in a variety of contexts, including crossing the street, making a friend, investing in the stock market, etc.

Another problem with Ms. Vetrano's examples surfaced when students answered her second question. After her instruction, students thought that all toys were red because all the examples used were red toys. Because children tend to **overgeneralize,** or draw too general a conclusion, Ms. Vetrano needed to prevent this error by showing the students **nonexamples** that were also toys. For example, after showing the students a red ball, she could have shown them a blue ball and said that it was *not* red. Similarly, she could have shown other toys of a different color and explained that they weren't red either. When he taught the word *cautious*, Mr. Lopez used nonexamples by showing a boy running across a busy city street and a distraught investor who lost all his money in the 1929 stock market crash. Ms. Vetrano's lesson on teaching red and Mr. Lopez's examples in teaching the word *cautious* demonstrate the importance of selecting examples from multiple contexts when directly teaching the meaning of vocabulary. Unless teaching examples and nonexamples are selected carefully, students may reach the wrong conclusions about the vocabulary you are teaching. To avoid these errors, always use a range of positive examples to broaden the concept being taught, as well as at least two nonexamples to rule out overgeneralizations.

Teaching Vocabulary by Modeling

When teaching vocabulary to younger students whose limited language makes it unlikely that they will understand verbal explanations, **model** examples and nonexamples as you directly teach the word. For example, if you were teaching the meaning of *next to*, you could not verbally explain this vocabulary term without showing the position of one object next to another as you said the phrase. For one of your examples you might put a book *next to* the wall. You might choose to move a chair *next to* the desk. You might stand *next to* a student. Each time you said the new vocabulary term, you would demonstrate, so that students could physically see the placement of the object. Modeling also helps you teach concepts that are difficult to define such as *plaid*, a concept that can only be explained by presenting visual examples.

When using this technique to directly teach vocabulary, the teacher first models a series of positive examples and nonexamples of the new vocabulary word or concept. When Ms. Robertson was teaching the adverb *slowly* to her kindergarten students, she modeled the following examples and nonexamples. During her demonstration she said the key word with extra emphasis, to be certain that students' attention was on that word.

1. Mrs. Robertson walked very slowly in the front of the room and said, "*I am walking **slowly**.*"
2. She then wrote the name of a student in the class very slowly on the board and said, "*I am writing **slowly**.*"
3. She also waved good-bye very slowly and said, "*I am waving good-bye **slowly**.*"
4. Next, she ran quickly in place and said, "*I am **not** walking **slowly**.*"
5. Finally, she quickly wrote a student's name on the board using exaggerated speed and said, "*I am **not** writing **slowly**.*"

After presenting examples and nonexamples, Mrs. Robertson then tested how well students knew the examples just presented. For this phase of the teaching process, Mrs. Robertson walked slowly in front of the room and asked, "*Am I walking **slowly** or **not slowly**?*" After students answered correctly, she wrote a name slowly on the board and asked, "*Am I writing **slowly** or **not slowly**?*" Once students can accurately answer the structured testing questions, the teacher asks the students to decide whether to say the new word or other review vocabulary words in response to open-ended questions. When Mrs. Robertson reached this part of the lesson, she wrote a name slowly on the board and asked, "*How am I writing?*" The students who knew to use the key vocabulary term in their responses answered, "*slowly.*" Mrs. Robertson then ran fast in place and asked the students, "*How am I running?*" The students responded, "*quickly,*" using a review word covered the previous week. If they had not already learned that term, they probably would have answered, "*not slowly.*" Each time students answered the question, they had the opportunity to practice saying the new vocabulary term and to apply its meaning to a new situation.

Some teachers who want to emphasize oral language in their classroom expect their students to answer vocabulary questions in complete sentences. In these cases, students would answer, *"No, you are **not** walking **slowly**,"* or *"Yes, you are walking **slowly**."* The more opportunities students have to say the word, the greater the likelihood that it will become a permanent part of their vocabulary. A format for teaching vocabulary through modeling is shown in Table 9.2.

When students answer in unison, a teacher substantially increases their active practice opportunities for saying the new word at least five times in one quick session. Follow these guidelines when developing your questions for modeling as well as for the synonym and definition formats that follow.

Guidelines for Developing Vocabulary Questions

Use the Names of Your Students in Your Examples Whenever Possible   Using the names of real students in your class can be very motivating. Also, integrating students' names into examples that are specifically tied to their lives in some way is a good way of tapping into your students' background knowledge.

> When she taught the vocabulary word *sniffing*, Ms. Carlstrom used the name of Titus, a student in her class who liked apple pie. *"Titus loves apple pie. When he walked in the door of his house the other day, he did this* (teacher makes a sniffing noise), *thinking that his grandmother had made an apple pie. Was Titus **sniffing** or **not sniffing**?"*
> *"Tell me again what **sniffing** means."*

End by Providing a Practice Opportunity   Even if the answer is "not (vocabulary word)," give your students the opportunity to respond. Ms. Carlstrom used the following nonexample when she presented the word *sniffing.*

> *"If a lion sounds like this* (teacher makes a lion's roar) *while he's chasing an elephant, is the lion **sniffing** or **not sniffing**?"* Her students laughed as they answered, *"**not sniffing**."*

Reflect the Students' Lives with Relevant Questions   Construct your questions so they reflect experiences in the students' lives, material they are learning at school, or popular media they have seen or heard. One question Ms. Carlstrom asked connected her example of sniffing to a unit she was doing about sources of energy.

> *"When Renauld went into his house, he did this* (teacher makes a sniffing sound), *because he thought he smelled natural gas, which has a smell when it is leaking. Was Renauld **sniffing** or **not sniffing**?"*

Use the Exact Vocabulary from the Story in Your Questions and as the "Correct" Responses   Always write your questions so that students will listen to and use the exact vocabulary word used in the story. If a word in the text is written in the past tense, ask your questions so that the students have to answer in the past tense. Many students who are at risk routinely do not use the past tense form of words in their conversations. Because the meaning of text is often affected by the tense of a verb, providing extra practice using past-tense verbs should also improve students' accuracy in comprehending text and writing about events that happened in the past. Sometimes the phrase "Tell me..." can help with the phrasing of these questions.

> In all of the examples for the word *sniffing* just described, the students were required to answer with the word *sniffing*, as opposed to *sniff* or *sniffed*. If the word had instead been *sniffed*, Ms. Carlstrom would have stated her question like this: *"Tell me whether I **sniffed**, or whether I did **not sniff**."*

TABLE 9.2   Teaching Vocabulary Through Modeling

Objective	Given 3 examples and 3 nonexamples of the new word, the students will say whether each is an example or nonexample, telling how they knew the answer, with 100% accuracy.
Materials Needed	Preparation for this activity includes selection of words. If objects are used for modeling, they should be readily available so instruction does not lag. Either prewrite the questions you will ask or jot notes about the questions on a sheet you can use for reference.
Signaling	Depending on the word, use one of these signals: Signal 1: Use finger snaps/hand claps to signal a unison response for your questions. Signal 2: Use a loop signal if asking a question about a picture.
Time	Between 2 and 5 minutes per word.
Rationale	Knowledge of vocabulary is important for reading comprehension.
Tips	✳ Although you will ask for unison answers during this activity, often you will want to ask individual students to answer *why* and *how do you know* questions, which have longer answers. ✳ Animate your questions with gestures and emotion related to the scenario. ✳ Always phrase questions so students have the opportunity to say the vocabulary word. Rather than answering with a simple "no," expect students to answer, "not (*vocabulary word*)."

Instructions	**Teacher**	**Student**
	1. Advance Organizer	
	2. My Turn	
	✳ If modeling a word, show students three positive examples and three nonexamples of the word. If teaching the word *eyebrow*, point to your eyebrow and say, "This is an eyebrow." For a nonexample, you might point to Jason's foot and say, "This is not an eyebrow."	
	3. Your Turn	
	Ask students direct questions about the vocabulary word related to positive and negative examples. Intermix your type of questions. Students should answer six questions correctly before moving on to the next step.	
	✳ If modeling the word *eyebrow*, you might point to Shondra's chin and ask this nonexample question: **"Is this an eyebrow or not an eyebrow?"** You might point to Kendra's eyebrow and ask this example question: **"Is this an eyebrow or not an eyebrow?"**	not an eyebrow an eyebrow
	4. Review of previously learned words (example- and nonexample-based questions) interspersed with questions about the new word.	
	5. Individual Student Checkout	
	Ask two or three students to answer questions about the new word and/or review words.	

Error Correction	If students make an error, immediately return to a My Turn–Your Turn pattern. Later in the lesson ask students about the word they missed to provide more practice. Only use a Together if students have difficulty pronouncing the vocabulary word and could use the practice saying it with you.
Perk Up Your Drill	✳ The use of students' names and the names of other staff in the building is motivating to students. ✳ Students are motivated by humorous questions and examples. They especially like absurd questions. ✳ Relate questions to events that have occurred in school life.

TABLE 9.2   Continued

Adaptations	※ If you expect students to answer in complete sentences, get them into the habit of consistently answering in this way. In the beginning, some classes will answer in a complete sentence if after they answer in one or two words, you simply say to them, "Tell me in a complete sentence." In other classes where students have fewer language skills, in the beginning you will need to model the complete sentence before they repeat it. If you are consistent in expecting a complete sentence, the students will soon learn the patterns so they can do that.
	※ You will want to use more Togethers with ESL students who could use practice articulating words.
	※ Make sure when you use your students' names that your questions do not reflect discriminatory stereotypes. For example, when asking questions about words related to feats of strength, use girls' names as well as boys' names.

Source: This script is based on one originally developed and field-tested by Carnine, D. W., Silbert, J., Kame'enui, E. J., & Tarver, S. (2010). *Direct instruction reading* (5th ed.). Boston: Merrill Prentice Hall.

Mix in *Why* Questions After Example and Nonexample Questions   Students' answers to *why* questions give you a good idea about whether they understand the meaning of the word. After Ms. Carlstrom was sure that her students knew the definition of *sniffing,* she asked a *why* question to gauge her students' understanding of the word:

> *"This word is **sniffing**. What's the word?"*
>
> *"**Sniffing** means smelling with short breaths. What does **sniffing** mean?"*
>
> *"Watch me."* (Make a **sniffing** noise.) *"Was I **sniffing** or **not sniffing**?"*
>
> *"Why do you say that?"*

Using Synonyms to Teach New Vocabulary Directly

In this teaching strategy, teachers use a known word to teach students an unknown word having the same meaning. For example, if students don't know the meaning of the word *residence,* but know the meaning of *home, home* can be used to teach *residence.* Let's look at how a teacher uses synonyms to teach the meaning of a new word:

> Mr. Gilman first told his students, *"A residence is a home."* He then proceeded to present a series of examples and nonexamples of residence. For example, he held up a photo of a house and asked, *"This is a picture of Condy's home. Is it her **residence** or **not** her **residence**?"* After his students answered, he asked, *"Aquanetta went to the mall. Is the mall her **residence**, or **not** her **residence**? How do you know?"* After six or seven examples and nonexamples, he moved into the next phases of his teaching and reviewed the new word *residence* with other vocabulary words that students had learned in the past few weeks. Mr. Gillman pointed to a picture of a hotel and asked, *"Is this a **residence**? How do you know?"*

A sample series of teaching examples for the word *timid* is shown in Figure 9.1.

Using Definitions to Teach New Vocabulary Directly

The first step in teaching vocabulary using definitions is to have a clear, understandable definition. In most cases you cannot select definitions straight from the dictionary without adapting them. Beck et al. (2002) point out that dictionary definitions are constructed

> **Synonyms: Examples and nonexamples for teaching the word *timid*:**
>
> 1. Before presenting examples and nonexamples, have students look at the word and repeat the synonym after you until they can easily say it:
>
>   timid "*Timid* means easily frightened or shy. What does *timid* mean?"
>
> 2. Ask students questions based on examples and nonexamples of *timid*.
>
>   * The new student was shy on the first day of school. Was the new student timid or not timid? How do you know?
>   * Gabriel enjoys making everyone laugh. Is Gabriel timid or not timid? Why?
>   * Sara is not afraid to talk in front of the class. Is Sara timid or not timid?
>   * Marissa became easily frightened during the play and forgot her lines when she saw all the people in the audience. Did Marissa become timid or not timid? Why?
>   * William is very friendly and outgoing. He can make friends with anyone. Is William timid or not timid?
>   * A deer is a shy animal. Is a deer timid or not timid?
>   * (Teacher makes a scared face with matching body posture.) Do I look timid or not timid?
>   * On the first day of camp, Jorie was so afraid that she could hardly talk. Was Jorie timid or not timid? How do you know?
>   * Lionel always raises his hand in class because he likes to explain the answer. Is Lionel timid or not timid? Why?
>   * (Teacher swaggers around the room with an "I am cool look" on his face.) Do I look timid or not timid?
>   * A robin will fly away as soon as a person comes close to it. Is a robin timid or not timid? Why?
>   * A grizzly bear will growl and run after a human who is trying to escape from him. Is a grizzly bear timid or not timid? Why?
>
> 3. Ask students to tell you the definition for the word *timid* one more time. Ask review questions about previously learned words.
>
>   * What does *timid* mean? What does *nonsense* mean? Kendra moved from Swan Hillman School to Lewis Lemon School when she was in first grade. Would you say that Kendra *transferred* or *did not transfer* to another school?

FIGURE 9.1   Direct Teaching: Synonyms

Source: Adapted from Carnine, D. W., Silbert, J., Kame'enui, E. J., & Tarver, S. (2010). *Direct instruction reading* (5th ed.). Boston: Merrill Prentice Hall.

primarily to meet space limitations. Because of this constraint, dictionary definitions can be vague and misleading. Consider the problems with these dictionary definitions as described by these authors.

Conspicuous: easily seen

Typical: being a type

Exotic: foreign; strange; not native

Devious: straying from the right course; not straightforward

The definition for *conspicuous* fails to communicate that something can be easily seen, yet not be conspicuous. *Conspicuous* is something that pops out at you and that is not conveyed by the definition presented here. The definition for *typical* is so vague that it sheds little light on what the word means. The definition for *exotic* includes three possible meanings, but it is unclear whether all, some, or one have to be present for something to be exotic. The definition for *devious* could be easily misinterpreted. A young learner may conclude that *devious* has to do with crooked walking or getting lost. (Beck et al., 2002, p. 34)

Dictionary definitions may also contain difficult words that students may be unable to decode or may not know the meaning of. Take, for example, the definition of *illusion:* a mistaken perception of reality. This definition includes a number of words that may be unfamiliar to students, including *perception* and *reality.* The definition "to believe something is true when it is not" would be much easier to understand.

Sometimes the definitions provided in students' reading series are clearer than dictionary definitions, but there are no guarantees. Therefore, when using definitions to teach words, it is recommended that you write your own definitions or modify dictionary or basal definitions to make them clearer. Carnine, Silbert, Kame'enui, and Tarver (2010) suggest a helpful strategy for writing a clear, comprehensive definition. They describe definitions as having two key elements: a small class to which the word belongs, and a statement of how the word differs from other members of the class. For example, take the word *sniffing.* Its class is *smelling,* and it differs from other ways of smelling because it is smelling using short breaths. Another example would be the word *south.* South is a direction (class) and it differs from other directions in that it is the direction opposite north. Beck et al. (2002) suggest using student-friendly definitions that define words using everyday language. For example, taking the word *sniffing* that was just defined, a student-friendly definition might read: when someone is smelling something using short breaths. Another example of a student-friendly definition is this definition for the word *chores:* small jobs that have to be done every day or every week. Finally, consider this student-friendly definition for the word *recipe:* a set of directions for how to cook something.

Once your definition is developed, begin teaching your students the new vocabulary word. As you point to the word on the board, assess its readability and determine whether to ask students to read the word or tell them what it says. Next say the definition, having them repeat it after you. Then, present a series of examples and nonexamples in the form of questions. As suggested earlier, use at least two positive examples of the word, making sure these examples have enough range to prevent misconceptions, as well as two nonexamples to help students rule out inappropriate generalizations. Figure 9.2 lists examples and nonexamples for the word *permanent.* Your examples should be presented in an unpredictable order.

Using *Text Talk* to Teach New Vocabulary Directly

Text Talk is a research-based direct teaching strategy and curriculum that teaches vocabulary in context using definitions (Beck & McKeown, 2007). Students actively process the meaning of each designated vocabulary word including its connection to other words, an approach shown to be superior to traditional read-alouds in which specific words are either not called out at all or merely clarified briefly while reading (Coyne et al., 2009). Use these steps when using *Text Talk* with your students.

1. Describe the word in the context of the text (e.g., *"In this story, the ogre is opposed to everything that the people want to do; he's opposed to their wanting a holiday; he's opposed to their wanting more rest from work; and he's opposed to letting the kids play."*)
2. Explain the meaning of the word.
3. Ask the children to repeat the word so that they create a phonological representation of it.
4. Provide examples of the word in contexts other than the one used in the story.

Teaching Definitions: Examples and nonexamples for teaching the word *permanent*

1. Before presenting examples and nonexamples, have students look at the word and repeat the definition after you. Say the definition slowly and with emphasis so students can easily repeat it. With more difficult definitions, you may need to inject some "Togethers" when teaching the definition. You and the students will repeat the definition together until they are able to say it by themselves.

   "Permanent means 'meant to last for a long time.' What does *permanent* mean?"

2. Ask students questions based on examples and nonexamples of *permanent.*

   ※ Molly bought an ice cream cone on a hot day. Is an ice cream cone permanent or not permanent? Why?

   ※ The mayor of Chicago paid the artist Pablo Picasso to build a large concrete sculpture that sits in the plaza. Is the sculpture permanent or not permanent? Why?

   ※ Patrick put his old plastic action figures into a box when he left for college. The action figures are made out of strong plastic and will probably last until his grandchildren are old enough to play with them. Are these action figure toys permanent or not permanent? Why?

   ※ Stuart wrote a secret spy note to his friend on paper and told his friend to destroy it after reading the message. Is the note permanent or not permanent? Why?

   ※ After Maria's baby teeth fell out, new, larger teeth grew in her mouth. Maria's mother told her that if she brushed these new teeth every day, she would have them for the rest of her life. Were the new teeth permanent or not permanent? Why?

3. Ask students to tell you the definitions for the word one more time. Ask review questions. "Tell me one more time what *permanent* means."

FIGURE 9.2 Direct Teaching: Definitions

Source: Adapted from Carnine, D. W., Silbert, J., Kame'enui, E. J., & Tarver, S. (2010). *Direct instruction reading* (5th ed.). Boston: Merrill Prentice Hall.

5. Have the children make judgments about examples.
6. Ask the children to construct their own examples.
7. Reinforce the word's phonological and meaning representations by asking students to say it again. Have the students read the word if they have the skills to do that.
8. Reinforce the words on subsequent days by (a) keeping charts of the words from several stories posted on the wall; (b) placing a tally mark next to the word if children hear or use one of the words; (c) attempting to use the words in regular classroom activities that occur each day such as the morning message: *"Today is Monday. Jamal wants a **feast** for his birthday."* (p. 256)

Read how an example of *Text Talk* can be applied to a children's story at **http://bit.ly/g7WWu.**

An example of how to use these steps to teach vocabulary directly is shown in Figure 9.3.

Using Semantic Maps to Teach New Vocabulary Directly

Semantic maps are visual representations of vocabulary that help students organize subject matter by having them categorize, label the categories, and discuss concepts related to a target word. The parts of the map are used to teach the class of words to which it belongs (*"What is it?"*), its characteristics (*"What is it like?"*), and some examples. A sample semantic map for *spider* is shown in Figure 9.4. When teaching the word *spider,* the teacher first presents the word to the students and places the word *spiders* into the center of the

---

Feast

Explain

In the story, it said that the animals found the robbers' tale full of good things to eat, and so they had a *feast*.

A *feast* is a big special meal with lots of delicious food.

Say the word with me: *"feast"*

People usually have a *feast* on a holiday or to celebrate something special. We all have a *feast* on Thanksgiving Day.

Discuss and Summarize

❋ Let's think about some examples of feasts. I will name some things and if they are examples of a feast, say yum! If they are not, don't say anything.

   ❋ Eating an ice cream cone. no response

   ❋ Eating at a big table full of all kinds of food. yum!

❋ If you wanted to eat a feast, what kind of food would you want?

❋ What's the word that means a big special meal?

FIGURE 9.3   Text Talk

Source: Adapted from Beck, I. L, & McKeown, M. G. (2007). Increasing young low-income children's oral vocabulary repertoires through rich and focused instruction. *The Elementary School Journal, 107*(3), 251–271.

FIGURE 9.4   Semantic Map

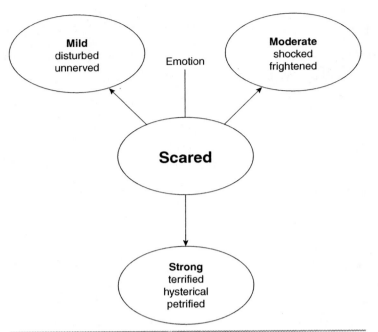

FIGURE 9.5 Emotional Word Web

Source: From Barton, J. (1996). Cited in H. W. Catts & A. G. Kamhi (2005), *Language and reading disabilities* (2nd ed.). Boston: Allyn & Bacon, p. 191.

FIGURE 9.6 Vertical and Horizontal Semantic Maps

Source: Foil, C. R., & Alber, S. R. (2002). Fun and effective ways to build your students' vocabulary. *Intervention in School and Clinic, 37*(3), 134.

map. The teacher then presents some information about spiders by describing them to students, having students read from their texts, or showing a video or DVD on spiders. If *spider* is a review word, the teacher skips the presentation of information and proceeds directly to constructing the map, asking students to supply the information, and providing support when they have forgotten details. Under the "What is it?" category, the teacher writes the larger class of living things to which spiders belong as *arachnid*. When she asks students, *"What is it like?"* the teacher helps students identify the characteristics of spiders: that they have eight legs, are up to 3 inches long, and eat insects or small vertebrates. Examples of different types of spiders are identified and written on the map. If the prior discussion went into more detail, she might lead the students to list the individual spiders as being either *ground spiders* or *web spiders.* For a follow-up activity, students complete blank semantic maps of spiders as independent work in class or as homework.

Semantic maps can also be used to show the relationships between words. Note the "emotional map" developed by Barton (1996) for the word shown in Figure 9.5, and the horizontal map developed by Foil and Alber (2002) for the word *music* shown in Figure 9.6.

Using Keywords to Teach New Vocabulary Directly

The **keyword method** (Jitendra et al., 2004) uses mnemonics to make vocabulary more meaningful to students and hence easier to understand and remember. This method involves two key components, the keyword and a visual depiction of the vocabulary word. First the teacher selects a keyword that sounds similar to some part of the vocabulary word. The keyword should be familiar to the students, concrete, and easily pictured. For example, Mastropieri (1988) taught the word *apex*, meaning the highest point, by first associating it with the keyword *ape.* For the visual that ties together the keyword, *ape,* with the definition of *apex,* Mastropieri and colleagues showed students a picture of an ape sitting on the highest point of a rock. Students were more apt to readily recall the definition of *apex* by thinking of the keyword (*ape*) and picturing that ape sitting on the highest point of a rock. An example of the keyword image for *apex* is shown below in Figure 9.7. The keyword method is most effective for students who are at risk when the keywords and corresponding visual images are generated by the teacher rather than the students (Bos & Vaughn, 2008).

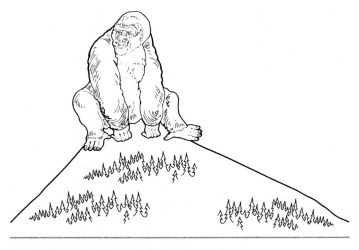

FIGURE 9.7 Keyword for Apex

What Methods Do I Use to Teach Students to Learn New Vocabulary Independently?

Using Context to Teach Independent Word-Learning Strategies

While the direct instruction of vocabulary is an essential part of reading instruction, students learn most new vocabulary on their own through independent reading. Students who are at risk may be cut off from this rich source of vocabulary for a number of reasons. Certainly, problems with reading accuracy and fluency are the most serious impediments to independent reading. Also, the meaning of vocabulary words is not always made accessible by authors whose primary intention is to tell a story or explain a phenomenon (Beck et al., 2002). Thus, reading to learn requires strategies that students who are at risk may lack. You need to teach these strategies systematically and explicitly, just as you teach word-reading skills.

Using context clues to figure out the meaning of new words is one important independent vocabulary strategy students need to know. Ruddell (1999) has identified five types of context clues that can help students learn the meaning of new vocabulary within natural contexts. These clues are defined in Table 9.3 and include synonyms, definitions, antonyms, examples, and general clues. Learning to identify all of the various types of context clues is likely to be overwhelming for younger students, so it may be more appropriate for older students (Baumann, Edwards, Boland, Olejnik, & Kame'enui, 2003).

Teaching students to use context clues, especially when the context clues are definitions, examples, or more general clues, is a difficult skill for beginning teachers who will need to preplan how to indirectly teach vocabulary this way. Later, when they have more experience, teachers learn how to teach these clues more naturally on the spot during the first reading of a story. Figure 9.8 provides an example format a teacher can use when teaching vocabulary words this way. In this format, the teacher presents a small section of the passage that contains the new word, as well as words before and after that word to help students figure out its meaning. In the example shown here, students are led to figure out the meaning of the word *logical.* They first read the passage and then the targeted word, which is underlined. The teacher then asks questions that lead the students to figure out

TABLE 9.3 Types of Context Clues

Context Clue	Example
1. Definition	The author gives you a definition for the word *zenith* in the sentence.
	When the sun hit its **zenith,** which means *right overhead,* I could tell it was noon by the tremendous heat.
2. Synonym	The author uses another word that means about the same as the word you are trying to understand.
	Captain Jackson's uniform was **impeccable.** In fact, it was so *perfect* that she always had the highest score during inspection.
3. Antonym	The author uses another word that means the opposite or nearly the opposite of the word you are trying to understand.
	The soldier was very **intrepid** in battle, in contrast to the person next to him, who was quite *cowardly.*
4. Example	The author gives you several words or ideas that are examples of the word you are trying to understand.
	Tigers, lions, panthers, and leopards are some of the most beautiful members of the **feline** family.
5. General	The author gives you some general clues to the meaning of a word, often spread over several sentences.
	Patriotism was a *very strong force* in the South. People *loved their part of the country* and were *very proud to be Southerners.*

Note: In Context Clue section, italicized words provide context clues for bold words.

Source: Baumann, J., Edwards, E.., Boland, E., Olejnik, S., & Kame'enui, E. (2003). Vocabulary tricks: Effects of instruction in morphology and context on fifth-grade students' ability to derive and infer word meanings. *American Educational Research Journal, 40*(2), 447–494.

the word. In the example, the teacher asks, *"How did Lincoln prove his side of an argument?"* In the final step the students read the passage with the same word, *logical,* and then read it again, substituting a synonym or definition that means the same thing.

Although the strategy of using context clues to learn new vocabulary is helpful, it also has its limitations. First, some context clues may be easier to uncover than others. As Carnine and colleagues (2010) point out, using the context is made more difficult when the defining words are separated from the target word by other words not related to its meaning, or when the definition of the word is stated negatively. Notice how *imprint* is defined in context below.

Sometimes a fossil is only an *imprint* of a plant or animal. Millions of years ago, a leaf fell off a fernlike plant. It dropped onto the swampy forest soil, which is called peat. The leaf rotted away. But it left the mark of its shape in the peat. The peat, with the *imprint* of the leaf, hardened.

The words that explain *imprint,* "mark of its shape," come well after the first reference to it and before the second reference, thus rendering the context clues less accessible than if they had come right after *imprint.* This means that the teacher may need to provide more support if students are to learn this new word. One suggestion would be to use the following think-aloud technique.

"Let's see. The word **imprint** *is underlined. That means it's important and probably a word I'll need to figure out. What does it mean when a word is underlined in the story? Now I need to look at the words around* **imprint** *to see if I can figure it out. Hmm, sometimes the meaning of the word isn't right next to it in the story."* (Reads next part starting with Millions.) *"This sentence tells how a fossil is made. I don't see the meaning*

1. Give students a short reading passage of several sentences that contain a vocabulary word you have decided to teach. Select a passage where context clues are provided in the text.

   Example: It was while he was serving in the Illinois legislature that Lincoln decided he'd like to study to become a lawyer. He had a lawyer's <u>logical</u> mind, and he had a special knack for proving his side of an argument. Step by step, he could lay out the facts in a clear and uncomplicated way until soon enough he'd have everyone convinced.

2. Ask one student to read the passage before identifying the underlined word.

   Teacher: **"Kyle, read this passage about Lincoln."**

3. Ask another student(s) to find either the synonym or the definition of the underlined word in the passage.

   Teacher: **"How did Lincoln prove his side of an argument, Cyndie?"**

   Cyndie: "Step-by-step, he laid out the facts in a clear and uncomplicated way."

   Teacher: **"Yes, Lincoln explained all of the facts of a case *step-by-step in a clear and uncomplicated way.* That is how his mind worked. Everybody, let's read that last sentence together."**

   Class: "Step-by-step, he laid out the facts in a clear and uncomplicated way until soon enough he'd have everyone convinced."

   Teacher: **"Greg, what is a logical mind?"**

   Greg: "A mind that lays out the facts step-by-step in a clear and uncomplicated way."

4. Ask students to reread the sentence and substitute the synonym or definition for the vocabulary word.

   Teacher: **"So I could read, 'He had a lawyer's *mind that laid out the facts step-by-step in a clear and uncomplicated way.*' That's how a logical mind thinks. Everyone, let's read the entire second sentence together, but instead of reading *logical,* use the definition."**

   Class and
   Teacher: "He had a lawyer's mind that lays out the facts step-by-step in a clear and uncomplicated way and he had a special knack for proving his side of an argument."

   Teacher: **"Kwame, it's your turn to read the second sentence with the definition for *logical.*"**

   Kwame: "He had a lawyer's mind that lays out the facts step-by-step in a clear and uncomplicated way and he had a special knack for proving his side of an argument."

Notes:

- Synonym context clues are easier to teach than definition context clues. You will need to provide more support through questions and Togethers for longer definitions.

- Use regular error correction strategies when students make an error. Often students who are at risk will have difficulty with verb tense and pronouns when substituting a definition for the vocabulary word. In these cases, use more Togethers, and model the way to say the revised sentence before asking students to do the same.

FIGURE 9.8   Indirect Teaching: Context Clues

Source: Adapted from Carnine, D. W., Silbert, J., Kame'enui, E. J., & Tarver, S. (2010). *Direct instruction reading* (5th ed.). Boston: Merrill Prentice Hall.

> yet. Wait—now it says the leaf left the mark of its shape in the peat. That's what an imprint is—a mark of something's shape."

In this next example, deriving the meaning of the word *swamp* is complicated by the presence of the word *not* included in a negative definition.

> "Back when the dinosaurs lived here, my town was a big swamp. The land was not dry like it is now."

In this example, the teacher might ask the following questions to guide students to the meaning of *swamp*:

"Read the passage. What's the underlined word?" (swamp) *"It says the land was not dry like it is now. If land is not dry, then what is it?"* (wet) *"Yes, wet. So, what kind of land do you think a swamp is?"* (wet land) *"Don't forget, when you see a word explained using the word* **not,** *you have to think extra carefully about what it means. You can get tricked."*

Using Morphemic Analysis to Teach Independent Word-Learning Strategies

Unfortunately, not all words are explained by the words around them, so students need other strategies to figure out new words. Another strategy teaches students to figure out new words using morphemes. Morphemes can be whole words such as *spell,* or they may be word parts such as the prefix *re-* or the suffix *-less.* To demonstrate how morphemes can be used to figure out the meaning of new vocabulary words, let's look at the word *careless,* which consists of two morphemes: *care* and *less.* If students know that *less* means *without,* they know that *careless* means doing something without care or without being careful. Similarly, the word *misspell* can be broken into the parts of *mis* and *spell.* If they know that *mis* means *not,* then they know that *misspell* means to *not spell* or *spell incorrectly.*

For morphemes to be helpful to students in figuring out vocabulary, they must be clearly recognizable in a word and be readily translatable into a meaningful definition. Both *misspell* and *careless* fit those criteria. Unfortunately, not all words with morphemes are so clear-cut. The meanings of many words are difficult to determine using morphemes alone, as in these examples:

The word *epidermis* is composed of two morphemes: *epi,* which means *beside* or *upon,* and *dermis,* which means *skin.* The literal definition of *epidermis,* based on its morphemes, is *upon the skin.*

The word *irreducible* is composed of four morphemes: *ir,* which means *not; re,* which means *back* or *gain; ducere,* which means *to lead;* and *ible,* which means *capable of being.* The literal definition of *irreducible,* based on its morphemes, is *not capable of being led back (to the original).*

Ducere is difficult to translate into a meaningful definition. Other morphemes have multiple meanings or are not readily recognizable. Because the utility of using morphemes varies, it is suggested that you teach your students the morphemes that are most useful. A table of common morphemes, their meanings, and example words was shown in Table 4.3 (p. 127). Strategies for teaching students to use word parts to both decode words and discern their meaning were also described under "Applying Structural Analysis to Reading Regular Words" in Chapter 4 (p. 125).

Using the Dictionary to Teach Independent Word-Learning Strategies

The definitions listed in a dictionary are often vague or contain words that students can neither decode nor understand. Perhaps that is why in studies where students were handed a dictionary and asked to create sentences, 63% of the sentences were judged to be "odd," and students frequently interpreted one or two words from a definition as being the entire meaning of a word (Beck et al., 2002). We recommend that students use learner-friendly dictionaries that are often developed for English language learners and thus use language that is accessible for any student who struggles with language. The *Collins COBUILD Learner's Dictionary* (Cobuild, 2005) and the *Easy English Dictionary* (Baker & Bettino, 1988) are effective examples. The *Easy English Dictionary,* designed for younger children and those with lower vocabularies, includes a higher proportion of black-and-white line drawings to illustrate the more concrete words. Both dictionaries contain clear sentences about each key word to help students understand the word in context. Still, caution when using any dictionary is advised, since even the best dictionaries include definitions that need to be rewritten in a more reader-friendly manner.

Besides containing unclear definitions, dictionaries often present multiple word meanings. Multiple meanings are difficult to comprehend for students who are at risk. An example of teaching students multiple meanings using the dictionary is shown in Table 9.4.

TABLE 9.4   Teaching Multiple Meanings Using the Dictionary

Teacher	Students
1. The teacher reads the word in context.	
"The doctor gave the sick boy a *shot* of very strong medicine."	
2. The teacher asks students to find the word in their dictionaries.	
"Let's see if we can figure out the meaning of the word *shot* using the dictionary. Everyone, find the word *shot* in your dictionaries and raise your hand when you have found it."	Students raise hands
3. The teacher helps students think through selecting the correct definition.	
"There are three definitions in the dictionary. We know that dictionaries often have more than one definition for a word. Let's see if we can figure out which one fits our sentence from the story.	
I'm going to read each definition and we'll try to figure out which one fits our sentence about the sick boy.	
1. The sound of firing a gun.	
2. A kick, throw, or hit in some games to score points.	
3. Medicine placed under the skin by a needle.	
Let's talk about the first one: the sound of firing a gun. Does that fit what the doctor is doing to the boy?"	Everyone: No
"Why doesn't it fit, Simone?"	Simone: The doctor isn't shooting a gun or something at the boy.
"Let's look at the next one: a kick, throw, or hit in some games to score points. Everyone, does that fit what the doctor is doing?"	Everyone: No
"How do you know, Latrese?"	Latrese: The doctor isn't playing a game with the boy, he's trying to make him feel better.
"Let's look at the last definition: medicine placed under the skin by a needle. Everyone, does that fit what the doctor is doing?"	Everyone: Yes
"Manny, how do you know?"	Manny: He's putting medicine in him to make him feel better.
"So, everyone, what definition fits our sentence?"	Everyone: Medicine placed under the skin by a needle.
"Yes. Now, when we talk about the Old West in social studies today, we'll talk about a different definition for *shot.* Which one do you think will fit into that story, Garth?"	Garth: The sound of firing a gun.

Before students can look up words in the dictionary, they need to learn several preskills. These preskills include the following:

1. Identifying letters.
2. Saying letters in an a–z sequence.
3. Knowing the concepts of *before* and *after.*
4. Knowing alphabetic order for the first letter.
5. Determining the position of letters relative to each other: When you call out a letter, students should be able tell you which letter comes after and which letter comes before the named one. When a student opens the dictionary to the *o* page, looking for the word *dirigible,* he needs to know that *d* comes before *o,* so he needs to jump ahead to the front quarter of the dictionary.
6. Knowing alphabetic order to the second letter.
7. Knowing alphabetic order to the third letter.
8. Scanning a dictionary page to locate a given word.
9. Knowing what guide words are, and how to locate words using them.
10. Knowing how to interpret the most common abbreviations used in dictionary entries.
11. Knowing how to interpret the most common pronunciation tips.

You have learned a number of strategies for increasing student vocabulary knowledge both directly and indirectly. In its summary of the research on vocabulary instruction, the report of the National Reading Panel (2000) stated that "dependence on a single vocabulary instruction method will not result in optimal learning" (p. 427). The *In Your Classroom* feature describes a research-based strategy that combines several of the vocabulary-teaching strategies covered in this text.

In Your Classroom

Vocabulary Instruction

Baumann and colleagues (2003) combined two methods of independent word learning, context clues and morphemic analysis, to successfully teach previously unknown vocabulary words to fifth-grade students. They taught students the following three-part strategy called the "vocabulary rule" (Figure 9.9).

When you come to a word, and you don't know what it means, use:

1. **Context Clues:** Read the sentences around the word to see if there are clues to its meaning.

2. **Word-Part Clues:** See if you can break the word into a root word, prefix, or suffix to help figure out its meaning.

3. **Context Clues:** Read the sentences around the word again to see if you have figured out its meaning.

FIGURE 9.9 Vocabulary Rule

Source: Baumann, J., Edwards, E., Boland, E., Olejnik, S., & Kame'enui, E. (2003). Vocabulary tricks: Effects of instruction in morphology and context on fifth-grade students' ability to derive and infer word meanings. *American Educational Research Journal, 40*(2), 447–494.

In order to carry out Step 2 of the vocabulary rule, Baumann and colleagues taught their fifth graders this strategy for identifying word parts and using them to figure out the meaning of a new word. Figure 9.10 lists the steps to finding word-part clues.

1. Look for the **Root Word,** which is a single word that cannot be broken into smaller words or word parts. See if you know what the root word means.

2. Look for a **Prefix,** which is a word part added to the beginning of a word that changes its meaning. See if you know what the prefix means.

3. Look for a **Suffix,** which is a word part added to the end of a word that changes its meaning. See if you know what the suffix means.

4. Put the meaning of the **Root Word** and any **Prefix** or **Suffix** together and see if you can build the meaning of the word.

FIGURE 9.10   Word-Part Clues

Source: Baumann, J., Edwards, E., Boland, E., Olejnik, S., & Kame'enui, E. (2003). Vocabulary tricks: Effects of instruction in morphology and context on fifth-grade students' ability to derive and infer word meanings. *American Educational Research Journal, 40*(2), 447–494.

Before learning the "vocabulary rule" strategy, students were taught essential preskills for applying it. They learned to identify common affixes and state their meanings, as well as to identify and describe the five types of context clues: definitions, synonyms, antonyms, examples, and general context clues.

How Can I Teach My Students to Answer Vocabulary Questions on High-Stakes Tests?

Given increased accountability, your students will take high-stakes tests in the early primary grades. Students who read accurately and fluently on grade-level material are likely to perform at or above standard on high-stakes tests. Nonetheless, being test-wise can have a favorable impact on performance. Being test-wise means that students are familiar with the test formats and are able to apply strategies that increase their chances of getting correct answers, even when they are unsure of the correct answers. Vocabulary questions are an important part of the reading portion of most high-stakes tests. This section identifies question types your students are likely to encounter on their high-stakes tests and describes strategies to help them answer vocabulary correctly. Three of the most common types of vocabulary items on high-stakes tests include using the context, synonyms, and multiple-meaning formats (Educational Resources Inc., 2004). Examples of each of these types of item follow.

Using the Context

Alonzo thinks the stars are beautiful. He likes to *gaze* at them for hours. When he is in the country, the sky is very black so he can see the stars well.

A person who *gazes* at the stars:

A. dislikes them.
B. draws them.
C. looks at them.
D. talks to them.

Synonyms

An *incredible* story is:

A. boring.
B. unbelievable.
C. unhappy.
D. long.

Multiple Meanings

When Dashika finished the 10-mile race, she was _dead_.

In which sentence does the word _dead_ mean the same thing as in the sentence above?

    A. The roses in my garden are _dead_.
    B. The beach is _dead_ in the wintertime.
    C. The soldier was a _dead_ shot with the rifle.
    D. The camper was _dead_ after climbing uphill for 2 miles.

Strategies for teaching students to answer each of these types of vocabulary question are described in Table 9.5. Note that first the steps involved in answering the questions are clearly specified. The examples described employ think-alouds to make it clear to students not only what they have to do to answer a question, but what they need to be thinking about as they do so. Think-alouds have been shown to be an effective strategy for teaching comprehension to students who are at risk (Gersten, Fuchs, Williams, & Baker, 2001).

How Can I Provide Extra Vocabulary Practice for My Students?

Thus far, a number of effective strategies for the initial teaching of vocabulary to students who are at risk have been described. While these strategies are effective in introducing vocabulary to students, by themselves they are not enough. Reading research is quite clear that "multiple encounters are required before a word is really known, that is, if it is to affect comprehension and become a useful and permanent part of the students' vocabulary repertoire" (Beck et al., 2002, p. 73). Beck stresses that these repeated exposures must be rich, meaning that students are actively involved in "using and thinking about word meanings and creating lots of associations among words" (p. 73). This extra practice must extend beyond the classroom and into community environments as well.

Practice Activities for New Words

This section describes strategies for providing students with multiple exposures to new words. Remember that you need to provide more support and return to explicit teaching if students cannot complete these activities with at least 80% success. Student errors on these assignments provide you with an opportunity to give feedback and use an error-correction strategy. If students are old enough or you can quickly scan the worksheets, correct them on the spot so that students will profit from the immediate feedback.

Preprinted Response Cards and Write-On Response Boards These two practice activities recommended by Foil and Alber (2002) can be carried out with large groups, because both involve the use of unison response. As stated elsewhere in this text, because everyone is participating, unison-response formats help students pay attention and increase the opportunities for practice. The teacher distributes cards that have the vocabulary word printed in large letters on the front side and the definition and an example sentence printed on the back.

After every student has several cards, the teacher tells everyone a definition and students hold up the correct vocabulary word. In another adaptation of this same activity, the

TABLE 9.5 Strategies for Answering Vocabulary Questions on High-Stakes Tests

Question Type 1: Using Context Clues to Determine Meaning

Example	Alonzo thinks the stars are beautiful. He likes to *gaze* at them for hours. When he is in the country, the sky is very black so he can see the stars well.
	A person who *gazes* at the stars—
	A. dislikes them.
	B. draws them.
	C. looks at them.
	D. talks to them.
Strategy	Read only the underlined vocabulary word and try to pick out the correct definition based on what you already know.
	If you can't figure out the correct definition, go back and read the sentence. Underline the clue words that can help you find the definition and try again.
	If you still can't find the definition, substitute each of the choices into the sentence and pick the one that makes sense.
	If you still can't answer the question, guess one of the answers you think might be right.
Applied Strategy	**"Let's see. The underlined vocabulary word is *gaze*. Let's see if any of the choices means *gaze*. Hmm . . . Dislikes them? Draws them? Looks at them? Talks to them? I'm not sure what the answer is."**
	"I'm going to read the sentence and see if I can find words that might give me a clue about the meaning of *gaze*. I think the words *see the stars well* are important, so I will underline them in the sentence. But I'm still not quite sure of what the answer is."
	"Okay. Now I'm going to substitute each choice word in the sentence and see which makes sense."
	"'He likes to dislike them for hours.' That doesn't make sense at all. 'He likes to draw them for hours.' I don't think he would be able to draw the stars at night. It couldn't be that one. 'He likes to look at them for hours.' That one seems to make sense since it talks about being able to see the stars in the dark. I'll check the last one out just to be sure, but I think the answer is *look*. 'He likes to talk to them for hours.' That doesn't make sense. So, I think the answer is C, *looks at*."

Question Type 2: Multiple Meaning Formats

Example	**When Dashika finished the 10-mile race, she was *dead*.**
	In which sentence does the word *dead* mean the same thing as in the sentence above?
	A. The roses in my garden are *dead*.
	B. The beach is *dead* in the wintertime.
	C. The soldier was a *dead* shot with the rifle.
	D. The camper was *dead* after climbing uphill for 2 miles.
Strategy	Read the underlined vocabulary word.
	Read the **bolded** sentence containing the word and think of a simple definition or words that mean the same thing.
	Read each of the four possible answer sentences, substituting your definition instead of the word.
	After each sentence, ask yourself, "Does this make sense?" If not, cross out that choice and repeat for the other choices.
	If you still can't come up with the answer, take a guess by picking one of the choices you think might be right.
Applied Strategy	**"The underlined word is *dead*. *Dead* has many meanings. I need to figure out what it means in the bolded sentence. First I'll read that sentence. 'When Dashika finished the 10-mile race, she was *dead*.' Well, even though a 10-mile race is very long, I don't think Dashika is likely to die from it. I think she would be *very tired*. So I think *dead* here means very tired. Let me put *very tired* in each sentence and see which one makes sense."**

Continued

TABLE 9.5   Continued

Applied Strategy (Continued)	"'The roses in my garden are very tired.' That doesn't make sense. Roses don't get tired. I'm going to move to the next one. 'The beach is very tired in the wintertime.' That doesn't make any sense either. Then how about next one? 'The soldier was a very tired shot with the rifle.' That doesn't make sense either. Let's try the last one. 'The camper was very tired after climbing uphill for 2 miles.' That makes sense. The camper would be tired after that climb. So the answer is D."

Question Type 3: Synonyms

Example	An _incredible_ story is: A. boring. B. unbelievable. C. unhappy. D. long.
Strategy	Ask yourself what the word means without looking at the definitions given below. See if your definition is one of the four choices. If your definition is not one of the four choices, try to put each choice in a sentence and ask yourself, "Is that **incredible**?" If you still can't come up with an answer that makes sense, make a guess on one of the choices you think might be right.
Applied Strategy	"What does _incredible_ mean? I think it means _funny_. Let's see if that is a choice. Hmm . . . It isn't. Now I'm going to try to put each of the choices into a sentence and see if I can figure out the meaning of _incredible_ that way." "An incredible story. A boring story? Incredible and boring don't mean the same thing." "An incredible story. An unbelievable story? That seems right. I remember my brother talking about an incredible band. He said they were so good, he couldn't believe it. I'll look quickly at the other two choices, but I think B is the right answer. Let's see—_unhappy_? No—_long_? No, that isn't right either. I'm going to answer B for this question."

teacher distributes dry-erase boards to each student along with dry-erase markers. The teacher then establishes the word bank by writing a list of vocabulary words on the board. As with the preprinted word cards, the teacher tells a definition, and students answer by writing the appropriate word from the word bank on their slates. To maintain momentum, the teacher must maintain a perky pace and use a clear signal throughout the lesson (e.g., _"Boards up."_ or _"Card up."_). Foil and Alber (2002) point out that the whiteboards don't allow for as many student answers because writing on the slates takes more time than just holding up a preprinted card. However, they state that the activity may be just as worthwhile because writing the words reinforces spelling skills.

Classwide Peer Tutoring   Another way to provide extra vocabulary practice is through structured peer tutoring. In this approach, used by Miller, Barbetta, and Heron (1994), the teacher provides each student with a folder that has two pockets attached on the inside. The teacher prints "go" on one pocket, and "stop" on the other pocket. The teacher also provides students with index cards on which a vocabulary word is written on one side and its definition on the other. The students work in pairs in which they take turns being the tutor. The tutor shows each vocabulary word to his partner and asks the partner to restate the definition. Praise is given for correct answers, and corrective feedback in the form of a My Turn–Your Turn is provided for incorrect answers. Words mastered (three consecutive days correct) are put in the "stop" pocket. Words that have yet to be mastered are placed in the "go" pocket. After a predetermined time, usually around 5 minutes, the students switch roles. After both students have had their turn, they chart the number of words they have mastered on a graph taped to the inside of the folder. Words in the "stop" pile are reviewed periodically in subsequent days. As with any peer-tutoring procedure, tutors need to be carefully trained, and their teaching tactics closely monitored.

Never Too Many Questions   After teaching a vocabulary word, teachers need to find every opportunity to ask questions about the new word. They can ask questions immediately after students know the definition, they can ask questions before lunch, they can ask questions when the word surfaces in the story. *Who, what, where, why, when,* and *which* questions like the following provide extra opportunities for students to use the new words they have learned:

* *"What would you do if your best friend let you use a **delicate** glass to drink out of and you broke it? Have you ever broken anything that was **delicate,** and what was it?"*
* *"What are some things that make you **anxious?** Why?"*
* *"When have you seen a **procession,** and what kind of **procession** was it?"*

Making Choices   This activity recommended by Beck and colleagues (2002, p. 56) forces students to think about the precise definition of the word as applied to authentic descriptions. Even better, students answer in unison, so everyone is engaged in responding to the questions:

> If any of the things I mention is a *competition,* say "competition." If not, don't say anything at all.

> * a relay race
> * the Olympics
> * lunch with a friend
> * the school spelling bee
> * watching a movie

> If any of the things I mention is something that might make you *chuckle,* say "chuckle." If any of the things I mention might make you *sob,* say "sob."

> * your mom tickling your toes
> * burning your hand on a hot plate
> * watching a cartoon show where a mouse fools a cat
> * seeing a clown pull a quarter out of someone's ear
> * losing your money for lunch

Word Associations   In another activity, Beck and colleagues (2002, p. 44) have students make a connection between a new vocabulary word and a word that they already know and then describe why they made it. If a teacher had directly taught the words *glitter,* *pessimist, rubbish, arid,* and *antonyms,* he would write the five words on the board and ask the class to answer the following questions in unison:

* *"Tell me the word that goes with gold."* (answer: *glitter*)
* *"Tell me the word that goes with opposites."* (answer: *antonyms*)
* *"Tell me the word that goes with parched."* (answer: *arid*)
* *"Tell me the word that goes with negative."* (answer: *pessimist*)
* *"Tell me the word that goes with garbage."* (answer: *rubbish*)

Thumbs Up–Thumbs Down   This adaptation of a self-reflection activity in *Bringing Words to Life* (Beck et al., 2002; p. 45) provides review for descriptive words previously taught in class. The teacher asks students to hold their thumbs up if a trait she calls out describes them and to hold their thumbs down if the trait does not describe them. Individual students are asked to tell why they selected their answer.

* *"Are you independent? Why?"*
* *"Are you mischievous? Why?"*
* *"Are you gullible? Why?"*
* *"Are you assertive? Why?"*
* *"Are you loyal? Why?"*

Narrow Reading   An adjunct to directly teaching a "big concept" vocabulary word is **narrow reading,** where the teacher can assign different texts on the same topic so that the learner encounters the word in different contexts (Schmitt & Carter, 2000). If students have just learned the meaning of *circuit* and *electrical current,* the teacher might have everyone read the book *The Magic School Bus and the Electric Field Trip,* by Joanna Cole; photocopies of pages 41–44 of *Electricity and Magnetism Fundamentals,* by Robert Wood; and a choice of either the section on circuits in *All About Electricity,* by Melvin Berger, or the section on circuits in *The First Book of Electricity,* by Sam and Beryl Epstein.

Practice Activities for Review Words: Coordinating Vocabulary with Writing Activities

When students have the opportunity to write vocabulary words they have learned, they are more apt to remember a word when they read it in text. If the word is a spelling word, design the activity so that students practice independently spelling the word. If the word is not a spelling word, provide a written model on the board, overhead projection, or paper so students write it correctly. These are some activities you can use for vocabulary review practice:

Fill-In-the-Blank Stories   Vocabulary words are listed at the top of the page unless they are also spelling words, and students fill in the blanks of a story with appropriate words.

Dictionary "Race-and-Rite"   Each student needs a dictionary, pencil, and paper for this activity. Students are divided into three teams. If students are expected to know the spelling of the word, the teacher says the word; if students do not know the spelling, the teacher points to the word and asks students to read it. When the teacher says, "Look it up," the students race to look up the word in the dictionary. As soon as they have found the word, they write it along with the dictionary page number. Then they immediately write a complete sentence using the word. When a student has completed the task, she holds up her thumb. At a set time, the teacher says, "Stop," and quickly scans the papers of whichever team has the most thumbs raised. That team gets one point for every person who wrote the correct page number as well as a complete sentence.

The Good-bye List   The teacher keeps a list of vocabulary words that have been taught on a chart that is titled the "Good-bye List." Each morning he writes between 5 and 10 vocabulary words on the board. When students enter the room, they know that they are supposed to write the word, a definition of the word, and a sentence showing correct usage of the word. They can earn three points per vocabulary word toward their language arts grade for doing this activity correctly. If 90% of students get all three points for a word two days in a row, the word is taken off the Good-bye List. Students are encouraged to shrink the list so that the teacher is "forced" to teach even more words because he cannot keep up with his hardworking class.

Vocabulary Words as Themes   When students are asked to write a paragraph, story, or descriptive paper, the assignment should be structured so that they use targeted vocabulary words. If students have just read *Cloudy with a Chance of Meatballs*, ask them to write several sentences about what would happen if they were walking outside in the *hail*. If students have been studying about the early American *colonists*, ask them to write a page about what hardships they would face as a *colonist* on the moon.

Grids   The teacher prepares a worksheet using the table function of a word processing program. Vocabulary words are listed in the first column and students are asked to write synonyms and/or antonyms in the next column(s). The teacher needs to determine whether a dictionary or textbook is necessary for student success.

Word Journals   Once your students know basic word processing, they can use their computer lab time to make personal dictionaries using the vocabulary words you have taught them.

> Activities for teaching vocabulary are found at: **www.readingfirst.virginia. edu/index.php/elibrary/C11/.**

How Do I Teach the Language of Learning?

Teachers of younger students who are at risk are often frustrated when teaching vocabulary, because many of their students come to school unable to speak using more than three- or four-word utterances, use prepositions, or answer *where, what,* and *why* questions. Given that oral language deficits are a risk factor for later reading problems (Catts, 1991; Wilson & Risucci, 1998), these teachers' concerns are well placed. Students' oral language skills, along with listening comprehension skills, affect their ability to comprehend text. Although teaching vocabulary is essential, it is often not sufficient. Louisa Moats describes what is needed to overcome the language gap that presents additional challenges for so many students from poverty:

> From the time they enter preschool, students must experience language stimulation all day long if they are to compensate for their incoming linguistic differences. Teachers must immerse them in the rich language of books. Children need to rehearse the rules of discourse, such as staying on topic, taking turns, and giving enough information so the listener understands. Children must learn how to speak in discussions, to question, paraphrase, retell and summarize, as the recently developed standards for listening and speaking now specify. Teachers must teach directly the form, meaning, and use of words, phrases, sentences, and texts. Everything from the articulatory features of /k/ and /g/ to the construction of an organized essay is grist for the instructional mill. (Moats, 2001)

Because teachers do not have the training of speech pathologists, they often feel at a loss in developing their students' oral language skills, a loss that is substantiated by research. Close examination of typical school curricula and methods reveals that classroom exposure to literature, use of an informal language experience approach, infrequent opportunities to talk, and infrequent feedback and correction of oral language have little impact on developing students' language skills (Beimiller, 2003). By the second year of Project PRIDE, we realized that all of the kindergarten students needed a more structured language curriculum providing extensive practice. An account of the program *Language for Learning* is given in the *Research Note* section. If students who are at risk are going to comprehend written text at grade level, their classroom curriculum must ensure that the following language skills essential for learning are developed at as early an age as possible. Language curricula used in preschool and kindergarten should teach these skills.

* Answers simple "wh-" questions (who, what, where, when, and why) in a full sentence.
* Understands and answers questions for sentences that include a subject + action + object (e.g., "The girl makes cookies.") and a subject + action + location (e.g., "The camel walks on the hill.").
* Uses prepositions (on, on top of, over, in front of, in between, into, inside, beside, under, beneath, behind, in back of, through, out of).
* Understands quality (alike, same, different), amount (all, more, few), size (big, little, short), opposites (hot-cold, big-little, up-down), and categories (containers, vehicles, months, food, numbers).
* Uses articles (the, a, an) in conversation.
* Answers yes/no questions in a complete sentence.
* Knows colors, shapes, and numbers.
* Uses possessives (his, hers) and personal pronouns (we, she).
* Answers more complex "wh-" questions (e.g., "What can you do with a shovel?" "Why do you go to school?").
* Follows three-part sequence of directions (e.g., "Put your crayons in your desk, put your papers in your cubbies, and get your coats.").
* Uses *and* to chain together two concepts or actions.
* Relates information about an experience that happened in the past in more than one complete sentence.
* Uses irregular-tense verbs in conversation (hit, caught, sat).
* Speaks in complex sentences of more than four words.
* Tells what happens *first, middle,* and *last* in a sequence of events.
* Tells a story about an event or experience.
* Understands and describes the difference between things that are the same and things that are different, such as the difference between children and grown-ups.
* Uses all parts of speech in conversation.
* Uses plurals, past tense verbs, and present progressive (-ing) in speech.

Learn more about *Language for Learning* at: **https://www.sraonline.com/ products_main.html.**

How Important Is Vocabulary for Older Learners?

When an older student does not derive meaning from what she is reading, the teacher needs to assess the student's benchmark skills to determine whether she has developed alphabetic principle, can decode multisyllabic words, can read fluently, and has acquired an adequate vocabulary to read grade-level text. Whether assessment shows that reading

Research Note

Language Development

The year before Project PRIDE started, we observed kindergarten classes in all three schools and took data on students to assist in our decision making the next fall when we started coaching in the classrooms. During the observations, we noticed that although teachers read to students every day and engaged in language experience activities such as cooking, growing plants, and constructing objects related to thematic units, the language poverty of students persisted. Many students' discourse when answering teachers' questions, conversing on the playground, or describing what happened the night before was more typical of a three-year-old than an end-of-year kindergartner. Simply teaching phonemic awareness, letter sounds, and beginning decoding would be inadequate unless we could also develop the students' language skills, so necessary for comprehension.

We decided to supplement the already-established classroom language experience with the *Language for Learning* direct instruction curriculum (Engelmann & Osborn, 1999). The *Language for Learning* curriculum just described was selected because it incorporates explicit and systematic instruction of listening comprehension and oral language, provides many opportunities for each child to answer questions throughout the lessons, and introduces a careful sequence of skills. When we gave the kindergartners the curriculum pretest, our observations about their low language skills were confirmed; approximately 40% of the students had such low language skills that they tested into the beginning lessons of the program. These children were not yet using prepositions; they could not repeat a six-word sentence; they did not use articles in conversation or use the word *not* in a complete sentence, such as "He is not driving a car." Some still did not know the difference between their *chin* and *cheek* and could not differentiate between their first and last name. How could we hope to get them to fully develop reading comprehension when their language was so impoverished?

The children lowest in oral language were to receive *Language for Learning* for a half hour in groups ranging between two and eight children. In order to do this, special education teachers, student teachers, paraprofessionals, and Title I teachers were trained to teach the language groups. The teachers expressed their surprise at discovering what difficulty so many of the children had with "first" and "next" and how much practice they needed to learn those concepts. Talking about "*an* elephant" in contrast to "*a* book" and selecting the right article doesn't come easily when a child hasn't picked up that convention from the environment. After Christmas, the kindergarten teachers noticed that many of the children in *Language for Learning* were beginning to surpass their peers. The children were sequentially naming the days of the week and seasons of the year, identifying more body parts, and using plurals. It looked as if the intensive half hour of talking and more talking while sustaining attention to wait for the teacher's signal was helping these children learn language concepts more efficiently.

That year we gave the *Slingerland Listening Skills Comprehension* test to all of our kindergarten students at the beginning and end of the school year. We were interested in seeing whether the children who received *Language for Learning* made progress in listening comprehension and whether they were able to catch up to their classmates who entered kindergarten with higher language skills. The results showed that the *Language for Learning* group made significant gains in listening comprehension and that the gap between them and their peers was virtually gone. The teachers told us they felt as if they were teaching language appropriately for the first time, and that until they taught the program, they had not been aware of the many critical sequential language skills needed for more expressive conversation. They also found themselves integrating the *Language for Learning* skills into other activities throughout the day.

deficits include earlier reading skills or just vocabulary deficits, instruction should always include the direct teaching of vocabulary. An older student has not had access to the indirect learning of new words through extensive reading, and thus his reading deficit results in a smaller vocabulary.

Design of Vocabulary Instruction

Vocabulary instruction will incorporate many of the same direct and indirect teaching strategies as used with younger students, but can be more directly connected to text as the teacher discusses the author's selection of words and how the choice of a word affects the author's communication with the reader. Vocabulary instruction should rely less on synonyms and more on teaching similarities and differences between words. Beck and colleagues (2002) recommend that the teaching of vocabulary at this level incorporate four design elements: frequency, richness, extension of words beyond the classroom, and choice of vocabulary words.

Frequency   Because of the content area demands for older students, the teacher should plan on directly teaching at least 10 words per week. Words taught during previous weeks should be repeatedly reviewed.

Richness   A variety of activities should actively involve students in writing, speaking, and associating each word with other words. Activities should be designed so that students use critical thinking skills in applying what they have learned about the meaning of the word. The authors recommend that rather than have students memorize definitions, the teacher should "provide opportunities for students to use the words, explore facets of word meaning, and consider relationships among words" (Beck et al., 2002, p. 74). Answering timed true/false questions also helps students clarify and refine the meaning of new words as well as develop fluency.

Extension of Words Beyond the Classroom   The use of a *Word Wizard* chart or wall area helps students use active listening to hear new vocabulary words outside the classroom. Students earn points on the *Word Wizard* chart by bringing in evidence that they heard, saw, or used one of their assigned vocabulary words outside the classroom—in other classes, at home, in the mall, watching TV, in a book, or from any other source. McEwan (2009) describes how one middle school teacher motivated her students to use new vocabulary outside the classroom:

> I have my English students for study hall, which is a perfect time to have our little "word chats." Students have to describe when they used the word, to whom they were speaking, and exactly what they said. They can only get credit for one word per day. Amazingly, with just this little motivation, my students are using words we studied weeks ago and even other teachers are noticing their vocabulary usage. One of my C students found this activity so appealing that he is on target to be the first one to reach the 30-word prize. Javier's latest example featured his mother: "I was talking to my mom, and she was getting all dressed up to go to the movies. I told her she looked luminous." (p. 100)

Choice of Vocabulary   The choice of vocabulary words taught presents additional challenges when teaching vocabulary to older learners. A larger proportion of the words selected are from expository rather than the narrative text emphasized in the primary grades. The teacher's word selections include different considerations in content area subjects. For example, in expository text, selecting words related to the content being studied is more important than selecting those appearing more frequently in print (Marzano, 2004). Marzano and Pickering (2005) suggest a systematic process for selecting terms needed to understand expository text. First, for each subject area you teach, estimate the number of new terms that you think you can reasonably cover each week. As was earlier recommended, about two terms per day, ten per week appears to be the norm for direct vocabulary teaching, though that number may be reduced for content area instruction. For example, Marzano and Pickering recommend starting with as few as four terms per week. In a 36-week school year, the teacher would then instruct 144 words for that subject area. Next, identify the terms that you believe are critically important to the content taught. These are terms necessary for understanding the big ideas of the subject, which should also match national and state standards for the content area in question. If the number of words you select is greater than the number originally estimated, remember that Marzano's suggestion of four words per week is just a recommendation, and your students may be able to learn more words each week. If not, carefully deliberate about the importance of each word before deleting some. Finally, whenever possible, work to develop school-wide efforts to select and teach key terms in content areas (Berne & Blachowicz, 2009; Marzano, 2004). Students who are at risk benefit when instructional efforts are consistent and systematic, both within and across classrooms.

> Marzano and Pickering (2005) have compiled lists of 7,923 key vocabulary words for 11 subject areas in Grades K–12 in their book *Building Academic Vocabulary*.

How Can I Teach Vocabulary to English Language Learners?

Many vocabulary words that readers encounter have **literal,** or actual, **meanings,** such as the word *creek* in a story where Laurel, a main character, says, "I'm getting my pole and going fishing in the *creek.*" The reader can picture Laurel casting for fish in a shallow creek at the bottom of the hill where she is going fly-fishing. Other words or phrases, such as **idioms,** have **figurative meanings** where the meaning is not literal, implying more than what is said on the surface. When Stephano says, "I crashed my car and am *up a creek,*" the idiom *up a creek* means *in trouble.*

Idioms that have figurative meanings present additional challenges for English language learners. Phrases such as "to smell a rat" or "hot under the collar" must be learned as a whole, because they cannot be understood from the meanings of the separate words within them. While some idioms are regarded as slang and typically heard in oral language, other idioms are regarded as formal or informal. They are liberally sprinkled through much fiction and narrative reading, and comprehension of the text depends on the reader perceiving them as a whole and knowing their meaning.

The same recommendations given for teaching vocabulary also apply to teaching idioms. Teachers should ignore the more obscure idioms and focus their teaching on ones that students are more likely to encounter in their reading. Idioms with clear meanings should be taught first. When first teaching an idiom, teachers should consider whether learning the literal meaning of the idiom will help the student remember it. For example, the idiom "roll with the punches" means to make it through times of hardship. This phrase came to be used because rolling with the punches is a technique used in boxing where the objective is to avoid receiving a direct hit. The boxer tries to move away from the punch in an attempt to avoid the blow or at least take a less painful, glancing blow. Because this example helps the reader make sense of the idiom, the teacher could explain it when she introduces the word.

Whether the teacher refers to the literal background of the phrase or not, each idiom has a figurative meaning that the student can apply to text. Irugo (1986) recommends that teachers portray the meaning of the idiom as concretely as possible. Pictures that depict the meaning of the idiom can help the student remember the phrase, as can stories in which the phrase is used in a humorous context. Unless an idiom is supported by context in the beginning, English language learners are less likely to remember it, so having students role-play the idiom or act out sentences containing the idiom are effective teaching techniques. If the

FIGURE 9.11 A Drop in the Bucket

Source: www.goenglish.com/adropinthebucket.asp.

students' first language has a similar idiom, connecting the English idiom to that one will help the students' retention of the new phrase. Mr. Swiggums displayed the picture in Figure 9.11 on the SMART Board in front of his classroom and explained that "a drop in the bucket" is something that is not very important because it is small. He asked his students to look at the picture and see how small the water drop looked in the much larger bucket. A drop in a large bucket isn't important because you would need so many drops to fill the bucket. Next Mr. Swiggums asked his students to read in unison "A drop in the bucket," which was written next to the picture. He wanted to be sure that everyone clearly heard the new idiom and could read it. Mr. Swiggums explained that when Charlotte broke her pencil she said, "It's just a drop in the bucket," because Charlotte's dog was sick, her mom had yelled at her that morning for ripping her dress, and her best friend wasn't talking to her. Compared to the bigger problems of her dog's illness, her mom's anger, and losing her best friend, breaking a pencil was not important. Breaking the pencil was a very little problem. Breaking the pencil was just "a drop in the bucket." As Mr. Swiggums said "just a drop in the bucket," he shrugged his shoulders, threw out his hands, and made a facial expression reflecting that breaking the pencil was not important. He then asked his students to mimic his body language as they said "just a drop in the bucket" together.

In order to help develop students' understanding of English idioms, Celce-Murcia, Brinton, and Goodwin (2002) recommend that teachers use idioms for controlled practice activities when students are learning to use correct rhythm patterns and word stress in connected speech phrases. The following idioms, all containing the word *talk,* are recommended for an oral speech practice session:

> all talk and no action
> talk is cheap
> talk a blue streak
> talk shop
> talk through your hat
> talk someone's head off (Celce-Murcia et al., 2002, p. 170)

> For English as a Second Language resources and activities related to teaching vocabulary, visit **http://ucaeliteachers.pbworks.com/Websites+and+Online+Resources+for+Students.**

> To learn the origins of some of the most common idioms used in the United States, visit **http://www.pride-unlimited.com/probono/idioms3.html#q** and **http://www.goenglish.com/Idioms.asp.**

A teacher using this strategy would go through the list, first saying each phrase before students repeated it, imitating the teacher as closely as possible. Although students would not yet know the meaning of many of these idioms, they would be gaining familiarity with hearing the key words used within the larger idioms.

A number of Internet websites have defined idioms and illustrate them with descriptive or humorous pictures. Downloading the pictures from these sites gives the teacher easy access to instant demonstration materials. In the general reference section of larger bookstores, teachers can also find worksheets and explanations about how common idioms originated.

Fortunately, preliminary research suggests that strategies that are effective for teaching vocabulary to English-only students are also effective for English language learners (Silverman, 2007). In fact, Silverman's research suggests that English language learners' progress in response to systematic, explicit vocabulary instruction may be even greater than their English-only counterparts. Ways that effective vocabulary instruction can be delivered to both English language learners and English-only learners are described in the *Technology* section.

Technology

Using Technology to Teach Vocabulary

The National Reading Panel report (2000) indicates that computer technology can benefit the development of reading vocabulary. Several research studies investigating computer-aided vocabulary instruction for students who are at risk report increased scores on vocabulary assessments given after the conclusion of the computer intervention (Horton, Lovitt, & Givens, 1988; Segers & Verhoeven, 2003). However, too few rigorous studies have been conducted to determine what type of computer instruction is most effective in teaching reading vocabulary. Because software programmers have used a number of different strategies in their reading vocabulary teaching programs, teachers can be confused by all of the options. We have identified some of the current instructional design features available in software programs for teaching vocabulary so you can be a more informed consumer when selecting a program.

The buyer must beware of spending money for a program that is little more than a standard vocabulary worksheet. In these programs the student either matches a definition to each vocabulary term or writes the word of a definition. If the answer is correct, a pleasant chime sounds or text on the screen indicates that the answer is correct. If the answer is not correct, an unpleasant beep sounds or text pops up indicating an error. Student errors do not affect the sequence of instruction, and the student is expected to begin answering the next question whether he was right or wrong. A score is displayed at the end of the activity.

Vocabulary computer programs with more sophisticated designs may include some of the following features. At this point in time, however, regardless of the feature involved, it appears that when adults are meaningfully involved in children's computer-based instruction, the effects are greater (Nir-Gal & Klein, 2004).

- **Immediate feedback for answers**—When students answer incorrectly, the program will either reteach the word or display the correct answer.
- **Effective error correction**—When students answer incorrectly, after leading the student to answer correctly, the program will ask the same question again so that the student has the opportunity to answer correctly one more time.
- **Digitized or synthesized speech**—A study by Hebert and Murdock (1994) showed that students learn more vocabulary when a computer program integrates speech with the computer instruction.

- **Pictures or animation for teaching**—Some programs teach initial vocabulary displaying pictures or animations to illustrate new words. For example, the word *locomotive* might be illustrated by a train chugging down a track. Programs for younger students who are not yet reading often require students to select pictures that match a word spoken by a story character.
- **A variety of student responses appropriate for students' age and developmental level**—Students may click a mouse or touch their finger to the screen to select a vocabulary word or picture, move an object to a picture of a vocabulary word, paint pictures of vocabulary words, type in letters of a vocabulary word, select multiple-choice options related to the vocabulary word (e.g., antonym, synonym, correct sentence with blank, definition), or select key vocabulary terms written in hypertext (see below). Students' hands are not large enough to learn word processing until third grade, so programs for younger students should utilize a mouse or point-touch screen.
- **Easy record keeping**—Some programs allow students to save their scores or the programs automatically save their scores so the teacher can monitor progress.
- **Number of new vocabulary words learned**—Some programs introduce large sets of vocabulary words; others limit the number of vocabulary words introduced and do not introduce more until students have success with the first set. In one study, Johnson, Gersten, and Carnine (1987) studied two groups of students in Grades 9 through 12. One group learned vocabulary from a computer program that introduced small sets of only seven words; the other group's program introduced a larger set of 25 words. At the end of the intervention, the researchers concluded that the students who learned from the program that introduced small sets of words learned the specified 50 vocabulary words more quickly.
- **Teacher selection of vocabulary words**—Some flexible programs allow the teacher to input up to 20 vocabulary words, definitions, and sentences. Other programs teach predetermined vocabulary words.
- **Motivation**—Software programs teaching vocabulary have a wide variety of motivational strategies. Some programs teach vocabulary words in the

Continued

context of playing games, including "Indiana Jones"–type adventures or Save the Planet mysteries; some teach vocabulary within the context of interesting stories; some attach success with the ability to earn clues to solve a mystery; some use percentage correct scores as a motivator. Always check to see that the motivator does not consume too much instructional time.

■ **Hypertext**—During the past fifteen years, **hypertext** has increasingly been used as one computer software strategy to teach vocabulary. With hypertext, the software designers link designated words (which are usually indicated by a different text color) to a database. Depending on their preferences, readers can select the designated words and bring on-screen the information in the database. Clicking on a word might link the reader to a definition of the word, to a picture of the word, to a clue for figuring out the word, or to a video of someone describing the word. Students reading electronic books on screen can select a word and immediately obtain information on it. More research is still needed to determine whether hypertext is an effective vocabulary-teaching strategy and, if so, which kinds of hypertext work best with what types of students. Note the visual aspects of the hypertext. Programmers indicate that hypertext of dark letters on a light background is less tiring for the reader than the reverse.

What Games and Activities Will Reinforce Students' New Vocabulary and Language Skills?

If students who are at risk are going to learn the vocabulary they need for success in reading more difficult text, vocabulary and language instruction must be ongoing throughout the school day, during transition periods between classes, and in science, math, art, social studies, and music classes.

Link to a free talking-picture dictionary at **www.languageguide.org/english.** Pictures are arranged into categories such as insects or colors. Running the mouse over the picture triggers a hypertext box containing the spelling of the word while a voice simultaneously says the word.

In Ms. DeMarco's class, vocabulary development is integrated into almost every daily activity. During morning announcements, the principal talks about the inspirational word of the week. After introducing the definition for the word *honorable*, the principal briefly uses the word in context to describe an individual who accomplished great things because he or she had honorable traits. The principal talks about an honorable action the person did. By the end of the week, everyone in the school knows the word *honorable*. After announcements, Ms. DeMarco, the teacher, tells students to think of someone who could be described by the mystery word. As students wait in line to go to the bathroom, she holds an impromptu discussion about individuals who the children believe have honorable characteristics.

When the literacy block of time begins, Ms. DeMarco directly preteaches three words that are in the story. A vocabulary word from last week is reviewed. As students practice reading new words that will be in the story, she selects one or two that are more difficult for the students to decode, because they don't know the meaning. Ms. DeMarco quickly gives the definition of the word and tells the meaning before asking everyone to say the meaning. She then asks several questions that force the students to use the new word in their answer. During the second reading of the story, she asks several questions requiring students to use their new vocabulary words. Students are expected to answer in complete sentences so they will get practice developing their language skills. Spelling instruction provides an opportunity to talk again about one of the words on the list, *straddle*. Because everyone needs a stretch, Ms. DeMarco asks everyone to straddle their desk chairs, to touch the floor, to stand up, and to straddle their chairs again before going back to work.

The time allotted for writing brings more opportunities to use new words. Ms. DeMarco asks the students to write about what the fox saw on his morning route to work. Besides asking students to use the vocabulary word *route* in their written paragraphs, Ms. DeMarco informs the students that she wants them to use two other vocabulary words, *creatures* and *enchanted*. Ms. DeMarco always has students work on grammar at the end of the literacy time block, and today's practice exercises using irregular past-tense forms of verbs are so difficult that she decides to have the students practice in unison so she can provide modeling and error corrections until they have more success with using these words in sentences. When students line up for lunch, they have to say the name of a friend and an adjective starting with the same letter as that name. Everyone had enjoyed this grammar activity so much earlier in the week that Ms. DeMarco used variations of it during free times.

The rest of the day is as vocabulary–language intensive as the morning. Ms. DeMarco misses no opportunities in math, science, or social studies to teach related vocabulary terms. She is always informed about what students are learning in art or music class, so she can reinforce new vocabulary learned in those classes. Ms. DeMarco anchors her direct teaching of vocabulary by having students read, spell, and write new vocabulary words as well as use them in oral communication. If there are a few moments when students are waiting to go home at the end of the day, she will throw in a quick vocabulary or language game. Some of the game activities she interjects at those times follow.

Absurdity Is Fun

What would happen if a cougar startled everyone at recess? Why aren't our shoes made of concrete? What would happen if our shoes were made of concrete? What would happen if a mouse made a thundering noise? Ms. DeMarco likes to ask absurd questions because they are excellent for getting children to think and express their ideas.

Thumbs-Up–Thumbs-Down

Ms. DeMarco's students needed more practice identifying complete sentences. First she taught her students to identify complete sentences by having them select the complete sentences from a list that included both complete and incomplete sentences. Then, Ms. DeMarco started doing the following activity. She put up a large picture on the board and asked students to describe in a complete short sentence what they saw (e.g., "There is a train." "There is a bridge."). Next, she had her students create more complex sentences using connectors (e.g., "There is a train, and there is a bridge," or better still, "There is a train crossing over a covered bridge."). In order to get everyone to participate, she had the other students in the class indicate if their classmate used a complete sentence or not by giving a soundless "thumbs-up" or "thumbs-down." When students gave incomplete sentences, she immediately moved into a My Turn correction and had everyone say the complete sentence after her. During this activity, she tried to use pictures that enabled students to use some of their new vocabulary words.

Plurals, Plurals, and More

Either because of dialect or because English was their second language, many students in Ms. DeMarco's class did not correctly use plurals, especially irregular ones, in formal syntax when answering questions or writing stories. She tried to include a plural–singular discrimination activity in her classroom schedule several times a week, even if for only a short time, to provide practice. When students made errors, she used an effective error correction.

Ms. DeMarco divided the class into two teams to play the plural game. Everyone on Team 1 was given a card with *yes* written on one side and *no* written on the other. Once the card was up, it couldn't be switched or the team didn't get a point. The members of Team 2 sat in a line, ready to walk up to the front and answer questions. Ms. DeMarco used a new vocabulary word the students had been learning or a word whose plural form needed practice. The first student on Team 2 walked up to the front and Ms. DeMarco said, *"I see one canyon."* She then said, *"Say it for six."* The same student had to answer, *"I see six canyons."* After the student said the sentence, the Team 1 members held up their cards to indicate whether the correct answer was given. Students on Team 1 got a point if the correct plural was used. Students on Team 2 got a point if every card (or 9 out of 10 cards) had the correct answer. Some questions that Ms. DeMarco asked included these:

> *"I see a **deer**. Say it for **eight**."*
>
> *"A **chime** rang today. Say it for **three**."*
>
> *"Kwame fought a **lion**. Say it for **two**."*

Strategies for motivating your students to do their best during reading class are described in *In Your Classroom.*

In Your Classroom

Motivating Your Students to Do Their Best

When you are conducting a challenging reading class, you cannot afford to waste a minute of instructional time dealing with disruptive behaviors. Before the school year begins, be proactive and plan the physical classroom environment to reflect environmental strategies supported by research as effective ways to help students stay on task, focused on their work. One of your first decisions should be determining where students will sit during large and small reading groups. Studies investigating the behavior of high-risk students showed that students have more on-task behavior and decreased disruptive behavior when they have more personal space. In classrooms where students have more space between each other, teachers are even rated by their students as more sensitive and friendly (Paine, Darch, Deutchman, Radicchi, & Rosellini, 1983). If students sit at desks, teachers often can reduce behaviors that are disruptive to the class by simply moving the desks farther apart.

In younger classrooms, students often sit on the rug during group reading time. In classrooms that are not physically large enough to have a large rug area, the wigglier children will often begin jostling each other with their elbows while invading each other's personal space. In these circumstances, teachers find themselves frequently correcting students to keep their hands and feet to themselves. In these smaller classrooms, chairs might present a better alternative for getting students to do their best work. Sometimes only one or two students in the class have a difficult time when the group is reading on the rug. For those stu-

dents, a carpet square, a taped-off area, or a chair often provides the structure needed to listen and participate in the group. If older students sit around tables, reducing the number of students at one table provides more space between them.

Use of frequent activity shifts and periodic physical movement to provide students with the opportunity to stretch will also help students' concentration. The younger the student, the more activity shifts are needed. For example, after students who were sitting on the rug practiced the sound for the letter *n*, one teacher inserted a 2-minute activity where every time she said the *n* sound, the students jumped up like frogs. Then, after a short practice session blending words, the teacher asked everyone to walk to their tables to write the letter *n*. The writing practice was followed by a game where everyone stood up and in unison answered *yes* or *no* to vocabulary questions the teacher asked. Although a teacher in an older classroom can stretch teaching activities out over longer periods of time, periodic 1- or 2-minute stretch breaks can still release energy before students begin the next activity.

Teachers should also be sensitive to students' need for water. If students are actively answering in unison, their throats become parched after a while, causing them to become uncomfortable. In order to avoid this distraction, some teachers allow their students to carry water bottles; others always stop for a moment at the water fountain when the class is in the hall en route to special activities.

APPLIED ACTIVITIES

1. Answer the following fact-or-fiction questions about vocabulary using references from research sources cited in the chapter or from information on the website resources listed in the sidebars.

   a. Research shows that children learn more words directly, from instruction in school, than they learn indirectly, from listening or conversing. Is this fact or fiction? Explain why.

   b. The meaning of most words can be discerned using the context. Is this fact or fiction? Explain why.

   c. It is important that students learn the meaning of all unknown words in the story before they read the story. Is this fact or fiction? Explain why.

2. The following vocabulary words have been identified in your reading series for the upcoming story about a farmer who planted a seed that grew into a large turnip: *granddaughter, planted, grew, strong, enormous,* and *turnip*. Assuming you have only enough time to teach your second-grade students the meaning of two of these words, which words would you choose to teach? Justify your selections.

3. For the next 48 hours, make a list of words that you don't know the meaning of and note where you encountered each word. For example, you may not know the meaning of a word used by a TV broadcaster, a word mentioned in a lecture, a word you read in the newspaper, or a word in the directions for your new software program.

4. Develop either a student-friendly definition or a synonym for each of the following vocabulary words: *survive, frontier, nearby, tame,* and *orchard*.

5. For two of the words above, one using a synonym and the other a definition, develop a series of student questions to teach the meaning of the word using examples and nonexamples. Model your questions after ones shown in Figures 9.1 and 9.2. For each word, include at least three positive and three negative examples.

6. Develop a keyword for one of the following words: *burly, cram, epic, enzyme,* or *powwow*. In developing the keyword, use a similar process to the one used for the word *apex* in Figure 9.7.

7. Develop a semantic map to teach students the range of words that can be used to represent the word *charismatic*. Your semantic map should help students better understand the concept of "charismatic" by categorizing its different qualities.

8. Shown below is a passage from a Grade 2 basal. Tell how you would teach students to use context clues to figure out the meaning of the word *lack*. The thick cloud of dust, rock, and smoke would swirl around the world, blocking the sunlight for months or even years. Without sunlight, the earth would grow very cold. Their idea is that the <u>lack</u> of sunshine caused dinosaurs and other life forms to die.

9. Identify the words below that you would teach using morphemic analysis. For one of these words, develop a mini-script telling what you would say to your students when teaching them to use morphemic analysis to figure out its meaning.

careless	bicolor	winless
confusing	demented	unspeakable
discouraged	useful	substandard
discipline	uncomfortable	revocable

10. Your students came across the following sentence in their readers: "The boys and girls made a *dash* for the playground." You had them look up the word *dash* in their dictionaries and they found the following three meanings:

    a. a rush: We made a *dash* for the bus.

    b. a small amount: Put in just a *dash* of pepper.

    c. a short race: He won the fifty-yard *dash*.

    d. Develop a mini-script that you could use to teach students to figure out which meaning of *dash* is used in the story.

11. After lunch you can squeeze in 10 more minutes of vocabulary instruction. This week you have directly taught the following vocabulary words: *slight, hull, reflected, curve, eclipse,* and *prairie*. Plan activities you could do during that time this week to provide more practice for your class.

12. Select two idioms that contain the same word and describe at least two concrete activities you could use to teach the idioms to English language learners.

13. Analyze the strengths and weaknesses of a vocabulary software program.

REFERENCES

Adams, M., & Bereiter, C. (1995). *Collections for young scholars*. Chicago: Open Court Publishing.

Allen, J. (1999). *Words, words, words: Teaching vocabulary in grades 4–12*. York, ME: Stenhouse.

Armbruster, B., Lehr, F., & Osborn, J. (2001). *Put reading first: The research building blocks for teaching children to read*. Washington, DC: Partnership for Reading.

Baker, D., & Bettino, C. (1988). *Easy English dictionary*. D. McCarr, J. McCarr, L. Eckert, & S. Natwick (Eds.). Austin, TX: Pro-Ed.

Barrett, J. (1978). *Cloudy with a chance of meatballs*. New York: Atheneum Books.

Barton, J. (1996). Interpreting character emotions for literature comprehension. *Journal of Adolescent & Adult Literacy, 40*(1), 22–28. Cited in H. W. Catts & A. G. Kamhi (2005), *Language and reading disabilities* (2nd ed.). Boston: Allyn & Bacon, p. 191.

Baumann, J., Edwards, E., Boland, E., Olejnik, S., & Kame'enui, E. (2003). Vocabulary tricks: Effects of instruction in morphology and context on fifth-grade students' ability to derive and infer word meanings. *American Educational Research Journal, 40*(2), 447–494.

Beck, I., McKeown, M., & Kucan, L. (2002). *Bringing words to life: Robust vocabulary instruction.* New York: The Guilford Press.

Beck, I. L., & McKeown, M. G. (2007). Increasing young low-income children's oral vocabulary repertoires through rich and focused instruction. *The Elementary School Journal, 107*(3), 251–271.

Beck, I. L., McKeown, M. G., & Kucan, L. (2008). *Creating robust vocabulary: Frequently asked questions and extended examples* (p. 35). New York: The Guilford Press.

Berger, M. (1995). *All about electricity.* New York: Scholastic.

Berne, J., & Blachowicz, C. L. (2009). What reading teachers say about vocabulary instruction: Voices from the classroom. *The Reading Teacher, 62,* 314–323.

Biemiller, A. (2001). Teaching vocabulary: Early, direct, and sequential. *American Educator, 25,* 24–28.

Biemiller, A. (2003). Oral comprehension sets the ceiling on reading comprehension. *American Educator, 27*(1), 23–25.

Bos, C. S., & Vaughn, S. (2008). *Strategies for teaching students with learning and behavior problems* (7th ed.). Boston: Allyn & Bacon.

Carey, S. (1978). The child as word learner. In M. Halle, J. Bresnan, & G. Miller (Eds.), *Linguistic theory and psychological reality* (pp. 264–293). Cambridge, MA: MIT Press.

Carnine, D. W., Silbert, J., Kame'enui, E. J., & Tarver, S. (2010). *Direct instruction reading* (5th ed.). New Jersey: Merrill Prentice Hall.

Catts, H. (1991). The relationship between speech-language impairments and reading disabilities. *Journal of Speech and Hearing Research, 36,* 948–958.

Celce-Murcia, M., Brinton, D., & Goodwin, J. (2002). *Teaching pronunciation: A reference for teachers of English to speakers of other languages.* Cambridge: Cambridge University Press.

Cobuild, C. (2005). *Collins COBUILD dictionary.* Florence, KY: Heinle ELT.

Cole, J. (1997). *The magic school bus and the electric field trip.* New York: Scholastic.

Collections for young scholars. (1995). Chicago: Open Court Publishing.

Coyne, D. M., Loftus, S., Zipoli, R., & Kapp, S. (2009). Direct vocabulary instruction in kindergarten: Teaching for breadth versus depth. *The Elementary School Journal, 110*(1), 1–18.

Educational Resources Inc. (2004). *Strategies for high-stakes tests.* Unpublished manuscript.

Ehri, L. (2000). Learning to read and learning to spell: Two sides of a coin. *Topics in Language Disorders, 20*(3), 19–49.

Ehri, L. (2005). Learning to read words: Theory, findings, and issues. *Scientific Studies of Reading, 9,* 167–188.

Engelmann, S., & Osborn, J. (1999). *Language for learning.* Columbus, OH: SRA/McGraw-Hill.

Epstein, S., & Epstein, B. (1977). *The first book of electricity.* New York: Franklin Watts.

Espin, C. A., Busch, T. W., Shin, J., & Kruschwitz, R. (2001). Curriculum-based measurement in the content areas: Validity of vocabulary-matching as an indicator of performance in social studies. *Learning Disabilities Research & Practice, 16*(3), 142–151.

Foil, C. R., & Alber, S. R. (2002). Fun and effective ways to build your students' vocabulary. *Intervention in School and Clinic, 37*(3), 131–139.

Gersten, R., Fuchs, L. S., Williams, J. P., & Baker, S. (2001). Teaching reading comprehension strategies to students with learning disabilities: A review of research. *Review of Educational Research, 71*(1), 279–320.

Hart, B., & Risley, T. R. (1995). *Meaningful differences in the everyday experiences of young American children.* Baltimore: Paul H. Brookes.

Hebert, B. M., & Murdock, J. Y. (1994). Comparing three computer-aided instruction output modes to teach vocabulary words to students with learning disabilities. *Learning Disabilities & Practice, 9*(3), 136–141.

Hirsch, E. D. (2003). Reading comprehension requires knowledge of words and the world: Scientific insights into the fourth-grade slump and the nation's stagnant reading comprehension scores. *American Education, 27,* 10–48.

Horton, S., Lovitt, T., & Givens, A. (1988). A computer-based vocabulary program for three categories of student. *British Journal of Educational Technology, 19*(2), 131–143.

Irugo, S. (1986). A piece of cake: Learning and teaching idioms. *ELT Journal, 40*(3), 236–242.

Jitendra, A. K., Edwards, L. L., Sacks, G., & Jacobson, L. A. (2004). What research says about vocabulary instruction for students with learning disabilities. *Exceptional Children, 70,* 299–322.

Johnson, G., Gersten, R., & Carnine, D. (1987). Effects of instructional design variables on vocabulary acquisition of LD students: A study of computer-assisted instruction. *Journal of Learning Disabilities, 20*(4), 206–213.

Joshi, R. M., Treiman, R., Carreker, S., & Moats, L. (2008–2009). How words cast their spell: Spelling is an integral part of learning the language, not memorization. *American Educator, winter,* 8–18, 42–43. http://www.aft.org/pubsreports/american_educator/issues/winter08_09/joshi.pdf

Klingner, J. K., Vaughn, S., & Boardman, A. (2007). *Teaching reading comprehension to students with learning difficulties.* New York: The Guilford Press, pp. 49–51.

Marzano, R. J. (2004). *Building background knowledge for academic achievement: Research on what works in schools.* Alexandria, VA: Association for Supervision and Curriculum Development.

Marzano, R. J., & Pickering, D. J. (2005). *Building academic vocabulary: Teachers manual.* Alexandria, VA: Association for Supervision and Curriculum Development.

Maslen, B., & Maslen, J. (2006). *Bob Books: Beginning readers.* New York: Scholastic.

Mastropieri, M. A. (1988). Using the keyword methods. *Teaching Exceptional Children, 20,* 4–8.

McEwan, E. (2009). *Teach them all to read: Catching kids before they fall through the cracks* (2nd ed.). Thousand Oaks, CA: Corwin.

McKeown, M., Beck, I., Omanson, R., & Pople, M. (1985). Some effects of the nature and frequency of vocabulary instruction on the knowledge and use of words. *Reading Research Quarterly, 20,* 522–535.

Miller, A. D., Barbetta, P. M., & Heron, T. E. (1994). START tutoring: Designing, training, implementing, adapting, and evaluating tutoring programs for school and home settings. In R. Gardner et al. (Eds.), *Behavior analysis in education: Focus on measurably superior instruction* (pp. 265–282). Monterey, CA: Brooks/Cole.

Moats, L. (Summer, 2001). Overcoming the language gap. *American Educator, 25*(2), 5, 8–9. http://www.aft.org/pubsreports/american_educator/summer2001/lang_gap_moats.html

National Reading Panel. (2000). *Teaching children to read: An evidence-based assessment of the scientific research literature on reading and its implications for reading instruction.* Washington, DC: National Institute of Child Health and Human Development.

Nir-Gal, O., & Klein, P. S. (2004). Computers for cognitive development in early childhood: The teacher's role in the computer learning environment. *Information in childhood education annual,* p. 97.

Paine, S., Darch, C., Deutchman, L., Radicchi, J., & Rosellini, L. (1983). *Structuring your classroom for academic success.* Champaign, IL: Research Press.

Pany, D., Jenkins, J. R., & Schreck, J. (1982). Vocabulary instruction: Effects on word knowledge and reading comprehension. *Learning Disability Quarterly, 5,* 202–215.

Ruddell, R. B. (1999). *Teaching children to read and write: Becoming an influential teacher* (2nd ed.). Boston: Allyn & Bacon.

Schmitt, N., & Carter, R. (2000). The lexical advantage of narrow reading for second language learners. *TESOL Journal, 9*(1), 4–9.

Scott, J. (2005). Opportunities to acquire new meaning from text. In E. Hiebert & M. Kamil (Eds.), *Teaching and learning vocabulary: Bringing research to practice* (pp. 45–68). Hillsdale, NJ: Erlbaum.

Segers, E., & Verhoeven, L. (2003). Effect of vocabulary training by computer in kindergarten. *Journal of Computer-Assisted Learning, 19,* 557–566.

Silverman, R. D. (2007). Vocabulary development of English-language and English-only learners in kindergarten. *The Elementary School Journal, 107*(4), 365–384.

Sousa, D. (2005). *How the brain learns to read.* Thousand Oaks, CA: Corwin.

Stahl, S. A., & Fairbanks, M. M. (1986). The effects of vocabulary instruction: A model-based meta-analysis. *Review of Educational Research, 56*(1), 72–110.

Stanovich, K. E. (1986). Matthew effects in reading: Some consequences of individual differences in the acquisition of literacy. *Reading Research Quarterly, 21,* 360–407.

Taylor, H. (1993). *Coyote places the stars.* New York: Simon & Schuster.

Wilson, B., & Risucci, D. (1998). The early identification of developmental language disorders and the prediction of the acquisition of reading skills. In R. Masland & M. Masland (Eds.), *Preschool prevention of reading failure* (pp. 187–203). Parkton, MD: York Press.

Wood, R. (1997). *Electricity and magnetism fundamentals.* New York: McGraw-Hill.

10 Comprehension

Objectives

After reading this chapter, you will be able to:

1. Describe the knowledge and skills students need to comprehend narrative and expository text and the four key factors that influence comprehension.

2. Identify effective general teaching methods and strategies for teaching students to comprehend text.

3. Implement strategies for teaching comprehension at the sentence, paragraph, and text level.

4. Describe instruction that incorporates multiple strategies to maximize student gains in reading comprehension and motivate students to read more widely.

5. Describe ways to screen, diagnose student needs, and monitor progress in reading comprehension in a multi-tier or RTI model.

6. Identify commercial reading programs that can give struggling readers in Tier 3 a more systematic, explicit approach to learning comprehension skills.

7. Prepare students for passing high-stakes tests in reading.

8. Implement strategies for teaching comprehension skills to older students and English language learners.

What Is Reading Comprehension, and Why Teach It?

When the principal distributed the state test results, Ms. Linder was eager to see her students' reading scores. Her fantasy was that everyone would meet the state standards, but reality was far from that. Ms. Linder noticed that most of the students in her class who met or exceeded standards on the test had also met benchmark on the most recent DIBELS assessment in Oral Reading Fluency. But that still left the 40% of her students who had not passed the state test! Not content with having 40% of her students not make AYP, Ms. Linder thought about each of the students who had not passed the state test. Several of the students had poor fluency skills and read text with longer words very slowly. Two children had poor oral language skills. One puzzle was Ricardo, a student whose primary language was Spanish and who scored above benchmark on the DIBELS Oral Reading Fluency assessment but still failed to meet standards on the state test. Benjamin, a student who was diagnosed with dyslexia, struggled with reading fluency but had strong oral language and reasoning skills. Although Benjamin scored below benchmark on the DIBELS, he surprised Ms. Linder by scoring above the standard on the state test.

What different kinds of reading problems did Ms. Linder's students exhibit?

How will the presence of these problems affect the way Ms. Linder teaches comprehension?

Reading comprehension is the active process of obtaining meaning from written text. As in Ms. Linder's class, students' comprehension problems result from a variety of factors. Shankweiler, Lundquist, and Dreyer (1999) studied a group of poor comprehenders and found that most of the students who could not comprehend had decoding problems of comparable magnitude; only about 10% of the poor comprehenders had comprehension problems even though they were good decoders. Often these poor comprehenders were English language learners such as Ricardo, who moved to this country two years ago. In contrast to the first group, a few students are always able to compensate for slow decoding, as Benjamin did. Just as with phonemic awareness, alphabetic principle, fluency, advanced word reading, and vocabulary, "one size does not fit all" when it comes to reading comprehension.

In its simplest form, reading is the ability to decode and understand the meaning of written words. However, the process of deciphering the meaning of written words is exceedingly complex because it is influenced by a number of important factors including the person who is reading, the text being read, the task the reader is trying to accomplish, and the context in which the reading is being done (RAND Reading Study Group, 2002). A visual display of these four factors is shown in Figure 10.1, followed by a more in-depth description. Effective comprehension instruction takes into account all four factors.

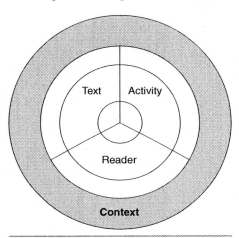

FIGURE 10.1 Factors That Affect Reading Comprehension

Text

Several characteristics of the text itself influence whether a reader comprehends text; these include text readability, text structure, and text organization. Traditionally, educators have looked to text readability as one gauge of text difficulty. Text readability formulae take into account factors such as sentence and word length as well as syntactic structure. For example, to calculate the projected grade level of a text, a teacher can use the Dale-Chall readability formula, which is based on an average sentence length and the number of unfamiliar words (Chall & Dale, 1995). The authors of this readability formula determined that readers typically find it easier to read, process, and recall a passage if the words are familiar and the sentences shorter. During the past two decades, the emphasis has shifted from classic readability formulae to other text features that also affect comprehension. The clarity of writing contributes to the ease of comprehending a text, including the presence of clear pronoun references, explicit or obvious connectives such as *because, since,* or *therefore,* and transition elements between ideas (Hiebert, 1999).

Text structure refers to the way certain types of text are organized to form a framework or pattern (Bos & Vaughn, 2008; Englert & Thomas, 1987). Students who can recognize these patterns have an easier time understanding what they read. The two broadest categories of text, **narrative text** (fiction) and **expository text** (nonfiction) are then broken down into subcategories. Science fiction, tall tales, and mystery stories are subgenres of narrative text. Examples of expository text include biographies, letters, and textbooks. Narrative text is generally much easier to comprehend than expository text, which is characterized by a greater density of technical vocabulary as well as concepts requiring considerable student background knowledge. Keep in mind that comprehension in one kind of reading matter does not automatically transfer to comprehension in others. Jahil's ease in understanding and remembering expository science text does not ensure that he will have the same facility with narrative text. If Jahil does not understand irony, he will have difficulty comprehending a narrative text that is satirical. Table 10.1 lists some differences between narrative and expository text.

It is important to teach your students what text structures are, how to recognize them in text, and how to use them to understand what they are reading. Narrative text, which has a **plot,** can be organized into meaningful parts called **story grammars** including **theme, setting,** character, problem, attempts at resolution, resolution, and reactions. Later in this chapter, visual organizers called story maps, which are used to help organize students' thinking about narrative text, will be discussed in more detail.

Expository text is also organized in specific ways, but unlike narrative text, each piece of expository text does not have the same structure. Expository text usually includes more than one text structure. Fortunately, there are key structures that occur with enough frequency to make manageable the assessing of common expository text structures and the teaching of their identification as a comprehension tool. Table 10.2 shows a list of the five common expository text structures, the ideas they communicate to the reader, and the key words that signal their presence.

Each of these expository text structures has a related graphic organizer or organizers that teachers can use to assist comprehension during or after reading. A sample of some of those organizers and how to teach them will be provided later in this chapter.

TABLE 10.1   Comparison of Narrative and Exposition

Narrative	Expository
Purpose to entertain.	Purpose to inform.
Consistent text structure; all narratives have same basic organization.	Variable text structures; different genres have different structure.
Focus on character motivations, intentions, goals.	Focus on factual information and abstract ideas.
Often require multiple perspective taking understanding points of view of different characters.	Expected to take the perspective of the writer of the text.
Can use pragmatic inferences, i.e., inference from similar experiences.	Must use logical-deductive inferences based on information in texts.
Connective words not critical—primarily *and, then, go.*	Connective words critical—wide variety of connectives, e.g., *because, before, after, when, if–then, therefore.*
Each text can stand alone.	Expected to integrate information across texts.
Comprehension is generally assessed informally in discussion.	Comprehension often assessed in formal, structured tests.

Source: Catts, H. W., & Kamhi, A. G. (1999). *Language and reading disabilities* (2nd ed.). Boston: Pearson Education, p. 159. Copyright © 1999 by Pearson Education. Reprinted by permission of the publisher.

TABLE 10.2   Expository Text Types and Characteristics

Text Type	Function	Signal Words
Descriptive	The text describes something or where something is.	**Description signals** let the reader know where: *above, over, under, outside, between, down, of, in front of, on top of, beside, to the right/ left, behind, across, along, outside, inside, near, appears to be, nearby*
Sequence/ procedural	The text tells how to do or make something. The text relates a sequence of events.	**Sequence** or **time signals** let the reader know information about *when* something is happening: *first . . . next . . . then, second . . . third, following this step, finally, initially, afterward, preceding, while, as, then, at last, now, ever since, in quick succession, eventually*
Cause/ effect	The text gives reasons why something happens. The text tells what might happen next.	**Cause/effect signals** let the reader know when one thing is the result of something else: *because, since, reasons, then, therefore, for this reason, results, effects, consequently, so, in order, thus, as a result, thus, hence*
Problem/ solution	The text states a problem and offers solutions to the problem.	**Problem/solution signals** let the reader know what the problem is or what the solution is
Comparison/ contrast	The text shows how two things are the same or different.	**Compare/contrast signals** let the reader know about how things are alike or different: *different, same, alike, similar, although, however, on the other hand, but yet, still, rather than, instead of, as opposed to*
Enumerative	The text gives a list of things that are related to the topic.	**Example signals** let the reader know that this is what something means: *an example is, for instance, another, next, finally, for example, in other words, such as, in the same way as, specifically, much like, similar to*

A third text characteristic that affects comprehension is *text organization.* Text that is clearly organized around "big ideas" explicitly communicated to the reader is easier to understand than text emphasizing smaller details. Big ideas are the major concepts in a text that give meaning to all the smaller details. For example, if, in the title or an introductory list of objectives, the author of a science article highlights the big idea that the flow of energy can be controlled by conductors and insulators, and then makes an explicit connection in the text between this big idea and smaller details, the reader will be more likely to understand the text and generate insightful questions about the content.

Comprehension involves understanding various types and levels of information. The ease with which children access information from text depends on how explicitly it is written. For example, information directly stated in the text is easier to understand than information that needs to be inferred. Because texts vary in explicitness, comprehension instruction should reflect that variability by including both explicit and implicit text (Bos & Vaughn, 2008). In explicit text, information is stated directly in the text and can be learned using a minimum of background knowledge. This type of text is the easiest to comprehend. In text that is implicit, students need to use their background knowledge and reasoning skills to infer or make sense of it. For example, Ms. Chao had her students read the following paragraph:

> Susan got a pretty doll for her birthday. The doll cost her parents a lot of money. She also got a new tennis racquet and two new CDs. But Susan still didn't feel happy.

First Ms. Chao asked her students, *"What did Susan get for her birthday?"* This question required explicit information because the answer was directly stated in the text. Next, Ms. Chao asked her students, *"Why was Susan unhappy?"* This question asked for implicit information since the answer was not directly contained in the text; the students needed to use their background knowledge and reasoning skills to answer it (Bos & Vaughn, 2008).

> You will find a number of articles on text elements at the TextProject website: **http://www.textproject.org/topics/ text.**

Reader

Prior knowledge, or the knowledge and skills that readers bring to the reading process, also strongly influence comprehension. First and foremost is a reader's ability to decode text accurately and fluently enough to allow him to think about what he is reading. It is often claimed that large numbers of students, called "word callers," can fluently read text but do not comprehend what they are reading. In reality, research shows that only about 2.5% of all readers fall into this category, thus emphasizing the strong relationship between fluency and comprehension (Shankweiler, 1999). Students who effortlessly read the words in a text usually have the resources needed to comprehend the information in comparison to students whose energy and attention are consumed by laborious decoding. Strategies for producing fluent, accurate readers were covered in Chapters 1 and 3–5.

A student's background, language, and vocabulary knowledge also affect comprehension. If Carla has visited the Southwest, she is more apt to understand a mystery that takes place in the Arizona desert. If Connor's grandmother talks about her homeland of Vietnam, he is likely to understand clearly a well-written expository text about the Vietnam War. Strategies for building student vocabulary and other oral language skills were described in Chapter 9. Because comprehension is "an active process that requires an intentional and thoughtful interaction between the reader and the text" (National Reading Panel, 2000, p. 13), readers must actively employ various comprehension strategies as they read. Good readers make predictions based on background knowledge, focus on looking forward and backward in the text to find important information, paraphrase, explain, summarize, and construct conclusions about what they read (Smith, 1999). They employ fix-up strategies such as underlining or using a dictionary when they recognize that they are not fully understanding the text (Keene, 2002).

Activity

The nature and purpose of the reading task also affect comprehension (Moats, 2005). Motivation to continue reading can depend on whether an individual is reading for pleasure or to acquire new information. Is the text voluntary reading or part of a job or school requirement? Before the reader starts, does she have prior interest or background knowledge about the reading? All of these factors can affect students' motivation to persist and continue reading until they achieve understanding. Finally, reading may be tied to extrinsic consequences that include grades or test scores, or intrinsic consequences that involve feelings of amusement, satisfaction, or enlightenment (Moats, 2005). Consequences can affect all aspects of comprehension, including whether students stick with a task and the desire to select the correct strategies, monitor understanding, and employ fix-up strategies if needed. Gato might not have had any interest in Antarctica before reading a book on that topic that his teacher has selected, but halfway through his reading he becomes so interested in learning more about the emperor penguins and how the ice is beginning to melt that he starts rereading the book again so he understands all the information.

Context

Finally, the context in which reading occurs can have a significant effect on comprehension, especially the amount of support provided for reading by peers and teachers. McEwan (2001) explains,

> Students must experience success if they are to progress in reading proficiency. Therefore, teachers must structure learning situations that ensure success. Success increases the willingness of students to work harder and to endure some frustration. Teachers can control a student's success in three ways: (a) selection and sequencing of instructional objectives (b) grouping of students for instruction and (c) instructional procedures and activities. (p. 84)

Specific strategies for carrying out each of these ways of building success are described throughout this chapter and text. When a student is expected to read frustration-level text, feelings of inadequacy for the task can consume her attention and diminish effort. The extent to which reading is valued at home or within a student's peer group also can affect the effort that goes into reading challenging material for understanding. If several third-grade girls are reading *The Baby-Sitters Club* or Harry Potter books and then at recess discussing the hair-raising stories, other third graders are likely to pick up the same books. Many schools have strengthened their reading culture by providing incentives to students who read a certain number of books by holding book fairs and by routinely encouraging parents to read to their children. Teachers and building principals who are readers themselves and have a personal passion for reading are more likely to convey that enthusiasm to students.

What Underlying Skills Do Students Need to Comprehend Text?

Oral Reading Fluency

We have often explained that students who can read text accurately and fluently are much more likely to be able to understand what they read. Therefore, systematic, explicit instruction in phonics and oral reading fluency is at the heart of any good instructional program in reading comprehension (Pressley, 2002).

Oral Language

Chapter 9 emphasized the importance of oral language skills, including knowledge of vocabulary and figurative language. Students who come to school deficient in oral language need direct instruction in those oral language skills essential for adequate listening, speaking, and, ultimately, reading. Most instruction in reading comprehension consists of students discerning the meaning of groups of paragraphs, or passages. Yet, students' ability to understand passages depends largely on their ability to understand sentences. Moats (2005) points out that because the structure of written language is different from oral language, many children may struggle in understanding written sentences even if they are able to understand oral ones. In addition, the ability to process sentence structure efficiently aids overall reading comprehension as well as written composition (Moats, 2005). For these reasons, effective comprehension instruction often needs to include some explicit instruction at the sentence level. In this section, ways to teach sentence repetition and how to answer who, what, where, when, and why questions are discussed. Later in the chapter, strategies for teaching students to make inferences at the sentence level are described.

Sentence Repetition Sentence repetition, or the ability to repeat verbatim a simple sentence pronounced by the teacher, is an important yet difficult skill for many young children who are at risk for reading difficulties. Both listening and reading comprehension depend on children being able to hold information in **working memory,** also called short-term memory, as they simultaneously process new information (Willingham, 2009). Carnine, Silbert, Kame'enui, and Tarver (2010) recommend providing 3 to 5 minutes of daily practice for students who cannot perform this skill. Practice can start with a simple My Turn where the teacher says the sentence, followed by a Your Turn. If students are unable to exactly repeat the sentence, the teacher can provide more support by saying the sentence and emphasizing the deleted or mispronounced part with a "pause and punch." In a pause and punch, the teacher increases her voice volume as she says the words that were

Read more about how working memory combines information from the environment and integrates it with information stored in long-term memory at **http://www.aft.org/pubs-reports/american_educator/issues/spring2009/index.htm.**

difficult for the students. If a pause and punch doesn't provide enough support, the teacher should move into a Together turn, saying the sentence together with students until they can say it independently (Kozloff, 2005). If students continue to struggle, the teacher should start with short three- to four-word sentences and gradually increase the length as students progress. When students are able to repeat longer sentences exactly and with normal intonation, they are ready to move to more advanced oral language skills.

Who, What, Where, When, and Why Questions   Many younger and ELL students also need to learn how to answer what Carnine and colleagues refer to as the question words: *who, what, when, where,* and *why* (Carnine et al., 2010). The authors recommend teaching *who* and *what* questions first, as these are the easiest. Instruction should follow a developmental sequence, next focusing on *when* and *where* questions before the more difficult *why* questions. To teach the question words, start instruction at the My Turn–Your Turn level as in this example of teaching *who* and *what.* As with sentence repetition, if students make errors while answering the questions, add the support of Together practice. In the beginning use a pause and punch when saying the critical question words, as in "The BIG rabbit hopped UNDER the fence."

> **My Turn**
>
> *Teacher:*   **"Sarah picked up the rabbit. WHO picked up the rabbit? Sarah."** (pause) **"WHAT did Sarah do? Picked up the rabbit."**
>
> **Your Turn**
>
> *Teacher:*   **"Tabitha ate a peach. Say that."**
> *Students:*   "Tabitha ate a peach."
> *Teacher:*   **"WHO ate a peach?"**
> *Students:*   "Tabitha."
> *Teacher:*   **"WHAT did Tabitha do?"**
> *Students:*   "Ate a peach."

Teachers should set high expectations for their students during oral language activities, requiring their students to use the correct past tense verb form of *ate* when they answer. Once students have learned to answer all five types of questions, teachers can provide cumulative review using one sentence as the basis for student answers and eliminate the pause and punch in their questions. Question words can be taught orally or using written text. As with any comprehension activity, be sure that the reading material can be read with at least 90% accuracy before using it for comprehension activities. Research-based methods for building reading-comprehension skills while reading aloud to children are explained in the *Research Note.*

Background Knowledge

The term "fourth-grade slump" describes a pattern of declining test scores that begins when many students reach fourth grade (Chall, Jacobs, & Baldwin, 1990). Students whose scores on reading tests decline do not regress in fourth grade; rather, they are expected to read increasingly difficult text that contains more specialized vocabulary and abstract ideas. Often they have no frame of reference to the topics or issues in the higher level text. Even more alarming, the gap between students unable to read increasingly difficult text and their peers only continues to widen until it becomes what has been described as the "eighth-grade cliff." In a downward spiral, these students are now cut off from the steadily increasing background knowledge or knowledge of the world that they could be learning through assigned and recreational reading.

Research Note

Using Interactive Read-Alouds to Build Comprehension Skills

A **read-aloud** is planned reading of text to students for a specific purpose. These oral-reading sessions have the potential to develop comprehension, oral language, vocabulary, core knowledge, and visualization skills, as well as to increase motivation for the subject or reading in general, but only if they are highly interactive. During highly interactive read-alouds, the teacher conducts prereading activities to prepare students to understand the context of the story. Throughout the story students have the opportunity to answer questions to clarify the meaning of the text. The teacher uses many of the comprehension strategies discussed throughout this chapter as students learn to predict, summarize what they are reading, answer critical-thinking questions, and draw conclusions. Sometimes pictures are shown to enable students to visualize the text. However, pictures are shown only after the reading to ensure that students are deriving meaning from the language. Highly interactive read-alouds have been shown to be more effective in teaching vocabulary than traditional read-alouds that follow a performance style (Beck & McKeown, 2007; Coyne, Simmons, Kame'enui, & Stoomiller, 2004). In performance-style read-alouds, teachers dramatically read the text while students passively listen to the performance. Conversation is limited to before and after the story, so students miss out on valuable opportunities to interact with the language of the text during the story. In short, simply reading aloud to children who are at risk is not enough, and caution is advised, as performance-based read-alouds take up valuable instructional time when children could be learning important reading skills (Brabham & Lynch-Brown, 2002).

Ironically, researchers have concluded that the "fourth-grade slump" results from a lack of background knowledge in the first place. Cognitive psychologists explain that adept readers connect their background knowledge to new knowledge that they read in a text. Constructing meaning from text is an active, dynamic process requiring the reader to use knowledge brought to the text. E. D. Hirsch (2000) described this process when he wrote, "It takes knowledge to gain knowledge" (p. 2). Remember a time when you read a text for which you had no background knowledge. For example, if you have little or no background in higher level European cultural history, the following paragraph makes little sense. If your background knowledge does not include the book mentioned in this text, you have few clues about the meaning of unknown vocabulary words. Hours later you will probably not remember this information you read:

> Since his death, Musil criticism has suffered from a polemical opposition between those who want to salvage Musil for a left-wing, Enlightenment tradition and those who are fundamentally apolitical and attracted primarily to his mysticism. The most basic level of this controversy concerns the philological problems of Musil's massive *Nachlass* and his intentions for the completion of *The Man Without Qualities*. The difficulty of resolving this debate lies not only in the open-endedness of Musil's work but also in his attempt to dissolve the polar style of thought which assumes the firm oppositions between romanticism and positivism, idealism and materialism. (Luft, 1980, p. 3)

Did you feel a rising tension as you tried to extract the meaning from this text? In a discussion of the relationship of prior knowledge to comprehension, the National Reading Panel report (2000) authors explain the relationship of background knowledge to reading comprehension:

> A reader must activate what he or she knows to use it during reading to comprehend a text. Without activation of what is known that is pertinent to the text, relevant knowledge may not be available during reading, and comprehension may fail; this is analogous to listening to someone speak an unknown foreign language.

If students who are at risk for reading difficulties are to move past the fourth-grade slump, they need an *information-rich* curriculum from the time they enter school. The information that students learn, whether it be the names of continents, information about the pyramids of Egypt, the origins of the early American civilization, or the properties of an alloy, are stored in long-term memory, available for use when reading books on related subjects.

The following strategies prepare students who are at risk to build their background knowledge and avoid the fourth-grade slump.

* Develop classroom libraries that have at least 50% nonfiction books. Although adults often assume that students prefer reading fiction, a study by Kletzien and Szabo (1998) indicated that when elementary students of both genders are given quality fiction and nonfiction books, they choose nonfiction at least 50% of the time.
* Use strategies described in Chapter 9 to teach vocabulary.
* Integrate gradual and cumulative teaching of information about the world we live in, starting in kindergarten. Young children enjoy learning important information about things they know nothing about, as long as it is taught well. Establish specific grade-level standards in each of the content areas that specify core factual information, and vocabulary students will learn so that teachers in upper grades can build on that foundational knowledge.
* Plan lessons so that students are reading as much expository text as narrative text during reading classes.
* Use *narrow reading* to develop students' depth of knowledge in a specific subject area. Planning an in-depth unit in science or social studies using multiple reading sources about the same subject is more effective than a less intensive approach. Lionel will know more about the Civil War if the teacher includes as part of the lesson plans a short story about Robert E. Lee, a book about Harriet Tubman and the Underground Railroad, a movie and discussion about President Lincoln, and a writing assignment about an article discussing a Yankee soldier's life.
* Weave background information into every subject area. If your third-grade students are drawing a picture of their school, teach them the meaning of *architecture* and *three-dimensional*. Everyone should be encouraged to use these same terms when they draw another building they have chosen.
* Use strategies to activate prior knowledge and use them as a check to indicate when you need to supply missing background knowledge.

> Investigate Core Knowledge lesson plans written by teachers who are developing an information-rich curriculum: **http://www.coreknowledge.org/CK/resrcs/lessons/index.htm.**

How Do I Teach Students to Comprehend Text?

Use Explicit Instruction

Research indicates that all students benefit when comprehension instruction is systematic and explicit. Lesson enhancements described in Chapter 1 are as important for teaching comprehension as they are for teaching more basic reading skills. Students need cumulative review to solidify background knowledge about the content they are reading and to continually refine their comprehension strategy skills. In order to maintain student interest, lessons need to move at a perky pace with enough reinforcement provided to bolster students' confidence. Teachers show students what reading comprehension "looks like" through **think-alouds (My Turn)** when they describe their own thought process in reading the text. This process enables students to "see" the teacher using a skill that could not otherwise be observed. Gradually teachers reduce support until students can independently vocalize their own think-alouds and are accustomed to actively thinking about what they are reading, whether for expository or narrative text (Rosenshine, 1997). McEwan (2009) refers to the process of starting instruction with strong scaffolding before gradually reducing it as "coaching" students. During the more heavily scaffolded My Turn phase, students observe their teacher applying comprehension strategies through think-alouds. Gradually the teacher carefully reduces her support by using Your Turns with feedback and close monitoring, until eventually the students independently apply those comprehension strategies.

Ask Questions

When teachers ask frequent, quality questions about text, their students retain information longer, understand the text with more clarity, integrate information from the text with their own knowledge, and become critical thinkers. We were surprised that in many classrooms we observed, teachers often waited to ask questions until after students read the text, even when student accuracy in reading the words was high. They worried that by asking questions during the story they would interrupt the students' concentration, so we reassured them that by asking frequent questions they would deepen students' understanding and thus increase attention paid to text.

Before planning what questions to ask, teachers need to determine how to divide a passage into manageable segments. Younger students who are at risk often are at the sentence-comprehension level, and unless questions are asked after every sentence, they do not integrate the information in the sentence they are reading with the preceding and forthcoming sentences. Usually older students are at the paragraph or page stage of questioning when they are learning how to pull together "big ideas" from longer text. Ankit is fortunate because his teacher asks frequent questions throughout the lesson. As the class reads a book on the Civil War, he is forced to actively think throughout the lesson because she might call on him at any time even if his hand is not raised. When Ankit answers questions supporting his answers with information from the text, he has more exposure to the content through this discussion. These exposures during discussion increase the likelihood that information about the Civil War will become a part of his long-term memory. When students were confused reading an introductory sentence about the Battle of Appomattox, the teacher's question-answer scaffolding helped Ankit understand the rest of the paragraph describing why this was such a critical battle.

Preplanning the questions that you will ask during the text reading ensures that you ask a variety of different types of questions and that the lesson moves at a perky pace. Because of design issues, packaged commercial reading programs such as those of Harcourt or Houghton Mifflin include questions that are scattered throughout the teacher manuals, often two or three pages away from where a teacher would logically ask them. In reading programs that depend on leveled texts, often the teacher has to shoulder the burden of writing out all the questions, or the recommended questions are in other source books. To help teachers remember to ask high-quality questions, we showed them how during preplanning they could write each question on a Post-it note which they then attached to the place in the book where they would ask it. Sometimes when teachers planned their lessons they put notes at the end of sentences, and sometimes they put them at the end of paragraphs, but they always asked at least one question per page.

Preplanning questions helps teachers ask quality questions that are relatively short, clear, and unambiguous. In order to plan your questions, you need to know the different types of questions teachers ask and some of the best practices related to matching questions to text. The two main categories of questions are literal and inferential questions:

1. Literal questions are questions that students can find the information for directly in the text. The questions are often facts, vocabulary, dates, times, and locations explicitly stated in the text. Some examples are: *What was the date when the war started? Who ate the beans? What city did they live in? What was the name of the first colony?*

2. Inferential questions are questions for which the answers are not explicitly stated in the text. Thus, students use hints and clues in the text along with their own knowledge and experience to answer them. Some examples are: *In what season did the story take place, and what clues let you know that? How did Stuart Little's size help his family? After reading this section, do you think that Rosetta's family is poor, middle class, or rich, and what clues let you know that?*

The National Reading Panel report (2000) indicates that answering questions is probably best used as part of a multiple-strategy teaching package. The question–answer relationship (QAR) is one strategy that helps students who have difficulty answering **inference** questions. Teachers introduce the QAR strategy by explaining to students that there are four types of questions they usually answer about what they have read. "Right there" questions are literal questions with the answer stated in the reading, usually in one sentence. Answers to the next three types of questions come from thinking about what they already know or from clues in the text. Students are then introduced to the four specific kinds of questions, depicted in Figure 10.2, that they answer during or after their reading.

In the Book QARs

Right There

The answer is in the text, usually easy to find. The words used to make up the question and words used to answer the question are **Right There** in the same sentence.

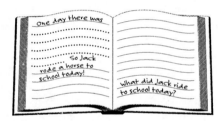

In My Head QARs

Author and You

The answer is *not* in the story. You need to think about what you already know, what the author tells you in the text, and how it fits together.

**Think and Search
(Putting It Together)**

The answer is in the story, but you need to put together different story parts to find it. Words for the question and words for the answer are not found in the same sentence. They come from different parts of the text.

On My Own

The answer is *not* in the story. You can even answer the question without reading the story. You need to use your own experience.

FIGURE 10.2 Four Types of Questions

Source: T. E. Raphael. Teaching question–answer relationships revisited. *The Reading Teacher, 391*(6), p. 519. Reprinted with permission of International Reading Associatin.

TABLE 10.3   Answers to Questions

Type of Question	Question	What Mrs. Garcia Said
Right There	What type of winter was it in Boston?	The first sentence tells me that it was a cold winter in Boston. The information is **right there** in that sentence.
Think and Search	Why did Peter and Thomas look like roly-poly cubs?	The second sentence tells me that the boys looked like roly-poly cubs because they wore so much clothing, and I remember that the first sentence told me that it was cold in Boston. If they were going outside in the cold, they needed to put on all those clothes, which made them look like little cubs. By **searching** through the first two sentences and using my brain **to think,** I found the answer.
On My Own	Do you think that the boys will deliver all the wood?	The story doesn't tell me anything about this, but I can figure something out **on my own.** I know that wood is heavy. If it's cold outside maybe it is snowing and the roads are slippery. The boys might fall in the snow and not be able to deliver those heavy logs to everyone.
Author and Me	What kind of transportation do you think the boys used when they went to deliver the soap and candles?	The **author** doesn't tell me anything about the kind of transportation they used. But the author does write that the story happened a long time ago back in 1774. I know that cars weren't invented then and that people either rode horses, rode in carriages pulled by horses, or walked. Since these were young boys, I imagine that they walked.

After introducing the four types of questions, the teacher then asks students to read three or four sentences displayed on an overhead projection and uses a My Turn to show how and why she would answer each of the questions. For example, Mrs. Garcia completed the example grid in Table 10.3 and explained to the class how she arrived at the answer to the four questions that were based on this passage.

> It was a cold winter in Boston back in 1774, but the cut wood had to be delivered. Ethan, who was 9 years old, and Jeb, who was 10, looked like roly poly cubs when they went out, they wore so much clothing. Mom, who was sick from the fever, stayed at home close to the fire.

Teachers ask older students a higher proportion of more difficult inferential questions than they do younger ones, although both groups need a combination of the four types. When a student is unable to answer a question, the "think-aloud" strategy discussed later in this section allows the teacher to show the student how she arrives at the answer (Cotton, 1989).

Calibrate Wait-Time Before Asking Questions

Wait-time, also called think-time, is the silent pause between the last word a teacher says in a question to students and the first word a student says when answering the teacher's question. Researchers have determined that teachers' wait-time is typically less than one second (Cotton, 1989). Even though maintaining a perky pace during reading lessons is important, extending wait-time to three seconds between the end of a question and the start of the answer gives students additional time to think about their answer. This additional think-time benefits students in a number of ways:

* Students give longer, more accurate answers.
* The number of times students don't respond decreases.

* Many more students volunteer answers.
* Academic achievement in the class generally increases.
* More students who are English language learners, have speech problems, or have learning disabilities will volunteer answers.
* A few more-capable students are unable to dominate class discussion.

Since three seconds is the absolute minimum for effective wait-time, if you are unaccustomed to having a longer period of silence between your question and an answer, take three slow steps around the room or count "1-100, 2-100, 3-100" on your fingers behind your back as a reminder cue. Let your students know that you are waiting to see many students raise their hands before calling on someone to answer your question so that they will habitually start to formulate answers immediately after your questions (Cotton, 1989; Stahl, 1990).

Scaffold Incorrect Answers and "No Responses"

Often students who are at risk will not attempt to answer questions because they are worried about making errors in front of their classmates or are unsure of their speech. Even when you increase your wait-time, some of these students will not volunteer answers and when you call on them will say, *"I don't know,"* or silently shrug their shoulders. Increase your support and use the following four-step "cue-clueing procedure" so that your students who routinely do not answer questions develop the confidence and skills to begin participating. For example, if you ask, *"What is one detail in this section that led me to decide the main idea was 'Mae was fascinated by science'?"* scaffold instruction for a student whose hand was not raised, as in this example:

1. First provide a cue: *"What are some of the things that Mae was doing in this section that showed she was fascinated with learning science?"*
2. Give the student a 3-second wait-time pause to formulate an answer. If he still can't answer, then move to step 3.
3. Increase your scaffolding and provide a clue that is so overt you are certain it will lead the student to the right answer: *"Look at sentence 4 and read it."* (Student reads: "Mae spent many hours at the library reading books about science and space.") Then ask, *"So where did she go to learn more about science?"* (Student answers, "The library.")
4. Reinforce and expand the student's answer to bolster confidence: *"Yes, that's absolutely right. The information in the book describing how Mae went to the library and spent all that time reading about science and space was a clue that she must really like science."*

Asking a student to reread the key sentence providing a clue to the information is always more effective than calling on another student or simply providing the answer. When Len is unable to describe how Jo is feeling about eating the food she made, Ms. Andrist points to the key sentence and asks him to read it again. *"Think about how Jo is feeling when you read this sentence,"* urges Ms. Andrist. Len reads, *"She was on the verge of crying when she met Laurie's eyes which looked merry."* If Len then answers, *"verge of crying,"* Ms. Andrist will probe further and ask, *"So how would she **feel** if she was on the verge of crying?"* If Len still cannot answer, Ms. Andrist will explain the clues that tell her the answer. Even though this sentence looks like a basic one, it is possible that a student

Learn about the different types of wait-time and think-time at **http://www. atozteacherstuff.com/pages/1884. shtml.**

does not know what "met Laurie's eyes" or "verge of crying" mean. These two phrases might be particularly problematic for English language learners. A student could also be confused by the clause in the sentence describing how *merry* Laurie is. Simply asking students to reread the sentence and then answer doesn't provide enough support for those problems. The teacher might need to clarify vocabulary or figurative language, as was discussed in Chapter 9, or use "think-alouds," which are described in more detail in the next section.

Model Comprehension Skills Through Think-Alouds

In a classroom, you can often tell which students are not actively thinking about what they are reading or what is read to them by the glazed look in their eyes. Many struggling readers do not naturally develop an ongoing dialogue with the text and author as they read. They haven't developed metacognition, which is the conscious awareness of their thought processes while reading. Because these students do not use **metacognitive skills,** they are unable to plan, monitor, and select effective strategies when there is a problem with their comprehension. The use of think-alouds is a strategy by which a teacher models the active thinking process that skilled readers use and teaches students these skills. A teacher might choose to verbalize his thoughts about a comprehension strategy he is using, how he determines the meaning of a vocabulary word, how he determines whether he understands what he is reading, or what he predicts will come next in the text and why. Think-alouds allow teachers to develop students' metacognitive skills by making their own explicit. When a student is unable to answer inferential questions, the teacher uses a think-aloud to draw his attention to the clues in the text or the background knowledge needed to answer the question.

Struggling readers benefit from observing what skilled readers think about while reading, and teacher modeling through think-alouds provides that insight. Mr. Gramble used a think-aloud to help students understand what an *assumption* was by using the following think-aloud: *"From the text and illustration, I can tell something about Alex. She says she is unhappy because her father isn't home. I can remember a time when I was disappointed with someone and I felt sad. I can also tell that Alex does not like dressing up and her mother wants her to wear her best dress. Because she misses her father and doesn't like to dress up, I'm going to make an assumption that Alex is not going to enjoy her birthday party."* By using a think-aloud, Mr. Gramble enabled his students to see a skill that could not otherwise be observed. Although initially teachers provide all the think-alouds, gradually they reduce their support and encourage students to use think-alouds as they read the text. You will learn more about how to do this when you read the section on reciprocal teaching. Some common think-aloud starters include:

* Think-aloud starters:

    "I predict that this next section will be about . . . because. . . ."

    "I want to learn more about. . . ."

    "I wonder why. . . ."

    "I have a picture in my mind of. . . ."

    "I don't understand this section so I'll read ahead a few lines to see if it becomes clearer. If not, I'll reread it."

    "The word _____ in the sentence gives me a clue that. . . ."

    "From what I know about . . . I can tell that. . . ."

> Try out one of the specific think-aloud activities at **http://bit.ly/XiEpy.**

Use Graphic Organizers with New Text

Graphic organizers such as the semantic maps discussed in Chapter 9 are visual representations of information that depict the relationships between facts, terms, and ideas within a learning task. Other examples of graphic organizers include tables, timelines, flowcharts, or diagrams used to record, organize, analyze, synthesize, and assess information and ideas. Students with limited working memory benefit from their use as memory aids during instruction. Students with attention or listening problems also benefit from having a completed graphic before, during, or after their reading. Graphic organizers can be completed by the teacher before, during, or after reading the text. They can also be completed by students with help from the teacher or independently as practice or review after instruction. However, having students complete graphic organizers prior to instruction can be problematic. Read the following description of Mrs. Whipple's lesson and think about why her use of a graphic organizer was ineffective.

> After students independently read a story about an oafish giant, Mrs. Whipple divided her class into groups and asked each group to complete a graphic organizer listing details about six characters' attitudes toward the giant.

Mrs. Whipple didn't realize that when graphic organizers are used for independent work, those students who have the best comprehension skills usually complete the graphic organizer for the group, while other students' engagement is limited

Note how Mrs. Palmer used My Turns to teach her students how to complete graphic organizers.

> Mrs. Palmer discussed the graphic organizer with the entire class after they had read the story. Each student had a copy of the graphic organizer, but she also projected a large copy on the board using a think-aloud to explain, *"Today we will find out what every character thought about the Giant and write that information on our chart. Watch me answer the first one. I'm going to start looking for the first character on page one where the author introduces Rabbit. I will read everything that Rabbit says and does to find out how he feels about Giant."* (Mrs. Palmer showed the students what scanning text looks like with her eyes and finger silently moving down the page.) *"Oh, look! On page 2, Rabbit runs away from Giant and hides. I know that when someone runs away and hides they are usually scared. I will write Rabbit's name in the first box and then write in the second box that he feels scared of the giant. I'd like everyone to write that on your chart as I write it on mine."*
>
> After modeling one answer, Mrs. Palmer wanted to see if the students were ready for a Together, so she reduced her scaffolding. *"Now, I want all of you to find the place where Bear first starts talking."* Mrs. Palmer scanned the class to make sure that everyone was scanning the text. *"Now read what Bear says and does to find out how he feels about the giant."* Mrs. Palmer provided enough wait-time so that more students figured out the answer. She then called on students to explain their answers and tell where they found them in the book. If students were able to fill in the information with Togethers, Mrs. Palmer continued to provide that support throughout the class session.
>
> At the end of the lesson, Mrs. Palmer reviewed the critical content again using the graphic organizer. She asked a student to summarize the text using the graphic organizer as a guide. Later, Mrs. Palmer had students complete a blank graphic organizer for homework or independent work.

Although older students need less support, using a graphic organizer while students are reading text stimulates interest, keeps students actively thinking, and organizes information for them so that they retain it longer. Archer and Gleason (2010) suggest the following guidelines for constructing graphic organizers when using them to help students comprehend expository text (pp. 339–342).

a. **Determine the critical content (e.g., vocabulary, concepts, ideas, generalizations, events, details, facts) that you wish to teach your students.** Helping students

Attribute	Native Americans	Colonists
Land	Shared	Owned
	Lived close to it without changing it	Cleared it
	Respected it	Used it

Summary

Native Americans and colonists had different ideas about the land. Native Americans shared the land, whereas the colonists owned individual pieces of it. Native Americans lived close to the land; they respected and did not change it. Colonists used the land for their own gain.

FIGURE 10.3   Comparison–Contrast Concept Map

Source: Friend, M., & Bursuck, W. (2006). *Including students with special needs: A practical guide for classroom teachers* (5th ed). Boston: Allyn & Bacon, p. 327.

focus on the most critical information is important for several reasons. First, struggling readers may have trouble identifying the most important information in an oral lesson or textbook chapter. In most cases this information will be content stressed in your state's standards. Second, it is easier for students to remember several main ideas than many isolated details. Third, putting too much information on a graphic organizer can make it so visually complex that students may have trouble interpreting it.

b. **Organize the concepts in a visual representation.** Because the purpose of a graphic organizer is to clarify interrelationships among ideas and information, you should keep the visual display as simple as possible. Figures 10.3 and 10.4 show two examples of completed graphic organizers.

c. **Design a completed concept map.** Completing the map before you teach with it ensures that the information is clear and accurate and can be presented to your students in a timely manner.

d. **Create a partially completed concept map (to be completed by students during instruction).** Requiring students to fill out the map as you present your lesson is an excellent way to keep them on task. Also, many students with special needs benefit from a multisensory approach; seeing the information on the graphic, hearing it from the teacher, and writing it on the map helps them retain the information presented.

e. **Create a blank concept map for students to use as a postreading or review exercise.** This structure for review provides more practice for students, who are then more likely to put the information in long-term memory.

> Download free graphic organizers from **http://www.eduplace.com/ graphicorganizer/index.html.**

The **story map** shown in Figure 10.4 is a graphic organizer that Ms. Barrows used to teach her students the story *The Funny Farola* (Miranda & Guerrero, 1986). This type of graphic organizer has been shown to help students with special needs read with better comprehension because it provides a visual guide to understanding and retelling stories. As the students read the story, Ms. Barrows guided their comprehension by asking the students questions about the various story elements and then recording the correct answers on the story map. As you read a description of her instruction, determine where she is using My Turns, Togethers, or Your Turns.

Ms. Barrows: Where do you think the story takes place? It's hard to tell, because the writers don't come right out and say it.

Lovell: I think it takes place in a city.

Ms. Barrows: Why do you think so, Lovell?

Lovell: Because it sounds like it's a big parade, and cities have big parades.

Characters	Setting
Dora Dora's mom and dad Dora's brother, Ramon, and her sister, Rosa	A city on the day of a parade.

Problems

Dora's brother and sister got lost at the parade.
Dora's family laughed at her farola.

Attempts

Dora got on her father's shoulders to see
whether she could find her brother and sister.

Resolution

Dora found her brother and sister because they were holding her funny farola and she was able
to see it.

Lesson

Just because other people think something is different, doesn't mean that it is not any good.

FIGURE 10.4   Story Map

Ms. Barrows: Good thinking, Lovell. When stories don't come out and say things, we have to figure it out by thinking hard, and that's what you did. Let's all fill in the setting on our maps. [They do.] Remember, we said last week that all stories have a problem that needs to be solved. Read the next four pages and find out what the problem is here. [The students read the passage.] What's the problem?

Justin: Well, Dora's little brother and sister got lost at the parade.

Ms. Barrows: Right. That's one problem. Write it on your maps. Now, does anyone see another problem?

Eliseo: I know. Dora made a farola that looked like a frog and everybody laughed at her.

Ms. Barrows: Eliseo, what's wrong with a farola that looks like a frog? I thought it looked cute.

Eliseo: I think it was because Dora's was different from everyone else's. In the pictures in the story, there were no farolas that looked like animals.

Ms. Barrows: That's right, Eliseo. Let's all put this problem on our maps. [They do.] Let's read the next page and find out what Dora and her mom and dad attempted to do to try to find her brother and sister. (Friend & Bursuck, 2008; pp. 342–343)

Teach Comprehension Before, During, and After Reading the Text

Comprehension strategies, content instruction, and question asking are integrated into all parts of a reading lesson occurring before, during, and after the reading. An effective way to differentiate instruction is through **frontloading** techniques used before reading to activate students' prior knowledge, discuss critical knowledge and vocabulary needed to understand the text, and provide information on text structure and comprehension strategies useful in understanding the text. English language learners benefit when pictures and objects are added to frontloading activities. Before reading a text about extreme weather, show students a two-minute video clip of a hurricane and tornado. Then discuss any related science principles necessary for understanding the text. Students from poverty who lack direct experiences that other classmates have, such as vacations at the beach or trips to Alaska, benefit from frontloading activities that fill in information they do not have (Buehl, 2008).

The most productive comprehension instruction occurs when a teacher asks a high percentage of questions requiring thought before, during, and after the reading, as shown in Table 10.4. When Mr. Hearn asks frequent questions as he is reading a biography to his students, he can readily determine whether they are accurately comprehending the information the author intends to convey. If students get lost in the text, he can help them apply strategies to fix the problem. When questions are strictly factual in nature and are left for after the reading, students fail to learn to apply comprehension strategies or use inference to answer questions.

How Do I Teach Comprehension at the Sentence Level?

Students who need sentence-level comprehension instruction the first time they read through text include younger students who are at risk, English language learners, and older, more skilled readers who are reading difficult text.

Sentences written in the **passive voice,** in which the subject of the sentence is the recipient of the action rather than the actor, are always more difficult to understand. For example, the sentence *The barking dog was chased by the yellow cat* is less clear than *The yellow cat chased the barking dog* because in the second sentence, which used the active voice, the main actor, the cat, clearly chased the barking dog. Carnine and colleagues (2010) suggest an effective strategy for teaching students to comprehend sentences written in the passive voice. The teaching format involves constructing a short sentence in the active voice and then rewriting or saying it in the passive voice. Initially the teacher begins with a My Turn, using a think-aloud, before asking questions to check for understanding. For example, in teaching passive voice, Mrs. Eckstein used the following minimally different sentences: *Allonzo screamed at Clarissa* and *Clarissa was screamed at by Allonzo.* First, she used a think-aloud and said, *"Clarissa was screamed at by Allonzo; that means Allonzo did the screaming and Clarissa was screamed at."* She then repeated each sentence, reduced support, and used a Your Turn, asking, *"Who was screamed at?"* and *"Who did the screaming?"* Students have mastered this skill when they can accurately answer questions about novel sentences without a My Turn.

Another aspect of written language that can make comprehension at the sentence level more difficult is the use of **pronoun referents**—the nouns to which pronouns refer. A

TABLE 10.4   Before, During, and After Reading

	Teachers set purpose and use frontloading techniques to:	Students learn to:	Metacognitive questions teachers ask to activate students' thinking about the text include:
Before Reading	※ connect new text information to prior knowledge. ※ provide a scaffold for instruction by preteaching words students might have difficulty decoding. ※ increase interest in reading the text. ※ teach one or two vocabulary words necessary to understand the text. ※ introduce a graphic organizer.	※ read the title and headings. ※ look at the pictures. ※ predict what the passage might be about. ※ ask themselves what they already know about the topic. ※ decode and read by sight any difficult words. ※ consider the purpose for reading the text.	※ What do you think the selection might be about? Why? ※ What do you know about (topic/story)? ※ What would you be interested in learning about (topic/story)? ※ What do you think it would be like to_____? ※ What clue(s) does the title give us about the main character?
During Reading	※ clarify unknown vocabulary, metaphors, and concepts. ※ use a graphic organizer to teach a specific comprehension strategy or to provide connections between ideas, concepts, characters and other pieces of information in text. ※ assess students' application of comprehension strategies.	※ think about what they are reading and if it makes sense. ※ stop sometimes and summarize what they've read so far. ※ visualize the people, places, and events they are reading about. ※ imagine talking with the author while reading. ※ question and predict. ※ seek clarification when there are questions. ※ make inferences. ※ make connections between ideas, concepts, and characters in the text. ※ evaluate the text.	※ What did you think about as you read this section? ※ Were there any parts that were hard to understand in this section? ※ What did you do when you came to parts that were hard to understand? ※ Were there any hard words in this section? ※ What did you do when you didn't know a word? ※ What do you predict will happen next and why? ※ What does the author want us to know about? ※ Does that make sense with what the author told us before? Why? ※ How did the author let you know something had changed?
After Reading	※ help students integrate information from text with their own core knowledge. ※ teach students to summarize main ideas in text. ※ ensure that students retain core information in long-term memory. ※ Provide the opportunity to apply critical thinking skills.	※ generate questions about the text. ※ think about what they read and review questions/predictions. ※ write or speak on a specified topic related to material read. ※ compare what was read with something already known. ※ summarize a reading selection. ※ outline the text.	※ Where did you find it difficult to understand what you were reading and what fix-up strategy did you use? ※ What is the main idea of what you just read? How did you come to that answer? ※ What picture did the author paint in your head? ※ Do you need to reread so that you understand? ※ Which of your predictions was right? ※ How would you judge the overall quality of other students' comments? Can you give an example?

general rule of thumb is that the closer the pronoun is to its referent, the easier it is to understand. Consider this section of text:

> Now life began to change. The Eskimo hunters could see that these tools were useful. So they became traders, too. They trapped more furs than their families needed. Then they brought the furs to the trading posts. There they could trade the furs for supplies they had never had before. Because the new tools helped Eskimo hunters get along better, they became part of the Eskimo environment. (Brandwein & Bauer, 1980; cited in Friend & Bursuck, 2008)

Many readers may have trouble figuring out who *they* refers to in this passage because the author did not clearly indicate the pronoun referent. Although the placement of most pronouns is not this problematic, they must be explicitly taught because even basic pronoun referents can be difficult for students who are at risk (Friend & Bursuck, 2008). As with other skills in this section, the teacher first must analyze the text students will be using, anticipate problems, and, through explicit instruction, prevent these problems from occurring, thus enhancing comprehension. Before students read, the teacher identifies unclear pronouns and asks students to underline those pronouns in a passage. Finally, a series of questions asked by the teacher shows students how to find out to whom or what the pronoun refers.

Chapter 9 described the problems many students have reading unfamiliar idioms (*She was dressed to kill.*) and metaphors (*He mirrors the dancer's fancy footwork and flowing arms while gyrating to the beat of the drums and guitars.*). When previewing a story or article during your lesson planning, carefully look for this figurative language and integrate the teaching suggestions in Chapter 9 into your comprehension instruction.

Moats (2005) identified four other problematic sentence structures that can impede student comprehension which are detailed in Figure 10.5. To help students with these problematic constructions, Moats suggested identifying them in advance of reading a story and then monitoring student understanding of them. Moats also suggested paraphrasing difficult sentences for students as well as engaging the students in *sentence coloring.* In sentence coloring, after several My Turns, students read the same sentence several times with different phrasing or intonation to "color" the meaning of the words (p. 23). For example, Ms. Battaglia's class came across the sentence *They will understand only this?* while reading a newspaper editorial on the street riots in France. Ms. Battaglia wanted to be sure her students understood the impact of the question mark on the meaning of the sentence. She read the sentence to her students, coloring it to emphasize the *question* by emphasizing the word *this* at the end and using intonation denoting a question: *They will understand only* **this?** To provide contrast, she colored the sentence in a different way, as it would be spoken without the question mark, emphasizing the word *they* this time: **They** *will understand only this.* Ms. Battaglia then had her students say the sentence each way, commenting on the different meaning of each, including what the original sentence meant within the context of the editorial.

Lengthy sentences like the following one from Dickens's *A Christmas Carol* pose problems because, besides taxing the reader's working memory, they typically have a compound or complex sentence structure, or both.

> *If we were not perfectly convinced that Hamlet's Father died before the play began, there would be nothing more remarkable in his taking a stroll at night, in an easterly wind, upon his own ramparts, than there would be in any other middle-aged gentleman rashly turning out after dark in a breezy spot—say Saint Paul's Churchyard for instance—literally to astonish his son's weak mind.* (Dickens, 1843)

---

a. Passive Voice

Summer clothes *are to be replaced* by winter clothes.
New ideas *are often misunderstood* by those with firmly held biases.
The white minivan *was hit* head-on by the motorcycle.

b. Double Negative

We had *no* reason to think she was *un*stable.
There was *no* evidence that the suspect was *not* at home as he had claimed on the night of
    the robbery.
It was *not* true that he *dis*liked the gift.
I did *not* advise him *never* to reveal his intentions to her.

c. Verb Tenses and Auxiliaries

Under orders, *we were to be patient* for hours.
Would it not have been easier to say "yes"?
What would he be doing if he were here?

d. Prepositions and Articles

He put the paper *aside* to read the book.
He put the paper *beside* the book.
He put the paper *inside* the book.
This is *the* major problem.
This is *a* major problem.

e. Ambiguous Phrases, Word Order, and Placement of Phrases

Folding diapers would be expensive.
Hanging plants would require light.
They will understand only this.
Only they will understand this.
The drunken driver with the VW struck the woman.
The drunken driver struck the woman with the VW.

FIGURE 10.5 Problematic Sentence Structures

Source: From Moats, L. C. (2005). *Language essentials for teachers of reading and spelling. Module 6: Digging for meaning: Teaching text comprehension* (p. 22). Boston: Sopris West.

Strategies that can be used for teaching students to comprehend complex sentences such as this and other kinds of sentences include the following:

- Read to children and teach them to comprehend complex syntax on a regular basis, asking frequent questions at the sentence level and using graphic organizers. Through listening comprehension you directly develop students' reading comprehension skills.
- Place students into an explicit language program in preschool or kindergarten such as *Language for Learning* (Chapter 9, pp. 308–309).
- "Play mom," and when younger students or English language learners use short sentences, be a model and gently expand their sentences as feedback.
- Expect students to answer in complete sentences, and use scaffolding to help them develop that habit. If John answers your question by explaining, "went uphill to dangerous forest," reply, "You are right. The brave soldier went uphill to the dangerous forest. Now tell me your answer in a complete sentence."
- Teach formal grammar and diagramming sentences. The Language! reading program integrates diagramming into reading instruction. In one of the first lessons, students identify a sentence subject by answering the question, "What did it?" and the sentence verb by answering, "What did they do?"
- Ask quality inferential "detective" questions more frequently than "What did you think?" or "What do you predict?" questions. Teachers are surprised how difficult inferential

questions are for students. To increase motivation, always ask what specific "clue" words or background information students found in the sentence. Examples of detective questions at the sentence level include these:

Sentence: Six chicks scratch in one patch. **Detective questions:** "Are a dozen chicks scratching?" "Do the animals scratching have four legs?" "Are the chicks scratching in different places around the farm?"

Sentence: The village residents will always remember how the mysterious dragon helped them. **Detective questions:** "Do you think the village residents will remember the dragon 20 years from now?" "Did the people learn everything that could be known about the dragon?" "Was the sentence about strangers in the village helped by the dragon?"

After students answer the question, ask them to identify the word or phrase in the sentence that provided the clue. Gradually, students learn to critically think as they read and independently notice clues that give meaning to the text.

What Comprehension Strategies Do I Need to Teach?

While every reader benefits from learning and refining comprehension strategies, many students who are at risk will never move past the fourth-grade slump unless they receive explicit instruction in using them. Up until about 20 years ago, the prevailing practice for teaching reading comprehension was to provide students with practice activities consisting largely of passages followed by written comprehension questions. Very little time was spent directly teaching reading comprehension skills until ground-breaking research in the field of cognitive psychology provided evidence that, as with decoding skills, comprehension strategies also need to be taught explicitly and systematically (Duffy, 1993). Research supports the position that students can be taught to monitor their strategic behavior and performance and that this training can improve their reading.

> Learn more about how to teach reading comprehension strategies at **http://teacher.scholastic.com/reading/bestpractices/comprehension/promptsthatguide.pdf.**

Summarizing

A **summary** is a synthesis of the important ideas in a text (Armbruster, Lehr, & Osborn, 2001). Summarizing helps students identify the main ideas in expository text and recognize important story elements in narrative text. Summarizing can also help students evaluate their understanding of what they have read, tell important and unimportant information apart, and better remember what they have read. Summarizing can be done periodically after each paragraph or section or at the end of the reading. For narrative text, students can use a story map, such as the one shown in the previous section for *The Funny Farola* in Figure 10.4, to summarize the story. Younger students need structure when summarizing or they will describe one or two unrelated details from the story. If throughout the lesson you use a graphic organizer, at the end of the story it can serve as a prompt when students summarize the story. Often in kindergarten and first grade, the teacher needs to model giving a summary before asking two or three students to summarize the same story just like the teacher did.

For expository text and more difficult fiction, a summary often involves stating the main idea and supporting details of several related paragraphs. For example, Ms. Tara's students came up with the following summary based on several paragraphs from their social studies textbook about the United States economy after World War II: "*A combination of the housing boom and baby boom had a positive effect on the economy. Jobs were plentiful, and wages were high. Still, not everyone shared in the good economic times of the 1950s."* Summarizing is a difficult comprehension strategy in which students need consistent daily practice. Opportunities for practice include summarizing a section of text from the day before, summarizing sections of text during the reading, and summarizing the entire article or story at the end.

Outlines can be helpful to students as they write summaries. Two groups of outlines for summary writing are described here. The first group of outlines can be used to write easier summaries, the second to write more difficult ones.

- Outlines for easier summaries
  - Describe the beginning, middle, and end of a story and the setting.
  - Describe the main problem in the story and the outcome.
- Outlines for more difficult summaries
  - Present concrete events and facts in sequence.
  - Supply missing information through appropriate inferences.
  - Include some explanation of the causes of events.

Teachers who have students summarize the text as part of group instruction, providing feedback on their group summary before asking everyone to write their own summary, help students generalize this important skill to their writing.

Main Ideas and Details

The **main idea** is the central idea around which a piece of text is organized. The confusion that students experience when they need to identify main ideas is revealed when they write disorganized papers filled with disjointed paragraphs about random details or when their oral book reports remind you of lists of unrelated, insignificant bits of information. For example, Mary's book report, which was supposed to last three minutes, stretches on and on as she recounted every small detail. It is difficult for students to identify main ideas when they are lost in the details. Even when students are explicitly taught to identify main ideas in the primary grades, in high school they still need to refine their ability to pick out and describe the main ideas of novels and longer articles. The main idea is easier to identify when it is expressed explicitly (written in a sentence) than when it is implied (suggested without being explicitly stated). Sometimes each paragraph in text contains a main idea. When the main idea of a paragraph is explicitly described in a sentence, that sentence is called the **topic sentence.**

At first, students are taught to identify main ideas from paragraphs, but later they expand that skill to larger segments of text. Since explicit main ideas are often found in the first sentence, students often try to pull the main idea out of that sentence whether it is there or not. When they have to figure out an implied main idea by making an inference from the information in the text, sometimes they are unable to see the big picture. Teachers can prevent these problems by using a variety of teaching examples—some explicit, some not—and selecting paragraphs having topic sentences in the beginning, middle, and end. Graphic organizers such as the one in Table 10.5 used during SAFER

TABLE 10.5 Main Idea and Details Chart

Main Idea	
Detail 1	
Detail 2	
Detail 3	

reading help students differentiate between main ideas and details. Main ideas are what the reading is mostly about; details are smaller pieces of specific information that tell the reader more about the main idea, the characters, new vocabulary terms, or other elements in text.

When students notice a detail, they tell the teacher the specific detail, and the teacher writes it on the large graphic. At the end of each paragraph, through the use of think-alouds and cues as prompts, the teacher leads the students to identify the main idea. Later, she might have students read each detail and main idea listed on the chart and ask, "Is this what the whole paragraph is about?"

Dixon, Boorman, and Muti (2008) use step-by-step scaffolding to teach students to identify the main idea. Students first learn to identify who or what is talked about most, and then they learn to classify what is said about that person or thing. Combining those two pieces of information provides a main idea sentence, but two preskills are needed so that students can readily pick out this information from text. In order to determine the main idea "Suzanne is freezing in the cold," Mrs. Whitlaw's students first must know *who or what was talked about the most.* Although Suzanne's name might be mentioned once or twice in the paragraph, the word "she" or "her" might also describe her. Students need to recognize that "the red-faced girl" and "the shivering huddled form" also refer to Suzanne. These pronouns or nouns that refer to another word or name are called **anaphora.** If Mrs. Whitlaw's students are unable to recognize that these different pronouns and phrases indicate one person, she will first teach them to underline all the words in a paragraph that refer to a specified person. Students practice that skill until they can identify who is being talked about the most in a paragraph. The second preskill that Mrs. Whitlaw's students need to develop is *classification.* If text in the paragraph mentions that Suzanne's lips were blue, she was outside on a freezing day, her face was red from the cold, blowing wind, and she couldn't wait for the warm bus to arrive, in order to identify what is said about the person (Suzanne), students must classify those four details and realize that she was freezing in the cold. After learning about anaphora and developing classification skills, students are ready to identify the main idea in a variety of texts.

> Watch a model lesson where a teacher uses think-alouds and cues to teach students how to identify the main idea in a reading passage: **http://www. linkslearning.org/reading_links/ 8_pgr/index.html.**

Comprehension Monitoring

For students to learn how to monitor their comprehension, teachers must teach them not only to use specific comprehension strategies, but also when to use them. If you have ever read and comprehended a nineteenth-century Russian novel by Tolstoy, you will remember that whenever you became confused about the character referred to in the text, you stopped your reading to check the character list and determine exactly who was speaking and what the relationship was to the main characters, then asked yourself whether the dialogue now made sense given the character clarification. When two characters had almost identical names, you stopped and double-checked the spelling to make sure you knew who was speaking. Proficient readers are aware when they do not know a word or when the text does not make sense, and they know how to apply the **fix-up strategies** described in Table 10.6, deciding which ones will help them with specific problems. When readers are self-monitoring, they are consistently asking themselves, "Is what I am reading making sense?" **Monitoring text** is not a natural process, but research demonstrates that it can be taught.

Armbruster and colleagues (2001) have described several comprehension-monitoring strategies that students may use.

Identify Where the Difficulty Occurs   "I don't understand the second paragraph on page 76."

TABLE 10.6 Fix-Up Strategies

Sounding out unknown words	Slowing down and rereading
Looking up a word or name (e.g., dictionary, encyclopedia, glossary, Google, Wikipedia)	Making a prediction and periodically checking whether the text corresponds to that prediction; adjusting the prediction if necessary
Reading the preface, the chapter summary, the back cover or looking for a review of the book	Taking notes during reading, making a graphic organizer, outlining the text
Reflecting on what the author is trying to say in the book	Talking to another person about a difficult section of the book
Thinking about how the book relates to background knowledge; to the reader's experiences	Creating a visual image about what the book is about
Checking the Internet for information related to a difficult section	Determining whether the information is necessary for understanding the text and ignoring it if not

Identify What the Difficulty Is   "I don't get what the author means when she says 'Arriving in America was a milestone in my grandmother's life.'"

Restate the Difficult Sentence or Passage in Their Own Words   "Oh, so the author means that coming to America was a very important event in her grandmother's life."

Look Back Through the Text   "The author talked about Mr. McBride in Chapter 2, but I don't remember much about him. Maybe if I reread that chapter, I can figure out why he's acting this way now."

Look Forward in the Text for Information That Might Help Them Resolve the Difficulty   "The text says, 'The groundwater may form a stream or pond or create a wetland. People can also bring groundwater to the surface.' Hmmm, I don't understand how people can do that . . . Oh, the next section is called 'Wells.' I'll read this section to see if it tells how they do it." (p. 50)

Self-Questioning

One way that readers become actively engaged with text is by asking themselves questions as they read. Through asking questions, students can reflect on what they are reading, asking why the author chose the words he did or let the character come to such a devastating end, why the main story character would fall in love with that rude person whose personality is so different, or whether the spurned lover has a chance of making a comeback. Kyle might notice while reading a social studies book that the authors didn't include enough information about foxholes during World War I. That observation might lead him to ask himself whether it's worth looking for another book that describes what daily life in the foxholes was like. Later, when Kyle begins reading about the Battle of Verdun, he might ask himself who it seems will be the victor of that battle. Once the information is provided in the text, he'll ask himself whether his prediction was correct. Kyle, like other competent readers, is not aware that he monitors his comprehension routinely by asking himself whether he has understood a section just read until he comes to a section where he has to answer "no." As soon as Kyle realizes he read the page or pages without complete understanding, he immediately goes back to the beginning of the section and rereads. Just as with other comprehension strategies, self-questioning can be explicitly taught and included in multiple-strategy instruction. Teachers can prompt students to ask questions at different points in the text by starting with the main question words: who, what, where, when, why, how.

Questioning the Author (QtA) is a strategy developed by Isabel Beck and colleagues that gets students started asking questions by providing them with strategy questions that they can eventually ask themselves when they read. The teacher gives the students one or more paragraphs to read and then asks them to answer these questions:

1. What is the author trying to tell you?
2. Why is the author telling you that?
3. Does the author say it clearly?
4. How could the author have said things more clearly?
5. What would you say instead? (Beck, McKeown, Hamilton, & Kucan, 1997)

Finally, strategic readers need to routinely ask additional questions as a part of self-monitoring. Questions such as "Does this make sense?" "What parts of this story are different from my reading predictions," and "Do I need to take notes to understand?" help students know when to apply fix-up strategies to increase their comprehension.

Making Inferences

Proficient readers are unaware they are inferring as they identify information in the text that is not directly provided by the author. Inferring is a difficult concept to teach to students who are at risk because it is so abstract. Since most comprehension strategies and question answering require the ability to infer, suggestions to make inferences are integrated throughout most sections of this chapter. The QAR strategy, identifying the main idea, and monitoring comprehension all require the ability to infer. An easy rule for students to remember is: *"Making an inference is using clues from the text and your own knowledge and experience to figure out what the author is trying to tell you."*

How Can I Use Multiple Strategies to Maximize Student Gains in Reading Comprehension?

You have just learned about reading comprehension strategies that are research-based. These strategies can be even more effective when used together. The National Reading Panel (2000) determined that readers benefit when multiple comprehension strategies are taught during the process of reading narrative or expository text. Multiple-strategy instruction should include teaching students when specific comprehension strategies are most effective—before, during, or after the reading, as already depicted in Table 10.4 (page 338).

One way to teach students to use multiple strategies at once is called reciprocal teaching (Palincsar & Brown, 1988). Friend and Bursuck (2008) describe reciprocal teaching as:

> [A] way to teach students to comprehend reading material by providing them with teacher and peer models of thinking behavior and then allowing them to practice these thinking behaviors with their peers. At first, the teacher leads the dialogue, demonstrating how the strategies can be used during reading. As instruction goes on, the teacher gives the students more and more responsibility for maintaining the dialogue. Eventually students are largely responsible for the dialogue, though the teacher still provides help as necessary. (p. 371)

In reciprocal teaching students are taught the skills of summarizing, self-questioning, predicting, and clarifying. In the example that follows this passage from a U.S. history text, Mr. Buerhle used reciprocal teaching with his students (Kinder, 1990).

Economic Benefits of the Colonies

The English government had many economic reasons for wanting to build colonies in the New World. One of these had to do with England's balance of trade. The balance of trade compares what a nation buys from other nations with what other nations buy from it. If other nations buy more from it than the nation buys from others the balance of trade is good.

England did not have a good balance of trade. It needed many goods that it did not make or grow. The English weather was too cold to grow sugar cane, and England did not have enough trees to supply the wood needed to build ships. As a result, England had to buy goods such as sugar and wood from other nations. In turn, other nations bought wool and other products from England. If England had colonies in the New World, they could supply raw materials to England. These products from nature, such as wood, were necessary if England were to improve its balance of trade.

The colonies could also become a new market, or place to sell products for English goods. The colonists would need many supplies, such as tools and cloth, and English merchants would provide them. This would create more business and more jobs in England.

In time, many English merchants grew rich from this trade with the colonies. The English government also grew rich by taxing the people who shipped the goods to the colonies. (Reich & Beiler, 1988)

After reading the passage, Mr. Buerhle demonstrated (My Turn) the skills of summarizing, self-questioning, predicting, and clarifying. He looked at his students and said, "I have

---

In Your Classroom

Reciprocal Teaching

The students in this class have just read a section of text that focuses on Loch Ness. They are now applying the POSSE strategy—**p**redict, **s**earch, **s**ummarize, and **e**valuate—as shown in the following example.

Teacher: What is the main topic the text is talking about?

Peg: The Loch Ness monster.

Teacher: What was this section about? What was the main idea?

Peg: Oh, the lake. I have two questions: "What is a lake?" and "What lives in it?"

Teacher: Do you mean this particular lake or any lake?

Peg: This lake. Joe?

Joe: It's foggy, it's deep, and it's long and narrow.

Peg: Don?

Don: The land beside the lake. You don't know if it is real soft and you could fall through it.

Teacher: So it could be soft and swampy.

Ann: I think the Loch Ness monster lives there.

Teacher: Is Ann answering your question, Peg?

Peg: No.

Teacher: What was your question?

Peg: I had two: "What is a lake?" and "What lives in the lake?"

Joe: But the book never answered that. I have a question about the main idea. Aren't we supposed to ask a question about the main idea?

Teacher: Just about what we read.

Joe: Yes, but Peg asked us, "What lives in the lake?" but it doesn't really mention that in the book.

Teacher: That's true. The major idea has to do with Loch Ness and what it looks like. A minor idea that we inferred rather than directly read in the article was that the Loch Ness monster lives in the lake.

Peg: Are there any clarifications?

Students: (No response.)

Teacher: I have a clarification. You had trouble reading some of these words and I wondered if you know what some of them mean. What does *ancestors* mean?

The teacher continues discussing vocabulary.

Source: From Englert & Mariage (1991).

Research Note

Which Should I Teach: Content or Strategies?

Educators debate whether reading comprehension instruction should emphasize teaching strategies as in this lesson or teaching content, with little evidence to support either position. Reading instruction that emphasizes content focuses students on the meaning of the text, while strategy instruction emphasizes explicit teaching of cognitive strategies. The difference between the two approaches was described by McKeown, Beck, and Blake (2009):

> For a sense of how the two approaches operate, consider a group of students who have just finished reading a short segment of text. In a strategies approach, the teacher might ask the students to summarize the text and recall what kind of information goes into a good summary. She might follow up a student's summary by asking other students if it was a good summary and why or why not. In a content approach, the teacher might ask what the portion of text had been about, and as students respond, follow up by asking how pieces of information that students contributed fit in with what is being read or why the information is important. (p. 28)

Research has shown that both types of comprehension instruction benefit learners who are at risk (Beck, McKeown, Sandora, Kucan, & Worthy, 1996; Duffy & Roehler, 1989; Palincsar & Brown, 1988), but questions remain. With regard to strategies instruction, clear guidelines for which strategies to use, and in what situations and combinations, do not exist (McKeown et al., 2009). Research-validated guidelines for how to effectively teach content are also lacking (McKeown et al., 2009). Few studies have directly compared strategies and content instruction within the same study, and for those that have (for example, McKeown et al.) the results were inconclusive. In the meantime, we recommend that comprehension instruction integrate both approaches. Students who have read expository text about a tsunami should be able to write or orally describe new knowledge they have acquired about the life-threatening waves. Activities teaching students to identify the main idea for sections of the text can be integrated within the same lesson. When a class studies *The Secret Garden* (Burnett, 2008), the teacher can emphasize content teaching so students learn to recognize and hypothesize the cause of the physical and mental changes that occurred in the characters; to identify the contrast between Mary's life, climate, and family in India and those in England; and to discuss ethical issues and their feelings about the father who abandoned his son, while also learning how to apply self-monitoring comprehension strategies.

---

a question. How could the colonies make England rich?" (self-questioning) "As I think about it, the British could sell their products to the colonies. They could also get raw materials from the colonies so they could manufacture goods to see and improve their balance of trade." (clarifying) "To summarize, the British want to be rich and powerful by having the colonists buy only from them, and by using the colonies' raw materials to manufacture goods for export." (summarizing) "I wonder what the colonists will think about England's trade policy. I also wonder what England will do to make the colonies trade only with them." (self-questioning) "I think that England will use its military to force the colonies to trade just with them." (predicting) The *In Your Classroom* shows another example of how to teach multiple reading comprehension strategies using reciprocal teaching. The *Research Note* discusses the issue of whether reading comprehension instruction should emphasize the teaching of strategies or content.

Table 10.7 summarizes research-based practices associated with teaching reading comprehension.

TABLE 10.7   Research-Based Comprehension Instruction

Components of Instruction	Research-Based	Not Research-Based
Comprehension	Structure of both narrative and expository text taught directly; strategies overtly modeled and practiced in a planned progression; subskills such as main idea and theme are taught and applied.	Instruction dominated by choral reading, shared reading and guided reading with undirected classroom discussion; teacher modeling (thinking aloud) the primary instructional strategy but with little scaffolding reduction; acceptance of student-constructed meanings over consensual meanings or those intended by author; student book choices emphasized often at expense of content.

Source: Adapted from Moats, L. C. (2007). *Whole language high jinks: How to tell when "scientifically-based reading instruction" isn't.* Washington, DC: Fordham Institute.

How Can I Assess and Monitor My Students' Progress in Reading Comprehension in a Multi-Tier or RTI Model?

As with any skill, you need to assess comprehension to learn which students are experiencing difficulty (screening), what specific problems they are having (diagnosis), and whether they are acquiring the reading skills you are teaching them (progress monitoring). Reading comprehension assessment should occur in the following areas: oral reading fluency, oral language, listening comprehension, basic literal and inferential comprehension, narrative comprehension, expository comprehension, and metacognitive skills.

Screening and Progress Monitoring

Maze and cloze curriculum-based assessments can be used to identify which students are having comprehension problems and to monitor their progress. Cloze or maze assessments require students to silently read a grade-level passage for three minutes. In the cloze assessment, after the initial sentence, every specified (e.g., seventh, tenth) word is deleted. Students write in the correct word that is missing. The maze is a multiple-choice variation on the cloze, but after the first sentence, every seventh word is replaced with a choice of three words inside parentheses. One of the supplied words is correct, one is the same part of speech (e.g., noun or verb), and the third does not make sense. Students circle the correct word as they silently read the test. After students complete the test, the number of words correctly circled is tallied. Teachers use a scoring template as a guide to score the assessments and put slashes through any incorrect answers before returning to the top and counting the number of correct words. The score is usually expressed as the total number of responses correct (RC) followed by the total number of errors (e.g., 37/3). As with the oral reading fluency assessments, for the benchmark assessment students read three passages and the median score is recorded as the benchmark score (Parker, Hasbrouck, & Tindal, 1992; Shinn, Deno, & Espin, 2000).

In order to accurately complete a maze or cloze assessment, students have to decode the text; apply their background knowledge; and understand basic word order (syntax), vocabulary, and sentence meaning in context (semantics). Maze assessments are preferred to cloze for English language learners because the target words are provided. Maze assessments are also the best choice for younger or at-risk students because of reduced demands

TABLE 10.8   Typical Percentile Chart for a Maze Assessment

	Percentile	Fall Benchmark RC	Winter Benchmark RC	Spring Benchmark RC
FIFTH GRADE	90	27	33	36
	75	23	26	30
	50	16	20	24
	25	10	16	16
	10	7	10	12

on fine motor skills, working memory, and spelling (Gunderson, 2008). For this reason, as well as the fact that it has established norms, the maze assessment is emphasized in the text. While both maze and cloze assessments have adequate validity for assessing comprehension, they should be given with other assessments of skills underlying comprehension, such as oral reading fluency or a word analysis assessment.

Table 10.8 depicts a benchmark table similar to one that might be used to interpret fifth-grade maze performance. Note that the data reported are the number of responses correct (RC).

The benchmark scores on a normed table like this one allow you to compare the score of a student with the scores of other students in the district or the country. This table tells you that in the fall, 75% of the students had scores of 23 RC or lower, and 25% of the students had scores of 10 RC or lower. Scores below the 50th percentile indicate that additional Tier 2 or Tier 3 support may be needed, depending on whether other reading scores reflect the same low performance. For example, Kareen is a student in Ms. Arno's class. To interpret Kareen's median RC score of 8 in August, Ms. Arno looked at the Fall Benchmark column, where she noticed that Kareen's median score of 8 was below the 25th percentile. If other reading scores mirror this one, Ms. Arno will recommend that Kareen receive Tier 3 support.

Normative growth rates similar to those you learned about in Chapter 5 for oral reading fluency are also available for maze assessments. If you are a special education teacher, these growth rates can be useful in writing meaningful IEP objectives. In Grades 1–6, the realistic weekly growth rate for maze RC is .4 per week, while an ambitious growth rate is .85 (Stecker & Lembke, 2005). When students are behind their peers, IEP projections should be based on ambitious growth rates. For example, if Kareen's teacher Ms. Arno were to set a 30-week IEP objective at the beginning of the year based on the beginning benchmark median score of 8 RC and the ambitious growth rate, she could set a 30-week objective as follows:

number of weeks _____ ×.85 RC = _____ + median score _____ = _____ RC

The computation for Kareen would look like this:

30 (number of weeks) × .85 RC (ambitious rate) = 25.5 RC + 8 RC (median score) = 33.5 RC

Before she wrote her IEP objective, Ms. Arno looked at how many responses Kareen answered incorrectly to determine her level of accuracy. Looking at accuracy can help her determine if Kareen scored below the 50th percentile because she is a slow reader or due to some other factor. Ms. Arno found that Kareen missed 4 responses, so her accuracy was 8/(8 + 4), or 8/12, equaling 67%. The percentage score indicates that Kareen is a slow and inaccurate reader. Ms. Arno decided to do further diagnostic testing to determine if poor decoding, poor fluency, or both were contributing to Kareen's comprehension deficit. She also decided to include accuracy as well as correct responses in developing this IEP objective for Kareen: "Given a grade-level maze reading passage and a 3-minute time limit, Kareen will circle the correct word choice, making 33.5 correct responses with 90% or

Norm tables for maze fluency are listed in the book *The ABC's of CBM: A practical guide to curriculum-based measurement* (Hosp, Hosp, & Howell, 2007) or can be purchased through AIMSweb and Edcheckup.

You can make your own maze sheets by visiting the Maze Passage Generator at **http://www.rti2.org/rti2/mazes.**

higher accuracy, on two out of three consecutive reading passages." Throughout the year, Ms. Arno can use the same kind of graph to monitor progress for maze as she uses for charting oral reading fluency.

You cannot conventionally assess reading comprehension for older learners or kindergarten or first-semester first-grade students who have limited decoding skills. For these students, the best option is to assess listening comprehension, which can be done in one of two ways. For younger students, use a measure specifically developed for assessing listening comprehension, such as the Texas Primary Reading Inventory (TPRI) described in Chapter 9. In this measure, students listen to a passage and then answer explicit and implicit comprehension questions about what they heard. The Early Reading Diagnostic Assessment (ERDA) is a similar listening comprehension instrument. In the ERDA, students in kindergarten listen to the teacher read passages, answer questions about the passage, and then retell the story in their own words; first-grade students look at a picture, listen to the teacher read a passage, and then answer comprehension questions about main ideas and supporting elements from the passage. For older students with limited decoding skills, use the comprehension assessment you are giving to the rest of the students and read it to them before asking the questions. While most tests haven't been standardized to account for oral administrations, giving the test orally should still provide you with an adequate basis for screening potential comprehension problems.

Diagnostic Assessment

Once you have determined that there is a comprehension problem, the next step is to identify the specific problems that contribute to poor reading comprehension. Assessing reading comprehension is difficult because of the great variance across tests as well as the multiplicity and complexity of the factors that contribute to reading comprehension performance. For example, student weaknesses in underlying skills such as decoding can have a significant effect on their comprehension scores. Sarah might have high-level comprehension skills, but if her decoding skills are weak and she has to read lengthy passages on a comprehension test, her scores will reflect low comprehension. The nature of the reading task used on a test can also limit the utility of the findings. For example, the comprehension section of the Wechsler Individual Achievement Test-II (WIAT) doesn't require students to read a large amount of text. Thus, students' scores on this test may not reflect the struggle they have reading longer expository text (Fletcher, Lyone, Ruchs, & Barnes, 2007). Researchers have revealed that a large proportion of questions on the Gray Oral Reading Test (GORT) can be answered with above-chance accuracy without reading the passage, with the final score reflecting reasoning from prior knowledge more than how accurately the student read and understood the passages (Keenan & Betjemann, 2006). For these reasons, it is recommended that teachers always validate performance on standardized tests of comprehension with curriculum-based assessments and observations of daily performance in class. When using tests of comprehension to make decisions related to eligibility for special education, we recommend synthesizing the results of two or three different reading comprehension tests (Keenan & Betjemann, 2006).

The fact that there are a variety of different comprehension problems presents another challenge for diagnostic assessment. For example, some students may lack the background, semantic, and/or syntactical knowledge needed to make inferences or glean information from the text that is not explicitly stated. Still others may be able to read accurately and fluently but don't think about what they are reading; they may need to learn how to ask themselves questions about key vocabulary and other story components as they read. Some students may have trouble monitoring their comprehension; these students cannot determine whether or not they are attaining the appropriate level of understanding, and, if not, employ fix-up strategies to improve their understanding. Finally, students may not understand how to use the organizational structures of both narrative and expository text. Described below are assessments that can be used to assess student strengths and weaknesses in the above areas.

Reading Accuracy and Fluency   As described in Chapter 5, student oral reading accuracy and fluency are strongly related to reading comprehension and can be measured using an Oral Reading Fluency measure.

Oral Language   A number of assessments used to screen and diagnose oral language problems were described in Chapter 9.

Background Knowledge   While there are some standardized tests that assess students' general level of background knowledge, background knowledge required for comprehension varies so much from text to text that it makes the most sense to assess student background knowledge at the beginning of each instructional activity. A strategy for determining how much knowledge students already have about a topic, so that you can decide how much background information to present in class prior to a reading assignment, is called the PReP (PreReading Plan) strategy (Friend & Bursuck, 2008; Langer, 1984). The PReP strategy has three major steps:

> 1. Preview the text or lesson and choose two to three important concepts. For example, for a science lesson, Mr. Amin, the teacher described in Step 2, chose the concept of photosynthesis and the key words *cycle* and *oxygen*.
>
> 2. Conduct a brainstorming session with students. This process involves three phases. In Phase 1 of brainstorming, students tell you what comes to mind when they hear the concept. This gives you a first glance at how much they already know about the topic. In Phase 2, students tell you what made them think of their responses in Phase 1. This information can help you judge the depth and basis for their responses and provides a springboard for students to refine their responses in Phase 3 of brainstorming. In Mr. Amin's class, two students mistakenly thought that photosynthesis had to do with photography because of the presence of *photo* in the word. This error provided an opportunity to build on students' knowledge. Mr. Amin explained that *photo* means "light" and that in photography, a camera takes in light and combines it with certain chemicals on film to make pictures. He then said that plants take in light, too, and when the light combines with chemicals in the plant, carbohydrates and oxygen are made. This process is called *photosynthesis.* In this way, Mr. Amin used what the students already knew to teach them a concept they did not know. In Phase 3, students can add to their responses based on the discussion in Phase 2.
>
> 3. Evaluate student responses to determine the depth of their prior knowledge of the topic. During this step, you can decide whether students are ready to read the text and/or listen to a lecture on photosynthesis, or they first need more information. In Mr. Amin's class, two students continued to have trouble understanding that photosynthesis was something plants did with light to make carbohydrates and oxygen. They needed more information before they were ready to read the chapter. Mr. Amin accommodated these students by showing them a video illustration of photosynthesis including concrete examples that weren't necessary to use with the rest of the class (Friend & Bursuck, 2008; p. 335).

Basic Literal and Inferential Comprehension   You can diagnose basic literal and inferential comprehension skills using the assessments listed on the next page.

Iowa Test of Basic Skills (ITBS) Form M

This assessment for Grades K and up can be given individually or in groups. Comprehension starts with Level 6, and the tasks require progressively more independence in reading as the test level increases.

Texas Primary Reading Inventory (TPRI)

In this individually given assessment for Grades 1 and 2, students read developmentally appropriate passages and answer five comprehension questions, three of which are explicit and two implicit.

Test of Reading Comprehension–Third Edition (TORC–3)

The TORC–3 measures comprehension in four ways: syntactical similarities, paragraph reading, sentence sequencing, and reading directions.

Woodcock Reading Mastery Test–Revised (WRMT–R)

In this individually administered assessment, students silently read a passage that has a word missing and then tell the examiner a word that could appropriately fill in the blank space. The passages are drawn from actual newspaper articles and textbooks.

Text Structure: Narratives   One way to assess student knowledge of narrative text structures is to turn information about **story grammars** into comprehension questions. Using story grammar questions to assess narrative comprehension skills has a number of advantages. First, focusing on story grammars ensures that the focus of the assessment is on the big ideas of stories as opposed to less important details. Second, writing clear comprehension questions that accurately measure the intended comprehension skill can be difficult. In our experience, when writing your own questions it is often difficult to discern whether students have a comprehension problem or the comprehension items simply weren't written clearly enough. For your primary readers, try these more basic story grammar questions (Carnine et al., 2010).

Who is the story about?
What is he/she trying to do?
What happens when he/she tries to do it?
What happens in the end?

For more intermediate readers, select among these possible questions for each essential story grammar (Carnine & Kinder, 1985).

Theme

What is the major point of the story?
What is the moral of the story?
What did _____ learn at the end of the story?

Setting

Where did _____ happen?
When did _____ happen?

Character

Who is the main character?
What is ____ like?

Initiating Events

What is _____'s problem?
What does _____ have to try to do?

Attempts

What did ____ do about _____?
What will _____ do now?

Resolution

How did _____ solve the problem?
How did _____ achieve the goal?
What would you do to solve _____'s problem?

Reactions

How did _____ feel about the problem?
Why did _____ do _____?
How did _____ feel at the end?
Why did _____ feel that way?
How would you feel about _____?

When assessing story grammars, first have the students read a story that they can read with at least 95% accuracy (Gunning, 2002). Older struggling readers benefit from reading the story silently, then orally. For older skilled students, the story can be read once silently. Younger students should only read the story orally (Klingner, Vaughn, & Boardman, 2004). For students with significant decoding problems, read the story as they listen. After students have heard or read the story, ask the story grammar questions and record student answers.

There are times when you might not wish to ask questions about a story. Specific questions can give students clues to the answers, and they especially help students identify the information you think is important to remember or the way you organize this information. One way to solve this problem is to have students retell stories after they read them, using a checklist during the retelling. Students then must organize the information they think is important so you can evaluate the completeness of their recall. Two requirements are necessary for effective evaluation of story retellings to occur: a standard set of criteria to evaluate the completeness of the **retelling,** and the opportunity to evaluate each student's retelling individually. Ms. Padilla used a Story Grammar Retelling Checklist to evaluate the story retelling for Chantille, a student in her class. While in this case Ms. Padilla had Chantille read the story, if Chantille had been unable to read the story with 95% accuracy, Ms. Padilla could have read it to Chantille before having her retell it.

Look at Chantille's scores shown in Table 10.9. As you can see, she had a good idea of who the main characters were and received a "+" for this component (Characters). Chantille named two problems in the story: Dora making a farola that her family laughed at, and Dora's brother and sister getting lost. Chantille identified the problem of the lost kids without being prompted, and the problem of the funny farola with prompts; thus a "+" and a "✓" were scored for Goal/Problem. It was unclear from Chantille's response exactly how the characters tried to solve their problem, so she received a minus (–) for Attempts. Chantille did say the problem was solved when Dora's brother and sister saw the frog; she received

TABLE 10.9   Story Grammar Retelling Checklist

Student Name	Story Elements Evaluated												
	Theme		Setting		Characters		Goal/ Problem		Attempts		Resolution		Reactions
Chantille	–		✓		+		+	✓	–		+	–	+	

Source: Friend, M., and Bursuck, W. (2008). *Including students with special needs: A practical guide for classroom teachers* (5th ed., pp. 134–135). Boston: Pearson Education.

a "+" for this element of Resolution. However, she did not say how this resolved the problem of her family laughing at the farola, so she received another minus (–). Chantille's reaction to the story was appropriate, so a "+" was scored. For Setting, Chantille received a "✓"; Ms. Padilla prompted her. Finally, Chantille received a minus (–) for Theme. This response was lacking, even after prompting.

Ms. Padilla's prompts included explicit references to the various story grammar components. For example, she asked, "You said that Dora's sister and brother got lost. What did they do to solve that problem?" as opposed to asking a more general question, such as "What happened to Dora's sister and brother?" This use of specific language makes the story grammar components more clear, a necessary structure for younger, more naïve learners.

Text Structure: Expository   Student knowledge and use of expository text structures can be assessed by having students read passages from one or more of their content-area textbooks. The passages should be at the students' independent reading level and should reflect common text structures that you want to assess. Passages from students' science or social studies books work well for this purpose. As with story grammars, students can read the passages orally, silently, or both, depending on reading skills. If students are unable to read the book with at least 95% accuracy, read the passages to them. Following reading, the student answers questions developed to assess text structure comprehension. For example, here is a brief passage from an eighth-grade social studies text (Buggey, Danzer, Mitsakos, & Risinger, 1985).

> **Striking Workers**
>
> As prices rose, labor unions demanded higher wages. Although many of these demands were met, some companies refused to give their workers adequate pay increases. The result was a number of strikes that soon threatened the stability of the American economy.

To assess overall comprehension of text, ask a main idea question based on the text structure. Here are two possible examples for this paragraph.

Why were there a number of union strikes after the war?

What happened as a result of a rise in prices after the war?

You can also use retellings to assess knowledge of text structures. Ask the student to "tell me in your own words as much information as you can remember from the selection you just read" (Gunning, 2002). If the student does not tell you enough information, ask, "Can you tell me anything more?" While the student is engaged in the retelling, note whether critical features are present in the recall. For example, you might note whether the student demonstrated knowledge of the cause-and-effect relationships among rising consumer prices, demands for higher wages, and strikes.

Metacognitive Skills   Despite their importance, most formal and informal reading assessments tend to ignore metacognitive skills, stressing pure recall or low-level inferences instead (Applegate, Quinn, & Applegate, 2002). Fortunately, you can assess metacognition by adding a metacognitive component to the assessment strategies just discussed. At first, students may engage in few or none of these metacognitive skills. However, over time, they will learn to use them as you model using think-aloud teaching strategies. One way to assess your students' metacognitive skills is to add a student think-aloud component to your comprehension assessment. In student think-alouds, students are asked occasionally to stop and voice their thoughts about the reading process while reading a text. Klingner, Vaughn, and Boardman (2004) referred to this process when they developed the Think-Along Passage (TAP) assessment method to assess the metacognitive strategies students use during reading to identify topics, predict what will happen next, monitor meaning, make inferences, and summarize. The kinds of questions that could be used in a Think-Along Passage assessment are shown in Figure 10.6.

Present child with book or reading passage (Example: *Too Many Tamales* by Gary Soto).

Identifying the Topic

1a. Look at this page. What do you think the story will be about?
    Ex: A surprise party; lots of tamales

1b. How do you know this?
    Ex: Their eyes look like this (points).

1c. If you don't know, how could you figure it out?
    Ex: Turn the pages; read the book.

Possible Strategies

Scans text
Looks at title
Refers to pictures
Refers to prior knowledge
Points out words
Other

Predicting
After a significant event in the story, stop the reading (e.g., after Maria tries on her mother's ring).

2a. What do you think will happen next?
    Ex: Her mom'll get mad.

2b. Why do you think that?
    Ex: 'Cause she shouldn't wear her mom's ring

2c. If you don't know, how could you find out?
    Ex: Read more of the story; look at the pictures.

Possible Strategies

Predicts based on prior knowledge
Predicts based on text cues
Rereads
Looks forward in the text
Uses context cues
Other

Monitoring Meaning
Choose a word that you think will be unfamiliar to the student.

3a. What do you think "masa" mean in the sentence you just read?
    Ex: Dough

3b. How could you tell?
    Ex: From the pictures; it's in a bowl.
    Ex: They kneaded it. That's what you do with dough.

3c. If you don't know, how could you find out?

Possible Strategies

Uses context cues
Substitutes something that looks
   or sounds similar
Mentions other resources
Mentions dictionary as resource
Relates personal experience
Other

Making Inferences
Select something that is not made explicit in the story.

4a. Why do you think they put the masa on corn husks?
    Ex: Cause they wanted to
    Ex: To keep all the stuff together

4b. How did you decide this?
    Ex: I just thought it.
    Ex: I know cause I help Gramma make tamales.

4c. If you don't know, how could you figure it out?

Possible Strategies

Infers based on text cues
Infers based on prior knowledge
Relates personal experience
Gives analogy
Scans forward
Rereads
Other

Summarizing
After you or the student has finished reading the book, ask for a summary.

5a. If you wanted to tell your friends about this story, what would you tell them?

5b. How did you decide what things to tell them?

5c. If you don't know, how do you think you could decide?

Possible Strategies

Retells mostly main ideas
Retells mostly details
Organizes ideas in recall
Summaries are disorganized
Expresses opinions or reactions
Connects to personal experiences
Uses genre structure to help recall
Other

FIGURE 10.6 Think-Along Passage Protocol for Assessing Strategic Reading

Source: Based on information from Paris, S. G. (1991), cited in H. W. Catts & A. G. Kamhi (2005). *Language and reading disabilities* (2nd ed., p. 187). Boston: Pearson Education.

In Your Classroom

Motivating Your Students to Read Widely

- Provide daily opportunities for students to independently read self-selected and teacher- and peer-recommended texts. All teacher-selected material should be at the students' independent levels so they can be read with at least 95% accuracy. See pages 172–173 in Chapter 5 for guidelines on how to select the appropriate reading material for students.
- Convey enthusiasm for the books your students are reading and talk about your own reading outside of class. If students' parents aren't modeling recreational and informational reading at home, the teacher can pass along the purpose of and excitement from her reading outside of school. One week Mrs. Rice told her class about a book she was reading about magnets, since she was going to teach them that subject and wanted to learn more. Two weeks earlier she described the exciting mystery novel she was reading and the adventures the main character had in the deserts of the Sahara.
- Allow students to select books from a classroom library when they have completed their work. This minimizes behavior problems that can arise from waiting and also provides more opportunities for students to self-select books of interest.

To meet the needs of all students, classroom libraries should contain a wide range of books, from easy decodable books to challenging chapter books without pictures. As recommended in Chapter 9, 50% of the books should be nonfiction.
- Honor and encourage students' outside reading. Some schools have developed motivational plans to encourage students to read a certain number of books in order to earn awards. Be a book detective and notice what your students are reading so you can comment briefly on their selections. Students will do more reading if it leads to more attention. When Mr. Bayer was teaching the continent of Africa in social studies, he turned to Lydia and asked her to tell the most interesting thing she had learned about Africa in a book about pyramids that he had noticed her reading the previous week. When the lunch line was backed up in the hall, Mr. Bayer turned to Shelley and said that he noticed she had been reading *Little House on the Prairie*, which was always a favorite book of his students.
- Encourage a classroom reading culture by having students write blogs and tweets to comment on books they enjoyed reading.

When your students are able to read accurately and fluently, as well as understand what they read, you will have given them a powerful tool to increase their learning over a lifetime. Still, reading is only empowering insofar as students do it. That is why it is so important for teachers to motivate their students to read widely to further their own learning. Strategies for motivating your students to read widely are described in the *In Your Classroom* feature above.

How Can I Give Struggling Readers in Tier 3 a More Systematic, Explicit Approach to Learning Comprehension Skills?

A key theme of this book is that some students struggle to acquire reading skills, despite receiving Tier 1 instruction that is enhanced and reasonably well executed. For the reading components of phonemic awareness, alphabetic principle, and fluency, struggling students were provided with extra support in Tiers 2 and 3. You may find that some of your students also struggle with reading comprehension. Described below are four reading comprehension programs designed for students who can benefit from more explicit, systematic instruction delivered within a smaller instructional group.

Corrective Reading (Engelmann et al., 2008) is an intensive direct-instruction reading program for students in Grades 4–12 who are reading one or more years below grade level. The program has two tightly sequenced strands—decoding and comprehension. At specified times in the connected text activities, students are asked literal and inferential questions that are scripted in the teacher presentation books. Throughout the program, students learn key comprehension strategies to help them understand what they read, including thinking operations, information skills, reasoning skills, and sentence-writing skills, as well as strategies for organizing information, operating on information, using sources of information, using information for directions, and communicating information (Marchand-Martella, Slocum, & Martella, 2004).

Reading Success: Effective Comprehension Strategies (Dixon et al., 2008) is a reading comprehension program designed to supplement your regular reading program. It can be used with individuals from fourth grade through high school who decode at a fourth-grade level or higher, but who struggle meeting state standards in reading comprehension. Lessons take approximately 15 to 20 minutes each and can be taught daily or three times per week. The authors recommend scheduling the lessons to ensure that students finish the program before any spring testing in reading comprehension. The program teaches key comprehension skills using the scientifically based components of explicit strategy instruction, scaffolding, and review. The principal outcomes of *Reading Success* are related to inference, main idea, fact and opinion, literal comprehension, author's purpose, paraphrasing, rewriting passages, word meanings, and figurative language. The program includes placement tests as well as quizzes or tests every five lessons to test mastery of key program skills.

Text Talk, a curriculum for Grades K–3 (Beck & McKeown, 2001) focuses on comprehension and vocabulary development through the use of read-alouds and open-ended questions. The teacher reads stories that contain challenging vocabulary and enough complexity of events for children to build meaning. Throughout the read-aloud sessions, the teacher asks questions designed to encourage children to elaborate on their initial answers and draw on their background knowledge to gain understanding from the text. After students have responded to the text, pictures are discussed, and a variety of activities relating to the new vocabulary words are completed.

In the *Language!* program (Greene, 2009), comprehension is taught through the use of decodable connected text containing phonemic/graphemic concepts, vocabulary, and words that have been directly taught in the program. Reading comprehension instruction is also coordinated with instruction in expressive writing. The program stresses two key comprehension strategies within a "before, during, and after" reading instructional routine. Each story is followed by questions related to different levels of Bloom's taxonomy; the levels are introduced gradually, beginning in Unit 3. Students are directly taught the signal words for each of the six levels of the taxonomy so they can recognize what is being asked of them and can respond accordingly. They are also taught to create questions using signal words from the taxonomy. Story grammars are introduced gradually through Level 1 and into Level 2. While the Bloom questions and story grammars are stressed, *Language!* incorporates other comprehension strategies into its teaching routines, including brainstorming to build background knowledge, paraphrasing/ summarization, and the use of graphic organizers to recognize story parts.

To learn more about RTI, go to the IRIS Center website and complete modules 3, 4, and 5. Compare their recommendations for using the RTI model with recommendations that you have read about in this book. **http:// iris.peabody.vanderbilt.edu/ rti03_reading/chalcycle.htm http://iris.peabody.vanderbilt.edu/ rti04_alltogether/chalcycle.htm http://iris.peabody.vanderbilt.edu/ rti05_tier3/chalcycle.htm.**

How Do I Prepare My Students to Pass High-Stakes Tests in Reading?

While the most important job we have as teachers of reading is to teach our students to read for their own enjoyment and learning, the realities of today's culture of school accountability dictates that we must also prepare our students to perform well on high-stakes reading assessments. In our estimation, the best way to prepare students for high-stakes tests in reading is to have an effective reading program in place when children start school. Scientifically based reading programs, much like those described in this text, enable students to pass state tests by providing them with the phonemic awareness, phonics, fluency, vocabulary, and comprehension skills needed to read a wide range of text with understanding. That said, your students can still benefit from teacher-directed instruction and practice geared specifically toward your particular state test. Here are some steps to assure that the practice you provide goes beyond basic test preparation and further develops comprehension skills.

Analyze Your State Test

a. What types of passages are students required to comprehend? Most high-stakes tests in reading use narrative, expository, or functional material from everyday life such as application forms, recipes, or advertisements.

b. What levels of understanding are measured? Usually there is a mix of literal and inferential questions. Questions also test student ability to analyze and evaluate information as well as use metacognitive strategies.

c. What kinds of information are tested and how are the questions asked? Educational Resources Inc. (2004) has compiled a list of key question types as well as typical questions for each type. These are shown in Figure 10.7. Additional items and questions related to narrative prose and poetry adapted from Goudiss, Hodges, and Margulies (1999) are also included.

Teach Students to Recognize the Various Question Types   The ability to determine what a question is asking is an important first step in answering it correctly. That is why students need to be directly taught the information shown in Figure 10.7, along with other question-answering comprehension strategies like the QAR. When Travis was able to recognize that a question was asking about sequencing, he was then reminded to look for key words to help answer the question, such as *beginning, last, next,* and *before.* When Abdul recognized a vocabulary question, he automatically looked at the words around the word in the passage to figure out what it meant.

Teach Strategies for Answering Question Types Systematically and Explicitly
Just as in teaching the reading comprehension strategies described earlier in this chapter, systematic, explicit instruction works best when teaching your students to answer items on high-stakes tests. You can be systematic by working on the various question types one at a time, gradually introducing new types of questions as other types are mastered. You can be explicit by adding think-alouds to your My Turn–Together–Your Turn teaching routine. Examples of how to use think-alouds for a main idea/summarization question and a metacognitive question are shown below.

Main Idea/Summarization

I bought my car seven years ago. I haven't driven it for a year because I've been away. Yesterday I thought I'd get it ready to take out on the road again. I had a real shock when I looked at it.

Main Idea/Summarization	Author's Purpose	Moral
※ This *story* is mostly about _____. ※ What is this *story* mainly about? ※ What is another good name/title for this *story*? ※ Another title/name for the *selection* might be _____.	※ This story was written mainly to _____. ※ The writer wrote this *story* mainly to _____. ※ The *article* was written in order to _____. ※ _____ was written in order to _____.	※ The important message in the *story* is _____. ※ What lesson can be learned from this *selection*? ※ What lesson did _____ need to learn? ※ This story suggests _____.

Mood/Feeling/Emotion	Fact and Opinion	Sequencing
※ At the end of the story, _____ probably felt _____. ※ What made (character) feel _____?	※ Which of these is a fact in the story? ※ Which of these is an opinion in the story? ※ Which of the following is NOT _____? ※ All of the above are opinions except _____ _____. ※ Which of these is a fact stated in the article?	※ The boxes show _____. ※ Which belongs in box _____? ※ What must be decided before _____? ※ In the beginning of the story _____. ※ Which of these happens last? ※ After (an event in the story), what must happen next?

Prediction	Vocabulary	Sources of Information
※ What will probably happen the next time _____? ※ What will probably happen next? ※ What probably happened after the story ended? ※ Which of these happens last? ※ What do you think will happen in the future?	※ In this story, _____ means _____. ※ In this story, a _____ is a _____. ※ What did the author mean when he said _____? ※ In this story, a _____ is like a _____. ※ In this article the phrase _____ means _____. ※ What words in the story show that _____?	※ If you wanted to find out more information, you should _____. ※ Look in a (source). ※ Look in a book called (title). ※ You would most likely find this story in a _____. ※ What is the best way to learn more about _____?

Metacognitive Questions	Miscellaneous Stems	Character Analysis
※ To skim this passage the reader would _____. ※ In order to answer question _____, the reader would _____.	※ Which question does the first paragraph answer? ※ If the author added a sentence in the story, what might he add? _____ ※ This story is a _____.	※ The most important character in the story is _____. ※ How would you describe _____? ※ How are _____ and _____ different? ※ What is the best word to describe _____?

FIGURE 10.7   Common Question Types on High-Stakes Reading Tests

Continued

Setting Analysis	Plot Analysis	Author's Point of View
⊗ The story takes place _____?	⊗ What is the problem in the story?	⊗ What does the author think of _____?
⊗ Where is the story set?	⊗ How is the problem resolved?	⊗ What does the author think people should do if _____?
⊗ What time do you think _____ takes place?		
⊗ Where is _____ at the end of the story?		
⊗ Where do you think _____ lives?		
⊗ How much time passes in the story?		

Poetry and Poetic Language
⊗ Which lines rhyme?
⊗ What does the author mean by _____?
⊗ Why do you think the author wrote that?
⊗ What do the words _____ describe?
⊗ What point is the author trying to make when she _____?

FIGURE 10.7 Continued

Source: Adapted from Educational Resources Inc. (2004). Strategies for taking high-stakes tests. Unpublished materials; and Goudiss, M., Hodges, V., & Margulies, S. (1999). *The ISAT coach: Grade 3 reading.* New York: Triumph Learning/Coach Books.

The back window was cracked. Two of the lights wouldn't go on. The motor needed a lot of work. The rear door wouldn't open. I don't think I can afford to fix it. It's a shame. I liked my old car.

What is this passage mainly about?

A. New cars are expensive.
B. The car lights don't work.
C. The car is in very bad shape.
D. The writer has been away. (Goudiss et al., 1999, p. 105)

Think-Aloud *Let's see. I need to figure out what this whole passage is about—not just one thing that is in the passage. Let me try the first choice, A, "New cars are expensive." That wasn't even mentioned in the story, so that can't be right. Choice B says the car lights don't work—that was in the story but it's only one thing in the story, not what the whole passage is about—so the answer can't be B. Choice C says the car is in very bad shape—that's what a lot of the sentences in the passage talked about, so it would make a good choice here. I'm going to pick C.*

How Do I Teach Comprehension to Older Learners?

Reading instruction should increasingly emphasize comprehension strategies once students are reading at a fourth- or fifth-grade level (Moats, 2001). Some students who are at risk will continue to increase their reading skills if they are in content classes with teachers who routinely weave the comprehensive strategies discussed earlier in this chapter into their instruction. A biology teacher who teaches his students to ask questions to check their understanding of the chapter on plant life, who uses think-alouds to show how to apply comprehension strategies, and who accompanies reading assignments with graphic organizers is teaching expository reading comprehension strategies along with biology. An English teacher who teaches students to answer inferential questions based on the novels they are studying, who models ways to differentiate between major events and added details, and who demonstrates how to summarize sections of the story is teaching students narrative reading comprehension strategies.

Other students who are at risk can benefit from a separate class of study skills where comprehension strategies are taught more explicitly and the teacher provides the opportunity to systematically apply those strategies to course material from their content classes. Unless they spend more time learning comprehension strategies, these students will not acquire higher reading levels. A third group of students is comprised of those who still need support in beginning or advanced word reading, some of it intensive. Because they are still advancing in their word reading skills, a smaller proportion of their instruction will include learning comprehension strategies. To help these students make the most progress, teach them to apply comprehension strategies to narrative and expository text at their independent or instructional reading level.

One of the greatest challenges for teachers of older struggling readers is finding text that is at the students' instructional level but still is interesting and content rich. In selecting text for comprehension instruction with these readers, teachers have several options. Spadorcia (2001) recommends that books be examined through many different lenses, recognizing the particular skills that less-skillful students need to learn to become better readers. If the student is past the beginning reading phase, Spadorcia recommends using balanced literacy books having a combination of many high-frequency words and some decodable words. Her analysis showed that these books had higher levels of sentence-level sophistication. *Swamp Furies* (Schraff, 1992) is an example of this type of book. Another type of book, the "high interest—low reading level decodable book," is also often appropriate for comprehension instruction. A science fiction book, *Deadly Double* (France, 1998), is a typical high–low book that falls into this category (Spadorcia, 2001). Some book series, like the *National Geographic Explorer* books, have differentiated instruction for the same topic. One set of books on the topic of lightning is written at the second- to third-grade level, while another set of books on that same topic is written at the fourth- to sixth-grade level.

Because your older readers must learn subject matter content in many of their classes, and because they are more likely to read expository text as adults, look for content books that are written at students' independent or instructional reading levels. Content books written at a lower readability or for students at a lower grade level can be used to teach comprehension strategies for expository text. If they are used for teaching content, the teacher has to be sure that all state standards for that content area are included or taught. Teaching content in social studies can be especially difficult. An explanation of why this is the case and what to do about it is in *The Reflective Teacher* feature.

The *ReadingQuest.org: Making Sense in Social Studies* website has hyperlinks to 27 reading strategies that can be integrated into social studies instruction: **http://www.readingquest.org/home.html.**

The Reflective Teacher

Why Is Social Studies Text More Difficult?

After third grade, students read a much higher proportion of nonfiction text in school. Social studies text presents greater challenges for students who are at risk. Teachers in our project noticed that students' DIBELS scores routinely dipped when they read social studies passages. Comprehending history is highly specialized reading requiring readers to critically think about evidence, the historical context of when events occurred, multiple perspectives of individuals at the time, and the significance of the events (Zarnowski, 2006). Other factors that make reading social studies, especially history, more difficult include the following:

- The text often contains vocabulary and ideas that students are not familiar with and that cannot be inferred. Students have to be skilled decoders for some of the new multisyllable words and have an adequate vocabulary for the historical and geographic terms that appear in the text. For adequate comprehension, students need to know the meaning of 95% of the words in a text, so preteaching vocabulary is critical *before* reading social studies text.
- Social studies text includes many reference words such as *this, those,* and *it.* In combination with complex sentences and difficult concepts, students can misinterpret what *this* or *those* actually refer to.
- Social studies text has a higher proportion of text written in the passive voice. Consider this sentence: "The sleds the Inuit used were made by lashing animal hides and a basket together with more animal hides." If students are unfamiliar with the word *Inuit*, they can become confused by questions such as "What was made?" and "Who rode in the sleds?"
- Unless the teacher clearly and with enthusiasm explains to students the benefits of learning the social studies information, the students may not relate to it.
- Social studies text routinely uses figurative language. If a student does not actively engage with the text or is an English language learner, visualizing the meaning of what they are reading can pose problems, as in this sentence: "In this rugged region of the country, low hills *snuggle up* to the mountains on the eastern shores."

Because social studies has its own unique challenges for struggling readers, always conduct prereading activities that clarify key vocabulary and provide students with the opportunity to read more-difficult words. After words are introduced, students need frequent, rich follow-up instruction requiring critical thinking so that they have the opportunity to use the new terms at a deeper level. Expect students to explore different facets of the new vocabulary word's meaning, use new words together, and ask questions that require them to apply meaning (e.g., teacher question: *"Which of the following situations demonstrates emancipation: 'The teenager was legally free from his parents when he turned 16' or 'The servant paid homage to the queen'?"*) Finally, the use of a variety of graphic organizers to organize key information provides a blueprint students can use to study core knowledge from social studies text.

As mentioned earlier in this chapter, if the readability of a book is at an older student's instructional level, teacher read-alouds become an important instructional strategy. Using read-alouds with books or taped CDs enables older struggling readers to participate in the equivalent comprehension strategy instruction as peers. Older students will eventually need to practice using these strategies when reading text, but in this way the teacher can at least model the reasoning she uses in strategically approaching a book.

Teachers who convey their passion for reading to students and make the effort to seek out books at the students' reading levels on topics of interest to them can start to penetrate through the walls of resistance older struggling readers have developed. By the time a student reading below grade level is in middle school, one of the biggest challenges is breaking through the anxiety related to reading. The struggling reader has had years of sitting in classes hoping to avoid the humiliation of reading aloud, hearing that if she just "tried harder" she could read the book. Rekindling enthusiasm for reading as the older student gains skills is a slow process and takes careful scaffolding during instruction so the student can be successful during discussions and any oral reading. The student needs to receive twice the amount of praise and encouragement that other students need, and should have books assigned that can be read with a high degree of accuracy. When the student does not have the skills to read the assigned book in a class, taped texts should be an available accommodation whether or not the students has an IEP.

How Can I Teach Reading Comprehension to English Language Learners?

Comprehension of narrative and expository text can be challenging for English language learners who have no real-life experience with common story themes. A story that involves a typical children's birthday party in the United States, or one that takes place while family members are watching an after-Thanksgiving dinner football game, might be unduly confusing unless the teacher has explained the larger context before the reading. Eskey (2002) provides an example of five questions that might be confusing for students who have no experience with the type of party described in the following paragraph:

> It was the day of the big party. Mary wondered if Johnny would like a kite. She ran to her bedroom, picked up her piggy bank, and shook it. There was no sound. (p. 6)

Eskey explains that without discussion before reading the passage, the following questions would be difficult for students who have no cultural experience with such birthday parties:

1. What is the nature of the party in the text?
2. Are Mary and Johnny adults or children?
3. How is the kite related to the party?
4. Why did Mary shake her piggy bank?
5. What was Mary's big problem?

Expository text presents other related challenges. Even students who have developed fluent social language in English still find that academic language, the formal language of textbooks and lectures, requires different skills. Academic language has longer sentences, more complex grammar, and more technical vocabulary than social language. Also, topics in academic contexts are often more abstract, and the clues that English language learners gain from gestures and expressions are absent. A student who is proficient with social language can take up to five more years to develop academic language. That is why English language learners have to be more assertive with their teachers, because cues such as raised eyebrows or puzzled looks are usually inadequate to convey confusion in situations in which academic language is used. Of course, being assertive can raise additional problems for English language learners. Some of these students may be from cultures whose respect for teachers precludes their need to be assertive.

As you learned earlier in the chapter (see Table 10.2), signal words in text provide clues to indicate relationships among ideas and to clarify content. However, signal words provide additional challenges for English language learners. Signal words such as *for example, because, like,* and *first* link sentences and paragraphs together. They are essential for comprehension because they give the reader an indication of what will be happening. In the following sentence, the signal word *as* indicates a time relationship, letting the reader know that the makeup of the wood changed at the same time that the mud and sand of the swamps slowly turned to stone.

> As the mud and sand of the swamps slowly turned to stone, the makeup of the wood changed. (*The DK Science Encyclopedia*, 1998, p. 238)

Explicit teaching of the signal words and their function enables English language learners to use them as a strategy for increasing comprehension (Short, 1994). Teachers can use think-alouds to demonstrate how signal words provide clues for understanding, ask students to locate specific signal words in text, describe how the words provide clues to the meaning of a passage, and construct writing activities that require students to use specified signal words.

Instruction in comprehension monitoring is one of the key comprehension strategies that English language learners need. The ability to carefully monitor comprehension and apply fix-up strategies is crucial for them, because additional linguistic obstacles routinely impede their comprehension. Even though English language learners need to learn all of the comprehension strategies discussed throughout this chapter, Yu-fen Yang (2002) cautions that the focus of reading comprehension instruction first must emphasize language knowledge:

> However, the truth is that if readers do not possess sufficient language skills, then no matter how many diversified reading strategies they are equipped with, and how much training in metacognitive strategy usage they receive, the process will turn out to be fruitless if they have no basic resources to access when attempting to solve problems. They must have extensive resources to monitor whether their understanding of the text is coherent and logical. (p. 37)

Text that is directly related to the English language learner's culture or experience can reduce comprehension challenges. When texts do not have that connection, several days of prereading activities related to the topic can provide that same foundation for new vocabulary and concepts. Teaching strategies discussed in both Chapters 9 and 10 directly apply to English language learners (Francis, Rivera, Lesaux, Kieffer, & Rivera, 2006; Goldenberg, 2008). Some of the most important include the following:

* Use graphic organizers with all new text.
* Present key information about lesson content through visual cues, pictures, and gestures several times.

Learn more about the fourth-grade slump for English language learners by watching the video clip at **http:// www. readingrockets.org/webcasts/2004.**

* Model how to summarize the text, or have another student do it, before providing practice.
* Emphasize vocabulary instruction and strategies discussed in Chapter 9 whenever you teach comprehension.
* Use interactive read-alouds that provide many opportunities to participate in structured discussions of the text.

All students, including English language learners, can benefit from accessing information on the Internet. The *Technology* feature discusses ways to help students maximize their learning on the Internet.

Technology

Reading for Understanding on the Internet

The lack of valid research investigating the different skills needed to read text in books versus Internet text has fueled ongoing debate. Teachers wonder whether their students need to substantially retool and learn additional skills to derive meaning from Internet text. When MacArthur, Ferretti, Okolo, and Cavalier (2001) reviewed studies comparing reading on paper to reading unenhanced text on screen, they found no indication that reading text on screen affected students' comprehension either positively or negatively. Other studies they investigated in which students read text containing enhancements such as hyperlinks providing definitions of difficult words or main ideas showed mixed results.

Since students increasingly use the Internet in place of or in addition to a library, teachers are responsible for critically evaluating claims about the best methods to improve reading comprehension online. Unique features of Internet text may place different demands on the reader. In the course of reading, students often have to make decisions about the large volume of information instantaneously available to them. Becoming overwhelmed with these decisions, many students have been observed to "snatch and grab" the information. Rather than taking the time to evaluate critically which information is most valid and related to their research needs, students quickly hyperlink without much thought (RAND, 2002). In one large study, half of the college students lacked the skills to evaluate how valid and reputable information on nutritional supplements was (Ivanitskaya, O'Boyle, & Casey, 2006).

Social networking has gained popularity since the last edition of this book, and with its advent literacy has evolved from a solitary pursuit into a collective one. Although adults grumble about young adults' lack of spelling and writing skills, increasingly those skills influence social status on websites where a permanent record remains on Google for future employers to mine. In an article about how the Internet saved literacy, Farrell describes two academics' analysis of the increased demand for skilled reading, writing, and spelling skills:

> "You aren't just a consumer of text anymore," says Margaret Mackey, a professor at the University of Alberta's Library and Information Studies Department. "Reading now demands an almost instantaneous response, whether through commenting on a blog or writing a review on Amazon. The Internet has shortened the feedback loop on writing and has made readers more active participants," says Matt Kirschenbaum, an assistant professor of English at the University of Maryland. "Reading is more intimately associated with writing," he says. (Farrell, 2006)

Today's Internet reader must be skilled at comprehending expository text since it comprises the majority of reading on the Internet. Students who have not learned or do not apply expository strategies to paper reading cannot be expected to use them when reading on the Internet. Because estimates indicate that 90% of what students read in elementary school is narrative, students will be unable to fully utilize Internet sources unless teachers have explicitly taught and expected students to read expository text. When Schmar-Dobler (2003) compared reading strategies used in reading books to those used on the Internet, she found no differences in how readers do these things:

- Activate prior knowledge
- Determine important ideas
- Synthesize to sift important from unimportant details
- Draw inferences, reading between the lines and using background knowledge to help fill in gaps

Differences that Schmar-Dobler noted included how readers do these things:

- Rely more on skimming and scanning techniques because of the volume of text.
- Place more emphasis on using guiding questions to stay focused and to avoid getting lost in the text options
- Use Internet basic skills in order to perform tasks such as downloading appropriate text and avoiding pop-up ads that interfere with text reading

Instruction in writing skills that are so important for Internet use should start early. The *In Your Classroom* feature describes ways that Project PRIDE teachers began writing instruction in kindergarten.

In Your Classroom

Beginning Writing in Kindergarten

Beginning in kindergarten, many of the Project PRIDE teachers integrated writing activities into lesson planning to further enhance their students' reading comprehension skills. Teachers found that because students had such strong phonemic awareness skills and had learned to sound-spell, their writing was readable even when they used words that they had not yet learned to spell. Some of the writing activities that teachers planned in connection with comprehension activities were these:

- Writing summaries of stories or expository text in their own words

- Retelling a story from another character's perspective
- Writing several sentences connecting the theme of the story to something they have personally experienced
- Using a key sentence from a story as the story prompt for their writing
- Using the same graphic organizers used for reading comprehension as prewriting organizers before writing stories or informational text
- Completing charts or workbook pages requesting more information about text just read

What Games and Activities Reinforce Reading Comprehension Skills?

Some of the following games can be adapted for younger or older students. Other games are more appropriate for older groups.

Find the Hot Spots

Give students several stick-on notes to use as they read a text. Ask them to mark the described hot spots. For example, ask students to do one or a combination of the following:

* Place pink stick-on notes on pages where there is a vocabulary word they do not know or where the text is confusing.
* Place green stick-on notes on pages where they were excited about what they were reading and thought that the author's writing was exceptionally interesting.
* Place orange stick-on notes on pages where the author makes a claim that is not substantiated by facts or valid, reliable sources.
* Place blue stick-on notes on pages where the author writes about a problem.
* Place purple stick-on notes on pages where they wish they could write like that.

Provide Evidence

Divide students into small groups and give each player six cards. On three cards are adjectives used to describe the personalities of a character, and on three cards are characters from books recently read in class. Students take turns taking and discarding cards until they have a character and an adjective that match. Once a student has a match, he names the story his character is in, describes why his character has the specific personality trait, and provides evidence from the story supporting that opinion. For example, a student might explain that Mr. McGregor in *The Tale of Peter Rabbit* was mean "because he chased Peter around the garden" (Richards & Gipe, 2000).

What Would Your Character Do?

Divide students into small groups. Each student selects a card designating a character from a recently read story. The teacher then presents a situation and asks the students to think about what they know about their character from the story and describe how he or she would respond in the situation. The following is a sample situation described by the authors of this game:

> Your character is transported to a foreign land for two weeks. No one speaks your character's language. English is the only language your character speaks, reads, and writes. Your character needs food, a place to sleep, and money. What would your character do? (Richards & Gipe, 2000, p. 77)

Students should explain what their designated character would do and what evidence from the story leads them to predict that action.

Try Out Your Test-Making Skills

Divide the class into four groups. After students read expository text about social studies or science, ask them to write a specified number of questions about the main ideas of the text. Design a rubric to evaluate their test, making sure to award each team extra points if every question is about a main idea. Once students are finished writing their tests, give each group another group's test and see how well they remember the information they read. Award team points for questions answered correctly.

How Well Do I Understand?

As you read short pieces of expository text to students, ask them to raise one finger if they understand the text being read and two fingers if they do not understand it. Stop when the majority of students have two fingers raised and discuss strategies to clarify understanding of the text.

The Text Detective

Before students read an assigned text, give them short-answer worksheets with key *wh*-questions you want them to answer. Some questions might include: "In what period of time is this biography set?" "What was the main problem this character encountered growing up?" "Where did this character live most of his life?" "Who was the most influential person in this character's life?" and "Why do people say that this character is a leader?"

While games and other activities are effective in reinforcing reading comprehension skills, there is no substitute for effective, teacher-led instruction like that described in *The Reflective Teacher*.

> Visit the Cultural Literacy Rocks website at **www.aft.org/pubs-reports/ american_educator/spring2004/ literacyroacks.html.**

The Reflective Teacher

A Model Comprehension Lesson

Ms. Cowen's second-grade class was going to read *It's Probably Good Dinosaurs Are Extinct* by Ken Raney (1993). Before they read the book, students practiced reading the new morphemes they had recently learned and were now frequently applying to more difficult words they encountered in their reading: *age, tion, ish,* and *dis*. Next they decoded the new words that were in this story. Because students did not know the meaning of the words *extinct, roamed, existed,* and *herd,* Ms. Cowen directly taught them as vocabulary words. Three dinosaur names, *apatosaurus, protoceratops,* and *stegosaurus,* initially presented decoding challenges. Ms. Cowen knew that if students couldn't read the story with adequate accuracy, they would not understand it, so she planned her reading lessons so that students did not read the story until the second day after they had more practice with these and other new words.

On the day that students read the story, Ms. Cowen told everyone the title and, pointing to her large flip chart, asked everyone to tell her what information they already knew about dinosaurs. She wrote the students' answers on a graphic organizer (see Figure 10.8) and extended discussion through questions.

When students pointed out that some dinosaurs ate just plants, Ms. Cowen linked this story to a previous one by reminding students that several weeks ago in a different story they had learned a word that they could use for animals that ate only plants. After a hint,

someone excitedly remembered, "herbivore." After the chart was completed, Ms. Cowen asked, "Where did the dinosaurs live?" That question stumped the class, and so she drew everyone's attention to a large dinosaur picture on the wall. "Caves, they lived in caves," a girl shouted out. Ms. Cowen expanded that answer and said, "Yes, they lived everywhere on Earth. They lived in every country. They've even found dinosaur bones in ice. Some lived in water. Where did others live?" Several students chimed in and explained that some lived on land and others in the air. Ms. Cowen used the moment to expand everyone's knowledge and, pointing to the globe, told the students that scientists believe that the continents were all connected at one time.

Looking deep in thought, another child asked the teacher, "How did the scientists discover the dinosaurs?" Ms. Cowen explained how they found the bones and came up with the name "terrible lizard," which is what *dinosaur* means. "But they only found the bones—nothing else," she explained as everyone nodded their heads. At that, a student volunteered information about how her dad had bought her a computer CD about dinosaurs. One of the dinosaurs on the CD had a hard skull. Another student asked Ms. Cowen if dinosaurs were alive when she was a girl. At first Ms. Cowen joked about all the dinosaurs she would see outside the school at recess, but then she switched into a more serious mode and admitted

Continued

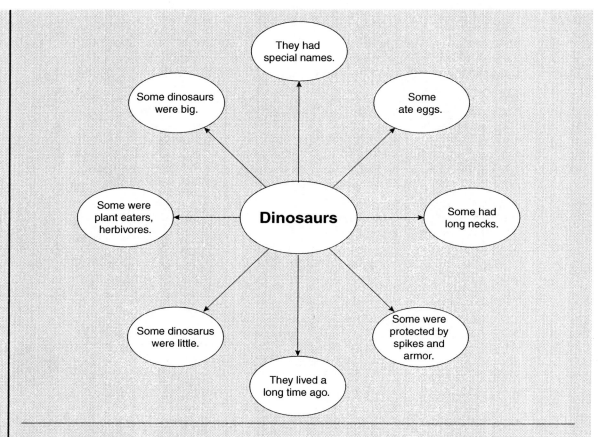

FIGURE 10.8 **Graphic Organizer for Dinosaur Story**

Source: Cowen, J. (2003). Unpublished materials. Rockford, IL: Rockford Public Schools.

that dinosaurs lived so long ago that there were none even when she was a baby. Most of the class seemed to enjoy the humor in this exchange.

After all the students had opened their books, Ms. Cowen explained that the new story was a fantasy story, and she asked what that meant. When one student replied, "not true," Ms. Cowen expanded the answer and explained, "Yes, the story was make-believe." Next everyone orally read the title in unison. Ms. Cowen asked students what "it's" was, since they had been studying contractions, and the class answered, "it is." One student then read two or three sentences while everyone else followed along with their fingers. At the end of that passage, Ms. Cowen asked several questions that the students enthusiastically answered:

"How does the boy feel about dinosaurs?"

"What does he wish he had?"

"How many of you wish you had a dinosaur for a pet?"

After the entire class raised their hands, one student explained why he wanted a dinosaur to help him. Then a second student read another two sentences. This

time Ms. Cowen stopped and asked, "Now the book says, 'It's probably good that dinosaurs are extinct.' What exactly does *extinct* mean?" Even though she had taught that word for two days, it took several hints for the class to remember what the difficult word meant. Wanting her students to use this word more, Ms. Cowen asked, "What would happen if dinosaurs were no longer extinct?" The students were appalled. "But they'd tear up our houses and eat our food," one answered. "They'd eat up our relatives," said another. A third girl chimed in, "They'd be very noisy at night and I couldn't sleep."

The first story reading continued with students reading passages followed by teacher questions. Information was clarified, connections drawn, understanding checked during this enjoyable story. Later, students would write and illustrate their work before it was displayed in the hallway. Two more dinosaur stories followed this one, one a narrative and the other expository. Decoding, oral-language expansion, writing, fluent reading, graphic organizers, storybook structure, and frequent questions all worked together to develop these students' reading comprehension.

APPLIED ACTIVITIES

1. Two fact-or-fiction questions about reading comprehension are included below. Pair up with a partner and take turns defending your position for one of these questions, using references from research sources cited in the chapter or from information on the website resources listed in the sidebars.

   a. While the research on developing phonemic awareness, alphabetic principle, and reading fluency is conclusive enough to guide teacher practice, we don't have a comparable knowledge base for reading comprehension. Is this fact or fiction? Explain why.

   b. Teaching reading comprehension requires that children first have a book in their hands that they are able to read. Is this fact or fiction? Explain why.

2. Shown here are the DIBELS Oral Reading Fluency and maze percentile scores for Ms. Redmond's Grade 3 class in May. Identify which children may be experiencing difficulty with reading comprehension. Determine whether any of these students is also below benchmark in ORF. Why do you think students who read slowly are more likely to also have trouble with comprehension? How would you account for Roberto's performance?

Student	ORF	Maze Percentiles
Alex	115	>75
Bruno	70	<25
Celia	100	<50
Roberto	110	<50
Aquanetta	93	<50

3. In this chapter you learned that the ability to comprehend is influenced by the person reading the text, the text being read, the task the reader is trying to accomplish, and the context in which the reading is being done. For each of the following reading problems, discuss the factor(s) that are contributing to the problem.

   a. Sharif is impulsive, and when given a reading assignment tends to rush through the text and not think about what he is reading.

   b. Margaret could not understand her library book because she always selects books that are too difficult for her.

   c. The reading assignment was difficult for Darren, but by trying extra hard he was able to get through it and answer the questions. Darren needed a good score on the assignment to get a passing grade for the marking period.

   d. Rinaldo refused to read in class because his classmates are critical of anyone who does what the teacher wants.

4. Think of a recent reading assignment for one of your classes. What metacognitive skills did you exercise in completing that assignment? How helpful were these skills for the successful completion of the assignment? How could you teach these skills to students who are unable to do them?

5. Shown here is a fable relating how slow and steady wins the race. Develop a graphic organizer that could be used to guide students as they read to comprehend the passage. Write a script showing what you would say if you were using My Turn–Together–Your Turn think-alouds to teach your students the key story grammar elements.

   One day the Rabbit made fun of the short legs and slow pace of the Turtle. The Turtle replied, laughing, "Though you may be fast as the wind, I will beat you in a race." The Rabbit, believing that to be simply impossible, agreed to the race. They agreed that their mutual friend the Fox should choose the course and fix the goal. On the day of the race the two animals started together. The Rabbit began running as fast as she could and soon got tired, lying down by the side of the trail. She fell fast asleep. The Turtle plodded along as he always did and never stopped for a moment, but went on with a slow but steady pace straight to the end of the course. Rabbit, at last waking up and moving as fast as she could, tried to catch up. Arriving at the end of the course, she saw the Turtle had reached the goal, and was comfortably resting. The Fox who had helped them laughed out loud and said, "It is true . . . slow but steady wins the race!"

6. Read the following passage taken from an eighth-grade social studies book. Identify the key text structure in the passage. Tell how you would use My Turn–Together–Your Turn think-alouds and a graphic organizer to teach students to recognize the text structure and understand the passage.

   Striking Workers

   As prices rose, labor unions demanded higher wages. Although many of these demands were met, some companies refused to give their workers pay increases. The result was a number of strikes that soon threatened the stability of the American economy.

   The rail strike was probably the most serious. The huge semitrailers and interstate highways we know today didn't exist then. Most of the nation's goods moved by rail. President Truman, who had worked feverishly to end the coal and auto strikes, was angry when the railway workers announced their strike. He said that he understood their problems, but that he couldn't allow a rail strike at the time. (Buggey et al., 1987)

7. Select a children's fiction story and generate 12 questions that you could ask students. Your questions should reflect story grammars as well as important vocabulary. Indicate which questions reflect explicit or implicit information in the text.

R E F E R E N C E S

Applegate, M., Quinn, B., & Applegate, A. (2002). Levels of thinking required by comprehension questions in informal reading inventories. *The Reading Teacher, 56*(2), 174–180.

Archer, A., & Gleason, M. (2010). Direct instruction in content-area reading. In D. W. Carnine, J. Silbert, E. J. Kame'enui, & S. Tarver (2010), *Direct instruction reading* (5th ed.). Boston: Merrill Prentice Hall.

Armbruster, B., Lehr, F., & Osborn, J. (2001). *Put reading first: The research building blocks for teaching children to read.* Washington, DC: Partnership for Reading.

Beck, I., & McKeown, M. (2001). *Text talk.* New York: Scholastic.

Beck, I. L., & McKeown, M. G. (2007). Increasing young low income children's oral vocabulary repertoires through rich and focused instruction. *Elementary School Journal, 107*(3), 251–271.

Beck, I., McKeown, M., Hamilton, R., & Kucan, L. (1997). *Question the author: An approach for enhancing student engagement with text.* Newark, DE: International Reading Association.

Beck, I. L., McKeown, M. G., Sandora, C., Kucan, L., & Worthy, J. (1996). Questioning the author: A yearlong classroom implementation to engage students with text. *The Elementary School Journal, 96,* 385–414.

Bos, C. S., & Vaughn, S. (2008). *Strategies for teaching students with learning and behavior problems* (7th ed.). Boston: Pearson Education.

Brabham, E. G., & Lynch-Brown, C. (2002). Effects of teacher's reading-aloud styles on vocabulary acquisition and comprehension of students in the early elementary grades. *Journal of Educational Psychology, 94*(3), 465–473.

Brandwein, P. F., & Bauer, N. W. (1980). *The United States, living in our world: Research, evaluation, and writing.* Barton R. Clark et al., consulting scientists. San Francisco and New York: Center for the Study of Instruction/Harcourt Brace Jovanovich.

Buehl, D. (2008). *Classroom strategies for interactive learning.* Newark, DE: International Reading Association.

Buggey, L., Danzer, G., Mitsakos, C., & Risinger, C. (1985). *America! America!* (2nd ed.). Upper Saddle River, NJ: Prentice Hall.

Burnett, F. H. (2008). *The secret garden.* Cambridge, MA: Candlewick Press.

Carnine, D., & Kinder, D. (1985). Teaching low-performing students to apply generative and schema strategies to narrative and expository material. *Remedial and Special Education, 6*(1), 20–30.

Carnine, D. W., Silbert, J., Kame'enui, E. J., & Tarver, S. (2010). *Direct instruction reading* (5th ed.). Boston: Merrill Prentice Hall.

Chall, J., & Dale, E. (1995). *Readability revisited: The new Dale-Chall readability formula.* Brookline, MA: Brookline Books.

Chall, J., Jacobs, V., & Baldwin, L. (1990). *The reading crisis: Why poor children fall behind.* Cambridge, MA: Harvard University Press.

Cotton, K. (1989). Classroom questioning. *School Improvement Research Series.* Northwest Regional Educational Laboratory. Retrieved June 17, 2009, from http://www.nwrel.org/scpd/sirs/3/cu5.html

Coyne, M. D., Simmons, D. C., Kame'enui, E. J., & Stoomiller, M. (2004). Teaching vocabulary during shared storybook readings: An examination of differential effects. *Exceptionality, 12,* 145–162.

Dickens, C. (1843). *A Christmas carol.* Retrieved June 17, 2009, from http://www.gutenberg.org/catalog/world/readfile?fk_files=93841&pageno=2

Dixon, R., Boorman, L., & Muti, K. (2008). *Reading success: Effective comprehension strategies.* Columbus, OH: McGraw-Hill/SRA.

DK Science Encyclopedia, The. (1998). C. Beattie et al. (Eds.). New York: DK.

Duffy, G. G., & Roehler, L. R. (1989). Why strategy instruction is so difficult and what we need to do about it. In C. B. McCormick, G. E. Miller, & M. Pressley (Eds.), *Cognitive strategy research: From basic research to educational applications* (pp. 133–157). New York: Springer-Verlag.

Duffy, G. G. (1993). Rethinking strategy instruction: Four teachers' development and their low achievers' understandings. *Elementary School Journal, 93,* 231–247.

Educational Resource Inc. (2004). *Strategies for taking high-stakes tests.* Unpublished materials.

Engelmann, S., Johnson, G., Carnine, L., Meyer, L., Becker, W., & Eisele, J. (2008). *Corrective reading.* Columbus, OH: McGraw-Hill/SRA.

Englert, C., & Mariage, T. (1991). Making students partners in the comprehension process: Organizing the reading "POSSE." *Learning Disability Quarterly, 14*(2), 123–138.

Englert, C., & Thomas, C. (1987). Sensitivity to text structure in reading and writing: A comparison between learning disabled and non-learning disabled students. *Learning Disability Quarterly, 10*(2), 93–105.

Eskey, D. E. (2002). Reading and the teaching of L2 reading. *Teachers of English to Speakers of Other Languages Journal (TESOL Journal), 11*(1), 5–9.

Farrell, M. (2006, December 1). How the Internet saved literacy. *Forbes.* Retrieved July 26, 2009, from http://www.forbes.com/2006/11/30/reading-literacy-internet-tech-media_cx_mf_books06_1201literacy_print.html

Fletcher, J., Lyone, G., Ruchs, L., & Barnes, M. (2007). *Learning disabilities: From identification to intervention.* New York: The Guilford Press.

France, M. (1998). *Deadly double.* Novato, CA: High Noon Books.

Francis, D. J., Rivera, M., Lesaux, N., Kieffer, M., & Rivera, H. (2006). Practical guidelines for the education of English language learners: Research based recommendations for instruction and academic interventions. Retrieved May 3, 2005, from http://www.centeroninstruction.org/files/ELL1-Interventions.pdf

Friend, M., & Bursuck, W. D. (2008). *Including students with special needs: A practical guide for classroom teachers* (5th ed.). Boston: Pearson Education.

Goldenberg, C. (2008). Teaching English language learners: What the research does—and does not—say. *American Education* (pp. 8–44). AFT publications and reports. Retrieved May 25, 2009, from www.aft.org/pubs-reports/american_educator/issues/summer08/goldenberg.pdf

Goudiss, M., Hodges, V., & Margulies, S. (1999). *The ISAT coach: Grade 3 reading.* New York: Triumph Learning/Coach Books.

Greene, J. F. (2009). *Language! A literacy intervention curriculum.* Longmont, CO: Sopris West.

Gunderson, L. (2008). *ESL literacy instruction: A guidebook to theory and practice* (2nd ed.). New York: Routledge.

Gunning, T. (2002). *Assessing and correcting reading and writing difficulties* (2nd ed.). Boston: Allyn & Bacon.

Hiebert, E. H. (1999). Text matters in learning to read. *The Reading Teacher, 52,* 552–568.

Hirsch, E. D. (2000, Spring). You can always look it up . . . or can you? *American Educator, 24*(1), 4–9.

Hosp, M., Hosp, J., Howell, K. (2007). *The ABCs of CBM: A practical guide to curriculum-based measurement.* New York: The Guilford Press.

Ivanitskaya, L., O'Boyle, I., & Casey, A. M. (2006). Health information literacy and competencies of information age students: Results from the Interactive Online Research Readiness Self-Assessment (RRSA). *Journal of Medical Internet Research, 8*(2), e6.

Keenan J., & Betjemann, R. (2006). Comprehending the Gray Oral Reading Test without reading it: Why comprehension tests should not include passage-

independent items. *Scientific Studies of Reading, 10*(4), 363–380.

Keene, E. (2002). From good to memorable: Characteristics of highly effective comprehension teaching. In C. Block, L. Gambrell, & M. Pressley (Eds.), *Improving comprehension instruction: Rethinking research, theory, and classroom practice* (pp. 80–105). San Francisco: Jossey-Bass.

Kinder, D. (1990). A reciprocal teaching example. Unpublished materials.

Kletzien, S., & Szabo, R. (1998). *Information text or narrative text? Children's preferences revisited.* Paper presented at the National Reading Conference, Austin, TX.

Klingner, J., Vaughn, S., & Boardman, A. (2004). *Teaching reading comprehension to students with learning difficulties.* New York: The Guilford Press.

Kozloff, M. (2005). Tips for effective teaching of language for learning. Retrieved July 14, 2009, from http://people.uncw.edu/kozloffm/tipsLanguageforLearning.DOC

Langer, J. (1984). Examining background knowledge and text comprehension. *Reading Research Quarterly, 19,* 468–481.

Luft, D. (1980). *Robert Musil and the crisis of European culture: 1880–1942.* Berkeley: University of California Press.

MacArthur, C., Ferretti, R., Okolo, C., & Cavalier, A. (2001, January). Technology applications for students with literacy problems: A critical review. *The Elementary School Journal, 101*(3), 73–301.

Marchand-Martella, N. E., Slocum, T. A., & Martella, R. C. (2004). *Introduction to direct instruction.* Boston: Allyn & Bacon.

McEwan, E. (2001). *Raising reading achievement in middle and high schools.* Thousand Oaks, CA: Corwin.

McEwan, E. (2009). *Teach them all to read: Catching kids before they fall through the cracks* (2nd ed.). Thousand Oaks, CA: Corwin.

McKeown, M., Beck, I., & Blake, R. (2009). Reading comprehension instruction: Focus on content or strategies. *Perspectives on Language and Literacy, 35*(2), 28–32.

Miranda, A., & Guerrero, M. (1986). The funny farola. In Adventures (pp. 42–53). Boston: Houghton Mifflin.

Moats, L. C. (March, 2001). When older students can't read. *Educational Leadership, 58*(6), 36–40.

Moats, L. C. (2005). *Language essentials for teachers of reading and spelling. Module 6: Digging for meaning: Teaching text comprehension.* Boston: Sopris West.

Moats, L. C. (2007). *Whole language high jinks: How to tell when "scientifically-based reading instruction" isn't.* Thomas B. Fordham Institute (ERIC Document Reproduction Service No. ED 4980005).

National Reading Panel. (2000). *Teaching children to read: An evidence-based assessment of the scientific research literature on reading and its implications for reading instruction.* Washington, DC: National Institute of Child Health and Human Development.

Palincsar, A. S., & Brown, A. L. (1988). Reciprocal teaching of comprehension-fostering and comprehension-monitoring activities. *Cognition and Instruction, 1,* 117–175.

Parker, R., Hasbrouck, J. E., & Tindal, G. (1992). The Maze as a classroom-based reading measure: Construction methods, reliability, and validity. *Journal of Special Education, 26,* 195–218.

Philbrick, R. (1998). *Max the mighty.* New York: Scholastic.

Pressley, M. (2002). Metacognition and self-regulated comprehension. In A. E. Farstrup & S. Samuels (Eds.), *What research has to say about reading instruction* (pp. 291–309). Newark, DE: International Reading Association.

RAND Reading Study Group. (2002). Reading for understanding: Towards an R&D program in reading comprehension. Retrieved August 10, 2009, from www.rand.org/publications/MR/MR1465

Raney, K. (1993). *It's probably good dinosaurs are extinct.* Seattle, WA: Green Tiger Press.

Reading Success Network, Southeast Comprehensive Assistance Center. (n.d.). Implications for teaching reading to English language learners: Participant materials. Retrieved August 7, 2009, from www.sedl.org/secac/rsn/ELL.pdf

Reich, J. R., & Beiler, E. L. (1988). *United States history.* Austin, TX: Holt, Rinehart & Winston.

Richards, J., & Gipe, J. (2000). Reading comprehension games for young students in mainstream settings. *Reading & Writing Quarterly, 16,* 75–80.

Rosenshine, B. (1997). Advances in research on instruction. In J. W. Lloyd, E. J. Kame'enui, & D. Chard (Eds.), *Issues in educating students with disabilities* (pp. 197–221). Mahwah, NJ: Erlbaum.

Schmar-Dobler, E. (September, 2003). Reading on the Internet: The link between literacy and technology. *Journal of Adolescent & Adult Literacy, 47*(1), 80–85.

Schraff, A. (1992). *Swamp furies.* Costa Mesa, CA: Saddleback Publishing, Inc.

Shankweiler, D. (1999). Words to meanings. *Scientific Studies of Reading, 3,* 113–127.

Shankweiler, D., Lundquist, E., & Dreyer, L. (1996). Reading and spelling difficulties in high school students: Causes and consequences. *Reading and Writing, 8*(3) 267–294.

Shinn, J., Deno, S. L., & Espin, C. (2000). Technical adequacy of the maze task for curriculum-based measurement of reading growth. *The Journal of Special Education, 34*(3), 164–172.

Short, D. (1994). Expanding middle school horizons: Integrating language, culture, and social studies. *TESOL Quarterly, 28,* 581–608.

Smith, M. (1999). Teaching comprehension from a multisensory perspective. In J. Birsh (Ed.), *Multisensory teaching of basic language skills.* Baltimore: Paul H. Brookes.

Sousa, D. (2005). *How the brain learns to read.* Thousand Oaks, CA: Corwin.

Spadorcia, S. (2001). Looking more closely at high-interest, low-level texts: Do they support comprehension? *Perspectives, 27*(2), 32–33. Retrieved March 25, 2009, from http://www.resourceroom.net/Comprehension/idahilocomp.asp

Stahl, Robert. (1990). *Using "think-time" behaviors to promote students' information processing, learning, and on-task participation: An instructional module.* Tempe: Arizona State University.

Stecker, P., & Lembke, E. (2005). Advanced applications of CBM in reading: Instructional decision-making strategies manual. Washington, DC: National Center on Student Progress Monitoring. Retrieved July 26, 2009, from http://nysrrc.monroe.edu/?q=node/43

Willingham, D. (2009). *Why don't students like school? A cognitive scientist answers questions about how the mind works and what it means for the classroom.* San Francisco: Jossey-Bass.

Yang, Y. (April, 2002). Reassessing readers' comprehension monitoring. *Reading in a Foreign Language, 14*(1). Retrieved Aug. 4, 2009, from http://nflrc.hawaii.edu/rfl/april2002/yang/yang.html

Zarnowski, M. (2006). *Making sense of history: Using high-quality literature and hands-on experiences to build content knowledge.* New York: Scholastic.

11 Developmental Word Knowledge

The Braid of Literacy

Literacy is like a braid of interwoven threads. The braid begins with the intertwining threads of oral language and stories. As children experiment with putting ideas on paper, a writing thread is entwined as well. As children move into reading, the threads of literacy begin to bond. Students' growing knowledge of spelling or **orthography**—the correct sequences of letters in the writing system—strengthens that bonding. The size of the threads and the braid itself become thicker as orthographic knowledge grows. See Figure 11.1.

During the primary years, children acquire word knowledge in a fundamentally aural way from the language that surrounds them. Through listening to and talking about life experiences and stories, children develop a rich speaking vocabulary. As they have opportunities to talk about and to categorize their everyday experiences, children begin to make sense of their world and to use language to negotiate and describe it.

As children observe parents, siblings, and caregivers writing for many purposes, they begin to experiment with pen and paper, gradually coming to understand the forms and functions of written language. The first written words students learn are usually their own names, followed by those of significant others. Words such as *Mom, cat, dog,* and phrases like *I love you* represent people, animals, and ideas dear to their lives.

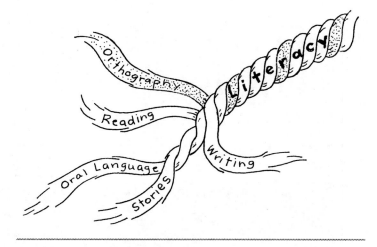

FIGURE 11.1 Braid of Literacy

As students mature as readers and writers, print becomes a critical medium for conceptual development. When purposeful reading, writing, listening, and speaking take place, vocabulary is learned along the way. Even more words are acquired when they are explicitly examined to discover the orthographic relationships among them and how these relationships represent sounds, patterns, and meanings.

The aim of this book is to demonstrate how an exploration of orthographic knowledge can lead to the lengthening and strengthening of the literacy braid. To do this, teachers must know a good deal about the way in which these threads join to create this bond so that they can direct children's attention to "words their way."

There are similarities in the ways learners of all ages expand their knowledge of the world. It seems that humans have a natural interest to find order, to compare and contrast, and to pay attention to what remains the same despite minor variations. Infants learn to recognize Daddy as the same Daddy with or without glasses, with or without a hat or whiskers. Through such daily interactions, we categorize our surroundings. Our students expand their vocabularies by comparing one concept with another. Gradually, the number of concepts they analyze increases, but the process is still one of comparing and contrasting. They may first call anything with four legs a dog until they attend to the features that distinguish dogs, cats, and cows, and later terriers, Labrador retrievers, border collies, and greyhounds. In the process they learn the vocabulary to label the categories.

Word study, as described in this book, occurs in hands-on activities that mimic basic cognitive learning processes: comparing and contrasting categories of word features and discovering similarities and differences within and between categories. For example, students often misspell words that end with the /k/ sound, spelling the word *snake* as *SNACK* or even *SNACKE*. By sorting words that end in *ck* and *ke* into two groups, as the student is doing in Figure 11.2, students discover the invariant pattern that goes with each (*ck* only follows a short vowel). The system is laid bare when words are sorted into categories.

During word study, words and pictures are sorted in routines that require children to examine, discriminate, and make critical judgments about speech sounds, spelling patterns, and mean-

FIGURE 11.2 Student Sorting Words

ings. Just as *Math Their Way* (Baretta–Lorton, 1968) uses concrete manipulatives to illustrate principles of combining and separating, so *Words Their Way*, uses concrete pictures and words to illustrate principles of similarity and difference.

Invented Spellings: A Window into Developing Word Knowledge

Students have probably been inventing their own spelling ever since paper and pencil have been available, but it was not until the early 1970s that research by Charles Read (1971) and Carol Chomsky (1971) took a serious look at young children's spelling attempts. Their work introduced the world of literacy to the notion of **invented spelling.** Read understood that preschooler's attempts were not just random displays of ignorance and confusion. To the contrary, his linguistic analysis showed that invented spelling provides a window into a child's developing word knowledge (Read, 1971, 1975). Read's research uncovered a systematic, phonetic logic to preschoolers' categorizations of English speech sounds. At about the same time, Edmund Henderson and his colleagues at the University of Virginia had begun to look for similar logic in students' spellings across ages and grade levels (Beers & Henderson, 1977; Gentry, 1981; Henderson, Estes, & Stonecash, 1972). Read's findings provided these researchers with the tools they needed to interpret the errors they were studying. The Virginia spelling studies corroborated and extended Read's findings upward through the grades and resulted in a comprehensive model of developmental word knowledge (Henderson, 1990; Templeton & Bear, 1992a; Templeton & Morris, 1999). The power of this model lies in the diagnostic information contained in students' spelling inventions that reveal their current understanding of how written words work (Invernizzi, Abouzeid, & Gill, 1994).

Henderson and his students not only studied the development of children's spelling, but also devised an instructional model to complement that development. They determined that an informed analysis of students' spelling attempts can cue timely instruction in phonics, spelling, and vocabulary that is essential to move students forward in reading and writing. By using students' invented spellings as a guide, teachers can differentiate efficient, effective instruction in phonics, spelling, and vocabulary. We call this instruction **word study.**

Why is Word Study Important?

Becoming fully literate is absolutely dependent on fast, accurate recognition of words and their meanings in texts, and fast, accurate production of words in writing so that readers and writers can focus their attention on making meaning. Letter-sound correspondences, phonics, spelling patterns, high-frequency-word recognition, decoding, word meaning, and other attributes are the basis of written word knowledge. Designing a word study program that explicitly teaches students necessary skills and engages their interest and motivation to learn about how words work is a vital aspect of any literacy program. Indeed, how to teach students these basics in an effective manner has sparked controversy among educators for nearly two hundred years (Balmuth, 1992; Smith, 2002; Mathews, 1967).

Many phonics, spelling, and vocabulary programs are characterized by explicit skill instruction, a systematic scope and sequence, and repeated practice. However, much of the repeated practice consists of rote drill, so students have little opportunity to manipulate word concepts or apply critical thinking skills. Although students need explicit skill instruction within a systematic curriculum, it is equally true that "teaching is not telling" (James, 1958).

Students need hands-on opportunities to manipulate word features in a way that allows them to generalize beyond isolated, individual examples to entire groups of words that are spelled the same way (Juel & Minden-Cupp, 2000). Excelling at word recognition, spelling, and vocabulary is not just a matter of memorizing isolated rules and definitions. The best way to develop fast and accurate perception of word features is to engage in meaningful reading and writing, and to have multiple opportunities to examine those same words out of context. The most effective instruction in phonics, spelling, and vocabulary links word study to the texts being read, provides a systematic scope and sequence of word-level skills, and provides multiple opportunities for hands-on practice and application. In a sense, word study teaches students how to look at words so that they can construct an ever-deepening understanding of how spelling works to represent sound and meaning. We believe that this word study is well worth 10 to 15 minutes of instruction and practice daily.

What Is the Purpose of Word Study?

The purpose of word study is twofold. First, students develop a *general* knowledge of English spelling. Through active exploration, word study teaches students to examine words to discover generalizations about English spelling. They learn the regularities, patterns, and conventions of English orthography needed to read and spell. This general knowledge is conceptual in nature and reflects what students understand about the nature of our spelling system. Second, word study increases *specific* knowledge of words—the spelling and meaning of individual words.

General knowledge is what we access when we encounter a new word, when we do not know how to spell a word, or when we do not know the meaning of a specific word. The better our knowledge of the system, the better we are at decoding an unfamiliar word, spelling correctly, or guessing the meaning of a word. For example, if you have knowledge of short vowels and consonant blends, you would have no trouble attempting the word *crash* even if you have never seen it or written it before. The spelling is unambiguous, like so many single-syllable short-vowel words. Knowledge of how words that are similar in spelling are related in meaning, such as *compete* and *competition,* makes it easier to understand the meaning of a word like *competitor,* even if it is unfamiliar. Additional clues offered by context also increase the chances of reading and understanding a word correctly.

To become fully literate, however, we also need specific knowledge about individual words. The word *rain*, for example, might be spelled *rane*, *rain*, or *rayne*—all are orthographically and phonetically plausible. However, only specific knowledge will allow us to remember the correct spelling. Likewise, only specific knowledge of the spelling of *which* and *witch* makes it possible to know which witch is which! The relationship between specific knowledge and knowledge of the system is reciprocal; that is, each supports the other. Ehri (1992) expressed this idea in the following manner.

> What students store in memory about specific words' spellings is regulated in part by what they know about the general system. Learners who lack this knowledge are left with rote memorization which takes longer and is more easily forgotten. Similarly, what students learn about the orthographic system evolves in part from the accumulation of experiences with specific word spellings. (p. 308)

The purpose of word study, then, is to examine words in order to reveal consistencies within our written language system and to help students master the recognition, spelling, and meaning of specific words.

What is the Basis for Developmental Word Study?

Word study evolves from three decades of research exploring developmental aspects of word knowledge with children and adults (Henderson, 1990; Henderson & Beers, 1980; Templeton & Bear, 1992a). This line of research has documented the convergence of certain kinds of spelling errors that tend to occur together in clusters and reflect students' confusion over certain recurring orthographic principles. These "clusters" of errors have been described in relationship to the types of errors noted, specifically (1) errors dealing with the alphabetic match of letters and sound (*BAD* for *bed*), (2) errors dealing with letter patterns (*SNAIK* for *snake*), and (3) errors dealing with words related in meaning (*INVUTATION* for *invitation*). The same cluster types of errors have been observed among students with learning disabilities and dyslexia (Sawyer, Lipa-Wade, Kim, Ritenour, & Knight, 1997; Worthy & Invernizzi, 1989), students who speak in nonstandard dialects (Cantrell, 1990), and students who are learning to read in different alphabetic languages (Helman, 2004; Bear, Templeton, Helman, & Baren, 2003; Yang, 2004). Longitudinal and cross-grade-level research in developmental spelling has shown that this developmental progression occurs for all learners of written English in the same direction and varies only in the rate of acquisition (Invernizzi & Hayes, 2004). The scope and sequence of word study instruction is based on research investigating the linguistic logic underlying students' spelling as they progress in literacy.

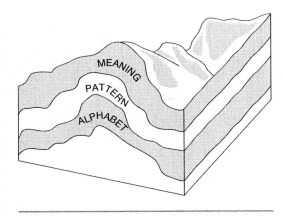

Word study also comes from what we have learned about the orthographic structure of written words. Developmental spelling researchers have examined the three layers of English orthography (Figure 11.3) in relation to the historical evolution of English spelling as well as developmental progressions from alphabet to pattern to meaning among learners of English. Each layer builds on the one before, and in mature readers and writers, there is interaction among the layers.

FIGURE 11.3 Three Layers of English Orthography

Alphabet

Our spelling system is **alphabetic** because it represents the relationship between letters and sounds. In the word *sat*, each sound is represented by a single letter; we blend the sounds for /s/, /a/, and /t/ to read the word *sat*. In the word *chin*, we still hear three sounds, even though there are four letters, because the first two letters, *ch*, function like a single letter, representing a single sound. So we can match letters—sometimes singly, sometimes in pairs—to sounds from left to right and create words. This **alphabetic layer** in English spelling is the first layer of information at work.

The alphabetic layer of English orthography was established during the time of Old English, the language spoken and written by the Anglo-Saxons in England between the Germanic invasions of the sixth century C.E. and the conquest of England by William of Normandy in 1066. Old English was remarkably consistent in letter–sound correspondence and used the alphabet to systematically represent speech sounds. The long vowels were pronounced close to the way they are in modern Romance languages today. The simplicity and consistency of the grapheme–phoneme correspondence in Old English were such that, armed with a phonetic guide to letters and sounds, modern readers can still read Abbot Aelfric's *Lord's Prayer* similar to the way Aelfric himself may have recited it over a thousand years ago (Henderson, 1990).

The history of the alphabetic layer reflected in the story of Old English is relevant to teachers today because beginners spell like little Saxons as they begin to read and write (Henderson, 1981). Armed with only a rudimentary knowledge of the alphabet and letter sounds, beginning spellers of all backgrounds use their alphabet knowledge quite literally. They rely on the sound embedded in the names of the letters to represent the sounds they are trying to represent (Read, 1971). This strategy works quite well for consonants when the names do, in fact, contain the correct corresponding speech sounds (*Bee, Dee, eF, eS,* etc). It works less well for letters that have more than one sound (C, G), and it does not work at all for consonants with names that do not contain their corresponding speech sounds (W: *double you*; Y: *wie*; and H: *aitch*). Short-vowel sounds are particularly problematic for novice spellers because there is no single letter that "says" the short-vowel sound. As a result, beginning readers choose a vowel whose pronounced name is closest by place of articulation to the targeted short-vowel sound (Beers & Henderson, 1977; Read, 1975). For example, a beginning reader might spell *BAD* for *bed*, or *bad*.

Pattern

What about words like *cape, bead,* and *light?* If we spelled these words with single letters, they would look like *cap, bed,* and *lit;* but of course these spellings already represent other words. The **pattern layer** therefore overlies the alphabetic layer. English does not have a single sound for each letter under all conditions. Single sounds are sometimes spelled with more than one letter or are affected by other letters that do not stand for any sounds themselves. When we look beyond single letter–sound match-ups and search for **patterns** that guide the groupings of letters, however, we find surprising consistency (Hanna, Hanna, Hodges, & Rudorf, 1966).

Take, for example, the *-ape* in *cape;* we say that the final *-e* makes the preceding vowel letter, *a*, stand for a long vowel sound. The *e* does not stand for a sound itself, but it plays an important role. The *-ape* group of letters therefore follows a pattern: when you have a vowel, a consonant, and a silent *-e* in a single syllable, this letter grouping forms a pattern that usually will function to indicate a long vowel. We refer to this pattern as the consonant-vowel-consonant-silent e (CVCe) pattern—one of several high frequency, long-vowel patterns.

The notion of pattern helps us talk more efficiently about the alphabetic layer as well. In a CVC pattern (*sat, chin, crash*), note that, regardless of how many consonant letters are on either side of the single vowel, the fact that there is but one vowel letter in that pattern means it will usually stand for a short vowel sound.

Words of more than one syllable also follow spelling patterns. These patterns are described with the same V and C symbols and also relate to the vowel sound within each syllable. Let's consider two of the most common syllable patterns. First is the VCCV pattern, such as in *robber* (the pattern is vowel and consonant to the left of the syllable break and consonant and vowel to the right). When we have this pattern, the first vowel is usually short. Second is the VCV syllable pattern, as in *robot, pilot,* and *limit.* This pattern will usually signal that the first vowel is long, but as in the case of *limit*, the first vowel also can be short. Overall, knowledge about patterns within single syllables, and syllable patterns within words, will be of considerable value to students in both their reading and their spelling.

Where did these patterns originate? The simple letter–sound consistency of Old English was overlaid by a massive influx of French words after the Norman Conquest in 1066. Because these words entered the existing language through bilingual Anglo-Norman speakers, some of the French pronunciations were adopted, too. Also, because the scribes who wrote the new words were biliterate, they applied French orthographic conventions to the spelling of some English words as well. Old English was thus overlaid with the vocabulary and spelling traditions of the ruling class, the Norman French. This complex interaction of pronunciation change on top of the intermingling of French and English spellings led to a proliferation of different vowel sounds represented by different vowel patterns. The extensive repertoire of vowel patterns today is attributable to this period of history, such as the various pronunciations of the *ea* vowel digraph in words like *bread, thread, great, break, meat,* and *clean.* To be sure, this merging of oral and written traditions disrupted the relatively consistent relationship between letters and sounds that existed in Old English. However, this second tier was superimposed on the alphabetic foundation—creating a pattern layer in which letter combinations reflected roughly the language of origin (Invernizzi & Hayes, 2004). It is uncanny that students moving out of the beginning phase spell like little Anglo-Normans when they write *taste* as *taist*, or *leave* as *leeve.*

Meaning

The third layer of English orthography is the **meaning layer.** When students learn that groups of letters can represent meaning directly, they will be much less puzzled when encountering unusual spellings. Examples of these units or groups of letters are prefixes, suffixes, Greek roots, and Latin stems.

As one example of how meaning functions in the spelling system, think of the prefix *re-*; whether we hear it pronounced "ree" as in *rethink* or "ruh" as in *remove*, its spelling stays the same because it directly represents meaning. Why is *composition* not spelled *compusition* since the second vowel sounds more like /uh/ than o? It is related in meaning to *compose*. The spelling of the second vowel in the related words, *compose* and *composition*, stays the same even though the pronunciation of the second syllable is different. Likewise, the letter sequence *photo* in *photograph, photographer,* and *photographic* signals spelling–meaning connections among these words, despite the changes in sounds that the letter *o* represents.

How did Greek roots like *photo* enter into English orthography? The explosion of knowledge and culture during the Renaissance required a new, expanded vocabulary to accommodate the growth in learning that occurred during this time. Classical roots and stems had the potential to meet this demand for meaning. Greek roots could be compounded or combined (e.g., *autograph* and *autobiography*) and prefixes and suffixes were added to Latin stems (*spectator, spectacular, inspect*). So, to the orthographic record of English history was added a third layer of meaning that built new vocabulary from elements that came from classical Greek and Latin. The spelling/meaning relations inherent in words brought into English during the Renaissance have important implications for vocabulary instruction today as students move through the intermediate grades and beyond (Templeton, 1991). As students explore how spelling visually preserves the semantic relationships among derivationally related words (e.g., *bomb* and *bombard*), vocabulary and spelling instruction become closely related. Chomsky and Halle (1968) used the word *muscle* to show how the seemingly arbitrary spelling of some words is, in reality, central to understanding the meaning of related words (*muscle,* from the Latin *musculus, muscular, musculature*). The silent *c* in the word *muscle* represents a **morphemic** aspect of written English that preserves its etymological history.

Organizing the phonics, spelling, and vocabulary curriculum according to historical layers of alphabet, pattern, and meaning provides a systematic guide for instruction and places the corpus of words to be studied in an evolutionary progression that mirrors the orthographic system itself. Anglo-Saxon words, the oldest words in English, are among the easiest to read and the most familiar. Words like *sun, moon, day,* and *night* are high-frequency, "earthy" words that populate easy reading materials in the primary grades. Anglo-Saxon words survive in high-frequency prepositions, pronouns, conjunctions, and auxiliary verbs (e.g., *have, was, does*) although the pronunciation is now quite different. More difficult Norman French words of one and two syllables—words like *chance, chamber, royal, guard,* and *conquer*—appear with great frequency in books suitable for the elementary grades. The most difficult words in English—words like *calculate, maximum, cumulus, nucleus, hemisphere, hydraulic,* and *rhombus*—are of Latin and Greek origin and appear most often in student reading selections in the middle grades and beyond. Thus, the history of English spelling reflects the frequency of written words as well as the appropriateness of studying certain kinds of words over others in relation to the learner (Henderson, 1992).

Alphabet, pattern, and meaning represent three broad principles of written English and form the layered record of orthographic history. Students' spelling attempts mirror the richness and complexity of this history. As students learn to read and write, they appear to literally reinvent the system as it was itself invented. As shown in Figure 11.4, beginners invent the spellings of simple words quite phonetically, just as the Anglo-Saxons did in 1000 C.E. As students become independent readers, they add a second layer of complexity by using patterns, much as the Norman French did in the latter part of the 14th century. Notice the overuse of the silent -*e* at the end of all of Antonie's words, much like Geoffrey Chaucer's!

	The Historical Development of Spelling	
	Anglo-Saxon	**Letter Name-Alphabetic**
Alphabet	WIF (wif) TODAEG (today) HEAFONUM (heaven) **(Lord's Prayer, 1000)**	WIF (wife) TUDAE (today) HAFAN (heaven) **(Tawanda, age 6)**
	Norman French	**Within Word Patterns**
Pattern	YONGE (young) SWETE (sweet) ROOTE (root) CROPPE (crops) **(Chaucer, 1440)**	YUNGE (young) SWETE (sweet) ROOTE (root) CROPPE (crop) **(Antonie, age 8)**
	Renaissance	**Syllables & Meaning**
Meaning	DISSCORD (discord) FOLOWE (follow) MUSSIKE (music) **(Elizabeth I, 1600)**	DISSCORD (discord) FOLOWE (follow) MUSSIC (music) **(Julian, age 14)**

FIGURE 11.4 Historical Development of English Orthography: Sound, Pattern, and Meaning from Past to Present

Source: Adapted from "Using Students' Invented Spellings as a Guide for Spelling Instruction that Emphasizes Word Study" by M. Invernizzi, M. Abouzeid, & T. Gill, 1994, *Elementary School Journal, 95*(2), p. 158. Reprinted by permission of The University of Chicago Press.

Intermediate and advanced readers invent conventions for joining syllables and morphemes, as was done during the Renaissance when English was first introduced to a Greco and Latinate vocabulary (Henderson, 1990). As Figure 11.4 shows, both Julian and Elizabeth I struggled with issues relating to consonant doubling where syllables meet.

What Students Need to Learn to Read and Spell English

Students discover the basic principles of spelling—alphabet, pattern, and meaning—when they read and write purposefully and are also provided with explicit, systematic word study instruction by knowledgeable teachers. Word study should give students the experiences they need to progress through these layers of information.

- For students who are experimenting with the alphabetic match of letters and sounds, teachers can contrast aspects of the writing system that relate directly to the representation of sound. For example, words spelled with short *e* (*bed, leg, net, neck, mess*) are compared with words spelled with short *o* (*hot, rock, top, log, pond*).
- For students experimenting with pattern, teachers can contrast patterns as they relate to vowels. For example, words spelled with *ay* (*play, day, tray, way*) are compared with words spelled with *ai* (*wait, rain, chain, maid*).
- For students experimenting with conventions of syllables, affixes, and other meaning units, teachers can contrast the stability of base words, roots, and affixes (prefixes and suffixes) across variations. Students can see that words with similar meanings are often spelled the same, despite changes in pronunciation. For example, *admiration* is spelled with an *i* because it comes from the word *admire*.

Word Study Is Developmental

When we say word study is developmental, we mean that the study of word features must match the level of word knowledge of the learner. Word study is not a one-size-fits-all program of instruction that begins in the same place for all students within a grade level. One unique quality of word study, as we describe it, lies in the critical role of differentiating instruction for different levels of word knowledge. Research spanning over 20 years has established how students learn the specific *features* of words as well as the *order* in which they learn them. Knowledgeable educators have come to know that word study instruction must match the needs of the child. This construct, called **instructional level,** is a powerful delimiter of what may be learned. Simply put, we must teach where the child "is at." To do otherwise results in frustration or boredom and little learning in either case. Just as in learning to play the piano students must work through book A, then book B, and then book C, learning to read and spell is a gradual and cumulative process. Word study begins with finding out what each child already knows and then starting instruction there.

One of the easiest ways to know what students need to learn is to look at the way they spell words. Students' spellings provide a direct window into how they think the system works. By interpreting what students do when they spell, educators can target a specific student's "zone of proximal development" (Vygotsky, 1962) and plan word study instruction that this student is conceptually ready to master. Further, by applying basic principles of child development, educators have learned how to engage students in learning about word features in a child-centered, developmentally appropriate way. When students are instructed within their own zone of proximal development—studying "words their way"—they are able to build on what they already know, to learn what they need to know next, and to move forward. With direct instruction and ongoing support, word features that were previously omitted or confused become amalgamated into an ever-increasing reading and writing vocabulary.

The Development of Orthographic Knowledge

Developmental spelling research describes students' growing knowledge of words as a continuum or a series of chronologically ordered stages or phases of word knowledge. In this book, we use the word *stage* as a metaphor to inform instruction. In reality, students grow in conceptual knowledge of the three general layers of information, and of specific word features, along a continuum and there is often an overlap in the layers and features students understand and use.

Students move hierarchically from easier, one-to-one correspondences between letters and sounds, to more difficult, abstract relationships between letter patterns and sounds, to even more sophisticated relationships between meaning units (**morphology**) as they relate to sound and pattern. Stages are marked by broad, qualitative shifts in the types of spelling errors students make as well as changes in the way they read words. It is not the case that students abandon sound once they move to the use of patterns, or abandon patterns once they move to the use of morphology. Rather, the names of the stages capture the key understandings that distinguish them among the layers of English orthography and among the levels of students' general knowledge of the orthography (Bryant, Nunes, & Bindman, 1997; Ehri, 1997, 2006; Templeton, 2002, 2003).

Because word study is based on students' level of orthographic knowledge, the word study activities presented in this book are arranged by stages of spelling. Knowing each student's stage of spelling will determine your choices of appropriate word study activities. This chapter presents an overview of these stages (see Figure 11.5).

Teachers can use the guidelines discussed in this chapter and the assessment procedures to determine the spelling stages of their students. By conducting regular spelling assessments, perhaps three times a year, teachers can track students' progress and

Alphabet - - - - - - ► **Pattern** - - - - - - ► **Meaning**

Emergent Stage
Emergent Reading
Pre-K to middle of 1

Letter Name–Alphabetic Stage
Beginning Reading
K to middle of 2

Within Word Pattern Stage
Transitional Reading
Grade 1 to middle of 4

Syllables and Affixes Stage
Intermediate Reading
Grades 3 to 8

Derivational Relations
Advanced Reading
Grades 5 to 12

FIGURE 11.5   Spelling and Reading Stages and
Grade Levels

development. An important prerequisite, however, is to know the continuum of orthographic development.

For each stage, students' orthographic knowledge is defined by three functional levels that are useful guides for knowing when to teach what (Invernizzi et al., 1994):

1. What students do correctly—an independent or easy level
2. What students use but confuse—an instructional level where instruction is most helpful
3. What is absent in students' spelling—a frustration level where spelling concepts are too difficult

By studying the stages of spelling development, it becomes obvious what sequence word study should take. In Vygotskian terms (1962), focus on the student's zone of proximal development by determining what the student uses but confuses. In this way, you will learn which orthographic features and patterns to explore, because this is where instruction will most benefit the student.

Stages of Spelling Development

Henderson described a developmental stage model of spelling acquisition after a decade of work at the University of Delaware and later at the University of Virginia (1981). He and his students examined the specific features students use to spell when they write. The discovery of Read's work (1971) in the linguistic arena helped Henderson and his students make sense of the spellings they had collected. Henderson and his students also found that students' spelling errors are not just random mistakes. Building on Read's discoveries, Henderson unearthed an underlying logic to students' errors that changed over time, moving from using but confusing elements of sound to using but confusing elements of pattern and meaning (Henderson et al., 1971). Subsequently, similar developmental changes in spelling have been observed across many groups of students, from preschoolers (Templeton & Spivey,

TABLE 11.1   Stages of Spelling Development

Current Stage Name	Henderson's Stages (1990)	Original Stage Names (Virginia Spelling Studies)
Emergent	Preliterate	Prephonetic
Letter Name–Alphabetic	Early Letter Name	Semi-Phonetic
	Letter Name	Phonetic
Within Word Pattern	Within Word	Transitional
Syllables & Affixes	Syllable Juncture	Correct
Derivational Relations	Derivational Constancies	

1980), through adults (Bear, Truex, & Barone, 1989; Worthy & Viise, 1996), as well as across socioeconomic levels, dialects, and other alphabetic languages (Cantrell, 2001; Yang, 2005). In addition, the analysis of students' spelling has been explored by other researchers independently (e.g. Bissex, 1980; Treiman, 1985; Ehri, 1992; Richgels, 1995, 2001).

By 1974, Henderson had formulated a description of increasingly sophisticated phases, or stages, of orthographic knowledge. Since then, he and his students have refined the description of these stages and reworked the labels to reflect their changing understanding of developmental word knowledge and to represent most appropriately what occurs at each level. For example, the label "syllable juncture" was broadened to include affixes. Table 11.1 displays the names of the stages currently in use compared to previous labels used by Henderson and his students at the University of Virginia. The stage names describe students' spelling behavior and make it easier to remember the basic strategies that students use to read and spell.

Stage I: Emergent Spelling

Emergent spelling encompasses the writing efforts of children who are not yet reading conventionally, and in most cases have not been exposed to formal reading instruction. Emergent spellers typically range in age from 0 to 5 years, although anyone not yet reading conventionally is in this stage of development. Most toddlers and preschoolers are emergent spellers, as are most kindergartners and even some first graders at the beginning of the year. Emergent spelling may range from random marks to legitimate letters that bear a relationship to sound. However, most of the emergent stage is decidedly **prephonetic.**

Emergent spelling may be divided into a series of steps or landmarks. In the early emergent stage, students may produce large scribbles that are basically drawings. The movement may be circular, and children may tell a story while they draw. At the earliest points in this stage, there are no designs that look like letters, and the writing is undecipherable from the drawing. As you can see in Figure 11.6A, Haley has drawn large scribble-like circles and simply called it writing, asserting that it says, "All the little birdies." There is little order to the direction in Haley's production; it goes up, down, and around, willy-nilly.

Gradually and especially when sitting next to other children or adults who write, children begin to use something that looks like script to "tell" about the picture. In the middle of the emergent stage, pretend writing is separate from the picture, although there is still no relationship between letters and sound. Writing may occur in any direction but is generally linear. In Figure 11.6B, the child labeled his drawing to the left of the picture as "Cowboy."

Throughout the emergent stage, children begin to learn letters, particularly the letters in their own names, and begin to pay attention to the sounds in words. Toward the end of the emergent stage, their writing starts to include the most prominent or salient sounds in a word. The ability to make a few letter-sound matches is evident in Figure 11.6C, where *Jasmin* is spelled JMOE. The movement from this stage to the next stage hinges on learning

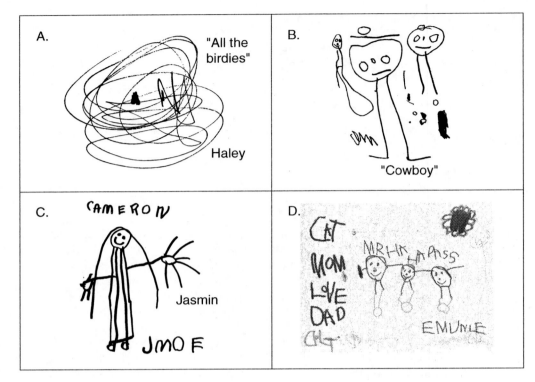

FIGURE 11.6   Early Emergent Writing

Source: Adapted with permission from Bloodgood, J.R (1996).

the **alphabetic principle:** Letters represent sounds in a systematic way, and words can be segmented into sequences of sound from left to right. Toward the end of emergent spelling, students start to memorize some words and write them repeatedly, such as the *cat, Mom, love,* and *Dad* in Figure 11.6D.

Stage II: Letter Name–Alphabetic Spelling

The **letter name–alphabetic spelling stage** is the second stage in the developmental model and encompasses that period of time during which students are formally taught to read, typically during the kindergarten and first-grade years and extending into the middle of second grade. Most letter name–alphabetic spellers are between the ages of 5 and 8 years, although a beginning reader at age 55 also can be a letter name–alphabetic speller (Bear, 1989; Viise, 1996). The name of this stage reflects students' dominant approach to spelling; that is, they use the *names* of the letters as cues to the sound they want to represent (Read, 1975). In Ellie's early letter–name alphabetic spelling shown in Figure 11.7, she used the letter *y* to represent the /w/ sound at the beginning of the word *when*, because the first sound in the pronounced letter name Y (wie) matches the first sound in the word *when*. The letter name for N includes the "en" sound to finish off the word *when*. Charles Read (1975) coined the term "letter name spelling" based on this predominant strategy of using letter names to represent speech sounds. Ellie used R and U to represent the entire words *are* and *you,* another early letter name strategy.

We divide this letter name–alphabetic stage into early, middle, and late periods because of the rapid and dramatic growth during this time. Throughout this stage, students learn to segment the sounds or **phonemes** within words and to match the appropriate letters or letter pairs to those sequences.

FIGURE 11.7   Early Letter Name–Alphabetic Spelling:
Ellie's Note to Her Sister, Meg—"When Are You Coming?"

Early Letter Name–Alphabetic Spelling   Students who are early in the letter name–alphabetic stage apply the alphabetic principle primarily to consonants as Ellie did in Figure 11.7. Often, students spell the first sound and then the last sound of single-syllable words. For example, *when* may be spelled *Y* or *YN*. The middle elements of syllables, the vowels, are usually omitted. Typically, only the first sound of a two-letter consonant blend is represented, as in FT for *float*. Early letter name–alphabetic writing often lacks spacing between words, which makes it hard to decipher unless you know something about the writer's message. This type of writing is **semiphonetic** because only some of the phonemes are represented.

When early letter name–alphabetic students use the alphabetic principle, they find matches between letters and the spoken word by how the sound is made or articulated in the mouth. For example, students may confuse the /b/ sound and /p/ sound because they are made with the lips in the same way except for one feature: In making the /b/, the vocal chords vibrate to produce a **voiced** sound. An early letter name–alphabetic speller might spell the word *pat* as BT.

Middle to Late Letter Name–Alphabetic Spelling   In her note in Figure 11.8, Kaitlyn shows mastery of most beginning and ending consonants. She spells many high-frequency words correctly, such as *will, love, have,* and *you,* but also makes spelling errors typical of a student in the middle letter name–alphabetic stage. What separates her from the early letter name speller is her consistent use of vowels. Long vowels, which "say their name," appear in *tim* for *time* and *hop* for *hope,* but silent letters are not represented. Short vowels are used but confused, as in *miss* spelled as *mes* and *much* as *mich.*

In the middle letter name–alphabetic stage, students are also learning to segment both sounds in a consonant blend and begin to represent the blends correctly, as in *GRAT* for *great.* Kaitlyn has also correctly represented the ch digraph in *much.* Because middle letter name–alphabetic spellers can segment and represent most of the sound sequences heard within single-syllable words, their spelling is described as **phonetic.**

By the end of this stage, late letter name-alphabetic spellers are able to consistently represent most regular short-vowel sounds, digraphs, and consonant blends because they have full **phonemic segmentation**. The letters *n* and *m* as in *bunk* or *lump* are referred to as **preconsonantal nasals** (nasals that come before a consonant) and are generally omitted by students throughout this stage when they spell them as *BUK* or *LUP.* Kaitlyn omitted the

FIGURE 11.8 Middle to Late Letter Name–Alphabetic Spelling: Kaitlyn's Farewell Note to her First Grade Teacher

nasal in her spelling of *don't* as *DOT* and used an interesting strategy to get the *n* in *want* by spelling it as *one + t*. Henderson (1990) recognized that the correct spelling of the preconsonantal nasal was a reliable and important watershed event that heralds the onset of the next stage of orthographic knowledge. By the end of the stage, students have mastered the alphabetic layer of English orthography and will now begin to use but confuse silent long-vowel markers such as the silent -*e* in the spelling of *rain* as *RANE*.

Stage III: Within Word Pattern Spelling

Students entering the **within word pattern spelling stage** can read and spell many words correctly because of their automatic knowledge of letter sounds and short-vowel patterns. This level of orthographic knowledge typically begins as students transition to independent reading toward the end of first grade, and expands throughout the second and third grades, and even into the fourth grade. Although most within word pattern spellers typically range in age from 7 to 10 years, many adult, low-skilled readers remain in this stage. Regardless, this period of orthographic development lasts longer than the preceding one, because the vowel pattern system of English orthography is quite extensive.

The within word pattern stage begins when students can correctly spell most single-syllable, short-vowel words correctly as well as consonant blends, digraphs, and preconsonantal nasals. Because these basic phonics features have been mastered, within word pattern spellers work at a more abstract level than letter name–alphabetic spellers (Zutell, 1994). They move away from the linear, sound-by-sound approach of the letter name–alphabetic spellers and begin to include patterns or chunks of letter sequences. Within word spellers can think about words in more than one dimension; they study words by sound and pattern simultaneously. As the name of this stage suggests, within word pattern spellers take a closer look at vowel patterns within single-syllable words (Henderson, 1990). They are sometimes referred to as transitional spellers because they are transitioning from the alphabetic layer to the meaning layer of English orthography through patterns.

Kim's writing in Figure 11.9 is that of an early within word pattern speller. She spells many short-vowel and high-frequency words correctly such as *hill, had, them, girl*, and *won*. She also spells some common long vowel patterns correctly in CVCe words like *time* and

My teme won the scoer game.
I was   the boll girl.
We   had to use cons
for the gowl. Evre time
the boll wintdowe Hill
I Had to Throwe   them a
nother boll.

FIGURE 11.9 Early Within Word Pattern Spelling: Kim's Soccer Game

game. Kim hears the long vowel sound in words like *team, goal,* and *throw,* but she selects the wrong pattern, spelling them as *TEME, GOWL,* and *THROWE*. She omits the silent *e* in *cones*. These are good examples of how Kim is using but confusing long vowel patterns.

During the within word pattern stage, students first study the common long-vowel patterns (long -*o* can be spelled with *o*–consonant–*e* as in *joke, oa* as in *goal,* and *ow* as in *throw*) and then less common patterns such as the VCC pattern in *cold* and *most*. The most difficult patterns are **ambiguous vowels** because the sound is neither long nor short and the same pattern may represent different sounds, such as the *ou* in *mouth, cough, through,* and *tough*. These less common and ambiguous vowels may persist as misspellings into the late part of the within word pattern stage.

Although the focus of the within word pattern stage is on the pattern layer of English orthography, students must also consider the meaning layer to spell and use **homophones** such as *bear* and *bare, deer* and *dear, hire* and *higher*. Sound, pattern, and meaning must be considered when spelling homophones. This introduces the spelling-meaning connection explored in the next two stages of spelling development.

Stage IV: Syllables and Affixes Spelling

The **syllables and affixes stage** is typically achieved in the upper elementary and middle school grades, when students are expected to spell many words of more than one syllable. This represents a new point in word study when students consider spelling patterns where syllables meet and meaning units such as affixes (prefixes and suffixes). Students in this fourth stage are most often between 9 and 14 years, though many adults with poor literacy skills may be found in this stage.

In Figure 11.10, a fourth-grader in the early syllables and affixes stage has written about his summer vacation. Xavier spelled most one-syllable short- and long-vowel words correctly (*went, west, drove, hike*). Many of his errors are in two-syllable words and fall at the place where syllables and affixes meet. Xavier has used—but confused—the conventions for preserving vowel sounds when adding an **inflected ending** in *stopped* and *hiking,* spelled as *STOPED* and *HIKEING*. The principle of doubling the consonant at the **syllable juncture** to keep the vowel short is used in *LITTEL* for *little,* but is lacking in his spelling of *summer* as *SUMER*. Syllable juncture patterns include the **open first syllable** in *hu-mor* (V/CV usually signals a long vowel in the first syllable) and **closed** first syllable in *sum-mer* and *cam-per* (VC/CV usually signals a short vowel sound in the first syllable). **Unaccented** final syllables give students difficulty, as shown in Xavier's spellings of *LITTEL* for *little* and *MOUNTIN* for *mountain*.

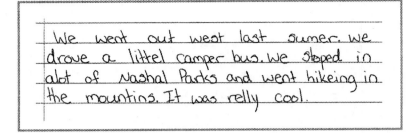

FIGURE 11.10   Syllables and Affixes Spelling: Xavier's Account of his Summer Adventures

Toward the end of the syllables and affixes stage, students grapple with affixes that change the meaning of the word. They may misspell affixes, such as in *desloyal* for *disloyal*, or *carefull* for *CAREFUL*. By studying base words and affixes as meaning units, these students anticipate the next stage, derivational relations, where they study the spelling–meaning connections of related words (Templeton, 2004). By studying base words and derivational affixes, students learn about English spelling at the same time they enrich their vocabularies.

Stage V: Derivational Relations Spelling

The **derivational relations spelling stage** is the last stage in the developmental model. Although some students may move into the derivational stage as early as grade 4 or 5, most derivational relations spellers are found in middle school, high school, and college. This stage continues throughout adulthood, when individuals continue to read and write according to their interests and specialties. This stage of orthographic knowledge is known as *derivational relations* because this is when students examine how words share common derivations and related base words and word roots. They discover that the meaning and spelling of parts of words remain constant across different but derivationally related words (Henderson & Templeton, 1986; Henry, 1988; Schlagal, 1989; Templeton, 1983). Word study in this stage builds on and expands knowledge of a wide vocabulary, often of Greek and Latin origin.

Early derivational relations spellers like Kaitlyn (Figure 11.11) spell most words correctly. However, some of her errors reflect a lack of knowledge about derivations. For example, *favorite* is spelled *FAVERITE* and does not show its relationship to *favor*, and *different* is spelled *DIFFRENT* and lacks a connection to *differ*. Her errors on final suffixes, such as the *-sion* in *division* and the *-ent* in *ingredients* are also very typical of students in this stage.

Frequent errors have to do with the **reduced vowel** in derivationally related pairs. For example, the vowel sound in the second syllable of the word *competition* is reduced to a **schwa** sound, as in *com-puh-ti–tion*. Students in the earlier part of the derivational relations stage might spell *competition* as *COMPUTIION* or *COMPOTITION* or even *COMPITITION*. A student who misspells *competition* may see the correct spelling more easily by going back to a base or root, as in *compete*, where the long vowel gives a clear clue to spelling. Knowing that the word *competition* is derivationally related to the word *compete* will help these students spell the derived form correctly.

Students' spelling errors often have to do with using but confusing issues of consonant doubling in **absorbed prefixes,** the convention of changing the last consonant of a prefix to the first consonant of the root word (e.g., *in* + *mobile* = *immobile*). For example, they may spell *immobile* as *IMOBILE* or *correspond* as *CORESPOND*. Other aspects of affixation students negotiate in the latter part of the derivational relations stage involve changing adjectives to nouns (*brilliant* to *brilliance; adolescent* to *adolescence*), and it is not uncommon to find students using but confusing these derivational endings (e.g., *ADOLESCANCE* for *adolescence; BRILLENCE* for *brilliance*).

FIGURE 11.11 Derivational Relations Spelling: Kaitlyn's 6th Grade Math Journal Reflection

The logic inherent in this lifelong stage can be summed up as follows: "Words that are related in meaning are often related in spelling as well, despite changes in sound" (Templeton, 1979, 1983, 2004). Spelling–meaning connections provide a powerful means for expanding vocabulary.

The Synchrony of Literacy Development

The scope and sequence of word study instruction is based on research that has described the developmental relationship between reading and spelling behaviors. When teachers conduct word study with students, they are addressing learning needs in all areas of literacy because development in one area relates to development in other areas. This harmony in the timing of development has been described as the **synchrony** of reading, writing, and spelling development (Bear, 1991b; Bear & Templeton, 1998). All three advance in stage-like progressions that share important conceptual dimensions.

Working independently, other researchers have described a remarkably similar progression of reading phases that cover the range from prereading to highly skilled, mature reading (Chall, 1983; Ehri, 1997; Frith, 1985; Juel, 1991; Spear-Swerling & Sternberg, 1997). There is converging evidence that reading, writing, and spelling development are integrally related. Figure 11.12 compares other researchers' descriptions of reading development to the spelling stages.

Individuals may vary in their rate of progress through these stages, but most tend to follow the same order of development. The synchrony that is observed makes it possible to bring together reading, writing, and spelling behaviors to assess and plan differentiated instruction that addresses students' developmental pace of instruction. The following discussion centers on this overall progression with an emphasis on the synchronous behaviors of reading and writing with spelling.

Emergent Readers

During the emergent stage, the child may undertake reading and writing in earnest, but adults will recognize their efforts as more pretend than real. Students may write with scribbles, letterlike forms, or random letters that have no phonetic relationship to the words they

Alphabet ──────────────────────────► Pattern ──────────────────────────► Meaning

Emergent Spelling
Emergent Reader

Prereading *(Chall, 1983)*
Logographic *(Frith, 1985)*
Prealphabetic *(Ehri, 1997)*
Selective Cue *(Juel, 1991)*

 Letter Name–Alphabetic Spelling
 Beginning Reader

 Stage 1: Initial Reading & Decoding *(Chall, 1983)*
 Alphabetic *(Frith, 1985)*
 Partial-to-Full Alphabetic *(Ehri, 1997)*
 Phonetic Cue *(Spear-Swerling & Sternberg, 1997)*

 Within Word Pattern Spelling
 Transitional Reader

 Stage 2: Confirmation & Fluency *(Chall, 1983)*
 Orthographic *(Frith, 1985)*
 Consolidated Alphabetic *(Ehri, 1997)*
 Automatic Word Recognition *(Spear-Swerling & Sternberg, 1997)*

 Syllables and Affixes Spelling
 Intermediate Reader

 Stage 3: Reading to Learn *(Chall, 1983)*
 Strategic Reading *(Spear-Swerling & Sternberg, 1997)*

 Derivational Relations Spelling
 Advanced Reader

 Stage 4: Multiple Viewpoints *(Chall, 1983)*
 Stage 5: Construction & Reconstruction *(Chall, 1983)*
 Proficient Adult Reading *(Spear-Swerling & Sternberg, 1997)*

FIGURE 11.12   Spelling and Reading Stages

confidently believe they are writing. These students may "read" familiar books from memory using the pictures on each page to cue their recitation of the text. For this reason, Chall (1983) called this stage of development *pre-reading*. Emergent readers may call out the name of a favorite fast food restaurant when they recognize its logo or identify a friend's name because it starts with a *t*, but they are not systematic in their use of any particular cue. During the emergent stage, children lack an understanding of the alphabetic principle or show only the beginning of this understanding. Ehri (1997) designated this as the *pre-alphabetic phase*; children's use of logos led Frith (1985) to name it the *logographic stage*. Juel (1991) uses the term *selective cue* to describe how children select nonalphabetic visual cues like the two *o*s in *look* to remember a word.

During the emergent stage, children can become quite attached to selected letters that they notice in their name. Upon entering preschool, Lee noticed that other children's names on their cubbies used some of the same letters that she used in her name. Perplexed and somewhat annoyed, she pointed to the letters that were also in her name. "Hey, that's MY letter!" she insisted. Children in the emergent stage also begin to see selected letters in their names in environmental print. Walking around the grocery store, Lee pointed to the box of Cheer detergent and said, "Look, Mommy! There's my name!" Lee's special relationship with the letters in her name is a living embodiment of the prealphabetic, logographic, and selective–cue strategy these researchers describe.

Beginning Readers

The understanding of the alphabetic nature of our language is a major hurdle for readers and spellers. The child who writes *light* as *LT* has made a quantum conceptual leap, having grasped that there are systematic matches between sounds and letters that must be made when writing. The early letter name–alphabetic speller is a beginning reader who has moved from pretend reading to real reading and begun to use systematic letter sound matches to identify and store words in memory. Just as early attempts to spell words are partial, so, too, beginning readers initially have limited knowledge of letter sounds as they identify words by phonetic cues. Ehri (1997) describes these readers and writers as being in the *partial alphabetic* phase. The kinds of reading errors students make during this phase offer insights into what they understand about print. Using context as well as partial consonant cues, a child reading about good things to eat might substitute *candy* or even *cookie* for *cake* in the sentence, "The cake was good." Readers in this stage require much support in the form of predictable, memorable texts.

As readers and writers acquire more complete knowledge of letter sounds in the later part of the letter name–alphabetic stage, they will include, but often confuse, vowels in the words they write and read. Students who spell *BAD* for *bed* may make similar vowel errors when they read *hid* as *had* in "I hid the last cookie." These students resemble Ehri's (1997) *full alphabetic* readers who begin to use the entire letter string to decode and store sight words. Nevertheless, the reading of letter name–alphabetic spellers is often disfluent and word by word, unless they have read the passage before or are otherwise familiar with it (Bear, 1992). If you ask such spellers to read silently, the best they can do is to whisper. They need to read aloud to vocalize the letter sounds. Readers in this stage continue to benefit from repeated readings of predictable texts, but also from the reading of text with many phonetically regular words. These "decodable" texts support the development of decoding strategies and the acquisition of sight words (Juel & Roper-Schneider, 1985; Mesmer, 2006). Not surprisingly, Chall (1983) referred to this stage as a period of *initial reading and decoding* when students are "glued to print."

Transitional Readers

Transitional readers and spellers move into the within word pattern spelling stage when single letter–sound units are consolidated into patterns or larger chunks and other spelling regularities are internalized. Longitudinal research on spelling development has identified the progressive order in which students appear to use these larger chunks. After automating basic letter sounds in the **onset** position (initial consonants, consonant blends, and consonant digraphs), students focus on the vowel and what follows (Ganske, 1994; Invernizzi, 1985, 1992; Viise, 1996). Short-vowel **rimes** are learned first with consonant blends in the context of simple word families or **phonograms** such as *h-at*, *ch-at*, or *fl-at*. These chunks come relatively easily in the letter name–alphabetic stage, probably as a result of their frequency in one-syllable words. Once the rime unit is solidified as a chunk, students appear to use but confuse the various long-vowel patterns of English (Invernizzi, 1992). Other stage models of reading acquisition describe this chunking phenomenon as an *orthographic* stage in which readers use progressively higher-order units of word structures to read and spell (Chall, 1983; Frith, 1985; Gibson, 1965). Ehri and McCormick (1998) call this the *consolidated alphabetic phase* in which students' reading is supported by familiarity with frequently occurring letter pattern units.

From the beginning to the end of this stage, students move from needing support materials and techniques to being able to pick from various texts and reading them independently—from the Sunday comics to easy chapter books such as *Freckle Juice* and *Superfudge*, both by Judy Blume, and *Ramona the Pest*, by Beverly Cleary. With easy, independent-level material, students stop fingerpointing and, for the first time, read silently (Bear, 1982; Henderson, 1990). Their reading moves from halting word-by-word reading to more expressive phrasal reading, and they can read fluently at their instructional level (Zutell & Rasinski, 1989). During this stage, students integrate the knowledge and skills acquired in the previous two stages, so Chall (1983) described this stage as one of *confirmation and fluency*. Advances in word knowledge affect students' writing, too. Their sizable sight word vocabulary allows them to write more quickly and with greater detail. Writing and reading speeds increase significantly between the letter name–alphabetic stage and the transitional within word pattern stage (Bear, 1992; Invernizzi, 1992).

Intermediate and Advanced Readers

Two additional stages of word knowledge characterize **intermediate** and **advanced readers:** syllables and affixes and derivational relations as shown in Figure 11.13. These two periods of literacy development are generally accompanied by the ability to solve abstract problems and to reflect metacognitively on experiences. Students operating within the meaning layer of English orthography have relatively automatic word recognition, and thus their minds are free to think as rapidly as they can read. They can use reading as a vehicle for learning new information from texts, and their vocabulary grows with their reading experience. Intermediate and advanced readers are also fluent writers. The content of their writing displays complex analysis and interpretation, and reflects a more sophisticated, content-oriented vocabulary.

Syllable and affix spellers read most texts with good accuracy and speed, both orally and silently. For these students, success in reading and understanding is related to familiarity and experience with the topic being discussed. Students in this intermediate stage acquire, through plenty of practice, a repertoire of reading styles that reflects their experience with different genres. They may obsess on reading fantasy or historical fiction and voraciously consume all of the books in a series, such as the Harry Potter books by J. K. Rowling or *His Dark Materials* by Philip Pullman. The same is true for writing. Students who are in this stage of word knowledge delight in writing persuasive essays, editorials, poetry, or their own versions of fantasy or realistic fiction.

Derivational relations spellers have a broader experience base that allows them to choose among a variety of reading styles to suit the text and their purposes for reading. They read according to their own interests and needs and they seek to integrate their knowledge with the knowledge of others. The same picture is evidenced in their writing. With purpose and practice, derivational relations students develop and master a variety of writing styles.

These two stages of word knowledge correspond roughly to Chall's (1983) *multiple viewpoints* and *construction and reconstruction* stages. Others refer to this period as one during which students learn to become *strategic readers* and ultimately become *proficient adult readers* (Spear-Swerling & Sternberg, 1997). Still others lump these two stages of reading together as the *automatic* stage (Gough & Hillinger, 1980), even though much is still not automatic. Syllable and affixes spellers continue to struggle with issues such as how to pronounce the name of the main character in *Caddie Woodlawn*, sometimes calling her "Cadie." Derivational relations spellers may have seen the word *segue* in print but never have heard it pronounced, and read it as *seck* or *seck-que*. Vocabulary and word use plays a central role in the connections that intermediate and advanced readers forge between reading and writing. From adolescence on, most of the new vocabulary students learn—except perhaps for slang—comes from reading and reflects new domains of content-specific knowledge that students explore (Beck, McKeown, & Kucan, 2002). Studying spelling–meaning connections is central to maximizing this vocabulary growth (Templeton, 1979, 1992).

Layers of the Orthography

ALPHABET/SOUND

PATTERN

MEANING

Reading and Writing Stages:

	Emergent	Beginning	Transitional	Intermediate	Advanced
Pretend read		Read aloud, word-by-word, fingerpoint reading	Approaching fluency, phrasal, some expression in oral reading. Wright Brothers of reading	Read fluently, with expression. Develop a variety of reading styles. Vocabulary grows with experience reading.	
Pretend write		Word-by-word writing, writing moves from a few words to paragraph in length	Approaching fluency, more organization, several paragraphs	Fluent writing, build expression and voice, experience different writing, styles and genre, writing shows personal problem solving and personal reflection.	

Spelling Stages:

Word	Emergent → (Early Middle Late)	Letter Name–Alphabetic → (Early Middle Late)	Within-Word Pattern → (Early Middle Late)	Syllables and Affixes → (Early Middle Late)	Derivational Relations → (Early Middle Late)
bed	MST · E	bd · bad	*bed*		
ship	TFP · S	sp · sep	*ship* · shep		
float	SMT · F	ft · fot · flot	flowt · floaut · flott	flote · *float*	
train	FSMP · G	jn · jan · chran	teran · traen · tran	trane · *train*	
bottle	· · B	bt · botl · bodol	· botel	bottel · botel · botal · *bottle*	
cellar	· · S	slr · salr · celr	seler · celer	seler · celer · seler · *cellar*	
pleasure	· · P	pjr · plasr · plager	plejer · pleser	pleser · plesher · plesher · plesour	plesour · *pleasure*
confident				confedent · confident · confiednet	confedent · confident · *confident*
opposition				opasishan · oppasishian · oppasishion	oposition · oposisian · oposision · *opposition*

Emergent examples include scribble/early writing forms.

FIGURE 11.13   The Synchrony of Literacy Development

Source: From The Synchrony of Literacy Development: A Guide to Instruction by D. Bear, 1998.

Research to Support the Synchrony of Spelling and Reading

Significant correlations between spelling and various measures of word recognition and decoding have been reported. For example, Ehri (2000) reviewed six correlational studies in which students of various ages (first grade through college) were asked to read and spell words and reported correlations ranging from .68 to .86. In other studies, spelling measures have accounted for as much as 40% to 60% of the variance in oral reading measures (Zutell, 1992; Zutell & Rasinki, 1989). Intervention studies exploring the added value of supplemental spelling instruction have repeatedly found that students who receive additional spelling instruction perform better on reading tasks such as oral reading, silent reading comprehension, and other reading-related measures in addition to spelling (Berninger et al., 1998; Goulandris, 1992; Graham, Harris, & Chorzempa, 2002; McCandliss, Beck, Sandak, & Perfetti, 2003). Notably, Perfetti (1997) observed that practice at spelling helps reading more than practice at reading helps spelling.

Students' spelling attempts also provide a powerful medium for predicting reading achievement (Cataldo & Ellis, 1988). Morris and Perney (1984) found that first graders' invented spellings were a better predictor of end-of-grade reading than a standardized reading readiness test. In a two-year study following students from first through third grade, Ellis and Cataldo (1992) reported spelling to be the most consistent predictor of reading achievement. Sawyer et al. (1997) reported that a child's score on a developmental spelling inventory (Ganske, 1999) was a more powerful predictor of decoding than phonemic awareness tasks such as segmentation. Moreover, the spelling inventory identified the exact word elements students had already mastered and those currently under negotiation. Thus, establishing levels of development in spelling and reading has enormous potential for guiding instruction.

Integrated Phonics, Spelling, and Reading Instruction

Henderson (1981) devised the concept of **word study** because he was convinced that understanding how children learned to spell words could also provide insight on how they read them. He believed that children's growing word knowledge encompassed phonological, syntactic, semantic, and orthographic information, and that categorizing written words enabled them to sort out the relationships among these linguistic sources. Henderson's instructional approaches (for example, *word sorts, word hunts, writing sorts*) were shaped by his belief that both linguistic and orthographic aspects of written words were critical factors in learning to read and write. His work, and the work of his colleagues and students, demonstrated that written word knowledge is developmental and advances progressively and in synchrony in relation to cognitive development, exposure to print, and instruction.

Figure 11.13 presents an integrated model of how reading, writing, and spelling progress in synchrony. In parent-teacher conferences, teachers might refer to this figure in discussing each student's development when they share his or her writing or show a collection of books that illustrates the range of instructional reading levels that correspond to the developmental levels in the figure. Parents can better understand where their children are along the developmental continuum and across reading, writing, and spelling by looking at the described behaviors and the spelling samples.

Word study activities in this book are organized around this model. If you can identify your students by the stages of reading, writing, and spelling, then you will know which chapters contain the activities that are most relevant to their development, as shown in Figure 11.5 on page 382.

As described throughout this chapter, developmental spelling theory suggests that invented spelling is a window into a child's knowledge of how written words work and can be used to guide instruction. Specific kinds of spelling errors at particular levels of orthographic knowledge reflect a progressive differentiation of word elements that determine how quickly students can read words and how easily they can write them. Insight into students' conceptual understanding of these word elements helps teachers direct their efforts as students learn to read and spell.

In this book, we suggest that orthographic knowledge plays a central role in a comprehensive language arts program that links reading and writing. Word knowledge accumulates as students develop orthographic understand-

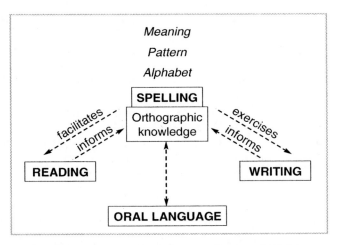

FIGURE 11.14   Word Study: Reading and Writing

ings at the alphabetic level, the pattern level, and the meaning level in overarching layers of complexity. Our complete understanding of phonics, word recognition, spelling, vocabulary, and even the grammar of words (syntax) is part of our word knowledge. Reading provides the corpus of words and defines the parameters of what may be studied. Through word study, students learn how the spelling system, or orthography, works to represent sound, pattern, and meaning. Writing then exercises that word knowledge. Figure 11.14 illustrates the theory of developmental word knowledge and shows how word study links reading and writing.

Where Do I Begin Word Study?

Students acquire word knowledge implicitly as they read and write, and also through explicit instruction orchestrated by the teacher. However, it is impossible to know exactly what to teach and when to teach it until we have a living child before us. An informed interpretation of students' reading and writing attempts shows us which words they can read and spell, and of those, which they might learn more about. There is more to pacing instruction than plugging students into a sequence of phonics or spelling features. Instructional *pacing* must be synonymous with instructional *placing*. That is, we must fit our instruction to what our students are using but confusing. How do we know what they are using but confusing? A good deal of what students know about orthography is revealed in their invented spellings produced in uncorrected writing.

Words Their Way

To help students explore and learn about words their way, instruction must be sensitive to two fundamental tenets:

1. Students' learning of phonics, spelling, and vocabulary is based on their developmental or instructional level.
2. Students' learning is based on the way they are naturally inclined to learn: through comparing and contrasting word features and discovering consistencies.

When these two tenets are honored, students learn *their* way—building from what is known about words to what is new. Rather than rote memorization activities designed only to ensure repeated mechanical practice, word study encourages active exploration and examination of word features that are within a student's stage of literacy development. Word study is active, and by making judgments about words and sorting words according to similar features, students construct their own understandings about how the features work. Active, thoughtful practice helps students internalize word features and become automatic in using what they have learned.

Table 11.2 summarizes the characteristics of each stage of development to help you understand the reading and writing context for the word study instruction that is appropriate for each stage.

TABLE 11.2 Developmental Stages, Characteristics, and Word Study Instruction

I. Emergent Stage

Characteristics
1. Scribbles letters and numbers
2. Lacks concept of word
3. Lacks letter-sound correspondence or represents most salient sound with single letters
4. Pretends to read and write

Reading and Writing Activities
1. Read to students and encourage oral language activities
2. Model writing using dictations and charts
3. Encourage pretend reading and writing

Word Study Focus
1. Develop oral language with concept sorts
2. Play with speech sounds to develop phonological awareness
3. Plan activities to learn the alphabet
4. Sort pictures by beginning sound
5. Encourage fingerpoint memory reading of rhymes, dictations, and simple pattern books
6. Encourage invented spelling

II. Letter Name–Alphabetic Stage

Early Letter Name–Alphabetic
Characteristics
1. Represents beginning and ending sounds
2. Uses letter names to invent spellings
3. Has rudimentary or functional concept of word
4. Reads word by word in beginning reading materials

Reading and Writing Activities
1. Read to students and encourage oral language activities
2. Secure concept of word by plenty of reading in predictable books, dictations, and simple rhymes
3. Record and reread individual dictations
4. Label pictures and write in journals regularly

Word Study Focus
1. Collect known words for word bank
2. Sort pictures and words by beginning sounds
3. Study word families that share a common vowel

TABLE 11.2 Continued

  4. Study beginning consonant blends and digraphs
  5. Encourage invented spelling

Middle to Late Letter Name–Alphabetic Stage
Characteristics
  1. Correctly spells initial and final consonants and some blends and digraphs
  2. Uses letter names to spell vowel sounds
  3. Spells phonetically, representing all salient sounds in a one-to-one, linear fashion
  4. Omits most silent letters and preconsonantal nasals in spelling (*bop* or *bup* for *bump*)
  5. Fingerpoints accurately and can self-correct when off track
  6. Reads aloud slowly in a word-by-word manner

Reading and Writing Activities
  1. Read to students
  2. Encourage invented spellings in independent writing, but hold students accountable for features and words they have studied
  3. Collect two- to three-paragraph dictations that are reread regularly
  4. Encourage more expansive writing and consider some simple editing procedures for punctuation and high-frequency words

Word Study Focus
  1. Sort pictures and words by different short vowel word families
  2. Sort pictures and words by short vowel sounds and CVC patterns
  3. Continue to examine more difficult consonant blends with pictures and words
  4. Study preconsonantal nasals and digraphs at the end of words
  5. Sort pictures comparing short and long vowel sounds
  6. Collect known words for word bank (up to 200)

III. Within Word Pattern Stage

Characteristics
  1. Spells most single-syllable, short vowel words correctly
  2. Spells most beginning consonant digraphs and two-letter consonant blends
  3. Attempts to use silent long vowel markers
  4. Reads silently and with more fluency and expression
  5. Writes more fluently and in extended fashion
  6. Can revise and edit

Reading and Writing Activities
  1. Continue to read aloud to students
  2. Guide silent reading of simple chapter books
  3. Write each day, writers' workshops, conferencing, and publication

Word Study Focus
  1. Complete daily activities in word study notebook
  2. Sort words by long- and short-vowel sounds and by common long-vowel patterns
  3. Compare words with *r*-influenced vowels,
  4. Explore less common vowels, diphthongs (*oi, oy*), and other ambiguous vowels (*ou, au, ow, oo*)
  5. Examine triple blends and complex consonant units such as *thr, str, dge, tch, ck*
  6. Explore homographs and homophones

IV. Syllables and Affixes

Characteristics
  1. Spells most single-syllable words correctly
  2. Makes errors at syllable juncture and in unaccented syllables

Continued

TABLE 11.2   Continued
_____

3. Reads with good fluency and expression
4. Reads faster silently than orally
5. Writes responses that are sophisticated and critical

Reading and Writing Activities
1. Plan read-alouds and literature discussions
2. Include self-selected or assigned silent reading of novels of different genres
3. Begin simple note taking and outlining skills, and work with adjusting reading rates for different purposes
4. Explore reading and writing styles and genres

Word Study Focus
1. Examine plural endings
2. Study compound words
3. Study consonant doubling and inflected endings
4. Study open and closed syllables and other syllable juncture issues
5. Explore syllable stress and vowel patterns in the accented syllable, especially ambiguous vowels
6. Focus on unaccented syllables such as *er* and *le*
7. Explore unusual consonant blends and digraphs (*qu, ph, gh, gu*)
8. Study base words and affixes
9. Focus on two-syllable homophones and homographs
10. Join spelling and vocabulary studies; link meaning and spelling with grammar and meaning
11. Explore grammar through word study
12. Sort and study common affixes (prefixes and suffixes)
13. Study stress or accent in two-syllable words

V. Derivational Relations
Characteristics
1. Has mastered high frequency words
2. Makes errors on low frequency, multisyllabic words derived from Latin and Greek
3. Reads with good fluency and expression
4. Reads faster silently than orally
5. Writes responses that are sophisticated and critical

Reading and Writing Activities
1. Include silent reading and writing, exploring various genres
2. Develop study skills, including textbook reading, note taking, adjusting rates, test taking, report writing, and reference work
3. Focus on literary analysis

Word Study Focus
1. Focus on words that students bring to word study from their reading and writing
2. Join spelling and vocabulary studies; link meaning and spelling with grammar and meaning
3. Examine common and then less common roots, prefixes, and suffixes (e.g., *ion*)
4. Examine vowel and consonant alternations in derivationally related pairs
5. Study Greek and Latin word roots and stems
6. Focus on abstract Latin suffixes (*ence/ance; ible/able; ent/ant*)
7. Learn about absorbed or assimilated prefixes
8. Explore etymology, especially in the content areas
9. Examine content-related foreign borrowings
_____

REFERENCES

Balmuth, M. (1992). *The roots of phonics: A historical introduction.* Austin, TX: Pro-Ed.

Baretta-Lorton, M. L. (1968). *Math their way.* Reading, MA: Addison-Wesley.

Bear, D. (1982). *Patterns of oral reading across stages of word knowledge.* Unpublished manuscript, University of Virginia, Charlottesville.

Bear, D. (1989). Why beginning reading must be word-by-word. *Visible Language, 23*(4), 353–367.

Bear, D. (1991b). "Learning to fasten the seat of my union suit without looking around": The synchrony of literacy development. *Theory into Practice, 30*(3), 149–157.

Bear, D. (1992). The prosody of oral reading and stage of word knowledge. In S. Templeton & D. Bear (Eds.), *Development of orthographic knowledge and the foundations of literacy: A memorial Festschrift for Edmund H. Henderson* (pp. 137–186). Hillsdale, NJ: Lawrence Erlbaum.

Bear, D., & Templeton, S. (1998). Explorations in developmental spelling: Foundations for learning and teaching phonics, spelling and vocabulary. *The Reading Teacher, 52,* 222–242.

Bear, D., Templeton, S., Helman, L., & Baren, T. (2003). Orthographic development and learning to read in different languages. In G. Garcia (Ed.), *English learners: Reaching the highest level of English literacy* (pp. 71–95). Newark, DE: International Reading Association.

Bear, D., Truex, P., & Barone, D. (1989). In search of meaningful diagnoses: Spelling-by-stage assessment of literacy proficiency. *Adult Literacy and Basic Education, 13*(3), 165–185.

Beck, I. L., McKeown, M. G., & Kucan, L. (2002). *Bringing words to life: Robust vocabulary instruction.* New York: Guilford Press.

Beers, J. W., & Henderson, E. H. (1977). A study of developing orthographic concepts among first grade children. *Research in the Teaching of English, 11,* 133–148.

Berninger, V. W., Vaughn, K., Abbott, R. D., Brooks, A., Abbott, S. P., Rogan, L., Reed, E., & Graham, S. (1998). Early interventions for spelling problems: Teaching functional spelling units of varying size with a multiple-connections framework. *Journal of Educational Psychology, 90,* 587–605.

Bissex, G. L. (1980). *Gnys at wrk.* Cambridge, MA: Harvard University Press.

Bryant, P., Nunes, T., & Bindman, M. (1997). Backward readers' awareness of language: Strengths and weaknesses. *European Journal of Psychology of Education, 12*(4), 357–372.

Cantrell, R. J. (2001). Exploring the relationship between dialect and spelling for specific vocalic features in Appalachian first-grade children. *Linguistics and Education, 12*(1), 1–23.

Cataldo, S., & Ellis, N. (1988). Interactions in the development of spelling, reading, and phonological skills. *Journal of Research in Reading, 11,* 86–109.

Chall, J. S. (1983). *Stages of reading development.* New York: McGraw-Hill.

Chomsky, C. (1971). Write first read later. *Childhood Education, 47,* 296–299.

Chomsky, N., & Halle, M. (1968). *The sound pattern of English.* New York: Harper & Row.

Ehri, L. (1992). Review and commentary: Stages of spelling development. In S. Templeton & D. Bear (Eds.), *Development of orthographic knowledge and the foundations of literacy: A memorial Festschrift for Edmund H. Henderson* (pp. 307–332). Hillsdale, NJ: Lawrence Erlbaum.

Ehri, L. C. (1997). Learning to read and learning to spell are one and the same, almost. In C. A. Perfetti, L. Rieben, & M. Fayol (Eds.), *Learning to spell: Research, theory, and practice across languages* (pp. 237–269). Mahwah, NJ: Lawrence Erlbaum.

Ehri, L. C. (2000). Learning to read and learning to spell: Two sides of a coin. *Topics in Language Disorders, 20,* 19–36.

Ehri, L. C. (2006). Alphabetics instruction helps children learn to read. In R. M. Joshi & P. G. Aaron (Eds.) *Handbook of orthography and literacy* (pp. 649–678). Mahwah, NJ: Lawrence Erlbaum.

Ehri, L., & McCormick, S. (1998). Phases of word learning: Implications for instruction with delayed and disabled readers. *Reading and Writing Quarterly: Overcoming Learning Difficulties, 14,* 135–164.

Ellis, N., & Cataldo, S. (1992). Spelling is integral to learning to read. In C. M. Steriing & C. Robson (eds). *Psychology, spelling, and education* (pp 112–142). Clevedon, UK: Multilingual Matters.

Frith, U. (1985). Beneath the surface of developmental dyslexia. In K. Patterson, J. Marshall, & M. Coltheart (Eds.), *Surface dyslexia: Neuro psychological and cognitive studies of phonological reading* (pp. 301–330). London: Lawrence Erlbaum Associates.

Ganske, K. (1994). Developmental spelling analysis: A diagnostic measure for instruction and research (University of Virginia). *Dissertation Abstracts International, 55*(05), 1230A.

Ganske, K. (1999). The developmental spelling analysis: A measure of orthographic knowledge. *Educational Assessment, 6,* 41–70.

Gentry, J. (1980). Learning to spell developmentally. *Reading Teacher, 34,* 378–381.

Gibson, E. J. (1965). Learning to read. *Science, 148,* 1006–1072.

Gough, P. B., & Hillinger, M. L. (1980). Learning to read: An unnatural act. *Bulletin of the Orton Society, 20,* 179–196.

Goulandris, N. K. (1992). Alphabetic spelling: Predicting eventual literacy attainment. In C. M. Sterling & C. Robson (Eds.) *Psychology, Spelling, and Education* (pp. 143–158). Clevedon, UK: Multilingual Matters.

Graham, S., Harris, K. R., & Chorzempa, B. F. (2002). Contribution of spelling instruction to the spelling, writing, and reading of poor spellers. *Journal of Educational Psychology, 94,* 669–686.

Hanna, P. R., Hanna, J. S., Hodges, R. E., & Rudorf, H. (1966). Phoneme-grapheme correspondences as cues to spelling improvement. Washington, DC: United States Office of Education Cooperative Research.

Helman, L. (2004). Building on the sound system of Spanish. *The Reading Teacher, 57,* 452–460.

Henderson, E. H. (1981). *Learning to read and spell: The child's knowledge of words.* DeKalb: Northern Illinois Press.

Henderson, E. H. (1990). *Teaching spelling* (2nd ed.). Boston: Houghton Mifflin.

Henderson, E. H. (1992). The interface of lexical competence and knowledge of written words. In S. Templeton & D. R. Bear (Eds.), *Development of orthographic knowledge and the foundations of literacy: A memorial Festschrift for Edmund H. Henderson* (pp. 1–30). Hillsdale, NJ: Lawrence Erlbaum Associates.

Henderson, E. H., & Beers, J. (Eds.), (1980). *Developmental and cognitive aspects of learning to spell.* Newark, DE: International Reading Association.

Henderson, E. H., Estes, T., & Stonecash, S. (1972). An exploratory study of word acquisition among first graders at midyear in a language experience approach. *Journal of Reading Behavior, 4,* 21–30.

Henderson, E. H., & Templeton, S. (1986). The development of spelling ability through alphabet, pattern, and meaning. *Elementary School Journal, 86,* 305–316.

Henry, M. (1988). Beyond phonics: Integrated decoding and spelling instruction based on word origin and structures. *Annals of Dyslexia, 38,* 258–275.

Invernizzi, M. (1985). *A cross-sectional analysis of children's recognition and recall of word elements.* Unpublished manuscript, University of Virginia, Charlottesville.

Invernizzi, M. (1992). The vowel and what follows: A phonological frame of orthographic analysis. In S. Templeton & D. Bear (Eds.), *Development of orthographic knowledge and the foundations of literacy: A memorial Festschrift for Edmund H. Henderson* (pp. 106–136). Hillsdale, NJ: Lawrence Erlbaum.

Invernizzi, M., Abouzeid, M., & Gill, T. (1994). Using students' invented spellings as a guide for spelling instruction that emphasizes word study. *Elementary School Journal, 95*(2), 155–167.

Invernizzi, M., & Hayes, L. (2004). Developmental-spelling research: A systematic imperative. *Reading Research Quarterly, 39,* 2–15.

James, W. (1958). *Talks to teachers on psychology and to students on some of life's ideals.* New York: Norton. (Original work published 1899.)

Juel, C. (1991). Beginning reading. In R. Barr, M. Kamil, P. Mosenthal, & P. D. Pearson (Eds.), *Handbook of reading research* (Vol. II, pp. 759–788). New York: Longman Press.

Juel, C., & Minden-Cupp, C. (2000). Learning to read words: Linguistic units and instructional strategies. *Reading Research Quarterly, 35,* 458–492.

Juel, C., & Roper-Schneider, D. (1985). The influence of basal readers on first grade reading. *Reading Research Quarterly, 18,* 306–327.

Mathews, M. (1967). *Teaching to read: historically considered.* University of Chicago Press.

McCandliss, B., Beck, I., Sandak, R., & Perfetti, C. (2003). Focusing attention on decoding for children with poor reading skills: Design and preliminary tests of the word building intervention. *Scientific Studies of Reading, 7,* 75–103.

Mesmer, H. A. E. (2006). Text decodability and the first-grade reader. *Reading & Writing Quarterly, 21,* 61–86.

Morris, D., & Perney, J. (1984). Developmental spelling as a predictor of first-grade reading achievement. *The Elementary School Journal, 84,* 441–457.

Perfetti, C. A. (1997). The psycholinguistics of spelling and reading. In C. A. Perfetti, L. Rieben, & M. Fayol (Eds.), *Learning to spell: Research, theory, and practice across languages* (pp. 21–38). Mawah, NJ: Lawrence Erlbaum Associates.

Read, C. (1971). Pre-school children's knowledge of English phonology. *Harvard Educational Review, 41*(1), 1–34.

Read, C. (1975). *Children's categorization of speech sounds in English.* Urbana, IL: NCTE Research Report No. 17.

Richgels, D. J. (1995). Invented spelling ability and printed word learning in kindergarten. *Reading Research Quarterly, 30,* 96–109.

Richgels, D. J. (2001). Invented spelling, phonemic awareness, and reading and writing instruction. In S. B. Neuman & D. K. Dickenson (Eds.), *Handbook of Early Literacy Research* (pp. 142–155). New York: The Guilford Press.

Sawyer, D. J., Lipa-Wade, S., Kim, J., Ritenour, D., & Knight, D. F. (1997). *Spelling errors as a window on dyslexia.* Paper presented at the 1997 annual convention of the American Educational Research Association, Chicago.

Sawyer, D. J., Wade, S., & Kim, J. K. (1999). Spelling errors as a window on variations in phonological deficits among students with dyslexia. *Annals of Dyslexia, 49,* 137–159.

Schlagal, R. (1989). Constancy and change in spelling development. *Reading Psychology, 10*, 207–232.

Smith, N. B. (2002). *American Reading Instruction* (special edition). Newark. DE: International Reading Association.

Spear-Swerling, L., & Sternberg, R. J. (Contributor) (1997). *Off track: When poor readers become "learning disabled."* Boulder, CO: Westview Press.

Templeton, S. (1979). Spelling first, sound later: The relationship between orthography and higher order phonological knowledge in older students. *Research in the Teaching of English, 13*, 255–264.

Templeton, S. (1983). Using the spelling/meaning connection to develop word knowledge in older students. *Journal of Reading, 27*(1), 8–14.

Templeton, S. (1991). Teaching and learning the English spelling system: Reconceptualizing method and purpose. *Elementary School Journal, 92*, 183–199.

Templeton, S. (1992). Theory, nature, and pedagogy of higher-order orthographic development in older children. In S. Templeton & D. Bear (Eds.), *Development of orthographic knowledge and the foundations of literacy: A memorial Festschrift for Edmund H. Henderson* (pp. 253–278), Hillsdale, NJ: Lawrence Erlbaum.

Templeton, S. (2002). Effective spelling instruction in the middle grades: It's a lot more than memorization. *Voices from the Middle, 9*(3), 8–14.

Templeton, S. (2003). Spelling. In J. Flood, D. Lapp, J. R. Squire, & J. M. Jensen (Eds.), *Handbook of research on teaching the English language arts* (2nd ed., pp. 738–751). Mahwah, NJ: Lawrence Erlbaum Associates.

Templeton, S., & Bear, D. (Eds.). (1992a). *Development of orthographic knowledge and the foundations of literacy: A memorial Festschrift for Edmund H. Henderson.* Hillsdale; NJ: Lawrence Erlbaum.

Templeton, S., & Morris, D. (1999). Questions teachers ask about spelling. *Reading Research Quarterly, 34*, 102–112.

Templeton, S., & Spivey, E. M. (1980). The concept of "word" in young children as a function of level of cognitive development. *Research in the Teaching of English, 14*(3), 265–278.

Treiman, R. (1985). Onsets and rimes as units of spoken syllables: Evidence from children. *Journal of Educational Psychology, 77*(4), 417–427.

Viise, N. (1996). A study of the spelling development of adult literacy learners compared with that of classroom children. *Journal of Literacy Research, 28*(4), 561–587.

Vygotsky, L. S. (1962). *Thought and language.* Cambridge, MA: MIT Press.

Worthy, M. J., & Invernizzi, M. (1989). Spelling errors of normal and disabled students on achievement levels one through four: Instructional implications. *Bulletin of the Orton Society, 40*, 138–149.

Worthy, M., & Viise, N. M. (1996). Morphological, phonological and orthographic differences between the spelling of normally achieving children and basic literacy adults. *Reading and Writing: An Interdisciplinary Journal, 8*, 138–159.

Yang, M. (2005). Development of orthographic knowledge among Korean children in grades 1 to 6. (Doctoral Dissertation, University of Virginia). *Dissertation Abstracts International*, 66/05, 1697.

Zutell, J. (1992). An integrated view of word knowledge: Correlational studies of the relationships among spelling, reading, and conceptual development. In S. Templeton & D. Bear (Eds.), *Development of orthographic knowledge and the foundations of literacy: A memorial Festschrift for Edmund H. Henderson* (pp. 213–230). Newark, DE: International Reading Association.

Zutell, J. (1994). Spelling instruction. In A. C. Purves, L. Papa, & S. Jordan (Eds.), *Encyclopedia of English studies and language arts* (Vol. 2, pp. 1098–1100). New York: Scholastic.

Zutell, J., & Rasinski, T. (1989). Reading and spelling connections in third and fourth grade students. *Reading Psychology, 10*, 137–156.

12 Reading and Writing

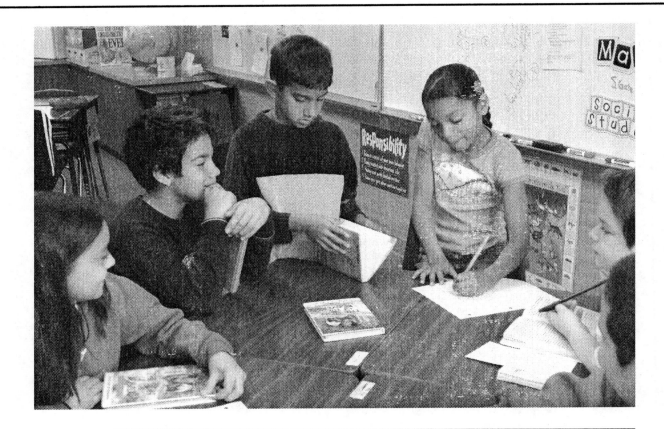

Introduction

Research has consistently shown that strong ties exist between reading and writing (Johnston, 1997; Tierney, 1990). Of particular interest to those who work with students with reading problems is the support that writing provides for reading development and the influence of reading on students' writing. This chapter discusses the writing process and how it relates to reading and gives many strategies to foster the development of writing. Some instructional strategies that help students connect reading and writing are included. Finally, suggestions are presented for teaching spelling and handwriting.

Importance of Teaching Writing

Why should a reading teacher focus on writing? The process of writing is highly related to the process of reading because readers and writers are both constructing—or composing—meaning. Readers construct meaning from the author's text; writers compose or construct meaning as they create text.

The reading-writing relationship begins in early literacy and continues throughout a student's literacy development (Richgels, 2003; Jacobs, 2002; Greene, 1995). In early literacy, the relationship focuses on sound-symbol relationships and concepts about print (Gentry, 2007; Dyson, 2003; Goswami, 2003; Richgels, 2003; Castle, Riach, & Nicholson, 1994). As students mature, the relationship between reading and writing becomes more complex. As students read a wider variety of texts, the influence of those texts can be observed in their writing (Calkins, 2004; Fletcher & Portalupi, 2001; Lancia, 1997; Sitler, 1995; Wollman-Bonilla & Werchadlo, 1995). Sharing good models of writing through reading provides the support students need to improve their writing (Saddler & Graham, 2008). As students engage in more mature writing, they begin to relate to authors' perspectives, and this relationship leads to a deeper understanding of text (Greene, 1995; White, 1995; Calkins, 1994, 2000; Weech, 1994). Students who perceive themselves to be writers are motivated to improve their writing, and they want to use models of written text to help them; thus, students' efforts to improve their writing foster improvement in the reading (Glenn, 2007).

In early literacy, writing helps students understand that print progresses from left to right and from the top of the page to the bottom. In beginning reading, writing provides students with the practice they need to pay attention to individual words and helps them match letters and sounds in words (Gentry, 2007; Richgels, 2003; Clay, 1998, 2002).

Throughout the phases of literacy development, practice in writing increases the understanding of how authors compose text (Olness, 2005; Calkins, 2004). Tierney (1990) interviewed students and found that those who identified themselves as authors viewed reading in a new light. These students expressed more enthusiasm for both reading and writing, and they read more critically. They viewed reading as a resource for new ideas and information for their writing.

Students also use writing to clarify their understanding of what they read. When they make written responses to reading, they increase comprehension (Freeman, 2003; Jacobs, 2002; White, 1995; Weech, 1994; Wells, 1992–1993; Jennings, 1991; Wittrock, 1984). Writing can help students master information in science, social studies, and other subjects (Jacobs, 2002; Cawley & Parmar, 2001; Button & Welton, 1997; Mayher, Lester, & Pradl, 1983). Writing can be a powerful tool in supporting students' learning (Unrau, 2008).

Using writing in instruction offers important sources of success and motivation for struggling readers. Students just learning to read may write or dictate messages and read their own words. Freed from the burden of trying to determine what another author meant, these students now have an opportunity to create, read, and display their own meanings.

For more advanced students with reading problems, writing can be used to deepen comprehension responses and to stimulate more reading. These students enjoy the permanence of responding in writing to books they have read, and their responses can be referred to later and shared with others. In addition, students who identify a topic to write about are often motivated to use reading as a way to find information.

Assessing Writing

In their preliminary diagnosis of students, teachers in our reading center collect five or six writing samples and analyze the students' writing across those samples. They try to collect different genres of writing to measure students' abilities to match genres to purposes for writing: description, informational, expository, and a personal narrative of an event. For students in the early phases of literacy development, they include at least one piece of dictation, using an adapted language experience approach (LEA). The LEA provides the opportunity to compare students' abilities to compose and effectively convey meaning through print when the constraints of physically producing letters and sounds are removed. This helps the teachers focus their attention on what students already know about using written language and how to support their continued development (Johnston & Rogers, 2003).

First, the teachers collect background information about students; then they determine students' reading levels using an informal reading inventory and analyze the results. As they are collecting this information, the teachers ask students to write for several different purposes, and then evaluate the writing samples based on the students reading levels. Thus, the writing samples from an eighth-grade student reading at a fourth-grade level would be evaluated using the criteria for a student at the intermediate level.

In the early phases of literacy development, reading teachers examine students' writing for conventions of print: left-to-right progression, top-to-bottom arrangement on the page, separation of individual words, and phonological representations of words. They also examine students' use of print versus drawing or scribbling. Examples of the forms used to analyze students' writing are included on the website for this text.

For students reading at a primer level through level 2, examine their abilities to present ideas in sequential order or in logical sequence. Also, consider their abilities to organize words into sentences and beginning paragraph organization, including appropriate punctuation.

For students reading at levels 3 through 5, examine their abilities to select appropriate genres of writing for different purposes. Also, consider paragraph organization, including topic sentences and supporting details. At these levels, teachers should expect conventional representation of spelling patterns and varied punctuation.

For students reading at levels 6 through 12, expect appropriate genre selection, conventional spelling, varied sentence structure, and correct punctuation. Also, expect paragraphs to include topic sentences and supporting details. Teachers should expect students to provide main ideas with subordinate sentences and to present a logical argument with supportive positions.

Interactive assessment should occur throughout instruction to monitor students' progress and to provide guidance for instructional decisions (Johnston & Rogers, 2003). Thus, as students write summaries of what they have read, write new endings to stories, or write their own stories, periodically compare their writing to their previous samples to ensure that instruction is meeting their needs and resulting in progress commensurate with their progress in reading.

Writing Instruction

Many instructional strategies can be used successfully with students who have reading problems. Students learn that a person writes for different purposes and for different audiences. For example, you use lists to organize your life and letters, email, or text messages to communicate with friends and family and you use reports to convey information.

This section first describes the writing process that students may use as they develop thoughts into finished written pieces. It then explores three more specific types of personal writing: written conversations, personal correspondence, and personal journals.

Writing Process

Teachers use the writing process to help students become joyful, proficient composers of text. This process has several stages, which range from a first idea to the creation of a formal product. In completing these stages, students in the reading center have come to write more easily and naturally. They have also become proud authors of written pieces that are now part of our library.

Selecting Topics   Topic selection is a key feature of good writing. Students are more willing to write if they choose what to write about. In shaping their content, they also think about the audience who will listen to or read their pieces.

At first, students tend to do personal writing about their own experiences. Topics may include someone they know, a special event, or themselves. Ideally, students should select their own topics; however, struggling readers often have little confidence in themselves as writers. Teachers can help these students by asking them to make lists of people who are special to them. While students were creating their lists, Ms. Grant, a third-grade teacher wrote her own list on the board:

Special People

Granddaddy

Mother

Betty, my sister

Dad

Next, Ms. Grant shared her list with the students and explained briefly why she chose these people. Finally, she encouraged students to share their lists. Then, she asked students to choose one person to write about. While students wrote about their topic, she wrote about hers. When beginning the writing process, you may want to stop periodically to support students in their efforts.

Of course, some students may wish to write reports or letters rather than doing personal writing. Because topic selection is important, you should honor these choices.

Writing Drafts   After topic selection, students begin writing drafts. Encourage your students to write what comes to mind about their topics. Students need not worry about spelling, punctuation, or the other mechanical aspects of writing as they draft their thoughts.

Next, give students opportunities to share their writing with a few of their classmates. Remind the classmates that they should only tell their friends what they like about their writing at this point.

You may devote several writing sessions to topic selection, drafting, and responding positively to students' writing. This procedure helps students develop the habit of writing on a regular basis and builds their confidence in an accepting environment.

Making Revisions   As ideas become clearer, writers revise their pieces. Mature writers do this constantly, making many insertions, deletions, and other changes. However, students with problems in reading and writing are often reluctant to revise. Sometimes, just writing a draft has required extensive effort and making revisions seems overwhelming.

Teachers can use several strategies to encourage revision. First, teachers can model revision in dictated stories and in their own work so that students view revision as a natural part of the writing process. Share one of your unfinished pieces and ask students for suggestions. Use their responses to make changes in your own writing and share the revised version with students in the next lesson.

When students meet to share their drafts, revision is often fostered through suggestions. Writers may find that others have questions about things that are unclear or suggestions for improvement. However, sharing drafts should also be a positive experience. First, have students identify something they like about the draft that is being shared. Only then should they ask questions and make suggestions. To model the concept that it is acceptable to question each others' writing and to make suggestions, have students ask questions of an author of a book you have read to them.

For your more reluctant revisers, try transforming an existing text into another genre. For example, you might alter a fairy tale from its narrative version to create a play. In this process, students must revise the text to create a script. After trying this activity with well-known stories, students are usually better able to write their own stories and are more willing to make revisions.

Editing   When students are satisfied with the content, they are ready to focus on mechanics (spelling, punctuation, and grammar), which are important so that someone else can easily read their pieces. Do not overburden students with changes. Guidelines that foster editing include:

* Focus on items that can be changed immediately.
* Limit suggestions to items that have been presented in instruction.
* Make no more than three suggestions to younger students and no more than five to older students.

Make notes about items that cannot be changed easily and save these for later instruction. Explicit instruction that addresses revision or editing concerns can be given as short minilessons during writing time.

Publishing   When the editing process is complete, the writing is ready to be shared with a wider audience. Graves (1994) refers to this as "publishing." Publishing is not limited to binding a book and sharing it with the class or placing it in a classroom library. Publishing may consist of a presentation, a bulletin board display, a play, or even a puppet show. Opportunities to publish for audiences beyond the classroom are especially motivating for many students. School-wide or cross-school poetry slams and readers' theater can provide students with opportunities to share their writing as well as enhance their reading and reading fluency. District-wide writing fairs can be held for students to share their best writing. As students write throughout the year, they are aware that they may select one of their pieces to represent their best writing as part of the writing fair (Strickland, Ganske, & Monroe, 2002). As the writing process develops, students' contributions will fill your literacy environment.

Evaluation of Writing   In guiding students to improve their writing, teachers must be able to evaluate their pieces. The evaluation of writing should focus on several levels, including content, organization of ideas, structure, and mechanics. By evaluating each, they gain a broad overview of a student's writing capabilities. To permit organized evaluation, start with the most general level—the content—and work toward the most specific—mechanics.

As a teacher, first, focus on content, the ability of the student to communicate thought. Ask two questions about the student's piece: "Does this student have an understanding that writing is a means of communication?" and "Does this student use writing effectively to express his or her ideas?"

Second, focus on the student's ability to organize ideas. For students in the beginning stages of writing, organization may consist of the ability to write information in sentences. Later, evaluate primary students' ability to present ideas in sequential order. For intermediate-level writers, evaluate abilities to organize related ideas into paragraphs. For more mature writers, evaluate the ability to organize paragraphs and sections of papers by related ideas.

Third, evaluate structure—the ability to use different writing forms, or genres, appropriately. For older students, focus on the characteristics of specific formats, such as an essay or thesis. For students in the beginning stages of writing, focus on sentences and grammatical structure. For intermediate students, judge paragraph structure as well.

Finally, after a selection of writing has been evaluated for content, organization, and structure, focus on the mechanics. Mechanics include spelling, punctuation, and proper use of capitalization.

From this evaluation, you can make decisions about a student's instructional needs on several different levels. For example, students may need help on aspects of writing as broad as how to write a letter or as narrow as using an apostrophe.

Evaluation leads you to two instructional decisions. First, decide what the student should correct to make his or her writing more easily read by others. This decision depends on the level of the student's reading ability. In addition, limit your corrections to areas that the student has been taught previously. The second decision is what the student needs to learn next in instruction. From the second decision, formulate instructional plans and present minilessons, short lessons focused on specific aspects of writing.

Supporting Students' Writing

In the early phases of literacy development, much of students' writing focuses on developing concepts about print, phonological awareness, and word identification. However, teachers know that the concurrent development of students' understandings about stories and story grammar is also important. Thus, in early literacy development, teachers provide extensive support for the physical act of writing by assuming the role of scribe while students engage in composing texts. As students become more proficient in letter production and sound representation, teachers gradually release responsibility for more of the writing process to students. This approach to writing instruction and the gradual release of responsibility to students parallels the reciprocal teaching approach advocated in comprehension instruction (Shanahan, 2005; Palinscar & Brown, 1984). Teachers must constantly assess students' writing to determine levels of expectations and how much responsibility to relinquish. In other words, teachers want to make sure they are guiding students within their zones of proximal development (Vanderburg, 2006). The next section provides descriptions of varying levels of scaffolding provided in writing instruction.

Modeled Writing   We begin with modeled writing, often in the form of the morning message. In primary classrooms, teachers often start the day with a morning message to preview the day and to build background knowledge for the day's learning experiences. As students become more experienced, this activity shifts to incorporate more student input (Mariage, 2001).

Interactive Writing   As students gain experience and develop an understanding of the teacher's expectations for morning message as well as the day's routines, they begin to contribute to the content of the morning message (Figure 12.1). Although the process shifts to look more like language experience activity, with students dictating the content and teachers assuming the role of scribe, it differs in that the teacher knows some components of the morning message that the students don't yet know. For example, the students may

Today is Wednesday, April, 16 2008. This morning, we will read a story about a girl named Madlenka, who wants to tell all of her neighbors that she has a loose tooth.

Luis's grandfather will visit during story time today. He will read a story about his country, Puerto Rico.

In math, we will learn about adding numbers between 10 and 20. We will need our counters.

In science, we will read about volcanoes. We hope we will see pictures of red lava.

Carol has some news. Last week, Carol's mother had a baby. Carol has a new brother named Josh.

FIGURE 12.1   Morning Message

contribute to the "news" portion of the morning message while the teacher introduces the story and other learning experiences.

In this example, the teacher began the procedure with the first paragraph already written on the board as the students entered the room. She began the second paragraph, and Luis contributed the fact that his grandfather planned to read a story from Puerto Rico. The teacher asked the students if they could remember what she had told them they would begin studying in math, and the teacher and students constructed the first sentence together. The children added the sentence about needing their counters based on their experience with learning new concepts. The teacher contributed the first sentence of the paragraph about science, and one of the children added the sentence about hoping to see pictures of lava based on a television show he had seen. Then the teacher asked if the students had any news to add, and Carol added the information about her new brother.

Thus, the responsibility for composing the morning message flowed back and forth between the teacher and the students. Because this particular morning message occurred late in the year, the teacher carried the process a little further to "share the pen" (Rubadue, 2002). As the teacher was writing, she invited individual children to come to the board and write parts of the message. Luis wrote his own name. David used labels from bins in the classroom to help him write *counters*. Carol not only contributed the news paragraph, but she also wrote her own name as well as the word *baby* and the beginning letter of *Josh*.

Guided Writing   As students gain understanding and confidence, more of the responsibility for writing is relinquished to them. Guided writing may occur in whole group, small group, or individual instruction. In guided writing, the students do the actual writing, but the teacher provides support as needed. Teachers may model topic selection or offer "limited choice" topic selection. Especially when relating reading and writing, teachers may guide the prewriting component of organizing by providing a graphic organizer to help students plan their writing. Teachers also establish classroom routines for sharing, responding to peers, revising, and editing. Guided writing occurs with all kinds of writing: stories, letters, journal entries, or reports. It is a gradual release of responsibility to foster students' independent writing (Olness, 2005).

Independent Writing   As with reading, the goal of writing instruction is independence. In independent writing, students initiate writing, provide their own structures for moving through the process, and engage writing as a natural part of the learning process as well as an avenue for reflection and pleasure. Students may reach independence in writing for some purposes while needing guidance in writing for other purposes. Often, students who are struggling in reading continue to need support in writing throughout their school years (Olness, 2005; Strickland, et al., 2002).

Personal Communication

Writing provides a means of sharing information about our personal lives with each other. As mature writers, we text, email, send cards and letters, and leave notes for family members. Students should emulate the purposes for written communication.

Written Conversations

In the written conversations strategy, developed by Carolyn Burke (Anderson, 1984), two students, or a student and a teacher, sit beside each other and communicate. The partners cannot speak; writing is the only communication allowed. If one person's message is unclear, the partner must ask for clarification in writing. Using this activity on a regular basis helps students learn to record their thoughts in writing.

This strategy is often used in the reading center as a way of "catching up on the news" with students. Instead of asking how things are going, the teacher writes a greeting and question to the student; the student, in turn, responds in writing. You can use different colored pens or pencils and date each page.

Some teachers like to have both partners writing at the same time. Other teachers prefer to have participants use one paper and take turns writing. Each session can include two or three exchanges.

If a teacher and a student form a partnership, the teacher can model correct spellings and grammatical structures in his or her responses. Over several weeks, you often notice significant improvements in a student's writing. Figure 12.2 presents an example of a written conversation between a teacher and her student in the reading center.

Of course, students also enjoy forming partnerships with one another. When two students are paired, they may form friendships and share interests and everyday experiences with their partners.

In a variation of written conversations called *personal correspondence,* students are assigned a pen pal to communicate with over a longer period of time. Partners may be in the same school, but they should not be in the same class. This activity is especially nice for establishing cross-grade partnerships. The older students' writing models the patterns the younger students need to learn, and older students become more aware of making their writing clear for their younger pen pals. The teacher can serve as the "mail carrier," or a student can be assigned the job.

Personal Journals

In personal journals, students reflect on events or experiences as is done in diaries; they practice recording personal experiences in writing. Usually, journals provide day-to-day records of events in their lives and how they felt about them.

When students maintain personal journals, they create a record of their own thoughts and feelings, which they can later read. To begin, each student needs a personal journal, usually a notebook of lined paper. Students may want to include titles for their journals or decorate them. Time is set aside, usually three or four periods a week, to record personal thoughts in journals. Ask students to write only on one side of a page.

After writing, a few students may choose to read their reflections to their classmates and ask for their responses. In addition, the teacher can collect journals, read them, and write responses. However, students may not want to share all of their journal entries. To preserve privacy, students can simply fold a page in half, lengthwise, to cover it; the teacher should not read folded pages. In responding to journals, teachers should be careful not to correct grammatical and spelling errors, because this practice undermines the student's confidence and may lessen the amount of writing. Instead, try to respond personally to the content of

You are doing such a nice job at clinic. How was school today? It was fine.

Tell me what you are studying in Science, or Social Studies. In science we are studing bats.

What are you studying in Social Studies? In social studies we are studing about animils from the jungel.

What types of animals live in the jungle? Wild monkys and chetas.

FIGURE 12.2   A Written Conversation

the student's message. Try to use words the student originally misspelled in your responses so that the student can see the words spelled correctly.

Sometimes, students with reading problems have such low self-esteem that they lack the confidence to maintain journals. They often feel that their lives are not important enough to deserve recording. Teachers can help students overcome this problem by modeling journal writing about everyday issues they address.

Students with reading problems sometimes have difficulty thinking of journal topics. To help them, supply one category for each of the first six journal writing sessions and ask them to brainstorm a list within this category. Then, they choose one idea from their list and write about it. Topics might include favorite places, special people, favorite stories, things I like to do, things I don't like to do, things that make me angry, and things I do well. To help them keep a record of these ideas, students create an "Ideas to Write About" page in their journals.

After engaging in journal writing using this technique six times, students are ready to choose their own topics without guidance. Then, if students have trouble thinking of a topic, suggest they use one of the topics from their "ideas" page.

Strategies for Integrating Reading and Writing

This section discusses ways to incorporate writing into reading instruction. Included are strategies for responding to narrative and informational text. Students need opportunities to reflect about their reading and to respond to it thoughtfully. Writing their thoughts about materials they are reading helps students to organize the ideas presented in the text and increases their comprehension (Fletcher & Portalupi, 2001; Calkins, 1994, 2000). As they formulate these responses, they also improve their writing skills.

Writing and Reading Narrative Text

Many motivating formats can be used to help students with reading problems. These formats include writing as a prereading experience, scripted stories, rewritten stories, and reader response journals.

Writing as a Prereading Experience   Teachers often use writing prior to reading stories to provide support for students' reading. In the story impressions strategy (Blachowicz & Fisher, 2002; Fisher, 1998; McGinley & Denner, 1987), teachers present students with a list of words and phrases from a story and have the students construct sentences that predict the plot. A teacher in the reading center presented the following list of words from *The Knight Who Was Afraid of the Dark* (by Hazen) to her student:

Dark Ages

Sir Fred

knight

afraid

darkness

bully

Melvin the Miffed

spy

Lady Wendylyn

love

banner

secret meeting

The student wrote the following possible sentences:

Long ago in the Dark Ages, there lived a knight named Sir Fred.

Sir Fred was the bravest knight in the land, but he was afraid of one thing—darkness.

One day a big bully came to the village, Melvin the Miffed.

Melvin was mad because he wanted to marry Lady Wendylyn, but she said no.

One night Melvin decided to spy on Lady Wendylyn.

He wanted to see if she was in love with someone else.

Melvin saw Lady Wendylyn making a banner for the village fair.

The banner had a picture of Sir Fred on his horse.

Melvin went to Sir Fred and told him that Lady Wendylyn wanted to meet him.

But they had to have a secret meeting at the castle at midnight.

Sir Fred was afraid, but he loved Lady Wendylyn.

Would he be brave enough to meet her?

Two other strategies that have proved successful in supporting students' understanding of narrative text include writing the story before reading and autobiographical prewriting.

Using these two strategies has helped engage students in their reading and has deepened their appreciation for and understanding of text (Weech, 1994; White, 1995).

White (1995) used writing to help ninth-grade students relate to stories to be read. Students were asked to respond to questions that were designed to help them activate background knowledge and personal experiences relevant to the stories to be read. White found this strategy to be highly effective in increasing students' engagement in the story, identification with characters, and understanding of the concepts presented.

Weech (1994) uses another kind of prereading strategy in which she has students write the story before reading it. She presents the students with scenarios, actions they must assume to have committed. These scenarios are related to events in the story to be read. For example, in preparing students to read *The Rime of the Ancient Mariner* (by Coleridge), Ms. Weech had students respond to three different situations: (1) Some were friends who revealed a secret they had promised to keep; (2) some were to assume they had lost a precious family heirloom but were to pretend they hadn't; and (3) some were to assume they had accidentally killed a mother bird leaving the babies in the nest. Having students assume these roles and substantiate or defend their actions helped them relate to literature that sometimes seems irrelevant to contemporary adolescents.

Scripted Stories   Patterned, or scripted, writing is a good strategy for beginning readers. In this strategy, the teacher shares a predictable book or poem with students. Then the students write their own version, altering the author's version slightly. This activity gives them the security of a writing frame that they can use to form their own, personalized response. Children love to substitute people and objects from their own experiences in response to Bill Martin's *Brown Bear, Brown Bear, What Do You See?*

Scripted writing encourages students to use their imaginations and practice words they meet in reading as they build their own confidence as writers. Good books to use for scripted writing include *Goodnight, Mr. Fly* (Jacobs), *Polar Bear, Polar Bear* (Martin), and *Alligator Pie* and *Jump Frog, Jump* (Lee). Useful poems are contained in *Beneath a Blue Umbrella, Poems by A. Nonny Mouse, Zoo Doings,* and *Laughing Out Loud* (Prelutsky); *Honey, I Love* (Greenfield); *The Pocketbook Book of Ogden Nash* (Nash); *Sing a Soft Black Song* (Giovanni); and *The Big O, The Missing Piece, Where the Sidewalk Ends,* and *A Light in the Attic* (Silverstein).

A group of kindergarten children dictated their own version of *Alligator Pie* presented in Figure 12.3.

Following the dictation, the teacher wrote each line on a page, and the students chose their favorites and illustrated them. Then the teacher bound the book and it became a favorite in the classroom library.

Alligator sandwich, alligator sandwich
If I don't get some, I think I'm gonna itch
Alligator drink, alligator drink
If I don't get some, I might turn pink
Alligator ice cream, Alligator ice cream
It's so good, it's like a happy dream

FIGURE 12.3   Scripted Story in Response to *Alligator Pie*

Source: Adapted from *Alligator Pie* by Lee (2008).

Rewritten Stories   Having students rewrite stories is invaluable in providing a model for story structure, enhancing language development, and comprehending text. This activity can be used along with comprehension strategies, such as the directed reading-thinking activity or story grammar.

After your students have read a story, ask them to recreate it in their own words. Young children who have difficulty with the mechanics of writing may prefer to dictate a story version to the teacher. Older students are usually able to write their own versions. In creating their own rewritten versions of stories, students need to reflect upon the structure of the story they have read. You can provide guidance for this activity in several ways:

* Use a story grammar and have students identify a character, setting, problem, and events. Then have students make sure they include these elements as they reconstruct the story. Thus, they become familiar with the story grammar elements and begin to use them as they create their own stories.
* Students can tell or write about a story they have read but take another point of view. As an example, you might use *The True Story of the Three Little Pigs* (by Sciesza), which retells the classic fairy tale from the wolf's point of view. Then students can create their own versions of classics, for example, rewriting *Snow White* from the stepmother's perspective.
* Students can rewrite by assuming a role within a story they have read. Lauren, a sixth grader in the reading center, read the book *If You Grew Up with George Washington* (Fritz) and then rewrote it, casting herself as the main character. A selection from the resulting book, "If You Grew Up with Lauren Lang," is shown in Figure 12.4.

We've all read stories with disappointing or surprising endings. Students may be asked to write their own endings to such stories. After reading "The Garden Party" (Mansfield), Karen, a high school student, wanted to change the ending (see Figure 12.5).

Reader Response Journals   A reading journal is used to write personal reactions to reading. Reading journals provide students with opportunities to connect reading to their own experiences.

These journals can also provide teachers with valuable feedback about students' understanding of ideas presented in text. When students respond to a story in writing, the teacher can tell whether they understood the story (Cahill, 2004; Farr, Lewis, Fasholz, Pinsky, Towle, Lipschutz, & Faulds, 1990).

To introduce reading journals, start by writing about something you and your students have read together, such as a short story. Try to connect the story to the students' own experiences. Students also like to use reading journals as opportunities to critique stories. At times, you can ask students to give "stars" in their journals to something they have read, ranging from one ("I hated it") to four ("I loved it"). Then, beneath the stars, ask them to explain why a chapter or story received this rating.

Teachers may also ask students to write about their favorite characters. Asking students to write about why they think the author had a character act in a certain way helps to make them more aware of how authors create stories. This awareness helps students when they write their own stories. Keeping a record of their own reactions to a character's development in a reading journal fosters students' literary appreciation.

Some teachers write responses to students' reading journals, thus making them into reading dialogue journals. Through these written responses, teachers can enhance a student's understanding, correct misunderstandings, offer a different perspective, or simply share a mutual appreciation for a story.

A special kind of response journal, the dialogue journal, provides an excellent opportunity for students and teachers to interact about text. In dialogue journals, students use a

> Do We Have Lights
> in Our House?
>
> We have a lot of lights
> in our house in all of
> our rooms. We do not have
> candles in the house. We
> have electricity in the
> house.
>
> Do We Have any
> Showers in the House?
>
> We have 2 showers in
> our house. We have
> shampoo and cold and
> hot water. We have water
> to brush our teeth, and
> we have tooth paste.

FIGURE 12.4 A Rewritten Story of "If You Grew Up with Lauren Lang"

Source: Adapted from *If You Grew Up with George Washington* by Ruth Belov and Emily Arnold McCully © (1993), published by Scholastic, Inc.

I think Laura would have said, "Isn't life a learning experience?" The reason why I think Laura would have said this is because Laura has learned that life isn't always joy and happiness, but pain and sorrowful.

Karen's new ending caused her to reflect more on the story, and she gained further insight into the story and wrote more:

I think Laura also learned about her own life. She has lived a sheltered life. Now she realizes that people don't have to dress nicely to be good. She realizes this when she apologizes for her hat.

FIGURE 12.5 Karen's Ending to "The Garden Party" by Mansfield letter format to respond to materials read. Teachers can initiate the interaction by writing a letter to a student asking about a particular character or about the student's favorite event in the story.

When using dialogue journals, students should have opportunities to write not only to teachers but to one another as well. Students write differently to different audiences. When writing to teachers, students usually provide more thorough retellings, perhaps to show the teacher they have actually read the story. However, when writing to classmates, students usually write abstracts of the stories and focus more attention on evaluating and recommending books they have read (Wells, 1992–1993).

We have used an adaptation of the dialogue journal with students in book clubs. First, we established book clubs at the primary, intermediate, and middle-level grades. At the first meeting of each club, we collected information about the students, including email addresses. Then we established a listserv for each book club. After the second meeting, when students were engaged in conversations about the books, we initiated a discussion thread for students' responses. These discussion threads have maintained active participation between book club meetings and provided an avenue for ongoing support as students read outside of meeting time.

Writing and Reading Informational Text

This section presents strategies for responding to informational texts that students read. In using these written responses, students are able to absorb, organize, and reflect on information more effectively and fully.

Learning Journals   In a learning journal or log, teachers ask students to write the most important things that they learned from a content area, such as social studies or science. Students may respond to a chapter in a textbook, an article, or a lesson. Students are also free to ask questions in their journals, and if a teacher notices a misunderstanding, he or she may clarify it for the student. Learning journals are especially helpful in content areas (Strickland, et al., 2002; Giacobbe, 1986). By asking students to describe what they have learned, teachers can see which concepts need reteaching. In this way, writing can help content-area teachers teach diagnostically. Unrau (2008) found that his responses to students' logs and his sharing of good examples precipitated improved writing as well as improved comprehension. Figure 12.6 presents a sample of a learning journal entry by a student in the reading center. This entry was written in response to a science article about peccaries.

RAFT   This strategy helps students to develop imaginative responses by assuming different roles and tasks in writing (Santa, Havens, & Harrison, 1989). RAFT stands for:

Role—who is writing

Audience—who is being written to

Format—the type of writing being done

Topic—what is being written about

Each of these four parts of writing can vary. For example, a role may include any character or object that has been studied. Students may write from the point of view of a participant in a historical event or of a cell in a biological function. In addition, any other character or object can form an audience. A student may write to another cell or to a historical figure on the opposing side. Formats can also vary. Students can write a letter, poetry, an invitation, a television script, a telegram, or a complaint. Finally, students can choose any one of a number of topics to write about.

THE PECCARY

Today I read about a peccary. I read that peccaries eat thorns, weeds, roots, cactus, and nuts. They live in Arizona, Texas, New Mexico, North America, South America, and Central America. The paper said they make sounds like a dog. They look like a pig and on their neck it is white and then it turns brown.

FIGURE 12.6   Robin's Learning Journal Entry

One middle school teacher of struggling students was having difficulty teaching the scientific concepts of matter. To enliven this subject, she asked each student to choose one of three roles: a solid water molecule, a liquid water molecule, or a gas molecule. Students were also free to choose their audiences, formats, and topics. One student, for example, chose to be a liquid water molecule writing to the cloud from which he had come. His format was a letter, and the topic concerned what it felt like to be in a raindrop. The RAFT activity dramatically increased learning and enthusiasm in this science classroom.

Teachers may assign RAFT tasks or let the students choose them. The more varied the RAFT choices, the more students will develop an appreciation for other points of view and possibilities. Santa, Havens, and Harrison (1989) suggest that teachers avoid the word write and instead use more precise words, such as describe, convince, or explain, in assignments. These terms encourage students to be more precise in their writing and to develop the ability to write persuasively.

Figure 12.7 shows a RAFT written by a fifth-grade student during a unit on the fight for independence. In this RAFT, the student has assumed the role of an American officer. The audience was not specified because the format was a personal journal entry. However, the student indicated that he thought the officer would like to keep a journal to give to his children after the war. The topic as provided by the section of the chapter being studied: "Winning the War."

> Part J Winning the War / Journal of an American Officer
>
> December 19th, 1778 Valley Forge. We are having a very hard winter here in Valley Forge. While the British are in Philidelpheia in people's homes, we are starving and freezing to death. Even in my cabin its cold. We are suffering heavy losses. My favorite soldier, Robert Price has died. Not only he died 2,999 others died too. We are having very hard time. But we are getting better. Baron Von Steuben of Prussia is helping us in many ways. He is turning our group of poorly trained men into a well-trained Prussian army!

FIGURE 12.7   Murray's RAFT about "Winning the War"

Writing with Poetry

When students write poetry, they use language actively and express themselves in imaginative ways. However, students with reading problems have difficulty writing poetry that rhymes because imposing rhyming patterns on your thoughts requires almost professional-level skill. For this reason, you should encourage students to write poetry that doesn't rhyme.

To be effective in teaching students to write poetry, teachers must be willing to become poets as well. They should write their own poetry and write collaboratively with their students. Parr and Campbell (2006) offer these suggestions for teaching poetry in your classrooms:

1. Look at any preconceived notions that you and your students may have about poetry.
2. Develop a poetry-rich environment to share your love and respect for poetry.
3. Discover poetry in everyday experiences.
4. Focus on process rather than product; this will foster students' enjoyment.
5. Be a poet and engage your students in writing poetry; accept your current level and move forward.
6. Support students' writing and move them forward gradually. Take risks yourself and encourage your students to do so.
7. Create a comfortable environment for sharing poetry.
8. Keep it fun!

Students with reading problems often feel more comfortable creating poetry from structured formats. Character poems provide a high comfort level as well as an opportunity for getting acquainted. One of the formats the reading center students enjoy is presented in Figure 12.8.

In Strategy Snapshot 12.1, teacher Mary Welch uses the poetic formats of haiku and rap to help Eddie, a disabled high school student, record his interests.

A third-grade class with many low-achieving students read "Sarah Cynthia Sylvia Stout Would Not Take the Garbage Out," a poem by Shel Silverstein in *Where the Sidewalk Ends*, about the fate that befell a child who refused to take out garbage. Students were asked to use each of their five senses to describe what they thought the garbage would be like. The class created a book consisting of five pages, one for each sense.

Examples of what the garbage felt like included:

It's gooey around you.

Gook

Mashed potatoes

Mud

Yuck

Nasty stuff

A soft chicken

The class book was decorated with illustrations by several students and placed in the classroom library.

Format for Character Poem	Jennifer's Character Poem
First name	Jennifer
Three words describing yourself	Shopper, athlete, pretty
Sister/brother/daughter/son of . . .	Sister of Steven
Who likes . . .	Who likes birds and basketball
Who fears . . .	Who fears the dark
Lives in . . .	Lives in Chicago
Last Name	Smithers

FIGURE 12.8   Character Poem

Strategy Snapshot 12.1

Eddie Writes Poetry

Mary Welch (Shapiro & Welch, 1991) used poetry to motivate and instruct Eddie, a 15-year-old boy classified as severely learning disabled and reading five years below his grade level. He wrote poems with different forms. Eddie extended his expertise into haiku, a poem of three lines, using the following format:

Line 1: What or who (5 syllables)
Line 2: Feeling, action, or description (7 syllables)
Line 3: A summative phrase (5 syllables)

Eddie wrote about his favorite motorcycle:

Harley Davidson
Ride into the setting sun
Stay with their design.

Eddie also wrote raps:

Harleys are cool, especially when they're blue
They look so fine, all of the time
When I go for a ride, everybody wants a ride
If I say no, you'll say go!
So bye-bye, it's time to fly

To help Eddie use his interest in music to improve his reading, Mary used *The Poetry of Rock* (Goldstein, 1969), which features the lyrics to popular songs. One of the best outcomes of Eddie's program was his growing sense of power as he taught Ms. Welch important facts about cars and motorcycles.

Developing the Ability to Spell

To make their writing more easily read by others, students need to learn to spell. Spelling is best developed by practice; daily writing experiences develop good spelling abilities. This writing should be done for genuine purposes and specific audiences rather than just being writing "exercises" (Gentry & Gillet, 1993). In addition to writing, however, many students with reading problems need more explicit instruction in spelling.

Spelling is challenging for many people, even some who read well. Students who have reading problems are almost always poor spellers. Spelling is certainly more difficult than reading. The context, structural analysis, and meaning clues that help you to read a written word are not present when you want to spell it. In reading, you can sometimes substitute a word for an unfamiliar one and maintain meaning for the text. In spelling, only one pattern of letters is accepted as correct; no substitutions are allowed. Finally, the correspondence between spoken sounds and written forms in English is not always consistent.

Reading, writing, and spelling are closely related. Learning letter-sound associations in reading helps you use them in spelling. As children read, they repeatedly see words spelled correctly. As their reading and writing develop, students learn regular sound-letter patterns, which they use to read new words and to spell (Gentry, 2004; Ehri, 2000; Wong, 1986; Henderson, 1985).

Spelling Development

Just as children go through stages when learning to talk, they go through stages in learning to communicate in print. Much research has focused on the concept of invented spelling. For example, Read (1971, 1975) has documented that preschool children use the sounds of letter names to write words before formal instruction. Children follow similar sequences as they learn to spell, although they may go through phases at different rates (Gentry, 2004; Morrow, 2004; Gentry & Gillet, 1993; Henderson, 1981).

Drawing and Scribbling   Children in early stages of literacy may draw pictures to communicate ideas. As they become aware that adults communicate through lines and squiggles on paper, they begin to do so too.

Precommunicative Stage   When children become aware that writing uses letters, they begin to make strings of letters. They may make no connection between letter sounds and names. Instead, children simply write letters they have seen in their environment, such as a cursive K made the way it appears on a cereal box. Adults usually cannot read what children have written at this stage. In fact, children themselves often cannot reread what they have written unless they read it immediately.

Semiphonetic Stage   When children become aware that letters are associated with sounds, they begin to use letter names to help them in their writing. They may write only one letter (usually the first sound) to represent an entire word. Frequently, one string of letters, without spaces, represents an entire sentence or several sentences. Although children can often immediately reread what they write, teachers seldom can. Thus, having the child read the message to you is important so that you are aware of instructional needs.

Phonetic Stage   Once children understand what words are, they can identify sounds within them. At the phonetic stage, students write all the sounds they hear in words. Although these "invented" spellings may not look like the English spellings, they are systematic and phonetically correct. Students at this stage still use letter names to determine which letters to write, but each sound is represented, and adults can often read them.

Transitional Stage   As students receive reading and writing instruction, they become aware that print represents visual characteristics of words as well as sounds. For example, rather than writing the *r* that they hear for the last syllable in letter, they now begin to use the conventional English *er* to represent this final syllable. Frequently, students will overgeneralize patterns. After students learn the word *enough*, they may overuse the letters *gh* to represent the *f* sound in other words. Most students now separate words by spaces. Often students in the transitional stage become reluctant to take risks in writing and use only words they know how to spell.

Conventional Stage   In this stage, students use all aspects of print to represent words. They know that letters represent specific sound patterns. They are also aware that some patterns differ from the typical English letter-sound correspondence.

Based on research by Ehri (1997, 2004), Gentry (2007) espouses a phase theory to describe early literacy development. Gentry (2004) describes five levels of early writing as presented in Figure 12.9. The terms for the levels are attributed to Ehri (1997).

Spelling Assessment

Teachers can learn a great deal about students' word knowledge by analyzing samples of their writing. However, students with reading problems often choose only familiar words in

Level	Characteristics
Non-Alphabetic	Writer may scribble in letter-like forms but does not use real alphabetic letters.
Pre-Alphabetic	Writes random letters with no letter-sound correspondence
Partial Alphabetic	Uses letters to represent sounds
	Sometimes uses vowels, but not consistently
	May mix some memorized conventional spelling with developmental spelling
Full Alphabetic	Almost all sounds in words are represented by letters, but some may be represented by letter sounds rather than conventional patterns. For example, the letter *r* may represent an entire syllable: the student may write *batr* for the word *batter*.
	Quite a few sight words (from reading) may be mixed with developmental spelling
Consolidated Alphabetic	Begins to use patterns, syllables, and chunks of letters to represent sounds. Can spell most *consonant-vowel-consonant* patterns conventionally. Uses known words to represent unfamiliar chunks of words. For example, may use the word *you* to represent the long *u* sound.

FIGURE 12.9   Gentry's Writing Scale Levels of Early Spelling

their writing. For this reason, spelling tests provide valuable tools for analyzing students' word knowledge.

Spelling, writing, and reading develop concurrently and provide support for each other as students engage in literacy experiences. Thus, in the early stages of spelling, instruction should provide connections between phonemic awareness and spelling. As students advance in reading and writing, their spelling instruction should reflect the morphophonemic aspects of word knowledge as they learn base words and affixes. Finally, the focus should be bases and derivatives.

To assess students' abilities to apply phonics skills, ask them to write unfamiliar words. In *Teaching Kids to Spell* Gentry and Gillet (1993) designed a developmental spelling test for primary children that includes 10 words:

monster	human
united	eagle
dress	closed
bottom	bumped
hiked	type

Gentry says to pronounce each word, give a sentence using that word, and repeat the word. Teachers should tell their students that the words are too difficult for most first and second graders to spell but that they are to write their best guesses. In analyzing the spellings, teachers should classify the students' responses and analyze specific patterns to determine instructional needs (Gentry & Gillet, 1993).

Gillet and Temple (2000) have more recently designed two spelling inventories to analyze students' spelling and document progress. Developmental Spelling Inventory I is for use with Grades K through 2. This test consists of 16 words, presented in two sessions. In the first session, teachers present eight words:

fish	learned
bend	shove
jumped	witch
yell	piece

At the second session, the teacher presents eight additional words:

late	chirped
bench	neck
drive	trained
wet	tick

The directions for administration and analysis are similar to those presented by Gentry and Gillet (1993). The analysis provides the basis for planning for word study instruction. Using the pretest as the baseline, teachers can develop a systematic assessment plan to monitor students' progress as part of their school's response-to-intervention plan.

There are many published spelling assessments so it is recommended that you select one that aligns well with your reading instruction. There are spelling tests and directions for analysis in *Words Their Way* by Bear, Invernizzi, Templeton, and Johnston (2004) and in *Word Matters: Teaching Phonics and Spelling in the Reading/Writing Classroom,* by Pinnell and Fountas (1998). Both of these books provide suggestions for analyzing the results, placing students along a developmental continuum, and providing developmentally appropriate instruction. For young children, teachers in the reading center use the spelling portion of the Early Literacy Assessment available on the website for this text.

Spelling Instruction

Many different formats and strategies can be used for spelling instruction. Gentry (2004) provides guidelines for successful word knowledge instruction:

1. Follow a specific curriculum to provide consistency and continuity.
2. Use techniques that are grounded in research.
3. Select developmentally appropriate words and patterns for instruction. Remember that spelling levels lag behind reading levels. Students can read words before they can spell them. Indeed, much of our learning and visual memory for spelling is derived from our reading.
4. Provide differentiated instruction. Just as teachers differentiate their reading instruction, they should differentiate spelling instruction so that they can provide developmentally appropriate instruction as described in number three above.
5. Make connections between spelling and word study and reading/writing. While struggling readers and writers may need intensive, explicit instruction in word analysis and spelling, teachers should take every opportunity to demonstrate the connections between recognizing words and spelling and how those skills are applied in reading and writing. Words that have been learned in reading provide patterns for spelling instruction. Writing provides opportunities to practice newly learned words. Good spelling helps to make writing more readily accessible to audiences.

Spelling Workshop   Gentry and Gillet (1993) recommend a workshop approach to teaching spelling similar to that used in teaching the writing process. This approach includes several steps:

1. To foster ownership, students select their own words to study for a week. These words may be selected from their writing folders, or they may be words from stories or topics being studied. Young children should select only four or five new words. Older children may choose 10 or more. In addition, teachers may add words for study based on student needs. Sometimes, the class may decide to focus on a specific pattern, such as a word ending.
2. Students keep their own records as they progress through the week's activities. They may also monitor their progress on end-of-week tests and select missed words for another week's study. They may keep a spelling log to record their new words.
3. Students work together to learn their words. They may play games, work on common patterns, practice with one another to improve visual memory, and help provide feedback for one another.

Visual Memory   In spelling, students need to visualize patterns in words. This visualization becomes even more important in later spelling development, because they must visualize root words to help them in spelling derivatives (e.g., *nation, nationality, nationalize*). Visual memory can be developed in many ways. Visualizing words and writing them allows students to learn words independently. It also avoids the useless step of merely having students copy words.

In tactile writing, students use their fingers to trace words cut from felt, sandpaper, or other textured paper. This technique is a good way to help very disabled students remember words and patterns. Using these aids, ask students to trace words within one word family (*rate, mate, skate*).

Look-Cover-Write-Check   The look-cover-write-check strategy has been used successfully for years. The steps include:

1. Look at a spelling word.
2. Cover the spelling word.
3. Visualize the covered word in your mind.
4. Write the spelling word from memory.
5. Check your writing with the uncovered spelling word.

Word Walls   Cunningham (2000, 2005) suggests the use of word walls to support students' spelling and writing. Teachers can write the words being studied on word cards, order them according to their beginning letter, and attach them to the wall. Word walls are helpful both in giving students ideas for writing and in supporting their spelling. Encourage students to visualize words and try to write them before they look at the wall.

Structural Patterns   Students need to develop an awareness of root words and combining affixes to create more complex words. Compound words provide a good introduction to structural patterns.

Gentry and Gillet (1993) suggest beginning with a compound word from a story or content area lesson. For example, reading the book *Snow* (Keats) can serve as a springboard to a lesson on such compound words as *snowfall*; then brainstorm words to combine with snow to create other compound words (*snowbank, snowmobile*).

Students can also study root words and the prefixes and suffixes that can be added to create derived words. To explore such spelling patterns, students can create lists of words that end with *-tion, -ic,* or *-ence* or begin with *anti-* or *pre-*.

A variation of the game Concentration can help students focus on root words and derivatives (Gentry and Gillet, 1993). To play this game, write sets of derived words on cards. One set might include *confide, confidence, confidential, confidante*. Another set could be *remind, remember, memory, reminisce*. To play the game, students try to make pairs of related words (for example, *remind* and *reminisce*).

Handwriting

Despite the growing popularity of computers, the physical act of handwriting remains basic to many school and life activities. A student with difficulties in handwriting is greatly hampered. Many students who do not read well also suffer from problems that result in poor handwriting. These problems include poor eye-hand coordination, deficient motor development, and limited spatial judgment (Lerner & Kline, 2006; Lerner & Johns, 2009). Because the writing system is adapted to right-handed students, those who are left-handed often have difficulties.

Most children begin writing in manuscript (or printing), which is relatively easy to construct and similar to the typeface in printed material. Students learn cursive writing in second or third grade. Even students without reading problems sometimes have difficulty making the transition from manuscript to cursive writing. Cursive letters are complex and require a greater variety of lines, curves, loops, and transitions.

Many teachers report easier transitions from manuscript to cursive writing if the D'Nealian method is used in beginning writing instruction. In this method, students are taught to write in manuscript, but the manuscript letters are written at a slant and the end strokes end in upward curves rather than straight lines. However, in D'Nealian, the difference between the appearance of their written words and the printed words in books is greater.

Some simple suggestions, if practiced regularly, may help improve handwriting.

- Have students practice on the chalkboard before using paper. They can make large circles, lines, geometric shapes, letters, and numbers with large, free movements using the muscles of arms, hands, and fingers.
- Some students need to trace printing and writing. Make heavy black letters on white paper and clip a sheet of onionskin (thin) paper over the letters. Have students trace letters with crayons or felt-tip pen.
- Put letters on transparencies and use an overhead projector to project the image on a chalkboard or large sheet of paper. The student can then trace over the image.
- Guide students verbally as they write. For example, say "down, up, and, around" as children form letters.
- Because writing is a matter of habit, monitor proper posture and ways to hold writing implements. Students may need lines on a desk to show them how to position paper.

Summary

Reading and writing are related processes that involve constructing, or composing, meaning. Writing strengthens reading by giving insight into spelling for early readers, by helping students to understand how text is organized, and by serving as a springboard to reading as students need to collect information about the pieces they compose.

Writing instruction should incorporate the writing process: selecting topics, writing drafts, making revisions, editing, and publishing. In this process, students choose and develop their own topics and are not evaluated on mechanics until near the end of the process. To evaluate writing, focus, in this order, on content, organization, format (the ability to use genre properly), and mechanics. Some writing strategies include written conversations (or conversing in writing), personal correspondence with another student, and journals that record personal reactions.

Teachers can help students to integrate reading and writing by using writing to support students' reading. Several ways to integrate writing and reading are to use writing as a prereading activity, to organize information during reading, and to respond to reading. Students can explore imaginative aspects of writing by composing poetry.

Spelling development occurs in stages beginning with the precommunicative stage and moving through the semiphonetic, phonetic, transitional, and conventional stages. Students' writing throughout these stages should be viewed as a natural developmental process. Spelling assessment instruments can provide insight into students' abilities to apply phonics principles and enable teachers to plan for instruction as well as to monitor progress. Spelling instruction should include connections between phonics and visual memory as well as the derivational aspects of structural patterns in more complex words.

REFERENCES

Anderson, S. (1984). *A Whole-Language Approach to Reading*. Landham, MD: University Press of America.

Bear, D. R., Invernizzi, M., Templeton, S., & Johnston, F. (2004). *Words Their Way: Word Study for Phonics, Vocabulary, and Spelling Instruction* 3rd ed. Upper Saddle River, NJ: Pearson Education.

Blachowicz, C. L. Z., & Fisher, P. J. (2002). *Teaching Vocabulary in All Classrooms* (2nd ed.). Upper Saddle River, NJ: Pearson Education, Inc.

Borman, G. D., & D'Agostino, J. V. (1996). Title I and student achievement: A meta-analysis of federal evaluation results. *Educational Evaluation and Policy Analysis, 4,* 309–326.

Brown, A. L., & Palincsar, A. S. (1982). Inducing strategic learning from texts by means of informed, self-control training. Technical Report No. 262. Champaign: Center for the Study of Reading, University of Illinois.

Button, K., & Welton, D. (1997). Integrating literacy activities and social studies in the primary grades. *Social Studies and the Young Learner, 9,* 15–18.

Cahill, B. (2004). Return to sender: Stories in letters. *Writing,* November, 24–27.

Calkins, L. M. (2004). *The Art of Teaching Writing*. Portsmouth, NH: Heinemann.

Castle, J. M., Riach, J., & Nicholson, T. (1994). Getting off to a better start in reading and spelling: The effects of phonemic awareness instruction within a whole language program. *Journal of Educational Psychology, 86,* 350–359.

Cawley, J. F., & Parmar, R. S. (2001). Literacy proficiency and science for students with learning disabilities. *Reading and Writing Quarterly, 17,* 105–125.

Clay, M. M. (1998). *By Different Paths to Common Outcomes*. York, ME: Stenhouse Publishers.

Clay, M. M. (2002). *An Observation Survey of Early Literacy Achievement* (2nd ed.). Portsmouth, NH: Heinemann Educational Books.

Cunningham, P. M. (2000). *Phonics They Use: Words for Reading and Writing* (3rd ed.). New York: Longman.

Cunningham, P. M. (2005). *Phonics They Use: Words for Reading and Writing* (4th ed.). Boston: Allyn & Bacon.

Dyson, A. H. (2003). Writing and children's symbolic repertoires: Development unhinged. In S. B. Neuman & D. K. Dickinson (Eds.), *Handbook of Early Literacy Research.* New York: Guilford Press.

Ehri, L. C. (2000). Learning to read and learning to spell: Two sides of a coin. *Topics in Language Disorders, 20,* 19–36.

Ehri, L. C. (1997). *The Development of Children's Ability to Read Words.* Paper presented at the convention of the International Reading Association, Atlanta, GA.

Farr, R., Lewis, M., Fasholz, J., Pinsky, E., Towle, S., Lipschutz, J., & Faulds, B. P. (1990). Writing in response to reading. *Educational Leadership, 47,* 66–69.

Fisher, P. J. (1998). Teaching vocabulary in linguistically diverse classrooms. *Illinois Reading Council Journal, 26,* 16–21.

Fletcher, R., & Portalupi, J. (2001). *Nonfiction Craft Lessons: Teaching Information Writing K–8.* Portland, ME: Stenhouse Publishers.

Freeman, M. S. (2003). Using writing to assess student understanding of informational text. *New England Reading Association Journal, 39,* 21–28.

Gentry, J. R. (2004). *The Science of Spelling: The Explicit Specifics that Make Great Readers and Writers (and Spellers!).* Portsmouth, NH: Heinemann.

Gentry, J. R. (2007). *Breakthrough in Beginning Reading and Writing: The Evidence-Based Approach to Pinpointing Students' Needs and Delivering Targeted Instruction.* New York: Scholastic.

Gentry, J. R., & Gillet, J. W. (1993). *Teaching Kids to Spell.* Portsmouth, NH: Heinemann.

Giacobbe, M. E. (1986). Learning to write and writing to learn in the elementary school. In A. R. Petrosky & D. Bartholomae (Eds.), *The Teaching of Writing: Eighty-Fifth Yearbook of the National Society for the Study of Education,* pp. 131–147. Chicago: University of Chicago.

Gillet, J. W., & Temple, C. (2000). *Understanding Reading Problems: Assessment and Instruction* (5th ed.). New York: Longman.

Glenn, W. J. (2007). Real writers as aware readers: Writing creatively as a means to develop reading skills. *Journal of Adolescent & Adult Literacy, 51,* 10–20.

Goswami, U. (2003). Early phonological development and the acquisition of literacy. In S. B. Neuman & D. K. Dickinson (Eds.), *Handbook of Early Literacy Research.* New York: Guilford Press.

Graves, D. H. (1994). *A Fresh Look at Writing.* Portsmouth, NH: Heinemann.

Greene, B. G. (1995). Exploring the reading-writing relationship. *Reading Psychology: An International Quarterly, 16,* 261–268.

Henderson, E. H. (1985). *Teaching Spelling.* Geneva, IL: Houghton Mifflin.

Jacobs, V. A. (2002). Reading, writing, and understanding. *Educational Leadership, 60,* (3), 58–61.

Jennings, J. H. (1991). A comparison of summary and journal writing as components of an interactive comprehension model in social studies. In *The Fortieth Yearbook of the National Reading Conference,* pp. 67–82. Chicago: National Reading Conference.

Johnston, P. H. (1997). *Knowing Literacy: Constructive Literacy Assessment.* York, ME: Stenhouse Publishers.

Johnston, P. H., & Rogers, R. (2003). Early literacy development: The case for "informed assessment." In S. B. Neuman & D. K. Dickinson (Eds.), *Handbook of Early Literacy Research.* New York: Guilford Press.

Lancia, P. (1997). Literacy borrowing: The effects of literature on children's writing. *The Reading Teacher, 50,* 470–475.

Lerner, J. W. & Johns, B. (2009). *Learning Disabilities: Theories, Diagnosis, and Teaching Strategies.* Boston: Houghton Mifflin Co.

Lerner, J. W. & Kline, F. (2006). *Learning Disabilities and Related Disorders: Characteristics and Teaching Strategies.* Boston: Houghton-Mifflin Co.

Mayher, J. S., Lester, N. B., & Pradl, G. M. (1983). *Learning to Write/Writing to Learn.* Upper Montclair, NJ: Boynton/Cook.

McGinley, W. J., & Denner, P. R. (1987). Story impressions: A prereading/writing activity. *Journal of Reading, 31,* 248–253.

Morrow, L. M. (2004). *Literacy Development in the Early Years: Helping Children Read and Write* (5th ed.). Boston: Allyn & Bacon.

Olness, R. (2005). Using literature to enhance writing instruction: A guide for K–5 teachers. Newark, DE: International Reading Association.

Palincsar, A., & Brown, A. L. (1984). Reciprocal teaching of comprehension: Fostering and comprehension-monitoring activities. *Cognition and Instruction, 1,* 117–175.

Parr, M., & Campbell, T. (2006). Poets in practice. *The Reading Teacher, 60,* 36–46.

Pinnell, G. S., & Fountas, I. C. (1998). *Word Matters: Teaching Phonics and Spelling in the Reading/Writing Classroom.* Portsmouth, NH: Heinemann.

Read, C. (1971). Preschool children's knowledge of English phonology. *Harvard Educational Review, 41,* 1–34.

Read, C. (1975). Children's categorization of speech sounds in English. NCTE Research Reports, No. 17. Urbana, IL: National Council of Teachers of English.

Richgels, D. J. (2003). Phonemic awareness, and reading and writing instruction. In S. B. Neuman & D. K. Dickinson (Eds.), *Handbook of Early Literacy Research.* New York: Guilford Press.

Rubadue, M. (2002). Sharing the pen. www.Teaching K-8.com.

Saddler, B., & Graham, S. (2008). The relationship between writing knowledge and writing performance among more and less skilled writers. *Reading and Writing Quarterly, 23,* 231–247.

Santa, C., Havens, L., & Harrison, S. (1989). Teaching secondary science through reading, writing, studying, and problem solving. In D. Lapp, J. Flood, & N. Farnan (Eds.), *Content Area Reading and Learning: Instructional Strategies.* Upper Saddle River, NJ: Prentice Hall.

Shanahan, T. (2005). *The National Reading Panel: Practical Advise for Teachers.* Naperville, IL: Learning Point Associates.

Shapiro, S., & Welch, M. (1991). Using poetry with adolescents in a remedial reading program: A case study. *Reading Horizons, 31,* 318–331.

Sitler, H. (1995). Letters from Emily: Writing-reading connection. *Language Arts, 72,* 360–365.

Strickland, D. S., Ganske, K., & Monroe, J. K. (2002). *Supporting Struggling Readers and Writers: Strategies for Classroom Intervention 3–6.* Newark, DE: International Reading Association.

Tierney, R. J. (1990). Redefining reading comprehension. *Educational Leadership, 47,* 37–42.

Unrau, N. (2008). *Content Area Reading and Writing: Fostering Literacies in Middle and High School 2nd ed.* Upper Saddle River, NJ: Pearson.

Vanderburg, R. M. (2006). Reviewing research on teaching writing based on Vygotsky's theories: What we can learn. *Reading and Writing Quarterly, 22,* 375–393.

Weech, J. (1994). Writing the story before reading it. *Journal of Reading, 37,* 364–367.

Wells, M. C. (1992–1993). At the junction of reading and writing: How dialogue journals contribute to students' reading development. *Journal of Reading, 36,* 294–302.

White, B. F. (1995). Effects of autobiographical writing before reading on students' responses to short stories. *Journal of Educational Research, 88,* 173–184.

Wittrock, M. C. (1984). Writing and the teaching of reading. In J. M. Jensen (ed.), *Composing and Comprehending,* pp. 77–83. Urbana, IL: ERIC Clearinghouse on Reading and Communication Skills.

Wollman-Bonilla, J. E., & Werchadlo, B. (1995). Literature response journals in a first-grade classroom. *Language Arts, 72,* 562–570.

Wong, B. Y. (1986). A cognitive approach to teaching spelling. *Exceptional Children, 53,* 169–172.

13 Literacy Instruction for Diverse Populations

Multicultural Diversity, English Language Learners, Parents and Families, Adolescents, and Adults with Reading Problems

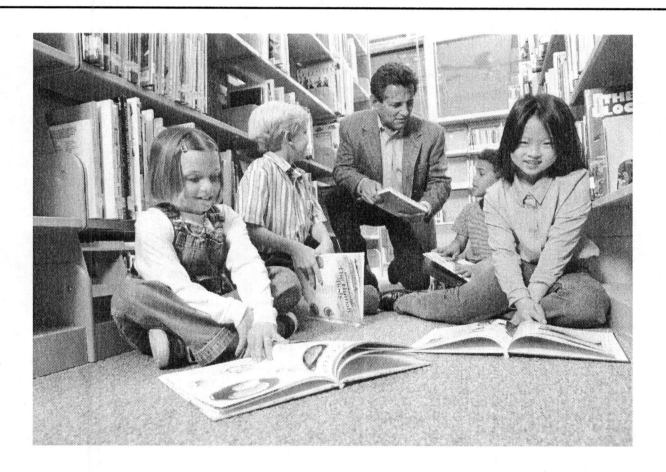

Introduction

Literacy in a Multicultural Society

Diverse Cultural Views about Reading
Teaching Children from Diverse
Cultures

English Language Learners

Who Are ELLs?
Methods for Teaching ELLs
Teaching Reading to ELLs
Strategies for Teaching Reading to
ELL Students

Introduction

In this chapter, we look at literacy instruction for several different populations. We review literacy in today's diverse multicultural society, examine English Language Learners (ELLs), analyze the important role of the family and parents in developing literacy, and discuss adolescents and adults with reading problems.

Literacy in a Multicultural Society

The value of diverse cultures and the benefits of linguistic and cultural diversity are well recognized in today's society. Each cultural, racial, and linguistic population makes unique and immeasurable contributions to the U.S. society. The term *cultural pluralism* reflects this philosophy. Today's society appreciates the values that stem from different cultural populations.

Society is becoming increasingly pluralistic and diverse. As immigrant groups come to North America with their own languages, cultures, and traditions, the U.S. society increasingly appreciates it's rich cultural resources. Schools are called on to meet the challenges of increasing diversity and to respond vigorously and flexibly to these new challenges. Teachers have the responsibility to offer the best instruction they can to all students.

Diverse Cultural Views about Reading

Diverse cultures may hold different views about many issues that affect reading and literacy learning. For example, a student's family may view reading very differently than the school or the teacher. Schools traditionally expect children to have the kinds of literacy background experiences that middle-class, English-speaking parents traditionally provide. For example, middle-class parents frequently read and discuss stories with their children (often at bedtime) and discuss them. Through these literacy experiences, children become aware of what a book is, how to handle books, how print and speech match, and how a story is constructed. Middle-class parents frequently ask their children questions for which the parents already know the answer. Such literary activities are also are common school experiences in kindergarten and first grade. This practice is, again, an experience frequently repeated in school, when a teacher questions children about material they have read (Armbruster, Lehr, & Osborn, 2006; Lerner, Lowenthal, & Egan, 2003; Jiménez, 2002).

However, these types of early literacy experiences may not occur within all cultures and families. For example, in some cultures, storybook reading to children is uncommon; in others, parents read stories to their children but do not follow up with the adult-child interactions that foster the ability to handle books or talk about stories. Thus, children come to school with different kinds of background experiences with books and with reading. Teachers must honor the experiences that children already have while providing experiences that children do not have.

Cultural differences also are seen in children's oral language and styles of verbal interactions. In some cultures, children are not encouraged to speak in an extended fashion until they develop enough competence to "hold their own" on a topic (Cazden, 1988). The child may conclude that a good child is a quiet child. If children are not encouraged to display extended language use at home, they may be fearful of offering opinions or engaging in conversations in class.

Teachers should realize that some children from diverse cultures may be reluctant to express themselves in class. Teachers should not underestimate the extent of children's knowledge about a subject, even though they are reluctant to speak in class. It is important that children be encouraged to talk to build language and reading skills.

Decades of research shows that children in all cultures need to have the following building blocks of reading and writing (Armbruster, et al., 2006). All children need to:

* have many experiences in talking and listening
* learn about print and books
* become aware of sounds in spoken language, such as rhyming words and individual sounds in word and language
* have knowledge about the letters of the alphabet
* have many experiences of parents and others reading stories aloud
* have opportunities to expand their vocabulary and knowledge of words

Teaching Children from Diverse Cultures

There are many ways for teachers to encourage children to share their linguistic and cultural heritage. Some activities include:

* **Use volunteers from the child's culture.** Ask grandparents, other relatives, or community members to visit or donate time to a school. Community volunteers can relate successfully to the children.
* **Explain expectations.** Fully explain the expectations and routines when working with all students. For example, provide explicit instruction in how to choose a book, what happens during quiet time, how to take turns, and how to listen as the teacher reads a story.
* **Have students make and share contributions from their own cultures.** One teacher had children write raps that summarize their learning in U.S. history and science as well as novels (Spinelli, 2006).
* **Have children from a diverse culture and the mainstream culture teach each other.** For example, in one school Hispanic children in a bilingual class were paired with children from a mainstream class. Each child taught five words on different topics such as sports or food from their culture. English-speaking children learned Spanish words, and Spanish-speaking children learned English words. This activity culminated in the second grade's participation in the annual bilingual celebration of the school as well as the communal breaking of a stubborn piñata to celebrate the holiday Cinco de Mayo.
* **Have families from different cultures share experiences.** Families from different cultures often can share experiences and feelings orally or in writing. In one

classroom, the children's older brothers and sisters were asked to write the story of how their families came to the United States. The following story was written by an older brother:

My Family's Trip to America

This story all began when my family was in the war suffering. Lots of people were pushing and shoving. They pushed and shoved because they wanted to escape from the Communists. If they were caught, they would die or would be their prisoner and would be put in jail. Thee jail is a cark, damp. dreary dungeon. Most were killed by gun shots. My family cam to America. My mom and dad came from Vietnam. Freedom is what my father and mother came for. They chose the right place, America. They were glad they made it.

* **Display pictures that show people from diverse backgrounds and communities.**   Include people from culturally diverse backgrounds at work, at home, and in leisure activities.
* **Use seating arrangements and class organization to encourage students to try new ways of interacting and learning.**   Students from different cultural groups enjoy sharing ideas and experiences. This environment is best fostered if students have a variety of opportunities in which to sit, talk, and work with others.
* **Use books about cultural traditions.**   Books representing the child's cultural traditions can contribute to a rich and accepting atmosphere. Table 13.1 provides some book titles to foster multicultural understanding.

Table 13.2 provides some principles for teachers to support cultural diversity in the classroom.

TABLE 13.1   Multicultural Children's Books

African and African American

A Is for Africa by I. Onyefufo. Photographs in alphabet book provide a stunning view of life in a Nigerian village.

Afrobets series by S. Willis Hudson. Preschool concepts (colors, shapes, numbers) presented with African animals, artifacts, and everyday objects.

Amazing Grace by M. Hoffman. Can an African English girl play Peter Pan in a school play? This story concerns racial awareness and self-esteem.

Mary Had a Little Lamb by S. Hale (illus. by B. McMillan). Photographs of an African American Mary offer a unique interpretation of this classic nursery rhyme.

The People Could Fly by V. Hamilton. Anthology of 24 folktales focus on the black experience in the southern United States.

Pink and Say by P. Polacco. In this true story, a black Union soldier nurses a wounded Confederate soldier.

Native American

Dancing with the Indians by A. S. Medearis. An African American author tells of her ancestors' participation in a Seminole Indian celebration.

Encounter by J. Yolen. Set in 1492, a Taino Indian child recounts the visit of Columbus, highlighting differences between Native Americans and Europeans.

Ikomi and the Boulder by P. Goble. Lively trickster tale explains why the Great Plains are covered with rocks and bats and have flat faces.

TABLE 13.1 Continued

Knots on a Counting Rope by B. Martin, Jr., & J. Archambault. Wise grandfather helps a Native American boy to face his blindness.

Maii and Cousin Horned Toad by S. Begay. This Navaho fable explains why coyotes stay away from horned toads.

Momma Do You Love Me? by B. Joosse. An Eskimo child questions mother about "What if I . . . ?" Many Eskimo terms are explained.

Sunpainters by Baje Whitethorne. According to Navajo legend, the sun must be repainted after an eclipse.

Hispanic

Diego by J. Winter. The life of the famous muralist Diego Rivera is depicted in simple bilingual text with artwork that mirrors his own.

Everybody Has Feelings by C. Abery. A bilingual (Spanish-English) exploration of people and their feelings.

First Day of School by M. Deru. Young foxes hunting for chickens make friends with them instead.

Gathering the Sun by A. F. Ada. A poem for each letter of the Spanish alphabet celebrates farmworkers and their products. Poems are translated into English.

Let's Go (Vamos) by E. Emberley. This book explores the four seasons in bilingual text.

Moon Rope by L. Elhert. This Peruvian folktale (Spanish-English) about why there is a moon features a fox.

Radio Man by A. Dorros. A child of a migrant worker family sends a message to his friend by radio. Text is bilingual.

Un Cuento de Queztalcoatl by M. Parke & S. Panik. Part of the Mexican and Central American legends series in which each of several tales is told (in separate short books) in English and Spanish. This tale tells of a game among the Aztec gods.

Asian

Baseball Saved Us by K. Mochizuki. A Japanese-American boy interned during World War II finds solace in baseball.

The Dragon's Robe by D. Nourse. A Chinese girl weaves a beautiful silk robe to save her father's life.

Grandmother's Path, Grandfather's Way by L. Vang & J. Lewis. Lore and legends of the Hmong Southeast Asian tribe (Hmong-English).

Jar of Dreams by Y. Uchida. Rinko, a Japanese-American girl, tells about her family life in California.

The Little Weaver of Thai-Yen Village by Tran-Khanh-Yuyet. One of the Fifth World Tales series, in Vietnamese and English. A Vietnamese girl comes to the United States for an operation. Other books in this series feature different Asian groups.

Source: This list was compiled by Susan Ali.

TABLE 13.2 Strategies to Support Cultural Diversity

※ Be responsive to cultural and individual diversity.
※ Create an open, accepting classroom environment to ensure all students from all cultural and linguistic backgrounds feel comfortable in class.
※ Include books and stories in the curriculum to enhance understanding of other cultures.
※ Teach about sensitivity and acceptance issues.
※ Share personal experiences about cultural issues.

English Language Learners

English Language Learners (ELLs) are students whose first language is not English and who are not yet proficient in English. Understandably, ELL students may experience difficulty in understanding or speaking English or in reading or writing in English.

Who Are ELLs?

In today's diverse society, the number of students who come from homes in which a language other than English is spoken is rapidly increasing. Today, one in five students speaks a language other than English in his or her home (International Reading Association, 2007). The number of English Language Learners rose to three-quarters of a million in the year 2000 (Jiménez, 2002). The Hispanic population increased to 44.3 million in 2006, making it the largest language group in the United States (U.S. Census Bureau, 2006). Spanish speakers represent 76 percent of the non-English language population, However, there are more than 100 distinct language groups served in U.S. schools (Jiménez, 2002). Common languages of ELL students include Spanish, Russian, Vietnamese, Hmong, Creole, Korean, Cantonese, Chinese, and Arabic. To make the task of teaching ELL students even more challenging, some ELL students also have a basic learning disability in addition to their limited English proficiency. If a language disorder is present in the primary language, it also will be present in the secondary language (McCardle, 2005). Over 15 percent of the students with learning disabilities are identified as Hispanic (U.S. Department of Education, 2006).

Several federal laws affect ELL students. The No Child Left Behind (NCLB) Act of 2001 requires that ELL students take the state standards tests taken by all students in U.S. schools. Further, the scores of ELL students are grouped and reported separately. Understandably, many ELL students have difficulty with these tests and their low scores can negatively impact the standing of their school.

The second law that can impact ELL students is the Individual with Disabilities Education Improvement Act of 2004 (IDEA-2004). This law requires that all students with disabilities take the state standards tests. The scores of students with disabilities also are grouped and reported separately. Individualized education programs (IEPs) must consider their language needs. IDEA-2004 also requires that states report the number of children with disabilities served by race or ethnicity (Lerner & Johns, 2009; Klingner, Artiles, & Barletta, 2006).

Methods for Teaching ELLs

Several different methods are used for teaching students who are ELLs. These methods include:

* **English as a second language (ESL).**   This method is used in classes that have students who come from many different language backgrounds. Students learn through carefully controlled oral repetitions of English language patterns. This approach often is used in schools where children come from many different language backgrounds and providing instruction in all native languages is not feasible.
* **Bilingual instruction.**   This method is used when all of the students in the class are from one language background. Instruction is provided in two languages. Students use their native language for part of the school day and use the second language (English) for the other portion of the school day. Academic subjects are often taught in the student's native language and the student receives oral practice in

English. The objective of bilingual instruction is to strengthen school learning through the native language and gradually to add the secondary language.

* **Instruction through immersion.** In this method, students are immersed in, or receive extensive exposure to, the second language. In fact, where no formal instruction is available for a person learning a second language, immersion is usually what occurs naturally. Individuals simply learn English as they live in the mainstream of an English-speaking society. Immersion is widely employed with schoolchildren in Canada, where it is used to teach French to English-speaking children by enrolling them in French-speaking schools.

Teaching Reading to ELLs

Students who are ELLs often have difficulty in learning to read in English. They are not yet proficient in English, yet must learn to read in English. The following methods can help build reading skills for ESL students (August & Shanaham, 2006; Jiménez, 2002; Hudson & Smith, 2002; Ortiz, 2001):

* **Provide abundant oral language practice.** Reading is connected to listening and speaking. By providing opportunities for students to speak in English and to converse with one another, students can improve their oral language skills in English, which helps provide a basis for reading in English.
* **Use easy-to-read English language books.** Practice with English language books offers opportunities to strengthen abilities in English. When ESL students read high-interest, easy-to-read storybooks in English, they improve in reading and in reading comprehension.
* **Build reading fluency.** Reading fluency refers to the ability of students to read easily quickly, without labored hesitancy. The strategy of repeated reading is a useful method for building fluency in reading. Have students re-read orally from books they have previously read.
* **Incorporate writing into the lesson.** Have students write a story about a selection that they have just read. Reading and writing are strongly connected, and the process of writing can strengthen reading. (See Chapter 12 for more strategies for integrating reading and writing.)

Strategies for Teaching Reading to ELL Students

The school settings in which students spend so much time should reflect their language backgrounds. The following strategies are examples of ways to make classrooms and materials reflect their language backgrounds:

* **Encourage ELL students to use their first language around the school.** For example, books in the classroom and library, bulletin boards, and signs can be in the students' native language. Students can also help each other. For example, Jerzy, a child whose native language was Polish, was paired with Irena, a child who had just immigrated from Warsaw. This pairing increased the self-esteem and language skills of both students.
* **Help students to understand that reading is based on language.** They should understand that to read in English, they must understand the English words and sentence structures they meet in books. ELL students should be free to learn sophisticated information and concepts in the language they are most comfortable using. Information and abilities can be learned first in any language and then transferred to another language.

- **Build oral language skills.** As noted, reading is connected to listening and speaking. Reading in English can strengthen all language abilities in English. If students have some proficiency in English, reading English books will further all English language skills.

- **Use English books.** Reading books in English can be an excellent way to improve general mastery of English. When students learning English are given an abundance of high-interest storybooks in English, their progress in reading and listening comprehension increases. Use books that have repetition in language structures. For example, predictable books, which repeat refrains over and over, are excellent for learning English. Well-known folktales and fairy tales with familiar plots are also useful. Fairy tales typically have repeated phrases that children enjoy hearing and saying. Also, attractively illustrated books, in which pictures support the text, are excellent for ELL students. Some good books to use for developing concepts include *The Toolbox* (Rockwell); *Circles, Triangles, and Squares; Over, Under, Through, and Other Spatial Concepts*; and *Push-Pull, Empty-Full: A Book of Opposites* (Hoban); *Bread, Bread, Bread* (Morris); *People* (Spier); and *Growing Vegetable Soup* (Ehlers). Books that invite talk include *A Taste of Blackberries* (Smith) and *The Biggest House in the World* (Lionni); *Nana Upstairs, Nana Downstairs* (De Paola); *The Keeping Quilt* (Polacco); and *The Story of Ferdinand* (Leaf).

- **Use books that focus on language use.** ELL students who are more advanced in English language skills profit from using books focusing on language use, such as *Amelia Bedelia* and its sequels (Parish), which feature common idioms in amusing situations, and *Many Luscious Lollipops* and its sequels (Heller), which focus on parts of speech, such as adjectives, nouns, and adverbs. Finally, the increasing number of books written in two languages allows students to match their native language patterns with corresponding English ones.

- **Provide numerous opportunities to use English.** ELL students must be given many opportunities to move from learning and producing limited word translations and fragmented concepts to using longer sentences and expressing more complex ideas and feelings. Engage students in increasingly complex reading and writing experiences; check to make sure that they understand the concepts.

- **Find opportunities to use more complex English.** These situations will vary according to the level of students. In one kindergarten class of Russian-speaking children, a game of "Simon Says," complete with gestures, provided an active response to English. At a more advanced level, a third-grade bilingual Spanish class listened to the hilarious "twisted" fairy tale, *The True Story of the Three Little Pigs* (Scieszka) in both English and Spanish, and then acted it out. Later that year, the class listened to *Charlotte's Web* (White) read in English, chose their favorite words, and then matched these words in Spanish.

- **Use conversation about books to foster natural language usage.** In fostering a discussion of a story, the teacher can ask such questions as the following: "What do you think this story will be about?", "What do you think will happen next?", "Why do you think that?", "Tell me more about . . . ", "What do you mean by . . . ?" Encourage students by giving them time to respond. In addition, students may respond in pairs to make the activity less threatening. Conversation about personal reactions to stories is excellent for giving meaning-based practice in using English. Students enjoy discussing their favorite characters and the best parts of a story. To aid them, the teacher may list helpful English adjectives on the board.

- **Foster home-school collaboration.** Establishing communication with the parents and other family members such as siblings is important. More can be accomplished when the school and home work together. Parents should be contacted frequently to

Literacy Instruction for Diverse Populations **435**

communicate students' successes as well as the problems their children encounter. Remember that parents often have valuable information and insights that can be useful in the teaching process. Families can also make valuable contributions to school programs. In one fourth-grade bilingual room, two mothers sewed all the costumes for 36 fifth-grade children who sang Venezuelan songs. In helping the school's celebration, parents, school staff, and students gained a sense of community involvement (Spinelli, 2006).

* **Develop units for reading and language arts that use literature from a variety of linguistic and cultural backgrounds to reflect the diversity in U.S. society.** Table 13.1 lists books suitable for students from many different backgrounds. Students of all backgrounds enjoy reading them but, of course, they are especially important for the self-esteem of students in the groups they feature.

The Important Role of Families and Parents in Fostering Literacy

Learning to read starts at home, long before the child goes to school. Parents and family members play a key role in early literacy and preparing the child for reading. Children begin to understand the nature of written language when parents read stories to them (Armbruster, et al., 2006).

When the child fails to learn to read, the parents react with feelings of frustration and anxiety. It is important for teachers to talk regularly to parents of children with reading problems. Devoting time to understanding the needs of these families is important because it shows the teacher's willingness to help. When parents realize how hard the teacher is trying, the parents will often match the teacher's efforts by reading with their children at home or buying books for them. Of course, during these encounters with parents, teachers must be respectful of parents' perspectives. In fact, by listening to the parents' experiences with their children, teachers often gain information that is important for instruction (Spinelli, 2006).

One useful strategy that parents can use is the "You Read to Me, I'll Read to You" strategy described in Table 13.3.

TABLE 13.3 You Read to Me, I'll Read to You Strategy

In the You Read to Me, I'll Read to You Strategy, a child places two books in a large bag. One is to be read by the parent to the child; the other is to be read by the child to the parent. Primary children are expected to engage in 15 minutes of personal reading and to listen to a parent read for an additional 15 minutes. For older children, the times are extended to 20 minutes. To verify that the reading has occurred, parents use a form to list the books read and the number of minutes spent reading and then initial the form.

In this strategy, parents become participants in the reading process. This also acquaints parents with a variety of reading formats. Parents may read a high-level book to their children to provide language development. Parents and children may read different books at the same time, silently, so each enjoys a private reading experience, or parents and children may read the same book and then discuss it after reading. Parents may read a book to a child, and the child can "echo read" each page that the parent has read. Parents and children can also take turns reading the same book or read a book as a play by taking the parts of different characters. Easy books and tapes can be provided to parents who are uncertain of their own reading abilities.

TABLE 13.4 Activities for Parents

- Make family message boards to encourage literacy.
- Read a favorite book over again.
- Display books in theme baskets (e.g., Halloween, spring).
- Provide suggestions on how to choose books at libraries and bookstores.
- Model thinking about what you learned after reading a book.
- Suggest ways to purchase discount or used children's books.

Parent Workshops

Being the parent of a child with a reading problem can be frustrating and discouraging. Workshops for parents provide a way to involve parents. Parents need to share their feelings and experiences with others and perhaps get useful ideas from them. They also need information about the best placement for their child and their rights under the law. Perhaps most important, parents need to share positive literacy experiences they have had with their children.

The parent workshops typically meet once per week for about 10 sessions. During the workshop sessions, parents share experiences and ideas with one another and often develop close relationships with other parents. Parents often ask for information concerning laws on special education and educational placement. They also seek ways to foster reading in their children.

One activity is to ask parents to bring a favorite book that they remember reading as a child. The books they bring are usually easy and entertaining and fun to share at the parent workshops. Parents can also be asked to relate the affectionate experiences that they and their own parents shared during reading. Parents can discuss ways to foster similar warm experiences with their own children.

One activity for the parent workshop is to encourage parents to write. A writing activity deepens the parents' own understanding of literacy and helps them understand how difficult writing can be for children. Parents come to understand the nature of the writing process and how spelling and punctuation should be a last step in writing rather than the first step.

At the end of the series of workshops, a piece of writing from each child and participating parent can be bound into a book and read at a final celebration. Each parent and child can receive a copy of this joint book as a memento of a positive experience.

Additional activities that can be used during the parent workshops are listed in Table 13.4.

Adolescents with Reading Problems

Adolescence (the 13- to 20-year-old age range) is a well-documented period of social, emotional, and physical change. Adolescents must resolve conflicts between their desires for freedom and security, as they are torn between wishing for independence and yet not being ready for the responsibilities of full adulthood. Adolescents must cope with rapid physical changes in growth, appearance, and sexual drive. Peer pressure greatly affects adolescents; they seek group acceptance and are increasingly aware of how their peers are doing. All these characteristics of adolescence present challenges that may negatively affect learning.

Characteristics of Adolescents with Reading Problems

Teenagers with reading problems not only have difficulty in school, but they must also cope with the normal challenges and adjustments presented by adolescence. Trying to deal with this combination creates special burdens for teenagers, such as:

* **Passive learning.** Adolescents with reading and learning problems often develop an attitude of *learned helplessness* and dependence. They wait for teacher direction instead of active learning (Deshler, Schumaker, Lenz, Bulgren, Hock, Knight, et al., 2001).
* **Poor self-concept.** Low self-esteem and other emotional problems result from years of failure (Smith, 1992).
* **Poor social skills.** Adolescents with academic problems often have difficulty making and keeping friends during a period when friendships and peer approval are important (Bryan, 1991; Vaughn, 1991).
* **Difficulty with attention.** Poor attention and concentration are common in teenagers who read poorly (Lerner, Lowenthal, & Lerner, 1995). Because long periods of concentration are required for high school work, attention problems can be quite serious.
* **Lack of motivation.** After years of failure, many teenagers feel that they are dumb and that their efforts to learn are useless. Adolescents can learn only if they are motivated and can attribute success to their own efforts (Lenz & Deshler, 2003).

Special Considerations at the Secondary Level

Adolescents who have reading problems face many challenges in the secondary school. Secondary schools require all students to pass statewide performance tests, and adolescents with reading problems often have difficulty taking these statewide tests. Poor performance on these statewide tests can jeopardize their graduation from high school. States now require that high school students pass state standards tests to receive their diplomas. Only 57 percent of students with learning disabilities (many of whom have reading problems) receive high school diplomas (U.S. Department of Education, 2006). Many of these students drop out of school and often face grim futures in the streets. Unless students with reading problems are given opportunities to learn, holding them to higher standards will only victimize these students (Lerner & Johns, 2009).

In addition, many content-area secondary teachers are not oriented to working with low-achieving readers. The training and orientation of secondary teachers is typically in their area of specializations (history, science, English literature, etc.). Content-area secondary teachers may not have not been trained to adjust their teaching for poor readers.

There are many strategies to help adolescents with reading problems. If the student has a severe reading problem, the teacher might be able to tape lessons. Books recorded for the blind can be made accessible to low-achieving readers. During examinations, students might be allowed to give answers orally, to tape answers, or to dictate answers to someone else. Students who do write could be allowed additional time.

Components of Effective Secondary Programs

Effective components for poor readers in the secondary schools include (Zigmond, 1997):

* **Intensive instruction in reading.** Students with reading problems need rigorous individualized instruction.
* **Direct instruction in high school "survival" skills.** Training may be needed for successful functioning in a high school. For example, training in behavior control

helps students learn how to stay out of trouble in school. Training students in teacher-pleasing behaviors allows students to acquire behavior patterns (look interested, volunteer responses) that make teachers view them more positively. Strategies such as organizing time, previewing textbooks, taking notes from a lecture or text, organizing information, and taking tests are needed for academic success.

- **Successful completion of courses.**   Students with reading problems may cut classes, come late, and not complete assignments. Empathetic, caring teachers and counselors can foster course completion. Success in the ninth grade is particularly critical for high school.
- **Planning for life after high school.**   Adolescents with reading problems need to prepare for a successful transition to higher education or the world of work.

Adults with Reading Problems

For many individuals, a reading disability is a lifelong problem, a problem that does not disappear when schooling has been completed.

Adult literacy presents an ever-growing challenge. Some adults with problems in reading have dropped out of school and now find themselves blocked from employment. Others may be employed but want to advance in their jobs or enhance their personal skills. Some adults have been denied opportunities because they lived in countries that did not provide a free education. Still other adults are concerned with learning to speak and write in English.

Postsecondary and College Programs

Postsecondary education includes community colleges, vocational-technical training, and colleges. Programs in a variety of settings at a growing number of colleges and other postsecondary institutions serve adult learners with reading problems.

Accommodations for students with disabilities for colleges have been triggered by Section 504 of the Rehabilitation Act (1973). This law requires educational institutions that receive federal funds to make reasonable accommodations for students who are identified as having a disability. Many such individuals suffer from reading problems.

Some strategies for helping adult students in postsecondary education cope with academic demands are:

- Give students course syllabi 4 to 6 weeks before class begins and provide time to discuss them personally with students.
- Begin lectures and discussions with systematic overviews of the topic.
- Use a chalkboard or overhead projector to outline lecture material and orally read what is written on the board or transparencies.
- Use a chalkboard or overhead projector to highlight key concepts, unusual terminology, or foreign words.
- Clearly identify important points, main ideas, and key concepts orally in lectures.
- Give assignments in writing and orally; be available for further clarification.
- Provide opportunities for student participation, question periods, and discussion.
- Provide time for individual discussion of assignments and questions about lectures and readings.
- Provide study guides for the text, study questions, and review sessions to prepare for exams.

* Allow oral presentations or tape-recorded assignments instead of requiring students to use a written format.
* Modify evaluation procedures: Include untimed tests, wide-lined paper for tests, and alternatives to computer-scored answer sheets.

Needs of Adults with Reading Problems

Although some adults are lucky enough to get higher education, many adults with reading problems have great difficulty finding their niche in the world. They have trouble working, socializing, and even coping with daily tasks. Many adults with reading problems have ingenious strategies for avoiding, hiding, and dealing with their problems.

One story of an adult with significant problems in reading was a man whose wife had died a few years before and was caught in a social dating whirl. He coped with his poor reading by routinely entering a restaurant with his lady friend, putting down the menu, and saying, "Why don't you order for both of us, dear? Your selections are always perfect." This man hired professionals to handle all of his personal matters, including his checkbook. His friends attributed his actions to wealth and never suspected his inability to read.

Instructional Programs for Adults

Adults who seek help with their reading problems are likely to be highly motivated to learn and to demand an explanation of the goals and purposes of their programs. This commitment enables them to succeed.

More and more adults seek help that goes beyond the basic stages of literacy. As a result, the field of adult literacy has expanded its original responsibilities from basic functional literacy to a high-technical level (approximately twelfth-grade reading level). Some instructional options for adult reading programs include the following:

* Adult Basic Education (ABE) and General Education Development (GED) programs provide adult basic education (from elementary levels through eighth grade) and a high school level education with a general education diploma. Both the ABE and GED are funded by the federal government and require group instruction. Approximately two-and-a-half-million adults are enrolled in these programs (Gottesman, 1994).
* Literacy Volunteers of America (www.proliteracy.org), a private organization training volunteers to work with adults, serves the needs of more than 52,000 people. Instruction is individual, and programs are aimed at the illiterate and semiliterate adult. A component for teaching English as a second language is available.
* Laubach Literacy Action is the U.S. division of Laubach Literacy International. Frank Laubach, a missionary, developed a program to teach literacy to people worldwide. This program uses volunteers and currently serves more than 150,000 adults. Materials, including initial instruction in a pictorial alphabet, are available through New Readers' Press.
* ELL adult literacy programs concentrate on English as a second language. Federal funding comes from the Adult Education and Family Literacy Act (1998). These programs currently serve more than one million limited-English-proficient adults. As more immigrants enter the U.S. workforce, ESL services are expected to increase (Newman, 1994).

Adults with reading problems express their wishes for a wide variety of life skills. They express needs for improving social skills, career counseling, developing self-esteem and confidence, overcoming dependence, survival skills, vocational training, job procurement and retention, reading, spelling, management of personal finances, and organizational skills. They often express a particular need for help in coping with jobs.

Summary

The diversity of U.S. culture is one of the country's most important strengths. As new immigrant groups continue to come to the United States with their own languages, cultures, and traditions, U.S. society is increasingly enriched in cultural resources. Although cultures differ in their views about literacy and language, teachers can make school a welcome place where all children can share their linguistic and cultural backgrounds.

English Language Learners (ELL) are students whose native language is not English. ELL students may have limited proficiency in English. The number of ELL students is increasing in U.S. schools. About 80 percent of ELL students speak Spanish. The No Child Left Behind Act of 2001 and the Individual with Disabilities Education Improvement Act of 2004 are two laws that are impacting ELL students. Models for teaching English as a second language include the bilingual or native language model, the English as a second language (ESL) model, sheltered English, and immersion. Several research projects are currently under way to determine the most effective ways to teach reading to ELL students, especially Spanish-speaking students. Currently, recommended strategies for teaching reading to ELL students include using literature from various linguistic and cultural backgrounds, using interactive seating arrangements, using language-based instruction, building oral language skills, using predictable, repetitive books, using conversations about books, and using cooperative learning.

Parents and families play an important role in fostering literacy. Early reading begins in the home.

Many adolescents have reading problems. Secondary programs should focus on content-area reading.

Many individuals have reading problems that continue into adulthood. Programs for adults in postsecondary and college programs include ABE and GED classes, Literacy Volunteers of America, Laubach Literacy Action, and ELL programs for adults.

REFERENCES

Armbruster, B., Lehr, F., & Osborn, J. (2006). *A Child Becomes a Reader: Proven Ideas from Research for Parents.* Washington, DC: National Institute for Literacy.

August, D., & Shanaham, T. (Eds). (2006). *Developing Literacy in Second-Language Learners: Report of the National Literacy Panel on Language-Minority Children and Youth.* Mahwah, NJ: Lawrence Erlbaum Associates.

Bryan, T. (1991). Social problems and learning disabilities. In B. Wong, (Ed.) *Learning about Learning Disabilities* (pp. 195–231). San Diego: Academic Press.

Cazden, C. (1988). *Classroom Discourse: The Language of Teaching and Learning.* Portsmouth, NH: Heinemann.

Deshler, D., Schumaker, J., Lenz, B., Bulgren, J., Hock, M., Knight, J., et al. (2001). Ensuing content learning by secondary students with learning disabilities *Learning Disabilities Research and Practice, 16*(2), 96–108.

Gottesman, R. (1994). The adult with learning disabilities: An overview. *Learning Disabilities: A Multidisciplinary Journal, 5*(1), 1–13.

Hudson, R., & Smith, S. (2002). Effective reading instruction for struggling Spanish-speaking readers: A combination of two literatures. Available at www.ldonline.org.

International Reading Association. (2007). *Key Issues and Questions in English Language Learners Literacy research.* Newark, DE: International Reading Association and Washington, DC: International Institute of Child Health and Human Development.

Jiménez, R. (2002). Fostering literacy development of Latino students. *Focus on Exceptional Children, 34*(6), 1–10.

Klingner, J., Artiles, A., & Barletta, L. (2006). English language learners who struggle with reading: Language acquisition or LD? *Journal of Learning Disabilities, 39*, 2, 108–128.

Lenz, B., & Deshler, D. (2003). *Teaching Content to All: Evidence-Based Inclusive Practice in Middle and Secondary Schools.* Boston: Pearson.

Lerner, J. W., Lowenthal, B., & Lerner, S. (1995). *Attention Deficit Disorders: Assessment and Teaching.* Pacific Grove, CA: Brooks/Cole.

Lerner, J. W., & Johns, B. (2009). *Learning Disabilities and Related Mild Disabilities: Characteristics, Teaching Strategies, and New Directions.* Boston: Houghton Mifflin.

Lerner, J., Lowenthal, B., & Egan, R. (2003). *Preschool Children with Special NeEds: Children At-Risk and Children with Disabilities.* Boston: Allyn & Bacon.

McCardle, R. (2006). Bilingual literacy research. The DELSS Research Network and beyond. *The International Dyslexia Association Perspectives, 32*(2), 1–5.

Newman, A. P. (1994). Adult literacy programs: an overview. *Learning Disabilities: A Multidisciplinary Journal, 5*(1), 51–61.

Ortiz, A. (2001). English language learners with special needs: Effective instructional strategies. Available at www.ldohline.org/aticle/5622.

Spinelli, C. (2006). *Classroom Assessment for Students in Special and General Education.* Columbus, OH: Pearson Merrill/Prentice Hall.

U.S. Census Bureau. (2006). Washington, DC: U.S. Department of Congress, Bureau of the Census.

U.S. Department of Education. (2006*). To assure the free appropriate public education of all children with disabilities.* Twenty-fifth Annual Report to Congress on the Implementation of the Individuals with Disabilities Education Act. Washington, DC: U.S. Department of Education.

Vaughn, S. (1991). Social skills enhancement in students with learning disabilities. In B. Wong, (Ed.). *Learning about Learning Disabilities* (pp. 408–440). San Diego: Academic Press.

Zigmond, N. (1990). Rethinking secondary school programs for students with learning disabilities. *Focus on Exceptional Children, 23,* 1–22.

Zigmond, N. (1997). Educating students with disabilities: The future of special education. In. J. Lloyd, E. Kame euni., & D. Chard (Eds.). *Issues in Educating Students with Disabilities* (pp. 275–304, 377–391). Mahwah, NJ: Erlbaum.

A Early Reading Assessment Batteries Used for Screening

	Dynamic Indicators of Basic Skills (DIBELS)	AIMSweb	Phonological Awareness Literacy Screening (PALS)	Texas Primary Reading Inventory (TPRI)
Type of Test	Curriculum-based measurement	Curriculum-based measurement	Criterion-referenced assessment	Criterion-referenced assessment
Score Reports	Benchmark goals represent minimum levels of performance for students to reach in order to be considered on track for becoming a reader. Scores are based on research indicating the predictive validity of a score related to a student meeting the next benchmark. Students' scores are reported as: 1. Benchmark or Established (student has an 80%–100% probability of reaching the next benchmark if no supplemental support is given). Usually designated as Tier 1. 2. Some Risk or Emerging (student has a 50% probability of achieving the next benchmark goal if no supplemental support is given). Usually designated as Tier 2. 3. At Risk or Deficit (student has a 0%–20% probability of achieving the next benchmark goal if no supplemental support is given). Usually designated as Tier 3.	Scores at the 90th, 75th, 50th, 20th, and 10th percentile are reported based on district and national norms. Generally, students whose scores are below the 50th percentile would need some level of additional support. Percentiles are also given for "rate of improvement," indicating expected progress for a student over the course of a year. "State prediction lines," which vary from state to state depending upon the difficulty of the state test, provide information about specific scores that students need to pass state reading tests with 70% and 80% probability. Because the difficulty level of state test scores differs quite significantly, in one state a third-grade student might need to read 95 words correct per minute to have an 80% probability of passing the state reading test, and in another state a student would need to read 120 words correct per minute to have that same probability of passing the state test.	Predetermined benchmark scores indicate that a student has met the level of minimum competency necessary to benefit from typical classroom literacy instruction. For reading text, a student's independent, instructional, and frustration reading levels are based on the percentage of words read correctly.	Students are given short screening assessments BOY and EOY. The screening test results determine which test items are given to the student from a more in-depth inventory assessment, which is given three times a year (BOY, MOY, and EOY). Test items on the inventory get progressively more difficult, and the goal is for students to eventually score "developed" on all of them by the end of the year. For reading text, a student's independent, instructional, and frustration reading levels are based on the percentage of words read correctly. Predetermined benchmark scores indicate that a student has "developed" or is "still developing" skills assessed on the screening. Students who have "still developing" scores on the TPRI at the beginning of grade 2 will be one-half year or more below grade level at the end of Grade 2 if more reading intervention is not provided.
Progress-Monitoring Forms Available	Yes, and because this is a CBM test, aimlines are used to determine whether students are on track to meet the end-of-the-year goal.	Yes, and because this is a CBM test, aimlines are used to determine whether students are on track to meet the end-of-the-year goal. The slope of student progress is also computed based on "rate of improvement" information.	Quick-checks, which are short, task-targeted assessments, are available for progress monitoring. Tasks on the quick-checks differ from tasks on screening tests, and quick-checks for the same skill get progressively more difficult.	Progress-monitoring passages are available for progress monitoring oral reading fluency every 2 to 6 weeks.

Continued

	Dynamic Indicators of Basic Skills (DIBELS)	AIMSweb	Phonological Awareness Literacy Screening (PALS)	Texas Primary Reading Inventory (TPRI)
Time Required to Give to One Child	Each assessment takes between 1 and 5 minutes. Typically between two and five assessments are given.	Each assessment takes between 1 and 5 minutes. Typically between two and five assessments are given.	Assessment battery takes between 20 and 60 minutes.	Assessment battery takes between 10 and 25 minutes.
Specific Interventions Tied to Test Scores	No, but teachers can get more information on the performance of the student by doing an informal error analysis.	No, but teachers can get more information on the performance of the student by doing an informal error analysis.	Yes; the Instructional Resources link on the PALS website provides recommended activities for each area tested.	A student's reading errors are linked to related activities in state-adopted basals and activities from an intervention activity guide.
Specific Subtests in the Screening Assessment Battery	※ Initial Sound Fluency (BOY* K–MOY* K) ※ Letter Naming Fluency (BOY K–BOY first) ※ Phoneme Segmentation Fluency (MOY K–EOY* first) ※ Nonsense Word Fluency (MOY K–BOY second) ※ Oral Reading Fluency (MOY first–EOY sixth) ※ Retell Fluency (first–third)	※ Letter Naming Fluency (BOY K–BOY first) ※ Letter–Sound Fluency (BOY K–BOY first) ※ Phoneme Segmentation Fluency (MOY K–EOY first) ※ Nonsense Word Fluency (MOY K–EOY first) ※ Oral Reading Fluency (BOY first–EOY eighth) ※ Spelling (BOY first–EOY eighth) ※ Maze (BOY first–EOY eighth)	<u>Kindergarten:</u> ※ Individual rhyme awareness ※ Individual beginning sound awareness ※ Lowercase alphabet recognition ※ Letter–sounds ID ※ Spelling ※ Concept of word ※ Word recognition in isolation <u>First–third grade:</u> Level A: Entry level ※ Spelling inventory ※ Word recognition in isolation ※ Letter sounds ※ Oral reading in context Level B: Alphabetics ※ Alphabet recognition ※ Letter sounds ※ Concept of word Level C: Phonemic awareness ※ Blending ※ Sound-to-letter ※ Concept of word	<u>Kindergarten screening:</u> ※ Letter name–sound (sound is scored) ※ Blending onset-rime <u>Kindergarten inventory:</u> ※ Book and print awareness ※ Phonemic awareness: rhyming, blending word parts, blending phonemes, deleting initial sounds, & deleting final sounds ※ Graphophonemic: letter name knowledge & letter-to-sound linking ※ Listening comprehension <u>First-grade screening:</u> ※ Letter–sound task (only BOY) ※ Word reading ※ Blending phonemes <u>First-grade inventory:</u> ※ Phonemic awareness: blending word parts, blending phonemes, deleting initial sounds, & deleting final sounds ※ Graphophonemic: initial consonant substitution, final consonant substitution, middle vowel substitution, initial blend substitution, & final blend substitution ※ Reading accuracy, fluency, and comprehension <u>Second- & third-grade screening:</u> ※ Word list reading <u>Second- & third-grade inventory:</u> ※ Graphophonemic: spelling tests ※ Reading accuracy, fluency, and comprehension

*BOY = Beginning of year   MOY = Middle of year   EOY = End of year

B Beginning Phonics Diagnostic Assessment

Student Copy

m	B	tap
f	G	beg
l	L	cot
n	N	pin
s	R	dug
y	D	
r		flat
v	a	snip
qu	o	slim
w	u	
x	e	plum
z	i	drip
		stem
b	on	scan
c	at	
d	if	last
g	up	bent
h		gift
j	fed	
k	lip	stomp
p	sun	craft
t	man	trust
	rot	plant

Teacher's Score Sheet and Analysis Sheet for Beginning Phonics Diagnostic Assessment

Directions: Place a plus (+) by each correct answer, mark no response as NR, and place a minus (−) by each incorrect answer. Write what the child said next to incorrect answers. If the student says the name of a letter say, "That's the name of the letter, now say its sound." If it is obvious that the student cannot complete the test, discontinue it.

Student:_____   Date:_____

Consonants: Continuous Letter-Sounds	**Short Vowel Letter-Sounds**	**CCVC words with beginning blends (just continuous sounds)**
m	a	
f	o	flat
l	u	snip
n	e	slim
s	i	
y		**CCVC words with beginning blends (least one stop sound)**
r	**Vowel-Consonant Words (VC)**	
v		
qu	on	
w	at	plum
x	if	drip
z	up	stem
		scan
Consonants: Stop Letter-Sounds	**CVC words beginning with continuous sounds**	
b		**CVCC words ending with final blends**
c	fed	
d	lip	last
g	sun	bent
h	man	gift
j	rot	
k		**CCVCC words with beginning and ending blends**
p	**CVC words beginning with stop sounds**	
t		
	tap	stomp
Upper Case Letter-Sounds	beg	craft
	cot	trust
B	pin	plant
G	dug	
L		
N		
R		
D		

C Advanced Word-Reading Diagnostic Assessment

Student Copy

flight	crowd	payable
dawn	shouldn't	antifreeze
roast	we're	coastal
peach	pillow	devotion
batch	subway	dismissive
stain	nephew	dreadful
pound	bother	intermix
broom	hooky	prejudge
kneel	handle	ability
shine	fried	inspire
tube	hoped	politic
wrung	traded	barely
haunt	hauling	midterm
knock	praises	goodness
boil	mocked	mistake
hawk	moaning	return
fudge	grassiest	noxious
lurks	fencing	semicircle
grown	tallest	toxic
thorn	whipping	
barges	joyless	

Teacher's Score Sheet and Analysis Sheet for Advanced Word-Reading Diagnostic Assessment

Directions: Place a plus (+) by each correct answer, mark no response as NR, and place a minus (−) by each incorrect answer. Write what the child said next to the incorrect answer.

Student: _____   Date: _____

flight _____	crowd _____	payable _____
dawn _____	shouldn't _____	antifreeze _____
roast _____	we're _____	coastal _____
peach _____	pillow _____	devotion _____
batch _____	subway _____	dismissive _____
stain _____	nephew _____	dreadful _____
pound _____	bother _____	intermix _____
broom _____	hooky _____	prejudge _____
kneel _____	handle _____	ability _____
shine _____	fried _____	inspire _____
tube _____	hoped _____	politic _____
wrung _____	traded _____	barely _____
haunt _____	hauling _____	midterm _____
knock _____	praises _____	goodness _____
boil _____	mocked _____	mistake _____
hawk _____	moaning _____	return _____
fudge _____	grassiest _____	noxious _____
lurks _____	fencing _____	semicircle _____
grown _____	tallest _____	toxic _____
thorn _____	whipping _____	
barges _____	joyless _____	

Advanced Word-Reading Diagnostic Assessment 1: Decoding Error Pattern Chart

Name: _____ Date: _____

After you have given the test, circle the letter combination or affix for each misread part of the word.

Analyze the Entire Word	No Try	Short Vowel	Long Vowel	-r Controlled Vowel (ar, er, ir, ur, are, ire, ere, ore, ure)	Consonant Digraph (e.g., sh, th, ch, ph, ng)	Blend (e.g., st, sl, nd, nt, lf, ld, ct, pr)	Other Letter Combination (e.g., dge, kn, al, ss)	Contraction	Inflectional Ending (plurals, -ed, -ing, -'s, -er, -est)	C or g rule	Prefix	Suffix
flight	NT		igh			fl-						
dawn	NT						aw					
roast	NT		oa			-st						
peach	NT		ea		ch							
batch	NT	ă					tch					
stain	NT		ai			st-						
pound	NT					-nd	ou					
broom	NT					br-	oo					
kneel	NT		ee				kn					
shine	NT		i_e		sh							
tube	NT		u_e as oo									
wrung	NT	ŭ			ng		wr					
haunt	NT					-nt	au					
knock	NT	ŏ					kn, ck					
boil	NT						oi					

Continued

449

Continued

Analyze the Entire Word	No Try	Short Vowel	Long Vowel	-r Controlled Vowel (ar, er, ir, ur, are, ire, ere, ore, ure)	Consonant Digraph (e.g., sh, th, ch, ph, ng)	Blend (e.g., st, sl, nd, nt, lf, ld, ct, pr)	Other Letter Combination (e.g., dge, kn, al, ss)	Contraction	Inflectional Ending (plurals, -ed, -ing, -'s, -er, -est)	C or g rule	Prefix	Suffix
hawk	NT						aw					
fudge	NT	ŭ					dge					
lurks	NT			ur		-ks			s			s
grown	NT		ow			gr-						
thorn	NT			or	th							
barges	NT			ar					es	g(e)		es
crowd	NT					cr-	ow					
shouldn't	NT				sh	-nt		shouldn't				
we're	NT		ē					we're				
pillow	NT	ĭ	ow				==					
subway	NT	ŭ	ay								sub	
nephew	NT	ĕ					ph, ew					
bother	NT	ŏ		er	th							
hooky	NT						oo					y
handle	NT	ă					le					
fried	NT		ī			fr-			ed			ed (d)
hoped	NT		o_e						ed			ed (t)

Continued

Analyze the Entire Word	No Try	Short Vowel	Long Vowel	-r Controlled Vowel (ar, er, ir, ur, are, ire, ere, ore, ure)	Consonant Digraph (e.g., sh, th, ch, ph, ng)	Blend (e.g., st, sl, nd, nt, lf, ld, ct, pr)	Other Letter Combination (e.g., dge, kn, al, ss)	Contraction	Inflectional Ending (plurals, -ed, -ing, -'s, -er, -est)	C or g rule	Prefix	Suffix
traded	NT		a_e			tr-			ed			ed
hauling	NT						au		ing			ing
praises	NT		ai						es			es
mocked	NT	ŏ					ck		ed			ed (t)
moaning	NT	oa							ing			ing
grassiest	NT	ă				gr-	ss		est (y to i)			est
fencing	NT	ě							ing (delete e)	c(i)		ing
tallest	NT						all		est			est
whipping	NT	ĭ			wh		pp		ing (dbl. cons.)			ing
joyless	NT						oy					less
payable	NT		ay									able
antifreeze	NT		ee			fr-					anti	
coastal	NT		oa			-st-						al
devotion	NT		ō in *vo*								de	tion
dismissive	NT	ĭ in *miss*					ss				dis	ive
dreadful	NT					dr-	ea					ful
intermix	NT	ĭ in *mix*		er in *inter*							inter	

Continued

451

Continued

Analyze the Entire Word	No Try	Short Vowel	Long Vowel	-r Controlled Vowel (ar, er, ir, ur, are, ire, ere, ore, ure)	Consonant Digraph (e.g., sh, ph, ng)	Blend (e.g., st, sl, nd, nt, lf, ld, ct, pr)	Other Letter Combination (e.g., dge, kn, al, ss)	Contraction	Inflectional Ending (plurals, -ed, -ing, -'s, -er, -est)	C or g rule	Prefix	Suffix
prejudge	NT	u					dge				pre	
ability	NT	ĭ in *bil*									a	ity
inspire	NT			īre		sp					in	
politic	NT	ŏ, ĭ										ic
barely	NT			āre								ly
midterm	NT			er							mid	
goodness	NT						oo					ness
mistake	NT		a_e								mis	
return	NT			ur							re	
noxious	NT	ŏ in *nox*										ious
semicircle	NT			ir			le			c(i)	semi.	
toxic	NT	ŏ										ic
Total Errors	/61	/22	/20	/10	/7	/17	/29	/2	/13	/6	/12	/26

D Diagnostic Spelling Assessment for Advanced Readers

Administration

Administer the spelling inventory the same way you would a spelling test. Use the words in a sentence to be sure students know the exact word. Sentences are provided after the word list. Assure students that this activity is not for a grade, but to help you plan for their needs. Seat students so as to minimize copying. You might want to give this test over a two-day period.

Analysis

This test assesses:

1. students' application of the 10 outlined spelling rules.
2. spelling of common word parts.

Use the Error Guide and circle each error or write in the student's spelling. Total the number of errors in a column at the bottom of the column to determine if there are distinct error patterns. Each rule number on the Error Guide corresponds to the numbered rules listed below.

Ten of the Most Helpful Spelling Rules:

1. Because words don't usually end in *v*, always add an *e* after a final *v*, such as in *dove.*
2. When words end in *ack, eck, ick, ock,* and *uck,* the /k/ is spelled *ck.*
3. When words end in *adge, edge, idge, odge,* and *udge,* the /j/ is spelled *dge.*
4. When words end in *atch, etch, itch, otch,* or *utch,* the /ch/ is spelled tch.
5. The floss rule: A final *f, s,* or *l* that appears after a short vowel is doubled.
6. Final *e* rule: When a word ends in *e* and you add a common word part that begins with a vowel, drop the *e.*
7. Doubling rule: When a short word ends CVC and the next morphograph begins with a vowel, double the final consonant.
8. Plural variation rule: When a word ends in a "hissing" sound (*-s, -z, -x, -ch, -sh*), add an *-es* to form the plural.
9. Changing *y* to *i* rule: When a word ends in a consonant and *y,* change the *y* to *i* before adding *-ed, -es, -er,* and *-est.*
10. Changing *f* rule: Some words that end in the /f/ sound change the letter *f* to *ves* in the plural form. You can always hear the sound /v/ in the plural.

Sentences to Use with Diagnostic Spelling Test

1. **Shove.** Do not **shove** anyone in the hallway.
2. **Fried.** I **fried** a fish yesterday before eating it.
3. **Enjoyment.** I get **enjoyment** from playing games.
4. **Impossible.** It's **impossible** to climb that mountain in sandals.
5. **Sharing.** The two children are **sharing** their candy.
6. **Flexible.** He is so **flexible** that he can do a backbend.
7. **Enable.** Don't **enable** his hitting by laughing at it.
8. **Tension.** After the fight, you could feel the **tension** in the air.
9. **Glorious.** What a **glorious** day it is with the sun shining.
10. **Slimy.** The worm was too **slimy.**
11. **Stormiest.** On the **stormiest** day of the year thunder roared.
12. **Portable.** I just hate to use **portable** toilets.
13. **Dustier.** The room was **dustier** than last year and I sneezed.
14. **Judging. Judging** from your frown, you are unhappy.
15. **Tireless.** The garden had no weeds because of his **tireless** work.
16. **Honesty.** Because I never lied, I was known for my **honesty.**
17. **Mocking.** They were **mocking** her for wearing a purple tie to school.
18. **Creation.** His **creation** in art class was a painting of a lizard.
19. **Grumpier.** Today I'm **grumpier** because I didn't eat breakfast.
20. **Reasonable.** Any **reasonable** kid would want 3 meals a day.
21. **Presses.** Mom **presses** our clothes with an iron.
22. **Brightly.** I smiled **brightly** after getting chocolate.
23. **Prejudge.** Don't **prejudge** my attitude until you know me better.
24. **Swelled.** His fist **swelled** after he hit the cement block.
25. **Antifreeze.** In winter I put **antifreeze** in the car.
26. **Ducking.** Sheila was **ducking** under a tree in the rain.
27. **Creative.** Juan's drawing was the most **creative** one in the class.
28. **Halves.** After I cut the orange, I gave both **halves** to Joe.
29. **Clutched.** She **clutched** her child's hand so he wouldn't get lost.
30. **Gloves.** When it gets cold, he puts on his **gloves.**
31. **Dental.** I am scared of any **dental** procedures on my teeth.
32. **Tinier.** The mouse was **tinier** than the big rat.
33. **Festive.** I made sure that the party was **festive.**
34. **Grimly.** He **grimly** walked to the principal's office.
35. **Nonsense.** I thought the eel cartoon was a lot of **nonsense.**
36. **Pledge.** Juliet will **pledge** her heart to Romeo.
37. **Quizzes.** I hope there are no **quizzes** in school the whole week.
38. **Hateful.** She's so mean that everyone thinks she's **hateful.**
39. **Helpful.** Thomas is always so **helpful** that he's very likable.
40. **Stretcher.** He went to the hospital on a **stretcher.**
41. **Snobby.** She has so much money and acts **snobby** because of it.
42. **Skinniest.** That thin boy was the **skinniest** boy I'd seen.
43. **Pennies.** I don't like **pennies** because they aren't worth anything.
44. **Novelty.** The glow worm toy that gave off sparks was a **novelty.**

Student's Score Sheet

Name: **Date:**

	RULES										Prefix	Suffix	Base/Root Word
	1	2	3	4	5	6	7	8	9	10			
1. shove	ve												shove
2. fried									y to i			ed	fry
3. enjoyment											en	ment	enjoy
4. impossible											im	ible	possible
5. sharing						drop e						ing	share
6. flexible												ible	flex
7. enable											en		able
8. tension						drop e						ion	tense
9. glorious									y to i			ous	glory
10. slimy						drop e						y	slime
11. stormiest									y to i			est	storm
12. portable												able	port
13. dustier									y to i			er	dusty
14. fudging		udge				drop e						ing	fudge
15. tireless												less	tire
16. honesty												y	honest
17. mocking		ock										ing	mock
18. creation						drop e						tion	create
19. grumpier									y to i			er	grumpy
20. reasonable												able	reason
21. presses					ss			es				es	press
22. brightly												ly	bright
23. prejudge		udge									pre		judge
24. swelled					ll							ed	swell
25. antifreeze											anti		freeze
26. ducking		uck										ing	duck
27. creative						drop e						ive	create
28. halves									ves			es	half
29. clutched			utch									ed	clutch
30. gloves	ve + s											s	glove
31. dental												al	dent-
32. tinier									y to i			er	tiny
33. festive												ive	fest
34. grimly												ly	grim
35. nonsense											non		sense
36. pledge		edge											pledge
37. quizzes							dbl	es				es	quiz
38. hateful												ful	hate
39. likable						drop e						able	like
40. stretcher			etch									er	stretch
41. snobby							dbl					y	snob
42. skinniest							dbl		y to i			y +est	skin
43. pennies									y to i			es	penny
44. novelty												ty	novel
Totals	/2	/2	/3	/2	/2	/7	/3	/2	/8	/1	/6	/38	/44

E Tests of Vocabulary

Name of Test	Aspect of Language Assessed	Norms	Administered	Time	Comments
Peabody Picture Vocabulary Test-4 (PPVT-4)	Receptive	2.6–adult	Individually	15 minutes	Pointing format useful for young children
Expressive Vocabulary Test (EVT-2)	Expressive	2.6–adult	Individually	3–8 minutes per subtest	Designed to be expressive companion to PPVT-4
Test of Language Development-4 (TOLD)	Receptive and expressive	Primary: 4.0–8.11 Intermediate: 8.0–17.4	Individually	Level 1: ≈30 minutes; Level 2: 65 minutes	Subtests include picture vocabulary, relational vocabulary, and multiple meanings
Test of Word Knowledge (TOWK)	Receptive and expressive	5–17	Individually	10–20 minutes	Diagnostic: multiple subtests within two levels
Wechsler Individual Achievement Test (WIAT-11)	Expressive	4–8.5	Individually	10–30 minutes	Students identify pictures that match a spoken word and provide a word that matches a picture
Woodcock Reading Mastery Test Revised (WRMT-R)	Receptive	5–7.5+ Grades K–1.6	Individually	Less than 30 minutes	Reading task involving synonyms and antonyms
Iowa Test of Basic Skill (ITBS)	Receptive	Grades K–8	Individually or group	Levels 5 and 6: 20 minutes; Levels 7 and 8: 15 minutes; Levels 9–14: 15 minutes	For Grades K & 1 (levels 5–6): picture word matching; for Grades 1 and 2 (levels 7–8): picture or stimulus word followed by set of multiple-choice definitions read orally; for Grades 3–8 (levels 9–14): multiple-choice

Continued